CRITIQUES *and* ESSAYS

on

MODERN FICTION

1920-1951

REPRESENTING THE ACHIEVEMENT OF MODERN AMERICAN AND BRITISH CRITICS

Selected By

JOHN W. ALDRIDGE
UNIVERSITY OF VERMONT

WITH A FOREWORD BY

MARK SCHORER

THE RONALD PRESS COMPANY · NEW YORK

Copyright, 1952, by

THE RONALD PRESS COMPANY

5VR

Library of Congress Catalog Card Number: 52-6180

PRINTED IN THE UNITED STATES OF AMERICA

PREFACE

This book has been designed for use as a primary text in courses in the criticism of modern fiction, and as a collateral text in courses in the survey of modern fiction. Its strong formalist bias may fit it for further use as a reference text for courses in the aesthetics of fiction and in the writing of the short story and novel. But the governing intention of the book is that it should meet the needs of the increasing numbers of serious students who are interested in fiction as an art rather than as a model, and who may be expected to be concerned with the element which most clearly distinguishes it as an art, its technique or form.

It is hoped that the instructor will find here satisfactions, at least in the first instance, of a more utilitarian kind. The collection into one volume of such a great variety of key critical material, much of it never before published in book form and most of it no longer readily obtainable in periodical form, should serve to lighten the burden which the teaching of the textless course in fiction criticism or survey has hitherto placed upon his research energies. It should afford him convenient access to the best results of the sustained effort by which, in recent years, our criticism of fiction has at last begun to catch up with that of poetry; and when used with an assigned selection of the works treated in each of the studies, it should help him to establish with his students the basis for an enlightened standard of critical judgment and approach. But that it will not release him from his rightful employment altogether will be clear to him as soon as he examines Mr. Robert W. Stallman's bibliography, which is undoubtedly the most complete listing of critical publications on modern fiction now available, and an effective reminder of the limits within which a book of this kind must necessarily operate.

The arrangement of the studies into an organic pattern is not intended to suggest a continuity of purpose or approach where, it may be felt, none may be supposed to exist; although it may well serve to suggest one which until now has not been fully appreciated. Its first purpose is to give practical form to a body of material written for a variety of separate occasions but chosen for use here because of its appropriateness to the single occasion of this book. If that occasion is, for the most part, to do honor to the study of technique in fiction, it is so because that is where our achievement lies and where, if we are serious, we are compelled to go. But I should be doing less than justice to the scope of this volume if I did not add that the technical bias, while it has been everywhere informing, has nowhere been rigidly enforced, and that of the several approaches known to modern criticism, the best have here found representation.

In selecting the contents and determining their arrangement, I have tried, in so far as possible, to anticipate the needs of the typical course in the criticism or survey of modern fiction. The arrangement whereby the student is exposed, first, to studies of technique as principle, next, to critiques in which principle is illustrated in the method of single works, and, finally, to analyses of the general modes of individual authors, would seem to be the most logical one for the purposes of the classroom. The choice of studies has been governed by two considerations: the scope and nature of the subject matter presented in the typical course and the necessity that this volume should meet the requirement of manageable length. In deference to both I have chosen to represent the achievement of the major British and American critics only, in so far as it is revealed in their investigations into the work of those modern British and American authors most likely to be taught in the university today. This decision has been uniformly respected except in the few instances where the study of technique in the novel has necessarily evoked comment on the practices of nineteenth-century and Continental authors. In all instances my aim has been to present material which will stand not only as the most informative and teachable of the available studies of a given work or author but as a prime example of the critical method in action. My introductory notes to each of the three parts may serve to suggest to the instructor a possible approach to the task of organizing and preparing this material for effective classroom use.

It cannot be asserted too often that the criticism here represented is hardly the work of a school, the fruit of a movement, or the evidence of a prophecy come untimely true. The prophecy to which I refer is one made not long ago by Mr. Blackmur when, in the course of his remarks for the *Kenyon Review* on the critic's business, he suggested that we are undoubtedly in for a little "new criticism" of the novel. The criticism in this volume is not the fulfilment of his prophecy, and yet it may serve to reduce it from the level of prophecy to the level of correct inference where it more rightly belongs. For Mr. Blackmur did not argue that we have not already had a criticism of the novel that might reasonably be called new. He meant that we have not yet formulated it or codified its insights or dignified it with a term, as we certainly shall do, and as we have already done with the criticism of poetry.

What we have already done with the novel has been to treat it as a form and as an art and not as the indiscriminate bolus of sensation, polemic, and psychology which it was formerly thought to be. We have arrived at this by much the same process as we have arrived at it in poetry—simply by learning to read all over again, and by learning to keep separate in our minds what we have read and what we have merely lived. But perhaps as the price we have had to pay for our wisdom, we have too often been guilty of a vagrant scrupulosity, an overweening eagerness, at all costs, to be pure. We may have thrown out the bolus only to be forced to bring it back in again as soon as we have learned how to use it. We may one day find, as Mr. Blackmur says, that we can no longer be "so verbal, nor so imagistic, nor so 'symbolic' (in the logical senses) in our analyses" of fiction, that we can continue to be so only at the risk of losing both the bolus and the art. It will undoubtedly be on that day that the "new criticism" of the novel which Mr. Blackmur prophesied will begin to be written.

What we have not yet done, and presumably will not do until this criticism can be written, is take into proper account those elements other than form which, because we are dealing with fiction, make far greater demands upon our attention than they would if we were dealing with poetry. In our concern with form we have neglected the question of source, which would take us back to both society and the mystery of the creative process, and the question of end, which would take us forward to both society and ethics. Probably for this reason the criticism we now have functions best in relation to works in which rigid adherence to form and thematic complexity rules these questions safely out of order. We have at hand distinguished studies of the James novel, the Joyce novel, the Dostoevski novel, the Kafka novel, the Conrad novel, the Hemingway novel, and the Faulkner novel; and we have them, at least to a certain extent, because these novels readily lend themselves to the kind of performance which our critics are best able to give. But we must not forget that they are also the novels which are most deserving of our time and of our criticism; and if it were not for the fact that, because they are so deserving, they threaten to produce a criticism which has forgotten how to judge, we should be ready to forgive them altogether.

The judging we are inclined to leave to the injudicious, just as we are inclined to leave the naturalistic and more directly experiential novel to critics whose interests are more in sociology than in art, more in the man than in the artist. I do not say that these interests are wrong: I say simply that they are what we have. It is my impression that they have given us just about everything we know about the novels of Fitzgerald, Dos Passos, Crane, Anderson, Lawrence, Wolfe, Dreiser, and Farrell. The interests of our more formalist critics have certainly not given us much about these novels; and they are not likely to so long as they are of a nature not to be aroused by anything less than perfection.

But it is not the function of a volume of this kind to act as an agent either of conciliation or of dispute for the critical interests which it sets out to serve. As an anthology, it will be doing its proper job if it manages to suggest the range and variety of the achievement which has called it into being. I should like to propose that this achievement has already begun to have as considerable an effect on our reading of fiction as the achievement of the "new criticism" has had on our reading of poetry, and that with time it will be expanded and deepened to include all those levels of insight of which, at the back of our minds, we are aware, but which our present reading of fiction cannot open to us.

——

I wish to thank the several persons who so graciously gave time and study to the prospectus of this volume, as well as those who, in conversation or in correspondence, gave criticism and advice by which the selection of material has benefited: Mr. Malcolm Cowley and Professors Warren Beck, R. P. Blackmur, Richard Chase, David Daiches, Francis Fergusson, Leslie A. Fiedler, Frederick J. Hoffman, Lewis Leary, H. M. McLuhan, Arthur Mizener, Norman Holmes Pearson, Philip Blair Rice, Harry K. Russell, Mark Schorer, Robert W. Stallman, Allen Tate, Lionel Trilling, Austin Warren, and Philip Wheelwright. I owe an additional debt to Mr. Schorer for providing the foreword, and to Mr. Stallman for his many kindnesses as well as for his bibliography. Finally, I should like to express to my wife, Lanice Dana Aldridge, my deep appreciation of her assistance at all stages in the work of preparing the manuscript.

Burlington, Vermont   JOHN W. ALDRIDGE
January, 1952

NOTE: Footnotes introduced by asterisks are the editor's; those introduced by numerals are the authors', and are reproduced from the original texts.

CONTENTS

PART III
THE MODE OF THE NOVELIST

CONTENTS

FOR LANICE

FOREWORD

WHEN T. S. Eliot wrote that "the novel ended with Flaubert and with James," and Allen Tate wrote that "Flaubert created the modern novel," they were probably making not an opposite but an identical assertion. They were saying that even in 1856 the great spacious days of the nineteenth-century novel were coming to a close. If in her essay "Modern Fiction," Virginia Woolf moved the date with arch precision to December, 1910, it was only because she forgot for the moment that those Georgian novelists whom she called "spiritualists" had had their predecessors in James and Flaubert, through the latter of whom the novel had, according to Mr. Tate, "at last caught up with poetry." At last caught up with poetry, or been lost to it? That is the difference between Mr. Tate's observation and Mr. Eliot's, and on this difference hangs the continuing debate on the present state and the future possibilities of the novel.

The difference between what the novel *had been,* and what poetry always *is* or what the modern novel has often tried to *be,* is brought home to us when we consider such a piece of analysis as Joseph Frank's in "Spatial Form in the Modern Novel," where there is no longer any assumption of a radical generic difference between novels and poems. There was a time when the novel was written in greater comfort than can possibly have been felt as her native possession by such a novelist as the author of *Nightwood*. Lionel Trilling says that "the novel was better off when it was more humbly conceived than it is now; the novelist was in a far more advantageous position when his occupation was misprized, or when it was estimated by simpler minds than his own, when he was nearly alone in his sense of wonder at the possibilities of his genre, at the great effects it might be made to yield. The novel was luckier when it had to compete with the sermon, with works of history, with philosophy and poetry and with the ancient classics, when its social position was in question and like one of its own poor or foundling or simple heroes it had to make its way against odds. Whatever high intentions it had, it was permitted to stay close to its own primitive elements from which it drew power. Believing this," Mr. Trilling concludes, he has no wish "to join in the concerted effort of contemporary criticism to increase the superego of the novel." But is this imputation fair to criticism?

Sometimes slowly but always finally, criticism follows—can only follow—upon the genre that it inspects, and therefore in some degree it takes its colors from the colors of the genre. As there was no very conscious "art of the novel" before Flaubert (which is not in the least the same as saying that there were not many great novels and a great novelistic art), so there was no criticism of the novel at all. But with the appearance of such a novelist of the increased superego as Flaubert, and, in England, as James, as Conrad, and as Ford, the criticism of the novel could begin, and for better or worse it was necessarily a criticism of the increased superego. The modern criticism of the novel begins in the modern novel, in the works of Flaubert, James, Conrad, among others, and in their utterances, especially James's, about their works. Would we have any criticism of fiction without such clues to its pursuit as were thrown out by James, when, for example, he said of Conrad that he showed himself "absolutely alone as a votary of the way to do a thing that shall make it undergo the most doing," or, for example, of Flaubert, that *"Madame Bovary,* subject to whatever qualification, is absolutely the most literary of novels, so literary that it covers us with its mantle. It shows us once for all that there is no *intrinsic* call for a debasement of the type. The mantle I speak of is wrought with surpassing fineness, and we may always, under stress of whatever charge of illiteracy, frivolity, vulgarity, flaunt it as the flag of the guild"? What was the flag for the masters was no less the workbench and the tools upon it of the apprentices, or whatever secondary title one wishes to assign to critics. It need not surprise us that James was already dead for sixteen years before that flag was officially raised in Percy Lubbock's *The Craft of Fiction,* the first systematization in criticism of James's own methods and insights into method.

It need not surprise us, because criticism always lags. Recently it was my unhappy experience to read through the contemporary critical evaluations of Ford Madox Ford's *The Good Soldier,* which was published in 1915. It is a highly self-conscious performance, told in the first person, and absolutely depending for even a glimmer of intelligibility on a recognition of the limitations of that person. For over twenty-five years, Henry James had been exploring the possibilities of the dramatized point of view in the novel, yet in 1915 *The Good Soldier* could still be read by critics as though the narrator were to be taken, if not indeed for the author himself, at least as seriously as the author. Thus character, method, style, and meaning were all lost at once, and what is really a considerable comedy was treated as though it were a tragedy *manqué.* A critic for the *Nation* complained of the "disjointed, cumulative" method, by which the "episodes themselves, after being worked up with care, are not exploited for their own sake, but disposed of with a kind of negligence," so that "somehow the whole thing fails to focus." The method is in fact an immediate representation of the narrator's moral cowardice, and that *is* the focus; but in 1915 it did not occur to most readers, critics included, what later criticism has made so clear, and, in the words of John Peale Bishop, even admonitory: that "the meaning of a novel should be [not in the words, or the words alone, but] in its structure." In the *New Republic,* Theodore Dreiser complained of the inconsistency of Ford's central character, whereas Dowell's report of his own inconsistency is the dramatization of his astigmatism. What an occasion for heartbreak! A British reviewer explained the method of the novel by assuring his readers that the author "sees plainly that the whole thing is too unpleasant to form the subject of a direct narrative, so we are asked to become listeners whilst Dowell gives his reminiscences in broken and spasmodic gusts." To a man, therefore, the reviewers found the novel "unreal," even as they commented on "the skill which went to writing" it.

Like many another modern novel, *The Good Soldier* is a work of enormous skill, but it is a great deal more besides. What it is besides the critic cannot know unless he can examine the operations of the skill, and how can he possibly know even whether a novel is skilful if he cannot see beyond its first technique to the meaning that that technique is analyzing and establishing? Whatever its limitations, modern criticism has at least overcome certain crude dualisms, as that between matter and method, which many novelists ever since Flaubert have assured us does not exist for them, and today, I suppose, such a Jamesian notion of "form" in the novel as this proposed by Percy Lubbock is generally assumed by critics: "The best form is that which makes the most of its subject—there is no other definition of the meaning of form in fiction. The well-made book is the book in which the subject and the form coincide and are indistinguishable—the book in which the matter is all used up in the form, in which the form expresses all the matter." Thirty years ago, such a notion was not assumed, and what, one may fairly ask, would have happened to later novels generally so different as *Ulysses, The Plumed Serpent, A Passage to India, Light in August, Between the Acts, The Death of the Heart, All the King's Men,* and *The Middle of the Journey* if one could imagine these as having fallen into the exclusively insensitive critical hands that grasped and buried Ford's *The Good Soldier* for thirty-five years? We are reminded of Lionel Trilling's remembrance of *Winesburg, Ohio* in the old Modern Library edition: "... the brown oilcloth binding, the coarse paper, the bold type crooked on the page, are dreadfully evocative. Even the introduction by Ernest Boyd is rank with the odor of the past, of the day when criticism existed in heroic practical simplicity, when it was all truth against hypocrisy, idealism against philistinism, and the opposite of 'romanticism' was not 'classicism' but 'realism,' which—it now seems odd—negated both." But the greatest philistinism, we should remind ourselves further, was in criticism itself, and whatever charges we may wish to bring against more recent criticism—its constrictiveness, its monotony, its tenuousness, its Lord's Prayer engravings on pennies—must we not also say that it will not, with such egregious confidence in its stupidity, break great hearts?

II

The novel now is modern. Such reminders of the particulars of our contemporary esthetic experience in general as are provided in, for example, Harry Levin's discussion of Joyce, called "Montage," show us in what exact detail it is modern. And as the novel itself no longer exists in "heroic practical simplicity," so criticism of the novel can hardly be expected to. How, then, shall we describe it, this body of criticism not more than about thirty years old, and so generously represented in this volume? Can we describe it at all, if one description means to imply a homogeneous body of work? Certainly many critics are here present who, at the mention of the names of many others who are also present, strain back with a harassed cry of *noli me tangere*. And perhaps that cry is our clue to terms sufficiently general to include nearly all the criticism that appears here: the criticism of modern fiction is an unusual combination of the humble and the arrogant, and each quality is both a virtue and a vice.

Modern critics are arrogant toward one another and humble before their authors. It is a matter of relative unimportance, I should think, if critics can or cannot bring themselves to speak to others of their kind, but only *of* them; yet such hostility is surely wasteful. There can be no doubt that modern critics have devoted an excess of their energies, of thought as of wit and malice, to the appraisal of other critics, with what one might regard as a geometric regression in rewards for which an assertion of self-esteem can hardly be expected to compensate. The criticism of criticism, and, even, the criticism of criticism of criticism, have become a common mirror game in our day, and are manifestations of this quality; a certain self-protective and anticipatory dogmatism of tone that is to be detected in much of even our more primary criticism is another. The effect of this tone on the prose in which much contemporary criticism is written is assuredly among its least attractive traits and is at least one that militates against much of it in itself achieving the conditions of literature, as certain less austerely critical, more leisurely and belletristic efforts of the earlier twentieth century and of the nineteenth century are literature. Yet this same hostility suggests something of the vigor of modern criticism—the vigor that is to be found in a bristling variety of view, in opposition and conflict. There is a tendency in certain quarters to lump together all serious contemporary discussion of literature, and especially of fiction, in a non-existent cult or coterie, to treat it as though it were some kind of single-minded conspiracy against any simple pleasure, any unpretentious delight in the literary arts, or against the scholarly investigation of the historical development of these arts. But persons who are alarmed by this hypothesis of their own construction need only glance through the contents of this volume to see that modern criticism encourages many approaches, and that these approaches are not exclusive of one another. General agreement prevails not in method of analysis but in the assumption that one is not performing an analysis or a critical act at all if one is not talking about the literary work, and on its evidence, as it exists before one. Modern criticism is above all determined to read well.

It is in this sense that one may say that modern critics are humble before their authors if not among themselves. They are determined above all to grant their novelists seriousness, and to take the novel seriously, to take it, that is to say, not as amusement but as art.

This, again, is a point of view that has not always prevailed in the discussion of the novel. For fiction is, of course, constantly and peculiarly susceptible to being read as though it were not art at all but an immediate transcript of life, a journalistic form of history. In most of its types, it comes to us looking like life—concerned with people who have names like our own, who talk in some ways as we talk, who are involved in the various activities that do constitute our own daily lives. These are some of the materials of the novel but they are no more the novel itself than images are a poem or colors a picture. The "life-like" materials of the genre have generally been viewed, however, as somehow commensurate with the genre itself. The reasons for such a confusion are not difficult to find and we must presently indicate them, but for the moment let us point out only that when the novel is viewed in this way, it gives the critic nothing to talk about but its "reality," on the one hand, and then, on the other, those more or less superfluous "techniques" or "skills" that are necessarily regarded as, at best, little more than enhancements of "reality," at worst, intrusions upon it. Very few critics in the present collection will be found to write from this point of view. "If art contrives to give the illusion of reality, it is done—as they say—with mirrors, and we are concerned with how it is done," writes Harry Levin. Interestingly enough, those critics here who confound "the illusion of reality" with "reality" itself are critics of naturalistic novels. It is more tempting to take the naturalistic novel as a form of non-art than any other kinds of novels, but even here, another kind of critic will recognize that there is a difference between life and "a slice of life." The difference lies in the act of slicing, which is the act of selecting, and therefore, really, the act of ordering, or at any rate, the basis upon which ordering becomes a possibility.

Modern critics are humble in the presence of the novelist in this sense, that they assume that the novel is like other arts in that it, too, is a symbolic presentation of an attitude toward experience. A novelist inevitably utilizes experience, but he utilizes it in such a way that, according to Martin Turnell, it is transformed into a pattern, and "this pattern *is* the novel." When John Peale Bishop writes of "The Sorrows of Thomas Wolfe," he shows us a novelist unwilling or unable to transform the welter of his experience into a pattern that is expressive of values—and therefore he shows us a failure. For the possession of life in the novel is imaginative or it is no possession at all.

A novel is not life but an image of life, an author's selective interpretation concretely embodied. Every selection from the whole of actuality is an interpretation of the whole of actuality, and the novel differs from journalism first of all in that this selection rests not on partisan bias or theoretical judgment but on the bias of a whole temperament, in which intellect and imagination, the senses and the passions, are one. The novel next differs from journalism in the primary importance of style—the agent that unifies the image, gives it its body, presents that body, and in doing so, casts its evaluative light back on the chaos of actuality from which it came. The novel differs from journalism finally in that all its materials—prose, people, plots, and whatever else may go into it—are elements included not for the sake of a full report of action but as the elements necessary to a symbolically organized image of action. When Norton R. Girault writes about the characters in a novel by Robert Penn Warren, and when Richard Chase writes about the "symbolic texture" of a novel by William Faulkner, and when Ray B. West, Jr., writes of the imagery in a story by Katherine Anne Porter, their basic assumption is the same: that whatever single element in a novel one may select for analysis, a novel in itself is an integration of an attitude which the study of any single element will reveal. Modern criticism pursues these integrations, and when its humility fails it and becomes at least a bore if not a vice, it is when its pursuit becomes overingenious, and we lose sight of the novel for the arduous effort that the critic makes in reading it aloud to us. We hear not the novelist's words but the critic's labored breathing.

III

Percy Lubbock's "well-made book" is a sound concept but an unfortunate phrase, for it suggests not a work of art but an artifact. "... even when we are so queerly constituted as to be ninety-nine parts literary," Henry James said, "we are still a hundredth part something else. This hundredth part may, once we possess the book—or the book possesses us—make us imperfect as readers, and yet without it should we want or get the book at all?" It was the considerably more than hundredth part of the "something else" in James that always left him uneasy before and sometimes plainly unsatisfied with Flaubert. Of *L'éducation sentimentale*, he asked, "Why did Flaubert choose, as special conduits of the life he proposed to depict, such inferior and in the case of Frederic such abject human specimens?" He might have asked the same question of the work that involves Emma Bovary, for when James spoke of the "amount of felt life" that goes into a work of art, he had in mind, it would seem, the quantity of experience of a certain *quality;* or if he did not, why should he have introduced the word "moral" into his proposition? "There is, I think, no more nutritive or suggestive truth than that of the perfect dependence of the 'moral' sense of a work of art on the amount of felt life concerned in producing it." The novel can *feel* life (and its own life) in a variety of ways, and each of these has its own depths and heights, and, if I understand the point of James's remark, I should think that the peculiar task of the critic would be to measure these depths and heights. Philip Rahv says, "Experience ... is the substructure of literature above which there rises a superstructure of values, ideas, and judgments—in a word, of the multiple forms of consciousness." All the "skills" or "techniques" that go into the novel are the means by which these values, these "multiple forms of consciousness," are, first, expressed, and, then, judged. The critic measures the novelist's judgments.

In vital ways, the judgments of novelists change as the novel itself undergoes historical changes. "But this base and summit," Mr. Rahv continues, "are not stationary: they continually act and react upon each other." This statement implies a good deal about the central history of the novel as a genre, and, consequently, about the ways in which criticism has estimated the novel.

Let us consider for a moment the impact of one of Virginia Woolf's "materialists," John Galsworthy, upon one of her "spiritualists," D. H. Lawrence. "Nauseated ... up to the nose," as he said, Lawrence was contemplating the characters of *The Forsyte Saga,* and he asked his readers, "Why can't we admit them as human beings? Whence arises this repulsion from the Forsytes, this refusal, this emotional refusal, to have them identified with our common humanity? Why do we feel so instinctively that they are inferiors? It is because they seem to us to have lost caste as human beings, and to have sunk to the level of the social being, that peculiar creature that takes the place in our civilization of the slave in the old civilizations. ... the fatal change today is the collapse from the psychology of the free human individual into the psychology of the social being, just as the fatal change in the past was a collapse from the freeman's psyche to the psyche of the slave. The free moral and the slave moral, the human moral and the social moral: these are the abiding antitheses."

Lawrence's remarks are illuminating if only, as is not unusual with him, because they are overstated. Our experience of novels would seem to suggest a necessary mitigation of his terms as he here sets them: the free human being inalterably opposed to the bound social being, the free moral forever different from what he calls, in this unnecessary extremity, the slave moral. Actually, it was such a mitigation that his own novels struggled in the course of their twenty years to achieve, and that is why they sometimes seem more like the ten parts of one novel than like ten different novels. His critical terms are ideal terms, yet, paradoxically, they bring us nearly into the heart of those conditions that seem to be essential to the novel.

The very first of these, I should say, is that the novel must find a form that will hold together in some firm nexus of structure the individual human being and the social being. These may be shown to be *nearly* one, they may be shown to be different but harmonious, they may be shown to be different and totally at odds; but the two *together* must be there, and the form must provide for their presence. Isolate one from the other and the resulting fiction will flow away from the novel into another genre. Isolate the individual consciousness and we will have pure lyric or pure philosophy; isolate the social being and we will have pure narrative or chronicle or history. In neither will we find the kind of morality (the kind of "felt life") that it is the peculiar province of the novel to analyze; for it is in the connection, in the structural nexus, of the self-responsible individual and the socially related individual that the moral springs of action lie, that moral choice can work. The novel seems to exist at a point where we can recognize the intersection of the stream of history and the stream of soul.

If we consider the novel in these terms, it is not difficult to mark the limits of the genre, and to find examples of those limits. Put *Moll Flanders* at one end and *The Waves* at the other, and we have something like an approximate framework. Or we can reverse the framework and put *Rasselas* at one end and John Hersey's *Hiroshima* at the other, and we will still be just outside the novel. *Moll Flanders* makes no pretense to formal organization and is all social surface; *The Waves,* intent on pure psychic life, sacrifices everything to its elaborately patterned design and is all undifferentiated sensibility. So, too, Johnson's book is all informal philosophy, Hersey's, all informal sociology. None is a novel. But if the novel begins where *Moll Flanders* and *Rasselas,* in their different ways, leave off, it has left off where *The Waves* and *Hiroshima,* in their different ways, begin. The two novels by Defoe and Virginia Woolf are like the mouth of the snake and the tail that it bites: social surface is sensibility, sensibility is a section of London. We may take these two books as marking the limits just outside the genre that is the novel, and ask how the novel came to exist within them.

The novel as we know it—certainly as we know it in English—had very humble origins. It was thought of, first of all, as fact; it was not only new, it was news. It developed in a thoroughly rationalistic age to meet the requirements of a newly literate class. It came out of history and popular religion and political scandal and social reform. It came out of essays and letters; it came immediately out of books like *A Journal of the Plague Year* and *Moll Flanders:* faked history, faked biography. And the elements that were faked pushed simple narrative on into the novel. Beginning in the spirit of anti-romance, of journalism, of experience, of the socially realistic, the early forms of fiction inevitably laid down generic laws for the novel, and even modern novelists must continue to work within those laws of genre; but all the time the thing that was to be the novel was pulling away from the purely social and secular traits of the thing out of which it was coming. When, finally, a novel emerged, it showed itself to be a work in which individual human relationships were dramatized through events within a social context, and the dynamics of the novel, the poles of its possible tensions, were thus established. The novel was a form of prose fiction that was concerned with the relationships of character and class, and in two hundred years, for all its proliferations of technique, it has developed no techniques that are not concerned with the expression of these relationships. As the relationships change in fact, the genre changes in form.

The novel is not journalism, philosophy, poetry; not politics, theology, sociology; not even morality. But if it finds its proper structure, a structure that can hold together both the individual human being and the social being, it can include, in some sense, the interests of all of these. It stands halfway between poetry and history, between the invocation of psychic consciousness and the exposition of social movement, between evocation and narration.

If, in recent times, the novel has struggled more and more toward the condition of poetry, has become more and more concerned with internal states, has become more evocative and less documentary, that is because the gap between the individual human being and the social circumstances in which he exists has itself become hazardously wide. The novel documents this alteration. In its primitive form—in *Moll Flanders,* for example—the individual is still buried completely in the first massive dominance of emerging class consciousness; in the novel of the mid-eighteenth century, the two merge and interact, are separable but not at odds, and the art of Jane Austen carries this relationship to its point of finest discrimination. In the great mid-nineteenth century novels, the balance between the claims of the individual and of the social being still holds, but the polarity is greater. We can view it in the distance between Dickens's malign and benign forces, as, in *Middlemarch,* we can see it in the distance between Bulstrode, conventional value at its worst in social hypocrisy, and Dorothea Brooke, individual aspiration and idealism at their highest but most completely divorced from social circumstance. With Hardy, a new relationship develops;

the individual interest is seen as opposed to the social interest, and in this figuration, Sue Bridehead's tragedy is the defeat of the neurotic individual under social pressure. In Conrad, the same relationship shows itself in the isolation of the individual from the social scene at large, and in James, in the rarity of his social scene, even when it is full of people. Joyce's very subject is this relationship, the drawing apart of the two interests. In Lawrence, the relationship is clearest because most extreme: the individual struggling to leap beyond the social boundaries entirely, yet always being drawn back into community circumstance, and, finally, into communal idealism. In Virginia Woolf we cross over the line again, and the novel leaves by the door opposite the door it had entered—the individual usurping the whole scene, social responsibility eliminated.

As the individual finds an ever diminishing social authority with which to identify himself, the novel more and more moves toward the extremities of poetry and history, and the criticism of fiction becomes either more and more complex or less and less critical. The difference between Stendhal's idea of the novel as "a mirror dawdling down a lane" (which no novel ever was, least of all his own inestimably great works), and James's idea of a novel as a dramatization of that "which groups," is tremendous, and the two notions imply quite different functions for the criticism of the novel. Most of the criticism presented in the following pages takes its start from the Jamesian implication, but James himself, we are always reminded, felt that much of human experience was so incoherent, in the moral tongue, that no means—no skill, technique, style, method, form—could give it more than the appearance of a language—that is, of grouping, of having moral meaning. Those "values, ideas, and judgments" to which Philip Rahv refers and which comprise that morality of which the novel as novel is capable, must continue to find their source in the social material that makes the novel possible in the first place. In essays like R. P. Blackmur's on James and D. S. Savage's on Aldous Huxley, as in T. S. Eliot's now famous review of Joyce's *Ulysses,* we observe critics searching out potentialities for the expression of values in the novel within its own generic permissions. If Flaubert "created" the modern novel, and the modern novel created the criticism of the novel, perhaps criticism has now reached the point at which it can turn and truly measure Flaubert, and then suggest ways in which a more and more spurious form of poetry can push on to an authentic form of prose that is not only history. But perhaps this really is sunset, and then, of course, criticism must pull down the flag.

MARK SCHORER

Berkeley, California
October 1951

PART I
THE TECHNIQUE OF FICTION

THE ESSAYS in Part I deal in general terms with the principle of technique or form in modern fiction. It is appropriate that they should be introduced by selections from that great seminal work of formalist criticism, Percy Lubbock's *The Craft of Fiction,* which stands, together with the critical writings of Henry James, from whose Prefaces Lubbock derived his central bias, at the source of what we may, if we are not careful, yet come to call a "new criticism" of fiction. Lubbock's achievement consists not merely in his having taken literally and asserted explicitly certain insights which James took as his natural novelist's endowment and asserted piecemeal and at random. It consists most particularly in his having elevated the products of both James's critical and his creative sensibility to the status of a closely reasoned esthetic of literary form, an esthetic that, in its application to the art of fiction, is, to use Allen Tate's words, "successful in the same sense, and to no less degree than the famous lecture notes on the Greek drama taken down by an anonymous student at the Lyceum in the fourth century B.C."

The comparison with the *Poetics* suggests much more than mere identity of achievement and kind; for in contemplating the form of the Jamesean novel Lubbock came upon a way of re-phrasing, for the special purposes of the novel, the ancient truth of Aristotle's principle of dramatic action. "All literary art," he might have said, "strives toward the condition of drama, toward the fullest and most exact *rendering* of its subject in terms of the concrete fact or event, which in the play is gesture and speech, in the novel gesture, speech, image, and symbol, and in the poem image and symbol." But Lubbock takes pains throughout his book to make clear the inclusiveness of his use of the term dramatic. The weakness of such a novel as *The Awkward Age,* which in its form most closely resembles the play, is precisely that it is not dramatic enough. Its content consists almost entirely of only that which can be rendered through the medium of gesture and speech. The strength, on the other hand, of such a novel as *The Ambassadors,* which in its form least resembles the play, is that it achieves a maximum rendering of its subject not only through gesture and speech but through a concrete pictorialization of Strether's inner life and sensibility. The drama of mere surface action is, thus, in Lubbock's terms, subordinated to that ultimate

3

drama which directs the most penetrating light of scrutiny upon its subject and discovers it the most thoroughly to our view.

This approach to the question of drama in fiction constitutes one of the great illuminating ideas of modern criticism. Lubbock expresses it with customary succinctness in an early paragraph of *The Craft of Fiction:* "The best form is that which makes the most of its subject ... The well-made book is the book in which the subject and the form coincide and are indistinguishable—the book in which the matter is all used up in the form, in which the form expresses all the matter." It is clearly what T. S. Eliot had in mind when, in pondering the problem of emotion in art, he delivered his famous verdict: "The more perfect the artist, the more completely separate in him will be the man who suffers and the mind which creates"; or when he spoke, in connection with Shakespeare, of "the struggle—which alone constitutes life for a poet—to translate his personal and private agonies into something rich and strange, something universal and impersonal." It is the idea whose urgent demand for precise definition undoubtedly caused him to formulate his principle of the "objective correlative"; and it appears finally as the shaping insight behind such primary dicta of his critical program as "convention" and "classicism." Other writers and critics have stated it similarly and from the point of view of one or more of its several aspects. Joyce proclaimed it through Stephen Dedalus in his *Portrait of the Artist* and then went on to construct his entire theory of art around it. "The dramatic form is reached," says Stephen, "when the vitality which has flowed and eddied round each person fills every person with such vital force that he or she assumes a proper and intangible esthetic life ... The esthetic image in the dramatic form is life purified in and reprojected from the human imagination." And the late C. H. Rickword was thinking of James and paraphrasing Joyce when he said in "A Note on Fiction" that "it is the problem of objectifying and setting in disciplined motion the subjective narrative that has occupied nearly all English novelists of importance since Fielding, and Richardson before him."

In one way or another all the essays in Part I—and, indeed, the vast majority of the essays in the remainder of the book—draw illumination and force from Lubbock's informing idea. They have been arranged so as to trace the process of the symbolization of reality—which is the core of Lubbock's thought in its simplest terms—back through the novel and the single scene to its proper source in the language of fiction itself.

Allen Tate pays his respects to Lubbock and then, as if to do him double honor, invites us to consider a scene from Flaubert in terms of its "fullness of rendition," its capacity to make us *see,* precisely as James was able to make us see the working sensibility of Strether, through the enactment of hidden emotion in the concrete, visible event. As Emma Bovary, in her moment of despair, feels herself impelled toward suicide, "the humming vertigo" which seems to draw the street to her and which she alone can know is "rendered audible to us by the correlative sound of the lathe" turning below her. By means of such a method Flaubert manages to get the impression he wishes to create wholly inside the action; he performs "the complete imaginative job himself," and provides us with an *exemplum* of the finest dramatic technique of which fiction is capable.

Joseph Frank begins his essay with a discussion of yet another scene from Flaubert, the county fair scene in *Madame Bovary.* Here, as action proceeds simultaneously at three levels, each playing upon the others with an enlivening irony, we are obliged, Frank tells us, to perceive the totality of movement and meaning reflexively in an instant of time. We are forced to pause amid the flow of narrative sequence and see all that is happening all at once. This does not seem unreasonable when we recognize that the scene, on its three levels of action, is happening all at once and that what we are doing is simply placing ourselves completely inside the scene and participating in its irony from the position of the characters. Nothing is at this point told to us: the simultaneity of the cross-cutting movements is rendered in space before our eyes.

This principle of reflexive reference must be put to work in such a novel as *Ulysses* where the time-flow of the narrative is deliberately halted and the effort of the entire book is to create an "impression of simultaneity for the life of a whole teeming city" and, what is more remarkable, to maintain it "through hundreds of pages that must be read as a sequence." To meet this problem, Joyce "presented the elements of his narrative . . . in fragments, as they are thrown out unexplained in the course of casual conversation, or as they lie embedded in the various strata of symbolic reference." Thus, at any one moment of time, the reader has at hand "the same instinctive knowledge of Dublin life, the same sense of Dublin as a huge, surrounding organism" which the characters, as Dubliners, possess. By the end of the novel the reader has, in fact, become a Dubliner, and through the same process that he has become a participant in Flaubert's scene, through a unified spatial apprehension of the totality of Dublin as it is created around and within him.

In an attempt to translate to the level of esthetic form certain "quasi-mystical experiences . . . which enabled him to escape what he considered to be time's domination," Proust, in the scene describing the reception at the Princesse de Guermantes', struck upon the same spatializing principle. Instead of presenting his characters in time, which would have been the same as presenting them in a continuous line of development, he confronted the reader with various snapshots of them " 'motionless in a moment of vision,' taken at different stages of their lives; and the reader, in juxtaposing these images, experiences the effects of the passage of time exactly as the narrator had done." Like Flaubert with his whirring lathe, Proust discovered in these images a correlative in dramatic action to a state or vision of the consciousness which was, by itself, unknowable; but he went beyond Flaubert in evolving a technique that would not only transcend the impurity of time but arrest its passage in a single "revelatory moment" of rendered fact.

As Frank, in the concluding section of his essay, focuses his general statement of spatial form upon the technique of a single novel, so Mark Schorer, in the two concluding essays of Part I, gathers up the germinal views of the preceding essays and applies them, in a new synthesis of the old form-content dichotomy, to the problem of language in fiction. In his summary remarks on the significance of an approach to technique as the discovering, defining, and, ultimately, the evaluating principle of fiction, Schorer carries the dramatic or correlative view of art about as far as it can be carried before it must end its course in what Eliot called "the desert of exact likeness to the reality which is perceived by the most commonplace mind." Specifically, he thinks of technique in two respects: "the uses to which language, as language, is put to express the quality of the experience in question; and the uses of point of view not only as a mode of dramatic delimitation, but more particularly, of thematic definition. Technique is really what T. S. Eliot means by 'convention'—any selection, structure, or distortion, any form or rhythm imposed upon the world of action; by means of which—it should be added—our apprehension of the world of action is enriched and renewed." We are confronted here with most of the determinations that have invigorated the formalist study of fiction since its beginning—"expression" or rendition, "point of view" as a mode of "thematic definition," "convention" or form as a means by which "our apprehension of *the world of action* is enriched and renewed." "Technique objectifies," says Schorer and, in speaking of the stories and early novels of Hemingway, "technique was the perfect embodiment of the subject and gave that subject its astounding largeness of effect and meaning." "The best form is that which makes the most of its subject," it is instructive to recall

Lubbock's saying; or simply, as James put it, "questions of art are questions (in the widest sense) of execution."

Having set down his view of the delineating value of technique, Schorer undertakes in his next essay to estimate that value in terms of the metaphorical function of language in three distinguished novels. He begins with an assumption with which the best modern criticism of poetry has always begun but which the standard criticism of fiction has attempted, and largely failed, to survive without: "fiction is a literary art." Even though the novel, because of its form and content, easily opens itself to "first questions about philosophy or politics" and to "first questions about conduct," it remains "an image of life; and the critical problem is first of all to analyze the structure of the image."

To the job of work which such an analysis demands of the critic, Schorer brings a method of the most exacting scrutiny. Technique now is viewed as the texture of metaphors which, by their quality, determine the theme and even the structure of a novel, its symbolic properties, and, ultimately, the special character of the mind behind it. It is from the kind of conceptions this mind habitually entertains that the metaphors derive their quality; but the meaning which they cause a novel to have is not necessarily the meaning the mind intends. Metaphorical language is both the embodiment of intention or theme and its discoverer. It may serve as the vehicle of the author's chosen subject; but it may also serve as the means by which the chosen subject is refuted and the true subject revealed.

Thus while Emily Brontë seemed to be writing, and thought she was writing, in *Wuthering Heights,* to instruct Lockwood "in the nature of a grand passion," she succeeded in writing to instruct herself, through her metaphors, "in the vanity of human wishes." As the instruments of her edifying intention, she chose metaphors of animal and elemental violence. "Human conditions are like the activities of the landscape, where rains *flood,* blasts *wail,* and the snow and wind *whirl wildly* and *blow* out lights," and human character is analogous, in its inflated passion, to the savagery of beasts. "Heathcliff is a 'fierce, pitiless, *wolfish* man.' He is also 'a *bird* of bad omen' and 'an evil *beast*' prowling between a 'stray sheep' 'and the fold, waiting his time to spring and destroy.' "

But such violence demands exhaustion. "The passions of animals," Schorer tells us, "have meaning in that they are presumably necessary to survival; Heathcliff's passion destroys others, himself, and at last, itself. The tumult of the elements alternates with periods of peace, and the seasons are not only autumn and winter. The *fact* of alternation enables nature to endure. The singleness of Heathcliff's tempestuous and wintry emotional life dooms it." What began as a novel intended "to dramatize with something like approval . . . 'the sense of a stupendous self and an insignificant world' " ends as a novel which signifies "the impermanence of self and the permanence of something larger." For by the end, the grand passion has burned out, and only the elements remain.

It is through the revelation of such an irony that Emily Brontë's metaphors instruct her and Schorer instructs us. His study of the function of metaphor in *Wuthering Heights* and the other novels provides us with an exact, almost clinical definition of his "technique as discovery" principle, of the way in which meaning enters and is rendered in fiction. The source of this meaning is not at the moment his concern, as it has not been the concern of the great critical tradition from which his views derive. Yet in contemplating the metaphors of commerce and property in *Persuasion* and the metaphors of religious yearning in *Middlemarch*, particularly as they exist in dramatic opposition to metaphors of sentiment, on the one hand, and metaphors of material restraint on the other, one is impelled to ask the final question: from what peculiar social and moral circumstances do these metaphors derive their substance and, more importantly, to what extent does the dramatic opposition between them depend on the presence, within the society which produced them, of a correlative moral opposition? This question is raised throughout Schorer's study but is never explicitly stated or explored. It is the question of how, in the broadest sense, the values of life become the values of art; and the struggle of critics to answer it satisfactorily provides a natural link between the discussions of the technique of fiction with which this book begins and the discussions of fiction, personality, and society with which it ends.

THE STRATEGY OF POINT OF VIEW *

Percy Lubbock

I

THE WHOLE intricate question of method, in the craft of fiction, I take to be governed by the question of the point of view—the question of the relation in which the narrator stands to the story. He tells it as *he* sees it, in the first place; the reader faces the story-teller and listens, and the story may be told so vivaciously that the presence of the minstrel is forgotten, and the scene becomes visible, peopled with the characters of the tale. It may be so, it very often is so for a time. But it is not so always, and the story-teller himself grows conscious of a misgiving. If the spell is weakened at any moment, the listener is recalled from the scene to the mere author before him, and the story rests only upon the author's direct assertion. Is it not possible, then, to introduce another point of view, to set up a fresh narrator to bear the brunt of the reader's scrutiny? If the story-teller is *in* the story himself, the author is dramatized; his assertions gain in weight, for they are backed by the presence of the narrator in the pictured scene. It is advantage scored; the author has shifted his responsibility, and it now falls where the reader can see and measure it; the arbitrary quality which may at any time be detected in the author's voice is disguised in the voice of his spokesman. Nothing is now imported into the story from without; it is self-contained, it has no associations with anyone beyond its circle.

Such is the first step towards dramatization, and in very many a story it may be enough. The spokesman is there, in recognizable relation with his matter; no question of his authority can arise. But now a difficulty may be started by the nature of the tale that he tells. If he has nothing to do but to relate what he has seen, what anyone might have seen in his position, his account will serve very well; there is no need for more. Let him unfold his chronicle as it appears in his memory. But if he is himself the subject of his story, if the story involves a searching exploration of his own consciousness, an account in his own words, after the fact, is not by any means the best imaginable. Far better it would be to see him while his mind is actually at work

---

* "The Strategy of Point of View" (Editor's title) originally appeared as chaps. xi, xiii, and xvii of *The Craft of Fiction*, by Percy Lubbock (Jonathan Cape: Charles Scribner's Sons, 1921; Peter Smith, 1947). It is reprinted here in rearranged (xvii, xi, xiii) and slightly emended form by permission of Mr. Peter Smith.

in the agitation, whatever it may be, which is to make the book. The matter would then be objective and visible to the reader, instead of reaching him in the form of a report at second hand. But how to manage this without falling back upon the author and *his* report, which has already been tried and for good reasons, as it seemed, abandoned? It is managed by a kind of repetition of the same stroke, a further shift of the point of view. The spectator, the listener, the reader, is now himself to be placed at the angle of vision; not an account or a report, more or less convincing, is to be offered him, but a direct sight of the matter itself, while it is passing. Nobody expounds or explains; the story is enacted by its look and behaviour at particular moments. By the first stroke the narrator was brought into the book and set before the reader; but the action appeared only in his narrative. Now the action is there, proceeding while the pages are turned; the narrator is forestalled, he is watched while the story is in the making. Such is the progress of the writer of fiction towards drama; such is his method of evading the drawbacks of a mere reporter and assuming the advantages, as far as possible, of a dramatist. How far he may choose to push the process in his book—that is a matter to be decided by the subject; it entirely depends upon the kind of effect that the theme demands. It may respond to all the dramatization it can get, it may give all that it has to give for less. The subject dictates the method.

And now let the process be reversed, let us start with the purely dramatic subject, the story that will tell itself in perfect rightness, unaided, to the eye of the reader. This story never deviates from a strictly scenic form; one occasion or episode follows another, with no interruption for any reflective summary of events. Necessarily it must be so, for it is only while the episode is proceeding that no question of a narrator can arise; when the scene closes the play ceases till the opening of the next. To glance upon the story from a height and to give a general impression of its course—this is at once to remove the point of view from the reader and to set up a new one somewhere else; the method is no longer consistent, no longer purely dramatic. And the dramatic story is not only scenic, it is also limited to so much as the ear can hear and the eye see. In rigid drama of this kind there is naturally no admission of the reader into the private mind of any of the characters; their thoughts and motives are transmuted into action. A subject wrought to this pitch of objectivity is no doubt given weight and compactness and authority in the highest degree; it is like a piece of modelling, standing in clear space, casting its shadow. It is the most finished form that fiction can take.

But evidently it is not a form to which fiction can aspire in general. It implies many sacrifices, and these will easily seem to be more than the subject can usefully make. It is out of the question, of course, wherever the main burden of the story lies within some particular consciousness, in the study of a soul, the growth of a character, the changing history of a temperament; there the subject would be needlessly crossed and strangled by dramatization pushed to its limit. It is out of the question, again, wherever the story is too big, too comprehensive, too widely ranging, to be treated scenically, with no opportunity for general and panoramic survey; it has been discovered, indeed, that even a story of this kind *may* fall into a long succession of definite scenes, under some hands, but it has also appeared that in doing so it incurs unnecessary disabilities, and will likely suffer. These stories, therefore, which will not naturally accommodate themselves to the reader's point of view, and the reader's alone, we regard as rather pictorial than dramatic—meaning that they call for some narrator, somebody who *knows,* to contemplate the facts and create an impression of them. Whether it is the omniscient author or a man in the book, he must gather up his experience, compose a vision of it as it exists in his mind, and lay *that* before the reader. It is the reflection of an experience; and though there may be all imaginable diversity of treatment within the limits of the reflection, such is its essential character. In a pictorial book the principle of the structure involves a point of view which is not the reader's.

It is open to the pictorial book, however, to use a method in its picture-making that is really no other than the method of drama. It is somebody's experience, we say, that is to be reported, the general effect that many things have left upon a certain mind; it is a fusion of innumerable elements, the deposit of a lapse of time. The straightforward way to render it would be for the narrator—the author or his selected creature—to view the past restrospectively and discourse upon it, to recall and meditate and summarize. That is picture-making in its natural form, using its own method. But exactly as in drama the subject is distributed among the characters and enacted by them, so in picture the effect may be entrusted to the elements, the reactions of the moment, and *performed* by these. The mind of the narrator becomes the stage, his voice is no longer heard. His voice *is* heard so long as there is narrative of any sort, whether he is speaking in person or is reported obliquely; his voice is heard, because in either case the language and the intonation are his, the direct expression of his experience. In the drama of his mind there is no personal voice, for there is no narrator; the point of view becomes the reader's once more. The shapes of thought in the man's mind tell their own story. And that is the art of picture-making when it uses the dramatic method.

But it cannot always do so. Constantly it must be necessary to offer the reader a summary of facts, an impression of a train of events, that can only be given as somebody's narration. Suppose it were required to render the general effect of a certain year in a man's life, a year that has filled his mind with a swarm of many memories. Looking into his consciousness after the year has gone, we might find much there that would indicate the nature of the year's events without any word on his part; the flickers and flashes of thought from moment to moment might indeed tell us much. But we shall need an account from him too, no doubt; too much has happened in a year to be wholly acted, as I call it, in the movement of the man's thought. He must narrate—he must make, that is to say, a picture of the events as he sees them, glancing back. Now if he speaks in the first person there can, of course, be no uncertainty in the point of view; he has his fixed position, he cannot leave it. His description will represent the face that the facts in their sequence turned towards *him;* the field of vision is defined with perfect distinctness, and his story cannot stray outside it. The reader, then, may be said to watch a reflection of the facts in a mirror of which the edge is nowhere in doubt; it is rounded by the bounds of the narrator's own personal experience.

This limitation may have a convenience and a value in the story, it may contribute to the effect. But it need not be forfeited, it is clear, if the first person is changed to the third. The author may use the man's field of vision and keep as faithfully within it as though the man were speaking for himself. In that case he retains this advantage and adds to it another, one that is likely to be very much greater. For now, while the point of view is still fixed in space, still assigned to the man in the book, it is free in *time;* there no longer stretches, between the narrator and the events of which he speaks, a certain tract of time, across which the past must appear in a more or less distant perspective. All the variety obtainable by a shifting relation to the story in time is thus in the author's hand; the safe serenity of a far retrospect, the promising or threatening urgency of the present, every gradation between the two, can be drawn into the whole effect of the book, and all of it without any change of the seeing eye. It is a liberty that may help the story indefinitely, raising this matter into strong relief, throwing that other back into vaguer shade.

And next, still keeping mainly and ostensibly to the same point of view, the author has the chance of using a much greater latitude than he need appear to use. The seeing eye is with somebody in the book, but its vision is reinforced; the picture contains more, becomes richer and fuller, because it is the author's as well as his creature's, both at once. Nobody notices, but in fact there are now two brains behind that eye; and one of them is the author's, who adopts and shares the *position* of his creature, and at the same time supplements his wit. If you analyse the picture that is now presented, you find that it is not all the work of the personage whose vision the author has adopted. There are touches in it that go beyond any sensation of his, and indi-cate that some one else is looking over his shoulder—seeing things from the same angle, but seeing more, bringing another mind to bear upon the scene. It is an easy and natural extension of the personage's power of observation. The impression of the scene may be deepened as much as need be; it is not confined to the scope of one mind, and yet there is no blurring of the focus by a double point of view. And thus what I have called the sound of the narrator's voice (it is impossible to avoid this mixture of metaphors) is less insistent in oblique narration, even while it seems to be following the very same argument that it would in direct, because another voice is speedily mixed and blended with it.

So this is another resource upon which the author may draw according to his need; sometimes it will be indispensable, and generally, I suppose, it will be useful. It means that he keeps a certain hold upon the narrator *as an object;* the sentient character in the story, round whom it is grouped, is not utterly subjective, completely given over to the business of seeing and feeling on behalf of the reader. It is a considerable point; for it helps to meet one of the great difficulties in the story which is carefully aligned towards a single consciousness and consistently so viewed. In that story the man or woman who acts as the vessel of sensation is always in danger of seeming a light, uncertain weight compared with the other people in the book—simply because the other people are objective images, plainly outlined, while the seer in the midst is precluded from that advantage, and must see without being directly seen. He, who doubtless ought to bulk in the story more massively than any one, tends to remain the least recognizable of the company, and even to dissolve in a kind of impalpable blur. By his method (which I am supposing to have been adopted in full strictness) the author is of course forbidden to look this central figure in the face, to describe and discuss him; the light cannot be turned upon him immediately. And very often we see the method becoming an embarrassment to the author in consequence, and the devices by which he tries to mitigate it, and to secure some reflected sight of the seer, may even be tiresomely obvious. But the resource of which I speak is of a finer sort.

It gives to the author the power of imperceptibly edging away from the seer, leaving his consciousness, ceasing to use his eyes—though still without substituting the eyes of another. To revert for a moment to the story told in the first person, it is plain that in that case the narrator has no such liberty; his own consciousness must always lie open; the part that he plays in the story can never appear in the same terms, on the same plane, as that of the other people. Though he is not visible in the story to the reader, as the others are, he is at every moment *nearer* than they, in his capacity of the seeing eye, the channel of vision; nor can he put off his function, he must continue steadily to see and to report. But when the author is reporting *him* there is a margin of freedom. The author has not so completely identified him-self, as narrator, with his hero that he can give him no objective weight whatever. If necessary he can allow him something of the value of a detached and phenomenal personage, like the rest of the company in the story, and that without violating the principle of his method. He cannot make his hero actually visible—there the method is un-compromising; he cannot step forward, leaving the man's point of view, and picture him from without. But he can place the man at the same distance from the reader as the other people, he can almost lend him the same effect, he can make of him a dramatic actor upon the scene.

And how? Merely by closing (when it suits him) the open con-sciousness of the seer—which he can do without any look of awkward-ness or violence, since it conflicts in no way with the rule of the method. That rule only required that the author, having decided to share the point of view of his character, should not proceed to set up another of his own; it did not debar him from allowing his hero's act of vision to lapse, his function as the sentient creature in the story to be intermitted. The hero (I call him so for convenience—he may, of course, be quite a subordinate onlooker in the story) can at any mo-ment become impenetrable, a human being whose thought is sealed from us; and it may seem a small matter, but in fact it has the result that he drops into the plane of the people whom he has hitherto been seeing and judging. Hitherto subjective, communicative in solitude, he has been in a category apart from them; but now he may mingle with the rest, engage in talk with them, and his presence and his talk are no more to the fore than theirs. As soon as some description or discussion of them is required, then, of course, the seer must resume his part and unseal his mind; but meanwhile, though the reader gets no direct view of him, still he is there in the dialogue with the rest, his speech (like theirs) issues from a hidden mind and has the same dramatic value. It is enough, very likely, to harden our image of him, to give precision to his form, to save him from dissipation into that luminous blur of which I spoke just now. For the author it is a resource to be welcomed on that account, and not on that account alone.

For besides the greater definition that the seer acquires, thus de-tached from us at times and relegated to the plane of his companions, there is much benefit for the subject of the story. In the tale that is quite openly and nakedly somebody's narrative there is this inherent weakness, that a scene of true drama is impossible. In true drama nobody *reports* the scene; it *appears,* it is constituted by the aspect of the occasion and the talk and the conduct of the people. When one of the people who took part in it sets out to report the scene, there is at once a mixture and a confusion of effects; for his own contribution to the scene has a different quality from the rest, cannot have the same crispness and freshness, cannot strike in with a new or unexpected note. This weakness may be well disguised, and like everything else in the whole craft it may become a positive and right effect in a particular story, for a particular purpose; it is always there, however, and it means that the full and unmixed effect of drama is denied to the story that is rigidly told from the point of view of one of the actors. But when that point of view is held in the manner I have described, when it is open to the author to withdraw from it silently and to leave the actor to play his part, true drama—or something so like it that it passes for true drama—is always possible; all the figures of the scene are together in it, one no nearer than another. Nothing is wanting save only that direct, unequivocal sight of the hero which the method does indeed absolutely forbid.

Finally there is the old, immemorial, unguarded, unsuspicious way of telling a story, where the author entertains the reader, the minstrel draws his audience round him, the listeners rely upon his word. The voice is then confessedly and alone the author's; he imposes no limitation upon his freedom to tell what he pleases and to regard his matter from a point of view that is solely his own. And if there is anyone who can proceed in this fashion without appearing to lose the least of the advantages of a more cautious style, for him the minstrel's licence is proper and appropriate; there is no more to be said. But we have yet to discover him; and it is not very presumptuous in a critic, as things are, to declare that a story will never yield its best to a writer who takes the easiest way with it. He curtails his privileges and chooses a narrower method, and immediately the story responds; its better condition is too notable to be forgotten, when once it has caught the attention of a reader. The advantages that it gains are not nameless, indefinable graces, pleasing to a critic but impossible to fix in words; they are solid, we can describe and recount them. And I can only conclude that if the novel is still as full of energy as it seems to be, and is not a form of imaginative art that, having seen the best of its day, is preparing to give place to some other, the novelist will not be willing to miss the inexhaustible opportunity that lies in its treatment. The easy way is no way at all; the only way is that by which the most is made of the story to be told, and the most was never made of any story except by a choice and disciplined method.

II

And now for the method by which the picture of a mind is fully dramatized, the method which is to be seen consistently applied in *The Ambassadors* and the other later novels of Henry James. How is the author to withdraw, to stand aside, and to let Strether's thought tell its own story? The thing must be seen from our own point of view and no other. Author and hero, Thackeray and Esmond, Meredith and

Harry Richmond, have given their various accounts of emotional and intellectual adventure; but they might do more, they might bring the facts of the adventure upon the scene and leave them to make their impression. The story passes in an invisible world, the events take place in the man's mind; and we might have to conclude that they lie beyond our reach, and that we cannot attain to them save by the help of the man himself, or of the author who knows all about him. We might have to make the best of an account at second hand, and it would not occur to us, I dare say, that anything more could be forthcoming; we seem to touch the limit of the possibilities of drama in fiction. But it is not the final limit—there is fiction here to prove it; and it is this further stroke of the art that I would now examine.

The world of silent thought is thrown open, and instead of telling the reader what happened there, the novelist uses the look and behaviour of thought as the vehicle by which the story is rendered. Just as the writer of a play embodies his subject in visible action and audible speech, so the novelist, dealing with a situation like Strether's, represents it by means of the movement that flickers over the surface of his mind. The impulses and reactions of his mood are the players upon the new scene. In drama of the theatre a character must bear his part unaided; if he is required to be a desperate man, harbouring thoughts of crime, he cannot look to the author to appear at the side of the stage and inform the audience of the fact; he must express it for himself through his words and deeds, his looks and tones. The playwright so arranges the matter that these will be enough, the spectator will make the right inference. But suppose that instead of a man upon the stage, concealing and betraying his thought, we watch the thought itself, the hidden thing, as it twists to and fro in his brain—watch it without any other aid to understanding but such as its own manner of bearing may supply. The novelist, more free than the playwright, could of course *tell* us, if he chose, what lurks behind this agitated spirit; he could step forward and explain the restless appearance of the man's thought. But if he prefers the dramatic way, admittedly the more effective, there is nothing to prevent him from taking it. The man's thought, in its turn, can be made to reveal its own inwardness.

Let us see how this plan is pursued in *The Ambassadors*. That book is entirely concerned with Strether's experience of his peculiar mission to Europe, and never passes outside the circle of his thought. Strether is despatched, it will be remembered, by a resolute New England widow, whose son is living lightly in Paris instead of attending to business at home. To win the hand of the widow, Strether must succeed in snatching the young man from the siren who is believed to have beguiled him. The mission is undertaken in all good faith, Strether descends upon Paris with a mind properly disposed and resolved. He comes as an ambassador representing principle and duty, to treat with the young man, appeal to him convincingly and bear him off. The task before him may be difficult, but his purpose is simple. Strether has reckoned, however, without his imagination; he had scarcely been aware of possessing one before, but everything grows complicated as it is touched and awakened on the new scene. By degrees and degrees he changes his opinion of the life of freedom; it is most unlike his pre-vision of it, and at last his purpose is actually inverted. He no longer sees a misguided young man to be saved from disaster, he sees an exquisite, bountiful world laid at a young man's feet; and now the only question is whether the young man is capable of meeting and grasping his opportunity. He is incapable, as it turns out; when the story ends he is on the verge of rejecting his freedom and going back to the world of commonplace; Strether's mission has ended success-fully. But in Strether's mind the revolution is complete; there is nothing left for him, no reward and no future. The world of commonplace is no longer *his* world, and he is too late to seize the other; he is old, he has missed the opportunity of youth.

This is a story which must obviously be told from Strether's point of view, in the first place. The change in his purpose is due to a change in his vision, and the long slow process could not be followed unless his vision were shared by the reader. Strether's predicament, that is to say, could not be placed upon the stage; his outward be-haviour, his conduct, his talk, do not express a tithe of it. Only the brain behind his eyes can be aware of the colour of his experience, as it passes through its innumerable gradations; and all understanding of his case depends upon seeing these. The way of the author, there-fore, who takes this subject in hand, is clear enough at the outset. It is a purely pictorial subject, covering Strether's field of vision and bounded by its limits; it consists entirely of an impression received by a certain man. There can accordingly be no thought of rendering him as a figure seen from without; nothing that any one else could discern, looking at him and listening to his conversation, would give the full sense of the eventful life he is leading within. The dramatic method, as we ordinarily understand it, is ruled out at once. Neither as an action set before the reader without interpretation from within, nor yet as an action pictured for the reader by some other onlooker in the book, can this story possibly be told.

Strether's real situation, in fact, is not his open and visible situa-tion, between the lady in New England and the young man in Paris; his grand adventure is not expressed in its incidents. These, as they are devised by the author, are secondary, they are the extension of the moral event that takes place in the breast of the ambassador, his change of mind. That is the very middle of the subject; it is a matter that lies solely between Strether himself and his vision of the free world.

It is a delightful effect of irony, indeed, that he should have accomplished his errand after all, in spite of himself; but the point of the book is not there, the ironic climax only serves to bring out the point more sharply. The reversal of his own idea is underlined and enhanced by the reversal of the young man's idea in the opposite sense; but essentially the subject of the book would be unchanged if the story ended differently, if the young man held to his freedom and refused to go home. Strether would still have passed through the same cycle of unexpected experience; his errand might have failed, but still it would not have been any the more impossible for him to claim his reward, for his part, than it is impossible as things are, with the quest achieved and the young man ready to hasten back to duty of his own accord. And so the subject can only be reached through Strether's consciousness, it is plain; that way alone will command the impression that the scene makes on him. Nothing in the scene has any importance, any value in itself; what Strether sees in it—that is the whole of its meaning.

But though in *The Ambassadors* the point of view is primarily Strether's, and though it *appears* to be his throughout the book, there is in fact an insidious shifting of it, so artfully contrived that the reader may arrive at the end without suspecting the trick. The reader, all unawares, is placed in a better position for an understanding of Strether's history, better than the position of Strether himself. Using his eyes, we see what *he* sees, we are possessed of the material on which his patient thought sets to work; and that is so far well enough, and plainly necessary. All the other people in the book face towards him, and it is that aspect of them, and that only, which is shown to the reader; still more important, the beautiful picture of Paris and springtime, the stir and shimmer of life in the Rue de Rivoli and the gardens of the Tuileries, is Strether's picture, *his* vision, rendered as the time and the place strike upon his senses. All this on which his thought ruminates, the stuff that occupies it, is represented from his point of view. To see it, even for a moment, from some different angle—if, for example, the author interposed with a vision of his own—would patently disturb the right impression. The author does no such thing, it need hardly be said.

When it comes to Strether's treatment of this material, however, when it is time to learn what he makes of it, turning his experience over and over in his mind, then his own point of view no longer serves. How is anybody, even Strether, to *see* the working of his own mind? A mere account of its working, after the fact, has already been barred; we have found that this of necessity is lacking in force, it is statement where we look for demonstration. And so we must see for ourselves, the author must so arrange matters that Strether's thought will all be made intelligible by a direct view of its surface. The immediate flaw or ripple of the moment, and the next and the next, will then take up the tale, like the speakers in a dialogue which gradually unfolds the subject of the play. Below the surface, behind the outer aspect of his mind, we do not penetrate; this is drama, and in drama the spectator must judge by appearances. When Strether's mind is dramatized, nothing is shown but the passing images that anybody might detect, looking down upon a mind grown visible. There is no drawing upon extraneous sources of information; Henry James knows all there is to know of Strether, but he most carefully refrains from using his knowledge. He wishes us to accept nothing from him on authority—only to watch and learn.

For suppose him to begin sharing the knowledge that he alone possesses, as the author and inventor of Strether; suppose that instead of representing only the momentary appearance of Strether's thought he begins to expound its substance: he must at once give us the whole of it, must let us into every secret without delay, or his exposition is plainly misleading. It is assumed that he tells all, if he once begins. And so, too, if the book were cast autobiographically and Strether spoke in person; he could not hold back, he could not heighten the story of his thought with that touch of suspense, waiting to be resolved, which stamps the impression so firmly into the memory of the onlooker. In a tale of murder and mystery there is one man who cannot possibly be the narrator, and that is the murderer himself; for if he admits us into his mind at all he must do so without reserve, thereby betraying the secret that we ought to be guessing at for ourselves. But by this method of *The Ambassadors* the mind of which the reader is made free, Strether's mind, is not given away; there is no need for it to yield up all its secrets at once. The story in it is played out by due degrees, and there may be just as much deliberation, refrainment, suspension, as in a story told scenically upon the stage. All the effect of true drama is thus at the disposal of the author, even when he seems to be describing and picturing the consciousness of one of his characters. He arrives at the point where apparently nothing but a summary and a report should be possible, and even there he is precluded from none of the privileges of a dramatist.

It is necessary to show that in his attitude toward his European errand Strether is slowly turning upon himself and looking in another direction. To announce the fact, with a tabulation of his reasons, would be the historic, retrospective, undramatic way of dealing with the matter. To bring his mind into view at the different moments, one after another, when it is brushed by new experience—to make a little scene of it, without breaking into hidden depths where the change of purpose is proceeding—to multiply these glimpses until the silent change is apparent, though no word has actually been said of it: this is Henry James's way, and though the *method* could scarcely be more devious and roundabout, always refusing the short cut, yet by these very qualities and precautions it finally produces the most direct impression, for the reader has *seen*. That is why the method is adopted. The author has so fashioned his book that his own part in the narration is now unobtrusive to the last degree; he, the author, could not imaginably figure there more discreetly. His part in the effect is no more than that of the playwright, who vanishes and leaves his people to act the story; only instead of men and women talking together, in Strether's case there are innumerable images of thought crowding across the stage, expressing the story in their behaviour.

But there is more in the book, as I suggested just now, than Strether's vision and the play of his mind. In the *scenic* episodes, the colloquies that Strether holds, for example, with his sympathetic friend Maria Gostrey, another turn appears in the author's procedure. Throughout these clear-cut dialogues Strether's point of view still reigns; the only eyes in the matter are still his, there is no sight of the man himself as his companion sees him. Miss Gostrey is clearly visible, and Madame de Vionnet and little Bilham, or whoever it may be; the face of Strether himself is never turned to the reader. On the evening of the first encounter between the elderly ambassador and the young man, they sat together in a café of the boulevards and walked away at midnight through quiet streets; and all through their interview the fact of the young man's appearance is strongly dominant, for it is this that first reveals to Strether how the young man has been transformed by his commerce with the free world; and so his figure is sharply before the reader as they talk. How Strether seemed to Chad—this, too, is represented, but only by implication, through Chad's speech and manner. It is essential, of course, that it should be so, the one-sided vision is strictly enjoined by the method of the whole book. But though the seeing eye is still with Strether, there is a noticeable change in the author's way with him.

In these scenic dialogues, on the whole, we seem to have edged away from Strether's consciousness. He sees, and we with him; but when he *talks* it is almost as though we were outside him and away from him altogether. Not always, indeed; for in many of the scenes he is busily brooding and thinking throughout, and we share his mind while he joins in the talk. But still, on the whole, the author is inclined to leave Strether alone when the scene is set. He talks the matter out with Maria, he sits and talks with Madame de Vionnet, he strolls along the boulevards with Chad, he lounges on a chair in the Champs Elysées with some one else—we know the kind of scene that is set for Strether, know how very few accessories he requires, and know that the scene marks a certain definite climax, wherever it occurs, for all its everyday look. The occasion is important, there is no doubt about that; its importance is in the air. And Strether takes his part in it as though he had almost become what he cannot be, an objective figure for the reader. Evidently he cannot be that, since the centre of vision is still within him; but by an easy sleight of hand the author gives him almost the value of an independent person, a man to whose words we may listen expectantly, a man whose mind is screened from us. Again and again the stroke is accomplished, and indeed there is nothing mysterious about it. Simply it consists in treating the scene as dramatically as possible—keeping it framed in Strether's vision, certainly, but keeping his consciousness out of sight, his thought unexplored. He talks to Maria; and to us, to the reader, his voice seems as much as hers to belong to somebody whom we are *watching*—which is impossible, because our point of view is his.

A small matter, perhaps, but it is interesting as a sign, still another, of the perpetual tendency of the novel to capture the advantages which it appears to forego. *The Ambassadors* is without doubt a book that deals with an entirely nondramatic subject; it is the picture of an *état d'âme*. But just as the chapters that are concerned with Strether's soul are in the key of drama, after the fashion I have described, so too the episode, the occasion, the scene that crowns the impression, is always more dramatic in its method than it apparently has the means to be. Here, for instance, is the central scene of the whole story, the scene in the old Parisian garden, where Strether, finally filled to the brim with the sensation of all the life for which his own opportunity has passed, overflows with his passionate exhortation to little Bilham— warning him, adjuring him not to make *his* mistake, not to let life slide away ungrasped. It is the hour in which Strether touches his crisis, and the first necessity of the chapter is to show the sudden lift and heave of his mood within; the voices and admonitions of the hour, that is to say, must be heard and felt as he hears and feels them himself. The scene, then, will be given as Strether's impression, clearly, and so it is; the old garden and the evening light and the shifting company of people appear as their reflection in his thought. But the scene is *also* a piece of drama, it strikes out of the book with the strong relief of dramatic action; which is evidently an advantage gained, seeing the importance of the hour in the story, but which is an advantage that it could not enjoy, one might have said.

The quality of the scene becomes clear if we imagine the story to be told by Strether himself, narrating in the first person. Of the damage that this would entail for the picture of his brooding mind I have spoken already; but suppose the book to have taken the form of autobiography, and suppose that Strether has brought the story up to this point, where he sits beside little Bilham in Gloriani's garden. He describes the deep and agitating effect of the scene upon him, calling to him of the world he has missed; he tells what he thought and felt; and then, he says, I broke out with the following tirade to little Bilham—

and we have the energetic outburst which Henry James has put into his mouth. But is it not clear how the incident would be weakened, so rendered? That speech, word for word as we have it, would lose its unexpected and dramatic quality, because Strether, arriving at it by narration, could not suddenly spring away from himself and give the impression of the worn, intelligent, clear-sighted man sitting there in the evening sun, strangely moved to unwonted eloquence. His narration must have discounted the effect of his outburst, leading us up to the very edge of it, describing how it arose, explaining where it came from. He would be *subjective,* and committed to remain so all the time.

Henry James, by his method, can secure this effect of drama, even though his Strether is apparently in the position of a narrator throughout. Strether's are the eyes, I said, and they are more so than ever during this hour in the garden; he is the sentient creature in the scene. But the author, who all through the story has been treating Strether's consciousness as a play, as an action proceeding, can at any moment use his talk almost as though the source from which it springs were unknown to us from within. I remember that he himself, in his critical preface to the book, calls attention to the way in which a conversation between Strether and Maria Gostrey, near the beginning, puts the reader in possession of all the past facts of the situation which it is necessary for him to know; a *scene* thus takes the place of that "harking back to make up," as he calls it, which is apt to appear as a lump of narrative shortly after the opening of a story. If Strether were really the narrator, whether in the first person or the third, he could not use his own talk in this manner; he would have to tell us himself about his past. But he has never *told* us his thought, we have looked at it and drawn our inferences; and so there is still some air of dramatic detachment about him, and his talk may seem on occasion to be that of a man whom we know from outside. The advantage is peculiarly felt on that crucial occasion at Gloriani's, where Strether's sudden flare of vehemence, so natural and yet so unlike him, breaks out with force unimpaired. It strikes freshly on the ear, the speech of a man whose inmost perturbations we have indeed inferred from many glimpses of his mind, but still without ever learning the full tale of them from himself.

The Ambassadors, then, is a story which is seen from one man's point of view, and yet a story in which that point of view is itself a matter for the reader to confront and to watch constructively. Everything in the novel is now dramatically rendered, whether it is a page of dialogue or a page of description, because even in the page of description nobody is addressing us, nobody is reporting his impression to the reader. The impression is enacting itself in the endless series of images that play over the outspread expanse of the man's mind and memory. When the story passes from these to the scenes of dialogue—

from the silent drama of Strether's meditation to the spoken drama of the men and women—there is thus no break in the method. The same law rules everywhere—that Strether's changing sense of his situation shall appeal directly to the onlooker, and not by way of any summarizing picture-maker. And yet *as a whole* the book is all pictorial, an indirect impression received through Strether's intervening consciousness, beyond which the story never strays. I conclude that on this paradox the art of dramatizing the picture of somebody's experience touches its limit. There is indeed no further for it to go.

III

What, then, is a dramatic subject? In big chronicles like Thackeray's it is clear that the controlling point of view can only be that of the chronicler himself, or of some one whom he sets up to tell the story on his behalf. The expanse of life which the story covers is far too great to be shown to the reader in a series of purely dramatic scenes. It is absolutely necessary for the author or his spokesman to draw back for a general view of the matter from time to time; and whenever he does so the story becomes *his* impression, summarized and pictured for the reader. In *Esmond* or *The Virginians* or *The Newcomes,* there are tracts and tracts of the story which are bound to remain outside the reader's direct vision; only a limited number of scenes and occasions could possibly be set forth in the form of drama. A large, loose, manifold subject, in short, extensive in time and space, full of crowds and diversions, is a pictorial subject and can be nothing else. However intensely it may be dramatized here and there, on the whole it must be presented as a conspectus, the angle of vision being assigned to the narrator. It is simply a question of amount, of quantity, of the reach of the subject. If it passes a certain point it exceeds the capacity of the straight and dramatic method.

Madame Bovary and *The Ambassadors,* again, are undramatic in their matter, though their reach is comparatively small; for in both of them the emphasis falls upon changes of mind, heart, character, gradually drawn out, not upon any clash or opposition resolved in action. They *might* be treated scenically, no doubt; their authors might conceivably have handled them in terms of pure drama, without any direct display of Emma's secret fancies or Strether's brooding imagination. But in neither case could that method make the most of the subject or bring out all that it has to give. The most expressive, most enlightening part of Strether's story lies in the reverberating theatre of his mind, and as for Emma, the small exterior facts of her story are of very slight account. Both these books, therefore, in their general lines, are pictured impressions, not actions—even though in *Bovary* to some extent, and in *The Ambassadors* almost wholly, the picture is itself dramatized in the fashion I have indicated. That last effect

belongs only to the final method, the treatment of the surface; under-
neath it there is in both the projection of a certain person's point of
view.

But now look at the contrast in *The Awkward Age,* a novel in which
Henry James followed a single method throughout, from top to bottom,
denying himself the help of any other. He chose to treat this story
as pure drama; he never once draws upon the characteristic resource
of the novelist—who is able, as the dramatist is not able, to give a
generalized and foreshortened account of the matter in hand. In *The
Awkward Age* everything is immediate and particular; there is no
insight into anybody's thought, no survey of the scene from a height,
no resumption of the past in retrospect. The whole of the book passes
scenically before the reader, and nothing is offered but the look and
the speech of the characters on a series of chosen occasions. It might
indeed be printed as a play; whatever is not dialogue is simply a kind
of amplified stage-direction, adding to the dialogue the expressive effect which might be given it by good acting. The novelist, using this
method, claims only one advantage over the playwright; it is the advantage of ensuring the very best acting imaginable, a performance in
which every actor is a perfect artist and not the least point is ever
missed. The play is not handed over to the chances of interpretation—
that is the difference; the author creates the manner in which the words
are spoken, as well as the words themselves, and he may keep the
manner at an ideal pitch. Otherwise the novelist completely ties his
hands, submitting to all the restraints of the playwright in order to
secure the compactness and the direct force of true drama.

What is the issue of a certain conjunction of circumstances? The
subject of the book is in the question. First of all we see a highly
sophisticated circle of men and women, who seem so well practised in
the art of living that they could never be taken by surprise. Life
in their hands has been refined to a process in which nothing appears
to have been left to chance. Their intelligence accounts for everything;
they know where they are, they know what they want, and under a
network of discretion which they all sustain they thoroughly understand each other. It is a charmed world, altogether self-contained,
occupying a corner of modern London. It is carefully protected within
and without; and yet oddly enough there is one quite common and
regular contingency for which it is not prepared at all. Its handling of
life proceeds smoothly so long as all the men and women together are
on a level of proficiency, all alike experienced in the art; and they can
guard themselves against intruders from elsewhere. But periodically
it must happen that their young grow up; the daughter of the house
reaches the "awkward age," becomes suddenly too old for the school-
room and joins her elders below. Then comes the difficulty; there is
an interval in which she is still too young for the freedom of her elders'

style, and it looks as though she might disconcert them not a little, sitting there with wide eyes. Do they simply disregard her and continue their game as before? Do they try to adapt their style to her inexperience? Apparently they have no theory of their proper course; the difficulty seems to strike them afresh every time that it recurs. In other such worlds, not of modern London, it is foreseen and provided for; the young woman is married and launched at once, there is no awkward age. But here and now—or rather here and *then,* in the nineteenth century—it makes a real little situation, and this is the subject of Henry James's book.

It is clearly dramatic; it is a clean-cut situation, raising the question of its issue, and by answering the question the subject is treated. What will these people do, how will they circumvent this awkwardness? That is what the book is to show—action essentially, not the picture of a character or a state of mind. Mind and character enter into it, of course, as soon as the situation is particularized; the girl becomes an individual, with her own outlook, her own way of reaching a conclusion, and her point of view must then be understood. But whatever it may be, it does not constitute the situation. That is there in advance, it exists in general, and the girl comes upon the scene, like the rest of the people in the book, to illustrate it. The subject of the book lies in their behaviour; there are no gradual processes of change and development to be watched in their minds, it is their action that is significant. By clever management the author can avoid the necessity of looking inside their motives; these are betrayed by visible and audible signs. The story proceeds in the open, point by point; from one scene to another it shows its curve and resolves the situation. And very ironic and pleasing and unexpected the resolution proves. It takes everybody by surprise; no one notices what is happening till it is over, but it begins to happen from the start. The girl Nanda, supposably a helpless spectator, takes control of the situation and works it out for her elders. She is the intelligent and expert and self-possessed one of them all; they have only to leave everything to her light manipulation, and the awkwardness—which is theirs, not hers—is surmounted. By the time she has displayed all her art the story is at an end; her action has answered the question and provided the issue.

The theme of the book being what it is, an action merely, and an action strictly limited in its scope, it requires no narrator. In a dozen scenes or so the characters may set it forth on their own account, and we have only to look on; nobody need stand by and expound. The situation involves no more than a small company of people, and there is no reason for them to straggle far, in space or time; on the contrary, the compactness of the situation is one of its special marks. Its point is that it belongs to a little organized circle, a well-defined incident in their lives. And since the root of the matter is in their behaviour, in

the manner in which they meet or fail to meet the incident, their behaviour will sufficiently express what is in their minds; it is not as though
the theme of the story lay in some slow revulsion or displacement of
mood, which it would be necessary to understand before its issue in
action could be appreciated. What do they *do?*—that is the immediate
question; what they think and feel is a matter that is entirely implied
in the answer. Obviously that was not at all the case with Strether. The
workings of his imagination spread over far more ground, ramified
infinitely further than anything that he *did;* his action depended upon
his view of things and logically flowed from it, but his action by itself
would give no measure at all of his inner life. With the people of *The
Awkward Age,* on the other hand, their action fully covers their motives
and sentiments—or can be made to do so, by the care of a dexterous
author.

And so the story can be rendered with absolute consistency, on one
method only, if the author chooses. And he does so choose, and *The
Awkward Age* rounds off the argument I have sought to unwind—the
sequence of method and method, each one in turn pushing its way
towards a completer dramatization of the story. Here at any rate is one
book in which a subject capable of acting itself out from beginning
to end is made to do so, one novel in which method becomes as consistent and homogeneous as it ever may in fiction. No other manner of
telling a story can be quite so true to itself. For whereas drama, in this
book, depends not at all upon the author's "word of honour," and
deals entirely with immediate facts, the most undramatic piece of
fiction can hardly for long be consistent in its own line, but must seek
the support of scenic presentation. Has anyone tried to write a novel
in which there should be no dialogue, no immediate scene, nothing at
all but a diffused and purely subjective impression? Such a novel, if
it existed, would be a counterpart to *The Awkward Age.* Just as Henry
James's book never deviates from the straight, square view of the passing event, so the other would be exclusively oblique, general, retrospective, a meditation upon the past, bringing nothing into the foreground,
dramatizing nothing in talk or action.

The visionary fiction of Walter Pater keeps as nearly to a method of
that kind, I suppose, as fiction could. In *Marius* probably, if it is to be
called a novel, the art of drama is renounced as thoroughly as it has
ever occurred to a novelist to dispense with it. I scarcely think that
Marius ever speaks or is spoken to audibly in the whole course of the
book; such at least is the impression that it leaves. The scenes of the
story reach the reader by refraction, as it were, through the medium
of Pater's harmonious murmur. But scenes they must be; not even
Pater at his dreamiest can tell a story without incident particularized
and caught in the act. When Marius takes a journey, visits a philosopher or enters a church, the event stands out of the past and makes

an appeal to the eye, is presented as it takes place; and this is a movement in the direction of drama, even if it goes no further. Pater, musing over the life of his hero, all but lost in the general sentiment of its grace and virtue, is arrested by the definite images of certain hours and occasions; the flow of his rumination is interrupted while he pauses upon these, to make them visible; they must be given a kind of objectivity, some slight relief against the dim background. No story-teller, in short, can use a manner as strictly subjective, as purely personal, as the manner of *The Awkward Age* is the reverse.

But as for this book, it not only ends one argument, it is also a turning-point that begins another. For when we have seen how fiction gradually aspires to the weight and authority of the thing acted, purposely limiting its own discursive freedom, it remains to see how it resumes its freedom when there is good cause for doing so. It is not for nothing that *The Awkward Age* is as lonely as it seems to be in its kind. I have seized upon it as an example of the dramatic method pursued *à outrance,* and it is very convenient for criticism that it happens to be there; the book points a sound moral with clear effect. But when it is time to suggest that even in dealing with a subject entirely dramatic, a novelist may well find reason to keep to his old familiar mixed method—*circumspice:* it would appear that he does so invariably. Where are the other *Awkward Ages,* the many that we might expect if the value of drama is so great? I dare say one might discover a number of small things, short dramatic pieces which would satisfy the requirement; but on the scale of Henry James's book I know of nothing else. Plenty of people find their theme in matters of action, matters of incident, like the story of Nanda; it is strange that they should not sometimes choose to treat it with strict consistency. How is one to assert a principle which is apparently supported by only one book in a thousand thousand?

I think it must be concluded, in the first place, that to treat a subject with the rigour of Henry James is extremely difficult, and that the practice of the thousand thousand is partly to be explained by this fact. Perhaps many of them would be more dramatically inclined if the way were easier. It must always be simpler for a story-teller to use his omniscience, to dive into the minds of his people for an explanation of their acts, than to make them so act that no such explanation is ever needed. Or perhaps the state of criticism may be to blame, with its long indifference to these questions of theory; or perhaps (to say all) there is no very lively interest in them even among novelists. Anyhow we may say from experience that a novel is more likely to fall below its proper dramatic pitch than to strain beyond it; in most of the books around us there is an easy-going reliance on a narrator of some kind, a showman who is behind the scenes of the story and can tell us all about it. He seems to come forward in many a case without doing the story any

particular service; sometimes he actually embarrasses it, when a matter
of vivid drama is violently forced into the form of a narration. One
can only suspect that he then exists for the convenience of the author.
It *is* helpful to be able to say what you like about the characters and
their doings in the book; it may be very troublesome to make their
doings as expressive as they might be, eloquent enough to need no
comment.

Yet to see the issue slowly unfolding and flowering out of the middle
of a situation, and to watch it emerge unaided, with everything that
it has to say said by the very lines and masses of its structure—this is
surely an experience apart, for a novel-reader, with its completeness
and cleanness and its hard, pure edge. It is always memorable, it fills
the mind so acceptably that a story-teller might be ready and eager to
aspire to this effect, one would think, whenever his matter gives him
the chance. Again and again I have wished to silence the voice of the
spokesman who is supposed to be helping me to a right appreciation of
the matter in hand—the author (or his creature) who knows so much,
and who pours out his information over the subject, and who talks
and talks about an issue that might be revealing itself without him.
The spokesman has his way too often, it can hardly be doubted; the
instant authority of drama is neglected. It is the day of the deep-
breathed narrator, striding from volume to volume as tirelessly as the
Scudéries and Calprenèdes of old; and it is true, no doubt, that the
novel (in all languages, too, it would seem) is more than ever inclined
to the big pictorial subject, which requires the voluble chronicler; but
still it must happen occasionally that a novelist prefers a dramatic
motive, and might cast it into a round, sound action and leave it in
that form if he chose. Here again there is plenty of room for enterprise
and experiment in fiction, even now.

But at the same time it must be admitted that there is more in the
general unwillingness of story-tellers to entrust the story to the people
in it—there is more than I have said. If they are much less dramatic
than they might be, still it is not to be asserted that a subject will
often find perfect expression through the uncompromising method of
The Awkward Age. That book itself perhaps suggests, if it does no
more than suggest, that drama cannot always do everything in a novel,
even where the heart of the story seems to lie in its action. The story
of Nanda drops neatly into scenic form—that is obvious; it is well
adapted for treatment as a row of detached episodes or occasions,
through which the subject is slowly developed. But it is a question
whether a story which requires and postulates such a very particular
background, so singular and so artificial, is reasonably denied the
licence to make its background as effective as possible, by whatever
means. Nanda's world is not the kind of society that can be taken for
granted; it is not modernity in general, it is a small and very definite

tract. For the purposes of her story it is important that her setting should be clearly seen and known, and the method of telling her story must evidently take this into account. Nanda and her case are not rendered if the quality of the civilization round her is left in any way doubtful, and it happens to be a very odd quality indeed.

Henry James decided, I suppose, that it was sufficiently implied in the action of his book and needed nothing more; Nanda's little world would be descried behind the scene without any further picturing. He may have been right, so far as *The Awkward Age* is concerned; the behaviour of the people in the story is certainly packed with many meanings, and perhaps it is vivid enough to enact the general character of their lives and ways, as well as their situation in the foreground; perhaps the charmed circle of Mrs. Brookenham and her wonderful crew is given all the effect that is needed. But the question brings me to a clear limitation of drama on the whole, and that is why I raise it. Here is a difficulty to which the dramatic method, in its full severity, is not specially accommodated, one that is not in the line of its strength. To many of the difficulties of fiction, as we have seen, it brings precisely the right instrument; it gives validity, gives direct force to a story, and to do so is its particular property. For placing and establishing a piece of action it is paramount. But where it is not only a matter of placing the action in view, but of relating it to its surroundings, strict drama is at once at a disadvantage. The seeing eye of the author, which can sweep broadly and generalize the sense of what it sees, will meet this difficulty more naturally. Drama reinforcing and intensifying picture we have already seen again and again; and now the process is reversed. From the point of view of the reader, the spectator of the show, the dramatic scene is vivid and compact; but it is narrow, it can have no great depth, and the colour of the atmosphere can hardly tell within the space. It is likely, therefore, that unless this close direct vision is supplemented by a wider survey, fronting the story from a more distant point of view, the background of the action, the manner of life from which it springs, will fail to make its full impression.

It amounts to this, that the play-form—and with it fiction that is purely dramatic in its method—is hampered in its power to express the outlying associations of its scene. It *can* express them, of course; in clever hands it may seem to do so as thoroughly as any descriptive narration. But necessarily it does so with far more expense of effort than the picture-making faculty which lies in the hand of the novelist; and that is in general a good reason why the prudent novelist, with all his tendency to shed his privileges, still clings to this one. It is possible to imagine that a novel might be as bare of all background as a play of Racine; there might be a story in which any hint of continuous life, proceeding behind the action, would simply confuse and distort the right effect. One thinks of the story of the Princesse de Clèves, floating serenely in the void, without a sign of any visible support from a furnished world; and there, no doubt, nothing would be gained by bringing the lucid action to ground and fixing it in its setting. It is a drama of sentiment, needing only to be embodied in characters as far as possible detached from any pictured surroundings, with nothing but the tradition of fine manners that is inherent in their grand names. But wherever the effect of the action depends upon its time and place, a novelist naturally turns to the obvious method if there is no clear reason for refusing it. In *The Awkward Age*, to look back at it once more, it may be that there is such a reason; the beauty of its resolute consistency is of course a value in itself, and it may be great enough to justify a *tour de force*. But a *tour de force* it is, when a novelist seeks to render the general life of his story in the particular action, and in the action alone; for his power to support the drama pictorially is always there, if he likes to make use of it.

TECHNIQUES OF FICTION *
ALLEN TATE

THERE must be many techniques of fiction, but how many? I suppose a great many more than there are techniques of poetry. Why this should be so, if it is, nobody quite knows, and if we knew, I do not know what use the knowledge would have. For the great disadvantage of all literary criticism is its practical ignorance, which in the very nature of its aims must be incurable. Even the aims of criticism are unknown, beyond very short views; for example, in the criticism of the novel, Mr. Percy Lubbock tells us that the secret of the art is the strategy of "point of view"; Mr. E. M. Forster that the novelist must simply give us "life," or the illusion of "bouncing" us through it—which looks like a broader view than Mr. Lubbock's, until we pause to examine it, when it turns out to be worse than narrow, since to look at everything is to see nothing; or again Mr. Edwin Muir holds that "structure" is the key to the novelist's success or failure. There is no need here to explain what these critics mean by "point of view," or "life," or "structure"; but they all mean something useful—in a short view, beyond which (I repeat) critics seem to know little or nothing.

What the novelists know may be another thing altogether, and it is that knowledge which ought to be our deepest concern. You will have to allow me the paradox of presuming to know what the novelists know —or some of them at any rate—while as a critic I profess to know nothing. The presumption might encourage us to predict from the very nature of the critic's ignorance the nature and quality of the knowledge possible to good writers of fiction. The novelist keeps before him constantly the structure and substance of his fiction as a whole, to a degree to which the critic can never apprehend it. For the first cause of critical ignorance is, of course, the limitations of our minds, about which we can do little, work at them as we will. It is the special ignorance by which we, as critics, are limited in the act of reading any extended work of the imagination. The imaginative work must always differ to

* From *On the Limits of Poetry*, by Allen Tate, copyright 1944 by the *Sewanee Review*, copyright 1948 by Allen Tate, by permission of The Swallow Press and William Morrow and Company, Inc. "Techniques of Fiction" was originally presented as a lecture in the Coolidge Auditorium of the Library of Congress under the auspices of the Writers Club, October 25, 1943. It was first printed in the *Sewanee Review*, Spring, 1944, and later included, in its present revised form, in *The Hovering Fly*, by Allen Tate (The Cummington Press, 1948) and *On the Limits of Poetry*, by Allen Tate (The Swallow Press and William Morrow & Co., Inc., 1948).

such a great degree as almost to differ in kind from philosophical works, which our minds apprehend and retain almost as wholes through the logical and deductive structures which powerfully aid the memory. Who can remember, well enough to pronounce upon it critically, all of *War and Peace,* or *The Wings of the Dove,* or even *Death in Venice,* the small enclosed world of which ought at least to do something to aid our memories? I have reread all three of these books in the past year; yet for the life of me I could not pretend to know them as wholes, and without that knowledge I lack the materials of criticism.

Because Mr. Lubbock seems to know more than anybody else about this necessary ignorance of the critic, and for other important reasons, I believe him to be the best critic who has ever written about the novel. His book, *The Craft of Fiction,* is very nearly a model of critical procedure. Even in so fine a study as Albert Thibaudet's *Gustave Flaubert* there is nothing like the actual, as opposed to the merely professed, critical modesty of numerous statements like this by Lubbock: "Our critical faculty may be admirable; we may be thoroughly capable of judging a book justly, if only we could watch it at ease. But fine taste and keen perception are of no use to us if we cannot retain the image of the book; and the image escapes and evades us like a cloud." Where, then, does Lubbock get the material of his criticism? He gets as much of it as any critic ever gets by means of a bias which he constantly pushes in the direction of extreme simplification of the novel in terms of "form," or "point of view" (after James's more famous phrase, the "post of observation"), or more generally in terms of the controlling intelligence which determines the range and quality of the scene and the action. It is the only book on fiction which has earned unanimous dislike among other critics (I do not know three novelists who have read it), and the reason, I think, is that it is, in its limited terms, wholly successful; or, if that is too great praise, it is successful in the same sense, and to no less degree than the famous lecture notes on the Greek drama taken down by an anonymous student at the Lyceum in the fourth century B.C. The lecture notes and *The Craft of Fiction* are studies of their respective arts in terms of form; and I think that Lubbock had incomparably the more difficult job to do. The novel has at no time enjoyed anything like the number and the intensity of objective conventions which the drama, even in its comparatively formless periods, has offered to the critic. The number of techniques possible in the novel are probably as many as its conventions are few.

Having said so much in praise of Mr. Lubbock, I shall not, I hope, seem to take it back if I say that even his intense awareness of what the novelist knows fails somehow, or perhaps inevitably, to get into his criticism. Anybody who has just read his account of *Madame Bovary* comes away with a sense of loss, which is the more intense if he has also just read that novel; though what the loss is he no more than Mr.

Lubbock will be able to say. Yet no critic has ever turned so many different lights, from so many different directions, upon any other novel (except perhaps the lights that are called today the social and the historical); and yet what we get is not properly a revelation of the techniques of *Madame Bovary* but rather what I should call a marvelously astute chart of the operations of the central intelligence which binds all the little pieces of drama together into the pictorial biography of a silly, sad, and hysterical little woman, Emma Bovary. It is this single interest, this undeviating pursuit of one great clue, this sticking to the "short view" till the last horn blows and night settles upon the hunting field, which largely explains both the greatness of Mr. Lubbock's book and the necessary and radical ignorance of criticism. We cannot be both broad and critical, except in so far as knowledge of the world, of ideas, and of man generally is broadening; but then that knowledge has nothing to do specifically with the critical job; it only keeps it from being inhuman. That is something; but it is not criticism. To be critical is to be narrow in the crucial act or process of judgment.

But after we gather up all the short views of good critics, and have set the limits to their various ignorances, we are confronted with what is left out or, if you will, left over: I have a strong suspicion that this residue of the novel or the story is what the author knew as he wrote it. It is what makes the little scenes, or even the big ones, "come off." And while we no doubt learn a great deal about them when, with Mr. Muir, we study the general structure, or the relation of scenes, or, with Mr. Lubbock, follow the godlike control of the mind of Flaubert or of James through all the scenes to the climax—while this knowledge is indispensable, I should, myself, like to know more about the making of the single scene, and all the techniques that contribute to it; and I suspect that I am not asking the impossible, for this kind of knowledge is very likely the only kind that is actually within our range. It alone can be got at, definitely and at particular moments, even after we have failed, with Mr. Lubbock (honorable failure indeed), to "retain the image of the book."

It sounds very simple, as no doubt it is essentially a simple task to take a scene from a novel apart, and to see what makes it tick; but how to do it must baffle our best intentions. Suppose you want to understand by what arts Tolstoy, near the beginning of *War and Peace*, before the ground is laid, brings Peter, the bastard son of old Count Bezuhov, into the old Count's dying presence, and makes, of the atmosphere of the house and of the young man and the old man, both hitherto unknown to us, one of the great scenes of fiction: you would scarcely know better than I where to take hold of it, and I have only the merest clue. Suppose you feel, as I do, that after Rawdon Crawley comes home (I believe from jail—it is hard to remember

Thackeray) and finds Becky supping alone with Lord Steyne—suppose you feel that Thackeray should not have rung down the curtain the very moment Becky's exposure was achieved, but should have faced up to the tougher job of showing us Becky and Rawdon alone after Lord Steyne had departed: Is this a failure in a great novelist? If it is, why? The negative question, addressed to ourselves as persons interested in the techniques of an art, may also lead us to what the novelists know, or to much the same thing, what they should have known. And, to come nearer home, what is the matter with Ty Ty Walden's philosophical meditations, towards the end of *God's Little Acre,* which freezes up our credulity and provokes our fiercest denial? It is surely not that Ty Ty is merely expressing as well as he can the doctrine of the innate goodness of man in the midst of depravity. That doctrine will do as well as any other in the mouth of a fictional character provided his scene and his experience within the scene entitle him to utter it; but before we can believe that Ty Ty is actually thinking anything whatever, we have got in the first place to believe that Ty Ty is a man— which is precisely what Mr. Caldwell evidently did not think it important to make us do.

How shall we learn what to say about particular effects of the story, without which the great over-all structure and movement of the human experience which is the entire novel cannot be made credible to us? The professional critics pause only at intervals to descend to these minor effects which are of course the problems without which the other, more portentous problems which engage criticism could not exist. The fine artists of fiction, I repeat, because they produce these effects must understand them. And having produced them, they are silent about the ways they took to produce them, or paradoxical and mysterious like Flaubert, who told Maupassant to go to the station and look at the cab-drivers until he understood the typical cab-driver, and then to find the language to distinguish one cab-driver from all others in the world. It is the sort of *obiter dicta* which can found schools and movements, and the schools and movements often come to some good, even though the slogan, like this one, means little.

I suppose only the better novelists, like Defoe, Madame de La Fayette, Turgenev, Dickens, Flaubert, many others as great as these, some greater, like Tolstoy and Dostoevsky, knew the special secrets which I am trying, outside criticism, so to speak, to bring before you. There is almost a masonic tradition in the rise of any major art, from its undifferentiated social beginnings to the conscious aptitude which is the sign of a developed art form. Doubtless I ought to repeat once more that for some reason the moment the secrets of this aptitude come within the *provenance* of formal criticism, they vanish. They survive in the works themselves, and in the living confraternity of men of letters, who pass on by personal instruction to their successors the "tricks of the trade." The only man I have known in some twenty years of literary experience who was at once a great novelist and a great teacher, in this special sense, was the late Ford Madox Ford. His influence was immense, even upon writers who did not know him, even upon other writers, today, who have not read him. For it was through him more than any other man writing in English in our time that the great traditions of the novel came down to us. Joyce, a greater writer than Ford, represents by comparison a more restricted practice of the same literary tradition, a tradition that goes back to Stendhal in France, and to Jane Austen in England, coming down to us through Flaubert, James, Conrad, Joyce, Virginia Woolf and Ernest Hemingway.

It is a tradition which has its own secrets to offer; yet in saying that I am not claiming for it greater novelists than some other school can produce or novelists greater than those who just happen. There is Meredith (for those who, like Ramon Fernandez, can read him); there is Thomas Hardy, there is even the early H. G. Wells. But there is not Arnold Bennett; there is not John Galsworthy; not Hugh Walpole nor Frank Swinnerton. This is prejudice, not criticism. And these are all Britons, not Americans. I have no desire to play 'possum on the American question. Yet I am convinced that among American novelists who have had large publics since the last war, only Dreiser, Faulkner, and Hemingway are of major importance. There are "good" popular novelists who have done much to make us at home physically in our own country; they have given us our scenes, our people, and above all our history; and these were necessary to the preliminary knowledge of ourselves which we have been a little late in getting and which must be got and assimilated if we are going to be a mature people. Possibly the American novel had to accomplish the task that in Europe had been done by primitive chronicle, mémoire, ballad, strolling player. The American novel has had to find a new experience, and only in our time has it been able to pause for the difficult task of finding out how to get itself written. That is an old story with us, yet beneath it lies a complexity of feeling that from Hawthorne down to our time has baffled our best understanding. The illustration is infinite in its variety. At this moment I think of my two favorite historians, Herodotus and Joinville, and I am embarrassed from time to time because Herodotus, the pagan, seems nearer to my experience than Joinville, the Christian chronicler of St. Louis. It is perhaps easier for us to feel comfortable with the remote and relatively neutral elements of our culture. Those experiences of Europe which just precede or overlap the American experience bemuse us, and introduce a sort of chemical ambivalence into our judgment. Joinville is both nearer to me than Herodotus, and less immediate. What American could not be brought to confess a similar paradox? To our European friends who are now beginning to know us, and who in all innocence may subscribe to the popular convention of The Simple American Mind, I would say, if it is not too impolite: Beware.

But the American novel is not my present subject, nor, thank heaven, the American mind. My subject is merely the technique of fiction which now at last I feel that I am ready to talk about, not critically, you understand, but as a member of a guild. Ford used to say that he wrote his novels in the tone of one English gentleman whispering into the ear of another English gentleman: how much irony he intended I never knew; I hope a great deal. I intend none at all when I say that these remarks are set down by an artisan for other artisans.

Gustave Flaubert created the modern novel. Gustave Flaubert created the modern short story. He created both because he created modern fiction. I am not prepared to say that he created all our fictional forms and structures, the phases of the art of fiction that interest Mr. Lubbock and Mr. Muir. He did not originate all those features of the short story which interest historians and anthologists. These are other matters altogether. And I do not like to think that Flaubert created modern fiction because I do not like Flaubert. It was the fashion in France, I believe, until the Fall, to put Stendhal above Flaubert. I am not sure but I suspect that a very tired generation felt more at ease with a great writer whose typical heroes are persons of mere energy and whose books achieve whatever clarity and form that they do achieve as an accident of the moral ferocity of the author. But without *Le Rouge et Le Noir,* or without what it put into circulation in French literary *milieu* after 1830, Flaubert could not have written *Madame Bovary.* I do not like to think that Stendhal did this because I do not like Stendhal. Both Stendhal and Flaubert had the single dedication to art which makes the disagreeable man. Doubtless it would be pleasanter if the great literary discoveries could be made by gentlemen like Henry James, who did make his share, and who, of course, was a greater novelist than either of these Frenchmen; or by English squires; but we have got to take them, as Henry James would not do in the instance of Flaubert, as they come, and they often come a little rough.

A moment ago I introduced certain aspersions upon a few English novelists of the recent past, but it was with a purpose, for their limitations, sharply perceived by the late Virginia Woolf in her famous essay *Mr. Bennett and Mrs. Brown,* will make quite clear the difference between the novelist who, with Mr. Forster, merely bounces us along and the novelist who tries to do the whole job, the job that Flaubert first taught him to do. Mrs. Woolf is discussing Hilda Lessways, Arnold Bennett's heroine, and she says:

But we cannot hear her mother's voice, or Hilda's voice; we can only hear Mr. Bennett's voice telling us facts about rents and freeholds and copyholds and fines. What can Mr. Bennett be about? I have formed my own opinion of what Mr. Bennett is about—he is trying to make us imagine for him. . . .

"Trying to make us imagine for him"—the phrase erects a Chinese wall between all that is easy, pleasant, and perhaps merely socially useful in modern fiction, and all that is rigorous, sober, and self-contained. Mrs. Woolf, again, in speaking of the novels of Galsworthy, Bennett and Wells, says: "Yet what odd books they are! Sometimes I wonder if we are right to call them books at all. For they leave one with a strange feeling of incompleteness and dissatisfaction. In order to complete them it seems necessary to do something—to join a society, or, more desperately, to write a cheque."

That is very nearly the whole story: the novelist who tries to make us imagine for him is perhaps trying to make us write a check—a very good thing to do, and I am not sure that even the socially unconscious Flaubert was deeply opposed to it, though I shall not attempt to speak for him on the question of joining societies. Let us see this matter as reasonably as we can. All literature has a social or moral or religious purpose: the writer has something that he has got to say to the largest public possible. In spite of Flaubert's belief that he wrote only for himself, this is as true of *Madame Bovary* as of *Uncle Tom's Cabin.* Is there a real difference between these books that might justify us in setting apart two orders of literature? Perhaps; for the difference is very great between getting it all inside the book and leaving some of it irresponsibly outside. For even though the check be written in a good cause it is the result of an irresponsible demand upon the part of the novelist. But the distinction is not, I think, absolute, nor should it be. And I am sure that Sainte-Beuve was right when he wrote in his review of *Madame Bovary* that not all young married women in Normandy were like Emma: was there not the case of the childless young matron of central France who, instead of taking lovers and then taking arsenic, "adopted children about her . . . and instructed them in moral culture"? Very good; for it is obvious that persons who join societies and write checks for moral culture are proper characters of fiction, as indeed all human beings of all degrees of charity or misanthropy are. But that is not the point at issue.

That point is quite simply that Flaubert, for the first time consciously and systematically, but not for the first time in the history of fiction, and not certainly of poetry—Flaubert taught us how to put this overworked and allegorical check *into* the novel, into its complex texture of scene, character and action: which, of course, is one way of saying that he did the complete imaginative job himself, and did not merely point to what was going on, leaving the imaginative specification to our good will or to our intellectual vanity. (I pause here to remark the existence of a perpetual type of critic who prefers inferior literature, because it permits him to complete it. Flaubert understood the critics who, committed to the public function of teacher, resent being taught.) This completeness of presentation in the art of fiction was not, I repeat, something new, but I gather that it had previously appeared only here and there, by the sheer accident of genius: I think of Petronius; a few incidents in Boccaccio; half a dozen scenes by the Duke of Saint-Simon (the memorialists shade imperceptibly into the novelists); the great scene in which the Prince de Clèves tells his wife that he has refrained from expressing his love for her because he wished to avoid conduct improper to a husband; Emma Woodhouse with Mr. Knightley at the parlor table looking at the picture-album; countless other moments in early prose literature; but most of all that great forerunner, *Moll Flanders,* which is so much all of a piece in the Flaubertian canon that sometimes I think that Flaubert wrote it; or that nobody wrote either Defoe or Flaubert. For when literature reaches this stage of maturity, it is anonymous, and it matters little who writes it.

This is extravagant language. Or is it? It is no more than we are accustomed to when we talk about poetry, or music, or most of all the classical drama. The fourth-century lecture notes, to which I have already referred, sometime ago licensed the most pretentious claims for the stage, and for poetry generally. I am only saying that fiction can be, has been, and *is* an art, as the various poetries are arts. Is this an extravagant claim? Only, I am convinced, in the minds of the more relaxed practitioners of this art, who excuse something less than the utmost talent and effort, and in the minds of critics who find the critical task more exacting than historical reporting, which reduces the novel to a news supplement. Was, as a matter of fact, Emma typical of young Norman womanhood? Are the Okies and Arkies just as Steinbeck represents them? What a triumph for the historians when it was found that there had actually been a young man whose end was like Julien Sorel's! And is it true what Mr. Faulkner says about Dixie? If it is, is what Mr. Stark Young says also true? This, I submit, is the temper of American criticism of fiction, with rare exceptions of little influence.

It is time now, towards the end of this *causerie,* to produce an image, an *exemplum,* something out of the art of fiction that underlies all the major problems of "picture and drama," symmetry, foreshortening, narrative pattern, pace and language—all those complexities of the novelist's art which Henry James, alone of the great fictionists, tried to explain (how much he coyly evaded!) in his famous Prefaces: problems that laid the ground for Mr. Lubbock's beautiful study. I am looking for something very simple and, in its direct impact, conclu-

sive; a scene or an incident that achieves fullness of realization
in terms of what it gives us to see and to hear. It must offer us
fullness of rendition, not mere direction or statement. Don't state, says
James, time and again—render! Don't tell us what is happening, let
it happen! So I would translate James. For our purposes here it cannot
be too great a scene, if we would see all round it: it must be a scene
that will give us the most elementary instruction in that branch of the
art of which the critics tell us little. What shall it be? Shall it be
Prince André lying wounded under the wide heavens? Shall it be Moll
Flanders peeping out of the upstairs window of the inn at her vanishing fourth (or is it fifth?) and undivorced husband, slyly avoiding him
because she is in the room with her fifth or is it sixth? I could find
perfect *exempla* in James himself. What could be better than Milly
Theale's last soirée before she becomes too ill to appear again? Then
there are James's fine "sitting-room scenes," the man and the woman
talking out the destiny of one or both of them: Lambert Strether and
Maria Gostrey, John Marcher and May Bartram, Merton Densher and
Milly Theale. Or there is Strether looking down upon the boat in
which Chad Newsome and Madame de Vionnet, unaware of Strether's
scrutiny, betray that air of intimacy which discloses them for the first
time to Strether as lovers.

Yet about these excellent scenes there is something outside our purpose, a clue that would sidetrack us into the terms of form and structure which I have virtually promised to neglect. Let us select an
easy and perhaps even quite vulgar scene, a stock scene, in fact, that
we should expect to find in a common romantic novel, or even in a
Gothic story provided the setting were reduced to the bourgeois scale.
Let the situation be something like this: A pretty young married
woman, bored with her husband, a small-town doctor, has had an affair
of sentiment with a young man, who has by this time left town. Growing more desperate, she permits herself to be seduced by a neighboring
landowner, a coarse Lothario, who soon tires of her. Our scene opens
with the receipt of his letter of desertion. He is going away and will
not see her again. The young woman receives the letter with agitation
and runs upstairs to the attic, where having read the letter she gives
way to hysteria. She looks out the window down into the street, and
decides to jump and end it all. But she grows dizzy and recoils. After
a moment she hears her husband's voice; the servant touches her arm;
she comes to and recovers.

It is distinctly unpromising: James would not have touched it;
Balzac, going the whole hog, might have let her jump, or perhaps left
her poised for the jump while he resumed the adventures of Vautrin.
But in any case there she stands, and as I have reported the scene you
have got to take my word for it that she is there at all: you do not see
her, you do not hear the rapid breathing and the beating heart, and

you have, again, only my word for it that she is dizzy. What I have done here, in fact, is precisely what Mrs. Woolf accused the Georgian novelists of doing: I am trying to make you imagine for me, perhaps even covertly trying to make you write a check for the Society for the Improvement of Provincial Culture, or the Society for the Relief of Small Town Boredom, or for a subscription to the Book of the Month Club which would no doubt keep the young woman at improving her mind, and her mind off undesirable lovers. I hope that we shall do all these good things. But you must bear in mind that the Book of the Month Club would probably send her the kind of literature that I have just written for you, so that she too might take to writing checks. Is there any guarantee that they would be good checks? The question brings us up short against certain permanent disabilities of human nature, which we should do well to see as objectively as possible, in the language of a greater artist; which is just what we shall now proceed to do:

> Charles was there; she saw him; he spoke to her; she heard nothing, and she went on quickly up the stairs, breathless, distraught, dumb, and ever holding this horrible piece of paper, that crackled between her fingers like a plate of sheet-iron. On the second floor she stopped before the attic-door, that was closed.
> Then she tried to calm herself; she recalled the letter; she must finish it; she did not dare to. And where? How? She would be seen! "Ah, no! here," she thought, "I shall be all right."
> Emma pushed open the door and went in.
> The slates threw straight down a heavy heat that gripped her temples, stifled her; she dragged herself to the closed garret-window. She drew back the bolt, and the dazzling light burst in with a leap.
> Opposite, beyond the roofs, stretched the open country till it was lost to sight. Down below, underneath her, the village square was empty; the stones of the pavement glittered, the weathercocks on the houses were motionless. At the corner of the street, from a lower story, rose a kind of humming with strident modulations. It was Binet turning.
> She leant against the embrasure of the window, and reread the letter with angry sneers. But the more she fixed her attention upon it, the more confused were her ideas. She saw him again, heard him, encircled him with her arms, and the throbs of her heart, that beat against her breast like blows of a sledge-hammer, grew faster and faster, with uneven intervals. She looked about her with the wish that the earth might crumble into pieces. Why not end it all? What restrained her? She was free. She advanced, looked at the paving-stones, saying to herself, "Come! Come!"
> The luminous ray that came straight up from below drew the weight of her body towards the abyss. It seemed to her that the floor dipped on end like a tossing boat. She was right at the edge, almost hanging, surrounded by vast space. The blue of the heavens suffused her, the air was whirling in her hollow head; she had but to yield, to let herself be

taken; and the humming of the lathe never ceased, like an angry voice calling her.

"Emma! Emma!" cried Charles.

She stopped.

"Wherever are you? Come!"

The thought that she had just escaped from death made her faint with terror. She closed her eyes; then she shivered at the touch of a hand on her sleeve; it was Félicité.

"Master is waiting for you, madame; the soup is on the table."

And she had to go down to sit at table.

The English translation is not good; its failure to convey the very slight elevation of tone is a fundamental failure. It is not a rhetorical elevation, but rather one of perfect formality and sobriety. We are not looking at this scene through Emma's eyes. We occupy a position slightly above and to one side, where we see her against the full setting; yet observe that at the same time we see nothing that she does not see, hear nothing that she does not hear. It is one of the amazing paradoxes of the modern novel, whose great subject is a man alone in society or even against society, almost never with society, that out of this view of man isolated we see developed to the highest possible point of virtuosity and power a technique of putting man wholly into his physical setting. The action is not stated from the point of view of the author; it is rendered in terms of situation and scene. To have made this the viable property of the art of fiction was to have virtually made the art of fiction. And that, I think, is our debt to Flaubert.

But we should linger over this scene if only to try our hands at what I shall now, for the first time, call sub-criticism, or the animal tact which permits us occasionally to see connections and correspondences which our rational powers, unaided, cannot detect. What capital feature of the scene seems (if it does) to render the actuality more than any other? The great fact, I think, is the actuality, and your sense of it is all that is necessary. Yet I like to linger over the whirring lathe of old Binet, a lay figure or "flat character" who has done little in the novel and will never do much, and whose lathe we merely noted from the beginning as a common feature of a small town like Yonville. I should like to know when Flaubert gave him the lathe, whether just to tag him for us; whether writing the present scene, he went back and gave it to him as a "plant" for use here later; or whether, having given him the lathe, he decided it would be useful in this scene.

What is its use? James said that the work of fiction must be "a direct impression of life," a very general requirement; but in the perspective of nearly ninety years since the publication of *Madame Bovary* and the rise of the Impressionist novel through Henry James, James Joyce, and Virginia Woolf, the phrase takes on a more specific sense. Mind you the phrase is not "direct representation," which only the stage can give us. But here, using this mechanic's tool, Flaubert gives us a direct *impression* of Emma's sensation at a particular moment (which not even the drama could accomplish), and thus by rendering audible to us what Emma alone could hear he charged the entire scene with actuality. As Emma goes to the window she merely notes that Binet's lathe is turning—*C'était Binet qui tournait*. Then she looks down at the street which seems to rise towards her—*Allons! Allons!* she whispers, because she cannot find the will to jump. We have had rendered to us visually the shock of violent suicide. Now comes the subtle fusion of the reaction and of the pull toward self-destruction, which is the humming in her head: how can Flaubert *render* it for us? Shall we not have to take his word for it? Shall we not have to imagine for him? No: *l'air circulait dans sa tête creuse,* he says; and then: *le ronflement du tour ne discontinuait pas, comme une voix furieuse qui l'appelait*—"the whirring of the lathe never stopped, like a voice of fury calling her." The humming vertigo that draws the street towards her is rendered audible to us by the correlative sound of the lathe.*

That is all, or nearly all, there is to it; but I think it is enough to set up our image, our *exemplum.* I leave to you, as I constantly reserve for myself, the inexhaustible pleasure of tracing out the infinite strands of interconnection in this and other novels, complexities as deep as life itself but ordered, fixed, and dramatized into arrested action. If I have made too much of Flaubert, or too much of too little of Flaubert, I can only say that I have not willfully ignored men as great, or greater. It is proper to honor France, and to honor the *trouvère,* the discoverer; for it has been through Flaubert that the novel has at last caught up with poetry.

---

* The principle of correlative action is, of course, common to all fiction of the first order, although one supposes it to be most common—in the sense that Allen Tate speaks of it here—to the so-called impressionistic fiction which, in our day, stems from Flaubert. Ernest Hemingway, perhaps because his dramatic sense is so closely related to his tactile, is exceptionally skillful in using it. In *The Sun Also Rises* the death of the gored Spaniard serves as a correlative in action to the spiritual murder of Robert Cohn, just as the savage frenzy of the entire Pamplona celebration serves to dramatize the feeling of nightmare unreality which takes possession of all the characters as Cohn's bad behavior begins to destroy the code which has previously held them together. In *A Farewell to Arms* Frederick Henry's loss of code finds a dramatic correlative, first, in the Isonzo bombardment when he is wounded and feels his soul leave his body, and, second, in the retreat from Caporetto when his sense of nightmare is equated with the madness of the convoy movement through the mud and rain.

A great many of the essays in this book are concerned with the problem of dramatic correlation, although most of them have to do with the writer's struggle to find dramatic means to express his own emotion rather than with his struggle to find parallels in the action of scene or setting for the unknowable emotions of his characters. (See particularly the essays by Joseph Frank, Irene Hendry, Robert W. Stallman, Francis Fergusson, Arthur Mizener, Lionel Trilling on Anderson, and John Peale Bishop.)

SPATIAL FORM IN THE MODERN NOVEL *

Joseph Frank

For a study of esthetic form in the modern novel, Flaubert's famous county-fair scene in *Madame Bovary* is a convenient point of departure. This scene has been justly praised for its mordant caricature of bourgeois pomposity, its portrayal—unusually sympathetic for Flaubert—of the bewildered old servant, and its burlesque of the pseudo-romantic rhetoric by which Rodolphe woos the sentimental Emma. At present, it is enough to notice the method by which Flaubert handles the scene—a method we might as well call cinematographic, since this analogy comes immediately to mind. As Flaubert sets the scene, there is action going on simultaneously at three levels, and the physical position of each level is a fair index to its spiritual significance. On the lowest plane, there is the surging, jostling mob in the street, mingling with the livestock brought to the exhibition; raised slightly above the street by a platform are the speech-making officials, bombastically reeling off platitudes to the attentive multitudes; and on the highest level of all, from a window overlooking the spectacle, Rodolphe and Emma are watching the proceedings and carrying on their amorous conversation, in phrases as stilted as those regaling the crowds. Albert Thibaudet has compared this scene to the medieval mystery play, in which various related actions occur simultaneously on different stage levels; but this acute comparison refers to Flaubert's intention rather than to his method. "Everything should sound simultaneously," Flaubert later wrote, in commenting on this scene; "one should hear the bellowing of the cattle, the whisperings of the lovers and the rhetoric of the officials all at the same time." [1]

But since language proceeds in time, it is impossible to approach this simultaneity of perception except by breaking up temporal sequence. And this is exactly what Flaubert does: he dissolves sequence by cutting back and forth between the various levels of action in a

---

* "Spatial Form in the Modern Novel" (Editor's title) originally appeared as Sections 2 and 3 of "Spatial Form in Modern Literature," by Joseph Frank, which was printed in three parts in the *Sewanee Review*, Spring, Summer, and Autumn, 1945. It is used here by permission of the author and the magazine editors.

[1] This discussion of the county-fair scene owes a good deal to Albert Thibaudet's *Gustave Flaubert*, probably the best critical study yet written on the subject. The quotation from Flaubert's letter is used by Thibaudet and has been translated from his book.

slowly-rising crescendo until—at the climax of the scene—Rodolphe's Chateaubriandesque phrases are read at almost the same moment as the names of prize winners for raising the best pigs. Flaubert takes care to underline this satiric similarity by description, as well as by juxtaposition, as if he were afraid the reflexive relations of the two actions would not be grasped: "From magnetism, by slow degrees, Rodolphe had arrived at affinities, and while M. le Président was citing Cincinnatus at his plow, Diocletian planting his cabbages and the emperors of China ushering in the new year with sowing-festivals, the young man was explaining to the young woman that these irresistible attractions sprang from some anterior existence."

This scene illustrates, on a small scale, what we mean by the spatialization of form in a novel. For the duration of the scene, at least, the time-flow of the narrative is halted: attention is fixed on the interplay of relationships within the limited time-area. These relationships are juxtaposed independently of the progress of the narrative; and the full significance of the scene is given only by the reflexive relations among the units of meaning. In Flaubert's scene, however, the unit of meaning is not, as in modern poetry, a word-group or a fragment of an anecdote, but the totality of each level of action taken as an integer: the unit is so large that the scene can be read with an illusion of complete understanding, yet with a total unawareness of the "dialectic of platitude" (Thibaudet) interweaving all levels, and finally linking them together with devastating irony. In other words, the struggle towards spatial form in Pound and Eliot resulted in the disappearance of coherent sequence after a few lines; but the novel, with its larger unit of meaning, can preserve coherent sequence within the unit of meaning and break up only the time-flow of narrative. (Because of this difference, readers of modern poetry are practically forced to read reflexively to get any literal sense, while readers of a novel like *Nightwood,* for example, are led to expect narrative sequence by the deceptive normality of language sequence within the unit of meaning.) But this does not affect the parallel between esthetic form in modern poetry and the form of Flaubert's scene: both can be properly understood only when their units of meaning are apprehended reflexively, in an instant of time.

Flaubert's scene, although interesting in itself, is of minor importance to his novel as a whole, and is skillfully blended back into the main narrative structure after fulfilling its satiric function. But Flaubert's method was taken over by James Joyce, and applied on a gigantic scale in the composition of *Ulysses.* Joyce composed his novel of an infinite number of references and cross-references which relate to one another independently of the time-sequence of the narrative; and, before the book fits together into any meaningful pattern, these references must be connected by the reader and viewed as a whole.

Ultimately, if we are to believe Stuart Gilbert, these systems of reference form a complete picture of practically everything under the sun, from the stages of man's life and the organs of the human body to the colors of the spectrum; but these structures are far more important for Joyce, as Harry Levin has remarked, than they could ever possibly be for the reader. Students of Joyce, fascinated by his erudition, have usually applied themselves to exegesis. Unfortunately, such considerations have little to do with the perceptual form of Joyce's novel.

Joyce's most obvious intention in *Ulysses* is to give the reader a picture of Dublin seen as a whole—to re-create the sights and sounds, the people and places, of a typical Dublin day, much as Flaubert had re-created his provincial county fair. And, like Flaubert, Joyce wanted his depiction to have the same unified impact, the same sense of simultaneous activity occurring in different places. Joyce, as a matter of fact, frequently makes use of the same method as Flaubert—cutting back and forth between different actions occurring at the same time—and usually does so to obtain the same ironic effect. But Joyce had the problem of creating this impression of simultaneity for the life of a whole teeming city, and of maintaining it—or rather of strengthening it—through hundreds of pages that must be read as a sequence. To meet this problem, Joyce was forced to go far beyond what Flaubert had done; while Flaubert had maintained a clear-cut narrative line, except in the county-fair scene, Joyce breaks up his narrative and transforms the very structure of his novel into an instrument of his esthetic intention.

Joyce conceived *Ulysses* as a modern epic; and in the epic, as Stephen Dedalus tells us in *A Portrait of the Artist as a Young Man,* "the personality of the artist, at first sight a cry or a cadence and then a fluid and lambent narrative, finally refines itself out of existence, impersonalizes itself, so to speak . . . the artist, like the God of creation, remains within or beyond or above his handiwork, invisible, refined out of existence, indifferent, paring his fingernails." * The epic is thus synonymous for Joyce with the complete self-effacement of the author; and, with his usual uncompromising rigor, Joyce carries this implication further than anyone had dared before. He assumes—what is obviously not true—that his readers are Dubliners, intimately acquainted with Dublin life and the personal history of his characters. This allows him to refrain from giving any direct information about his char-

---

* In the passage referred to, Stephen is speaking, not of the epic, but of the dramatic form. In the epic form "the personality of the artist passes into the narration itself, flowing round and round the persons and the action like a vital sea." Mr. Frank is right in saying that "Joyce conceived *Ulysses* as a modern epic," incorrect in saying that the stage of ultimate impersonalization is the epic stage. It is actually much more rewarding to consider *Ulysses* as an example of the epic as Stephen defines it, and *Finnegans Wake* as an example of the form in which the artist is "refined out of existence."

acters: such information would immediately have betrayed the presence of an omniscient author. What Joyce does, instead, is to present the elements of his narrative—the relations between Stephen and his family, between Bloom and his wife, between Stephen and Bloom and the Dedalus family—in fragments, as they are thrown out unexplained in the course of casual conversation, or as they lie embedded in the various strata of symbolic reference; and the same is true of all the allusions to Dublin life, history, and the external events of the twenty-four hours during which the novel takes place. In other words, all the factual background—so conveniently summarized for the reader in an ordinary novel—must be reconstructed from fragments, sometimes hundreds of pages apart, scattered through the book. As a result, the reader is forced to read *Ulysses* in exactly the same manner as he reads modern poetry—continually fitting fragments together and keeping allusions in mind until, by reflexive reference, he can link them to their complements.

Joyce intended, in this way, to build up in the reader's mind a sense of Dublin as a totality, including all the relations of the characters to one another and all the events which enter their consciousness. As the reader progresses through the novel, connecting allusions and references spatially, gradually becoming aware of the pattern of relationships, this sense was to be imperceptibly acquired; and, at the conclusion of the novel, it might almost be said that Joyce literally wanted the reader to become a Dubliner. For this is what Joyce demands: that the reader have at hand the same instinctive knowledge of Dublin life, the same sense of Dublin as a huge, surrounding organism, which the Dubliner possesses as a birthright. It is such knowledge which, at any one moment of time, gives him a knowledge of Dublin's past and present as a whole; and it is only such knowledge which might enable the reader, like the characters, to place all the references in their proper context. This, it should be realized is practically the equivalent of saying that Joyce cannot be read—he can only be re-read. A knowledge of the whole is essential to an understanding of any part; but, unless one is a Dubliner, such knowledge can be obtained only after the book has been read, when all the references are fitted into their proper place and grasped as a unity. Although the burdens placed on the reader by this method of composition may seem insuperable, the fact remains that Joyce, in his unbelievably laborious fragmentation of narrative structure, proceeded on the assumption that a unified spatial apprehension of his work would ultimately be possible.

In a far more subtle manner than with Joyce and Flaubert, the same principle of composition is at work in Marcel Proust. Since Proust himself tells us that, before all else, his novel will have imprinted on it "a form which usually remains invisible, the form of

Time," it may seem strange to speak of Proust in connection with spatial form. He has, almost invariably, been considered the novelist of time *par excellence:* the literary interpreter of that Bergsonian "real time" intuited by the sensibility, as distinguished from the abstract, chronological time of the conceptual intelligence. To stop at this point, however, is to miss what Proust himself considered the deepest significance of his work. Obsessed with the ineluctability of time, Proust was suddenly visited by certain quasi-mystical experiences—described in detail in the last volume of his work, "Le temps retrouvé"—which, by providing him with a spiritual technique for transcending time, enabled him to escape what he considered to be time's domination. By writing a novel, by translating the transcendent, extra-temporal quality of these experiences to the level of esthetic form, Proust hoped to reveal their nature to the world—for they seemed to him a clue to the ultimate secrets of reality. And not only should the world learn about these experiences indirectly, by reading a descriptive account of them, but, through his novel, it would feel their impact on the sensibility as Proust himself had felt it.

To define the method by which this is accomplished, one must first understand clearly the precise nature of the Proustian revelation. Each such experience, Proust tells us, is marked by a feeling that "the permanent essence of things, usually concealed, is set free and our true self, which had long seemed dead but was not dead in other ways, awakes, takes on fresh life as it receives the celestial nourishment brought to it." This celestial nourishment consists of some sound, or odor, or other sensory stimulus, "sensed anew, simultaneously in the present and the past." But why should these moments seem so overwhelmingly valuable that Proust calls them celestial? Because, Proust observes, his imagination could only operate on the past; and the material presented to his imagination, therefore, lacked any sensuous immediacy. But, at certain moments, the physical sensations of the past came flooding back to fuse with the present; and, in these moments, Proust believed that he grasped a reality "real without being of the present moment, ideal but not abstract." Only in these moments did he attain his most cherished ambition—"to seize, isolate, immobilize for the duration of a lightning flash" what otherwise he could not apprehend, "namely: a fragment of time in its pure state." For a person experiencing this moment, Proust adds, the word "death" no longer has meaning. "Situated outside the scope of time, what could he fear from the future?"

The significance of this experience, though obscurely hinted at throughout the book, is made explicit only in the concluding pages which describe the final appearance of the narrator at the reception of the Princesse de Guermantes. The narrator decides to dedicate the remainder of his life to re-creating these experiences in a work of art;

and this work will differ essentially from all others because, at its
foundation, will be a vision of reality that has been refracted through
an extra-temporal perspective. Viewing Proust as the last and most
debilitated of a long line of neurasthenic esthetes, many critics have
found in his decision to create a work of art merely the final step in
his flight from the burdens of reality. Edmund Wilson, ordinarily so
discerning, links up this view with Proust's ambition to conquer time,
assuming that Proust hoped to oppose time by establishing something
—a work of art—impervious to its flux; but this somewhat ingenuous
interpretation scarcely does justice to Proust's own conviction, expressed with special intensity in the last volume of his work, that he
was fulfilling a prophetic mission. It was not the work of art *qua*
work of art that Proust cared about—his contempt for the horde of
faddish scribblers was unbounded—but a work of art which should
stand as a monument to his personal conquest of time. This his own
work could do not simply because it was a work of art, but because
it was at once the vehicle through which he conveyed his vision and
the concrete substance of that vision shaped by a method which compels
the reader to re-experience its exact effect.

The prototype of this method, like the analysis of the revelatory
moment, occurs during the reception of the Princesse de Guermantes.
After spending years in a sanatorium, losing touch almost completely
with the fashionable world of the earlier volumes, the narrator comes
out of seclusion to attend the reception. He finds himself bewildered
by the changes in social position, and the even more striking changes
in character and personality among his former friends. According to
some socially-minded critics, Proust intended to paint here the invasion
of French aristocratic society by the upper bourgeoisie, and the gradual
breakdown of all social and moral standards caused by the first World
War. No doubt this process is incidentally described at some length;
but, as the narrator takes great pains to tell us, it is far from being
the most important meaning of the scene. What strikes the narrator,
almost with the force of a blow, is this: in trying to recognize old
friends under the masks which, as he feels, the years have welded to
them, he is jolted for the first time into a consciousness of the passage
of time. When a young man addresses the narrator respectfully, instead of familiarly as if he were an elderly gentleman, the narrator
realizes suddenly that he has become an elderly gentleman; but for
him the passage of time had gone unperceived up until that moment.
To become conscious of time, the narrator begins to understand, it
had first been necessary to remove himself from his accustomed environment—or, what amounts to the same thing, from the stream of
time acting on that environment—and then to plunge back into the
stream after a lapse of years. In so doing, the narrator found himself
presented with two images—the world as he had formerly known it,

and the world, transformed by time, that he now saw before him; and when these two images are juxtaposed, the narrator discovers, the passage of time is suddenly experienced through its visible effects. Habit, that universal soporific, ordinarily conceals the passage of time from those who have gone their accustomed ways: at any one moment of time the changes are so minute as to be imperceptible. "Other people," Proust writes, "never cease to change places in relation to ourselves. In the imperceptible but eternal march of the world, we regard them as motionless in a moment of vision, too short for us to perceive the motion that is sweeping them on. But we have only to select in our memory two pictures taken of them at different moments, close enough together however for them not to have altered in themselves—perceptibly, that is to say—and the difference between the two pictures is a measure of the displacement that they have undergone in relation to us." By comparing these two images in a moment of time, the passage of time can be experienced concretely, in the impact of its visible effects on the sensibility, rather than as a mere gap counted off in numbers. And this discovery provides the narrator with a method which, in T. S. Eliot's phrase, is an "objective correlative" to the visionary apprehension of the fragment of "pure time" intuited in the revelatory moment.

When the narrator discovers this method of communicating his experience of the revelatory moment, he decides, as we have already said, to incorporate it in a novel. But the novel the narrator decides to write has just been finished by the reader; and its form is controlled by the method that the narrator has outlined in its concluding pages. The reader, in other words, is substituted for the narrator, and is placed by the author throughout the book in the same position as the narrator occupies before his own experience at the reception of the Princesse de Guermantes. This is done by the discontinuous presentation of character—a simple device which, nevertheless, is the clue to the form of Proust's vast structure. Every reader soon notices that Proust does not follow any of his characters through the whole course of his novel: they appear and re-appear, in various stages of their lives, but hundreds of pages sometimes go by between the time they are last seen and the time they re-appear; and when they do turn up again, the passage of time has invariably changed them in some decisive way. Instead of being submerged in the stream of time—which, for Proust, would be the equivalent of presenting a character progressively, in a continuous line of development—the reader is confronted with various snapshots of the characters "motionless in a moment of vision," taken at different stages in their lives; and the reader, in juxtaposing these images, experiences the effects of the passage of time exactly as the narrator had done.* As he had promised,

* See Tolstoy's *War and Peace* for a similar use of this device.

therefore, Proust does stamp his novel indelibly with the form of time; but we are now in a position to understand exactly what he meant by the promise.

To experience the passage of time, Proust learned, it was necessary to rise above it, and to grasp both past and present simultaneously in a moment of what he called "pure time." But "pure time," obviously, is not time at all—it is perception in a moment of time, that is to say, space. And, by the discontinuous presentation of character, Proust forces the reader to juxtapose disparate images of his characters spatially, in a moment of time, so that the experience of time's passage will be fully communicated to their sensibility. There is a striking analogy here between Proust's method and that of his beloved Impressionist painters; but this analogy goes far deeper than the usual comments about the "impressionism" of Proust's style. The Impressionist painters juxtaposed pure tones on the canvas, instead of mixing them on the palette, in order to leave the blending of colors to the eye of the spectator. Similarly, Proust gives us what might be called pure views of his characters—views of them "motionless in a moment of vision" in various phases of their lives—and allows the sensibility of the reader to fuse these views into a unity. Each view must be apprehended by the reader as a unit; and Proust's purpose is only achieved when these units of meaning are referred to each other reflexively in a moment of time. As with Joyce and the modern poets, we see that spatial form is also the structural scaffolding of Proust's labyrinthine masterpiece.

*   *   *

The name of Djuna Barnes is not unknown to those readers who followed, with any care, the stream of pamphlets, books, magazines and anthologies that poured forth to enlighten America in the feverish days of literary expatriation. Miss Barnes, it is true, must always have remained a somewhat enigmatic figure even to the most attentive reader. Born in New York State, she spent most of her time abroad in England and France; and the glimpses one catches of her in the memoirs of the period are brief and unrevealing. She appears in *The Dial* from time to time with a drawing or a poem; she crops up now and again in some anthology of advance-guard writers—the usual agglomeration of people who are later to become famous, or to sink into the melancholy oblivion of frustrated promise. Before the publication of *Nightwood,* indeed, one might have been inclined to place her name in the latter group. For, while she has a book of short stories and an earlier novel to her credit, neither of them prepares one for the maturity of achievement so conspicuous in every line of her latest work.

Of the fantastical quality of her imagination, of the gift for imagery which, as T. S. Eliot has said, gives one a sense of horror and doom akin to Elizabethan tragedy; of the epigrammatic incisiveness of her phrasing and her penchant, also akin to the Elizabethans, for dealing with the more scabrous manifestations of human fallibility—of all these there is evidence in *Ryder,* Miss Barnes's first novel. But all this might well have resulted only in a momentary flare-up of capricious brilliance, whose radiance would have been as dazzling as it was insubstantial. *Ryder,* it must be confessed, is an anomalous creation from any point of view. Although Miss Barnes's unusual qualities gradually emerge from its kaleidoscope of moods and styles, these qualities are still, so to speak, held in solution, or at best placed in the service of a literary *jeu d'esprit.* Only in *Nightwood* do they finally crystallize into a definitive and comprehensible pattern.

Many critics—not least among them T. S. Eliot himself—have paid tribute to *Nightwood's* compelling intensity, its head-and-shoulders superiority, simply as a stylistic phenomenon, to most of the works that currently pass for literature. But *Nightwood's* reputation at present is similar, in many respects, to that of *The Waste Land* in 1922— it is known as a collection of striking passages, some of breathtaking poetic quality, appealing chiefly to connoisseurs of somewhat gamey literary items. Such a reputation, it need hardly be remarked, is not conducive to intelligent appreciation or understanding. Thanks to critics like F. R. Leavis, Cleanth Brooks, and F. O. Matthiessen, we are now able to approach *The Waste Land* as a work of art, rather than as a battleground for opposing poetic theories or as a curious piece of literary esoterica; and it is time that such a process should be at least begun for *Nightwood.*

Before dealing with *Nightwood* in detail, however, we must make certain broad distinctions between it and the novels already considered. While the structural principle of *Nightwood* is the same as in *Ulysses* and *À la recherche du temps perdu*—spatial form, obtained by means of reflexive reference—there are marked differences in technique that will be obvious to every reader. Taking an analogy from another art, we can say that these differences are similar to the differences between the work of Cézanne and the compositions of a later abstract painter like Braque. What characterizes the work of Cézanne, above all, is the tension between two conflicting but deeply-rooted tendencies: on the one hand, a struggle to attain esthetic form—conceived of by Cézanne as a self-enclosed unity of form-and-color harmonies—and, on the other hand, the desire to create this form through the recognizable depiction of natural objects. Later artists, abandoning Cézanne's efforts to achieve form in terms of natural objects, took over only his preoccupation with formal harmonies, omitting natural objects altogether or presenting them in some distorted manner.

Like Cézanne, Proust and Joyce accept the naturalistic principle, presenting their characters in terms of those commonplace details, those descriptions of circumstance and environment, that we have come to regard as verisimilar. At the same time, we have seen, they intended to control the ebullience of their naturalistic detail by the unity of spatial apprehension. But in *Nightwood,* as in the work of Braque and the later abstract painters, the naturalistic principle is totally abandoned: no attempt is made to convince us that the characters are actual flesh-and-blood human beings. We are asked only to accept their world as we accept an abstract painting or, to return to literature, as we accept a Shakespearian play—as an autonomous pattern giving us an individual vision of reality, rather than what we might consider its exact reflection.

To illustrate the transition that takes place in *Nightwood* let us examine an interesting passage from Proust, where the process can be caught at a rudimentary level. In describing Robert de Saint-Loup, an important character in the early sections of the novel, the narrator tells us that he could see concealed "beneath a courtier's smile his warrior's thirst for action—when I examined him I could see how closely the vigorous structure of his triangular face must have been modelled on that of his ancestors' faces, a face devised rather for an ardent bowman than for a delicate student. Beneath his fine skin the bold construction, the feudal architecture were apparent. His head made one think of those old dungeon keeps on which the disused battlements are still to be seen, although inside they have been converted into libraries." When the reader comes across this passage, he has already learned a considerable number of facts about Saint-Loup. He is, for one thing, a member of the Guermantes family, one of the oldest and most aristocratic in the French nobility and still the acknowledged leaders of Parisian society. Unlike their feudal ancestors, however, the Guermantes have no real influence over the internal affairs of France under the Third Republic. Saint-Loup, for another thing, is by way of being a family black sheep: seemingly uninterested in social success, a devoted student of Nietzsche and Proudhon, we are told that his head was full of "socialistic spoutings," and that he was "imbued with the most profound contempt for his caste." Knowing these facts from earlier sections of the novel, the reader accepts the passage quoted above simply as a trenchant summation of Saint-Loup's character. But so precisely do the images in this passage apply to everything the reader has learned about Saint-Loup, so exactly do they communicate the central impression of his personality, that it would be possible to derive a total knowledge of his character solely from the images without attaching them to a set of external social and historical details.

Images of this kind are commoner in poetry than in prose—more particularly, since we are speaking of character description, in dramatic poetry. In Shakespeare and the Elizabethans, descriptions of character are not "realistic" as we understand the word today: they are not a collection of circumstantial details whose bare conglomeration is assumed to form a definition. The dramatic poet, rather, defined both the physical and psychological aspects of character at one stroke, in an image or series of images. Here is Antony, for example, as Shake-speare presents him in the opening scene of *Antony and Cleopatra:*

> Nay, but this dotage of our general's
> O'erflows the measure: those his goodly eyes
> That o'er the files and musters of the war
> Have glow'd like plated Mars, now bend, now turn,
> The office and devotion of their view
> Upon a tawny front: his captain's heart,
> Which in the scuffles of great fights hath burst
> The buckles on his breast, reneges all temper,
> And is become the bellows and the fan
> To cool a gipsy's lust.

And then, to complete the picture, Antony is contemptuously called "the triple pillar of the world transformed into a strumpet's fool." Or, to take a more modern example, from a poet strongly influenced by the Elizabethans, here is the twentieth-century everyman:

> He, the young man carbuncular, arrives,
> A small house agent's clerk, with one bold stare,
> One of the low on whom assurance sits
> As a silk hat on a Bradford millionaire.

As Ramon Fernandez has remarked of similar character descriptions in the work of George Meredith, images of this kind analyze without dissociating; they describe character but, at the same time, hold fast to the unity of personality, without splintering it to fragments in try-ing to seize the secret of its integration.

Writing of this order, charged with symbolic overtones, piercing through the cumbrous mass of naturalistic detail to express the essence of character in an image, is the antithesis to what we are accustomed in the novel. Ordinary novels, as T. S. Eliot justly observes in his preface to *Nightwood,* "obtain what reality they have largely from an accurate rendering of the noises that human beings currently make in their daily simple needs of communication; and what part of a novel is not composed of these noises consists of a prose which is no more alive than that of a competent newspaper writer or government official." Miss Barnes abandons any pretensions of this kind of veri-similitude, just as modern artists have abandoned any attempt at naturalistic representation; and the result is a world as strange to the reader, at first sight, as the world of abstract art was to its first spec-tators. Since the selection of detail in *Nightwood* is governed, not by the logic of verisimilitude, but by the demands of the *décor* necessary to enhance the symbolic significance of the characters, the novel has baffled even its most fascinated admirers. Perhaps we can clear up some of the mystery by applying our method of reflexive reference, instead of approaching the book, as most of its readers have done, expecting to find a coherent temporal pattern of narrative.

Since *Nightwood* lacks a narrative structure in the ordinary sense, it cannot be reduced to any sequence of action for purposes of explanation. One can, if one chooses, follow the narrator in Proust through the various stages of his social career; one can, with some difficulty, follow Leopold Bloom's epic journey through Dublin; but no such reduction is possible in *Nightwood*. As Dr. O'Connor remarks to Nora Flood, with his desperate gaiety, "I have a narrative, but you will be put to it to find it." Strictly speaking, the doctor is wrong— he has a static situation, not a narrative, and no matter how hard the reader looks he will find only the various facets of this situation explored from different angles. The eight chapters of *Nightwood* are like searchlights, probing the darkness each from a different direction, yet ultimately focusing on and illuminating the same entanglement of the human spirit. In the first four chapters we are introduced to each of the important persons—Felix Volkbein, Nora Flood, Robin Vote, Jenny Petherbridge, and Dr. O'Connor. The next three chapters are, for the most part, long monologues by the doctor, through which the developments of the earlier chapters begin to take on meaning. The last chapter, only a few pages long, has the effect of a coda, giving us what we have already come to feel is the only possible termination. And these chapters are knit together, not by the progress of any action —either physical action, or, as in a stream-of-consciousness novel, the act of thinking—but by the continual reference and cross-reference of images and symbols which must be referred to each other spatially throughout the time-act of reading.

Although, at first reading, Dr. O'Connor's brilliant and fantastic monologues seem to dominate the book, overshadowing the other characters, closer reading will show that the central figure—the figure around which the situation revolves—is Robin Vote. This creation—it is impossible to call her a character, since character implies humanity and she has not yet attained the level of the human—is one of the most remarkable figures in contemporary literature. We meet her first when the doctor, sitting and drinking with Felix Volkbein in a Paris bar, is summoned by a bellboy from a near-by hotel to look after a lady who has fainted and cannot be awakened. "The perfume that her body exhaled," Miss Barnes writes of Robin,

> ... was of the quality of that earth-flesh, fungi, which smells of captured dampness and yet is so dry, overcast with the odour of oil of amber, which is an inner malady of the sea, making her seem as if she had invaded a sleep incautious and entire. Her flesh was the texture of

plant life, and beneath it one sensed a frame, broad, porous, and sleep-worn, as if sleep were a decay fishing her beneath the visible surface. About her head there was an effulgence as of phosphorus glowing about the circumference of a body of water—as if her life lay through her in ungainly luminous deteriorations—the troubling structure of the born somnambule, who lives in two worlds—meet of child and desperado.

Taken by itself, this description is likely to prove more confusing than enlightening; but a few pages later another attempt is made to explain Robin's significance.

Sometimes one meets a woman who is beast turning human. Such a person's every movement will reduce to an image of a forgotten experience; a mirage of an eternal wedding cast on the racial memory; as insupportable a joy as would be the vision of an eland coming down an aisle of trees, chapleted with orange blossoms and bridal veil, a hoof raised in the economy of fear, stepping in the trepidation of flesh that will become a myth.

It is significant that we first meet Robin—*la somnambule,* the sleep-walker—when she is being awakened; before that moment we have no knowledge of her life. Her life might be said to begin with that moment, and the act of awakening to be, symbolically, the act of birth.

From these descriptions, we begin to realize that Robin symbolizes a state of existence which is before, rather than beyond, good and evil. She is both innocent and depraved—meet of child and desperado—precisely because she has not reached the human state, where moral values become relevant. Lacking responsibility of any kind, abandoning herself to wayward and perverse passions, she yet has the innocence and purity of a child. (Nora tells the doctor in the seventh chapter that Robin played "with her toys, trains, and animals and cars to wind up, and dolls and marbles and toy soldiers.") Gliding through life like a sleepwalker, living in a dream from which she has not awakened—awakening would imply a consciousness of moral value—Robin is at once completely egotistical and yet lacking in a sense of her own identity. "And why does Robin feel innocent?" Dr. O'Connor asks, when Nora, Robin's lover, comes to him with her agonizing questions. "Every bed she leaves, without caring, fills her heart with peace and happiness. . . . She knows she is innocent because she can't do anything in relation to anyone but herself." But at the same time the doctor tells Felix, Robin's erstwhile husband, that Robin had written from America saying, "Remember me." "Probably," he remarks, "because she has difficulty in remembering herself." By taking these passages together, we can understand what the doctor means when he says that "Robin was outside the 'human type'—a wild thing caught in a woman's skin, monstrously alone, monstrously vain."

The situation of the novel, as we have already said, revolves around this extraordinary creature. Robin, Felix eagerly confides to the doctor, "always seemed to be looking for someone to tell her that she was innocent.... There are some people who must get permisison to live, and if the Baronin [Robin] finds no one to give her that permission, she will make an innocence for herself; a fearful sort of primitive innocence." To be conscious of one's innocence, of course, implies a consciousness of moral value which, we have seen, Robin does not possess. If Robin could find someone to tell her she was innocent, that would mean she had found someone who had raised her to the level of the human—someone who had given her "permission to live" as a human being, not merely to exist as an amorphous lump of moral possibility. This situation is the nub of the novel—Robin's relation to the other characters centers around the question: Will any of them be able to give her a sense of identity—to raise her to the level of the human?

Once this fundamental problem is grasped, much of what we read in the rest of *Nightwood* becomes considerably clearer. At the beginning of the book we are introduced to Felix Volkbein, a Viennese half-Jew with a somewhat questionable title. What Miss Barnes says of Felix immediately elevates him to the same type of symbolic stature that Robin possesses.

> What had formed Felix from the date of his birth to his coming to thirty was unknown to the world, for the step of the wandering Jew is in every son. No matter where and when you meet him you feel that he has come from ... some secret land that he has been nourished on but cannot inherit, for the Jew seems to be everywhere from nowhere. When Felix's name was mentioned, three or more persons would swear to having seen him the week before in three different countries simultaneously.

Combined with this aspect of Felix, we find attributed to him a curious "obsession for what he termed 'Old Europe': aristocracy, nobility, royalty.... He felt that the great past might mend a little if he bowed low enough, if he succumbed and gave homage." Immediately after seeing Robin, Felix confesses to the doctor that he "wished a son who would feel as he felt about the 'great past.'" "To pay homage to our past," he says, "is the only gesture that also includes the future." He pays court to Robin and, since her "life held no volition for refusal," they marry. Felix, then, makes the first effort to shape Robin, to give her permission to live by informing her with his own sense of moral values. He does so precisely because he senses, almost instinctively, that with Robin "anything can be done."

Felix fails with Robin, just as do the others who try to provide her with a moral framework. But what exactly does Felix's failure imply?

What, in other words, is the sense of values which proves inadequate to lift Robin to the level of the human? Because Felix is so astonishingly individual a creation, despite the broader significance of his rôle in the novel, this is a particularly difficult question to answer. Some clue may be found if we remind ourselves of another Wandering Jew in modern fiction, Leopold Bloom. Seeking for a character to typify *l'homme moyen sensuel,* not only of our own time but through all history, Joyce chose the figure of a Wandering Jew, vainly trying to integrate himself with a culture to which he is essentially alien. The predicament of the Jew, in a certain sense, is merely a magnification of the predicament of modern man himself, bewildered and homeless in a mechanical wilderness of his own creation. If we view Felix in this light, understanding his dubious title, his abject reverence for the great tradition of the past, his frantic desire to assimilate this tradition to himself as so many examples of a basic need to feel at home in some cultural framework, we can begin to understand the deeper implications of his character.

Until his meeting with Robin, Felix's relationship to what he considered the great traditions of the European past had been completely negative. The first chapter of the novel, dominated by Felix, is appropriately entitled "Bow Down"—for this phrase defines Felix's attitude towards the great tradition, even towards its trivial and unworthy modern representatives. "In restaurants he bowed slightly to anyone who looked as if he might be 'someone,' making the bow so imperceptible that the surprised person might think he was merely adjusting his stomach." The doctor, by linking this blind, unthinking worship of the aristocratic traditions of the past with the attitude of the masses in general towards an aristocracy they have falsely deified, lights up in a flash the symbolic meaning of Felix's obsession. "Nobility, very well, but what is it?" The Baron started to answer him, but the doctor held up his hand. "Wait a minute! I know—the few that the many have lied about well and long enough to make them deathless." Felix, then, is in the position of the masses, the common men, desperately lying to themselves about an inherited sense of values of which they know only the external trappings. But by marrying Robin, the doctor realizes, Felix is staking his existence on the belief that these traditional values still have vitality—that they can and will shape the primeval chaos of Robin into order. (On Felix's first visit to court Robin, he carries two volumes on the life of the Bourbons.) Knowing that Felix's attempt is doomed to failure, the doctor makes an effort to warn him: "The last muscle of aristocracy is madness—remember that"—the doctor leaned forward—"the last child born to aristocracy is sometimes an idiot. . . ." And, a few paragraphs later, the doctor reiterates, "So I say beware! In the king's bed is always found, just before it becomes a museum piece, the droppings of the black sheep."

Robin does bear Felix a child, sickly, stunted, prematurely aged, possibly feeble-minded—the droppings of the black sheep. And, after unwillingly conceiving the child "amid loud and frantic cries of affirmation and despair," Robin leaves Felix when he discovers she did not want it. "You didn't want him," he said ... "It seems I could not accomplish that." Since, for Felix, the child had meant the creative re-affirmation of the great European aristocratic tradition, Felix's confession of defeat with Robin represents, at the same time, his final realization that this tradition is impotent. It contains nothing for the future except the wistful and precocious senility of Guido, Felix's child. This is the explanation of the enigmatic scene at the end of the sixth chapter, where Felix, after dropping out of sight, makes his last appearance. On entering a Viennese café, Felix saw instantly "a tall man in the corner who, he was sure, was the Grand Duke Alexander of Russia, cousin and brother-in-law of the late Czar Nicholas." At first, Felix refuses to look at the man, but later "with the abandon of what a madman knows to be his one hope of escape, disproof of his own madness," as he is leaving the café "he turned and made a slight bow, his head in his confusion making a complete half-swing, as an animal will turn its head away from a human, as if in mortal shame." Here we have the consequence of Felix's failure with Robin: for if Felix had succeeded in asserting his values positively, in shaping Robin, there would no longer have been any need for him to "bow down"—he would have created a living incarnation of these values, Guido, the combination of Robin's primitive vitality and his own sense of the past, who would have had far more right to represent these values than their merely passive inheritors. But since Felix failed, as the doctor foresaw —though Felix fights against the recognition of failure, for Guido's sake—he is compelled, finally, to bow down once more in defeated submission.

The next character to enter the lists with Robin is Nora Flood, who comes perhaps closest of all to giving Robin "permission to live." Nora, as a symbolic figure, is given meaning on a number of levels; but the title of the third chapter, "Night Watch," expresses the essence of her spiritual attitude. We are told that she keeps "a 'paupers' salon for poets, radicals, beggars, artists, and people in love; for Catholics, Protestants, Brahmins, dabblers in black magic and medicine"—this last, of course, being an allusion to the doctor. Nora was "by temperament an early Christian; she believed the word." As Miss Barnes explains, this meant that she "robbed herself for everyone. . . . Wandering people the world over found her profitable in that she could be sold for a price forever, for she carried her betrayal money in her own pocket." It is significant that Nora is described in images of the American West: "Looking at her, foreigners remembered stories they had heard of covered wagons; animals going down to drink; children's heads, just as far as the eyes, looking in fright out of small windows, where in the dark another race crouched in ambush." The connection between these images, Nora's "paupers' " salon and her early Christian temperament is this: they represent different crystallizations of the same spiritual attitude. Among the determinants of this attitude are a belief in the innate goodness of man, or at least in his capacity for moral improvement, a belief in progress, an indiscriminate approbation for all forms of ethical and intellectual unconventionality—in short, the complete antithesis to the world of values represented by Felix. Irving Babbitt would have called Nora a hopeless Rousseauist; and he would have been right.

Characteristically, while Felix was drawn to Robin because he could use her, Nora is drawn to her through pity. The scene in which Nora meets Robin is important not only for what it reveals of their relationship, but also because there is a passage that confirms our interpretation of Robin. Both Robin and Nora are watching a circus performance when,

> . . . as one powerful lioness came to the turn of the bars, exactly opposite the girl [Robin], she turned her furious great head with its yellow eyes afire and went down, her paws thrust through the bars and, as she regarded the girl, as if a river were falling behind impassable heat, her eyes flowed in tears that never reached the surface.

Being neither animal nor human, Robin evokes pity from both species. Nora, intuitively understanding Robin's perturbation at the lioness's stare, takes her by the hand and leads her outside. And, although strangers until that moment, Robin is soon telling Nora "her wish for a home, as if she were afraid she would be lost again, as if she were aware, without conscious knowledge, that she belonged to Nora, and that if Nora did not make it permanent by her own strength, she would forget." What Robin would forget was where she belonged, her own identity, given to her at least for a while by the strength of Nora's love and pity.

Nora's failure with Robin is already foreshadowed in Miss Barnes's first description of Nora: she "had the face of all people who love the people—a face that would be evil when she found out that to love without criticism is to be betrayed." While Felix had deliberately tried to shape Robin, Nora simply envelops her in an all-embracing love which, because of Nora's belief in natural goodness, has no room for praise or blame. "In court," Miss Barnes remarks, Nora "would have been impossible; no one would have been hanged, reproached or forgiven because no one would have been 'accused.' " With a creature like Robin, the result was inevitable—Nora's self-sacrificing devotion does succeed for a time in giving Robin a sense of identity; Robin's unconditional acceptance by Nora, exactly as she is, eases the tension between the animal and the human that is tearing Robin's life apart; but Nora, in the end, is not able to give Robin "permission to live" any more than Felix could. Most of the third chapter of the novel is given over to an analysis of the slow estrangement between Robin and Nora, an estrangement all the more torturous because, while desired by neither, it is recognized as inevitable by both.

Yet the quality of Robin's relation with Nora shows how much more closely Nora came to success than Felix. With Felix, Robin had been passive, almost disinterested, in conformity with her somnambulistic nature. Although her life was a frenzy of activity, she never really acted in more than an animal sense—human action implies thought and decision, while Robin's acts were always re-actions to obscure impulses whose meaning she did not understand. With Nora, however, there are moments when Robin realizes the terror of their inevitable separation; and in these moments, clinging to Nora like a child, Robin becomes almost human because her terror reveals an implicit moral choice.

> Yet sometimes, going about the house, in passing each other, they would fall into an agonized embrace, looking into each other's face, their two heads in their four hands, so strained together that the space that divided them seemed to be thrusting them apart. Sometimes in these moments of insurmountable grief Robin would make some movement, use a peculiar turn of phrase not habitual to her, innocent of the betrayal, by which Nora was informed that Robin had come from a world to which she would return. To keep her (in Robin there was this tragic longing to be kept, knowing herself astray) Nora knew now that there was no way but death.

As usual, the appropriate comment on this situation is made by the doctor, seeing Nora out roaming the streets at night in search of Robin. " 'There goes the dismantled—Love has fallen off her wall. A religious woman,' he thought to himself, 'without the joy and safety of the Catholic faith, which at a pinch covers up the spots on the wall when the family portraits take a slide; take that safety from a woman,' he said to himself, quickening his steps to follow her, 'and love gets loose and into the rafters. She sees her everywhere,' he added, glancing at Nora as she passed into the dark. 'Out looking for what she's afraid to find—Robin. There goes the mother of mischief, running about, trying to get the world home.' " Robin, it should be noticed, is identified with "the world"—which may mean that the world is really no better off than she is—and Nora's failure with Robin, or rather her derangement over this failure, is attributed to her lack of the Catholic faith. The doctor does not say that the Catholic faith would have allowed Nora to control Robin by giving her a framework of moral values, but he does say that, if Nora had been a Catholic, the eccentricities of Robin's nature would not have plunged Nora into an abyss of self-torture and suffering. It is Nora's faith in natural goodness, her uncritical acceptance of Robin because of this faith, which has caused her to suffer. As a Catholic, the doctor implies, she would have been able to rationalize Robin's nature in terms of the Catholic understanding of sin and evil; and while this would not have prevented the evil, it would certainly have eased the disillusionment and suffering. As we shall see later, this passage is crucial to an understanding of the book as a whole.

Nora realizes that Robin is lost to her when, at dawn, she looks out of her window and sees another woman "her arms about Robin's neck, her body pressed to Robin's, her legs slackened in the hang of the embrace." This other woman, Jenny Petherbridge, is the only person in the novel without a trace of tragic grandeur—and this is not surprising, for she is depicted as the essence of mediocrity, the incarnation of the second-hand and the second-rate. Chapter four, in which she makes her main appearance, is titled "The Squatter"—this is the keynote of her character. Her life is a continual infringement on the rights of other people, an infringement that becomes permanent merely by the power of persistence. "Her walls, her cupboards, her bureaux, were teeming with second-hand dealings with life. It takes a bold and authentic robber to get first-hand plunder. Someone else's marriage ring was on her finger; the photograph taken of Robin for Nora sat upon her table." Jenny, again, is the only person in the novel who might be called bourgeois: there is more than a touch of the *nouveau riche* in her ostentation and her lavishness with money. Wanting to possess anything that had importance for other people, because she was unable to make anything important herself, "she appropriated the most passionate love that she knew, Nora's for Robin." Jenny's relationship to Robin differs from those of Felix and Nora: she has no intuition of Robin's pathetic moral emptiness, as Nora had, nor does she seize on Robin as a teeming chaos of vitality through which to realize her own values, as Felix had done; she simply appropriates Robin as another acquisition to her collection of objects that other people have valued. Staking her claim to Robin immediately after Nora, Jenny's main function in the novel seems that of underlining the hopelessness of Robin's plight. To fall from Nora to Jenny—to exchange the moral world of one for the moral world of the other— is only too convincing a proof that Robin has still failed to acquire any standards of value.

When, at the conclusion of the fourth chapter, we learn that Robin and Jenny have sailed for America, the novel definitely shifts its focus. Until this point Robin had been its center, both spiritually and actually; but Robin now drops out of sight—though she is talked about at great length—and does not appear directly again until the brief concluding episode. The next three chapters are completely dominated by the doctor, "Dr. Matthew-Mighty-grain-of-salt-Dante-O'Connor," whose dialogues with Felix and Nora—or rather, his monologues, prompted by their questions—make up the bulk of these pages. The doctor serves as commentator on the events of the novel—if events they can be called; and, as T. S. Eliot says of Tiresias in *The Waste Land,* what he sees, in fact, is the substance of the novel. This comparison can bear closer application, for there is an evident—and probably not accidental— similarity between the two figures. Like the man-woman Tiresias, symbol of universal experience, the doctor has homosexual inclinations; like Tiresias he has "foresuffered all" by apparently being immortal —he claims to have a "prehistoric memory," and is always talking as if he existed in other historical periods. Like Tiresias, again, who "walked among the lowest of the dead," the doctor is father confessor to the creatures of the night world who inhabit the novel, and is himself an inhabitant of that world; and in his role of commentator, the doctor "perceived the scene, and foretold the rest." For these reasons, Nora comes to him with the burning question—the title of the fifth chapter —"Watchman, What of the Night?" The doctor understands, of course, that she really means: Why has Robin left me? Since there is no rational answer to this question, and the doctor knows it, he proceeds, as he always does, to talk about himself, "for he considered himself the most amusing predicament." But since, as he tells Felix, "no man needs curing of his individual sickness; his universal malady is what he should look to," he talks about his own maladies from this universal perspective; and his monologues, as a result, turn out to be a discussion of the maladies with which the other characters are also stricken. In the passionate and inexhaustible flow of his confessions, the doctor obliquely illuminates the central situation in the novel.

It is impossible to give any exact idea of the doctor's monologues except by quoting them at length; and that would unduly prolong an already protracted analysis. What can be said, however, is this: to find anything approaching their combination of ironic wit and religious humility, their emotional subtlety and profound human simplicity, their pathos, their terror, and their sophisticated self-consciousness, one has to go back to the religious sonnets of John Donne. It is these mono- logues which prove the main attraction of the novel at first reading, and their magnetic power has, no doubt, contributed to the miscon- ception that *Nightwood* is only a collection of magnificent fragments. Since the doctor always speaks about himself *sub specie aeternitatis,* it is difficult, at first, to grasp the relations between his monologues and the central theme of the novel. T. S. Eliot notes in his preface that he could place the doctor in proper focus only after a number of readings; and this is likely to be the experience of other readers as well. But, as Eliot rightly emphasizes, the book cannot be understood unless the doctor is seen as part of the whole pattern, rather than as an over- whelming individual creation throwing the others into the background by the magnitude of his understanding and the depth of his insight. Accordingly, we have concentrated our exposition almost entirely on the central pattern, using passages from the doctor's monologues only when the pattern could not have been intelligibly described without them. Now that the pattern has been made clear, however, we can safely approach the doctor a little more closely and explain, if we can, his individual spiritual attitude. It is this attitude which, in the end, dominates the book and gives it meaning.

"Man," the doctor tells Felix, "was born damned and innocent from the start, and wretchedly—as he must—on those two themes—whistles his tune." Robin, it will be remembered, was described as both child and desperado, that is, both damned and innocent; and since the doctor generalizes her spiritual predicament, we can infer that he views the condition of the other characters—and of himself—as, in essentials, no different from Robin's. The doctor, who calls himself "the god of darkness," is a good illustration of his own statement. He is damned by his excess of the knowledge of evil, which condemns him to a living death. "You know what none of us know until we have died," Nora tells him. "You were dead in the beginning." But beyond the doctor's knowledge, beyond his twisted bitterness, is the pathos of abused innocence. "No matter what I may be doing," he cries, "in my heart is the wish for children and knitting. God, I never asked better than to boil some good man's potatoes and toss up a child for him every nine months by the calendar." And after the wonderful Tiny O'Toole episode, in which the doctor reveals all his saint-like simplicity—his attitude towards animals, by the way, reminds one of St. Francis of Assisi—Nora says: "Sometimes I don't know why I talk to you. You're so like a child; then again I know well enough." Because of his knowledge of man's nature, the doctor realizes that he himself, and the other people in the novel, differ from Robin only in degree; they are all involved to some extent in her desperate dualism, and in the end, he knows, their doom is equally inescapable. "We are but skin about a wind," he says, " with muscles clenched against mortality. . . . Life, the permission to know death." Come to ask the "god of darkness" about that fabulous night-creature, Robin, Nora draws the only possible conclusion from the doctor's harangues: "I'll never understand her—I'll always be miserable—just like this?" To which the doctor responds by one of his tirades that seems to be about nothing in particular, and yet turns out to be about everything.

But the quality in the doctor which grows upon the reader is the practical futility of his knowledge, his own hopelessness and helplessness. In the early chapters he turns up occasionally, exhibiting an insight into the other people which they themselves do not possess, and seeming, for this reason, to stand outside their dilemmas. But as the doctor comes to the foreground, we find this impression completely erroneous. He talks because he knows there is nothing else to do—and because to stop talking would be to think, and to think would be unbearable. "Look here," said the doctor. "Do you know what has made me the greatest liar this side of the moon, telling my stories to people like you to take the mortal agony out of their guts . . . to stop them from . . . staring over their knuckles with misery which they are trying to keep off, saying, 'Say something, Doctor, for the love of God!' And me talking away like mad. Well, that, and nothing else, has made me the liar I am." And in another place he sums it up succinctly: "I talk too much because I have been made so miserable by what you're keeping hushed."

The doctor, however, cannot always maintain this rôle: he cannot always drown his own agony in a flood of talk for the benefit of others. And so, his own tension exacerbated by Nora's increasing hysteria, he bursts forth: "Do you think, for Christ's sweet sake, that I am so happy that you should cry down my neck? Do you think there is no lament in this world, but your own?" "A broken heart have you!" he says scornfully, a few sentences later. "I have falling arches, flying dandruff, a floating kidney, shattered nerves *and* a broken heart! . . . Am I going forward screaming that it hurts . . . or holding my guts as if they were a coil of knives? . . . Do I wail to the mountains of the trouble I have had in the valley, or to every stone of the way it broke my bones, or of every lie, how it went down into my belly and built a nest to hatch me my death there?" It is on this note that we take leave of the doctor, cursing "the people in my life who have made my life miserable, coming to me to learn of degradation and the night." His last pronouncement, made in a drunken frenzy, is one of utter despair: "I've not only lived my life for nothing, but I've told it for nothing—abominable among the filthy people—I know, it's all over, everything's over, and nobody knows it but me—drunk as a fiddler's bitch—lasted too long—." He tried to get to his feet and gave it up. "Now," he said, "the end—mark my words—now *nothing, but wrath and weeping!*" These words should be taken, not as the maudlin mouthings of a self-pitying degenerate, but as the judgment of a man who once asked, with masochistic exultation, "Have I not summed up my time?" knowing that the answer would be Yes. They are the words of a man whose experience comprehends all history, a man with a "prehistoric memory," who has to be admonished by a friend, after telling of an incident involving himself and Catherine the Great, "For Heaven's sake, remember your century at least!"

But although the doctor, as an individual, ends on a note of complete negation, this is not his final judgment on the total pattern of the novel—it is only his final verdict on himself. His attitude towards Robin and the people surrounding her is somewhat more complex. We have already indicated the nature of this complexity by quoting the doctor's remark, when he sees Nora wandering through the streets in search of Robin, that she was a religious woman "without the joy and safety of the Catholic faith, which at a pinch covers up the spots on the wall when the family portraits take a slide." There may be nothing to do about Robin's situation—man's attempts to achieve a truly human existence have always ended in failure—but there is, at least, the consolation of what the doctor calls "the girl that you love so much that she can lie to you"—the Catholic Church. Discussing the confessional with Felix, the doctor describes it as the place where, although a person may lack genuine contrition, "mischief unravels and the fine high hand of Heaven proffers the skein again, combed and forgiven." It would be unwise to bear down too heavily on this point and make the doctor's attitude far more positive than it actually is. His Catholicism, although deeply rooted in his emotional nature, can offer consolation but not hope; and even its consolation is a puny thing, compared to the realities of the human situation as the doctor knows it. "I, as good a Catholic as they make, he tells Nora, "have embraced every confection of hope, and yet I know well, for all our outcry and struggle, we shall be for the next generation not the massive dung fallen from the dinosaur, but the little speck left of the hummingbird." If the doctor can really be said to derive any consolation from his Catholicism, it is the type derived by Pascal from contemplating the wretchedness and insignificance of man, rather than the type derived by Thomas Aquinas from contemplating an orderly and rational moral universe. "Be humble like the dust, as God intended, and crawl," he advises Nora, "and finally you'll crawl to the end of the gutter and not be missed and not much remembered." What the doctor would like to attain is the spiritual attitude that T. S. Eliot prays for in *Ash Wednesday*:

> Teach us to care and not to care
> Teach us to sit still.

Although the doctor cannot reach this state because he is too deeply involved in the sufferings of others—"I was doing well enough," he says to Nora, "until you came and kicked my stone over, and out I came, all moss and eyes"—he recognizes it as the only attitude offering some measure of inner peace.

Since the doctor is not the center of the pattern in *Nightwood*, the novel cannot end merely with his last appearance. We know Robin's fate from his monologues, but we have not had it presented to us dramatically: all we know is that Robin has gone to America with Jenny. The brief last chapter fills this gap, and furnishes, with the inevitability of great tragedy, the only possible conclusion. In America, Robin soon leaves Jenny and, impelled by some animal instinct, makes her way to where Nora lives. Without Nora's knowledge she lives in the woods of Nora's estate—we are not told how, and it is of no importance—sleeping in a decaying chapel belonging to Nora's family. One night Nora's watchdog scents Robin, and Nora, hearing the dog bark, follows him to investigate. Entering the chapel, she is witness to this strange and horrible scene between Robin and the dog:

> Sliding down she [Robin] went . . . until her head swung against his [the dog's]; on all fours now, dragging her knees. The veins stood out in her neck, swelled in her arms, and wide and throbbing rose up on her fingers as she moved forward. . . . Then she began to bark also, crawling after him—barking in a fit of laughter, obscene and touching. The dog began to cry then . . . and she grinning and crying with him; crying in shorter and shorter spaces, moving head to head, until she gave up, lying out, her hands beside her, her face turned and weeping; and the dog too gave up then, his eyes bloodshot, his head flat along her knees.

What this indicates, clearly, is that Robin has abandoned her efforts to rise to the human and is returning to the animal state; the *somnambule* is re-entering her age-old sleep.

So ends this amazing book, which combines the simple majesty of a medieval morality play with the verbal subtlety and refinement of a Symbolist poem. Our exposition, of course, has barely skimmed its surface: there are ramifications of the various characters that need a detailed exegesis far beyond the scope of our intention. But, limited as it is, our discussion should have proved one point: *Nightwood* does have a pattern—a pattern arising from the spatial interweaving of images and phrases independently of any time-sequence. And, as in *The Waste Land,* the reader is simply bewildered if he assumes that, because language proceeds in time, *Nightwood* must be perceived as a narrative sequence. We can now understand why T. S. Eliot wrote that "*Nightwood* will appeal primarily to readers of poetry," and that "it is so good a novel that only sensibilities trained on poetry can wholly appreciate it." Since the unit of meaning in *Nightwood* is usually a phrase or sequence of phrases—at most a long paragraph—it carries the evolution of spatial form in the novel forward to a point where it is practically indistinguishable from modern poetry.

TECHNIQUE AS DISCOVERY *

Mark Schorer

I

Modern criticism, through its exacting scrutiny of literary texts, has demonstrated with finality that in art beauty and truth are indivisible and one. The Keatsian overtones of these terms are mitigated and an old dilemma is solved if for beauty we substitute form, and for truth, content. We may, without risk of loss, narrow them even more, and speak of technique and subject matter. Modern criticism has shown us that to speak of content as such is not to speak of art at all, but of experience; and that it is only when we speak of the *achieved* content, the form, the work of art as a work of art, that we speak as critics. The difference between content, or experience, and achieved content, or art, is technique.

When we speak of technique, then, we speak of nearly everything. For technique is the means by which the writer's experience, which is his subject matter, compels him to attend to it; technique is the only means he has of discovering, exploring, developing his subject, of conveying its meaning, and, finally, of evaluating it. And surely it follows that certain techniques are sharper tools than others, and will discover more; that the writer capable of the most exacting technical scrutiny of his subject matter will produce works with the most satisfying content, works with thickness and resonance, works which reverberate, works with maximum meaning.**

We are no longer able to regard as seriously intended criticism of poetry which does not assume these generalizations; but the case for fiction has not yet been established. The novel is still read as though its content has some value in itself, as though the subject matter of fiction has greater or lesser value in itself, and as though technique were not a primary but a supplementary element, capable perhaps of not unattractive embellishments upon the surface of the subject, but hardly of its essence. Or technique is thought of in blunter terms than those which one associates with poetry, as such relatively obvious mat-

---

* "Technique as Discovery" originally appeared in the *Hudson Review,* Spring 1948. It is reprinted here by permission of the author and the magazine editors.
** "The best form is that which makes the most of its subject—there is no other definition of the meaning of form in fiction. The well-made book is the book in which the matter is all used up in the form, in which the form expresses all the matter." (*The Craft of Fiction,* by Percy Lubbock. Jonathan Cape: Chas. Scribner's Sons, 1921; Peter Smith, 1947, p. 40.)

ters as the arrangement of events to create plot; or, within plot, of suspense and climax; or as the means of revealing character motivation, relationship, and development; or as the use of point of view, but point of view as some nearly arbitrary device for the heightening of dramatic interest through the narrowing or broadening of perspective upon the material, rather than as a means toward the positive definition of theme. As for the resources of language, these, somehow, we almost never think of as a part of the technique of fiction—language as used to create a certain texture and tone which in themselves state and define themes and meanings; or language, the counters of our ordinary speech, as forced, through conscious manipulation, into all those larger meanings which our ordinary speech almost never intends. Technique in fiction, all this is a way of saying, we somehow continue to regard as merely a means of organizing material which is "given" rather than as the means of exploring and defining the values in an area of experience which, for the first time *then,* are being given.

Is fiction still regarded in this odd, divided way because it is really less tractable before the critical suppositions which now seem inevitable to poetry? Let us look at some examples: two well-known novels of the past, both by writers who may be described as "primitive," although their relative innocence of technique is of a different sort—Defoe's *Moll Flanders* and Emily Brontë's *Wuthering Heights;* and three well-known novels of this century—*Tono Bungay,* by a writer who claimed to eschew technique; *Sons and Lovers,* by a novelist who, because his ideal of subject matter ("the poetry of the immediate present") led him at last into the fallacy of spontaneous and unchangeable composition, in effect eschewed technique; and *A Portrait of the Artist as a Young Man,* by a novelist whose practice made claims for the supremacy of technique beyond those made by anyone in the past or by anyone else in this century.

Technique in fiction is, of course, all those obvious forms of it which are usually taken to be the whole of it, and many others; but for the present purposes, let it be thought of in two respects particularly: the uses to which language, as language, is put to express the quality of the experience in question; and the uses of point of view not only as a mode of dramatic delimitation, but more particularly, of thematic definition. Technique is really what T. S. Eliot means by "convention" —any selection, structure, or distortion, any form or rhythm imposed upon the world of action; by means of which—it should be added—our apprehension of the world of action is enriched or renewed.* In this sense, everything is technique which is not the lump of experience itself, and one cannot properly say that a writer has no technique or that he

* See Eliot on "Four Elizabethan Dramatists" in his *Selected Essays* (Harcourt, Brace & Co., 1932), p. 94. Also his *"Ulysses,* Order, and Myth" in Part III of this volume.

eschews technique, for, being a writer, he cannot do so. We can speak of good and bad technique, of adequate and inadequate, of technique which serves the novel's purpose, or disserves.

II

In the prefatory remarks to *Moll Flanders,* Defoe tells us that he is not writing fiction at all, but editing the journals of a woman of notorious character, and rather to instruct us in the necessities and the joys of virtue than to please us. We do not, of course, take these professions seriously, since nothing in the conduct of the narrative indicates that virtue is either more necessary or more enjoyable than vice. On the contrary, we discover that Moll turns virtuous only after a life of vice has enabled her to do so with security; yet it is precisely for this reason that Defoe's profession of didactic purpose has interest. For the actual morality which the novel enforces is the morality of any commercial culture, the belief that virtue pays—in worldly goods. It is a morality somewhat less than skin deep, having no relation to motives arising from a sense of good and evil, least of all, of evil-*in*-good, but exclusively from the presence or absence of food, drink, linen, damask, silver, and time-pieces. It is the morality of measurement, and without in the least intending it, *Moll Flanders* is our classic revelation of the mercantile mind: the morality of measurement, which Defoe has completely neglected to measure. He fails not only to evaluate this material in his announced way, but to evaluate it at all. His announced purpose is, we admit, a pious humbug, and he meant us to read the book as a series of scandalous events; and thanks to his inexhaustible pleasure in excess and exaggeration, this element in the book continues to amuse us. Long before the book has been finished, however, this element has also become an absurdity; but not half the absurdity as that which Defoe did not intend at all—the notion that Moll could live a rich and full life of crime, and yet, repenting, emerge spotless in the end. The point is, of course, that she has no moral being, nor has the book any moral life. Everything is external. Everything can be weighed, measured, handled, paid for in gold, or expiated by a prison term. To this, the whole texture of the novel testifies: the bolts of goods, the inventories, the itemized accounts, the landlady's bills, the lists, the ledgers: all this, which taken together comprises what we call Defoe's method of circumstantial realism.

He did not come upon that method by any deliberation: it represents precisely his own world of value, the importance of external circumstance to Defoe. The point of view of Moll is indistinguishable from the point of view of her creator. We discovered the meaning of the novel (at unnecessary length, without economy, without emphasis, with almost none of the distortions or the advantages of art) in spite of Defoe, not because of him. Thus the book is not the true chronicle of

a disreputable female, but the true allegory of an impoverished soul—
the author's; not an anatomy of the criminal class, but of the middle
class. And we read it as an unintended comic revelation of self and of
a social mode. Because he had no adequate resources of technique to
separate himself from his material, thereby to discover and to define
the meanings of his material, his contribution is not to fiction but to
the history of fiction, and to social history.

The situation in *Wuthering Heights* is at once somewhat the same
and yet very different. Here, too, the whole novel turns upon itself, but
this time to its estimable advantage; here, too, is a revelation of what is
perhaps the author's secret world of value, but this time, through what
may be an accident of technique, the revelation is meaningfully accomplished. Emily Brontë may merely have stumbled upon the perspectives
which define the form and the theme of her book. Whether she knew
from the outset, or even at the end, what she was doing, we may doubt;
but what she did and did superbly we can see.

We can assume, without at all becoming involved in the author's life
but merely from the tone of somnambulistic excess which is generated
by the writing itself, that this world of monstrous passion, of dark and
gigantic emotional and nervous energy, is for the author, or was in
the first place, a world of ideal value; and that the book sets out to
persuade us of the moral magnificence of such unmoral passion. We
are, I think, expected, in the first place, to take at their own valuation
these demonic beings, Heathcliff and Cathy: as special creatures, set
apart from the cloddish world about them by their heightened capacity
for feeling, set apart, even, from the ordinary objects of human passion
as, in their transcendental, sexless relationship, they identify themselves
with an uncompromising landscape and cosmic force. Yet this is absurd,
as much of the detail that surrounds it ("Other dogs lurked in other
recesses") is absurd. The novelist Emily Brontë had to discover these
absurdities to the girl Emily; her technique had to evaluate them for
what they were, so that we are persuaded that it is not Emily who is
mistaken in her estimate of her characters, but they who are mistaken
in their estimate of themselves. The theme of the moral magnificence
of unmoral passion is an impossible theme to sustain, and what interests us is that it was device—and this time, mere, mechanical device—
which taught Emily Brontë that, the needs of her temperament to the
contrary, all personal longing and reverie to the contrary, perhaps
—that this was indeed not at all what her material must mean as art.
Technique objectifies.

To lay before us the full character of this passion, to show us how it
first comes into being and then comes to dominate the world about it
and the life that follows upon it, Emily Brontë gives her material a
broad scope in time, lets it, in fact, cut across three generations. And
to manage material which is so extensive, she must find a means of

narration, points of view, which can encompass that material, and, in
her somewhat crude concept of motive, justify its telling. So she chooses
a foppish traveller who stumbles into this world of passionate violence,
a traveller representing the thin and conventional emotional life of
the far world of fashion, who wishes to hear the tale: and for her teller
she chooses, almost inevitably, the old family retainer who knows
everything, a character as conventional as the other, but this one representing not the conventions of fashion, but the conventions of the
humblest moralism. What has happened is, first, that she has chosen
as her narrative perspective those very elements, conventional emotion
and conventional morality, which her hero and heroine are meant to
transcend with such spectacular magnificence; and second, that she has
permitted this perspective to operate throughout a long period of
time. And these two elements compel the novelist to see what her
unmoral passions come to. Moral magnificence? Not at all; rather, a
devastating spectacle of human waste; ashes. For the time of the novel
is carried on long enough to show Heathcliff at last an emptied man,
burned out by his fever ragings, exhausted and will-less, his passion
meaningless at last. And it goes even a little further, to Lockwood, the
fop, in the graveyard, sententiously contemplating headstones. Thus
in the end the triumph is all on the side of the cloddish world, which
survives.

Perhaps not all on that side. For, like Densher at the end of *The
Wings of the Dove,* we say, and surely Hareton and the second Cathy
say, "We shall never be again as we were!" But there is more point
in observing that a certain body of materials, a girl's romantic daydreams, have, through the most conventional devices of fiction, been
pushed beyond their inception in fancy to their meanings, their conception as a written book—that they, that is, are not at all as they were.

III

Technique alone objectifies the materials of art; hence technique
alone evaluates those materials. This is the axiom which demonstrates
itself so devastatingly whenever a writer declares, under the urgent sense
of the importance of his materials (whether these are autobiography, or
social ideas, or personal passions)—whenever such a writer declares
that he cannot linger with technical refinements. That art will not
tolerate such a writer H. G. Wells handsomely proves. His enormous
literary energy included no respect for the techniques of his medium,
and his medium takes its revenge upon his bumptiousness. "I have
never taken any very great pains about writing. I am outside the hierarchy of conscious and deliberate writers altogether. I am the absolute
antithesis of Mr. James Joyce. . . . Long ago, living in close conversa-
tional proximity to Henry James, Joseph Conrad, and Mr. Ford Madox
Hueffer, I escaped from under their immense artistic preoccupations

by calling myself a journalist." Precisely. And he escaped—he disappeared—from literature into the annals of an era.

Yet what confidence! "Literature," Wells said, "is not jewelry, it has quite other aims than perfection, and the more one thinks of 'how it is done' the less one gets it done. These critical indulgences lead along a fatal path, away from every natural interest towards a preposterous emptiness of technical effort, a monstrous egotism of artistry, of which the later work of Henry James is the monumental warning. 'It,' the subject, the thing or the thought, has long since disappeared in these amazing works; nothing remains but the way it has been 'manipulated.' " Seldom has a literary theorist been so totally wrong; for what we learn as James grows for us and Wells disappears, is that without what he calls "manipulation," there *is* no "it," no "subject" in art. There is again only social history.

The virtue of the modern novelist—from James and Conrad down—is not only that he pays so much attention to his medium, but that, when he pays most, he discovers through it a new subject matter, and a greater one. Under the "immense artistic preoccupations" of James and Conrad and Joyce, the form of the novel changed, and with the technical change, analogous changes took place in substance, in point of view, in the whole conception of fiction. And the final lesson of the modern novel is that technique is not the secondary thing that it seemed to Wells, some external machination, a mechanical affair, but a deep and primary operation; not only that technique *contains* intellectual and moral implications, but that it *discovers* them. For a writer like Wells, who wished to give us the intellectual and the moral history of our times, the lesson is a hard one: it tells us that the order of intellect and the order of morality do not exist at all, in art, except as they are organized in the order of art.

Wells's ambitions were very large. "Before we have done, we will have all life within the scope of the novel." But that is where life already is, within the scope of the novel; where it needs to be brought is into novels. In Wells we have all the important topics in life, but no good novels. He was not asking too much of art, or asking that it include more than it happily can; he was not asking anything of it— as art, which is all that it can give, and that is everything.

A novel like *Tono Bungay*, generally thought to be Wells's best, is therefore instructive. "I want to tell—*myself*," says George, the hero, "and my impressions of the thing as a whole"—the thing as a whole being the collapse of traditional British institutions in the twentieth century. George "tells himself" in terms of three stages in his life which have rough equivalents in modern British social history, and this is, to be sure, a plan, a framework; but it is the framework of Wells's abstract thinking, not of his craftsmanship, and the primary demand which one makes of such a book as this, that means be discovered whereby the dimensions of the hero contain the experiences he recounts, is never met. The novelist flounders through a series of literary imitations—from an early Dickensian episode, through a kind of Shavian interlude, through a Conradian episode, to a Jules Vernes vision at the end. The significant failure is in that end, and in the way that it defeats not only the entire social analysis of the bulk of the novel, but Wells's own ends as a thinker. For at last George finds a purpose in science. "I decided that in power and knowledge lay the salvation of my life, the secret that would fill my need; that to these things I would give myself."

But science, power and knowledge, are summed up at last in a destroyer. As far as one can tell Wells intends no irony, although he may here have come upon the essence of the major irony in modern history. The novel ends in a kind of meditative rhapsody which denies every value that the book had been aiming toward. For of all the kinds of social waste which Wells has been describing, this is the most inclusive, the final waste. Thus he gives us in the end not a novel, but a hypothesis; not an individual destiny, but a theory of the future; and not his theory of the future, but a nihilistic vision quite opposite to everything that he meant to represent. With a minimum of attention to the virtues of technique, Wells might still not have written a good novel; but he would at any rate have established a point of view and a tone which would have told us what he meant.

To say what one means in art is never easy, and the more intimately one is implicated in one's material, the more difficult it is. If, besides, one commits fiction to a therapeutic function which is to be operative not on the audience but on the author, declaring, as D. H. Lawrence did, that "One sheds one's sicknesses in books, repeats and presents again one's emotions to be master of them," the difficulty is vast. It is an acceptable theory only with the qualification that technique, which objectifies, is under no other circumstances so imperative. For merely to repeat one's emotions, merely to look into one's heart and write, is also merely to repeat the round of emotional bondage. If our books are to be exercises in self-analysis, then technique must—and alone can—take the place of the absent analyst.*

Lawrence, in the relatively late Introduction to his *Collected Poems,* made that distinction of the amateur between his "real" poems and his "composed" poems, between the poems which expressed his demon directly and created their own form "willy-nilly," and the poems which, through the hocus pocus of technique, he spuriously put together and could, if necessary, revise. His belief in a "poetry of the immediate

* See Francis Fergusson on "D. H. Lawrence's Sensibility" in Part III of this volume for a discussion of this failure as a problem in dramatic rendition.

present," poetry in which nothing is fixed, static, or final, where all is shimmeriness and impermanence and vitalistic essence, arose from this mistaken notion of technique. And from this notion, an unsympathetic critic like D. S. Savage can construct a case which shows Lawrence driven "concurrently to the dissolution of personality and the dissolution of art." The argument suggests that Lawrence's early, crucial novel, *Sons and Lovers,* is another example of meanings confused by an impatience with technical resources.

The novel has two themes: the crippling effects of a mother's love on the emotional development of her son; and the "split" between kinds of love, physical and spiritual, which the son develops, the kinds represented by two young women, Clara and Miriam. The two themes should, of course, work together, the second being, actually, the result of the first: this "split" is the "crippling." So one would expect to see the novel developed, and so Lawrence, in his famous letter to Edward Garnett, where he says that Paul is left at the end with the "drift towards death," apparently thought he had developed it. Yet in the last few sentences of the novel, Paul rejects his desire for extinction and turns toward "the faintly humming, glowing town," to life—as nothing in his previous history persuades us that he could unfalteringly do.

The discrepancy suggests that the book may reveal certain confusions between intention and performance.

The first of these is the contradiction between Lawrence's explicit characterizations of the mother and father and his tonal evaluations of them. It is a problem not only of style (of the contradiction between expressed moral epithets and the more general texture of the prose which applies to them) but of point of view. Morel and Lawrence are never separated, which is a way of saying that Lawrence maintains for himself in his book the confused attitude of his character. The mother is a "proud, *honorable* soul," but the father has a "small, *mean* head." This is the sustained contrast; the epithets are characteristic of the whole; and they represent half of Lawrence's feelings. But what is the other half? Which of these characters is given his real sympathy—the hard, self-righteous, aggressive, demanding mother who comes through to us, or the simple, direct, gentle, downright, fumbling, ruined father? There are two attitudes here. Lawrence (and Morel) loves his mother, but he also hates her for compelling his love; and he hates his father with the true Freudian jealousy, but he also loves him for what he is in himself, and he sympathizes more deeply with him because his wholeness has been destroyed by the mother's domination, just as his, Lawrence-Morel's, has been.

This is a psychological tension which disrupts the form of the novel and obscures its meaning, because neither the contradiction in style nor the confusion in point of view is made to right itself. Lawrence is merely repeating his emotions, and he avoids an austerer technical scrutiny of his material because it would compel him to master them. He would not let the artist be stronger than the man.

The result is that, at the same time that the book condemns the mother, it justifies her; at the same time that it shows Paul's failure, it offers rationalizations which place the failure elsewhere. The handling of the girl, Miriam, if viewed closely, is pathetic in what it signifies for Lawrence, both as man and artist. For Miriam is made the mother's scape-goat, and in a different way from the way that she was in life. The central section of the novel is shot through with alternate statements as to the source of the difficulty: Paul is unable to love Miriam wholly, and Miriam can love only his spirit. The contradictions appear sometimes within single paragraphs, and the point of view is never adequately objectified and sustained to tell us which is true. The material is never seen as material; the writer is caught in it exactly as firmly as he was caught in his experience of it. "That's how women are with me," said Paul. "They want me like mad, but they don't want to belong to me." So he might have said, and believed it; but at the end of the novel, Lawrence is still saying that, and himself believing it.

For the full history of this technical failure, one must read *Sons and Lovers* carefully and then learn the history of the manuscript from the book called *D. H. Lawrence: A Personal Record,* by one E. T., who was Miriam in life. The basic situation is clear enough. The first theme —the crippling effects of the mother's love—is developed right through to the end; and then suddenly, in the last few sentences, turns on itself, and Paul gives himself to life, not death. But all the way through, the insidious rationalizations of the second theme have crept in to destroy the artistic coherence of the work. A "split" would occur in Paul; but as the split is treated, it is superimposed upon rather than developed in support of the first theme. It is a rationalization made from it. If Miriam is made to insist on spiritual love, the meaning and the power of theme one are reduced; yet Paul's weakness is disguised. Lawrence could not separate the investigating analyst, who must be objective, from Lawrence, the subject of the book; and the sickness was not healed, the emotion not mastered, the novel not perfected. All this, and the character of a whole career, would have been altered if Lawrence had allowed his technique to discover the fullest meaning of his subject.

A Portrait of the Artist as a Young Man, like *Tono Bungay* and *Sons and Lovers,* is autobiographical, but unlike these it analyzes its material rigorously, and it defines the value and the quality of its experience not by appended comment or moral epithet, but by the texture of the style. The theme of *A Portrait,* a young artist's alienation from his environment, is explored and evaluated through three different styles and methods as Stephen Dedalus moves from childhood through boyhood into maturity. The opening pages are written in something like the stream of consciousness of *Ulysses,* as the environment impinges directly on the consciousness of the infant and the child, a strange opening world which the mind does not yet subject to questioning, selection, or judgment. But this style changes very soon, as the boy begins to explore his surroundings, and as his sensuous experience of the world is enlarged, it takes on heavier and heavier rhythms and a fuller and fuller body of sensuous detail, until it reaches a crescendo of romantic opulence in the emotional climaxes which mark Stephen's rejection of domestic and religious values. Then gradually the style subsides into the austerer intellectuality of the final sections, as he defines to himself the outlines of the artistic task which is to usurp his maturity.

A highly self-conscious use of style and method defines the quality of experience in each of these sections, and, it is worth pointing out in connection with the third and concluding section, the style and method evaluate the experience. What has happened to Stephen is, of course, a progressive alienation from the life around him as he progressed in his initiation into it, and by the end of the novel, the alienation is complete. The final portion of the novel, fascinating as it may be for the developing aesthetic creed of Stephen-Joyce, is peculiarly bare. The life experience was not bare, as we know from *Stephen Hero;* but Joyce is forcing technique to comment. In essence, Stephen's alienation is a denial of the human environment; it is a loss; and the austere discourse of the final section, abstract and almost wholly without sensuous detail or strong rhythm, tells us of that loss. It is a loss so great that the texture of the notation-like prose here suggests that the end is really all an illusion, that when Stephen tells us and himself that he is going forth to forge in the smithy of his soul the uncreated conscience of his race, we are to infer from the very quality of the icy, abstract void he now inhabits, the implausibility of his aim. For *Ulysses* does not create the conscience of the race; it creates our consciousness.

In the very last two or three paragraphs of the novel, the style changes once more, reverts from the bare, notative kind to the romantic prose of Stephen's adolescence. "Away! Away! The spell of arms and voices: the white arms of roads, their promise of close embraces and the black arms of tall ships that stand against the moon, their tale of distant nations. They are held out to say: We are alone—come." Might one not say that the austere ambition is founded on adolescent longing? That the excessive intellectual severity of one style is the counterpart of the excessive lyric relaxation of the other? And that the final passage of *A Portrait* punctuates the illusory nature of the whole ambition? *

For *Ulysses* does not create a conscience. Stephen, in *Ulysses,* is a little older, and gripped now by guilt, but he is still the cold young man divorced from the human no less than the institutional environment. The environment of urban life finds a separate embodiment in the character of Bloom, and Bloom is as lost as Stephen, though touchingly groping for moorings. Each of the two is weakened by his inability to reach out, or to do more than reach out to the other. Here, then, is the theme again, more fully stated, as it were in counterpoint.

But if Stephen is not much older, Joyce is. He is older as an artist not only because he can create and lavish his Godlike pity on a Leopold Bloom, but also because he knows now what both Stephen and Bloom mean, and *how much,* through the most brilliant technical operation ever made in fiction, they can be made to mean. Thus *Ulysses,* through the imaginative force which its techniques direct, is like a pattern of concentric circles, with the immediate human situation at its center, this passing on and out to the whole dilemma of modern life, this passing on and out beyond that to a vision of the cosmos, and this to the mythical limits of our experience. If we read *Ulysses* with more satisfaction than we read any other novel of this century, it is because its author held an attitude toward technique and the technical scrutiny of subject matter which enabled him to order, within a single work and with superb coherence, the greatest amount of our experience.

IV

In the United States during the last twenty-five years, we have had many big novels but few good ones. A writer like James T. Farrell apparently assumes that by endless redundancy in the description of the surface of American Life, he will somehow write a book with the scope of *Ulysses.* Thomas Wolfe apparently assumed that by the mere disgorging of the raw material of his experience he would give us at last our epic. But except in a physical sense, these men have hardly written novels at all.

The books of Thomas Wolfe were, of course, journals, and the primary role of his publisher in transforming these journals into the semblance of novels is notorious. For the crucial act of the artist, the unique act which is composition, a sympathetic editorial blue pencil and scissors were substituted. The result has excited many

* Readers to whom this seems to suggest too great a separation between Stephen and Joyce are referred to an excellent discussion of the matter in Hugh Kenner's "The Portrait in Perspective," first published in *James Joyce: Two Decades of Criticism,* edited by Seon Givens (Vanguard Press, Inc., 1948).

people, especially the young, and the ostensibly critical have observed
the prodigal talent with the wish that it might have been controlled.
Talent there was, if one means by talent inexhaustible verbal energy,
excessive response to personal experience, and a great capacity for auditory imitativeness, yet all of this has nothing to do with the novelistic
quality of the written result; until the talent is controlled, the material
organized, the content achieved, there is simply the man and his life.
It remains to be demonstrated that Wolfe's conversations were any
less interesting as novels than his books, which is to say that his
books are without interest as novels. As with Lawrence, our response
to the books is determined, not by their qualities as novels, but by
our response to him and his qualities as a temperament.

This is another way of saying that Thomas Wolfe never really knew
what he was writing *about*. Of Time and the River is merely a
euphemism for Of a Man and his Ego. It is possible that had his conception of himself and of art included an adequate respect for technique and the capacity to pursue it, Wolfe would have written a great
novel on his true subject—the dilemma of romantic genius; it was his
true subject, but it remains his undiscovered subject, it is the subject
which *we* must dig out for him, because he himself had neither the
lamp nor the pick to find it in and mine it out of the labyrinths of
his experience. Like Emily Brontë, Wolfe needed a point of view beyond his own which would separate his material and its effect.*

With Farrell, the situation is opposite. He knows quite well what
his subject is and what he wishes to tell us about it, but he hardly
needs the novel to do so. It is significant that in sheer clumsiness of
style, no living writer exceeds him, for his prose is asked to perform no
service beyond communication of the most rudimentary kind of fact.
For his ambitions, the style of the newspaper and the lens of the documentary camera would be quite adequate, yet consider the diminution
which Leopold Bloom, for example, would suffer, if he were to be
viewed from these, the technical perspectives of James Farrell. Under
the eye of this technique, the material does not yield up enough; indeed, it shrinks.

More and more writers in this century have felt that naturalism as
a method imposes on them strictures which prevent them from exploring through all the resources of technique the full amplifications of
their subjects, and that thus it seriously limits the possible breadth of
aesthetic meaning and response. James Farrell is almost unique in the
complacency with which he submits to the blunt techniques of naturalism; and his fiction is correspondingly repetitive and flat.

That naturalism had a sociological and disciplinary value in the
nineteenth century is obvious; it enabled the novel to grasp materials

* See John Peale Bishop on "The Sorrows of Thomas Wolfe" in Part III of this
volume.

and make analyses which had eluded it in the past, and to grasp them boldly; but even then it did not tell us enough of what, in Virginia Woolf's phrase, is "really real," nor did it provide the means to the maximum of reality coherently contained. Even the Flaubertian ideal of objectivity seems, today, an unnecessarily limited view of objectivity, for as almost every good writer of this century shows us, it is quite as possible to be objective about subjective states as it is to be objective about the circumstantial surfaces of life. Dublin, in *Ulysses,* is a moral setting: not only a city portrayed in the naturalistic fashion of Dickens' London, but also a map of the modern psyche with its oblique and baffled purposes. The second level of reality in no way invalidates the first, and a writer like Joyce shows us that, if the artist truly respects his medium, he can be objective about both at once. What we need in fiction is a devoted fidelity to every technique which will help us to discover and to evaluate our subject matter, and more than that, to discover the amplifications of meaning of which our subject matter is capable.

Most modern novelists have felt this demand upon them. André Gide allowed one of his artist-heroes to make an observation which considerably resembles an observation we have quoted from Wells. "My novel hasn't got a subject. . . . Let's say, if you prefer it, it hasn't got *one* subject. . . . 'A slice of life,' the naturalist school said. The great defect of that school is that it always cuts its slice in the same direction; in time, lengthwise. Why not in breadth? Or in depth? As for me I should like not to cut at all. Please understand; I should like to put everything into my novel." Wells, with his equally large blob of potential material, did not know how to cut it to the novel's taste; Gide cut, of course—in every possible direction. Gide and others. And those "cuts" are all the new techniques which modern fiction has given us. None, perhaps, is more important than that inheritance from French symbolism which Huxley, in the glittering wake of Gide, called "the musicalization of fiction." Conrad anticipated both when he wrote that the novel "must strenuously aspire to the plasticity of sculpture, to the colour of painting, and to the magic suggestiveness of music— which is the art of arts," and when he said of that early but wonderful piece of symbolist fiction, *Heart of Darkness,* "It was like another art altogether. That sombre theme had to be given a sinister resonance, a tonality of its own, a continued vibration that, I hoped, would hang in the air and dwell on the ear after the last note had been struck." The analogy with music, except as a metaphor, is inexact, and except as it points to techniques which fiction can employ as fiction, not very useful to our sense of craftsmanship. It has had an approximate exactness in only one work, Joyce's final effort, and an effort unique in literary history, *Finnegans Wake,* and here, of course, those readers willing to approach the "ideal" effort Joyce demands, discovering an inexhaustible wealth and scope, are most forcibly reminded of the primary importance of technique to subject, and of their indivisibility.

The techniques of naturalism inevitably curtail subject and often leave it in its original area, that of undefined social experience. Those of our writers who, stemming from this tradition, yet, at their best, achieve a novelistic definition of social experience—writers like the occasional Sherwood Anderson, William Carlos Williams, the occasional Erskine Caldwell, Nathaniel West, and Ira Wolfert in *Tucker's People,* have done so by pressing naturalism far beyond itself, into positively gothic distortions. The structural machinations of Dos Passos and the lyrical interruptions of Steinbeck are the desperate maneuvers of men committed to a method of whose limitations they despair. They are our symbolists *manqué,* who end as allegorists.*

Our most accomplished novels leave no such impression of desperate and intentional struggle, yet their precise technique and their determination to make their prose work in the service of their subjects have been the measure of their accomplishment. Hemingway's *The Sun Also Rises* and Wescott's *The Pilgrim Hawk* are works of art not because they may be measured by some external, neo-classic notion of form, but because their forms are so exactly equivalent with their subjects, and because the evaluation of their subjects exists in their styles.

Hemingway has recently said that his contribution to younger writers lay in a certain necessary purification of the language; but the claim has doubtful value. The contribution of his prose was to his subject, and the terseness of style for which his early work is justly celebrated is no more valuable, as an end in itself, than the baroque involutedness of Faulkner's prose, or the cold elegance of Wescott's. Hemingway's early subject, the exhaustion of value, was perfectly investigated and invested by his bare style, and in story after story, no meaning at all is to be inferred from the fiction except as the style itself suggests that there is no meaning in life. This style, more than that, was the perfect technical substitute for the conventional commentator; it expresses and it measures that peculiar morality of the stiff lip which Hemingway borrowed from athletes. It is an instructive lesson, furthermore, to observe how the style breaks down when Hemingway moves into the less congenial subject matter of social affirmation: how the style breaks down, the effect of verbal economy as mute suffering is lost, the personality of the writer, no longer protected by the objectification of an adequate technique, begins its offensive intrusion, and the entire structural integrity slackens. Inversely, in the stories and the early novels, the technique was the perfect embodiment

* For a discussion of naturalism, see the essays in Part III, Section 2, of this volume. Delmore Schwartz on "John Dos Passos and the Whole Truth" in Part II is also instructive.

of the subject and it gave that subject its astonishing largeness of effect and of meaning.*

One should correct Buffon and say that style is the subject. In Wescott's *Pilgrim Hawk,* a novel which bewildered its many friendly critics by the apparent absence of subject, the subject, the story, is again in the style itself. This novel, which is a triumph of the sustained point of view, is only bewildering if we try to make a story out of the narrator's observations upon others; but if we read his observations as oblique and unrecognized observations upon himself the story emerges with perfect coherence, and it reverberates with meaning, is as suited to continuing reflection as the greatest lyrics.

The rewards of such respect for the medium as the early Hemingway and the occasional Wescott have shown may be observed in every good writer we have. The involutions of Faulkner's style are the perfect equivalent of his involved structures, and the two together are the perfect representation of the moral labyrinths he explores, and of the ruined world which his novels repeatedly invoke and in which these labyrinths exist. The cultivated sensuosity of Katherine Anne Porter's style has charm in itself, of course, but no more than with these others does it have aesthetic value in itself; its values lie in the subtle means by which sensuous details become symbols, and in the way that the symbols provide a network which is the story, and which at the same time provides the writer and us with a refined moral insight by means of which to test it.** When we put such writers against a writer like William Saroyan, whose respect is reserved for his own temperament, we are appalled by the stylistic irresponsibility we find in him, and by the almost total absence of theme, or defined subject matter, and the abundance of unwarranted feeling. Such a writer inevitably becomes a sentimentalist because he has no means by which to measure his emotion. Technique, at last, is measure.

These writers, from Defoe to Porter, are of unequal and very different talent, and technique and talent are, of course, after a point, two different things. What Joyce gives us in one direction, Lawrence, for all his imperfections as a technician, gives us in another, even though it is not usually the direction of art. Only in some of his stories and in a few of his poems, where the demands of technique are less sustained and the subject matter is not autobiographical, Lawrence, in a different way from Joyce, comes to the same aesthetic fulfilment. Emily Brontë, with what was perhaps her intuitive grasp of the need to establish a tension between her subject matter and her perspective upon it, achieves a similar fulfilment; and, curiously, in the same way

* For an excellent discussion of the technical failure of Hemingway's later novels, see "Ernest Hemingway: The Failure of Sensibility," by Ray B. West, Jr., in the *Sewanee Review,* Winter, 1945.
** See Ray B. West, Jr., on "Katherine Anne Porter: Symbol and Theme in 'Flowering Judas' " in Part II of this volume.

and certainly by intuition alone, Hemingway's early work makes a moving splendor from nothingness.

And yet, whatever one must allow to talent and forgive in technique, one risks no generalization in saying that modern fiction at its best has been peculiarly conscious of itself and of its tools. The technique of modern fiction, at once greedy and fastidious, achieves as its subject matter not some singleness, some topic or thesis, but the whole of the modern consciousness. It discovers the complexity of the modern spirit, the difficulty of personal morality, and the fact of evil—all the untractable elements under the surface which a technique of the surface alone cannot approach. It shows us—in Conrad's words, from *Victory* —that we all live in an "age in which we are camped like bewildered travellers in a garish, unrestful hotel," and while it puts its hard light on our environment, it penetrates, with its sharp weapons, the depths of our bewilderment. These are not two things, but only an adequate technique can show them as one. In a realist like Farrell, we have the environment only, which we know from the newspapers; in a subjectivist like Wolfe, we have the bewilderment only, which we record in our own diaries and letters. But the true novelist gives them to us together, and thereby increases the effect of each, and reveals each in its full significance.

Elizabeth Bowen, writing of Lawrence, said of modern fiction, "We want the naturalistic surface, but with a kind of internal burning. In Lawrence every bush burns." But the bush burns brighter in some places than in others, and it burns brightest when a passionate private vision finds its objectification in exacting technical search. If the vision finds no such objectification, as in Wolfe and Saroyan, there is a burning without a bush. In our committed realists, who deny the resources of art for the sake of life, whose technique forgives both innocence and slovenliness—in Defoe and Wells and Farrell, there is a bush but it does not burn. There, at first glance, the bush is only a bush; and then, when we look again, we see that, really, the thing is dead.

FICTION AND THE "ANALOGICAL MATRIX" *

MARK SCHORER

I

IF THE novel, as R. P. Blackmur recently proposed, is now to enjoy the kind of attention from criticism that for the past twenty years has been the privilege of poetry, criticism must begin with the simplest assertion: fiction is a literary art. It must begin with the base of language, with the word, with figurative structures, with rhetoric as skeleton and style as body of meaning. A beginning as simple as this must overcome corrupted reading habits of long standing; for the novel, written in prose, bears an apparently closer resemblance to discursive forms than it does to poetry, thus easily opening itself to first questions about philosophy or politics, and, traditionally a middle-class vehicle with a reflective social function, it bears an apparently more immediate relation to life than it does to art, thus easily opening itself to first questions about conduct. Yet a novel, like a poem, is not life, it is an image of life; and the critical problem is first of all to analyze the structure of the image. Thus criticism must approach the vast and endlessly ornamented house of fiction with a willingness to do a little at a time and none of it finally, in order to suggest experiences of meaning and of feeling that may be involved in novels, and responsibilities to and for their style which novelists themselves may forget.

To choose, more or less at random and without premeditated end, one novel by each of only three novelists, and to examine in each only one element in the language, the dominant metaphorical quality—this, positively, is to work piecemeal, and merely to suggest. I emphasize not *metaphor* but *quality,* intending not only the explicit but the buried and the dead metaphors, and some related traits of diction generally, that whole habit of value association suggested in Scott Buchanan's phrase, the "analogical matrix." The novels are *Persuasion, Wuthering Heights,* and *Middlemarch.*

II

Persuasion is a novel of courtship and marriage with a patina of sentimental scruple and moral punctilio and a stylistic base derived

* "Fiction and the 'Analogical Matrix'" was originally presented in longer form as a lecture before the English Institute at Columbia and the Kenyon School of English. It was first printed in the *Kenyon Review,* Autumn, 1949, and is used here by permission of the author and the magazine editors.

from commerce and property, the counting house and the inherited estate. The first is the expression of the characters, the second is the perception of the author. And whether we should decide that a persistent reliance on commerce and property for concepts of value is the habit of Jane Austen's mind, the very grain of her imagination, or that it is a special novelistic intention, is for the moment irrelevant. It is probable that the essence of her comedy resides, in either case, in the discrepancy between social sentiment and social fact, and the social fact is to be discovered not so much in the professions of her characters as in the texture of her style.

We are told at once that the mother of the three Elliot girls felt in dying that in them she left "an awful *legacy* . . . an awful *charge* rather"; that Sir Walter Elliot is devoted to his eldest daughter, Elizabeth (who opens "every ball *of credit*" and is waiting to be "properly *solicited* by baronet-blood"), but feels that his two younger daughters, Mary and Anne, are "of very inferior *value*"—indeed, "Anne's word had no *weight*." Anne is befriended by Lady Russell, who "had a *value* for rank and consequence," and even though it was Lady Russell no less than Sir Walter who discouraged Anne's marriage, seven years before, to the propertyless Captain Wentworth, Anne "*rated* Lady Russell's influence highly." "Consequence," we are told, "has its *tax*," and for seven years Anne has been paying it. The problem of the novel is to relieve her of the necessity of paying it and at the same time to increase her value.

We are in a world of substance, a peculiarly material world. Here, indeed, changes are usually named "*material* alterings"—for example, in "style of living" and "degree of consequence." Perhaps the word is used most tellingly in the phrases "a face not materially *disfigured*" and "a material difference in the *discredit* of it"; for *figure* and *credit* suggest the two large areas of metaphorical interest—arithmetic and business.

Time is *divided*, troubles *multiply*, weeks are *calculated*, and even a woman's prettiness is *reckoned*. Thus, one's independence is *purchased*; one is *rendered* happy or unhappy; one is on *terms*, friendly or unfriendly, with others. Young Mr. Elliot has "nothing to *gain* by being on *terms* with Sir Walter," but Lady Russell is convinced that he hopes "to *gain* Anne" even though Anne cannot "know herself to be so *highly rated*." We are asked to "take all the charms and perfections of Edward's wife upon *credit*," and "to judge of the general *credit due*." Captain Wentworth thought that he had *earned* "every blessing." "I have *valued* myself on honourable toils and just *rewards*." So Mary is in the habit of *claiming* Anne's energies, and Anne does not feel herself "*entitled* to reward." Young ladies have a "*stock* of accomplishments." "Here were *funds* of enjoyment!" Anne does not wish "for the possibility of *exchange*." Experience is thought of as *venture*, *reversal, prospect, fortune,* and *allowance.* Anne *"ventured* to recommend a larger *allowance* of prose in" Captain Benwick's "daily study." The death of a wife leaves a man with *"prospects* ... blighted," and Anne contemplates "the *prospect* of *spending"* two months at Uppercross. In this metaphorical context, even the landscape takes on a special shimmer: "all the *precious* rooms and furniture, groves, and *prospects."* An "arrangement" is *prudent* or *imprudent,* and feelings must be *arranged* as prudently as accounts: no one's "feelings could *interest* her, till she had a little better *arranged* her own." One *pays* addresses, of course, but one is also *repaid* for the "trouble of exertion." "It had *cost* her something to encounter Lady Russell's surprise." A town has *worth,* a song is not *worth* staying for, and Anne "had the full *worth* of" tenderness in "Captain Wentworth's affection." Captain Wentworth's account of Captain Benwick ("whom he had always *valued highly")* *"stamped him* well in the esteem of every listener." "Ten minutes were enough *to certify that"* Mr. Elliot was a sensible man. Stamped, certified; and at last Anne's character is *"fixed* on his mind as perfection itself," which is to say that, like a currency, it has been stabilized.

Moral qualities are persistently put in economic figures: Mary "had no *resources* for solitude" and she had *inherited* "a considerable *share* of the Elliot self-importance." Love, likewise: if Elizabeth is hoping to be *solicited* by baronet-blood, Anne has had to reject the "declarations and proposals" of an improvident sailor. "Alliance" is a peculiarly appropriate word for such prudential arrangements as these, and at the end of the novel, when "the engagement" is *"renewed,"* one sees bonded documents. Anne need no longer suffer those fits of dejection in which she contemplates others' *"prosperous* love," for hers at last has prospered, too.

In this context certain colorless words, words of the lightest intention, take on a special weight. The words *account* and *interest* are used hundreds of times in their homeliest sense, yet when we begin to observe that every narration is an *account,* and at least once "an *account* ... of the *negotiation,"* we are reminded that they have more special meanings. When Anne's blighted romance is called "this little history of sorrowful *interest,"* we hardly forget that a lack of money was the blight. Is "a man of principle" by any chance a man of substance?

The significance of this metaphorical substructure is clearest, perhaps, not when Jane Austen substitutes material for moral or sentimental values, but when she juxtaposes them. "He had ... been nothing better than a thick-headed, *unfeeling, unprofitable* Dick Musgrove, who had never done anything to entitle himself to more than the abbreviation of his name, living or dead." More simply, these three from a single paragraph: "a *fund* of good *sense,"* "*leisure* to *bestow,"* "something that is *entertaining* and *profitable."* "I must endeavour," says Captain Wentworth, in another such juxtaposition near the end of the novel, "I must endeavour to subdue my *mind* to my *fortune.*" *Persuasion* is a novel in which sensibility—and I am not now raising the question whether it is the sensibility of the author or of her characters or of her characters except for her heroes—a novel in which sensibility is subdued to property.

The novel explicitly asks, what is "the value of an Anne Elliot" and where is the man who will "understand" it? Anne herself feels that her value has sunk:

> A few months hence, and the room now so deserted, occupied by her silent, pensive self, might be filled again with all that was happy and gay, all that was *glowing and bright* in *prosperous love,* all that was most unlike Anne Elliot!
>
> ...Anne felt her spirits not likely to be benefited by an increasing acquaintance among his brother-officers. "These would have been all my friends," was her thought; and she had to struggle against a great tendency to lowness.

"A great *tendency to lowness.*" The phrase clarifies her situation, for Anne's is finally the problem of a stock that has a debased value, and when she thinks of doing good in such a further phrase as "good of a lower standard," we can hardly escape the recognition that this is a novel about marriage as a market, and about the female as marketable, and that the novel makes the observation that to sentimental scruple and moral fastidiousness, as they are revealed to us in the drama, much property is not necessary but *some* is essential—and this is shown us primarily in the style. The basis of the comedy lies in the difference between the two orders of value which the metaphors, like the characters, are all the while busily equating. At the end, in the last sentence, a prosperous sailor's wife, Anne has been relieved of "the tax of consequence," but now "she must *pay the tax* of quick alarm for belonging to that profession which is, if possible, more distinguished in its domestic virtues than in its national importance."

III

The style of Jane Austen is so entirely without flamboyance or gesture, the cited illustrations are so commonplace, so perfectly within the order of English idiom, that, unless we remind ourselves that our own habits of speech are even more intimately involved in the life of cash than Jane Austen's, no case at all may appear. Yet the inevitability of individual imaginative habit, the impressive fact that every mind selects its creative gamut from the whole range of possible language, and in thus selecting determines its insights and their scope, in short, its character and the character of its creations, is at once apparent when we open some other novel. Emily Brontë is very different from

Jane Austen, yet both were unmarried provincial women, living in the same half of the same century, speaking the same language, both daughters of clergymen, and one might reasonably expect to encounter, even in *Wuthering Heights,* some of those perfectly normal figures with which *Persuasion* abounds. There are, I think, none of the same kind. Emily Brontë does not "divide the time" but, on the first page, "the desolation"; "time," when she mentions it, "stagnates," and "prudence" is "diabolical." If there are any figures of the same kind, they are so few, and in their own metaphorical context, function so differently, that the total quality owes nothing to them. Where Wentworth speaks of the "crown" of "all my other successes," Lockwood speaks of the "copestone on my rage and humiliation." Both *crown* and *copestone on* mean climax, but "crown" is drawn from rank and money, "copestone" from earth and building. If Nelly Dean's phrase, "the crown of all my wishes," suggests a kingdom at all, it is a heavenly kingdom, quite different from "all my other successes." The difference signifies. *Wuthering Heights* has its own sphere of significant experience, and its metaphors, like its epithets and verbs, tell us different things. They tell us, too, of a special problem.

Wuthering Heights, as I understand it, means to be a work of edification: Emily Brontë begins by wishing to instruct her narrator, the dandy, Lockwood, in the nature of a grand passion; she ends by instructing herself in the vanity of human wishes. She means to dramatize with something like approval—the phrase that follows is from *Middlemarch*—"the sense of a stupendous self and an insignificant world." What her metaphors signify is the impermanence of self and the permanence of something larger.

To exalt the power of human feeling, Emily Brontë roots her analogies in the fierce life of animals and in the relentless life of the elements—fire, wind, water. "Wuthering," we are told, is "a significant provincial adjective, descriptive of the atmospheric tumult to which its station is exposed in stormy weather," and, immediately after, that "one may guess the power of the north wind blowing over the edge, by the excessive slant of a few stunted firs at the end of the house; and by a range of gaunt thorns all stretching their limbs one way, as if craving alms of the sun." The application of this landscape to the characters is made explicit in the second half of the novel, when Heathcliff says, "Now, my bonny lad, you are *mine!* And we'll see if one tree won't grow as crooked as another, with the same wind to twist it!" This analogy provides at least half of the metaphorical base of the novel.

Human conditions are like the activities of the landscape, where rains *flood,* blasts *wail,* and the snow and wind *whirl wildly* and *blow* out lights. A serving woman *heaves* "like a sea after a high wind"; a preacher *"poured* forth his zeal in a *shower";* Mrs. Dean *rushes* to welcome Lockwood, "exclaiming *tumultuously"; spirits are "at high-water mark"; Linton's soul is as different from Heathcliff's "as a moonbeam from lightning, or frost from fire"; abuse is *lavished* in a *torrent,* or *pours forth* in a *deluge; illnesses are "weathered . . . through"; "sensa-tions" are felt in a *gush; "your veins are *full* of *ice water;* but mine are *boiling";* hair *flies,* bodies *toss* or *tremble* like reeds, tears *stream* or *rain down* among ashes; discord and distress arise in a *tumult;* Catherine Linton "was *struck* during a *tempest* of passion with a kind of fit" and *"flew off* in the *height* of it."

Faces, too, are like landscapes: "a *cloud* of meditation" hangs over Nelly Dean's *"ruddy* countenance"; Catherine had a "suddenly *clouded* brow; her humor was a mere *vane* for constantly varying caprices"; "the surface of" the boy Heathcliff's "face and hands was dismally *beclouded"* with dirt; later, his face *"brightened* for a moment; then it was *overcast* afresh." "His forehead . . . *shaded* over with a heavy *cloud";* and "the *clouded* windows of hell," his eyes, *"flashed."* Hare-ton, likewise, grows "black as a *thundercloud";* or *darkens* with a frown. The older Catherine experienced whole *"seasons* of gloom," and the younger Catherine's "heart was *clouded . . .* in double *dark-ness."* Her "face was just like the *landscape—shadows* and *sunshine* flitting over it in rapid succession; but the *shadows* rested longer, and the *sunshine* was more transient." Sometimes "her eyes are *radiant* with *cloudless* pleasure," and at the end, Hareton shakes off "the *clouds* of ignorance and degradation," and his *"brightening* mind *brightened* his features."

Quite as important as the imagery of wind and cloud and water is the imagery of fire. In every interior, the fire on the hearth is the center of pictorial interest, and the characters sit *"burning* their eyes out before the fire." Eyes *burn* with anguish but do not *melt;* they always *flash* and *sparkle.* Fury *kindles,* temper *kindles,* a *"spark* of spirit" *kindles.* Catherine has a *fiery* disposition, but so do objects and states: words *brand,* shame is *burning,* merriment *expires* quickly, fevers *consume* life; hot coffee and basins *smoke,* they do not steam; and Isabella shrieks "as if witches were running *red-hot* needles into her." Sometimes fire is identified with other elements, as when a serv-ant urges *"flakes* of *flame* up the chimney," or when Isabella complains that the fire causes the wound on her neck, first stopped by the icy cold, to stream and smart.

Metaphors of earth—earth takes more solid and durable forms than the other elements—are interestingly few. Twice Heathcliff is likened to "an arid wilderness of *furze* and *whinstone";* there is a reference to his *"flinty* gratification"; and once he speaks scornfully of "the *soil* of" Linton's "shallow cares." Earth and vegetation sometimes result in a happy juxtaposition of the vast or the violent and the little or the homely, as when Heathcliff says of Linton that "He might as well plant *an oak in a flowerpot*," or when he threatens to "crush his ribs in like *a rotten hazelnut*," which is like his saying that Catherine's passion could be as readily encompassed by Linton as "*the sea* could be . . . contained in that *horse-trough*."

Most of the animals are wild. Hareton's "whiskers encroached *bearishly* over his cheeks," and Heathcliff denies the paternity of "that bear." Hareton had been "cast out like an unfledged *dunnock*," and Heathcliff is a "fierce, pitiless, *wolfish* man." He is also "a *bird* of bad omen" and "an evil *beast*" prowling between a "stray *sheep*" and the fold, waiting his time to spring and destroy. He has a "*ferocious* gaze" and a *savage* utterance; he *growls* and *howls* "like a beast," and is many times named "a brute," "a beast," "a brute beast." He struggles like a *bear*, he has *sharp cannibal teeth* which *gleam* "through the dark," and "*basilisk* eyes . . . *quenched* by sleeplessness." He *gnashes* his teeth and *foams* like a *mad dog*. He is "like a *bull*" to Linton's "*lamb*," and only at the very end, the exhausted end, "he breathed as fast as a *cat*."

For the domestic and the gentler animals are generally used for purposes of harsh satire or vilification. Edgar, "the soft thing," "possessed the power to depart, as much as a *cat* possesses the power to leave a *mouse* half killed, or a *bird* half eaten." He is "not a *lamb*" but "a sucking *leveret*," and his sister is a "pitiful, slavish, mean-minded *brach*," she is among those *worms*, who, "the more they writhe, the more" Heathcliff yearns "to crush out their entrails." Hindley dies in a stupor, "snorting like a *horse*"; "flaying and scalping" would not have roused him, and when the doctor arrives, "the *beast* has changed to *carrion*." Hareton is "an infernal *calf*," and young Linton is a "*puling chicken*" and a "*whelp*." Like a dying dog, he "slowly *trailed* himself off, and lay down," or, like a cold one, he "*shrank* closer to the fire." He "had *shrunk* into a corner of the settle, as quiet as a *mouse*"; he is called "a little perishing *monkey*"; and "he achieved his exit exactly as a *spaniel* might." He is also "an abject *reptile*" and a "*cockatrice*." Hareton, who is capable on occasion of gathering "*venom* with reflection," is once called a "*magpie*," and once said to be "obstinate as a *mule*"—one of the few kindly animal references in the novel. To be sure, Isabella describes herself as though she were a deer: "I *bounded*, *leaped* and *flew* down the steep road; then . . . *shot* direct across the moor, *rolling* over banks, and *wading* through marshes." And Catherine, on the whole, is not abused. She is a "cunning little *fox*" and she runs "like a *mouse*," but chiefly she is "soft and mild as a *dove*."

Emily Brontë's metaphors color all her diction. As her epithets are charged with passion—"jealous guardianship," "vexatious phlegm," "importunate branch"—so her verbs are verbs of violent movement and conflict, both contributing to a rhetorical texture where everything is at a pitch from which it can only subside. The verbs *demand* exhaustion, just as the metaphors *demand* rest. And there is an antithetical chorus in this rhetoric, a contrapuntal warning, which, usually but not only in the voice of Nelly Dean, says, "Hush! Hush!" all through the novel, at the beginning of paragraph after paragraph. At the end, everything *is* hushed. And the moths *fluttering* over Heathcliff's grave and "the soft wind *breathing* through the grass" that grows on it have at last more power than he, for all his passion. These soft and fragile things paradoxically endure.

The passions of animals, if we may speak of them as passions, have meaning in that they are presumably necessary to survival; Heathcliff's passion destroys others, himself, and at last, itself. The tumult of the elements alternates with periods of peace, and the seasons are not only autumn and winter. The *fact* of alternation enables nature to endure. The singleness of Heathcliff's tempestuous and wintry emotional life dooms it. Thus there is a curious and ironic contrast between the condition and the destiny of Heathcliff, and the full facts of those areas of metaphor. When, at the end of the novel, Nelly remarks that "the same moon shone through the window; and the same autumn landscape lay outside" as eighteen years before, she is speaking with metaphorical accuracy; but Heathcliff is *not* the same. He has not indeed come into a "sober, disenchanted maturity"—that will be the privilege of Hareton and the second Cathy; but he has completely changed in the fashion that Joseph described much earlier—"so as by fire" "... there is a strange change approaching: I'm in its shadow at present," he declares when he has found that nothing is worth the feeling of it. At last, after all the windy tumult and the tempests, he says, "I have to remind myself to *breathe....*"

If his life, exhausted at the end, has not been, as he once said of it, "a moral teething," and the novel, therefore, no tragedy, the story of his life has been a moral teething for the author. Lockwood is instructed in the nature of a grand passion, but he and Emily Brontë together are instructed in its final fruits: even roaring fires end in a bed of ashes. Her metaphors instruct her, and her verbs. That besides these rhetorical means (which in their functioning make tolerable the almost impossibly inflated style), she should have found structural means as well which give her whole narrative the remote quality of a twice-told tale, the property of an old wife (and so make its melodrama endurable), should reinforce the point. At the end, the voice that drones on is the perdurable voice of the country, Nelly Dean's. No more than Heathcliff did Emily Brontë quite intend that homespun finality. Like the older Catherine, Emily Brontë could have said of her book, "I've dreamed in my life dreams that have stayed with me ever after, and changed my ideas: they've gone through and through me, like wine through water, and altered the color of my mind." Her rhetoric altered the form of her intention. It is her education; it shapes her insight.

IV

Middlemarch is a novel written on a much grander scale than either of these others, with many points of narrative interest, a much more complex structural pattern, and an important difference in its metaphorical language. Jane Austen's metaphors are generally of the "buried" kind, submerged, woven deep in the ordinary, idiomatic fabric of the language; Emily Brontë's are generally epithetical. George Eliot's tend always to be, or to become, explicit symbols of psychological or moral conditions, and they actually function in such a way as to give symbolical value to much action, as Dorothea's pleasure in planning buildings ("a kind of work which she delighted in") and Casaubon's desire to construct a "Key to all Mythologies." Their significance lies, then, not so much in the choice of area (as, "commerce," or "natural elements" and "animals") as in the choice of function, and one tests them not by their field, their content, but by their conceptual portent. I should like to suggest a set of metaphorical qualities in *Middlemarch* which actually represents a series apparent in the thinking that underlies the dramatic structure. First of all, there are metaphors of unification; then, of antithesis; next, there are metaphors which conceive things as progressive, and then, metaphors of shaping and making, of structure and creative purpose; finally, there are metaphors of what I should call a "muted" apocalypse.

George Eliot's metaphors of unification pivot on her most characteristic verbs—these are of conciliation and reconciliation, of unification, of course, and of inclusion, of mingling, of associating, of merging and mixing, of embracing and comprehending, of connecting, allying, binding together and making room for. The elements to be brought together are as various as the universe—they may be merely "mingled pleasures" or "associated facts which ... show a mysterious electricity if you touched them," or the relation of urban and rural areas, which "made fresh threads of connection"; again, they may be attitudes— "criticism" and "awe" *mixing,* or qualities *uniting,* as, presumably, "the glories of doctor and saint" in dreary Casaubon, or men themselves making more *energetic alliances* "with impartial nature"; or they may be those yearnings of one individual for another which find completion in love, the institution of marriage, and the literal embrace; or, most important, they may be "lofty conceptions" which embrace multitudinousness—for example, the daily life of Tipton parish and Dorothea Brooke's own "rule of conduct." If only we knew more and felt more, these metaphors insist; for there *is,* we are told, "a knowledge which ... traces out the suppressed transitions which unite all contrasts." This is religious yearning, and it finds occasional psuedo-religious fulfilment, as after Lydgate's successful cogitations on morphology: he finds himself "in that agreeable after-glow of excitement when thought lapses from examination of a specific object into a suffusive sense of its connections with all the rest of our existence," and one can "float with the repose of unexhausted strength."

The metaphors of unification imply the metaphors of antithesis; the first represent yearnings, the second a recognition of fact. Thus we have metaphors of reality vs. appearance, as: "the large vistas and wide fresh air which she had dreamed of finding in her husband's mind were replaced by anterooms and winding passages which seemed to lead no-whither"; or of chaos vs. order (humorously dramatized by Mr. Brooke's "documents," which need arranging but get mixed up in pigeon-holes) as Mary Garth's "red fire," which "seemed like a solemn existence calmly independent of the petty passions, the imbecile desires, the straining after worthless uncertainties, which were daily moving her contempt"; or of shapelessness vs. shape, as "a kind Providence furnishes the limpest personality with a little gum or starch in the form of tradition." There are other kinds, of outer *vs.* inner, for example: "so much subtler is a human mind than the outside tissues which make a sort of blazonry or clock-face for it." It is this, the outer-inner antithesis, which underscores one of George Eliot's favorite words—"inward" or "inwardly," a usage which is frequently annoying because it is tautological, applied to states which can *only* be inward under the circumstances of the fiction, but, for that reason, all the more symptomatic. There are metaphorical antitheses of fact to wish, imbalance to balance, restlessness to repose, and many other opposites. Most important, and perhaps most frequent, are the figures which oppose freedom to various forms of restraint—burdens, ties, bonds, and so on: "he replies by calling himself Pegasus, and every form of prescribed work 'harness,'" to which the answer is, "I shall let him be *tried* by the *test* of freedom." Another example of the restraint-freedom opposition illustrates the way that reported action, when conjoined with these metaphors, pushes both on to explicit symbolism: near the end, Dorothea observes on the road outside her window "a man with a bundle on his back and a woman carrying her baby," and, still nearer the end, when Lydgate has "accepted his narrowed lot," that is, the values of his child-bride, he thinks, "He had chosen this fragile creature, and had taken the burden of her life upon his arms. He must walk as he could, carrying that burden pitifully."

The oppositions in these metaphors of antithesis are the classic oppositions between Things as They Are and Things as They Should Be, between the daily realities of a community like Middlemarch and the "higher" realities of that "New Jerusalem" toward which Dorothea and others are "on the road."

Everyone and everything in this novel is moving on a "way." Life is a *progress,* and it is variously and inevitably described as road, stream, channel, avenue, way, journey, voyage, ride (either on horse or by carriage), vista, chain, line, course, path, and process. To these terms one should add the terms of *growth,* usually biological growth, which carry much the same value. There must be at least a thousand and possibly there are more metaphorical variations on the general idea of life as progress, and this progress is illimitable. At the end of the novel we are told, in words somewhat suggestive of a more ortho- dox religious spirit than George Eliot, that "Every limit is a beginning as well as an ending."

Everything strains forward. Consciousness is a stream. "In Doro- thea's mind there was a current into which all thought and feeling were apt sooner or later to flow—the reaching forward of the whole consciousness toward the fullest truth, the least partial good." "Char- acter, too," we are told, "is a process," and it is a process which we recognize by achievement—"the niceties of inward balance, by which man swims and makes his point or else is carried headlong." Like Leopold Bloom, George Eliot's characters think of their existence as "the stream of life in which the stream of life we trace," but with a difference: the personal life finally flows into the "gulf of death," but the general stream flows on, through vistas of endlessly unfolding good, and that good consists of individual achievements of "the fullest truth, the least partial good," of Lydgate's individually *made points.* This is a progressive, in no sense a cyclical view of human history.

These metaphors of progress, like the restraint-freedom antithesis, involve George Eliot in her many complementary metaphors of hin- drance to progress. The individual purpose is sometimes confused by "a social life which seemed nothing but a labyrinth of petty courses, a walled-in maze"; sometimes by the inadequacy of the purpose itself, as Casaubon, who "was lost among small closets and winding stairs"; experience and circumstance over and over become "yokes," which slow the progress, for there are those always "who carry a weight of trials"; one may *toil* "under the fetters of a promise" or move, like Lydgate, more haltingly than one had hoped under the *burden* of a responsibility.

These hindrances are, generally speaking, social, not moral. One submits to them in the interests of the whole procession, and when one does not submit—as Dorothea, refusing to devote herself to Casau- bon's scholarship after his death—it is because one has discovered that they are not in the interests of the whole procession. The particular interests of the procession are indicated by the extended metaphors drawn from nearly every known field of physical and medical science. It is by the "serene light of science" that we glimpse "a presentiment of endless processes filling the vast spaces planked out of" our "sight by that wordy ignorance which," in the past, we "had supposed to be knowledge." It is by the same light that we are able to recognize our social obligations, according to the Religion of Humanity.

Thus, quite smoothly, we come to that fourth group of prevailing metaphors, those having to do with purpose. They are of shaping, of forming, of making, of framing; they pivot on notions of pattern or rule, measure or structure. They are all words used in metaphors which, explicitly or by implication, reveal the individual directing his destiny by conscious, creative purpose toward the end of absolute human order. Opposed to them are the many metaphors of derogation of the unorganized, notably the human mind, which, at worst, like Mr. Brooke's, availing nothing perceptible in the body politic, is a *mass*.

At the end of this grand vista are the metaphors of what I have called the "muted" apocalypse. The frequency with which George Eliot uses the words *up, high,* and *higher* in metaphorical contexts is equalled only, perhaps, by her use of the word *light,* until one feels a special significance in "giving *up*" and in all the faces that *beam,* all the ideas that *flash* across the mind, and all the things that are all the time being "taken" in *that light* or *this light.* Fire plays a perhaps predictably important metaphorical role, and, together with light, or alternating with it, usually accompanies or is implied by those frequent metaphors in which things are *gloriously* transformed, transfused, or transfigured. Treating this complex of figures as I do, as a kind of apocalyptic drama which of course does not exist in the novel as such, but surely does in the imagination of George Eliot, we are, now, at the moment before climax, all those metaphors involving ideas of veneration and adoration, or worshipful awe; these, in my factitious series, are immediately followed by the climax itself, which is contained in endless use of the word "revelation" and figurative developments from it. Perception, in this novel, is indeed thought of as revelation, and minds and souls are always "opening" to the influx. Things are many times "manifested" or "made manifest," as if life were a perpetual epiphany. If perception is not a "revelation," it is a "divination," and for the ordinary verb, "to recognize," George Eliot usually prefers to use "to divine." It is here that we come upon her unquestionably favorite word, and the center of her most persistent metaphors. For the word "sight" or "feeling" she almost always substitutes the more portentous word "vision." Visions are of every possible kind, from *dim* to *bright* to *blinding,* from *testing* to *guiding.* The simplest sight of the physical detail may be a vision; every insight is of course a vision, usually an *inward* vision.

The experience now subsides. If perception is revelation, then it is, secondarily, nourishment, and the recurrence of metaphors in which perception is conceived as spiritual food and drink, and of all the metaphors of *fullness, filling,* and *fulfilment,* is perhaps predictable.

It is likewise energizing, in various figurative ways, and in moments of climactic understanding, significantly, a charge of electricity flows through the human organism.

Illumination, revelation, fulfilment. One step remains in this pattern of a classic religious experience; that is expectation. Metaphors of expectation are everywhere; I will represent them in their most frequent form, a phrase so rubbed by usage that it hardly seems metaphorical at all. It is "to look forward," and it appears on nearly every page of *Middlemarch,* a commonplace there too, yet more than that: it is the clue to the whole system of metaphor I have sketched out; it is the clue to a novel, the clue to a mind.

I have separated into a series a metaphorical habit which of course always appears in conflux, and it is only because these metaphors do constantly associate themselves in the novel, that one may justifiably hit upon them as representing George Eliot's selectivity. One of many such elaborate confluences is as follows:

> ... Mr. Casaubon's talk about his great book was *full* of *new vistas;* and this sense of *revelation,* this *surprise of a nearer introduction* to Stoics and Alexandrians, as people who had ideas not totally unlike her own, kept in abeyance for the time her usual eagernesss for a *binding theory* which could bring her own life and doctrine into *strict connection* with that amazing past, and give the remotest *sources* of knowledge some *bearing* on her actions ... she was *looking forward* to *higher initiation* in ideas, as she was *looking forward* to marriage, and *blending* her *dim* conceptions of both. ... All her eagerness for acquirement lay within that *full current of sympathetic* motive in which her ideas and impulses were habitually *swept along.* She did not want to deck herself with knowledge—to wear it loose from the *nerves and blood that fed her action*; and if she had written a book she must have done it as St. Theresa did, under the *command of an authority that constrained her conscience.* But something she yearned for by which her *life might be filled* with action at once rational and ardent: and since the time was gone by *for guiding visions* and spiritual directors, since prayer *heightened* yearning, but not instruction, *what lamp* was there but knowledge?

Here are nearly all of them: metaphors of unification, of antithesis (restraint-freedom), of progress, of the apocalypse: height, light, revelation, vision, nourishment, and, of course, the forward look. The passage is not in the least exceptional. In my analytical sketch of such persistent confluences, I separated the elements into a series to demonstrate how completely, step by step, they embody a pseudo-religious philosophy, how absolutely expressive is metaphor, even in fiction, and how systematic it can become. This is a novel of religious yearning without religious object. The unification it desires is the unification of human knowledge in the service of social ends; the antitheses that trouble it (and I observe in this otherwise classic series no antitheses either of Permanence and Change, or of Sin and Grace) are the anti theses between man as he is and man as he could be in this world; the hindrances to life as progress are man's social not his moral flaws; the purposive dedication of individuals will overcome those flaws; we see the fulfilment of all truly intellectual passions, for the greater glory of Man.

Our first observation on the function of metaphor in this novel should, then, be of its *absolutely* expressive character. The second is perhaps less evident, and we may call it the interpretive function of metaphor, the extent to which metaphor comments on subject. The subject of this novel may be Middlemarch, a community, but, as even the title metaphorically suggests, the theme is the nature of progress in what is probably meant to be the typical British community in the 19th Century. (Observe, too, these names: Brooke, a running course, and Lydgate, his progress blocked by his wife, twice-blocked by his name.) Or we can select subjects within the subject, as the clerical subject interpreted by the pseudo-religious theme: the true "religious" dedication of a Dorothea Brooke, and the characters around her falling into various "religious" postures: Casaubon as the false prophet, Bulstrode as the parody-prophet, Lydgate as the nearly true prophet—a "scientific Phoenix," he is called—somehow deflected from his prophecy; and Ladislaw as the true prophet. Indeed, given the metaphorical texture, one cannot escape the nearly systematic Christ analogy which George Eliot weaves around Ladislaw, omitting from her figure only the supremely important element of Christ's sacrifice, and the reason for which He made it. This is to be expected in a novel which is about progress without guilt. Here, even the heroic characters cannot be said to have inner struggles, for all their "inward visions." Here there is much illumination and nearly no self-doubt; much science, and never a sin. One recognizes from the metaphorical structure that this novel represents a decay of the full religious experience into that part of it which aspires alone: Christian optimism divorced from the basic human tragedy.

The metaphorical complex provides a third, and a more interesting function: a structural function. *Middlemarch* is concerned with nearly every important activity in community life—political, clerical, agricultural, industrial, professional, domestic, of course, even scholarly. It involves many different characters and groups of characters. The relations between some of these characters and even between some of these groups are often extremely tenuous, often merely accidental. The dramatic structure, in short, is not very taut, yet one feels, on finishing the book, that this is a superbly constructed work, that, indeed, as foolish Mr. Brooke observes, "We're all one family, you know

—it's all one cupboard." What makes it so is thematic rather than dramatic unity.

The measure of Middlemarch is Dorothea's *sublimity,* the interpretive height from which she judges. From her sublimity, everything shades off, all the way down to garrulous Mrs. Cadwallader and villainous Mr. Bulstrode. The metaphors of unification which George Eliot enjoyed to use, those images of intermingling and embracing, are important in a double sense: they express Dorothea's ethical sentiments, and, actually, they and the others bind the material together. They tell us *how to take* each Middlemarcher *in what light.* They do this chiefly through the creation of symbolic echoes of the major situations in the minor ones, echoes often ironic, sometimes parodies.

Thus, in the imagery of vision, Dorothea's remark, made so early as in Chapter III, has a special ring: "I am rather shortsighted." In the imagery of human progress, Mr. Garth's question about Bulstrode, the pious fraud,—"whether he shall settle somewhere else, as a lasting thing"—has such symbolic value. Mr. Garth's own attitude toward agriculture is a thematic parody of the exaltation of Dorothea, Lydgate, and Ladislaw: "the peculiar tone of fervid veneration, of religious regard in which he wrapped it, as a consecrated symbol is wrapped in its gold-fringed linen." In the imagery of structure, a special meaning seems to attach to the word "dwell," when it refers to characters experiencing some state of mind. Lydgate's morphological research is another such symbolic extension of the metaphors of structure. Dorothea's avenue of limes outside her window, leading toward the sunset, becomes, finally, a representation in the landscape of the idea of progress. The political newspapers, notably unenlightened, are called *The Pioneer* and *The Trumpet,* and these are surely parodies, one of the progress metaphors, the other of the apocalyptic. Even that humble rural tavern, the *Weights and Scales,* reminds us of more exalted concern, in this novel, with justice and with metaphors of balance. And so that wretched farm called Freeman's End, which has nearly destroyed its tenant and his family, is an eloquent little drama of the freedom-restraint metaphors.

"We all of us," says George Eliot, "grave or light, get our thoughts entangled in metaphors, and act fatally on the strength of them." If the writing of a novel is a deed, as Conrad liked to think, she spoke truer than she knew.

V

Four tentative proposals seem relevant:

1. Metaphorical language gives any style its special quality, and one may even suggest—only a little humorously—that this quality derives in part from the content of the metaphors, that quantity shapes quality. Certainly the particular "dryness" of Jane Austen's style is

generated in part by the content of her images of the counting house, and certainly the inflatedness of Emily Brontë's is generated in large part by the prominence of wind and of atmospheric tumult in her metaphors. I cannot, unfortunately, suggest that George Eliot's pleasure in "light" has any notable effect on the quality of her style, but we can say that the content of her conceptions as her metaphors express it predicts a style solemn always, heavy probably, and sodden perhaps.

2. Metaphorical language expresses, defines, and evaluates theme, and thereby demonstrates the limits and the special poise within those limits of a given imagination. We have seen three novels in which metaphors in effect answered questions that the novels themselves neglected to ask.

3. Metaphorical language, because it constantly strains toward symbolism, can be in novels as in poems the basis of structure, and it can even be counterposed to dramatic structure. We have observed the structural function in *Middlemarch*. In *Wuthering Heights* we may observe the more complicated contrapuntal function of metaphor in structure. Gerard Manly Hopkins, writing of Greek tragedy, spoke of "two strains of thought running together and like counterpointed," the paraphrasable "overthought," and the "underthought"

> conveyed chiefly in the choice of metaphors etc. used, and often only half realized by the poet himself, not necessarily having any connection with the subject in hand but usually having a connection and suggested by some circumstance of the scene or of the story.

The metaphors of *Wuthering Heights* comprise such an "underthought," for although they are equated in the work, the work itself yet somehow develops a stronger and stronger contrast between the obligations of the human and the non-human creation.

4. Finally, metaphorical language reveals to us the character of any imaginative work in that, more tellingly perhaps than any other elements, it shows us what conceptions the imagination behind that work is able to entertain, how fully and how happily. I mean to say that style *is* conception, and that, for this reason, rhetoric must be considered as existing within—importantly within, and, sometimes, fatally within—what we call poetic. It is really style, and style primarily, that first conceives, then expresses, and finally tests these themes, these subjects, even these "kinds"—Jane Austen's manners, Emily Brontë's passions, George Eliot's morals. "Symbolization," said Susanne Langer (and I could not comfortably close these observations without mentioning her excellent name), "Symbolization is both an end and an instrument." "The right word," said George Eliot, "is always a power, and communicates its definiteness to our action." And "The Eye," said William Blake, "sees more than the heart knows."

PART II

CRITIQUES: STUDIES IN THE METHOD
OF MEANING

THE STUDIES in Part II are illustrations of that method of close textual analysis by which modern critics, particularly critics of poetry, have placed themselves in the most rewarding proximity to the meaning of a work of literature. They are all based on the formalist assumption that fiction is a literary art to which the soundest approach is through its source in language, and that it is not to be taken, at least in the first instance, as the subject of history, biography, or psychiatry. They also serve to demonstrate, in terms of exegesis, the principles that were set forth as theory in the essays of Part I.

The studies have been arranged so as to indicate the tendency of this kind of criticism to move, through stages of gradual refinement, toward a closer and closer engagement of single elements in the technical design of fiction. Beginning with F. R. Leavis' study of the general problem of technique in Conrad's minor works— a study, incidentally, which, in its grace of style, is a model for a kind of polished critical discourse which threatens to disappear as the art of technical scrutiny improves—the discussion proceeds to Irene Hendry's analysis of Joyce's method in the broad terms of language, then narrows, in the work of Harry Levin, Edmund Wilson, and Delmore Schwartz, to the more specific study of the technique of three novels, and finally focuses on the still more specific study of the symbolic content of single novels and stories in the analyses of Faulkner's *Light in August* by Richard Chase, Warren's *All the King's Men* by Norton R. Girault, and Porter's "Flowering Judas" by Ray B. West, Jr.

This development from general considerations of method to specific considerations of symbolic content is balanced, in these studies, by an increasingly explicit concern with the dramatizing or "rendering" principle of fiction, as set down by Lubbock, Tate, Frank, and Schorer in Part I. For Leavis the crucial problem of Conrad's minor fiction consists in its occasional failure to ascend to a truly dramatic evocation of its subject. *Heart of Darkness* achieves its intensity, he tells us, by means of "objective correlatives." "The details and circumstances of the voyage to and up the Congo are present to us as if we were making the journey ourselves and . . . they carry specificities of emotion and suggestion with them." But when Conrad fails to be satisfied with these means and begins to feel "that there is, or ought to be, some horror, some significance he has yet to bring out," he lapses into a merely "adjectival and worse than supererogatory insistence on 'unspeakable rites,' 'unspeakable secrets,' 'monstrous passions,' 'inconceivable mystery,' " whose imprecision of statement is matched only by its poverty of dramatic effect. "If he cannot," Leavis concludes, "through the concrete presentment of incident, setting, and image, invest the words with the terrific something that, by themselves, they fail to convey, then no amount of adjectival and ejaculatory emphasis will do it." One notices here the importance of "presentment" or rendering through the medium of concrete "incident, setting, and image," the stern disavowal of mere self-expression. "Poetry," said T. S. Eliot, "is not a turning loose of emotion, but an escape from emotion; it is not the expression of personality, but an escape from personality." What is occasionally at fault in Conrad is not merely his intruding personality, but the character of the language into which it tries, and fails, to escape.

Miss Hendry views Joyce's epiphany technique, in its most refined form, as a method of achieving the effect which Conrad's "adjectival insistence" could not achieve—the depersonalization of the esthetic image in dramatic and symbolic terms. The defect of *Stephen Hero* is its self-expressiveness; the virtue of *A Portrait of the Artist* is its successful rendition of the forms into which Joyce's emotion escaped and became generalized. The labor of compression he performed on the material of the novel resulted in a fabling of what was formerly merely particular—Emma Clery, the healthy, middle-class girl of the earlier version, became an etherealized "E__C__," essence of Virginity; the worshipping poor, formerly revealed in all attitudes of submissive piety, became the essence of Faith; and Stephen's brothers and sisters, formerly seen as separate entities with separate life, became the essence of Childhood. In the performance of his labor Joyce progressed from things to epiphanies of things, from a world of recollected experience to a world of achieved meaning and design, rendered through the medium of symbolic language.

Harry Levin, Edmund Wilson, and Delmore Schwartz are all concerned in their studies with the great question which Leavis and Hendry suggest: In precisely what way does the novelist approximate and transmit in impersonal language the full meaning of his personal vision? The problem for Joyce in attempting to render, first, the "flux of undifferentiated experience" of a day in Dublin, and, finally, the "dream fantasies and the half-unconscious sensations" of a Dubliner asleep, is much the same as the problem for Dos Passos in attempting to render the "whole truth" of a nation. But the difference between the achievements of the two men is a difference in the quality of the rendering, or simply in the imaginative grasp of the subject to be rendered.

To Schwartz the formal failure of *U. S. A.* is inseparable from, and largely the result of, Dos Passos' failure to re-create in imaginative terms the naturalistic truth with which his experience and his literary tradition provided him. The unassimilated materials of the novel—the "camera eye" sections, the "newsreels," and the "biographies"—testify to his awareness of a larger truth; but because they are unassimilated, they have the effect of obstructing rather than completing those central passages of narrative in which his real vision operates and is imprisoned. In this sense, Dos Passos is the victim of the whole truth; for it is the disproportion between his knowledge of that truth and his power to render it that accounts for the imperfect character of his art.

Here, in this kind of comparison with Dos Passos, Joyce clearly reveals his superior artistry. "The imitation of life through the medium of language" is, for Joyce, a problem in total rendition; and he brings to it not only a strength of imaginative grasp that far exceeds Dos Passos' but a technical equipment which enables him to depict the whole truth of his subject entirely within the formal limits of his medium. *Ulysses* becomes a world as *U. S. A.* never does; Joyce's skilled use of *montage* becomes a way of rendering the play of impressions upon the consciousness of Bloom in terms of "exact verbal equivalents," which register upon us with the fidelity of life; in every detail of its form the novel mirrors its subject. The form, says Levin, is "an elusive and eclectic *Summa* of its age," employing "the *montage* of the cinema, impressionism in painting, *leitmotiv* in music, the free association of psychoanalysis, and vitalism in philosophy." Form, to paraphrase Mark Schorer, *is* the subject; and form, in the ultimate sense, is successful imaginative conception.

Wilson's *Finnegans Wake* essay, a rare combination of close textual analysis and perceptive evaluation, defines Joyce's progress toward a literature of supreme rendition. The gigantic epiphany which composes the novel is not merely that of a single sleeping unconscious but that of the thoroughly awakened consciousness of the race. Through Earwicker we have set before us "the processes of universal history: the languages, the cycles of society, the typical relationships of legend"; and as we immerse ourselves in the stream of Earwicker's unconscious, much as we immersed ourselves in the consciousness of Bloom, we find that we too have become part of history: the great rhythms of birth, death, and resurrection, the rise and fall of civilizations, the coming of the first light and the final darkness to the cosmos, have been re-created both within and before us. There is, as Lubbock would say, no further for the art of presentment in fiction to go.

But for a criticism which seeks to concern itself seriously with the precise nature of that art there is considerably further to go. There is, in particular, the large area of analysis which lies beyond the mere interpretation of difficulty and which takes into close account the function of language as the symbolic agent of theme in fiction. It is here in this area, which, in its narrowest reaches has formerly been almost exclusively the province of the critic of poetry, that the inseparability of form and content, technique and subject, in fiction is revealed most clearly and finally.

Richard Chase, Norton R. Girault, and Ray B. West, Jr., approach the question of symbolic texture in *Light in August, All the King's Men,* and "Flowering Judas" with much the same care, and from much the same point of view, that Mark Schorer approaches the question of metaphor in *Wuthering Heights, Persuasion,* and *Middlemarch.* Like Schorer, they conceive of technique as the means by which the true content of fiction is not only discovered but objectified or rendered to the reader. For the special purposes of these studies, however, they restrict themselves, for the most part, to that single aspect of the symbolizing function of technique which is isolable in the specific word and image.

The images of the line and curve and their several variants in *Light in August* are, for Chase, concrete representations of the major interacting themes of the novel. "The linear discrete image stands for 'modernism': abstraction, rationalism, applied science, capitalism, progressivism, emasculation, the atomized consciousness and its pathological extensions. The curve image stands for holistic consciousness, a containing culture and tradition, the cyclical life and death of all the creatures of earth." And not only do these images suggest the two warring cultures which form the moral basis of Faulkner's art, but their implications create the psychological tensions by which the characters are dramatized and understood.

Girault's study of Warren's novel amounts to a completely new reading of a work which has up to now been much too facilely interpreted. Its special virtue consists in its admirable demonstration of the thematic properties of point of view. The sensibility of Jack Burden functions in the novel not only as the medium through which the character of Willie Stark is presented to us, but as the vehicle of Warren's major symbolism. Burden's progress through the cycle of death and rebirth to a discovery of his own evil is, first, an ironic parallelism and, finally, a revelation of Stark's own tragedy. It creates, through the iteration of characteristic metaphors, a pattern of meaning in terms of which the dilemma of the novel is elevated to the level of myth; and myth, as the study of such writers as Joyce and Faulkner must make clear, is one of the superior means by which the art of fiction attains a maximum universalizing and rendering of its subject.

West's close scrutiny of "Flowering Judas" narrows the discussion of technique to the smallest unit of fiction—the short story. Through his analysis of Miss Porter's symbols West provides a key to the method by which the critic most successfully cuts through the apparent meaning of a work and places himself closest to its true meaning. What appears to be a simple story of revolutionary intrigue becomes, in West's hands, a complex allegory of moral and religious responsibility. Laura, the frigid American girl, becomes a symbol of Judas the betrayer; Braggioni, the revolutionary, takes on the character of a Marxist Christ; and the prisoner Eugenio is transformed, through his murder, into a symbol of Man. In achieving this analysis West makes it clear that symbolism in fiction is the true source of theme, that, in the largest sense, it is technique alone, as Mark Schorer said, which "objectifies the materials of art."

JOSEPH CONRAD

F. R. Leavis

Minor Works and *NOSTROMO* *

An announcement once appeared in a quarterly, against the name of the present writer, of an article to be entitled *Conrad, the Soul and the Universe.* The exasperation registered in this formula explains, perhaps, why the article was never written. For that Conrad has done classical work is as certain as that his classical status will not rest evenly upon his whole *œuvre,* and the necessary discriminations and delimitations, not being altogether simple, clearly oughtn't to be attempted in any but a securely critical frame of mind. He has, of course, long been generally held to be among the English masters; the exasperation records a sense that the greatness attributed to him tended to be identified with an imputed profundity, and that this "profundity" was not what it was taken to be, but quite other, and the reverse of a strength. The final abandonment of the article may have been partly determined by Mr. E. M. Forster's note on Conrad that appeared in *Abinger Harvest:*

> What is so elusive about him is that he is always promising to make some general philosophic statement about the universe, and then refraining with a gruff disclaimer. . . . Is there not also a central obscurity, something noble, heroic, beautiful, inspiring half-a-dozen great books, but obscure, obscure? . . . These essays do suggest that he is misty in the middle as well as at the edges, that the secret casket of his genius contains a vapour rather than a jewel; and that we needn't try to write him down philosophically, because there is, in this direction, nothing to write. No creed, in fact. Only opinions, and the right to throw them overboard when facts make them look absurd. Opinions held under the semblance of eternity, girt with the sea, crowned with stars, and therefore easily mistaken for a creed.

—This might well have gratified the exasperation, and made its expression seem unnecessary.

Mr. Forster, however, doesn't attempt discriminations or precisions (his note is a reprinted review of *Notes on Life and Letters*). And he doesn't suggest those manifestations of the characteristic he describes in which we have something simply and obviously deplorable—something

* "Joseph Conrad: Minor Works and *Nostromo*" appears as Section 1, chap. iv, of *The Great Tradition,* by F. R. Leavis (Chatto & Windus: George W. Stewart, 1948). It was first published in *Scrutiny,* June, 1941, and is used here by permission of Mr. George W. Stewart.

that presents itself, not as an elusively noble *timbre,* prompting us to analysis and consequent limiting judgments, but as, bluntly, a disconcerting weakness or vice. Consider, for instance, how *Heart of Darkness* is marred.

Heart of Darkness is, by common consent, one of Conrad's best things—an appropriate source for the epigraph of *The Hollow Men:* "Mistah Kurtz, he dead." That utterance, recalling the particularity of its immediate context, represents the strength of *Heart of Darkness:*

> He cried in a whisper at some image, at some vision—he cried out twice, a cry that was no more than a breath—
> "The horror! The horror!"
> I blew the candle out and left the cabin. The pilgrims were dining in the mess-room, and I took my place opposite the manager, who lifted his eyes to give me a questioning glance, which I successfully ignored. He leaned back, serene, with that peculiar smile of his sealing the unexpressed depth of his meanness. A continuous shower of small flies streamed upon the lamp, upon the cloth, upon our hands and faces. Suddenly the manager's boy put his insolent face in the doorway, and said in a tone of scathing contempt—
> "Mistah Kurtz—he dead."
> All the pilgrims rushed out to see. I remained, and went on with my dinner. I believe I was considered brutally callous. However, I did not eat much. There was a lamp in there—light, don't you know—and outside it was so beastly, beastly dark.

This passage, it will be recognized, owes its force to a whole wide context of particularities that gives the elements here—the pilgrims, the manager, the manager's boy, the situation—their specific values. Borrowing a phrase from Mr. Eliot's critical writings, one might say that *Heart of Darkness* achieves its overpowering evocation of atmosphere by means of "objective correlatives." The details and circumstances of the voyage to and up the Congo are present to us as if we were making the journey ourselves and (chosen for record as they are by a controlling imaginative purpose) they carry specificities of emotion and suggestion with them. There is the gunboat dropping shells into Africa:

> There wasn't even a shed there, and she was shelling the bush. It appears the French had one of their wars going on thereabouts. Her ensign dropped limp like a rag; the muzzles of the long six-inch guns stuck out all over the low hull; the greasy, slimy swell swung her up lazily and let her down, swaying her thin masts. In the empty immensity of earth, sky and water, there she was, incomprehensible, firing into a continent. Pop, would go one of the six-inch guns; a small flame would dart and vanish, a tiny projectile would give a feeble screech—and nothing happened. Nothing could happen. There was a touch of insanity in the proceeding, a sense of lugubrious drollery in the sight; and it was not dissipated by somebody on board assuring me earnestly

there was a camp of natives—he called them enemies!—hidden out of sight somewhere.

We gave her her letters (I heard the men in that lonely ship were dying of fever at the rate of three a day) and went on. We called at some more places with farcical names, where the merry dance of death and trade goes on in a still and earthy atmosphere as of an overheated catacomb. . . .

There is the arrival at the Company's station:

I came upon a boiler wallowing in the grass, then found a path leading up the hill. It turned aside for the boulders, and also for an undersized railway-truck lying there on its back with its wheels in the air. One was off. The thing looked as dead as the carcass of some animal. I came upon more pieces of decaying machinery, a stack of rusty nails. To the left a clump of trees made a shady spot, where dark things seemed to stir feebly. I blinked, the path was steep. A horn tooted to the right, and I saw black people run. A heavy, dull detonation shook the ground, a puff of smoke came out of the cliff, and that was all. No change appeared on the face of the rock. They were building a railway. The cliff was not in the way of anything; but this objectless blasting was all the work going on.

A slight clanking behind me made me turn my head. Six black men advanced in a file, toiling up the path. They walked erect and slow, balancing small baskets full of earth on their heads, and the clink kept time with their footsteps. Black rags were wound round their loins, and the short ends behind waggled to and fro like tails. I could see every rib, the joints of their limbs were like knots in a rope; each had an iron collar on his neck, and all were connected together with a chain whose bights swung between them, rhythmically clinking. Another report from the cliff made me think suddenly of that ship of war I had seen firing into a continent. It was the same kind of ominous voice; but these men could by no stretch of imagination be called enemies. They were called criminals. . . .

There is the grove of death:

At last I got under the trees. My purpose was to stroll into the shade for a moment; but no sooner within it than it seemed to me that I had stepped into the gloomy circle of some Inferno. The rapids were near, and an uninterrupted, uniform, headlong, rushing noise filled the mournful stillness of the grove, where not a breath stirred, not a leaf moved, with a mysterious sound—as though the tearing pace of the launched earth had suddenly become audible.

Black shapes crouched, lay, sat beneath the trees, leaning against the trunks, clinging to the earth, half coming out, half effaced within the dim light, in all the attitudes of pain, abandonment, and despair. Another mine of the cliff went off, followed by a slight shudder of the soil under my feet. The work was going on. The work! And this was the place where some of the helpers had withdrawn to die.

They were dying slowly—it was very clear. They were not enemies, they were not criminals, they were nothing earthly now,—nothing but black shadows of disease and starvation, lying confusedly in the greenish gloom.... These moribund shapes were free as air and nearly as thin. I began to distinguish the gleam of the eyes under the trees. There, glancing down, I saw a face near my hand. The black bones reclined at full length with one shoulder against the tree, and slowly the eyelids rose and the sunken eyes looked up at me, enormous and vacant, a kind of blind, white flicker in the depths of the orbs, which died out slowly.

By means of this art of vivid essential record, in terms of things seen and incidents experienced by a main agent in the narrative, and particular contacts and exchanges with other human agents, the overwhelming sinister and fantastic "atmosphere" is engendered. Ordinary greed, stupidity and moral squalor are made to look like behaviour in a lunatic asylum against the vast and oppressive mystery of the surroundings, rendered potently in terms of sensation. This mean lunacy, which we are made to feel as at the same time normal and insane, is brought out by contrast with the fantastically secure innocence of the young harlequin-costumed Russian ("son of an arch-priest ... Government of Tambov"), the introduction to whom is by the way of that copy of Tower's (or Towson's) *Inquiry into Some Points of Seamanship,* symbol of tradition, sanity and the moral idea, found lying, an incongruous mystery, in the dark heart of Africa.

Of course, as the above quotations illustrate, the author's comment cannot be said to be wholly implicit. Nevertheless, it is not separable from the thing rendered, but seems to emerge from the vibration of this as part of the tone. At least, this is Conrad's art at its best. There are, however, places in *Heart of Darkness* where we become aware of comment as an interposition, and worse, as an intrusion, at times an exasperating one. Hadn't he, we find ourselves asking, overworked "inscrutable," "inconceivable," "unspeakable" and that kind of word already?—yet still they recur. Is anything added to the oppressive mysteriousness of the Congo by such sentences as:

> It was the stillness of an implacable force brooding over an inscrutable intention?

The same vocabulary, the same adjectival insistence upon inexpressible and incomprehensible mystery, is applied to the evocation of human profundities and spiritual horrors; to magnifying a thrilled sense of the unspeakable potentialities of the human soul. The actual effect is not to magnify but rather to muffle. The essential vibration emanates from the interaction of the particular incidents, actions and perceptions that are evoked with such charged concreteness. The legitimate kind of comment, that which seems the inevitable immediate resonance of the recorded event, is represented here:

And then I made a brusque movement, and one of the remaining posts of that vanished fence leaped into the field of my glass. You remember I told you I had been struck at the distance by certain attempts at ornamentation, rather remarkable in the ruinous aspect of the place. Now I had suddenly a nearer view, and its first result was to make me throw my head back as if before a blow. Then I went carefully from post to post with my glass, and I saw my mistake. Those round knobs were not ornamental but symbolic; they were expressive and puzzling, striking and disturbing—food for thought and also for the vultures if there had been any looking down from the sky; but at all events for such ants as were industrious enough to ascend the pole. They would have been even more impressive, those heads on the stakes, if their faces had not been turned to the house. Only one, the first I had made out, was facing my way. I was not so shocked as you may think. The start back I had given was really nothing but a movement of surprise. I had expected to see a knob of wood there, you know. I returned deliberately to the first I had seen—and there it was, black, dried, sunken, with closed eyelids,—a head that seemed to sleep at the top of that pole, and, with the shrunken dry lips showing a narrow white line of the teeth, was smiling too, smiling continuously at some endless and jocose dream of that eternal slumber.

I am not disclosing any trade secrets. In fact, the manager said afterwards that Mr. Kurtz's methods had ruined the district. I have no opinion on that point, but I want you clearly to understand that there was nothing exactly profitable in those heads being there. They only showed that Mr. Kurtz lacked restraint in the gratification of his various lusts, that there was something wanting in him—some small matter which, when the pressing need arose, could not be found under his magnificent eloquence. Whether he knew of this deficiency himself I can't say. I think the knowledge came to him at last—only at the very last, but the wilderness had found him out early, and had taken on him a terrible vengeance for the fantastic invasion. I think it had whispered to him things about himself which he did not know, things of which he had no conception till he took counsel with this great solitude—and the whisper had proved irresistibly fascinating. It echoed loudly within him because he was hollow at the core. . . . I put down the glass, and the head that had appeared near enough to be spoken to seemed at once to have leaped away from me into inaccessible distance.

—That the "admirer of Mr. Kurtz," the companion of the narrator here, should be the fantastically sane and innocent young Russian is part of the force of the passage.

By such means as it illustrates we are given a charged sense of the monstrous hothouse efflorescences fostered in Kurtz by solitude and the wilderness. It is a matter of such things as the heads on posts—a direct significant glimpse, the innocent Russian's explanations, the incidents of the progress up the river and the moral and physical incongruities registered; in short, of the charge generated in a variety of highly specific evocations. The stalking of the moribund Kurtz, a skeleton crawling through the long grass on all fours as he makes his bolt towards the fires and the tom-toms, is a triumphant climax in the suggestion of strange and horrible perversions. But Conrad isn't satisfied with these means; he feels that there is, or ought to be, some horror, some significance he has yet to bring out. So we have an adjectival and worse than supererogatory insistence on "unspeakable rites," "unspeakable secrets," "monstrous passions," "inconceivable mystery," and so on. If it were only, as it largely is in *Heart of Darkness,* a matter of an occasional phrase it would still be regrettable as tending to cheapen the tone. But the actual cheapening is little short of disastrous. Here, for instance, we have Marlow at the crisis of the episode just referred to:

> I tried to break the spell—the heavy, mute spell of the wilderness—that seemed to draw him to its pitiless breast by the awakening of forgotten and brutal instincts, by the memory of gratified and monstrous passions. This alone, I was convinced, had driven him out to the edge of the forest, towards the gleam of the fires, the throb of drums, the drone of weird incantations; this alone had beguiled his unlawful soul beyond the bounds of permitted aspirations. And, don't you see, the terror of the position was not in being knocked on the head—though I had a very lively sense of that danger too—but in this, that I had to deal with a being to whom I could not appeal in the name of anything high or low ... I've been telling you what we said—repeating the phrases we pronounced—but what's the good? They were common everyday words—the familiar vague sounds exchanged on every waking day of life. But what of that? They had behind them, to my mind, the terrific suggestiveness of words heard in dreams, of phrases spoken in nightmares. Soul! If anybody had ever struggled with a soul, I am the man. And I wasn't arguing with a lunatic either.... But his soul was mad. Being alone in the wilderness, it had looked within itself, and, by heavens! I tell you, it had gone mad. I had—for my sins, I suppose—to go through the ordeal of looking into it myself. No eloquence could have been so withering to one's belief in mankind as his final burst of sincerity. He struggled with himself too, I saw it—I heard it. I saw the inconceivable mystery of a soul that knew no restraint, no faith, and no fear, yet struggling blindly with itself.

—Conrad must here stand convicted of borrowing the arts of the magazine-writer (who has borrowed his, shall we say, from Kipling and Poe) in order to impose on his readers and on himself, for thrilled response, a "significance" that is merely an emotional insistence on the presence of what he can't produce. The insistence betrays the absence, the willed "intensity" the nullity. He is intent on making a virtue out of not knowing what he means. The vague and unrealizable, he asserts with a strained impressiveness, is the profoundly and tremendously significant:

> I've been telling you what we said—repeating the phrases we pro-
> nounced—but what's the good? They were common everyday words—the
> familiar vague sounds exchanged on every waking day of life. But what
> of that? They had behind them, to my mind, the terrific suggestiveness
> of words heard in dreams, of phrases spoken in nightmares.

—What's the good, indeed? If he cannot through the concrete presentment of incident, setting and image invest the words with the terrific
something that, by themselves, they fail to convey, then no amount of
adjectival and ejaculatory emphasis will do it.

> "I saw the inconceivable mystery of a soul," etc.

—That, of course, is an ambiguous statement. I see that there is a
mystery, and it remains a mystery to me; I can't conceive what it is;
and if I offer this inability to your wonder as a thrilling affair of
"seeing an inconceivable mystery," I exemplify a common trait of
human nature. Actually, Conrad had no need to try to inject "significance" into his narrative in this way. What he shows himself to
have successfully and significantly seen is enough to make *Heart of
Darkness* a disturbing presentment of the kind he aimed at. By the
attempt at injection he weakens, in his account of Kurtz's death, the
effect of that culminating cry:

> He cried in a whisper at some image, at some vision—he cried out
> twice, a cry that was no more than a breath—"The horror! The horror!"

—The "horror" there has very much less force than it might have
had if Conrad had strained less.
This final account of Kurtz is associated with a sardonic tone, an
insistent irony that leads us on to another bad patch, the closing interview in Brussels with Kurtz's "Intended":

> The room seemed to have grown darker, as if all the sad light of the
> cloudy evening had taken refuge on her forehead. This fair hair, this
> pale visage, this pure brow, seemed surrounded by an ashy halo from
> which the dark eyes looked out at me. Their glance was guileless, pro-
> found, confident, and trustful. She carried her sorrowful head as though
> she were proud of that sorrow, as though she would say, I—I alone know
> how to mourn for him as he deserves.

It is not part of Conrad's irony that there should be anything ironical
in this presentment of the woman. The irony lies in the association of
her innocent nobility, her purity of idealizing faith, with the unspeakable corruption of Kurtz; and it is developed (if that is the word)
with a thrilled insistence that recalls the melodramatic intensities of
Edgar Allan Poe:

> I felt a chill grip on my chest. "Don't," I said in a muffled voice.
> "Forgive me. I—I—have mourned so long in silence—in silence...."

You were with him—to the last? I think of his loneliness. Nobody near to understand him as I would have understood. Perhaps no one to hear...."

"To the very end," I said shakily. "I heard his very last words...." I stopped in a fright.

"Repeat them," she murmured in a heart-broken tone. "I want—I want—something—something to live with."

I was on the point of crying at her "Don't you hear them?" The dark was repeating them in a persistent whisper all around us, in a whisper that seemed to swell menacingly, like the first whisper of a rising wind. "The horror! the horror!"

"His last words—to live with," she insisted. "Don't you understand I loved him—I loved him—I loved him!"

I pulled myself together and spoke slowly.

"The last word he pronounced was—your name."

I heard a light sigh and then my heart stood still, stopped dead short by an exulting and terrible cry, by the cry of inconceivable triumph and of an unspeakable pain.

"I knew it—I was sure!" ... She knew. She was sure.

Conrad's "inscrutable," it is clear, associates with Woman as it does with the wilderness, and the thrilling mystery of the Intended's innocence is of the same order as the thrilling mystery of Kurtz's corruption: the profundities are complementary. It would appear that the cosmopolitan Pole, student of the French masters, who became a British master-mariner, was in some respects a simple soul. If anyone should be moved to question the propriety of this way of putting it, perhaps the following will be found something of a justification:

Woman and the sea revealed themselves to me together, as it were: two mistresses of life's values. The illimitable greatness of the one, the unfathomable seduction of the other, working their immemorial spells from generation to generation fell upon my heart at last: a common fortune, an unforgettable memory of the sea's formless might and of the sovereign charm in that woman's form wherein there seemed to beat the pulse of divinity rather than blood.

This comes from a bad novel, one of Conrad's worst things, *The Arrow of Gold*. It is a sophisticated piece of work, with a sophistication that elaborates and aggravates the deplorable kind of naïvety illustrated in the quotation. Not that the author's talent doesn't appear, but the central theme—and the pervasive atmosphere—is the "unfathomable seduction" of the "enigmatic" Rita; a glamorous mystery, the evocation of which (though more prolonged and elaborated) is of the same order as the evocation of sinister significance, the "inconceivable" mystery of Kurtz, at the close of *Heart of Darkness*. If any reader of that tale had felt that the irony permitted a doubt regarding Conrad's attitude towards the Intended, the presentment of Rita should settle it.

"Woman" figures in *The Rescue,* the book that in publication preceded *The Arrow of Gold* (both came out just after the 1914 war,
though *The Rescue* belongs essentially to Conrad's early period). The
glamour here is a simple affair—less sophisticated and more innocent.
But if *The Rescue* lacks the positive badness of *The Arrow of Gold,* it
is, on a grand scale, boring in its innocence. The seduction of Woman
as represented by Mrs. Travers is less insistently and melodramatically
"unfathomable" than in the later book, but cannot sustain the interest
Conrad demands for it; so to say that it is, in the formal design,
adequate to balancing Heroic Action as represented by Lingard—King
Tom, idealized seaman-adventurer—is not to say anything very favour-
able about the whole. *The Rescue,* in short, is an Academy piece—
"sombre, colourful, undeniably a classic" the reviewers may have said,
and its Grand Style staging of the conflict between Love and Honour
(a kingdom at stake) against a sumptuously rendered *décor* of tropical
sea, sunset, and jungle is, in its slow and conscientious magnificence,
calculated to engender more deference than thrill, and so can't even
be recommended as good boy's reading—though it offers little to adults.
The book, in fact, is not altogether a surprising kind of thing to have
come from a sailor of pertinacious literary talent and French literary
education. The reason for bringing it in just here is to enforce the
point that Conrad, for all his sophistication, exhibits a certain simplicity of outlook and attitude. About his attitude toward women there
is perceptible, all the way through his literary career, something of the
gallant simple sailor.

The sailor in him, of course, is rightly held to be a main part of his
strength. It is not for nothing that *Heart of Darkness,* a predominantly
successful tale, is told by the captain of the steamboat—told from that
specific and concretely realized point of view: appraisal of the success
of the tale is bound up with this consideration. But the stress up till
now has fallen upon Conrad's weaknesses. It is time to ask where the
strength may be found in its purest form. There will, I think, be
general approval of the choice of *Typhoon* as a good example. But I
am not sure that there is as general a recognition of just where the
strength of *Typhoon* lies. The point may be made by saying that it
lies not so much in the famous description of the elemental frenzy
as in the presentment of Captain MacWhirr, the chief mate Jukes and
the chief engineer Solomon Rout at the opening of the tale. Of course,
it is a commonplace that Conrad's distinctive genius comprises a gift
for rendering the British seaman. But is it a commonplace that the
gift is the specific gift of a novelist, and (though the subtler artist
doesn't run to caricature and the fantastic) relates Conrad to Dickens?
Consider, for instance, this:

> He was rather below the medium height, a bit round-shouldered,
> and so sturdy of limb that his clothes always looked a shade too tight

for his arms and legs. As if unable to grasp what is due to the difference of latitudes, he wore a brown bowler hat, a complete suit of a brownish hue, and clumsy black boots. These harbour togs gave to his thick figure an air of stiff and uncouth smartness. A thin silver watch-chain looped his waistcoat, and he never left his ship for the shore without clutching in his powerful, hairy fist an elegant umbrella of the very best quality, but generally unrolled. Young Jukes, the chief mate, attending his commander to the gangway, would sometimes venture to say, with the greatest gentleness, "Allow me, sir,"—and, possessing himself of the umbrella deferentially, would elevate the ferrule, shake the folds, twirl a neat furl in a jiffy, and hand it back: going through the performance with a face of such portentous gravity, that Mr. Solomon Rout, the chief engineer, smoking his morning cigar over the skylight, would turn away his head in order to hide a smile. "Oh! aye! The blessed gamp.... Thank 'ee, Jukes, thank 'ee," would mutter Captain MacWhirr heartily, without looking up.

Consider the exchanges between Captain MacWhirr and Jukes over the Siamese flag, deplorably, poor Jukes feels ("Fancy having a ridiculous Noah's ark elephant in the ensign of one's ship"), substituted for the Red Ensign. Consider the accounts of the home backgrounds of MacWhirr and the chief engineer.

It is to be noted further that these backgrounds in their contrast with the main theme of the tale afford a far more satisfactory irony (it is, in fact, supremely effective) than that, in *Heart of Darkness,* of the scenes at Brussels. At the same time it is to be noted that there is in *Typhoon* no sardonic Marlow, commenting on an action that he is made to project; whereas, though *Heart of Darkness* is given from the point of view of the captain of the steamboat, that captain *is* Marlow—Marlow, for whom Conrad has more than one kind of use, and who is both more and less than a character and always something other than just a master-mariner. For comment in *Typhoon* we have the letters home of Solomon Rout, the chief engineer, and the letter of Jukes to his chum. In short, nothing in the story is forced or injected; the significance is not adjectival, but resides in the presented particulars—the actors, the incidents and the total action: we are given the ship, her cargo and her crew of ordinary British seamen, and the impact on them of the storm.

The ordinariness is, with a novelist's art, kept present to us the whole time; the particular effect of heroic sublimity depends on that.

And again he heard that voice, forced and ringing feeble, but with a penetrating effect of quietness in the enormous discord of noises, as if sent out from some remote spot of peace beyond the black wastes of the gale; again he heard a man's voice—the frail and indomitable sound that can be made to carry an infinity of thought, resolution and purpose, that shall be pronouncing confident words on the last day, when heavens fall, and justice is done—again he heard it, and it was crying to him, as if from very, very far—"All right."

—Conrad can permit himself this, because the voice is that of the unheroically matter-of-fact Captain MacWhirr, whose solid specific presence, along with that of particularized ordinary sailors and engineers, we are never allowed to forget:

> A lull had come, a menacing lull of the wind, the holding of a stormy breath—and he felt himself pawed all over. It was the boatswain. Jukes recognized these hands, so thick and enormous that they seemed to belong to some new species of man.
> The boatswain had arrived on the bridge, crawling on all fours against the wind, and had found the chief mate's legs with the top of his head. Immediately he crouched and began to explore Jukes' person upwards, with prudent, apologetic touches, as became an inferior.

Or take this:

> The boatswain by his side kept on yelling. "What? What is it?" Jukes cried distressfully; and the other repeated, "What would my old woman say if she saw me now?"
> In the alleyway, where a lot of water had got in and splashed in the dark, the men were still as death, till Jukes stumbled against one of them and cursed him savagely for being in the way. Two or three voices then asked, eager and weak, "Any chance for us, sir?"
> "What's the matter with you fools?" he said brutally. He felt as though he could throw himself down amongst them and never move any more. But they seemed cheered; and in the midst of obsequious warning. "Look out! Mind that manhole lid, sir," they lowered him into the bunker. The boatswain tumbled down after him, and as soon as he had picked himself up he remarked "She would say, 'Serve you right, you old fool, for going to sea.'"
> The boatswain had some means, and made a point of alluding to them frequently. His wife—a fat woman—and two grown-up daughters kept a greengrocer's shop in the East-end of London.

The seamen are their ordinary selves, the routine goes forward in the engine-room, and the heroic triumphs of the *Nan-Shan* emerge as matters-of-fact out of the ordinariness:

> "Can't have ... fighting ... board ship,"

says Captain MacWhirr through the typhoon, and down into the 'tween-deck, into the human hurricane of fighting coolies, go Jukes and his men as a routine matter-of-fact course, to restore order and decency:

> "We have done it, sir," he gasped.
> "Thought you would," said Captain MacWhirr.
> "Did you?" murmured Jukes to himself.

"Wind fell all at once," went on the Captain.
Jukes burst out: "If you think it was an easy job—"
But his captain, clinging to the rail, paid no attention.
"According to the books the worst is not over yet."

And the qualities which, in a triumph of discipline—a triumph of the spirit—have enabled a handful of ordinary men to impose sanity on a frantic mob are seen unquestionably to be those which took Captain MacWhirr, in contempt of "Storm-strategy," into the centre of the typhoon. Without any symbolic portentousness the Captain stands there, the embodiment of a tradition. The crowning triumph of the spirit, in the guise of a matter-of-fact and practical sense of decency, is the redistribution—ship devastated, men dropping with fatigue—of the gathered-up and counted dollars among the assembled Chinese.

In *The Shadow Line,* also in common recognition one of Conrad's masterpieces (it is, I think, superior to *Heart of Darkness* and even to *Typhoon*), we have the same art. It has been acclaimed as a kind of prose *Ancient Mariner,* and it is certainly a supremely sinister and beautiful evocation of enchantment in tropic seas. But the art of the evocation is of the kind that has been described; it is not a matter of engendering "atmosphere" adjectivally, by explicitly "significant" vaguenesses, insistent unutterablenesses, or the thrilled tone of an expository commentator, but of presenting concretely a succession of particulars from the point of view of the master of the ship, who, though notably sensitive, is not a Marlow, but just a ship's master; an actor among the other actors, though burdened with responsibilities towards the crew, owners and ship. The distinctive art of a novelist, and the art upon which the success of the prose *Ancient Mariner* essentially depends, is apparent in the rendering of personality, its reactions and vibrations; the pervasive presence of the crew, delicately particularized, will turn out on analysis to account for the major part of the atmosphere. The young captain, entering the saloon for the first time and sitting in the captain's chair, finds he is looking into a mirror:

> Deep within the tarnished ormolu frame, in the hot half-light sifted through the awning, I saw my own face propped between my hands. And I stared back at myself with the perfect detachment of distance, rather with curiosity than with any other feeling, except of some sympathy for this latest representative of what for all intents and purposes was a dynasty; continuous not in blood, indeed, but in its experience, in its training, in its conception of duty, and in the blessed simplicity of its traditional point of view on life. . . .
>
> Suddenly I perceived that there was another man in the saloon, standing a little on one side and looking intently at me. The chief mate. His long, red moustache determined the character of his physiognomy, which struck me as pugnacious in (strange to say) a ghastly sort of way.

The disobliging and disturbing oddity of the mate turns out to be due
to the sinister vagaries and unseemly end of the late captain:

> That man had been in all essentials but his age just such another man
> as myself. Yet the end of his life was a complete act of treason, the be-
> trayal of a tradition which seemed to me as imperative as any guide on
> earth could be. It appeared that even at sea a man could become the
> victim of evil spirits. I felt on my face the breath of unknown powers
> that shape our destinies.

The sinister spell that holds the ship is characteristically felt in terms of
contrast with the tradition and its spiritual values, these being embodied in the crew, a good one, who carry on staunchly against bad
luck and disease. The visiting doctor himself is "good" in the same
way. The story ends, it will be noted, on the unexpected parting with
the faithful Ransome, the exquisitely rendered seaman with a voice
that is "extremely pleasant to hear" and a weak heart:

> "But, Ransome," I said, "I hate the idea of parting with you."
> "I must go," he broke in. "I have a right!" He gasped and a look of
> almost savage determination passed over his face. For an instant he was
> another being. And I saw under the worth and the comeliness of the
> man the humble reality of things. Life was a boon to him—his pre-
> carious, hard life—and he was thoroughly alarmed about himself.
> "Of course I shall pay you off if you wish it."
>
> *   *   *   *   *   *
>
> I approached him with extended hand. His eyes, not looking at me,
> had a strained expression. He was like a man listening for a warning
> call.
> "Won't you shake hands, Ransome?" I said gently. He exclaimed,
> flushed up dusky red, gave my hand a hard wrench—and next moment,
> left alone in the cabin, I listened to him going up the companion stairs
> cautiously, step by step, in mortal fear of starting into sudden anger our
> common enemy it was his hard fate to carry consciously within his faith-
> ful breast.

These things are worth many times those descriptions of sunsets, exotic
seas and the last plunge of flaming wrecks which offer themselves to the
compilers of prose anthologies.

This is at any rate to confirm the accepted notion of Conrad to this
extent: that his genius was a unique and happy union of seaman and
writer. If he hadn't actually been himself a British seaman by vocation
he couldn't have done the Merchant Service from the inside. The cosmopolitan of French culture and French literary initiation is there in
the capacity for detachment that makes the intimate knowledge
uniquely conscious and articulate. We are aware of the artist by vocation, the intellectual who doubles the seaman, only when we stop to

take stock of the perfection of the rendering and the subtle finish of the art.

But this fine balance, this identity, isn't always sustained. In Marlow, who (as remarked above) has a variety of uses, the detachment is separated off. As a main participant in events though, by his specific rôle as such, a detached one, he gives his technical function a dramatic status in the action, and the author a freedom of presence that, as we have seen, constitutes a temptation. Elsewhere Marlow is frankly a method of projection or presentation—one that we learn to associate with Conrad's characteristic vices and weaknesses. In *Youth,* for instance, one of the best-known of the tales, though not one of the best, he goes with the cheap insistence on the glamour, and with that tone which, here and in other places, makes one recall the formula of the early reviewer and reflect that the prose laureate of the British seaman does sometimes degenerate into a "Kipling of the South Seas." (And this is the point at which to note that Conrad can write shockingly bad magazine stuff—see the solemnly dedicated collection called *Within the Tides.*)

In *Lord Jim* Marlow is the means of presenting Jim with the appropriate externality, seen always through the question, the doubt, that is the central theme of the book. Means and effect are unobjectionable; it is a different matter from the use of Marlow elsewhere to pass off a vaguely excited incomprehension as tremendous significance. But *Lord Jim* doesn't deserve the position of pre-eminence among Conrad's works often assigned it: it is hardly one of the most considerable. There is, in fact, much to be said in support of those reviewers who (Conrad tells us) "maintained that the work starting as a short story had got beyond the writer's control," so that what we have is neither a very considerable novel, in spite of its 420 pages, nor one of Conrad's best short stories. The presentment of Lord Jim in the first part of the book, the account of the inquiry and of the desertion of the *Patna,* the talk with the French lieutenant—these are good Conrad. But the romance that follows, though plausibly offered as a continued exhibition of Jim's case, has no inevitability as that; nor does it develop or enrich the central interest, which consequently, eked out to provide the substance of a novel, comes to seem decidedly thin.

The eking out is done mainly from the world of *Almayer's Folly, An Outcast of the Islands,* and *Tales of Unrest,* those excessively adjectival studies in the Malayan exotic of Conrad's earliest vein. Those things, it had better be said here, though they are innocuous, and no doubt deserved for their originality of setting some respectful notice when they came out, will not be urged by judicious admirers of Conrad among his claims to classical rank. In their stylistic eloquence, which suggests a descent from Chateaubriand, their wearying exoticism, and their "picturesque" human interest, they aren't easy to re-read.

No, *Lord Jim* is neither the best of Conrad's novels, nor among the best of his short stories. If, on the other hand, his most considerable work had had due recognition, it would be known as one of the great novels of the language. For *Nostromo* is most certainly that. And it complicates the account of Conrad's genius in that it doesn't answer to the formula arrived at above. He is not here the laureate of the Merchant Service, the British seaman happily doubled with the artist —an artist whose "outsideness" with regard to the Merchant Service is to be constated only in the essential degree of detachment involved in an adequately recorded art. In *Nostromo* Conrad is openly and triumphantly the artist by *métier,* conscious of French initiation and of fellowship in craft with Flaubert. The French element so oddly apparent in his diction and idiom throughout his career (he learnt French before English) here reveals its full significance, being associated with so serious and severe a conception of the art of fiction.

The controlling conception of the novelist's art is severe, but the novel is luxuriant in its magnificence: it is Conrad's supreme triumph in the evocation of exotic life and colour. Sulaco, standing beneath snow-clad Higuerota, with its population of Indians, mixed-bloods, Hidalgos, Italians and English engineers, is brought before us in irresistible reality, along with the picturesque and murderous public drama of a South American State. This aspect of Conrad's genius in *Nostromo* has had full recognition; indeed it could hardly be missed. What doesn't seem to be a commonplace is the way in which the whole book forms a rich and subtle but highly organized pattern. Every detail, character and incident has its significant bearing on the themes and motives of this. The magnificence referred to above addresses the senses, or the sensuous imagination; the pattern is one of moral significances.

Nostromo has a main political, or public, theme, the relation between moral idealism and "material interests." We see the Gould Concession become the rallying centre for all in Costaguana who desire peace and order—the constitutionalists, the patriotic idealists, the Robin Hood of the oppressed, the representatives of the financial power of Europe and North America. The ironical end of the book shows us a Sulaco in which order and ideals have triumphed, Progress forges ahead, and the all-powerful Concession has become the focus of hate for workers and the oppressed and a symbol of crushing materialism for idealists and defenders of the spirit. This public theme is presented in terms of a number of personal histories or, it might be said, private themes, each having a specific representative moral significance.

The Gould Concession is in the first place the personal history of its inheritor, Charles Gould—and the tragedy of his wife. He, like the other main characters, enacts a particular answer to the question that we feel working in the matter of the novel as a kind of informing and organizing principle: what do men find to live *for*—what kinds of motive force or radical attitude can give life meaning, direction, coherence? Charles Gould finds his answer in the ideal purpose he identifies with the success of the Gould Concession:

> What is wanted here is law, good faith, order, security. Anyone can declaim about these things, but I pin my faith to material interests. Only let the material interests once get a firm footing, and they are bound to impose the conditions on which alone they can continue to exist. That's how your money-making is justified here in the face of lawlessness and disorder. It is justified because the security which it demands must be shared with an oppressed people. A better justice will come afterwards. That's your ray of hope.

Charles Gould's faith is parodied by his backer, the American financier Holroyd, whose interest in furthering a "pure form of Christianity" and whose rhetorical faith in the manifest destiny of the United States cannot without irony be said to give ideal significance to his love of power. Charles himself is absorbed by the Concession that killed his father, and Emilia Gould, standing for personal relations and disinterested human sympathy, looks on in starved loneliness at the redeeming triumph that is an ironical defeat of the spirit.

Nostromo, picturesque indispensable to his patrons and popular hero, has no ideal purpose. He lives for reputation, "to be well spoken of"—for his reflection in the eyes of others, and when, tempted by the silver, he condemns himself to clandestine courses the mainspring of his life goes slack. His return to find the new lighthouse standing on the lonely rock hard by his secret, and his consequent betrayal into devious paths in love, are magnificent and characteristic triumphs of symbolism. His appropriately melodramatic death is caused by the silver and occurs during a stealthy visit to it.

Martin Decoud, intellectual and "dilettante in life," Nostromo's companion in that marvellously rendered night of the Gulf (it is one of the most vivid pieces of sensuous evocation in literature), also has no ideal purpose. The voice of sceptical intelligence, with "no faith in anything except the truth of his own sensations," he enjoys conscious advantages, and has no difficulty in summing up Nostromo:

> Decoud, incorrigible in his scepticism, reflected, not cynically but with general satisfaction, that this man was made incorruptible by his enormous vanity, that finest form of egoism which can take on the aspect of every virtue.

He can also place Charles Gould, that "sentimental Englishman" who

> cannot exist without idealizing every simple desire or achievement. He could not believe his own motives if he did not make them first a part of some fairy tale.

Decoud himself, contemptuously free from the "sentimentalism of the
people that will never do anything for the sake of their passionate
desire, unless it comes to them clothed in the fair robes of an ideal,"
is frankly moved by his passion for Antonia Avellanos, and that alone,
when he initiates the step through which the mine is saved and the
aims of the patriots and idealists achieved. In this respect he provides
a criticism of Charles Gould's subtle infidelity to his wife. Yet, even
apart from his passion, he is not quite self-sufficient. At a moment when
we might have expected him to be wholly engrossed in practical considerations we find him, significantly, illustrating an essential human
trait:

> all the objectless and necessary sincerity of one's innermost life trying to
> react upon the profound sympathies of another's existence.

For

> In the most sceptical heart there lurks at such moments, when the
> chances of existence are involved, a desire to leave a correct impression
> of the feelings, like a light by which the action may be seen when per-
> sonality is gone, gone where no light of investigation can ever reach the
> truth which every death takes out of the world. Therefore, instead of
> looking for something to eat, or trying to snatch an hour or two of sleep,
> Decoud was filling the pages of a large pocket book with a letter to his
> sister.

Marooned on the Great Isabel (site of the subsequent lighthouse)
he discovers that his self-sufficiency is indeed radically qualified:

> Solitude from mere outward condition of existence becomes very
> swiftly a state of soul in which the affectations of irony and scepticism
> have no place. It takes possession of the mind, and drives forth the
> thought into the exile of utter unbelief. After three days of waiting for
> the sight of some human face, Decoud caught himself entertaining a
> doubt of his own individuality. It had merged into the world of cloud
> and water, of natural forces and forms of nature. . . .
> . . . He had recognized no other virtue than intelligence and had
> erected passions into duties. Both his intelligence and his passion were
> swallowed up easily in the great unbroken solitude of waiting without
> faith.

He shoots himself. The whole episode is given in painful immediacy.
Of all the characters the one nearest to self-sufficiency is Dr.
Monygham, the disliked and distrusted, and he, for all his sardonic
scepticism about human nature, does hold to an ideal. His scepticism
is based on self-contempt, for his ideal (he is, in fact, a stronger and
quite unequivocal Lord Jim) is one he has offended against; it is an
exacting ideal of conduct. He offers a major contrast with Nostromo
too. since his success in the desperate venture that saves the situation

and rehabilitates him (in his own eyes—he expects death) depends upon his having no reputation except for "unsoundness" and a shady past, and his being ready to be ill-spoken of and ill-thought of. His ideal, of course, isn't merely personal—it is of the same order as the moral idea of the Merchant Service (he is "an officer and a gentleman"): it owes its strength to a traditional and social sanction; and he has an outer stay in his devotion to Mrs. Gould.

Perhaps the completest antithesis to Decoud is Giorgio Viola, the serene old Garibaldino, also self-sufficient, or very near it—he by reason of his libertarian idealism, the disinterestedness of which is above all question. He represents with monumental massiveness the heroic age of the liberal faith—of *Songs before Sunrise* and the religion of humanity, and so provides a contrasting background for the representatives of Progress in Costaguana politics (by the end of *Nostromo* the Marxists are on the scene). He is commandingly real; but it is part of the irony of the book that the achievements he stands for should have produced the South America we are shown.

Captain Mitchell represents the Merchant Service. He is sane and stable to the point of stupidity. His inability to realize that he, Joe Mitchell ("I am a public character, sir"), has anything to fear from a ridiculously menacing Dago whose ruffians have stolen his presentation pocket-chronometer actually cows the all-powerful Dago into restoring both chronometer and freedom:

> The old sailor, with all his small weaknesses and absurdities, was constitutionally incapable of entertaining for any length of time a fear of his personal safety. It was not so much firmness of soul as the lack of a certain kind of imagination—the kind whose undue development caused intense suffering to Señor Hirsch; that sort of imagination which adds the blind terror of bodily suffering and of death, envisaged as an accident to the body alone, strictly—to all the other apprehensions on which the sense of one's existence is based. Unfortunately, Captain Mitchell had not much penetration of any kind; characteristic, illuminating trifles of expression, action, or movement, escaped him completely. He was too pompously and innocently aware of his own existence to observe that of others. For instance, he could not believe that Sotillo had been really afraid of him, and this simply because it would never have entered into his head to shoot anyone except in the most pressing case of self-defence. Anybody could see he was not a murdering kind of man, he reflected quite gravely.

These traits, it will be seen, qualify him for an essential function in the presentment of the action, to which he is related in a way symbolized by his triumphant sense—a sense uninformed by any comprehension of what is going forward—of being at the centre of things, whence history is directed, as he sits, an *habitué,* in Mrs. Gould's drawing-room.

On the significance of the other characters there is no need to enlarge: Señor Avellanos, the liberal idealist, who dies of disappointment, and the sheets of whose *Fifty Years of Misrule* are "fired out as wads for trabucos loaded with handfuls of type" during the "democratic" *émeute;* the fanatical Father Corbelàn; Hirsch, the embodiment of fear, and so on. Instead, a negative point had better be made by way of stressing the distinctive nature of the impressiveness of *Nostromo.* The impressiveness is not a matter of any profundity of search into human experience, or any explorative subtlety in the analysis of human behaviour. It is a matter rather of the firm and vivid concreteness with which the representative attitudes and motives are realized, and the rich economy of the pattern that plays them off against one another. To suggest, as Edward Garnett does in his introduction to *Conrad's Prefaces,* that perhaps this or that character wouldn't really have behaved just as he does in the book is misdirected criticism. The life-like convincingness of Conrad's persons (which is complete as we read, and undisturbed by properly critical reflection) doesn't entitle us to psychologize them as lives existing outside the book. I am reminded of certain remarks of T. S. Eliot's:

> A "living" character is not necessarily "true to life." It is a person whom we can see and hear, whether he be true or false to human nature as we know it. What the creator of character needs is not so much knowledge of motives as keen sensibility; the dramatist need not understand people, but he must be exceptionally aware of them.

It is an Elizabethan dramatist Eliot has in front of him; and it strikes me that there is something that recalls the strength of Elizabethan drama about the art of *Nostromo*—something Shakespearean, in fact. The keen sensibility and the exceptional awareness are apparent in the vividness with which we see and hear Conrad's persons, and there is nothing about them that, on reflection, we find untrue to human nature as we know it. But the seeing and hearing is adequate understanding: they are present to us and are plainly what they are; and to try, by way of appreciation or criticism, to go behind that is to misunderstand what the book offers us. There is plainly no room in *Nostromo* for the kind of illustrated psychology that many critics think they have a right to demand of a novelist (and of Shakespeare). Consider the number of personal centres of moral interest, and the variety of themes. Consider the number of vivid dramatic scenes and episodes. Consider the different strands that go to the totality of the action. There is the private tragedy of the Goulds; there is Nostromo's history, involving that of the Viola family; there is the story of Decoud and Antonia; there is that of Dr. Monygham and his self-rehabilitation; and all these and so much else are subsumed in the public historical drama—the study, concretely rendered, of the play of moral and material forces, political and personal motives, in the founding of the Occidental Republic.

Clearly, Conrad's study of motives, and of the relation between the material and the spiritual, doesn't depend for its impressiveness on any sustained analytic exhibition of the inner complexities of the individual psyche. The impressiveness lies in the vivid reality of the things we are made to see and hear, and the significance they get from their relations in a highly organized and vividly realized whole. It lies in such effects as that of the presence of Decoud and Nostromo in the lighter as it drifts with its load of silver and of Fear (personified by the stowaway Hirsch) through the black night of the Gulf; and that of the unexpected nocturnal encounter between Nostromo and Dr. Monygham, two sharply contrasted consciousnesses, in the vast deserted Custom House, and their discovery that the "shapeless high-shouldered shadow of somebody standing still, with lowered head" seen on the wall through a doorway, is thrown by the hanging body of the tortured Hirsch. We have it characteristically when Charles Gould, going out from his interview (consummate satiric comedy) with Pedrito Montero, would-be Duc de Morny to the new Napoleon, runs into the "constitutionalist" deputation he has refused to support ("The acceptance of accomplished facts may save yet the precious vestiges of parliamentary institutions"):

> Charles Gould on going out passed his hand over his forehead as if to disperse the mists of an oppressive dream, whose grotesque extravagance leaves behind a subtle sense of bodily danger and intellectual decay. In the passages and on the staircases of the old palace Montero's troopers lounged about insolently, smoking and making way for no one; the clanking of sabres and spurs resounded all over the building. Three silent groups of civilians in severe black waited in the main gallery, formal and helpless; a little huddled up, each keeping apart from the others, as if in the exercise of a public duty they had been overcome by a desire to shun the notice of every eye. These were the deputations waiting for their audience. The one from the Provincial Assembly, more restless and uneasy in its corporate expression, was overtopped by the big face of Don Juste Lopez, soft and white, with prominent eyelids and wreathed in impenetrable solemnity as if in a dense cloud. The President of the Provincial Assembly, coming bravely to save the last shred of parliamentary institutions (on the English model), averted his eyes from the Administrador of the San Tomé mine as a dignified rebuke of his little faith in that only saving principle.

Charles Gould's quiet unyieldingness in the face of Pedrito's threats and blandishments has already invested him for the moment with a larger measure of our sympathy than he in general commands. The brush with the deputation confirms this effect, while at the same time reinforcing dramatically that pattern of political significance which has a major part in *Nostromo*—a book that was written, we remind ourselves in some wonder, noting the topicality of its themes, analysis and illustrations, in the reign of Edward VII.

Again, we have the symbolic pregnancy of Conrad's dramatic method in such a representative touch as this (the context is the flight of aristocrats and adherents of "law and order" to the protection of the "master of the Campo"):

> The emissary of Hernandez spurred his horse close up.
> "Has not the master of the mine any message to send the master of the Campo?"
> The truth of the comparison struck Charles Gould heavily. In his determined purpose he held the mine and the indomitable bandit held the Campo by the same precarious tenure. They were equals before the lawlessness of the land. It was impossible to disentangle one's activities from its debasing contacts.

There is—the adjective proposes itself at this point—something rhetorical, in a wholly laudatory sense, about Conrad's art in *Nostromo*. One might add, by way of insisting further on the Elizabethan in it, that it has a certain robust vigour of melodrama. The melodrama, of course, is completely controlled to the pattern of moral significance. Consider, for instance, how the climax of the public drama is given us: it is a thrilling nick-of-time *peripeteia,* but it is given in retrospect through the pompous showmanship and uncomprehending importance of Captain Mitchell ("Fussy Joe"). The triumphs of the Progress he hymns are already assured and commonplace, and already (a few pages on) Dr. Monygham is asking:

> "Do you think that now the mine would march upon the town to save their Señor Administrador? Do you think that?"

He has just pronounced:

> "There is no peace and no rest in the development of material interests. They have their law, and their justice. But it is founded on expediency, and it is inhuman; it is without rectitude, without the continuity and the force that can be found only in a moral principle."

This is only one instance of that subtle play of the order of presentment against the time-order which the reader finds himself admiring in the book as a whole—subtle, yet, once taken stock of, appreciated as inevitable. It is characteristic of Conrad's method, to take another instance, that we should have seen, in a prospective glimpse given us at the very opening of the book, the pitiable *débâcle* of the Ribierist dictatorship of "reform" before we are invited to contemplate the hopes and enthusiasms of its supporters at the inauguration.

It will probably be expected, after so much insistence on the moral pattern of *Nostromo,* that something will be said about the total significance. What, as the upshot of this exhibition of human motive and attitude, do we feel Conrad himself to endorse? What are his positives? It is easier to say what he rejects or criticizes. About the judgment on Decoud's scepticisms we can have no doubt. And even Decoud concedes that the illusions "those Englishmen" live on "somehow or other help them to get a firm hold of the substance." To this concession we can relate the observations of the engineer-in-chief:

> "Upon my word, doctor, things seem to be worth nothing by what they are in themselves. I begin to believe that the only solid thing about them is the spiritual value which everyone discovers in his own form of activity—"
> "Bah!" interrupted the doctor.

The engineer has in mind Holroyd the millionaire and his preoccupation with a "pure form of Christianity." But although Dr. Monygham, himself devoted to a moral idea, is as such clearly not disapproved by the author, he is made to seem Quixotic, and it is difficult to feel that the ironic light in which the "spiritual values" discovered by the other main characters in their forms of activity are shown is less essentially dissociating than the irony focussed upon Holroyd. In fact, though Decoud is so decisively dealt with in the action, he remains at the centre of the book, in the sense that his consciousness seems to permeate it, even to dominate it. That consciousness is clearly very closely related to the author's own personal *timbre*, that which becomes representable in quotation in such characteristic sardonic touches as:

> They had stopped near the cage. The parrot, catching the sound of a word belonging to his vocabulary, was moved to interfere. Parrots are very human.
> "Viva Costaguana!" he shrieked. . . .

It is not a question of a "philosophy"; Conrad cannot be said to have one. He is not one of those writers who clear up their fundamental attitudes for themselves in such a way that we may reasonably, in talking of them, use that portentous term. He does believe intensely, as a matter of concrete experience, in the kind of human achievement represented by the Merchant Service—tradition, discipline and moral ideal; but he has also a strong sense, not only of the frailty, but of the absurdity or unreality, in relation to the surrounding and underlying gulfs, of such achievement, a sense so strong that it often seems very close to Decoud's radical scepticism, which is, in the account of those last days, rendered with such significant power. In fact, Decoud may be said to have had a considerable part in the writing of *Nostromo;* or one might say that *Nostromo* was written by a Decoud who wasn't a complacent dilettante, but was positively drawn towards those capable of "investing their activities with spiritual value"—Monygham, Giorgio Viola, Señor Avellanos, Charles Gould.

At any rate, for all the rich variety of the interest and the tightness of the pattern, the reverberation of *Nostromo* has something hollow about it; with the colour and life there is a suggestion of a certain emptiness. And for explanation it is perhaps enough to point to this reflection of Mrs. Gould's:

> It had come into her mind that for life to be large and full, it must contain the care of the past and of the future in every passing moment of the present.

That kind of self-sufficient day-to-dayness of living Conrad can convey, when writing from within the Merchant Service, where clearly he has known it. We are made aware of hostile natural forces threatening his seamen with extinction, but not of metaphysical gulfs opening under life and consciousness: reality on board ship is domestic, assured and substantial. "That feeling of life-emptiness which had made me so restless for the last few months," says the young captain of *The Shadow-Line,* entering on his new command, "lost its bitter plausibility, its evil influence." For life in the Merchant Service there is no equivalent in *Nostromo*—no intimate sense conveyed of the day-by-day continuities of social living. And though we are given a confidential account of what lies behind Dr. Monygham's sardonic face, yet on the whole we see the characters from the outside, and only as they belong to the ironic pattern—figures in the futilities of a public drama, against a dwarfing background of mountain and gulf.

This kind of vision, this sense of life, corresponds, there can be no doubt, to something radical in Conrad. All his readers must have noticed how recurrent and important the theme of isolation is in his work. And they must have noticed too the close relation between the Decoud consciousness and the sympathetic hero of *Victory,* the English-speaking Swede, Axel Heyst.

JOYCE'S EPIPHANIES *
IRENE HENDRY

I

By an epiphany he meant a sudden spiritual manifestation, whether in the vulgarity of speech or of gesture or in a memorable phase of the mind itself. He believed that it was for the man of letters to record these epiphanies with extreme care, seeing that they themselves are the most delicate and evanescent of moments.—Stephen Hero.

STEPHEN DEDALUS' esthetic in *A Portrait of the Artist as a Young Man* has the same specious quality as his Hamlet thesis in *Ulysses* and is a product of the same talent for parody; as Stephen's friend Lynch remarks, it has "the true scholastic stink." Both theories are, of course, more than parody: the speculations on Hamlet serve to crystallize Stephen's broodings on his spiritual parentage, and the esthetic is actually Joyce's, which he followed faithfully and in his own literary method. Just how closely method and principle were related in Joyce's work is shown by his little-noticed theory of epiphanies, which is mentioned fleetingly in *Ulysses* but is given explicit statement only in *Stephen Hero,* the fragmentary first draft of the *Portrait* recently published in book form for the first time.[1]

The theory of epiphanies, presented as Stephen's, is bound up with the three cardinal esthetic principles, or conditions of beauty, that he expounds to Lynch in one of their dialogues in the *Portrait.* (In *Stephen Hero,* the passive listener is Cranly, a character apparently based on Joyce's own college friend Byrne.) These principles have a respectable philosophic origin in the *integritas, consonantia,* and *claritas* of Aquinas. *Integritas* Stephen explains in pseudo-scholastic language as "wholeness"—the perception of an esthetic image as *one* thing, "self-bounded and self-contained upon the immeasurable background of space or time which is not it." *Consonantia,* similarly, is symmetry and rhythm of structure, the esthetic image conceived as "complex, multiple, divisible, separable, made up of its parts and their sum, harmonious"; "the synthesis of immediate perception is followed by the analysis of apprehension." The third principle, *claritas,*

* "Joyce's Epiphanies" originally appeared in the *Sewanee Review,* Summer, 1946. It is used here by permission of the author and the magazine editors.

[1] James Joyce, *Stephen Hero, A Part of the First Draft of A Portrait of the Artist as a Young Man,* edited from the manuscript in the Harvard College Library by Theodore Spencer (New York: New Directions, 1944).

is given the approximate meaning of "radiance" and equated with another Thomistic term, *quidditas,* or the "whatness" of a thing. *Quidditas* is the link with the theory of epiphanies, in this case, the definition in *Stephen Hero* is the more revealing:

> *Claritas* is *quidditas.* After the analysis which discovers the second qual-
> ity the mind makes the only logically possible synthesis and discovers the
> third quality. This is the moment which I call epiphany. First we recog-
> nise that the object is *one* integral thing, then we recognise that it is an
> organized composite structure, a *thing* in fact: finally, when the relation
> of the parts is exquisite, when the parts are adjusted to the special point,
> we recognise that it is *that* thing which it is. Its soul, its whatness, leaps
> to us from the vestment of its appearance. The soul of the commonest
> object, the structure of which is so adjusted, seems to us radiant. The
> object achieves its epiphany.

Joyce's epiphanies are mentioned by Harry Levin, who had access
to the manuscript of *Stephen Hero* in preparing his New Directions
study, and by Theodore Spencer, who edited and wrote the preface
to the published version of the fragment. Both Levin and Spencer,
however, emphasize only the obvious aspect of the epiphany: its effect
on the observer and his relation to the object "epiphanized." Spencer
calls the theory one which "implies a lyrical rather than a dramatic
view of life," thinking apparently of Stephen's definition of the
"lyrical" form of art as "the form wherein the artist presents his
image in immediate relation to himself." Levin takes the stories in
Dubliners as pure examples of epiphany, the collection of which
Stephen resolves (in *Ulysses*) to leave to all the libraries of the
world; Joyce's later works, he says, are "artificial reconstructions of
a transcendental view of experience," and his "dizzying shifts" of technique attempt "to create a literary substitute for the revelations of
religion."

But these descriptions do justice to neither the concept nor Joyce's
use of it. In the first place, of course, the epiphany is not peculiar to
Joyce alone. Virtually every writer experiences a sense of revelation
when he beholds a fragment of his ordinary world across what Bullough
has called "psychic distance"—dissociated from his subjective and practical concerns, fraught with meaning beyond itself, with every detail
of its physical appearance relevant. It is a revelation quite as valid as
the religious; in fact, from our present secular viewpoint, it perhaps
would be more accurate to say that the revelation of the religious
mystic is actually an esthetic revelation into which the mystic projects
himself—as a participant, not merely as an observer and recorder—
and to which he assigns a source, an agent and an end, called God.
What Joyce did was give systematic formulation to a common esthetic
experience, so common that few others—writers, if not estheticians—
have thought it worth considering for its own sake.

Again, many writers use "revelation" as a technical device in achieving their effects; Joyce, however, used it more consciously and with greater variation than anyone with whom he can be compared. More than a "transcendental view of experience" is involved in Joyce's application of his theory of epiphanies, just as there is more than mysticism in religion, particularly the Roman Catholicism that shaped his whole outlook as a young man. The theory furnished Joyce with a technique of characterization which evolved generally in the "lyrical-epical-dramatic" progression that Stephen describes: from the first person to the third, from the personal to the impersonal, from the kinetic to the static. It is a technique in which *integritas* and *consonantia* are always necessary to *claritas,* and *claritas* itself comes more and more to reside in *quidditas,* the soul, the essential identifying quality of the thing, than in a mystic, emotional exhilaration on the part of someone who looks on. *Claritas* is *quidditas* is the key the theory itself gives us.

In *Dubliners, claritas* is achieved most often, although not always, through an apparently trivial incident, action, or single detail which differs from the others making up the story only in that it illuminates them, integrates them, and gives them meaning. It is like the final piece which is added to the child's pile of lettered blocks and completes the spelling of a word or gives form to the "house" or "tower" he is building. Farrington's treatment of his son attaches to himself the petty tyranny we recognize first in his employer. Little Chandler's brief rebellion against domesticity frightens his child, and his dreams of being a poet are swept away by his remorse. After a drinking bout, Mr. Kernan is persuaded by his friends to take part in a retreat, at which Father Purdon's metaphor of the "spiritual accountant" crystallizes a businessman's religion that is only a reflection of their daily lives. And in "The Dead," the artistic highpoint of the collection, the conviviality of the banquet, Gabriel Conroy's confident rejection of the dead past, his scorn for Irish nationalism, and his desire of his wife are ironically drawn together and then dispersed by the story of Michael Furey.

Joyce used the *Dubliners* "block" technique again, with some modification, in the Nausicaa episode in *Ulysses,* where, after having sexually aroused Leopold Bloom and indulged in erotic daydreams of her own, Gerty MacDowell walks away with a limp. It is a technique that is obvious to us because it is familiar; although their origin is probably Katherine Mansfield or Chekhov rather than Joyce, similar "revelations" of character are vouchsafed regularly by the *New Yorker* and its imitators. Such stories are usually considered to be "objective" because the author offers no overt interpretation of his material but merely arranges it so that its meaning is "revealed" directly to the reader. The *Dubliners* stories seem to conform to Stephen's definition of "dramatic" art as the form in which the artist "presents his image in immediate relation to others"; "life purified in and reprojected from the human imagination." Joyce was not satisfied with such an easy attainment of the esthetic stasis, however, and this may have been because the "block" technique did not fulfill equally all three of his basic principles of art. *Claritas* is achieved, but the *quidditas* that constitutes it is dilute; *consonantia,* the parts and their sum, is in evidence, but *integritas* is not, at least to the same degree.

II

The example of epiphany which Joyce employs in *Stephen Hero*—a fragment of conversation between a girl and a young man, overheard on Mr. Bloom's own Eccles Street—is actually the final "block" of the *Dubliners* method without the foundation; one may guess that the foundation in each story was laid down later, in an effort to insure the impersonality of the epiphany Joyce originally experienced in a very personal fashion. It may be, too, that the collection of epiphanies Stephen wishes to leave to posterity is not *Dubliners* at all but a collection of just such fragments as the one he acknowledges.

A number of these "most delicate and evanescent of moments" occur throughout both *Stephen Hero* and the *Portrait,* taking up residence in Stephen's consciousness with neither elucidation nor relation to anything beyond themselves: factory girls and boys coming out to lunch; the witless laughter of an old woman; the screeching of a mad nun; a servant singing; the salutation of a flower girl. In *Ulysses,* too, the peregrinations of Bloom and Stephen about Dublin are rich in epiphanies of this sort; the shout Stephen hears in the street and calls a "manifestation of God" is only the most obvious.

Occasionally we are given a suggestion of what is "revealed" in Joyce's epiphanies. The black straw hat and the greeting of the prostitute in *Stephen Hero* have an inordinate fascination for Dedalus; "mustn't the devil be annoyed to hear her described as an evil creature?" he asks. In order to fill in the background of an epiphany, he sometimes makes a reconstruction of an event in the past: a forgotten medical student cutting the word *Foetus* in the wooden surface of his desk, or an imagined incestuous meeting in the rain, suggested by the dwarfish reader in the library and the rumors about his birth. And in at least three instances an epiphany helps Stephen to decide on the future course of his life: the snatch of song from the street, contrasting suddenly with the unsmiling face of the Jesuit who has been urging him to enter a novitiate; the vision of the girl wading at the shore; and the flight of birds about the college library, symbolizing the "fabulous artificer" after whom he is named.

The moment of revelation without its narrative base is the most conventional of Joyce's epiphanies; we find it elsewhere even in fiction which does not make use of revelation as a specific technique in the *Dubliners*-Chekhov-Mansfield-*New Yorker* manner. This is particularly true among writers who, like Virginia Woolf and John Dos Passos, have modified Joyce's stream-of-consciousness method. And in poetry the isolated moment of revelation dates at least from Wordsworth's experiences in the presence of mountains, leech-gatherers, and the lights about Westminster Bridge. The epiphanies in Joyce's own poetry, in such pieces as "The twilight turns from amethyst," "My love is in a light attire," "A Flower Given to My Daughter," "On the Beach at Fontana," fit so well into the familiar lyric pattern that the poetry is usually dismissed as something outside the main stream of his work.

Joyce's second epiphany technique does quite clearly conform to Stephen's definition of lyrical art. Although *claritas* is ultimately generated by *quidditas,* we are first aware of an effect on the beholder—Stephen, or ourselves through Stephen—not of an objectively apprehensible quality in the thing revealed; if we are to penetrate through to the *quidditas,* we must try to identify ourselves with Stephen or wrest a meaning of our own from the revelation. From the standpoint of eliminating the artist's personality from his work, this particular technique was a retrogression from the method of *Dubliners,* but it did have the advantage—in Joyce's esthetic theory, an extremely important one—of realizing the three principles, *integritas, consonantia,* and *claritas,* in a single image. The next step toward impersonal creation was to modify the image so that its *quidditas* would be unmistakable, with its radiance attached to itself rather than to a perceiving consciousness: Joyce's third epiphany technique, which explains the differences between *Stephen Hero* and *A Portrait of the Artist.*

In the *Portrait,* which covers in 93 pages events that require 234 pages in the *Hero* fragment, the original elements of Joyce's first novel, particularly the characters, are subjected to a process of compression and distillation that rejects all irrelevancies, all particularities and ambiguities, and leaves only their pure essence. In *Stephen Hero,* the common people at the Good Friday service are diverse in their submissive ignorance and their unquestioning respect for the clergy; the old women scrape their hands over the dry bottom of the holy-water font and speak in broad, realistic dialect. But in the *Portrait* the simple faithful are represented by pious sighs and a peasant smell "of air and rain and turf and corduroy," or by kneeling forms and whispering voices in the confessional box—"soft whispering cloudlets, soft whispering vapour, whispering and vanishing." In the first draft of the novel, Maurice and Isabel Dedalus appear specifically as characters; in the *Portrait,* Stephen's brothers and sisters are merely voices at the teatable, replying to his questions in pig Latin or singing with an "overtone of weariness behind their frail fresh innocent voices."

"He heard the choir of voices in the kitchen echoed and multiplied through an endless reverberation of the choirs of endless generations of children: and heard in all the echoes an echo also of the recurring note of weariness and pain. All seemed weary of life even before entering upon it."

The character of Stephen itself undergoes a transformation. The *Hero* draft is often marred by adolescent particularities: Stephen baiting his cruder classmates, sneering at his mother's pious superstitions, or trying to convert his parents to Ibsen. In the *Portrait,* however, the Ibsen episode is omitted entirely, the intellectual distance between Stephen and his contemporaries is given less emphasis, and the quarrel with his mother over his failure to do his Easter duty is mentioned only indirectly. The details of Stephen's debauches similarly remain obscure; what we are shown, in the boy's dreams of temptation, the sermons he listens to during the retreat, and his hallucinations of damnation and punishment, is actually an apotheosis—or epiphany— of sin and repentance, far removed from the adventures of the Eugene Gants who for a generation have been storming the brothels of the world in imitation of Stephen.

But the most striking attenuation occurs in the character of Emma Clery. In the *Hero* fragment, she is a healthy, middle-class girl who studies Gaelic with enthusiasm, flirts with priests, and is only confused and offended by Stephen's unconventional offer of himself. In the *Portrait,* however, we are told nothing of her appearance and are never allowed a clear conception of her as an individual. The Gaelic lessons shrink to an Irish phrasebook, the flirtation becomes a bitter recollection in Stephen's mind, associated with the scorn he feels for the Church, and there is only the barest hint of the circumstances of the rejection. The girl herself is never more than a shadowy presence —a provocative glance or speech, a shawled head, "fresh warm breath," laughter and tapping footsteps, a sash or a nodding hair ornament. Her etherealization extends even to her name, which in the *Portrait* becomes "E— C—."

In Stephen's discussion of *quidditas,* the necessary condition to radiance is a perfection of formal organization, or *consonantia* itself; "when the relation of the parts is exquisite, when the parts are adjusted to the special point, we recognize that it is *that* thing which it is." The formal adjustment in the examples of *quidditas* I have been citing is simpler and more tangible than the metaphors "distillation," "essence," and "etherealization" might suggest; it consists in nothing more mytserious than the division of a whole character into its separate parts, analogous to the "analysis of apprehension" Stephen matches up with *consonantia.* Although she represents an almost opposite conception of woman, Emma is an essence by virtue of the same process of formal disintegration as Molly Bloom, whom we know through most of *Ulysses* as drowsy breathing, untidily scattered garments, the rattling of the brass quoits on her bed, an odor, or a chance remark, when we know her directly, and as a collection of separate physical charms when we know her through Bloom. Stephen, only somewhat less than Bloom in his celebrated stream of consciousness, is the sum of fleeting memories, sense impressions, shifting thoughts, and associations, each "a memorable phase of the mind itself." The *integritas* of the character is sacrificed to the *integritas* of the esthetic image, and we are presented with generalities resynthesized from individuals: not the pious poor, but Faith; not Stephen's brothers and sisters, but Childhood; not Emma Clery, but Virginity. In *A Portrait of the Artist*, Stephen Dedalus and Emma already foreshadow the great male and female abstractions of Joyce's later work, which express on successively higher levels of sublimation the *quidditas* of each sex.

Emma's etherealization is, incidentally, suggested in other figures of women in Joyce's early work: Gretta Conroy in "The Dead"; the "memories of the girls and women in the plays of Gerhart Hauptmann" and "their pale sorrows," which the wet branches of trees call forth in Stephen's mind; the boyish figure of the Virgin in the liturgy, which Stephen visualizes as he listens to a servant singing "Rosie O'Grady." Joyce's feminine characters in general tend to become essences before his men. In fact, he conceived of only three types of woman, the Virgin, the Temptress, and the Mother—all curiously Catholic, all complementing the naïve misogyny of *Stephen Hero*, where Stephen sneers at the notion of "votes for the bitches" and refers to women inaccurately but with effective insult as "marsupials." Anna Livia Plurabelle ranges through all three essences; Molly Bloom combines the qualities of temptress and mother; and Emma is transformed into a temptress in Stephen's dreams, so that the boy's abortive passion becomes a conflict between carnal and spiritual love, centered in one object. This is the conflict that is made part of a "problem" formula in Joyce's play *Exiles*, with Bertha Rowan set off against the consumptive music teacher, who is significantly named Beatrice. (In at least one scene of the *Portrait*, incidentally, there is also a suggestion of *La Vita Nuova*, with ironic overtones: Emma standing silently in the school porch surrounded by her girl companions, while Stephen regards her from a distance, remembering her flirtatiousness in the presence of Father Moran.)

And when a character is broken down into its parts and resynthesized, what is the new integrating agent which assists the "synthesis of immediate perception" and serves both *consonantia* and *claritas*? Appropriately enough in Joyce's case, it is language itself. We are most familiar with the plays on etymology and multiple accretions of meaning in his later work, but at first he achieved his effects through

all the poet's or orator's traditional devices of cadence and balanced
period, metaphor and apostrophe, verbal connotation and subtle variation of sound. This is apparent in the examples of *quidditas* that have
been cited ("soft whispering cloudlets," "frail fresh innocent voices"),
where we are given auditory impressions rather than adequate visual
description. Epiphany is, in fact, one purpose of Joyce's amazing virtuosity of language, which grows as much between *Stephen Hero* and
the *Portrait* as between the *Portrait* and *Ulysses* or *Ulysses* and *Finnegans Wake*. It is not an attempt to "create a literary substitute for the
revelations of religion"; it is the vehicle of the radiant esthetic experience itself, and at the same time it is intimately related to the plan
of Joyce's work as a whole.

It has not been sufficiently emphasized, I think, that the three
major books, as well as the play and the poetry, together repeat on
the scale of the author's entire career the childhood-adolescence-
maturity pattern of the *Dubliners* stories. Youth—hope and rebellion;
maturity—disillusion and repentance; middle age—conformity and loneliness; age—resignation and death; in spite of palimpsests of Vico and
Homer, psychoanalysis, and Irish history, there is a clear and continuous line of development in Joyce's literal subject matter from his
first writings to his last. His theme is, quite simply, the life of man,
and his own life was devoted to writing piece by piece a vast Human
Tragedy, an epiphany of all mankind, in which a profound anthropological sense of the mystery and power of death takes the place of
the Christian's traditional faith in union with God and the life everlasting. It was mainly in the service of his theme, I believe, that Joyce
incorporated smaller "growth" patterns (often regarded as mere pedantic conceits) in his separate works: the passage of the day from
morning to night, a river flowing to the sea, a child growing to manhood. One of the most prominent of these is the Oxen of the Sun
episode in *Ulysses,* where the successive stages of the child's development in the womb are paralleled by successive stages of the development of the English language; but there are other examples of the
adaptation of linguistic techniques to his theme as well as to the
epiphany principle. Even in the early works there is a lyrical or
rhetorical passage wherever there is a climactic epiphany of particular
emotional significance, or where a generalized rather than an individual *quidditas* is revealed. In *Dubliners* we find the disillusion of
"Araby" and the elegiac closing pages of "The Dead." *Stephen Hero*
has Stephen's rhetorical outbursts against the Church and the "noc-
turne" scene just preceding Isabel's death, which in mood and setting
is very like Joyce's lyric "The twilight turns from amethyst," while
passage after passage in *A Portrait of the Artist,* some frankly dyed
with purple, make Joyce's first novel as much a vocal book as *Ulysses*
or *Finnegans Wake*.

The final epiphany in the *Portrait* is Stephen's famous journal entry marking the point at which the young man becomes an artist: "Welcome, O life! I go to encounter for the millionth time the reality of experience and to forge in the smithy of my soul the uncreated conscience of my race." Although we are supposed to think of it as written, this is pure oratory (Joyce refused to set off the written word from the spoken and exploited the possibilities of both to the utmost) and an exact formal counterpart of both Molly Bloom's remembered affirmation as she sinks into sleep and Anna Livia Plurabelle's valediction at dawn. Moreover, it is balanced by the fragmentary, unpersonalized impressions of the infant Stephen at the beginning of the book precisely as the soliloquies of Molly and Anna Livia are balanced by the impersonal narrative beginnings of *Ulysses* and *Finnegans Wake*. In a reversal of the progression in Stephen's theory (which actually describes the relation of the artist to his work rather than artistic form), Joyce moves from the third person to the first, and achieves in each case a simultaneous progression on another level. In the *Portrait,* the biological development from child to man becomes also a psychological and moral development, from passive receptivity to the self-conscious will. In *Ulysses,* with the progress of the day we are taken from the matter-of-fact blasphemies of Buck Mulligan to the nostalgia of middle age, a development away from the delusive optimism of the will. (For the eagerness of youth which Molly Bloom celebrates belongs as much to the past as the dead son Bloom himself has been seeking during the day, and Molly's memories—Anna Livia has them also—serve to bring into focus, or "reveal," what has gone before in much the same way as Gretta Conroy's story in "The Dead.") And in *Finnegans Wake* the concluding first-person passage is the final epiphany of the generalized human *quidditas,* the thinking and feeling soul (Joyce shows sensibility surviving will), before it enters a new cycle of existence and is dissolved in the inorganic beginnings we encountered on the first page of the book: "riverrun, past Eve and Adam's, from swerve of shore to bend of bay," the river flowing through the city. Here at last is a perfect unity of technique, theme, and esthetic principle, and a distillation of essence so complete that Being becomes quite literally the Word.

III

Joyce's work is a tissue of epiphanies, great and small, from fleeting images to whole books, from the briefest revelation in his lyrics to the epiphany that occupies one gigantic, enduring "moment" in *Finnegans Wake,* running through 628 pages of text and then returning upon itself. His major technique and the best illustration of his theory is the one just discussed, revelation through distillation of the pure, generalized *quidditas* from an impure whole, by which *consonantia* (here analysis of the whole into its parts) and *integritas* (resynthesis of the parts into a larger whole through the agency of language itself) interact to produce *claritas* directly. It is also his best-known technique (anyone who has grown up since the publication of *Ulysses* knows in advance, for instance, that Molly Bloom is female essence—Magna Mater and all that!) and in its high points it is his most spectacularly successful. It has, however, the defects of virtuosity. Usually the scale is too large to comprehend with ease, and the means to unity and diffusion, even in the intricate Joycean patterns of language, tend to become too mechanically ingenious, like Tchelitchew's devices for hiding children's figures among the images of trees. In spite of the author's intention, his method often separates from his meaning and actually becomes an obstacle to it, turning a serious work of art (which one cannot doubt *Finnegans Wake* is) into a parlor game.

Although it is less conspicuous and plays a fixed and minor role in the larger scheme of his work, Joyce makes use of one more epiphany technique which is worth considering because it is his closest approach to that austere impersonality of creation Stephen describes to Lynch: when "the artist, like the God of the creation, remains within or behind or above his handiwork, invisible, refined out of existence, indifferent, paring his fingernails." Under this, the intervention of a consciousness, even indirectly through the medium of language, is ruled out. A character is broken down into its separate parts, as it is under the "distillation" technique, but only one or two of the detached "parts"—"the vulgarity of speech or of gesture," a detail of figure or expression, an item of clothing—are recombined. Although it is free of irrelevancies, the *quidditas* represented by the recombination is not the *quidditas* of a generality but an individual; its function is to identify rather than to abstract.

In *Stephen Hero* to some degree, and especially in *A Portrait of the Artist,* we can watch this technique take form. A priest is invariably marked by the fluttering of his soutane. Father Dolan steadies Stephen's hand before administering the pandying, and the cruelty of his gesture extends to his "firm soft fingers," "his grey-white face and the no-coloured eyes behind the steel-rimmed glasses"; when the priest reappears in *Ulysses,* he is signified only by the pandybat. In the same way, Mr. Casey's three cramped fingers symbolize his activities as an Irish patriot and hence his loyalty to Parnell, which for the boy Stephen is the peculiar essence of his father's friend. Again, the humility and joylessness of the church office are represented in the movements of the Jesuit dean of studies as he lights the fire, in his old, lean body—literally *similiter atque senis baculus*—and his face, compared by Stephen to "an unlit lamp or a reflection hung in a false focus."

Gesture and clothing, in particular, are as important in creating an individual *quidditas* as voice and breathing in creating a generalized *quidditas*. "There should be an art of gesture," Stephen tells Cranly in *Stephen Hero*. In the *Portrait*, he finds his "image of the soul in prayer" in "the raised and parted hands, the parted lips and eyes of one about to swoon" of religious art, and during his period of repentance visualizes himself "accomplishing the vague acts of the priesthood which pleased him by reason of their semblance of reality and of their distance from it." Clothes, in their turn, are true repositories of the soul, as they are for Lévy-Bruhl's primitives. When he comes upon his schoolmates, swimming, Stephen thinks pityingly of their nakedness: "How characterless they looked! Shuley without his deep unbuttoned collar, Ennis without his scarlet belt with the snaky clasp, and Connolly without his Norfolk coat with the flapless sidepockets!" In *Stephen Hero*, he is first impressed by the prostitute's black straw hat, the outward and visible sign of her essence, and the clothes of the characters in Joyce's play *Exiles* are so important that they are not only described in the stage directions but are mentioned by the characters themselves, with a green velvet jacket playing a significant part in the action. Finally, in the nighttown episode of *Ulysses,* changes of costume are as frequent as in the charades in which Stephen takes part at Mr. Daniel's house (*Stephen Hero*), and the hallucinatory images of Bloom at successive stages of his past are all carefully dressed for their roles.

Gesture and clothing, details of physical appearance, peculiarities of speech, and intimate material appurtenances all serve to identify Stephen's friends in the *Portrait,* in dialogue passages which might be scenes from a play. Amid the profane, witty, or banal conversations of the students, the author intervenes only as a sort of property man, to mark each one with his objectified *quidditas,* which adheres to him from scene to scene virtually without change and in some instances even carries over into *Ulysses:* Cranly's "iron crown" of hair and priestly pallor, his profanity and Latin affectation of speech; Lynch's whinnying laugh, his habit of swearing "in yellow," and his gesture of putting out his chest; the shooting suit and fair goatee of McCann, the reformer; Davin's brogue and Dixon's signet ring; Heron's cane and smile; the pedant Glynn's umbrella. In these scenes Stephen himself, the individual Stephen, is often a participant; he has his ashplant, his "familiar," which he carries also in *Ulysses,* and his soul moves rapidly and elusively through a series of metamorphoses which never quite leave the realm of the literal: the lamp mentioned in his conversation with the dean of studies; Epictetus' bucketful of water; Cranly's handball; the louse he picks from his neck; the fig Cranly tosses into the gutter.

This technique represents the ultimate in "objective" characterization, "revealing" an individual essence by means of a detail or an object to which it has only a fortuitous relation; the pandybat expresses Father Dolan's soul not because it resembles him in any way but because it is associated with him in an act that marks him forever in Stephen's eyes. Through Joyce's fourth epiphany technique (in which *claritas* is a tiny, perfunctory flash, all but absorbed by *quidditas*) we can trace out a virtual iconography of the characters, like the systematic recurrence of emblems and attitudes among the figures in sacred art. This was probably intentional on the part of Joyce, who was curiously "influenced" by medieval concepts and methods, probably more so than any other writer of our time, and whose preoccupation with symmetry and correspondence and the-microcosm-within-the-macrocosm would have been worthy of Dante. (There are indications in the *Portrait* of his attraction to religious iconography, which itself had a literary origin in the Middle Ages. During his period of sin, the adolescent Stephen still delights in the traditional symbols of Mary, and saints and their emblems—St. Ignatius Loyola with his book, St. Francis Xavier indicating his chest, Lorenzo Ricci and his berretta—are noted with particular interest by Stephen the boy in the paintings at Clongowes.) In *Ulysses,* where the individual Mr. Bloom is signified variously by his hat, his newspaper and cigar, the lemon soap, the yellow flower, and the pork kidney, much of the medieval flavor of the Witches' Sabbath passages is due to the highly formalized iconography of the apparitions: King Edward with his bucket ("for identification bucket in my hand," the king explains himself), the dead Rudy with his Eton suit and his lambkin (a genuine epiphany to Bloom as he appears over the prostrate body of Stephen), Gerty Mac-Dowell with her bloody clout, Lord Tennyson and his Union Jack blazer, the corpse of Stephen's mother with her faded orange blossoms and torn bridal veil, her breath of "wetted ashes" and *Liliata rutilantium.*

The emblematic *quidditas* is used with greatest virtuosity in *Ulysses,* but it is a technique of characterization that runs through all of Joyce's work. There are remnants of it in *Finnegans Wake,* in the signatures (tree and stone, river and hill, H.C.E. and A.L.P.) of Anna Livia and Earwicker, and it appears even in *Dubliners.* Father Flynn's chalice and old Maria's saucer of clay are clear examples; in "Two Gallants," the coin takes part in the conventional narrative "revelation" and at the same time serves as the *quidditas* of the gallants; in "The Dead," the absent Michael Furey is represented obliquely and ironically by the snow, "The Lass of Aughrim," the overshoes, and the sore throat of Bartell D'Arcy, the vain concert tenor. In Joyce's poems we have the flower in "A Flower Given to My Daughter" and the snood "that is the sign of maidenhood" in "Bid adieu, adieu, adieu." *Exiles* has already been mentioned: its detailed descriptions of the dress and attitudes of the characters are not so much evidence of meticulous naturalistic accuracy as an effort to transmit to the actors the special objectified *quidditas* of each character as the author conceived it; the play is a failure largely because the stage directions cannot take the place of Joyce's own handling of the scenes. And finally, I think the same iconographic technique was ultimately responsible for the Joycean compound epithet that has now seeped down into Mr. Luce's editorial offices. In "shame-closing eyes," "dew-silky cattle," "saltwhite corpse," "snot-green sea," modeled on the "winedark sea" and "rosy-fingered dawn" that have been deified by scholars, a unique quality is wedded to its counterpart to produce a compact representation of *quidditas* in its smallest unit.

And so the individual *quidditas* is concentrated in a physical image, often, though not always, visual, as the generalized *quidditas* is diffused in a stream of sound. The soul of the thing, its whatness, truly "leaps to us from the vestment of its appearance." Basically, perhaps, there is no difference between Joyce's final epiphany technique and the symbolism of other writers—such as the *leitmotiv* of Thomas Mann —but in its development and its use there are very real differences. Following Freud, we have come to think of a symbol chiefly in terms of its representational qualities (Pribislav Hippe's pencil in *The Magic Mountain*); through a combination of experimental science and philosophical idealism, we tend also to find a value of their own in "things," which we conceive more or less as absolutes. Joyce's conception of the symbol is much closer to the conception of the medieval Church: a symbol has a specific function to perform in a given situation, and, when that function has been performed, nothing prevents the use of the symbol again in a totally different context. This flexibility results eventually in the intimate interpenetration of the parts and the whole that is one of the chief manifestations of Joyce's principle of *consonantia,* reaching a high degree of complexity in his later work. In *Finnegans Wake,* where, as the writers of exegeses remind us, every part presupposes every other part and their sum as well, it is difficult to separate out the individual threads of the pattern. But we can see its outlines already in the "Christmas" symbolism of the *Portrait,* where the significance of the velvet-backed brushes (maroon for the *quidditas* of Michael Davitt, green for the *quidditas* of Parnell) is expanded in Stephen's "red and green" impressions as he anticipates the school holiday, and the Irish church and Irish politics are ironically united at the dinner party on Christmas day in the violent quarrel between Aunt Dante and Mr. Casey; we see it also in the "bowl" symbolism in the early pages of *Ulysses,* where the bowl of shaving-lather.

introduced as the *quidditas* of Buck Mulligan, becomes successively the bay, the bowl of incense Stephen carried at Clongowes, and the bowl of green bile at his mother's deathbed. Although these are only minor examples of Joyce's method, few could illustrate it more effectively.

MONTAGE *

Harry Levin

THE IMITATION of life through the medium of language has never been undertaken more literally. *Ulysses* ignores the customary formalities of narration and invites us to share a flux of undifferentiated experience. We are not told how the characters behave; we are confronted with the *stimuli* that affect their behavior, and expected to respond sympathetically. The act of communication, the bond of sympathy which identifies the reader with the book, comes almost too close for comfort. The point of view, the principle of form which has served to integrate many amorphous novels, is intimate and pervasive. Joyce's efforts to achieve immediacy lead him to equate form and content, to ignore the distinction between the things he is describing and the words he is using to describe them. In this equation, time is of the essence. Events are reported when and as they occur; the tense is a continuous present. Joyce did not begin his *Portrait of the Artist,* as other autobiographers would, by summoning up a retrospective account of his earliest remembrances. Instead, the opening pages of the book are presented as an exact verbal equivalent of the opening impressions of his life.

The story of *Ulysses* takes no longer to happen than to read; acting time, as it were, is simultaneous with reading time. The plot of the novel is Mr. Bloom's schedule, which introduces us to divers places in Dublin at consecutive periods of the day. We have observed that Bloom's day lasts for sixteen waking hours, with some intermissions and interpolations, prefaced by a separate treatment of Stephen's morning and concluded with a tardy glimpse of Molly Bloom—eighteen hours and forty-five minutes by the final page. Bloom, on the whole, is our sensorium, and it is his experience that becomes ours. To record this experience, however, has not been a simple process of photography. Bloom's mind is neither a *tabula rasa* nor a photographic plate, but a motion picture, which has been ingeniously cut and carefully edited to emphasize the close-ups and fade-outs of flickering emotion, the angles of observation and the flashbacks of reminiscence. In its intimacy and in its continuity, *Ulysses* has more in common with the cinema than with other fiction. The movement of Joyce's

* "Montage" appears as Section 2, Part II, of *James Joyce,* by Harry Levin, copyright 1941 by New Directions. It is used here by permission of the author and the publisher, New Directions, 333 Sixth Avenue, New York City.

style, the thought of his characters, is like unreeling film; his method of construction, the arrangement of this raw material, involves the crucial operation of *montage*.

Joyce's unrewarded attempt to establish the first motion-picture theater in Ireland is only another chapter in the history of his misunderstandings with his country, but he fully understood the technical possibilities of the new medium. He keenly perceived—in spite of his defective vision—that the cinema is both a science and an art, and therefore the most characteristic expression of our time. His own technique shows the confluence of many modern developments in the arts and sciences. The impressionistic painters, by defining their object through the eyes of the beholder, gave Joyce an example which his physical handicap may have encouraged him to follow. The "ineluctable modality of the visible" was narrowed down for him, so that blurred sight looked for compensation in augmented sound. The Wagnerian school, with its thematic blend of music and ideas, had its obvious lesson for a novelist who had wanted to be a lyric poet or a professional singer.

The international psychoanalytic movement, under the direction of Jung, had its headquarters in Zurich during the war years while Joyce was writing *Ulysses*, and he could scarcely have resisted its influence. And, although philosophy could not have offered him much in the way of immediate data, it is suggestive to note that Bergson, Whitehead, and others—by reducing things-in-themselves to a series of organic relations—were thinking in the same direction. Thus the very form of Joyce's book is an elusive and eclectic *Summa* of its age: the *montage* of the cinema, impressionism in painting, *leitmotiv* in music, the free association of psychoanalysis, and vitalism in philosophy. Take of these elements all that is fusible, and perhaps more, and you have the style of *Ulysses*. To characterize this style, we must borrow a term from either German metaphysics or French rhetoric; we may conceive it as *Strom des Bewusstseins* or again as *monologue intérieur*. We shall find, however, that Joyce obtains his metaphysical effects by rhetorical devices, that the internal monologue lends itself more readily to critical analysis than the more illusory stream of consciousness.

The emergence of this method of fiction has been hailed as nothing less than a scientific discovery, and attributed to a half-remembered French symbolist, Edouard Dujardin. Joyce himself generously acknowledged his debt to a short novel of Dujardin's *Les lauriers sont coupés,* first published in 1887 and reprinted in the afterglow of Joyce's acknowledgment. Dujardin was not utterly unknown to the Dublin of *Ulysses,* since *Dana: A Magazine of Independent Thought* carried his defense of the excommunicated Catholic historian, Alfred Loisy, a month before Stephen tried to persuade the editor, John Eglinton, to accept an article on Shakespeare. The elderly innovator survived to promulgate a rambling definition of the style which he had invented and Joyce had perfected: "The internal monologue, in its nature on the order of poetry, is that unheard and unspoken speech by which a character expresses his inmost thoughts (those lying nearest the unconscious) without regard to logical organization—that is, in their original state—by means of direct sentences reduced to the syntactic minimum, and in such a way as to give the impression of reproducing the thoughts just as they come into the mind."

Dujardin's original experiment is something less than sensational. *Les lauriers sont coupés* is the sustained monologue in the present tense, without incident or consequence, of a naïve young man taking a beautiful actress out to dinner, interrupted by occasional fragments of dialogue and a few necessary stage-directions in the first person. The little book did not escape the sharp eye of Remy de Gourmont, who reviewed it as "a novel which seems in literature a transposed anticipation of the cinema." It seems to bear the same relation to ordinary fiction that the film does to the stage. For, to find ample literary precedent for the internal monologue, we need only turn to the theater. The conventions of Elizabethan drama permitted Shakespeare to marshal the arguments for and against suicide in Hamlet's soliloquy, or to mingle desperation with prose and song in the distractions of Ophelia's madness. Recent playwrights, like Eugene O'Neill, have renewed their license to soliloquize. Poets like Browning and T. S. Eliot have never abandoned this prerogative.

Even within the traditions of the novel, the internal monologue appears to be less of an innovation than Joyce or Dujardin would have liked to believe. André Gide has found instances in Dostoevsky's *House of the Dead*. Fanny Burney wrote tolerably conventional novels, a hundred years before Dostoevsky or Dujardin, but in the privacy of her diary she set down a page or two that ask demurely for comparison with the last words of Molly Bloom:

> Well, I am going to bed—Sweet dreams attend me—and may you sympathize with me. Heigh ho! I wonder when I shall return to London!—Not that we are very dull here—no, really—tolerably happy—I wish Kitty Cooke would write to me—I long to hear how my dear, dear, beloved Mr. Crisp does. My papa always mentions him by the name of my *Flame*. Indeed he is not mistaken—himself is the *only* man on earth I prefer to him. Well—I must write a word more—only to end my paper—so!—that's done—and now good night to you . . . . . .

James Fenimore Cooper, one of the least adroit novelists who ever won lasting fame, somehow flounders into the stream of consciousness. Cooper follows Scott in taking over a Shakespearean *entourage* of clowns and fools, one of whom is an old Negro retainer, Caesar, in

The Spy. When his young master takes leave of him, and jocosely suggests that Caesar convey a farewell kiss to the young ladies of the household, Cooper's racial feeling sinks into Caesar's subconsciousness:

> The delighted Caesar closed the door, pushing bolt after bolt, and turning the key until it would turn no more, soliloquizing the whole time on the happy escape of his young master.
> "How well he ride—teach him good deal myself—salute a young lady—Miss Fanny wouldn't let the old colored man kiss a red cheek."

This staccato diction, as the malice of Wyndham Lewis did not fail to observe, makes a startling appearance in the very first novel of Charles Dickens. *Pickwick Papers* is ordinarily evoked for other qualities than psychological subtlety. There are moments, nonetheless, when it would be hard to tell the silent meditation of Mr. Bloom from the laconic garrulity of Alfred Jingle, Esq. The flow of Mr. Jingle's discourse is also stimulated by the sight of local landmarks, and the movement of the stage-coach is registered in his spoken reactions:

> "Terrible place—dangerous work—other day—five children—mother—tall lady, eating sandwiches—forgot the arch—crash—knock—children look around—mother's head off—sandwich in her hand—no mouth to put it in—head of a family off—shocking, shocking! Looking at Whitehall, sir? fine place—little window—somebody's else's head off there, eh, sir?—he didn't keep a sharp look-out enough either—eh, sir, eh?"

Herman Melville's hero, in *Moby Dick,* is not psychoanalyzed but dramatized. Yet Ahab, lonely and absolute, scanning the sea from his cabin at sunset, has a curious resemblance to Stephen, in his self-conscious soliloquy by the shore. Their gestures are alike, if their speeches differ, and the difference is primarily a question of rhetoric. Ahab's speeches tend to fall into the natural meter of English tragedy:

> What I've dared, I've willed;
> and what I've willed, I'll do! They think me mad—
> Starbuck does; but I'm demoniac,
> I am madness maddened! That wild madness
> that's only calm to comprehend itself!
> The prophecy was that I should be dismembered;
> and—Aye! I lost this leg. I now prophesy
> that I will dismember my dismemberer.
> Now, then, be the prophet and the fulfiller one.
> That's more than ye, ye great gods, ever were.

It is no more true to say of Joyce, than of any other artist, that his work enlarges the domain of consciousness. *Ulysses* demonstrates no more about the processes of the mind than *Les Rougon-Macquart* proves about the laws of heredity. It is no service to Joyce to insist that his book is a scientific demonstration, and no disservice to recognize that his real originality is firmly grounded in literary tradition. We are so dazzled by the consummate craftsmanship that we forget to watch the conscientious craftsman. Though he may be more facile and complex than other writers, he conforms to the standards of their common craft. Though *Ulysses* employs the resources of the language to the extent of 29,899 different words, over half of these appear only once, and many of the rest serve some special purpose that seldom requires them to be repeated. Almost half of the 260,430 words in the book are drawn from a basic vocabulary of about a hundred mono-syllables, which—as Professor Hanley and his associates have shown in their index—closely coincide with the norms of colloquial usage. Occasionally there is a significant displacement: the word "street" is far more frequent in *Ulysses* than in ordinary speech. On the other hand, "is" and various verbal auxiliaries, because of the telegraphic syntax of internal monologue, are relatively infrequent with Joyce.

Joyce's habits of composition were Dædalean labors, to which his rewritten manuscripts and revised proofs bear formidable testimony. Collation of a casual page of printer's typescript with the final text of *Ulysses* indicates that sixty-five corrections have been made in proof —most of them mechanical details, to be sure, but at least ten contributions of some importance. There is little erasure or retrenchment; there is always addition, but never subtraction. Afterthought furnishes some of the most salient touches. For example, the mocking repetition in the Circe episode of Mulligan's taunt, "She's beastly dead," [565] * was pencilled in shortly before the typescript reached the printer. In some cases Joyce kept revising even after periodical publication. He could scarcely have composed his work by any other method than persistent accretion. He had first to compile an exhaustive and matter-of-fact *dossier,* on the plane of objective description that comes to the surface only in the Ithaca episode of the book; then to redistribute this material, with colored crayons and other mechanical aids, planting associations in the stream of consciousness and laying down coincidences according to his two keys; and finally to hope that this man-made chaos would synthesize in the reader's mind.

The exposition of *Ulysses* is necessarily circular; it plunges the reader, with epic vengeance, *in medias res.* Jung has declared that it has neither a beginning nor an end, that it can be read both forwards and backwards. The reader, entering the minds of the characters without the formality of an introduction, will encounter allusions long before they are explained. When Bloom puts on his hat to leave his house in the morning, he manifests concern over a slip of paper inside his hat-band.[56] Later, at the post office, we discover that this card contains the *nom de plume,* Henry Flower, under which he is secretly corresponding with Martha Clifford.[70] Throughout the remainder of the

* All page references are to the Modern Library edition of *Ulysses.*

book, the partly obliterated trade name inside the hat-band, "Plasto's high grade ha," becomes synonymous with Bloom's adulterous impulses.[275] Stephen's reactions are more imaginative, but equally furtive. When he meets his sister, Dilly, in a book-stall, he feels a painful sense of the decline of his family since their mother's death. The haunting image of his mother does not figure directly in his thoughts; self-reproach has found a purely verbal substitution: [240]

> She is drowning. Agenbite. Save her. Agenbite. All against us. She will drown me with her, eyes and hair. Lank coils of seaweed hair around me, my heart, my soul. Salt green death.
> We.
> Agenbite of inwit. Inwit's agenbite.
> Misery! Misery!

Joyce's literary sensibilities have endowed such passages with a peculiar poignance—not less peculiar nor poignant because they are difficult to communicate. That he should have seen fit to envelop the most genuine emotion in his book with the title of a treatise on the seven deadly sins by a fourteenth-century monk, Dan Michel of Northgate, carries mere pedantry to the point of paranoia. Bloom's psychology is coarser than Stephen's, but not less literary. As an advertising man, he is a man of letters in a small way. In lascivious mood, he conceives himself as Raoul, hero of the pornographic novel, *Sweets of Sin;* his messianic conscience addresses him as Elijah, straight off the handbill of the evangelist Dowie. Joyce's psychology is based on the *idée-fixe,* and tagged to appropriate echoes for every context. Ideas are put into words, and verbal themes are set to music. The note of blasphemy upon which the book opens, Mulligan's parody of the mass, is stridently repeated when Stephen enters the brothel. A whole liturgy is associated with the death of Mrs. Dedalus, and Bloom's cuckoldry is intermittently rehearsed in gems from his wife's operatic repertory. Church and state are celebrated in the ribald ballads of "Joking Jesus" and "Coronation Day." The texture of the internal monologue derives its richness and stiffness from a continuous thread of quotation.

We remember Stephen as a lyrical youth, trying his magic by attaching phrases to feelings. The pity of it, we remember, lay in the failure of words like "Araby" and "Grace" to cover the situations of *Dubliners.* We know that Joyce, with his highly developed auditory imagination and his unhappy estrangement from society, came to equate language and experience. We wonder whether his confidence in words was not overweening, whether he was not too articulate to achieve a really profound portrayal of human emotion. Could Joyce have apprehended the mute suffering in the eyes of the little princess, dying of childbirth in Tolstoy's *War and Peace,* or—in a different strain—the magnificent incoherence of Peeperkorn's speech, completely drowned out by the sound of a waterfall in Mann's *Der Zauberberg?* How far is language adequate to express the finer shadings and subtler modulations of the mind? "A permanently existing 'Idea' which makes its appearance before the footlights of consciousness at periodical intervals," William James tells us, "is as mythological an entity as the Jack of Spades." Internal monologue, for Joyce, is a way of dramatizing ideas that finds its logical climax in the external dialogue of the Circe episode. He did not bring literature any closer to life than perceptive novelists had already done; he did evolve his private mode of rhetorical discourse. He sought to illuminate the mystery of consciousness, and he ended by developing a complicated system of literary *leitmotiv.*

There is nothing to prevent the internal monologue from applying to things as well as to people. Stranger voices are to be heard, and the larger cadences of city life to be rendered. Joyce feels less and less committed to the point of view of either Stephen or Bloom. Having established their respective rhythms in the morning, and brought them together at noon, he feels free to break through their soliloquies and embark upon an independent series of self-conscious stylistic adventures. The episode at the office of the *Irish Freeman,* the cave of the winds, where both heroes put in their mid-day appearance, is punctuated by increasingly animated headlines. Each succeeding chapter becomes more involved in style, more distorted in shape, and more permeated by what Yvor Winters considers "the fallacy of imitative form." Joyce meets no serious obstacles in verbalizing the atmosphere of a newspaper office, or even in finding half-chewed syllables for the sounds of Bloom's lunch: "Table talk. I munched hum un thu Unchster Bunk un Munchday. Ha? Did you, faith?" [167] But Joyce's premise, that any given physical effect can be exactly duplicated by means of language, lures him into a confusing *mélange des genres.*

In the Siren scene, words and music are not simply associated; they are identified. Two pages, distracting and cryptic enough to have aroused the suspicions of the censorship during the last war, contain an initial statement of themes. It is easy to decode them, and to fit the fragments back into their narrative context; it is not easy to determine what song the sirens sang, or to pursue its musical pattern through the episode. When the program notes of Joyce's commentators classify the form as *fuga per canonem,* they do not make clear whether it is the language or the situation that is being treated fugally. Should we then accept each syllable as an interval in a melodic phrase? Or should we assume that the characters work out their own counterpoint, with Bloom as subject and Boylan as countersubject? In either case, the strict treatment of canon is unsatisfied, for there is an unlimited amount of variation. Polyphonic prose, short of the ambiguous harmonies of *Finnegans Wake,* is rarely more than a loose metaphor.

The Siren episode should not be expected to stand on its form alone, any more than any chapter in any novel. The whole passage is not a contrapuntal development of the opening phrases; the phrases are an impressionistic condensation of the passage. The introductory pages should be read as a thematic index to the following pages, but without the sequel they are meaningless. Like the lyrics in *Chamber Music,* the episode is a poem about music. The sound effects, it will be perceived, are sometimes obtained by the euphony or cacophony of words, and again—as with other objects of literary description—by the more conventional devices of quotation and reference. The banter of the barmaids and the songs of the concert room, the incessant tap of the blind man's stick and the absolute pitch of his tuning-fork, external and internal noises are duly observed and noted, sometimes by onomatopoeia and again by imagery: [252]

> Bronze by gold heard the hoofirons, steelyringing

The two barmaids, Miss Lydia Douce and Miss Mina Kennedy, listen to the sound of the viceregal procession.[253]

> Imperthnthn thnthnthn.

The lisping boot-boy mimics Miss Douce, when she threatens to complain of his "impertinent insolence." [254]

> Chips, picking chips off rocky thumbnail, chips.

Mr. Dedalus strolls into the bar.[257]

> Horrid! And gold flushed more.

Miss Kennedy coyly rebukes the giggling Miss Douce.[256]

> A husky fifenote blew.

Mr. Dedalus takes out his pipe.[257]

> Blew. Blue bloom is on the

Bloom calls for paper to write to Martha Clifford.[257]

> Gold pinnacled hair.

Miss Kennedy laughs with Miss Douce, before rebuking her.[256]

> A jumping rose on satiny breasts of satin, rose of Castille.

The description of the barmaids blends with Lenahan's pun: "What opera is like a railway line?" [260]

> Trilling, trilling: Idolores.

Miss Douce, polishing a tumbler, sings a song from *Floradora*.[257]

> Peep! Who's in the . . . peepofgold?

Lenahan is looking for Boylan.[258]

> Tink cried to bronze in pity.

The tink is the sound of a diner's bell. The pity is Miss Douce's, for the blind piano-tuner of whom she speaks.[259]

> And a call, pure, long and throbbing. Longindying call.

He has forgotten his tuning-fork.[260]

> Decoy. Soft word. But look! The bright stars fade. O rose! Notes chirruping answer. Castille. The morn is breaking.

Lenahan converses with the barmaid to the accompaniment of "a voiceless song." [260]

> Jingle jingle jaunted jingling.

Enter Boylan.[257]

> Coin rang. Clock clacked.

Boylan pays for his sloe-gin. It is almost time for his assignation.[261]

> Avowal. *Sonnez*. I could. Rebound of garter. Not leave thee. Smack. *La cloche!* Thigh smack. Avowal. Warm. Sweetheart, goodbye!

Miss Douce, to a musical background, puts on a teasing little performance for the benefit of Boylan and Lenahan.[262]

> Jingle. Bloo.

Bloom, with a sigh of relief, hears Boylan leave.[263]

> Boomed crashing chords. When love absorbs. War! War! The tympanum.

Simon Dedalus, Ben Dollard, and "Father" Cowley gather around the piano.[263]

> A sail! A veil awave upon the waves.

Cowley sings.[267]

> Lost. Throstle fluted. All is lost now.

Stephen's uncle, Richie Goulding, lunching with Bloom, attempts to whistle an air from *La Sonnambula*.[268]

> Horn. Hawhorn.

The breezy Boylan drives away in his carriage, with a symbolic jeer at Bloom's impending cuckoldry.[265]

> When first he saw. Alas!

Mr. Dedalus takes over, and begins to sing an air from *Martha:* "*M'appari.*" [269]

> Full tup. Full throb.

Music and food have a mixed effect upon Bloom's emotions.[270]

> Warbling. Ah, lure! Alluring.

Bloom associates the music with his wife's singing.[271]

> Martha! Come!

The climax of the song is a guilty reminder of his own correspondence with Martha Clifford.[271]

> Clapclop. Clipclap. Clappyclap.

Applause.[271]

> Goodgod he never heard inall

Richie Goulding reminisces about his brother-in-law's singing.[272]

> Deaf bald Pat brought pad knife took up.

The waiter brings writing materials.[273]

> A moonlit nightcall: far: far.

Mr. Dedalus attempts to recall some Italian music that he heard at Queenstown in his youth.[274]

> I feel so sad. P. S. So lonely blooming.

Bloom is answering Martha Clifford's letter.[275]

> Listen!

Miss Douce holds a sea-shell up to the ear of George Lidwell, Joyce's solicitor.[276]

> The spiked and winding cold seahorn. Have you the? Each and for other plash and silent roar.

The sound of the shell.[276]

> Pearls: when she. Liszt's rhapsodies. Hissss.

Bloom meditates on "chamber music." [278]

> You don't?

Miss Douce withdraws her arm from George Lidwell.[273]

> Did not: no, no: believe: Lidlyd. With a cock with a carra.

Boylan, meanwhile, is rapping at the door of 7 Eccles Street.[278]

> Black.

Cowley plays the opening chords of "The Croppy Boy." [278]

> Deepsounding. Do, Ben, do.

Dollard rises to sing.[278]

> Wait while you wait. Hee hee. Wait while you hee.

Bloom, in order to divert his mind from the subject of Boylan's appointment, jests desperately with himself about Pat, the waiter.[276]

> But wait!

The song is about to begin.[278]

> Low in dark middle earth. Embedded ore.

The opening chords are deep.[278]

> Nameinedamine. All gone. All fallen.

The hero of the song does penance *in nomine Domini;* he is "the last of all his race" and therefore prompts Bloom to think of himself and his dead son, Rudy.[279]

> Tiny, her tremulous fernfoils of maidenhair.

The song affects Miss Douce.[281]

> Amen! He gnashed in fury.

It reaches a climax.[281]

> Fro. To, fro. A baton cool protruding.

She manipulates the beer-pull, a symbol which synchronizes the present scene with what is happening at 7 Eccles Street.[281]

> Bronzelydia by Minagold.

Miss Douce and Miss Kennedy say farewell to a number of the company.[284]

> By bronze, by gold, in oceangreen of shadow. Bloom. Old Bloom.

Bloom, on his way out, passes by the sirens.[282]

> One rapped, one tapped with a carra, with a cock.

The sound of the cane of the blind piano-tuner, who is coming back to reclaim his tuning-fork, is answered by an echo of Boylan's crowing.[278]

> Pray for him! Pray, good people!

The song draws to a close.[282]

> His gouty fingers nakkering.

Dollard does a little Spanish dance on his way to the bar.[282]

> Big Benaben. Big Benben.

He is applauded.[282]

> Last rose Castille of summer left bloom I feel so sad alone.

Thoughts of Martha and of Lenahan's pun linger in Bloom's mind, as he goes his lonely way.[285]

> Pwee! Little wind piped wee.

He is digesting his lunch.[284]

> True men. Lid Ker Cow De and Doll. Ay, ay. Like you men. Will lift your tschink with tschunk.

Lidwell, Kernan, Cowley, Dedalus, and Dollard touch convivial glasses.[285]

> Fff! Oo!

Onomatopoeia.[285]

> Where bronze from anear? Where gold from afar? Where hoofs?

The echoes of the viceregal procession, and of the sirens, are dying out.[285]

> Rrrpr. Kraa. Kraandl.

Bloom's digestive noises are submerged in the sound of the passing tram.[286]

> Then, not till then. My eppripfftaph. Be pfrwritt.

A picture of Robert Emmet, in an antique shop outside, recalls to Bloom the last words of the dying patriot.[286]

> Done.

"When my country takes her place among the nations of the earth, then, and not till then, let my epitaph be written. I have done." [286]

Begin!

More and more, as the book proceeds, we are thrown back upon Joyce's talents for auditory observation. His ubiquitous ear is everywhere, and his mimicry is everybody. He is a hard-bitten hanger-on at Barney Kiernan's, gossiping of Bloom's discomfiture. He is a sentimental lady novelist, gushing over Gerty MacDowell. He is, in sudden succession, each of the principal stylists in the history of English literature. By this time, he has abandoned all pretense of adhering to the coign of vantage of certain characters. The narrative becomes clotted with Shandyan digression and inflated with sheer linguistic exuberance. The clinical small-talk of Stephen's friends, while Bloom awaits the birth of Mrs. Purefoy's child, is reported in language that recapitulates the evolution of English prose, from a primitive ritual to an American revival meeting, and that obliterates the point of the story—when Stephen gives up his key. These parodies, we are admonished, illustrate the principle of embryonic growth. We cannot take this admonition very seriously. To call in so many irrelevant authors as a middle term between the concepts of biology and the needs of the present narrative is to reduce Joyce's cult of imitative form to a final absurdity. For what organic reason, if any, must Lyly represent the fœtus in the third month, and Goldsmith in the sixth? And what's Bunyan to Mrs. Purefoy, or Mrs. Purefoy to Junius?

If the *pastiche* of the hospital episode is to be justified at all, it must be considered an intrinsic part of *Ulysses*. It does offer Joyce a fair field for his technical virtuosity, and allow him again to contrast the commonplaces of today with the splendors of the past. He does embrace with gusto the opportunities for further word-play. Yet he refuses to play the truly sedulous ape. Having subverted Homer and Shakespeare to his purposes, he is not anxious to submit to the limitations of lesser writers, but rather to extend his own. When a self-effacing parodist—a Max Beerbohm—takes off a writer, the result is acute criticism. When Joyce is dealing with others, he lacks this insight and precision. His parodies reveal himself—Joyce the Jacobean divine, Joyce the Restoration diarist, Joyce the Augustan essayist, Joyce the Gothic novelist. Here is Joyce as an Anglo-Saxon bard, no doubt the hapless Deor: [378]

> Some man that wayfaring was stood by housedoor at night's oncoming.
> Of Israel's folk was that man that on earth wandering far had fared.
> Stark ruth of man his errand that him lone led till that house.

Here is a Wardour Street approximation to the cloistered prose of Sir Thomas Malory: [384]

But sir Leopold was passing grave maugre his word by cause he still had
pity of the terrorcausing shrieking of shrill women in their labour and
as he was minded of his good lady Marion that had borne him an only
manchild which on his eleventh day on live had died and no man of art
could save so dark is destiny.

This is a highly concentrated version of Sir Thomas Browne: [387]

And as the ends and ultimates of all things accord in some mean and
measure with their inceptions and originals, that same multiplicit con-
cordance which leads forth growth from birth accomplishing by a retro-
gressive metamorphosis that minishing and ablation towards the final
which is agreeable unto nature so is it with our subsolar being.

This is Joyce in a suspiciously convincing impersonation of Dickens: [413]

And as her loving eyes behold her babe she wishes only one blessing
more, to have her dear Doady there with her to share her joy, to lay in
his arms that mite of God's clay, the fruit of their lawful embraces. He is
older now (you and I may whisper it) and a trifle stooped in the shoulders yet in the whirligig of years a grave dignity has come to the conscientious second accountant of the Ulster bank, College Green branch.

And this is Joyce in the congenial role of Carlyle: [416]

By heaven, Theodore Purefoy, thou has done a doughty deed and no
botch! Thou art, I vow, the remarkablest progenitor barring none in
this chaffering allincluding most farraginous chronicle.

Joyce's shifts from sober reality to bewildering richness, his transitions from the objective to the subjective and back—in the opinion of
Sergei Eisenstein, the film director and brilliant exponent of *montage*
—constitute one of the most effective applications of this technique.
In the internal monologue, which Eisenstein planned to use in his
unrealized production of Dreiser's *American Tragedy,* he saw a means
of going beyond the literal recording of surfaces that has so exclusively
preoccupied the film: "Presenting, as it were, the play of thought
within the *dramatis personæ*—the conflict of doubts, of bursts of passion, of the voice of reason, by quick movement, or slow movement,
emphasizing the difference in the rhythms of this one and that, and at
the same time contrasting the almost complete absence of outward action with the feverish inward debates behind the stony mask of the
face." An unyielding naturalism, in film or fiction, must be resigned
to the stalemate of total inaction. Flaubert sensed this dilemma and
set aside, in *La tentation de Saint-Antoine,* a realm of symbolic action.
Here the artist is still an observer, but he is also a tragic hero—a monk
in the desert who might be Flaubert at Croisset or Joyce in exile. Saint
Anthony is a spectator at his own tragedy, and the real actors are the

sphinxes and chimeras, the fathers of the church and decadent cities of the Mediterranean, that arise in his mind.

The climax of *Ulysses,* the Circe episode, achieves its action by a similar scene of introspective drama, which Middleton Murry has compared to the *Walpurgisnacht* episode in Goethe's *Faust.* Joyce, by this time, has set going enough trains of thought and accumulated enough contexts of experience to externalize his internal dialogue before the footlights of consciousness. Just as his mock-heroics confer grandeur upon little things, so his undramatic material insists upon dramatizing itself. To turn the mind inside out, presenting its ideas and emotions as allegorical *dramatis personæ,* is the procedure of the medieval morality play. It is also the program of the expressionist movement in the modern theater. In reaction from the naturalistic drama of Ibsen, the next generation was led by such playwrights as Strindberg in the direction of symbolism and psychic fantasy. Expressionism—as the Viennese dramatist, Hermann Bahr, defined it in 1916—sees through the eye of the mind and is active; impressionism saw through the eye of the body and was passive.

All the encounters and associations of the day—even the soap in Bloom's pocket—return for an expressionistic grand finale. In a dramatic dialogue extending through nearly a quarter of the book, to an accelerating tempo, against the backdrop of Dublin's "nighttown," Bloom and Stephen meet. At the establishment of Bella Cohen, the sorceress who turns men into beasts, the two streams of consciousness seem to converge. It was Stephen who read in a second-hand book a charm for winning a woman's love, *"Nebrakada femininum,"* [239] yet it is Bloom who hears those mystic words from his wife's apparition.[432] It was Bloom who noted at the funeral that Martin Cunningham's sympathetic face was like Shakespeare's,[95] yet it is now to Stephen that Shakespeare appears in the guise of Cunningham.[554] Both have their delusions of grandeur, as well as their anxiety-neuroses. Stephen is momentarily Cardinal Dedalus, Primate of all Ireland; Bloom is Lord Mayor, and ultimately Messiah. The incorporeal figments of both minds are strangely matched partners in a furious *danse macabre.*

There is a vulgar propriety in the musical accompaniment, Ponchielli's *Dance of the Hours,* upon which Bloom has already meditated that morning in the privy.[69] In honor of an English prostitute, Zoe,[489] there is also a *reprise* of the song played by a Scottish band that afternoon, "My Girl's a Yorkshire Girl." [250] Stephen is doing a *pas seul*— and tales are told of Joyce's own agility at this kind of performance —when he feels his mother's ashen breath and hears the Latin prayer he refused to say. His response is entirely in character: first an obscene monosyllable, then a phrase of expatriate French, next the echo of Lucifer's refusal, *Non serviam,* and finally a direct Wagnerian *leitmotiv,* the cry of Siegfried as he wields his sword, *Nothung!* The functioning of these literary reflexes, to the dismay of Madame Cohen and her *protégées,* impels Stephen to action. His operatic gesture is coupled, in the stage-direction, with a reminiscence of Blake that has been on his mind since his morning class. *(He lifts his ashplant high with both hands and smashes the chandelier. Time's livid final flame leaps and, in the following darkness, ruin of all space, shattered glass and toppling masonry.)* [567]

Within a few pages, it is Bloom's turn. He is able to get Stephen out of the brothel, but not to keep him from an argument with two British privates. The argument is part reality, part hallucination; Stephen is in no condition to discriminate. Lord Tennyson in his Union Jack blazer and King Edward with his bucket are on the other side, while Stephen is backed by Bloom's Sinn Feiner and his own milkwoman, "the old sow that eats her farrow." The hanging of the croppy boy, last of all his race, is re-enacted for Bloom's benefit; for Stephen the black mass is celebrated. The blow that knocks him unconscious is real enough. Bloom, with the aid of the genial undertaker, Corny Kelleher, disperses the crowd, says good-night to the watch, and is left alone with the prostrate figure of Stephen. It is the moment of Bloom's epiphany. Joyce, who has been at such pains to see that nothing happens all day, does not hesitate to pile one *dénouement* on top of the other. Having studiously refrained from presenting any complete human relationship, he now presents the most elementary feelings on the level of psychological melodrama. With calculated bathos, Bloom is made to feel his paternity. He addresses the pitiful spectre of his son, Rudy, who died at the age of eleven days; but there is no reply—only a stage-direction: [593]

> *(Gazes unseeing into Bloom's eyes and goes on reading, kissing, smiling. He has a delicate mauve face. On his suit he has diamond and ruby buttons. In his free left hand he holds a slim ivory cane with a violet bowknot. A white lambkin peeps out of his waistcoat pocket.)*

The continual effort of fiction to attain an impersonal reality seems, at first glance, to be reaching its fulfilment in *Ulysses.* Yet the more we read and reread the book, the larger it looms as a monument of personal artifice. Its scientific pretentions are sustained by the *trompe-l'œil* of literary technique. Its intellectual subtleties culminate in tried theatrical effects. This is no disparagement of Joyce, for all art is a synthesis, myth and cinema alike. If art contrives to give the illusion of reality, it is done—as they say—with mirrors, and we are concerned with how it is done. Perhaps it is because Joyce was so aware of the distinctions between art and life on the social plane, that he sought to merge them in the esthetic sphere. Perhaps he was insufficiently aware that, no matter how conscientiously experience is mirrored in literature, there will always remain something "which into words no virtue can digest." Bergson himself, the philosopher who held the fullest realization of the fluid nature of time and experience, also held that the intellect "spatializes." Consequently our imitations of life, no matter how complete and complicated we try to make them, are bound to be one-sided and over-simple.

THE DREAM OF H. C. EARWICKER *
Edmund Wilson

I

JAMES JOYCE's *Ulysses* was an attempt to present directly the thoughts and feelings of a group of Dubliners through the whole course of a summer day. *Finnegans Wake* is a complementary attempt to render the dream fantasies and the half-unconscious sensations experienced by a single person in the course of a night's sleep.

This presents a more difficult problem to the reader as well as to the writer. In *Ulysses,* the reader was allowed to perceive the real objective world in which the Blooms and Dedalus lived, and their situation and relationships in that world, so that its distortions or liquefactions under the stress of special psychological states still usually remain intelligible. But in *Finnegans Wake* we are not supplied with any objective data until the next to the last chapter, when the hero—and then only rather dimly—wakes up for a short time toward morning; and we are dealing with states of consciousness which, though they sometimes have something in common with the drunken imaginations of the nighttown scene in *Ulysses* or the free associations of Mrs. Bloom's insomniac reveries, are even more confused and fluid than these; so that it becomes on a first reading the reader's prime preoccupation to puzzle out who the dreamer is and what has been happening to him. And since Joyce has spent seventeen years elaborating and complicating this puzzle, it is hardly to be expected that one reading will suffice to unravel it completely.

Let me try to establish, however, some of the most important facts which provide the realistic foundation for this immense poem of sleep. The hero of *Finnegans Wake* is a man of Scandinavian blood, with what is apparently an adapted Scandinavian name: Humphrey Chimpden Earwicker, who keeps a pub called The Bristol in Dublin. He is somewhere between fifty and sixty, blond and ruddy, with a walrus mustache, very strong but of late years pretty fat. When embarrassed, he has a tendency to stutter. He has tried his hand at a number of occupations; has run for office and has gone through a bankruptcy. He is married to a woman named Ann, a former salesgirl, who is more or

* "The Dream of H. C. Earwicker" appears in *The Wound and the Bow,* by Edmund Wilson (Oxford University Press, 1947). It was first published in the *New Republic,* June 28, 1939, and July 12, 1939, and is used here by permission of the author.

less illiterate and whose maiden name seems to have begun with Mac. They are both Protestants in a community of Catholics, he an Episcopalian and she a Presbyterian; and by reason both of his religion and of his queer-sounding foreign name, he feels himself, like Bloom in *Ulysses,* something of an alien among his neighbors. The Earwickers have three children—a girl named Isobel, who has evidently passed adolescence, and two younger boys, twins: Kevin and Jerry. There are also a maid-of-all-work called Kate and a man about the place called Tom.

It is a Saturday night in summer, after a disorderly evening in the pub. Somebody—probably Earwicker himself—has been prevailed upon to sing a song: later, when it was closing time, he had to put a man outside, who abused him and threw stones at the window. There has also been a thunderstorm. Earwicker has been drinking off and on all day and has perhaps gone to bed a little drunk. At any rate, his night is troubled. At first he dreams about the day before, with a bad conscience and a sense of humiliation: then, as the night darkens and he sinks more deeply into sleep, he has to labor through a nightmare oppression.

He and his wife are sleeping together; but he has no longer any interest in her as a woman. He is preoccupied now with his children. His wife is apparently much younger than he, was only a girl when he married her; so that it is easy for him to confuse his first feelings for her with something like an erotic emotion which is now being aroused by his daughter. And his affection for his favorite son is even acquiring homosexual associations. Little Kevin is relatively sedate: named after the ascetic St. Kevin, he may be destined for the Catholic priesthood. Jerry (Shem) is more volatile and has given evidences of a taste for writing; and it is Jerry rather than Kevin (Shaun) with whom the father has tended to identify himself.

To tell the story in this way, however, is to present it the wrong way around. It depends for its dramatic effect on our not finding out till almost the end—pages 555-590,* in which Earwicker partially wakes up —that the flights of erotic fantasy and the horrors of guilt of his dream have been inspired by his feelings for his children. The pub is on the edge of the Phoenix Park, between it and the River Liffey and not far from the suburb of Chapelizod, which is said to have been the birthplace of Iseult. At the very beginning of the dream, we find Earwicker figuring as Tristram; and through the whole night he is wooing Iseult; he carries her off, he marries her. The Freudian censor has intervened to change *Isobel* into *Iseult la Belle*—as well as to turn the ana (upper)- Liffey, which figures in the dream as a woman, into *Anna Livia Plurabelle.* The idea of incest between father and daughter is developed on page 115; the transition from Isobel to Iseult is indicated in the "Icy-la-Belle" of page 246; and the sister of the twins is designated by her

* All page references are to the Viking Press edition of *Finnegans Wake.*

family nickname "Izzy" on page 431. But, though the boys have been given their real names and planted pretty clearly—on pages 26-27—it is not until almost the end—on page 556—that a definite identification of Earwicker's daughter with Iseult is made. In the same way, it is not until the passage on pages 564-565 that we are led to connect with Earwicker's son the homosexual motif which has first broken into his dream with the ominous incident of the father's accosting a soldier in the park and subsequently being razzed by the police, and which works free toward morning—page 474—to the idea, not related to actuality, of "some chubby boybold love of an angel."

In the meantime, the incest taboo and the homosexuality taboo have together—as in the development of Greek tragedy out of the old myths of cannibalism and incest—given rise, during Earwicker's effortful night, to a whole mythology, a whole morality. He is Tristram stealing Iseult, yes; but—at the suggestion of an Adam's mantelpiece in the bedroom where he is sleeping—he is also Adam, who has forfeited by his sin the Paradise of the Phoenix Park; at the suggestion of a copy of Raphael's picture of Michael subduing Satan which hangs on the bedroom wall, he is an archangel wrestling with the Devil. And he has fallen not merely as Adam but also as Humpty Dumpty (he is fat and his first name is Humphrey); as the hero of the ballad of *Finnegans Wake,* who fell off a scaffold while building a house (but came to life again at the sound of the word "Whisky"); and as Napoleon (an obelisk dedicated to Wellington is a feature of the Phoenix Park, though there is apparently no Wellington Museum). Since the landmarks of the life of Swift still keep their prestige in Dublin, he is Swift, who loved Stella and Vanessa with the obstructed love of a father and whose mind was finally blotted by madness: Swift's cryptic name for Stella, "Ppt," punctuates the whole book.

And Earwicker is also making up in sleep for an habitual feeling of helplessness due to his belonging to a racial and religious minority. He is sometimes the first Danish conqueror of Ireland, who sailed up that very Liffey; sometimes Oliver Cromwell, that other hated heathen invader.

But it is Joyce's further aim to create, through Earwicker's mythopœic dream, a set of symbols even more general and basic. He has had the idea of making Earwicker, resolved into his elemental components, include the whole of humanity. The river, with its feminine personality, Anna Livia Plurabelle, comes to represent the feminine principle itself. At one time or another all the women who figure in Earwicker's fantasy are merged into this stream of life which, always renewed, never pausing, flows through the world built by men. The daughter, still a little girl, is early identified with a cloud, which will come down to earth as rain and turn into the rapid young river; the Anna Livia Plurabelle chapter describes a lively woman's coming-of-age; in the end, the mature river, broader and slower now, will move toward her father, the sea. The corresponding masculine principle is symbolized by the Hill of Howth, which rises at the mouth of the Liffey; and the idea of the hill as a citadel and the idea of the city as a male construction associate themselves with this: the man is a hill that stands firm while the river runs away at his feet; he is a fortress, he is Dublin, he is all the cities of the world.

And if Earwicker is animated in sleep by the principles of both the sexes, he has also a double existence in the rôles of both Youth and Old Age. Canalizing his youthful impulses in a vision of himself as his favorite son, he dreams himself endowed with a resilience to go out and try life again; exalted by a purity of idealism which has not yet been tainted by experience, and yet bubbling with roguish drolleries, blithely beloved by the girls. On the other hand, foreshadowing his own decline, he sees the vision of a chorus of old men, who, drivelingly reminiscent, at the same time gloat and scold at the thought of the vigorous young Tristram kissing Iseult on the other side of the bushes, and exclaim in admiration—an expansion of Earwicker's feelings at the sight of his own sleeping son—over the form of the sleeping Earwicker (Shaun-Jerry). The old men are named Matthew Gregory, Marcus Lyons, Luke Tarpey and Johnny MacDougall; and they are identified variously with the four apostles, the Four Masters (early sages of Irish legend), the Four Waves of Irish mythology, the four courts of Dublin, and the four provinces of Ireland (Johnny MacDougall is evidently Ulster: he always follows at some distance behind the others). These fathers are always associated with a gray ass and sycamore trees, and have perhaps been suggested to Earwicker by four sycamore trees on the Liffey, among which a neighbor's donkey has been grazing. All of these major motifs are woven in and out from beginning to end of the book, and each at a given point receives a complete development: the woman-river in pages 196-216— the well-known Anna Livia Plurabelle chapter; the male city-fortress-hill in pages 532-554 (already published separately as *Haveth Childers Everywhere*); the Young Man in the chapters about Shaun, pages 403-473; and the Old Men, providing a contrast, just before, in 383-399.

There are also a stone and an elm on opposite sides of the Liffey, which represent the death principle and the life principle (Ygdrasil). The tree has several graciously rustling solos (a notable one at the end, beginning on page 619), and in the Anna Livia Plurabelle chapter she has a long conversation with the stone, which blends with the gossip of two old washerwomen drying clothes on the riverbank. This dialogue is only one of many dialogues which are really always the same disputation, and in which one of the parties, like the stone, is always hard-boiled, immobile and prosaic, while the other is sensitive, alive, rather light-mindedly chattering or chirping. The tougher of the two parties

in these interchanges is always browbeating or bullying the other. Sometimes they are Satan and Saint Michael; sometimes they are transmogri-
fied antitheses derived from Aesop's fables: the Mookse and the Gripes
(the Fox and the Grapes), the Ondt and the Gracehoper (the Ant and
the Grasshopper); but all these dualisms are evidently connected with
the diverse temperaments of Earwicker's twins (who sometimes appear
as Cain and Abel), and represent the diverse elements in the character
of Earwicker himself, as these struggle within his own consciousness, the
aggressive side sometimes reflecting certain powers in the external world
—the force of hostile opinion or the police—which he now fears, now
feels he can stand up to. The various pairs, however, shift their balance
and melt into one another so readily that it is impossible to give any
account of them which will cover all the cases in the book.

   Besides all this, just as Joyce in *Ulysses* laid the *Odyssey* under requi-
sition to help provide a structure for his material—material which, once
it had begun to gush from the rock of Joyce's sealed personality at
the blow of the Aaron's rod of free association, threatened to rise and
submerge the artist like the flood which the sorcerer's apprentice
let loose by his bedeviled broom; so in the face of an even more formidable danger, he has here brought in the historical theory of the
eighteenth-century philosopher, Giambattista Vico, to help him to organize *Finnegans Wake*. It was Vico's idea that civilizations always pass
through three definite phases: a phase when people imagine gods, a
phase when they make up myths about heroes, and a phase when they
see things in terms of real men. It will be noted that the figures mentioned above divide themselves among these three categories of beings.
Vico further believed that history moved in cycles and that it was always
repeating itself, which—to the frequent exasperation of the reader—
Finnegans Wake is also made to do. And there is also a good deal more
out of Vico, which you can find out about in *Our Exagmination* [1] but
which seems even more idle and forced than the most forced and idle
aspects of the Odysseyan parallel in *Ulysses*. The fact that there is a
Vico Road in the Dublin suburb Dalkey—"The Vico Road goes round
and round to meet where terms begin"—gives Joyce a peg in actuality
on which to hang all this theory.
   There is one important respect in which Joyce may seem to depart
from Vico. Vico, so far as is known, did not believe in progress: his
cycles did not spiral toward an earthly goal; his hope for salvation was

---

[1] *Our Exagmination Round His Factification for Incamination of Work in
Progress,* published by New Directions at Norfolk, Connecticut. This is a collection
of papers from *Transition,* the Paris magazine in which *Finnegans Wake* first appeared. The writers have taken their cues from Joyce himself, and he seems to have
chosen this way of providing the public with a key. It is, in fact, rather doubtful
whether without the work done by *Transition* it would be possible to get the hang
of the book at all. See also Mr. Max Eastman's account of an interview with Joyce
on the subject in Part III, Chapter III, of *The Literary Mind.*

in heaven. But the cycles of *Finnegans Wake* do result in a definite progression. As Earwicker lives through from darkness to light, he does slough off his feeling of guilt. By morning the Devil has been vanquished by Michael; Youth has bounded free of Age; the Phoenix of Vico and the Phoenix Park has risen from its ashes to new flight; Tristram has built a castle (Howth Castle) for his bride; and Iseult, once the object of an outlawed love, now married and growing older, turns naturally and comfortably at last into the lawful wife in the bed beside him, whom Earwicker is making an effort not to jab with his knees; the tumult and turbidity of Saturday night run clear in the peace of Sunday morning; the soul, which has been buried in sleep, is resurrected, refreshed, to life.

Yet if one looks at the book as a whole, one finds that the larger cycle does return upon itself. This will be seen when I discuss the last pages. In the meantime, let me merely point out that we do not find in *Finnegans Wake* any climax of exaltation comparable either to the scene where Stephen Dedalus realizes his artist's vocation or to Molly Bloom's great affirmative. The later book represents an aging phase in the constant human subject with which the series of Joyce's books has dealt. This subject—which must never be lost sight of, though in this case it is easy to do so—is the nexus of intimate relationships involved in a family situation. We find it first in the *Portrait of an Artist* in the attitude of Dedalus toward his family, and in the delicate but vital displacement in the relations of the young married couple who figure in the short story called *The Dead.* In *Exiles,* another young married couple come back from abroad with a son, and a more serious displacement takes place when the wife meets an old lover. In *Ulysses,* the relations of man and wife, by this time almost middle-aged, have been affected by more serious readjustments, and they are related in a complex way to the relations of the Blooms to their children, of Dedalus to his parents, and of both the Blooms to Dedalus. Now, in *Finnegans Wake,* the husband and wife have reached an age at which, from the emotional point of view, they seem hardly important to one another, and at which the chief source of interest is the attitude of the father toward the children—"the child we all love to place our hope in," as Earwicker thinks in the last moments before the rising sun wakes him up. (We have already had intimations of this relationship in the adoptively paternal instincts of Bloom toward the spiritually parentless Dedalus; in Joyce's little lyric poems, poignant to the point of anguish, that deal with his own children; and in the poem called *Ecce Puer,* in which the family cycle appears.)

Here this family situation has been explored more profoundly by Joyce than in any of his previous books. In sleep, the conventions and institutions with which we discipline and give shape to our lives are allowed partly to dissolve and evaporate, so as partly to set free the impulses of the common human plasm out of which human creatures are made; and then the sexual instincts of the man and the woman, the child's instinct and the parent's instinct, the masculine and feminine principles themselves, come into play in confusing ways, shadow forth disturbing relationships, which yet spring from the prime processes of life. *Finnegans Wake* carries even farther the kind of insight into such human relations which was already carried far in *Ulysses;* and it advances with an astounding stride the attempt to find the universally human in ordinary specialized experience which was implied in the earlier book by the Odysseyan parallel. Joyce will now try to build up inductively the whole of human history and myth from the impulses, conscious and dormant, the unrealized potentialities, of a single human being, who is to be a man even more obscure and even less well-endowed, even less civilized and aspiring, than was Leopold Bloom in *Ulysses*.

Finnegans Wake, in conception as well as in execution, is one of the boldest books ever written.

II

In order to get anything out of *Finnegans Wake,* you must grasp a queer literary convention. It has been said by T. S. Eliot that Joyce is the greatest master of language in English since Milton. Eliot has also pointed out that Milton is mainly a writer for the *ear.* Now Joyce through a large part of his adult life has been almost as blind as Milton; and he has ended, just as Milton did, by dealing principally in auditory sensations. There is as little visualization in *Finnegans Wake* as in *Samson Agonistes.* Our first criticism, therefore, is likely to be that nothing is *seen* in Earwicker's dream. It is, after all, not uncommon in dreams to have the illusion of seeing people and places as clearly as when we are awake; and in the dream literature with which we are already familiar—*Alice in Wonderland, The Temptation of Saint Anthony*—the dreamers are visited by plain apparitions, not merely by invisible voices. But we must assume with *Finnegans Wake* that Earwicker's imagination, like Joyce's, is almost entirely auditory and verbal. We have been partly prepared by *Ulysses,* in which we listen to the thoughts of the characters but do not see them very distinctly.

But there is another and more serious difficulty to be got over. We are continually being distracted from identifying and following Earwicker, the humble proprietor of a public house, who is to encompass the whole microcosm of the dream, by the intrusion of all sorts of elements—foreign languages, literary allusions, historical information—which could not possibly have been in Earwicker's mind. The principle on which Joyce is operating may evidently be stated as follows. If the artist is to render directly all the feelings and fancies of a sleeper, primitive, inarticulate, infinitely imprecise as they are, he must create a literary

medium of unexampled richness and freedom. Now it is also Joyce's
purpose in *Finnegans Wake* to bring out in Earwicker's consciousness
the processes of universal history: the languages, the cycles of society,
the typical relationships of legend, are, he is trying to show us, all implicit in every human being. He has, as I have indicated, been careful to
hook up his hero realistically with the main themes of his universal fantasia: the Bible stories, the Battle of Waterloo, Tristram and Iseult, and
so forth. But since Earwicker's implications *are* shown to be universal,
the author has the right to summon all the resources of his superior
knowledge in order to supply a vehicle which will carry this experience
of sleep. He has the same sort of justification for making the beings in
Earwicker's dream speak Russian in fighting the siege of Sebastopol
(which has got in by way of a picture hanging in Earwicker's house) as
Thomas Hardy has, for example, to describe in his own literary vocabulary a landscape seen by an ignorant person. If it is objected that
in *Finnegans Wake* the author is supposed to be not *describing,* but
presenting the hero's consciousness directly, Joyce might reply that his
procedure had precedent not only in poetry, but also in pre-naturalistic
fiction: even the characters of Dickens were allowed to make speeches
in blank verse, even the characters of Meredith were allowed to converse
in apothegms. Why shouldn't H. C. Earwicker be allowed to dream in a
language which draws flexibility and variety from the author's enormous reservoir of colloquial and literary speech, of technical jargons
and foreign tongues?

Yet here is where the reader's trouble begins, because here, in spite of
the defense just suggested, a convention that seems indispensable has
been disconcertingly violated. What Joyce is trying to do is to break out
of the Flaubertian naturalism into something that moves more at ease
and that commands a wider horizon, something that is not narrowly
tied down to the data about a certain man living in a certain year on
a certain street of a certain city; and the reaction is of course quite
natural: it was inevitable that the symbol and the myth, the traditional
material of poetry, should have asserted themselves again against the
formulas of scientific precision which had begun to prove so cramping.
But here the act of escaping from them shocks, just as it sometimes did
in Proust. Proust argues in an impressive way, in the final section of his
novel, the case against nineteenth-century naturalism; yet who has not
been made uncomfortable at finding that Proust's personal manias have
been allowed to affect the structure of his book: that a story which has
been presented as happening to real people should not maintain a consistent chronology, that it should never be clear whether the narrator of
the story is the same person as the author of the book, and that the author, who ought to know everything, should in some cases leave us in
doubt as to the facts about his hero? One had felt, in reading *Ulysses,*
a touch of the same uneasiness when the phantasmagoria imagined by

Bloom in the drunken nighttown scene was enriched by learned fancies which would seem to be more appropriate to Dedalus. And now in
Finnegans Wake the balloon of this new kind of poetry pulls harder at
its naturalistic anchor. We are in the first place asked to believe that a
man like H. C. Earwicker would seize every possible pretext provided
by his house and its location to include in a single night's dream a large
number of historical and legendary characters. And is it not pretty far-
fetched to assume that Earwicker's awareness of the life of Swift or the
Crimean War is really to be accurately conveyed in terms of the awareness of Joyce, who has acquired a special knowledge of these subjects?
Also, what about the references to the literary life in Paris and to the
book itself as Work in Progress, which take us right out of the mind of
Earwicker and into the mind of Joyce?

There are not, to be sure, very many such winks and nudges as this,
though the shadow of Joyce at his thankless task seems sometimes to fall
between Earwicker and us. Joyce has evidently set himself limits as to
how far he can go in this direction; and he may urge that since Earwicker is universal man, he must contain the implications of Joyce's
destiny as he does those of Swift's and Napoleon's, though he has
never heard of him as he has of them, and that to give these implications a personal accent is only to sign his canvas. Yet, even granting all
this and recognizing the difficulty of the task and accepting without res-
ervation the method Joyce has chosen for his purpose, the result still
seems unsatisfactory, the thing has not quite come out right. Instead
of the myths' growing out of Earwicker, Earwicker seems swamped in
the myths. His personality is certainly created: we get to know him and
feel sympathy for him. But he is not so convincing as Bloom was: there
has been too much literature poured into him. He has exfoliated into
too many arabesques, become hypertrophied by too many elements. And
not merely has he to carry this load of myths; he has also been all wound
round by what seems Joyce's growing self-indulgence in an impulse to
pure verbal play.

Here another kind of difficulty confronts us. There is actually a special kind of language which people speak in dreams and in which they
sometimes even compose poetry. This language consists of words and
sentences which, though they seem to be gibberish or nonsense from the
rational point of view, betray by their telescopings of words, their combinations of incongruous ideas, the involuntary preoccupations of the
sleeper. Lewis Carroll exploited this dream language in *Jabberwocky*,
and it has been studied by Freud and his followers, from whom Joyce
seems to have got the idea of its literary possibilities. At any rate,
Finnegans Wake is almost entirely written in it.

The idea was brilliant in itself, and Joyce has in many cases carried it
out brilliantly. He has created a whole new poetry, a whole new humor

and pathos, of sentences and words that go wrong. The special kind of equivocal and prismatic effects aimed at by the symbolist poets have here been achieved by a new method and on psychological principles which give them a new basis in humanity. But the trouble is, it seems to me, that Joyce has somewhat overdone it. His method of giving words multiple meanings allows him to go on indefinitely introducing new ideas; and he has spent no less than seventeen years embroidering *Finnegans Wake* in this way.

What has happened may be shown by the following examples. First, a relatively simple one from a passage about the Tree: "Amengst menlike trees walking or trees like angels weeping nobirdy aviar soar anywing to eagle it!" It is quite clear in the last seven words how an ornithological turn has been given to "nobody ever saw anything to equal it." Here is a more complex one: Earwicker, picturing himself in the chapter in which he partially wakes up, is made to designate his hair with the phrase "beer wig." This has as its basis *bar wig*, which has rushed into the breach as *beer wig* under the pressure of Earwicker's profession as a dispenser of drinks in his pub, of the fact that his hair is yellow, and of his tendency to imagine that his queer last name is being caricatured by his neighbors as "Earwigger"—a tendency which has led to his dream being impishly haunted by earwigs. There are thus four different ideas compressed in these two words. But let us examine—with the aid of the hints provided by the *Exagmination*—an even more complicated passage. Here is Earwicker-Joyce's depiction of the madness and eclipse of Swift: "Unslow, malswift, pro mean, proh noblesse, Atrahore, melancolores, nears; whose glauque eyes glitt bedimmed to imm; whose fingrings creep o'er skull: till quench., asterr mist calls estarr and graw, honath Jon raves homes glowcoma." This passage, besides the more or less obvious ones, contains apparently the following ideas: Laracor, Swift's living in Ireland, combined with the *atra cura, black care,* that rides behind the horseman in the first poem of Book Three of Horace's *Odes;* the Horatian idea that death comes to the mean and the noble alike; *proh,* the Latin interjection of regret, and *pro,* perhaps referring to Swift's championship of the impoverished Irish; *melancolores, melancholy* plus *black-colored; glauque,* French *gray-blue,* plus Greek *glaux, owl*—gray evening plus Swift's blue eyes, which also had an owlish appearance; in *glitt bedimmed to imm,* the doubled consonants evidently represent a deadening of the senses; *creep o'er skull,* French *crépuscule, twilight; asterr,* Greek *aster, star,* Swift's Stella, whose real name was Esther; Vanessa's real name was Hester—so Stella calls Hester a (q)wench; perhaps German *mist, dung, trash,* plays some part here, too—as well as German *starr, rigid; graw* evidently contains German *grau,* gray; *honath Jon* is *honest John* and *Jonathan; glowcoma* is *glaucoma,* a kind of blindness, plus the idea of a pale glow of life persisting in a coma. This passage has some beauty and power; but isn't it overingenious? Would anyone naturally think of Horace when he was confronted with "Atrahore"? And, even admitting that it may be appropriate to associate Latin with Swift, how does the German get in? Swift did not know German nor had he any German associations.[2]

In some cases, this overlaying of meanings has had the result of rendering quite opaque passages which at an earlier stage—as we can see by comparing the finished text with some of the sections as they first appeared—were no less convincingly dreamlike for being more easily comprehensible. You will find three versions of a passage in *Anna Livia Plurabelle* on page 164 of the *Exagmination;* and on page 213 of the book you will see that Joyce has worked up still a fourth. My feeling is that he ought to have stopped somewhere between the second and the third. Here is Version 1 of 1925: "Look, look, the dusk is growing. What time is it? It must be late. It's ages now since I or anyone last saw Waterhouse's clock. They took it asunder, I heard them say. When will they reassemble it?" And here is Version 4 of 1939: "Look, look, the dusk is growing. My branches lofty are taking root. And my cold cher's gone ashley. Fieluhr? Filou! What age is at? It saon is late. 'Tis endless now senne eye or erewone last saw Waterhouse's clogh. They took it asunder, I hurd thum sigh. When will they reassemble it?" There is a gain in poetry, certainly; but in the meantime the question and the answer have almost disappeared. Has it really made Anna Livia any more riverlike to introduce the names of several hundred rivers (*saon* is *Saône* doing duty as *soon,* and *cher* is the *Cher* for French *chair*)—as he also introduces in other sections the names of cities, insects, trees? And why drag in *Erewhon?* In the same way, the talk of the Old Men, which, when it first came out in *Navire d' Argent,* seemed almost equal in beauty to the Anna Livia Plurabelle chapter, has now been so crammed with other things that the voices of the actual speakers have in places been nearly obliterated.

Joyce has always been rather deficient in dramatic and narrative sense. *Ulysses* already dragged; one got lost in it. The moments of critical importance were so run in with the rest that one was likely to miss them on first reading. One had to think about the book, read chapters of it over, in order to see the pattern and to realize how deep the insight went. And *Finnegans Wake* is much worse in this respect. The main outlines of the book are discernible, once we have been tipped off as to what it is all about. It is a help that, in forming our hypothesis,

---

[2] I chose this passage because a partial exposition of it, which I take to be more or less authoritative, had appeared in the *Exagmination* (in the paper by Mr. Robert McAlmon). I did not remember to have read it in its place in *Finnegans Wake,* and was unable to find it when I looked for it. Since then I have been told by another reader who has been over and over the book that this sentence about Swift is not included. This is interesting because it indicates the operation of a principle of selection. Joyce suffered himself from glaucoma, and it may be that he eliminated the reference because he felt that it was too specifically personal.

the principle of Occam's razor applies; for it is Joyce's whole design and point that the immense foaming-up of symbols should be reducible to a few simple facts. And it must also be conceded by a foreigner that a good deal which may appear to him mysterious would be plain enough to anyone who knew Dublin and something about Irish history, and that what Joyce has done here is as legitimate as it would be for an American writer to lay the scene of a similar fantasy somewhere on Riverside Drive in New York and to assume that his readers would be able to recognize Grant's Tomb, green buses, Columbia University and the figure of Hendrik Hudson. A foreign reader of *Finnegans Wake* should consult a map of Dublin, and look up the articles on Dublin and Ireland in the *Encyclopaedia Britannica*.

Yet it seems to me a serious defect that we do not really understand what is happening till we have almost finished the book. *Then* we can look back and understand the significance of Earwicker's stuttering over the word *father* on page 45; we can see that "Peder the Greste, altipaltar" on page 344 combines, along with Peter the Great and *agreste, pederast* and *pater;* we can conclude that the allusion on page 373 about "begetting a wife which begame his niece by pouring her young-things into skintighs" refers back to the little story on pages 21-23, and that this whole theme is a device of the "dream-work" to get over the incest barrier by disguising Earwicker's own children as the children of a niece.

But in the meantime we have had to make our way through five hundred and fifty-four pages; and there is much that is evidently important that we still do not understand. How, for example, is the story of the "prankquean" just mentioned related to the motif of the letter scratched up by the chicken from the dump heap; and what is the point about this letter? The theme is developed at prodigious length in the chapter beginning on page 104; and it flickers all through the book. It turns up near the end—pages 623-624—with new emotional connotations. The idea of letters and postmen plays a prominent part all through. Little Kevin is represented as giving the postman's knock; and Earwicker—though he here seems to be identifying himself with the other son, Jerry—is caught up into a long flight of fantasy in which he imagines himself a postman. The letter comes from Boston, Massachusetts, and seems to have been written by some female relation, perhaps the niece mentioned above. One feels that there is a third woman in the story, and that something important depends on this. Yet a considerable amount of re-reading has failed, in the case of the present writer, to clear the matter up.

Finnegans Wake, in the actual reading, seems to me for two thirds of its length not really to bring off what it attempts. Nor do I think it possible to defend the procedure of Joyce on the basis of an analogy with music. It is true that there is a good deal of the musician in Joyce: his phonograph record of *Anna Livia* is as beautiful as a fine tenor solo. But nobody would listen for half an hour to a composer of operas or symphonic poems who went on and on in one mood as monotonously as Joyce has done in parts of *Finnegans Wake,* who scrambled so many motifs in one passage, or who returned to pick up a theme a couple of hours after it had first been stated, when the listeners would inevitably have forgotten it.[3]

I believe that the miscarriage of *Finnegans Wake,* in so far as it does miscarry, is due primarily to two tendencies of Joyce's which were already in evidence in *Ulysses:* the impulse, in the absence of dramatic power, to work up an epic impressiveness by multiplying and complicating detail, by filling in abstract diagrams and laying on intellectual conceits, till the organic effort at which he aims has been spoiled by too much that is synthetic; and a curious shrinking solicitude to conceal from the reader his real subjects. These subjects are always awkward and distressing: they have to do with the kind of feelings which people themselves conceal and which it takes courage in the artist to handle. And the more daring Joyce's subjects become, the more he tends to swathe them about with the fancywork of his literary virtuosity. It is as

[3] This essay was written in the summer of 1939, just after *Finnegans Wake* came out, and I have reprinted it substantially as it first appeared. Since then an article by Mr. John Peale Bishop in *The Southern Review* of Summer, 1939, and studies by Mr. Harry Levin in *The Kenyon Review* of Autumn, 1939, and in *New Directions* of 1939, have thrown further light on the subject; and I have also had the advantage of discussions with Mr. Thornton Wilder, who has explored the book more thoroughly than anyone else I have heard of. It is to be hoped that Mr. Wilder will some day publish something about *Finnegans Wake;* and in the meantime those interested in the book should consult the essays mentioned, upon which I have sometimes drawn in revising the present study.

One suggestion of Mr. Bishop's should certainly be noted here. He believes that the riddle of the letter is the riddle of life itself. This letter has been scratched up from a dung-heap and yet it has come from another world; it includes in its very brief length marriage, children and death, and things to eat and drink—all the primary features of life, beyond which the ideas of the illiterate writer evidently do not extend; and Earwicker can never really read it, though the text seems exceedingly simple and though he confronts it again and again.

I ought to amend what is said in this essay on the basis of a first reading by adding that *Finnegans Wake,* like *Ulysses,* gets better the more you go back to it. I do not know of any other books of which it is true as it is of Joyce's that, though parts of them may leave us blank or repel us when we try them the first time, they gradually build themselves up for us as we return to them and think about them. That this should be true is due probably to some special defect of *rapport* between Joyce and the audience he is addressing, to some disease of his architectural faculty; but he compensates us partly for this by giving us more in the long run than we had realized at first was there, and he eventually produces the illusion that his fiction has a reality like life's, because, behind all the antics, the pedantry, the artificial patterns, something organic and independent of these is always revealing itself; and we end by recomposing a world in our mind as we do from the phenomena of experience. Mr. Max Eastman reports that Joyce once said to him, during a conversation on *Finnegans Wake,* when Mr. Eastman had suggested to Joyce that the demands made on the reader were too heavy and that he perhaps ought to provide a key: "The demand that I make of my reader is that he should devote his whole life to reading my works." It is in any case probably true that they will last you a whole lifetime.

if it were not merely Earwicker who was frightened by the state of his emotions but as if Joyce were embarrassed, too.

Yet, with all this, *Finnegans Wake* has achieved certain amazing successes. Joyce has caught the psychology of sleep as no one else has ever caught it, laying hold on states of mind which it is difficult for the waking intellect to re-create, and distinguishing with marvelous delicacy between the different levels of dormant consciousness. There are the relative vividness of events reflected from the day before; the nightmare viscidity and stammering of the heavy slumbers of midnight; the buoyance and self-assertive vitality which gradually emerge from this; the half-waking of the early morning, which lapses back into the rigmaroles of dreams; the awareness, later, of the light outside, with its effect as of the curtain of the eyelids standing between the mind and the day. Through all this, the falling of twilight, the striking of the hours by the clock, the morning fog and its clearing, the bell for early mass, and the rising sun at the window, make themselves felt by the sleeper. With what brilliance they are rendered by Joyce! And the voices that echo in Earwicker's dream—the beings that seize upon him and speak through him: the Tree and the River, the eloquence of Shaun, the mumbling and running-on of the Old Men; the fluttery girl sweetheart, the resigned elderly wife; the nagging and jeering gibberish—close to madness and recalling the apparition of Virag in the Walpurgisnacht scene of *Ulysses,* but here identified with the Devil—which comes like an incubus with the darkness and through which the thickened voices of the Earwicker household occasionally announce themselves startlingly: "Mawmaw, luk, your beeftay's fizzin' over" or "Now a muss wash the little face." Joyce has only to strike the rhythm and the timbre, and we know which of the spirits is with us.

Some of the episodes seem to me wholly successful: the Anna Livia chapter, for example, and the end of *Haveth Childers Everywhere,* which has a splendor and a high-spirited movement of a kind not matched elsewhere in Joyce. The passage in a minor key which precedes this major *crescendo* and describes Earwicker's real habitations—"most respectable . . . thoroughly respectable . . . partly respectable," and so forth—is a masterpiece of humorous sordidity (especially "copious holes emitting mice"); and so is the inventory—on pages 183-184—of all the useless and rubbishy objects in the house where Shem the Penman lives. The *Ballad of Persse O'Reilly* (*perce-oreille,* earwig)—which blazons the shame of Earwicker—is real dream literature and terribly funny; as is also the revelation—pages 572-573—of the guilty and intricate sex relationships supposed to prevail in the Earwicker family, under the guise of one of those unintelligible summaries of a saint's legend or a Latin play. The waking-up chapter is charming in the passage—page 565—in which the mother comforts the restless boy and in the summing-up—

page 579—of the married life of the Earwickers; and it is touchingly and thrillingly effective in throwing back on all that has gone before the shy impoverished family pathos which it is Joyce's special destiny to express.

Where he is least happy, I think, is in such episodes as the voyage, 311 ff., the football game, 373 ff., and the siege of Sebastopol, 338 ff. (all in the dense nightmarish part of the book, which to me is, in general, the dullest). Joyce is best when he is idyllic, nostalgic, or going insane in an introspective way; he is not good at energetic action. There is never any direct aggressive clash between the pairs of opponents in Joyce, and there is consequently no real violence (except Dedalus' smashing the chandelier in self-defense against the reproach of his dead mother). All that Joyce is able to do when he wants to represent a battle is to concoct an uncouth gush of language. In general one feels, also, in *Finnegans Wake* the narrow limitations of Joyce's interests. He has tried to make it universal by having Earwicker take part in his dream in as many human activities as possible: but Joyce himself has not the key either to politics, to sport or to fighting. The departments of activity that come out best are such quiet ones as teaching and preaching.

The finest thing in the book, and one of the finest things Joyce has done, is the passage at the end where Ann, the wife, is for the first time allowed to speak with her full and mature voice. I have noted that Joyce's fiction usually deals with the tacit readjustment in the relationships between members of a family, the almost imperceptible moment which marks the beginning of a phase. In *Finnegans Wake,* the turning-point fixed is the moment when the husband and wife know definitely —they will wake up knowing it—that their own creative sexual partnership is over. That current no longer holds them polarized—as man and woman—toward one another; a new polarization takes place: the father is pulled back toward the children. "Illas! I wisht I had better glances," he thinks he hears Ann-Anna saying (page 626) "to peer to you through this baylight's growing. But you're changing, acoolsha, you're changing from me, I can feel. Or is it me is? I'm getting mixed. Brightening up and tightening down. Yes, you're changing, sonhusband, and you're turning, I can feel you, for a daughterwife from the hills again. Imlamaya. And she is coming. Swimming in my hindmoist. Diveltaking on me tail. Just a whisk brisk sly spry spink spank sprint of a thing theresomere, saultering. Saltarella come to her own. I pity your oldself I was used to. Now a younger's there." It is the "young thin pale soft shy slim slip of a thing, sauntering by silvamoonlake" (page 202 in the Anna Livia Plurabelle section) that she herself used to be, who now seems to her awkward and pert, and the wife herself is now the lower river running into the sea. The water is wider here; the pace of the stream is calmer: the broad day of experience has opened. "I thought you were all glittering with the noblest of carriage. You're only a bumpkin. I thought you the great in all things, in guilt and in glory. You're but a puny. Home!" She sees him clearly now: he is neither Sir Tristram nor Lucifer; and he is done with her and she with him. "I'm loothing them that's here and all I lothe. Loonely in me loneness. For all their faults. I am passing out. O bitter ending! I'll slip away before they're up. They'll never see me. Nor know. Nor miss me. And it's old and old it's sad and old it's sad and weary I go back to you, my cold father, my cold mad father, my cold mad feary father." ... The helpless and heartbreaking voices of the Earwicker children recur: "Carry me along, taddy, like you done through the toy fair."— for now she is herself the child entrusting herself to the sea, flowing out into the daylight that is to be her annihilation ... "a way a lone a last a loved a long the" ...

The Viconian cycle of existence has come full circle again. The unfinished sentence which ends the book is to find its continuation in the sentence without a beginning with which it opens. The river which runs into the sea must commence as a cloud again; the woman must give up life to the child. The Earwickers will wake to another day, but the night has made them older: the very release of the daylight brings a weariness that looks back to life's source.

In these wonderful closing pages, Joyce has put over all he means with poetry of an originality, a purity, and an emotional power, such as to raise *Finnegans Wake,* for all its excesses, to the rank of a great work of literature.

JOHN DOS PASSOS AND THE WHOLE
TRUTH *

DELMORE SCHWARTZ

IF WE think for a moment of the newspaper as a representation of American life, we get some idea of the basis of John Dos Passos' enormous novel.[1] It is not merely that one of the devices of this novel is the "newsreel" and consists of an arrangement of quotations from newspapers of the past thirty years; nor that another device is the "camera eye," and still another consists of biographies of Americans who have for the most part been prominent in the newspaper. It is in its whole sense of American life and in its formal character—its omnibus, omnivorous span—that Dos Passos' novel seems to at least one reader to derive from the newspaper. The sense of the unknown lives behind the wedding announcements and the obituaries, the immense gap between private life and public events, and between the private experience of the individual and the public experience represented in the newspaper as being constituted by accident, violence, scandal, the speeches of politicians, and the deliberations of Congress—all this would seem to have a good deal to do with determining Dos Passos' vision and his intention. There were concerts, club meetings, and lectures in St. Petersburg on the night in October, 1917, when the Russian Revolution occurred—it is such a curious mixture of the private worlds and the public world that seems to obsess Dos Passos.

Another and related way of characterizing his novels is through the names he has given them: *Three Soldiers,* a "picture" of the World War (which, curiously enough, delighted Amy Lowell), *Manhattan Transfer,* a "picture" of New York City, *The 42nd Parallel,* and *1919.* And thus it is interesting to remark that the name of *U.S.A.* apparently was chosen for Dos Passos by the reviewer in *Time* who said, when a part of the book appeared as a separate novel, that "Alone among U.S. writers, John Dos Passos has taken as his subject the whole U.S.A. and attempted to organize its chaotic high-pressure life into an understandable artistic pattern." The source of the title suggests that Dos Passos' way of grasping experience has a good deal, although not everything, in common not only with the triumvirate of *Time, Life,* and *Fortune,* but also with

* "John Dos Passos and the Whole Truth" originally appeared in the *Southern Review,* Autumn, 1938, and is used here by permission of the author and Louisiana · State University Press.

[1] *U.S.A.,* by John Dos Passos, Harcourt, Brace & Co., New York.

the whole tendency to get documents, to record facts, and to swallow
the whole rich chaos of modern life. The motion picture called *The
River,* with its mixture of lyricism and economic discourse, the picture-
and-text books, the Federal theater plays about housing and the AAA,
and even the poetry, in some of its aspects, of Mr. Horace Gregory and
Miss Muriel Rukeyser are like examples of a distinct method of attempting to take hold of experience in its breathless and disordered contemporaneity. How wide-spread the sense of life exemplified in Dos Passos
is, and what its basis is, can be seen in these words of a preface to a book
of short stories edited by a wholly different kind of writer:

> We were in Austria at the beginning of a desperately eventful year—
> a year that was to be characterized by almost universal unrest, by civil
> war, revolution, by strikes and unemployment figures reaching mon-
> strous proportions; a year which opened in France with the suicide or
> murder of Stavisky, throwing that country into chaos, causing two
> governments to fall; a year which saw the February slaughter in Vienna
> and the eventual murder of the Austrian Chancellor; a year which in
> one part of the world brought the tragedy of the Morro Castle and the
> expansion of the unprecedented and hotly disputed N.R.A., while an-
> other continent saw the King of Jugoslavia assassinated, the Blood
> Purge of Germany effected, and Hitler confirmed Leader-Chancellor of
> the Third Reich upon von Hindenburg's death; the year of a royal
> wedding in England, of Gandhi's retirement from politics, of civil strife
> in Spain, Austria, Bolivia; the year of the Chicago Fair, the devaluation
> of the dollar, the conclusion of the Holy Year at Vatican City, the year
> of the Great Drought—the year 1934.
> We decided then to compile a record in fiction form not only of that
> year's nationally or internationally important events but as well of the
> ordinary individual's life as it was being lived on the five continents
> throughout that period of time.[2]

The poetic fashioned by this kind of awareness can perhaps be stated
in this way: there are facts and things and processes continually going
on in the world and the writer intends nothing so much as to provide
portraits, even photographs, of them through the conventions of fiction
—and sometimes without those conventions. Of Dos Passos we can say—
and regard this as the best praise for anyone's intention—that his intention has been to tell the truth about the world in which he has had to
exist. But more than that, he has apparently gone from one end of the
world to the other in the effort to find the truth and not to permit the
Zeitgeist to evade him. So, at any rate, his travel book [3] indicates, providing an image of the author as the sensitive, unassuming, anonymous

[2] *365 Days,* Edited by Kay Boyle, Lawrence Vail, Nina Conarain. Harcourt, Brace
& Co., 1936.
[3] *Journey Between Two Wars,* by John Dos Passos, Harcourt, Brace & Co., New
York. This is a selection from Dos Passos' three previous travel books together with
some very interesting additions having to do with Spain in 1937.

observer who is intent upon seeing all that is to be seen—even when, as in Russia in 1928 and in Barcelona in 1937, he is compelled to see so much that will be contrary to his expectation and dearest hope.

At the conclusion of the last book of *U.S.A.* and after having written some 1400 pages, Dos Passos wrote a brief chapter to head the whole book and called the chapter *U.S.A.*, and here defined his intention, at the conclusion of his efforts, when he would know it best.

> The young man walks by himself through the crowd that thins into night streets . . . eyes greedy for warm curves of faces . . . mind a beehive of hopes . . . muscles ache for the knowledge of jobs. The young man walks by himself searching through the crowd with greedy eyes, greedy ears taut to hear, by himself, alone . . .
>
> The young man walks by himself, fast but not fast enough, far but not far enough (faces slide out of sight, talk trails into tattered scraps, . . .) he must catch the last subway, the streetcar, the bus, run up the gangplank of all the steamboats, register at all the hotels, work in the cities, answer the want-ads, live in all the boardinghouses . . . one job is not enough, one life is not enough.

And the only link, we are told, between the young man walking alone and the life he wished to know so fully was in the speech of the people. U.S.A. meant and was many things—a part of a continent, a group of holding companies, the soldiers who died for the U.S.A., the letters on an address, a stack of newspapers on file—"but mostly U.S.A. is the speech of the people." And Dos Passos has told us this before, in the introduction written to *Three Soldiers,* in 1932, when that book was canonized by The Modern Library. Again what he says is worth quoting for its expression of the utter honesty and clarity of his intention.

> You wake up one morning and find that what was to have been a *springboard into reality* [*my italics*] is a profession. Making a living by selling daydreams is all right, but few men feel it's much of a life for a man. . . . What I'm trying to get out is the difference in kind between the work of James Joyce, say, and that of any current dispenser of daydreams. . . . What do you write for, then? To convince people of something? That's preaching, and a part of the business of everyone who deals with words . . . but outside of preaching I think there is such a thing as straight writing. . . . The mind of a generation is its speech. A writer makes aspects of that speech enduring . . . makes of them forms to set the mind of tomorrow's generation. That's history. A writer who writes straight is the architect of history. . . . Those of us who have lived through [these times] have seen the years strip the bunting off the great illusions of our time. We must deal with the raw structure of history now, we must deal with it quick, before it stamps us out.

One may regret the slanging tone, as of Mr. Otis Ferguson (as if Dos Passos too were afraid that if he used abstract terms and an unconversational diction, he would be considered a sissy), and one may feel that an "architect of history" is rather a fancy claim, but one cannot deny that Dos Passos knows very well what he wants to do in his novels.

Naturally such motives have infected his style and method in every aspect. In *U.S.A.*, Dos Passos uses four "forms" or "frames," each of them deriving directly from his representative intention, his desire to get at the truth about his time with any available instrument. Each of these forms needs to be considered in itself.

There is the camera eye, an intermittent sequence of prose poems in an impressionist style: "all week the fog clung to the sea and cliffs . . . gray flakes green sea gray houses white fog lap of the waves against the wharf scream of gulls circling and swooping," or another brief example: "all over Tours you can smell the linden in bloom it's hot my uniform sticks the O.D. chafes me under the chin." Each impression is apparently autobiographical and dates from the childhood of the author to the 'twenties. The writing takes on the lyricism of a quasi-Joycean stream-of-consciousness and the emphasis is almost always upon the look and feel of things, mostly apart from any narrative context. At first glance the texture seems the crudity of an undergraduate determined to be modern, but upon examination this entirely disappears and one finds that all is based on faithful observation and is never pretentious, nor false. But these passages have no direct relation to the main story, although at times there is some link—just before a leading character goes to Havana, for example, the autobiographical impression is of a trip on a Spanish boat to Cuba.

Secondly, there are the newsreel passages which are inserted just as the camera eye panels are, between narratives. They consist of quotations from newspapers of a given time and period and also of its popular songs. Many amusing juxtapositions of headlines and stories are made by means of clever arrangements, and the lyrics are (where the present reader is able to judge) perfectly reminiscent. But the central intention of this form—to suggest the quality of various years and its public events—is not fulfilled for the most part. The newsreels are sometimes merely frivolous and trivial. One example may suffice to show this:

the first thing the volunteer firefighters did was to open the windows to let the smoke out. This created a draft and the fire with a good thirty-mile wind from the ocean did the rest

RECORD TURNOVER IN INSURANCE SHARES
AS TRADING PROGRESSES

Change all of your grey skies
Turn them into blue skies
And keep sweeping the cobwebs off the moon.

BROKERS' LOANS HIT NEW HIGH
MARKETS OPTIMISTIC

learn new uses for concrete. How to develop profitable concrete business. How to judge materials. How to figure jobs. How to reinforce
concrete. How to build forms, roads, sidewalks, floors, culverts, cellars.

The time, one would suppose, is 1927 or 1928. The stock market headlines indicate that time and are loosely relevant to the main narrative.
The first passage is a news story, however, and the last is an advertise-
ment. They are disjunct parts and they could with no difficulty be transposed to any other of the fifty-eight newsreels going back to the turn of
the century.

A third form is the "Biography." Here we are provided with concise
recitatives in a Whitmanesque diction which is used at times with
power. Each biography concerns a great figure of the period, and there
are twenty-six of them. Four leaders of the working class, Eugene V.
Debs, Joe Hill, Bill Haywood, and Wesley Everest; seven capitalists, An-
drew Carnegie, Henry Ford, William Randolph Hearst, J. P. Morgan,
Samuel Insull, and Minor C. Keith; four politicians, Robert La Follette
(Sr.), Theodore Roosevelt, Woodrow Wilson, and William Jennings
Bryan; four inventors, Luther Burbank, the Wright Brothers, Thomas
Edison, and Charles Steinmetz; three journalists, John Reed, Randolph
Bourne, and Paxton Hibben; an actor, Rudolph Valentino; a dancer,
Isadora Duncan; an efficiency expert, Frederick W. Taylor; an architect,
Frank Lloyd Wright; and one genuine intellectual, Thorstein Veblen.
One remarks that naturally enough there are no musicians, musical life
being what it is in America. But one regrets the omission of poets, un-
less John Reed be considered one—Harriet Monroe, Vachel Lindsay,
Amy Lowell, and even Hart Crane suggest themselves. There is no characteristic Broadway actor, such as Al Jolson. Professional sport, particularly major league baseball, which in fact prepossesses at least two million American souls for six months a year, might also have been represented, at least in the newsreels; and for biographies, one thinks of
Christy Matthewson, Connie Mack, Red Grange, and Gertrude Ederle.
But on the whole the biographies are as representative as one could wish
and are written with a fine power of generalization and concision—the
gist abstracted from the life of a man and presented in four or five pages,
concluding very well at times in the form of a simple contradiction,
Henry Ford's nostalgic desire for the horse-and-buggy days, which
his whole career, of course, worked to destroy, and Andrew Carnegie's
bestowal of millions for world peace, the millions being acquired, of
course, by the manufacture of steel used in munitions and battleships.

The major part of the novel, perhaps as much as 1200 pages, is, however, constituted by direct narratives of the lives of eleven leading char-

acters and perhaps three times as many minor ones who are notable. In creating a mode in which to present the lives of these characters, Dos Passos has definitely extended the art of narration. It is difficult to describe what he has accomplished because it is so much a matter of the digestion of a great many details and the use of facts which rise from the historical sense—all caught into a smooth-running story which, taken in itself, cannot fail to hold the reader's attention. The narratives are always in the third person and yet have all the warm interior flow of a story presented through the medium of a stream-of-consciousness first-person. One remarkable achievement is the way in which the element of time is disposed. With no break or unevenness at all, the narrative passes quickly through several years of the character's life, presenting much that is essential briefly, and then contracts, without warning, without being noted, and focuses for several pages upon a single episode which is important. It is an ability which an apprentice writer can best appreciate and comes from the indispensable knowledge of how very much the writer can *omit*—Hemingway knows this very well also—and a knowledge of how each sentence can expand in the reader's mind to include a whole context of experience. Another feature to be noted is Dos Passos' immense command of details which seem to come from a thousand American places and to be invested with a kind of historical idiom at all times. There is, for example, the story of Eleanor Stoddard, which begins:

> When she was small she hated everything. She hated her father, a stout red haired man smelling of whiskers and stale pipe tobacco. He worked in an office in the stockyards ... Nights she used to dream she lived alone with her mother in a big clean white house in Oak Park in winter when there was snow on the ground and she'd been setting a white linen table cloth with bright white silver ... When she was sixteen in highschool she and a girl named Isabelle swore together that if a boy ever touched them they'd kill themselves ... The only other person Eleanor liked was Miss Oliphant, her English teacher ... It was Miss Oliphant who induced Eleanor to take courses at the Art Institute. She had reproductions on her walls of pictures by Rossetti and Burne-Jones ... She made Eleanor feel that Art was something ivory white and very pure and noble and distant and sad ... She was reading through the complete works of George Eliot.

The whiskers and stale pipe smoke, the white house and the snow, the pictures of Rossetti and Burne-Jones, and the novels of George Eliot (as understood by such a person)—with such qualitative details a whole type of girlhood is summoned up and placed in time. The utterance, as if from the movement of the character's mind, is completely convincing and is achieved by a discreet use of speech diction and speech rhythms and words of direct feeling. Dos Passos has had to work for a long time to attain to this kind of mastery. In his earlier novels, the description was always thick, heavy, isolated, and the use of dialects at times approximated a vaudeville show. But these faults have been pursued to the point where they are magnificent virtues.

The thirteen leading characters who are presented through the medium of this kind of narrative are all members of the lower middle-class. The very rich and the working-class are not the subjects of direct attention, although they participate also in a variety of ways. It is true too that some of these characters are for all practical purposes reduced to the status of workers and most of them, on the other hand, desire to be rich, while three of them devote themselves to the cause of the working-class. But in the main, what we get is the typical life of the lower middle-class between 1900 and 1930. Typical indeed, for there is a constant "averaging," a constant effort to describe each character in terms which will reduce him to a type. The same motive seems to have dictated the kinds of character. There is an IWW typesetter, a Jewish radical leader, a movie star, an interior decorator, a publicity man, a stenographer, a Harvard aesthete, a sailor, an aviator, a social worker, a Red Cross nurse —all of them, I should add, might be characterized differently since they engage in other activities from time to time. Their chief values, which they do not examine or question in the least (except for the radicals), are "love" and "money." The accuracy of this presentation can be verified by examining a fair sample of advertising in order to see on what the advertisers are basing their appeals. And the fate of almost all the characters is defeat, inhuman, untragic defeat—either defeat of a violent death without meaning or the more complete degradation of "selling out"—selling one's friends, one's integrity, one's earnest ambition and hope, for nothing more than "the big money." By the conclusion of the book, every character with the exception of Ben Compton, the radical leader, has come to the point where self-respect is not remote, but a term as of a dead language. Compton has been thrown out of the Communist party for being an "oppositionist" (a note which would indicate a change of heart in Dos Passos, a loss of faith in the radical movement, which has occurred since the writing of *U.S.A.* was begun). The conclusion, to repeat, is that of utter loss, degradation, and hopelessness, the suicide of one character, the killing of another, the disgusting lives of the others, and the final contrast of a vagabond who has not eaten for some time waiting for a lift on the highway while a plane passes overhead, containing the rich, one of whom "sickens and vomits into the carton container the steak and mushrooms he ate in New York."

Whatever else we may say of American life as represented in these narratives, there is one statement which we must make first: it is so, it is true; we have seen this with our own eyes and many of us have lived in this way. This is a true picture of the lives of many Americans, and anyone who doubts the fact can learn for himself very quickly how accurate Dos Passos is. But there is, on the other hand, a great deal more to be said about the truth which the novel as a form is capable of presenting.

To begin the attempt at a thorough judgment, the formal inadequacy of *U.S.A.,* taken as a whole, is the direct experience of every reader. There is no need to summon up abstract canons, nor to make that very interesting approach which can be summed up in the question: what would Henry James say? No reader can go from page one to page 1449 without feeling that the newsreels, camera eyes, and biographies, however good they may be in themselves, are interruptions which thwart his interest and break the novel into many isolated parts.[4] Even in the central narratives, where, as in the greatest pure prose (that of Stendhal and Tolstoy, where the word is transparent as glass), the reader passes without an awareness of style to the intense, ragged actuality presented, even here the novel falls into separate parts, even though there is an occasional interweaving of lives. The unity, the *felt* unity, is only the loose grab-bag of time and place, 1919 and the U.S.A. The binding together of lives (and thus of the reader's interest and gaze) into the progress of a plot—an element present even in a work of the scope of *War and Peace*—is wholly lacking. This heaping together of fragments of valuable perception is a characteristic of the best poetry of our time and the connection is interesting. *The Waste Land,* Pound's *Cantos, The Bridge,* and *The Orators* of Auden are all examples. And as there is a separation or gap between the sensibility of the camera eye and the narrative form in *U.S.A.,* so in the history of modern poetry we can remark the converse phenomenon, how, since Coleridge wrote marginal summaries of the narrative to "The Ancient Mariner," the capacity for a narrative framework has gradually disappeared from poetry of the first order: modern poetic style can bear the utmost strain of sensibility, but it cannot tell a story. In the medium of poetry, however, a unity of tone and mood and theme can substitute, although imperfectly, for other kinds of unity. *U.S.A.* cannot be considered a poem, however, and even if it could, Dos Passos does not rise to the level of the poets in question. As a narrative, it becomes a suite of narratives in which panels without direct relation to the subject are inserted (one would suppose that Dos Passos in fact put the book together as a motion-picture director composes his film, by a procedure of cutting, arranging, and interposing parts). As a novel, it is not in any careful sense a novel, but rather an anthology of long stories and prose poems. And it is to be

---

[4] In his essay on Dos Passos, Malcolm Cowley insists that there is a sufficient connection between the narratives and the other forms. There is, for example, a biography of Wilson when the fictional persons are concerned with the aftermath of the World War, a biography of Rudolph Valentino when one of the characters is a movie star. The connection is thus general, tangential, and wholly external, and occurs to the reader only as a passing afterthought, if at all. This kind of connection can be compared with the *internal* unity of any biography or narrative in the book, and then the difference between a unified whole and a loose collection will be clear in terms of the book itself.

insisted that the unity and form in question are not the abstractions of the critic, but the generic traits of the actual experience of reading fiction.

But form is not, of course, applied to a novel as a press to a tennis racket. It is, on the contrary, the way in which the writer sees his subject, the very means of attempting to see. And thus it is obvious that the formal gaps in *U.S.A.* spring from Dos Passos' effort to see his world in conflicting ways. It has been observed that the stream-of-consciousness lyricism of the camera eye is an attempt to compensate for the flat naturalism of the narratives, and it is perhaps to this that Malcolm Cowley referred when he spoke of the remnants of "the Art Novel" in *U.S.A.* And T. K. Whipple, in his review of the book in *The Nation,* raises more serious questions and makes a much more negative judgment. Whipple remarks, with much insight, that there is an important contrast between the lives of the fictitious persons and the great persons in the biographies—the actual persons have "minds, consciousness, individuality, and personality" and especially the power to choose and to struggle, while these attributes are "reduced to a minimum" in the fictitious persons. This is very true, but, on the other hand, Dos Passos is not, as Whipple thinks, wrong and inaccurate—many American lives are of that quality and character.

And again, a like judgment, this time of *Manhattan Transfer,* was made by the Hungarian Marxist critic, Georg Lukacs, in a remarkable article in *International Literature* (which Howard Baker has already cited in *The Southern Review*). Lukacs is engaged in showing that the best novels of the past have depended a great deal on their ability to give their characters "intellectual physiognomies," that is, have made the ideas and beliefs of their characters a very important element of the substance and method. Of Dos Passos, Lukacs says with precision:

> he describes, for example, a discussion of capitalism and socialism. The place in which the discussion takes place is excellently, vigorously described. We see the steaming Italian restaurant with the spots of tomato sauce on the tablecloth, the tricolored remains of melted ice cream on a plate, and the like. The individual tones of the various speakers are well described. But what they say is perfect banality, the commonplace for and against that can be heard at any time and at any place.

But here again it ought to be replied, at least to begin with, that in actual life such conversations are for the most part banal. Dos Passos is nothing if not accurate.

Both Whipple and Lukacs are excellent witnesses, but neither of them names what seems to me to be the root of the inadequacy which they have variously observed. Whipple attributes the lack to a conception of the individual which is "one-sided" and not "dialectical," nor "the whole man." Lukacs would say that what is lacking is a philosophy, most of all, that of dialectical materialism. A third standpoint would be that which attributed the inadequacy and formal lack to a technical misconception, Mr. Winters' "the fallacy of imitative form," the error of naturalism for which art is merely a mirror of the disorder and incompleteness of life itself.

It seems to me, however, that one must dig much deeper to get to the basic reason for this novel's character as a novel. The root of the inadequacy is, I think, an inadequate conception of what the truth, the whole truth about the U.S.A., for example, is. The term, truth, is used merely in its common-sensical meaning, of an accurate report of that which is. The truth about the whole of experience is precisely what is more than the truth about any actual standpoint. It is merely the truth about the life of an individual person, as it appeared to the person himself, that we get from Dos Passos. The truth about the whole of experience is more than the sum of many or all standpoints, of many blind and limited lives. The whole truth includes what might have been and what may be and what is not (as not being). It includes the whole scale of imaginative possibilities and the nameless assumptions and values by which a society lives. It is exactly because the whole truth is so complex and various that the imagination is a necessity. And this is the reason why fiction is full of the fictitious and the imaginative. It ought to be said, to forestall the reader, that however sophisicated we are about the nature of truth, this statement of its *extent* (its formal width, apart from insisting on any particular truth) is incontestable. It does not depend upon any view of life, as of Montgomery Belgion,[5] but is rather involved in all views and all viewing. It is, moreover, presupposed in the very nature of literature.

But furthermore the whole truth is involved in literature in what seems to me a still more basic way. One fundamental postulate of literature seems to me to be here in question. It too cannot be argued about because it is the assumption by means of which we are enabled to speak.

---

[5] The most recent issue of *The Southern Review* contains an article by Belgion which proposes a notion of fiction directly contradictory to the above one. Mr. Belgion argues, and has argued for ten years, as if unable to persuade even himself, that literature is never a representation of the truth of actual life because (1) "actual life is too various and vast to be brought as a whole within the compass of a novel," and because (2) the writer is attempting to impose his own view of life upon the reader, is, in fact, "the irresponsible propagandist" for his own view of life (in that he decides the consequences of his character's acts, for example), and hence, since, in the last analysis, the truth about life cannot be established by a rigorous logical demonstration, no novel can be said to be true to life.

In answer to the first point, one need merely observe that it is not a question of *either* all of life *or* none of it—merely the whole truth about a part of life will suffice—and moreover the part can stand for the whole, the symbol being of the very essence of literature. In answer to the second point, one need merely observe that the truth of much in any fiction does not rest upon ultimate metaphysical decisions, but is common to all mankind and verifiable by them, just as the sciences are thus independent of "views" of life. One proof of this is the fact that we can and do admire works based on views directly opposed to our own.

One can merely point to examples—all literary judgment and analysis being, in the end, comparative—and as it happens, Dos Passos himself provides his own examples in this novel.

The unquestionable postulate—or presumption—of all literature is the individual of the fullest intelligence and sensibility—at least with respect to the circumstances of the work itself. Perhaps one can call this individual not the omniscient, but the multiscient individual. He is the one who in some one of many quite different fashions *transcends* the situation and the subject. Often the multiscient individual enters into the work only in the style of the author, and thus it is through the style that a mind of the fullest intelligence and sensibility is brought to bear on the subject. Another way of saying this is to observe that a story must have a hero and to say with Aristotle that the hero must be "superior" enough to make his fate significant—not as, for example, the death of a cow. Or again, one has to repeat with Aristotle that literature must concern itself not only with what men are, but with what they "ought" to be: ought is not used in its ethical sense (as of the didactic) for there is no Greek word equivalent to the ethical *ought;* but it is in the sense of the representation of the full scale of human potentialities that "what men ought to be" is meant. When literature concerns itself merely with what men are or have been, it is indistinguishable from history and journalism. But the multiscient individual takes other guises also: he is sometimes the ideas and beliefs by which a work is given its direction. Another method—the one which fulfills the need of transcending the subject best of all—is the use of the supernatural or the mythical, and this is perhaps the most characteristic convention of literature, occurring as it does not only in Shakespeare, when the ghosts or witches appear, and obviously in Dante and other descents into hell, but even in our time, in the hallucination scene of *Ulysses* and in such a play as *The Ascent of F6,* by Auden and Isherwood. The supernatural and the mythical tend to be the most obvious attributes of the imagination. In some form or other the subject is transcended by a superior standpoint, and the superior standpoint reduces itself to one thing, a human being of the greatest intelligence and sensibility, who views all that occurs and is involved in the action, and who is best able to grasp the whole truth of the subject.

What we want of literature is the truth, and the truth is the only intention of *U.S.A.* But, to repeat, the truth is not merely the way in which human beings behave and feel, nor is it wholly contained in their conscious experience. In Racine and in Henry James, to take extreme examples, many characters speak as no one has ever spoken, on land or sea. They speak so in order to contain many of the levels of truth present in any possible situation. The facts represented are always there, but a good many of them can never be consciously known by an actor involved up to his neck in the present moment, as the characters of *U.S.A.*

usually are. Only through the focus of the imagination can the relevant facts be brought into the narrative. In Dos Passos, however, there is a beautiful imaginative sympathy which permits him to get under the skin of his characters, but there is no imagination, and no Don Quixote. Dos Passos testifies to all this by his use of newsreels, just as he seeks the full sensibility in the impressions of the camera eye and the heroic character in the biographies; but in his central narratives the standpoint is always narrowed to what the character himself knows as the quality of his existence, life as it appears to him. And this leveling drags with it and tends to make rather crude and sometimes commonplace the sensibility shown in the other panels. If Dos Passos were not so wholly successful in grasping this level of experience, then, undoubtedly, he would be less aware of the need to jump back to the other levels of truth, and his novel would not break into four "eyes" of uncoördinated vision. Or to shift the metaphor, his novel attempts to achieve the whole truth by going rapidly in two opposite directions—the direction of the known experience of his characters, in all their blindness and limitation, and on the other hand, the direction of the transcendent knowledge of experience, the full truth about it. And thus the formal breakdown was scarcely avoidable.

The view of literature, of the truth, and of the individual assumed by Dos Passos may be attributed to two sources. First to the tradition of naturalism, a none too precise term, of which one need here observe only a few aspects. Naturalism has engaged the efforts of writers of the greatest gifts, such as Flaubert and Joyce, but each has managed to smuggle into the method of strict recording certain elements which are radically different. In Flaubert, it is a style of the greatest sensitivity; in Joyce, it is the style too, in a manifold way which seems at first mere virtuosity. Moreover, in these writers, as in the lesser examples of naturalism, one finds a most curious method of work, which alone is sufficient to indicate that the conception of the nature of literature and of the truth it can contain has altered very much. They deliberately observe experience; they seek out experience with a literary intention. Flaubert visited Carthage to get material for *Salammbô* and instructed Maupassant to sit in the park and write down all that he saw. Let us try, on the other hand, to conceive of Shakespeare, Cervantes, Dante, or Aeschylus engaging in such activities in order to write their works. They would say, one should suppose, that one writes from memory since one remembers what has deeply interested one, and one knows what has deeply interested one. And they would say that the imagination, with its compositional grasp, is the most important thing, the thing that one can get only from a work of art and nowhere else. The imagination which produces such figures as the Prince of Denmark and the Knight of the Doleful Countenance (apparently one of Dos Passos' favorite characters) is not derived from deliberate "research."

Moreover, we ought to remark that naturalism arose at the same time as the primacy of the physical sciences and industrialism; the intellectual and social relationship is this: the physical sciences and industrialism changed the conception of the nature of literature and truth in literature, and made writers of great genius attempt to compete with the scientist by adopting something of his special method. They thought, it would seem, that literature had changed or that its nature had been mistaken.

But naturalism and its external sources are merely effects of that society which has degraded the human being and his own conception of himself to the point where Dos Passos' presentation of him in his own terms is, in fact, perfectly true. One can only add that it is not the whole truth. The primary source of the formal breakdown of this novel is the U.S.A. It is only by distinguishing between the actual and the remotely potential that one can conceive of a different kind of life from that which Dos Passos accurately presents, on the part of most of the living. It is this mixture of the actual and the potential, however, which has made literature so precious to the human spirit.

One might, as a hypothesis, propose a brief theory of the relationship of the individual to the society as relevant to the contrast between Dos Passos' biographies and his narratives, and between the great imaginative figures of literature and the lives of most human beings as they are in any time and place. The elements, let us say, that constitute any person have their source in the society in which he lives and which produced him. The individual is always *in* the world and is inconceivable apart from it. But some individuals "prehend" these given, unavoidable elements in a new way—and this new way, new composition, alters the character of society. This individual, to refer only to Dos Passos' biographies, is usually the inventor, the artist, the intellectual—Socrates, St. Francis, Lenin. Not only do his acts provide part of the basis of historical change, but, to return to the above consideration of the fundamental postulate of literature, he is the hero, he is the one whose fate as an individual is not merely an incident; and he is above all the type of the highest intelligence and sensibility. This view need not be mistaken for the romantic one of the poet against the world, nor for a stale individualism, nor for a class judgment: its validity here rests upon what, in actuality, literature has been (although certain of the other arts have obviously not). What happens to such an individual, as hero, or what he sees, believes and imagines, as author, is, in fact, one criterion by which all societies are judged. He is our utmost concern and the object of our genuine curiosity when we go to literature, for it is only in literature that we can be sure of finding him. The lives of most individuals are undoubtedly matters of much interest for the author, and the truth about those lives is important. But the whole truth of experience (if past literature is not wholly nonsense) is more than the quality of most lives.

One is sure that Dos Passos knows this, since it is the reason for his four forms and his discontinuity. His novel is perhaps the greatest monument of naturalism because it betrays so fully the poverty and disintegration inherent in that method. Dos Passos is the gifted victim of his own extraordinary grasp of the truth. He is a victim of the truth and the whole truth.

THE STONE AND THE CRUCIFIXION: FAULKNER'S *LIGHT IN AUGUST* *

RICHARD CHASE

WITHOUT ado I wish to direct attention to the symbolic texture of *Light in August*. This texture is very much a matter of mechanics and dynamics—a poetry of physics. Repeatedly Faulkner presents appearance, event, and even character in the images of stasis, motion, velocity, weight, lightness, mass, line, relative position, circle, sphere, emptiness, fullness, light, and dark. The phrase "light in August" has at least two meanings. As Mr. Malcolm Cowley informs us in his *Portable Faulkner*, the phrase means "light" as opposed to "heavy" and refers to a pregnant woman who will give birth in August. And it also means "light" as opposed to "dark"—an affirmation of life and human spirit.** *Light in August* may be described, in Faulkner's own words (though he is describing something else), as "the mechanics, the theatring of evil." This is not a complete or fully fair description of Faulkner's novel, but it is complete and fair enough to demand that we look at the novel from this point of view—and that we finally ask, How successful is the author in extending his account of the mechanics and theatring of evil into an account of the human situation?

The reader of *Light in August* will be puzzled in the first few pages by what may be called "the string of beads image." We read that the wagon in which Lena Grove rides through the August afternoon is like "a shabby bead upon a mild red string of road" and that the village beside the railroad, from which she begins her long journey, is like "a forgotten bead from a broken string." Later our attention is called to the row of iron bars in the fence which surrounds the orphanage of Joe Christmas' childhood, to the identical windows of a street car, to a picket fence, and to the rows of identical white houses in which the lower-middle-class whites live. To these images of linear discreteness Faulkner opposes images of the curve. Lena Grove—searching for Lucas Burch, the father of her unborn child—passes through "a long monotonous succession of peaceful and undeviating changes from day to dark and dark to day"; but her mode of action and of consciousness is not of the order of the "string of beads." She is "like something moving forever and with-

* "The Stone and the Crucifixion: Faulkner's *Light in August*" originally appeared in the *Kenyon Review*, Autumn, 1948, and is used here by permission of the author and the magazine editors.

** See "An Introduction to William Faulkner" by Malcolm Cowley in Part III of this volume.

out progress across an urn." For her the road is not linear but like a string "being rewound onto a spool." These images of linear discreteness and curve are extended into one of the central images of the book: flight and pursuit.

We have already encountered the symbolic representation of two realms of being which are counterposed throughout the novel. The linear discrete image stands for "modernism": abstraction, rationalism, applied science, capitalism, progressivism, emasculation, the atomized consciousness and its pathological extensions. The curve image stands for holistic consciousness, a containing culture and tradition, the cyclical life and death of all the creatures of earth. Throughout the novel, Lena retains her holistic consciousness and she is strong, enduring, hopeful. All the other characters in one way or another are victims of the linear delusion. For Joe Christmas, in whom the linear consciousness becomes pathological, the curve image is a "cage" or a "prison" to be broken out of. Or it is something to be gashed from the outside so that whatever it contains will be spilled meaninglessly out. Joe gashes the whiskey tins he and Burch have buried in the woods as he has a vision of trees in the moonlight, standing like "a row of suavely shaped urns," each one cracked and extruding "something liquid, deathcolored, and foul." At the end, when Joe can no longer perform this symbolic act of urn smashing, the curve image becomes the fateful circle of repetition which he has never really either escaped or broken and which is the only path to the only kind of holism he will ever find: death. "I have never got outside that circle. I have never broken out of the ring of what I have already done and cannot ever undo." The tragic irony of the linear consciousness, Faulkner seems to say, is that it is an illusion; all consciousness is holistic, but it may be the holism of life (Lena) or of death (Joe). The remarkable symbol of the wheel in the passage describing the final madness of the Reverend Mr. Hightower presumably coincides with Joe's circle of doom, though here it may symbolize the completion in death of a cycle of legendary family history.

Faulkner's counterposing of motionlessness and motion seems to imply a fairly consistent deploying of polarity of character. Lena, Joe, and Hightower each has a certain kind of motionlessness. Lena, "her voice quite grave now, quite quiet," sitting "quite still, her hands motionless upon her lap," has the inner quiet of the wheel's axle, a stillness within movement. The stillness behind Joe's cold, contemptuous mask is the abstract stillness of separation, a schizoid disengagement from outer action. The motionlessness of Hightower, sitting "rigidly" behind his desk, his "forearms parallel upon the armrests of the chair," is the negation of the will and action by fear, "denial," and impotence.

The quality of Joe's action is simply a willed translation of his separateness. Whenever he is in motion, in fantasy or actuality, he is in flight; and this is true even of his many connections with women—these also he must turn into the pattern of flight whenever they threaten to bring him too close to the kind of central and holistic peace represented by Lena. Although Burch is throughout the book in a sense in flight from Lena, Byron Bunch, or the sheriff, his movements entirely lack Joe's willed abstract control. He is pure aimless motion, a rural poor white uprooted and cast adrift in an industrial-urban society. "He puts me in mind," says Byron Bunch, "of one of these cars running along the street with a radio in it. You can't make out what it is saying and the car ain't going anywhere in particular and when you look at it close you see that there ain't even anybody in it." A friend of Bunch's replies, "Yes, he puts me in mind of a horse. Not a mean horse. Just a worthless horse." This rude progression of metaphors will serve to indicate that Faulkner's imagination very frequently approaches the level of human character and consciousness beginning with the mechanical, and proceeding to the animal level through an intermediate level of dynamics.

The denouement of the novel can be conceived as the final resolution of several kinds of motion. Byron Bunch separates himself from his spiritual kinship with Hightower and his hitherto meaningless life finds its repose in Lena. Burch moves away from Lena, dooming himself, as it were, to aimless perpetual motion. The final flight of Joe to Hightower's house may seem too little explained as part of the plot. But it has a symbolic significance, since Joe, turning away for the last time from the realm of being which is represented by Lena and which he has tried to find in his various women, finds his ultimate refuge in the castration and death vouchsafed to him by Percy Grimm (only the last of all the symbolic castrations and deaths he has first sought and then endured). Hightower himself had turned away from the Lena-holism when years earlier he had in effect pursued his wife out of existence by believing in his fantasy that his "seed" had died with his grandfather in the Civil War.

II

Mr. Robert Penn Warren suggests that Faulkner's objection to the modern world is that it lacks the ability to set up "codes, concepts of virtue, obligations" by which man can "define himself as human" and "accept the risks of his humanity."[*] In *Light in August,* Faulkner seems to be concerned with showing that the codes modern man *does* set up do *not* allow him to define himself as human—that codes have become compulsive patterns which man clings to in fear and trembling while the pattern emasculates him. Byron Bunch, wondering why he lives to the split second by his big silver watch and works alone in the planing mill every Saturday afternoon and why the Reverend Mr. Hightower has re-

[*] See Robert Penn Warren's review of *The Portable Faulkner* in the *New Republic,* August 12, 1946.

fused to leave Jefferson, the scene of his ruin and disgrace, reflects, "It is because a fellow is more afraid of the trouble he might have than he ever is of the trouble he's already got. He'll cling to trouble he's used to before he'll risk a change." Byron and Hightower have for years been sustaining one anotner in their "patterns." Their relationship ends over the question of Bunch's aiding and courting Lena, pregnant with another man's child. The dilemma for each is whether to stick to a pattern of behavior which prohibits accepting "the risks of his humanity" or to become involved responsibly in a human situation. Byron chooses to break the pattern and accept the consequences of intervention. Hightower remains in the pattern (though he makes certain senile excursions from it), choosing to conspire in closing the circle of his destiny, choosing separation and madness. It is not true, as has been said, that all of Faulkner's characters are rigidly controlled by fate: Byron, for one, is left free to choose his own fate.

Joe Christmas is in many ways a masterful portrait of a man whose earliest years have been spent in an institution—an experience, as the psychiatrists show, which definitively affects not only the emotional centers of the victim but also the character of his conceptual thinking. In the forbidding orphanage (a true symbol of the conditions of modern life) Joe finds a surrogate mother—a cynical, suspicious and indeed almost paranoiac dietitian, a mockery of the Nursing Mother of the myths. His surrogate father is an obscenely fanatical inquisitor and peeping tom who functions as the janitor of the orphanage and who later turns out to be Joe's grandfather. The pattern of Joe's life is inexorably formed when the dietitian finds that he has been hiding in her closet eating tooth paste while she has been entertaining an interne on her bed (the tube of tooth paste is another urn symbol). The definitive event is not that Joe has seen the dietitian in the act but that she fails to punish him and instead offers him money not to tell. Having felt terribly guilty, having expected and even wanted to be punished, and having had no idea of giving away the secret, he is irretrievably shocked when she offers him the money. He had wanted the woman to engross him in her life, if only by beating him. Instead she denies him this engrossment and gives him a silver dollar, whose shining circumference forms a circle Joe will never break through. Joe's homosexuality is another theme symbolized by the "string of beads" image. The relationship between Joe and his guardian, McEachern, a fanatical apostle of a parochial and degenerate Presbyterianism who beats Joe with the impersonal violence of a machine, has for both McEachern and Joe the uneasy satisfaction of an abnormal but vehemently pure sexual alliance. McEachern has succeeded with Joe where the dietitian failed. Joe finds the relationship "perfectly logical and reasonable and inescapable," and he quickly learns to hate Mrs. McEachern because her proffered feminine kindnesses always threaten to taint an abstract and predictable re-lationship—just as the food she offers him makes him sick (all the women in Joe's life try to feed him; one of them is a waitress in a restaurant).

Joe's many adventures with women are attempts to escape the abstract quality of a latently homosexual life. As Joe pauses outside Miss Bur-den's house before keeping a tryst with her, Faulkner says, "The dark was filled with the voices, myriad, out of all time that he had known, as though all the past was a flat pattern. And going on: tomorrow night, all the tomorrows, to be part of the flat pattern, going on." "Then," says Faulkner, "it was time"—which seems to be a pun (the same one occurs in *The Sound and the Fury*) meaning that now Joe's existence can be measured by time (the urn consciousness) rather than by the abstraction of eternity. But the connection with Miss Burden, like all of Joe's con-nections with women, turns into a ritual reaffirmation that no such connection is possible, a circular path back to the compulsive pattern—as we see when after various ingenious phases of sexual flight and pur-suit, Miss Burden, before Joe kills her, is transmuted in appearance and behavior into a mocking likeness of McEachern. The sexual dilemma of Joe's life is nicely symbolized in the episode where he lolls in the woods (and gashes the whiskey tins) reading a magazine "of that type whose covers bear either pictures of young women in underclothes or pictures of men shooting one another with pistols." He reads as a man "walking along the street might count the cracks in the pavement, to the last final page, the last and final word." He goes through life with this same at-tachment to his pattern, hating the women in underclothes, longing for a purely masculine annihilation.

In symbolic polarity to the compulsive pattern we have Lena, who does not need to flee from involvement in human life, and Lucas Burch. Distantly adumbrating all the polarities of *Light in August,* the gay, irresponsible, aimless Burch symbolizes pure Chaos. Perhaps through the child in Lena's womb, Burch symbolizes the undetermined possibil-ity of a future the direction of which will be decided by the final reso-lution of forces among the other characters. If so, we may say that *Light in August* is a "hopeful" book. For the future is in the hands of Lena and Byron Bunch—a woman who endures and loves and a man who has decided to "accept the risks of his humanity."

III

Mr. Warren suggests that we ought not to think of Faulkner as an exclusively Southern writer but as a writer concerned with modern times in general. To this, one might add that Faulkner has many affini-ties with both Hawthorne and Melville. As Malcolm Cowley has said, the myth of a Southern society which emerges from Faulkner's work as a whole can be compared with Hawthorne's myth of New England. One might add that the dilemma with which Faulkner confronts Burch and Hightower—whether to take the responsibility of moral intervention in human affairs—is the same dilemma which confronts many of Hawthorne's characters (for example, the painter in "Prophetic Pictures"). Joe Christmas would be recognized by Hawthorne; for he is frightened and obsessed by the inescapable stain on every human life. There is never any real proof that Joe is part Negro, but Joe's gratuitous assumption that he is tainted is at the root of all his actions. He becomes as obsessed with his stain as does Aylmer with the blemish on his wife's face in Hawthorne's "The Birthmark" and with a purpose as relentless and immoral as Aylmer's he goes about removing the stain—an impulse which arises in the central figures of both "The Birthmark" and *Light in August* from what is, in the final moral terms, simply their inability to bear the burden of being human. (The word "burden," by the way, seems to have the same significance for the Southern writers as the pack of the peddler had for Hawthorne and Melville: the "burden" of one's history or of one's continually self-annihilating humanity. Miss Burden, in *Light in August,* is not the only character in Southern fiction so named.)

Faulkner and Melville share a liking for physical, dynamic, and animal images. Both abound in images of light and dark. In Faulkner's novel there is a persistent reference to white "blood" and black "blood," and Joe's ambiguous character is symbolized by the dark serge trousers and white shirt he invariably wears. Both Ahab and Joe Christmas are seeking an elusive *purity,* symbolized by whiteness. Both shape their doom by their sharp rejections of their own humanity. Both are "unmanned," to use Melville's word, by fate or by their own moral acts. Faulkner's manner of handling symbols and themes is like Melville's. His downright spiritual vehemence often produces a wonderful lyric or epic sense of life; but sometimes the symbols are crudely imagined or imperfectly assimilated in context. For example, the uneasy connection of Joe Christmas with Christ: several of Joe's acts take place on Friday, or "on the third day"; Mrs. McEachern washes his feet; Burch betrays him for a thousand pieces of silver; Hines, his grandfather and the only father Joe knows, imagines that he is God. Faulkner seems not to sense exactly how the Christ theme should be handled, sometimes making it too overt and sometimes not overt enough. His attempts to enlarge Joe's character by adducing a willed mythology remind one of Melville's similar attempts in *Pierre.* It may finally seem to us that Faulkner and Melville are most in control of their work when they approach the epic form, as in *As I Lay Dying* and *Moby Dick;* but that when they try novels of complex symbolic human relationships, their effort suffers from their uncertain power of grouping symbols into a close coherent statement.

IV

It has been said of Faulkner that his rhetoric and the actions it expresses are so terrific that they annihilate his characters, that his characters become mere targets for violent emotive bombardments. The measure of truth in this criticism does not destroy Faulkner as an artist. It simply indicates that he is one kind of artist—surely he is not a novelist of manners in quite the way that such a phrase as "the Balzac of the South" would imply. As if in self-criticism, Faulkner writes of Hines and his fanatical sermons: "So they believed that he was a little crazy. ... It was not that he was trying to conceal one thing by telling another. It was that his words, his telling, just did not synchronize with what his hearers believed would (and must) be the scope of a single individual." Yet in one of the utterances of the Reverend Mr. Hightower we find this idea translated into a true definition of tragedy: "Too much happens. That's it. Man performs, engenders, more than he can or should have to bear. That's how he finds that he can bear anything. That's it. That's what is so terrible." In such a statement as this Faulkner begins to justify the overplus of superhuman and subhuman violence in his novels. Nevertheless there remains a discrepancy between the theoretical justification and the artistic practice. We cannot avoid phrasing the aesthetic implication of Hightower's words in some such way as this: "Faulkner attributes more action and emotion to his characters than can meaningfully be attributed to them."

The alienation of man *via* language is a common theme in *Light in August*. The people who have beaten and robbed Joe and left him on the floor of a cheap boarding house, speak "in a language which he did not understand." The sermons of Hightower seem to have been expressly contrived to separate him from his congregation. As for Lena, her separation-by-language is always maintained only to the degree necessary to her total purpose. When she asks along the road for Burch, people direct her to "Bunch," but to her they always seem to say "Burch." She is purposefully separated from irrelevance and relaxed in her vision of reality. Separation by language is surely a fact of human life. But is Faulkner entirely in control of this theme? In the orphanage the dietitian and Hines meet "calm and quiet and terse as two conspirators" and then proceed to discourse in some pseudo-Old Testament language which is anything but calm, quiet, or terse. But perhaps it is another form of dissociation which makes this putatively powerful situation seem defective. Perhaps—in order that the dissociation might be in *his* mind, for it needs to be in *someone's* mind—the five-year-old Joe should have been present, watching and listening in awe to the terrible creatures, his mythical father and mother. It is simply a novelist's mistake to present us with a sharp dislocation between his characters and what they say, without accounting in context for the dislocation. One feels that Faulkner has missed a chance in this scene to form a profound associative human situation.

This leads us to a general question: What is the quality of consciousness displayed in *Light in August?* Surely, it is not a consciousness which broods over the whole range of action, associating people with each other or with a culture, establishing their manners and morals in a whole containment. It is a consciousness in flight and pursuit, wonderfully aware of fact, the physical and animal fact, wonderfully in possession of extreme emotions and the ecstasy of violence, cognizant too of the tender humorousness of love, and in general wonderfully fantastic and magical. *Par excellence,* it is the American folk-literary consciousness. When it seeks to interpret or enlighten the human situation, when Faulkner breaks off the humorous-tragical flow of rhetorical poetry and ventures an observation on human manners, he is likely to sound naïve. He will speak in the manner of the folk proverb: "Yes, sir. You just let one of them get married or get into trouble without being married, and right then and there is where she secedes from the woman race and spends the balance of her life trying to get joined up with the man race. That's why they dip snuff and smoke and want to vote." Or he will attempt a more intellectually formulated observation, with the following unhappy result: "the faces of the old men lined by that sheer accumulation of frustration and doubt which is so often the other side of the picture of hale and respected full years"—What a piece of philosophy! One can hardly help sensing an uncomfortable hiatus between Faulkner's poetic portrayal of manners and his explicit consciousness of them.[1]

Probably the episodes of family and cultural history which accompany Faulkner's account of Miss Burden and Hightower would mean more to a Southerner than they do to me. But especially in the case of Hightower there seems to be a failure of consciousness precisely at the point where we should understand the quality of the association between Hightower and his own history. Hightower has projected his sexual and spiritual impotence back upon a myth of his grandfather. Faulkner goes along with Hightower on this point, assuming too much that a fantasy projected from some center of real causation is the cause itself. He nearly allows Hightower to determine the quality of his (Faulkner's) consciousness. On the other hand, he is capable of involving Burch in a situation which calls for a degree of consciousness far above what seems possible, and then arbitrarily giving him the necessary consciousness; so that we have a dull country lout whose "rage and impotence is now almost ecstatic. He seems to muse now upon a sort of timeless and beautiful infallibility in his unpredictable frustrations" (the qualifiers "almost," "seems to," "a sort of" are significant). And a moment later we

---

[1] But the observations I have made in this paragraph would be substantially less true if applied to *The Sound and the Fury.*

find Burch (so it seems) reflecting that a Negro he is talking with "does not appear to have enough ratiocinative power to find the town." In *Anna Karenina* a dog conducts a humorous and anxious conversation with himself. But unlike the Burch episode, this does not seem in the least out of place, because Tolstoy with his great associative consciousness always gives one the feeling that he knows exactly when and how much to withdraw or extend his mind in the universe of his novel. I do not mean to imply that Faulkner's novel *lacks* consciousness, but only that the consciousness it displays is sometimes unhappily biased, bardic, parochial, and, in the societal or cultural sense, unmannered. Davy Crockett still screams in the Southern wilderness.

But of course any discussion which compares Faulkner unfavorably with a writer like Tolstoy must not be guilty of the assumption that Faulkner's Southern culture is as cohesive and knowable as Tolstoy's Russian culture was; obviously it is not. And Faulkner's claim to be the novelist of a culture (if that is his claim) must be judged on the basis of his whole work. Nevertheless the evidence of *Light in August,* though it shows that Faulkner is capable of very fine and very extensive and complex fictional constructions, also seems to indicate that he can fail us exactly at that level of existence where the subtle complications of human behavior have to be established. Faulkner works inward from the extremities, from the mechanics and the ecstasy of life. And this relentless, bardic-American bias often makes us wish he would reverse the procedure, that his consciousness would work through human manners into the human character and then outward toward the extremities it can contain or fail to contain. Human life submits itself to die at the hands of the artist so that it may be reborn in art, somewhat as Joe Christmas submits himself to the beatings of McEachern: "The boy's body might have been wood or stone; a post or a tower upon which the sentient part of him mused like a hermit, contemplative and remote with ecstasy and selfcrucifixion." One wants to know finally, What manner of man is this *between* the stone and the crucifixion?

v

But it is only one's high estimation of Faulkner which raises these questions at all. Like the author of *Moby Dick* Faulkner might say of himself, "I try everything; I achieve what I can." In these bad times, a serious venturesomeness must count heavily with us. But it is also a sense of Faulkner's achievement which makes me think him the equal of any American novelist of his generation. Perhaps *The Great Gatsby* is the only novel of the time which can be defended as superior to Faulkner's best work.

In the nineteen-thirties the liberal-progressive culture turned away from Faulkner for many of the same bad reasons which caused it, eighty years before, to turn away from Melville. If our liberal thought now begins to return from its disastrous wanderings of the last decades—that era of the great rejections—and to recover its vitality, it is because it grows capable of coming to terms with Faulkner, as it already learns again to come to terms with Hawthorne and Melville.

THE NARRATOR'S MIND AS SYMBOL:
AN ANALYSIS OF
ALL THE KING'S MEN *

Norton R. Girault

IF WE are to judge from many of the reviews, *All the King's Men* is a very difficult novel to "explain"—difficult, it appears, mainly because of the oblique first-person narrator point of view. There have been many comments about the irrelevance of Jack Burden, as if he were a sort of displaced person who had found his way into the novel through the servants' entrance, or an exhibit guide with an annoying habit of stopping in the middle of his discourse upon the exhibit to digress on his domestic problems. Actually the novel is a dramatic monologue on a grand scale, and Jack Burden is as much the protagonist as he is the commentator. But it is apparent that the story has not been read as a product of Jack's mind. Attempts to explain Willie Stark, for example, have often dodged the problem of taking Jack's statements in character; apparently it has been assumed that the reader sees Willie Stark at first hand and not through Jack's sensibility, and that Willie can be understood and interpreted whether Jack is or not. Such an assumption is enough to cause serious misreading, because out of the first-person narrator point of view grows an important aspect of the novel's theme—that an understanding of the world depends upon an understanding of the self: Jack Burden cannot understand Willie Stark until Jack understands himself. (There is a question, of course, as to whether Jack ever fully understands either himself or Willie Stark.) We can get at an understanding of Robert Penn Warren's interpretation of the Boss only through a perception of the way in which the Boss's story was experienced by Warren's first-person narrator.

I

Jack's story is so intimately related to Willie's that, as the narrative develops, their stories are told simultaneously. But phrases along the way like "at least that was the way I argued the case back then" remind the reader of the fact that Jack has lived through the actions he is describing and that he is trying to reorient himself in relation to them. It

* "The Narrator's Mind as Symbol: An Analysis of *All the King's Men*" originally appeared in *Accent*, Summer, 1947, and is used here by permission of the author and the magazine editors.

becomes more and more apparent as the story develops that Jack is telling it as a means of defining to himself what actually did happen to
him: the manner in which he reconstructs the story gives the reader an
insight into the nature of Jack's experience. For example, the fact that
Jack withholds his father's identity until he learns that Judge Irwin has
killed himself implies that he wants the discovery of the truth about his
paternity to make the same shocking impact upon the reader that it
made upon him; it is his way of dramatizing his reaction to the discovery. And when he attempts to describe subjective reactions to events that
are past, the metaphors he uses provide the reader with an insight into
why Jack Burden is an appropriate first-person narrator. A study of
those metaphors indicates that they support a basic symbolism of rebirth that runs through the novel and unifies it, and after our participation in the total experience of *All the King's Men,* we realize that it is
because Jack has been reborn, though not of woman (in a sense defined
by the symbolism), that he is qualified to tell us what happened to
Willie Stark.

The symbolic event that brings the rebirth symbolism into focus is
Jack's being awakened in the middle of the night by his mother's
screams. It is a "bright, beautiful, silvery soprano scream" that awakens
him, and his mother, hysterical, accuses him of having killed his father.
The accusation comes as the sudden revelation of the truth about his
paternity: Judge Irwin, not the Scholarly Attorney, suddenly becomes
his father. Jack has, as his mother charges, killed his father (his attempt
to blackmail the judge for the Boss results in the judge's suicide); but
he has also created a father, for it requires the violence of the suicide to
wring from his mother, out of her love for Judge Irwin, the long suppressed information which gives Jack self-definition. The scream signal-
izes Jack's rebirth (symbolically, it is a scream of labor pain) in that it
gives him a new mother and a new father, both of whom he can accept.
It disintegrates his conception of his mother as a woman motivated by
vanity and cupidity ("for years I had condemned her as a woman without heart"), because it reveals to him his mother's capacity for love; and
it disintegrates his conception of his father as the weak, pious Scholarly
Attorney, for in Judge Irwin Jack gains a father he can accept. The
scream seems to release something in him, to allow him to see the world
for the first time. It allows him to understand Willie Stark, but why it
does Jack cannot say. He simply knows that his knowledge of the Boss
and of himself grew, finally, out of the scream, that it marked the climax
of his story.

Jack's story builds toward his mother's scream in terms of his struggle
to resist rebirth. At the beginning of the novel, he sees the Boss's eyes
bulge as he begins a political speech and feels the "clammy, sad little
foetus" which is himself, huddled away up inside himself, cringing away
from "the cold hand in the cold rubber glove" reaching down to pull

him out into the cold. Jack feels that he is on the brink of a discovery about the Boss, but subconsciously he seeks the coziness of "not-knowing." His hesitation in his love affair with Anne Stanton results, in part, from the same sort of recoil from knowledge. And his dive and underwater embrace with her are an attempt to submerge himself along with Anne in a cozy womb-state of "not-knowing." (The medium will not retain them, of course, and they burst forth into their separateness.) Finally, this subconscious shrinking from a particular kind of knowledge becomes on Jack's part an attempt to repudiate his sensibility, an attempt begun as a result of his frustration in his love affair with Anne and of his dissatisfaction with his past (as symbolized by his parents). On the verge of the sexual act with Anne, he had sensed that to "know" Anne he would have to violate his image of her; he hesitates long enough to disrupt their love affair.

What Jack is searching for is a womb-state of innocence in nature in which his image of Anne will be preserved. And this search becomes a dominant motif leading up to his expulsion from the womb when he unwittingly causes the death of his father. Just before his discovery that Anne has become the Boss's mistress, he sits in his office and envies the jaybird perched in the tree outside his window:

> I could look down and think of myself inside that hollow chamber, in the aqueous green light, inside the great globe of the tree, and not even a jaybird there with me now, for he had gone, and no chance of seeing anything beyond the green leaves, they were so thick, and no sound except, way off, the faint mumble of traffic, like the ocean chewing its gums.

The associations with Jack's underwater dive with Anne are significant. Then, when this reverie is interrupted by his discovery of Anne's "infidelity" (of the Boss's violation of the image), Jack flies to California in an attempt to "drown himself in West." In all these struggles to lose himself in nature, there is a paradoxical struggle toward rebirth: the greater the struggle to resist rebirth, the greater the counter-struggle toward rebirth, as if Jack's nature, unformed, were enveloped by the womb of total nature, which reacts convulsively to reject him. Through his attempts to lose himself in nature, Jack is actually struggling, without realizing it, toward a discovery of his separateness in nature.

The significance of Jack's struggle to resist rebirth may be stated in these terms: Jack shrinks from the discovery of evil, of the taint in nature, of imperfection in the scheme of things. He has seen ugliness and imperfection and, with a cynical smugness, acknowledges their presence in nature, but he does not want to discover evil in himself. Subconsciously, he shrinks from the terrible knowledge that he is capable of good and evil, but until he is reborn through a revelation of the guilt he shares with humanity, he is not fully man, but rather embryonic and amoral. This aspect of the symbol's meaning is pointed up by a conversation Jack has with Lucy Stark about her son Tom's alleged fatherhood of an unborn child (it is significant in terms of the novel's structure that this conversation occurs just before Jack's rebirth):

> "It's just a baby," she almost whispered. "It's just a little baby. It's just a little baby in the dark. It's not even born yet, and it doesn't know what's happened. About money and politics and somebody wanting to be senator. It doesn't know about anything—about how it came to be—about what that girl did—or why—or why the father—why he—" She stopped, and the large brown eyes kept looking at me with appeal and what might have been accusation. Then she said, "Oh, Jack, it's a little baby, and nothing's its fault."
>
> I almost burst out that it wasn't my fault, either, but I didn't.

The irony, once the symbolism is understood, is obvious. The state of innocence Lucy has described is what Jack has been trying to discover in his attempts to drown himself in nature. He has been trying to hide in the dark where nothing will be his fault.

Fourteen pages later (about a week has passed), Jack is awakened by his mother's scream, and is shocked into the revelation that it has been his fault that his father has committed suicide. "At the moment," Jack says, "the finding out simply numbed me." On a literal level, he is referring to his discovery that Judge Irwin is his father. But, symbolically, what numbs him is the disintegration of his whole conception of himself. He has been sick with "the terrible division" of his age. His sensibility dissociated by his repeated attempts to escape into a womb-state of innocence, he has been living in a world out of time and divorced from experience, a world in which his actions have been neither good nor evil, but meaningless. Then suddenly, in one shocking experience, this illusory world is shattered, and he cannot define himself in relation to the new world (in which Judge Irwin is his father and a woman capable of love is his mother). When Jack's revelation of the truth about his paternity is taken along with all the examples in the novel of attempts to change various characters' conceptions of the world, it can be seen that his revelation is a commentary upon these other attempts to cure modern man of the sickness of his age. Jack himself, as the Boss's private detective, has tried to change other men's pictures of the world. He has tried to change Adam's by giving him "a history lesson"; and, ironically, he has caused his father's death by trying to change Judge Irwin's convictions about Willie Stark. Finally, in Adam Stanton's operation on the brain of the man suffering from catatonic schizophrenia, we have the attempt through surgery to change the picture of the world man carries around in his head; after the operation, Jack tells Adam, "Well, you forgot to baptize him—for he is born again and not of woman," and, ironically, baptizes the patient in the name of the Great Twitch, symbol of one of Jack's attempts to submerge himself in nature.

(Again, it is significant that this operation occurs before Jack's rebirth; Jack's wisecrack foreshadows the event and he does not realize the symbolic meaning it supports.) In one sense then, the whole novel depicts men "incomplete with the terrible division of their age," suffering from a schizophrenia they do not understand, men whose hope lies not in change from without (through surgery, "history lessons," and the like), but from rebirth from within. And because of the nature of Jack's malady, it is plausible that it should take some time for him to formulate a definition of what has happened to him.

The beginning of his reorientation is his discovery that he is, as his mother charges, guilty of his father's death. He realizes that by killing his father he has created him, and gradually he becomes aware of the fact that all of his detective work for the Boss has been a search for a father to replace the weak, pious fool he believed the Scholarly Attorney to be. The subconscious motive for his becoming the Boss's private detective is his attempt to find a father in Willie Stark, and his fidelity to the Boss is symbolic of his having substituted him for the alleged father with whom he is dissatisfied. But when, in Judge Irwin, Jack gains a father he can accept, he no longer requires the Willie Stark father-symbol; symbolically, the very detective work he has been hired by the Boss to do results in the end in the Boss's own death. In chapter nine, the day after the Judge's funeral, Jack walks into the Boss's office and refuses to do any more detective work for him. He wonders why, in fact, he does not quit the Boss's organization altogether. And, thinking of the Scholarly Attorney and Judge Irwin, he says, "True, since I had lost both fathers, I felt as though I could float effortlessly away like a balloon when the last cord is cut." But Jack has lost not two but three fathers—the Scholarly Attorney, the judge, and, though he does not realize it, the Boss—so, still numb from the disintegration of the conception of his father, he is unable to quit the Boss's machine.

Jack remains to discover, after the Boss's assassination, that it is he himself who has set the events in motion which culminate in the Boss's own death. After the Boss has died, Jack's independent detective work uncovers the complicity of Sadie Burke and Tiny Duffy (they are as responsible as Adam Stanton for the Boss's murder), but Jack discovers his own complicity too, for he sees that it is his earlier detective work that has produced the facts which led to the involvement of Anne and Adam Stanton in Willie Stark's enterprises and which made Sadie's revenge and Duffy's opportunism possible. But, ironically, the Boss has hired Jack to produce these facts. The Boss has engineered his own assassination. Guilt for the slaying seems to spread throughout the novel among all the characters. What shocks Jack is the discovery that his crime (as opposed to those of Sadie Burke, Tiny Duffy and Adam Stanton) is that his actions have been meaningless; the others have intended to kill the Boss, whereas he has intended to be the hired research man in search of objective fact, as faultless and amoral as Sibyl Frey's unborn baby. This perception of his spiritual sterility occurs when Jack is unable to go through with "the perfect duplication of what Duffy had done" (that is, effect the murder of Duffy by putting the idea in Sugar-Boy's head); Jack sees that he is as guilty as Duffy, that his murder of Duffy would, ironically enough, be as meaningless as Jack's unintended murder of the Boss. Jack is appalled by this discovery that he has been "caught in a monstrous conspiracy":

> I hated everything and everybody and myself and Tiny Duffy and Willie Stark and Adam Stanton ... They all looked alike to me then. And I looked like them.

But what saves Jack from this loathing for himself and the world is another discovery that grows out of his rebirth—the discovery of his capacity for love. When he learns that his mother is leaving the Young Executive, the scream is brought back to him in such a way that he is able to formulate a partial definition of its meaning; it releases him from his disgust with the world:

> The first hint was in the wild, silvery scream which filled the house when the word of Judge Irwin's death was received. That scream rang in my ears for many months, but it had faded away, lost in the past and the corruption of the past, by the time she called me back to Burden's Landing to tell me that she was going to go away. Then I knew that she was telling me the truth. And I felt at peace with her and with myself.

His mother's leaving (in that it is evidence of her love for Judge Irwin) makes him capable of loving her, and of loving the world (as his marriage to Anne indicates).

Jack Burden's reorientation grows out of a combination of events that begin with Judge Irwin's death. And after he has seen his friends die and his mother leave the Young Executive, he can see a justice in the injustice of a nature that man can never fully know. Like Cass Mastern, Jack has discovered that man cannot escape guilt, and he has discovered too that it is only through an acceptance of the evil in his nature that man can achieve good. He can even say that in his "own way" he is not certain that he does not believe the theological harangues of the Scholarly Attorney (symbol, perhaps, of the Christian tradition in the modern world). Through his rebirth, Jack has caught sight of the limits, and likewise the potentialities, of human knowledge. He had lived a long time in terms of a false conception of his paternity, and, through killing his father, had discovered his ignorance. He learns that man can never be sure of his knowledge: one can never fully know one's father. (There can be a pun in Warren's father-symbolism that equates man's knowledge of his temporal father with his knowledge of the Heavenly Father.) The only knowledge that Jack can be sure of is that tragic waste grows out of the limitations of human knowledge; therefore, man must strive constantly for that state *least* wasteful of human good. And so, as the novel ends, Jack Burden speaks of going into the "convulsion of the world" (the everchanging nature wherein he may be saved from the illusion of the absolute power of human knowledge) "and the awful responsibility of Time" (man's moral responsibility for the illusion of nature he creates).

II

Jack is qualified to tell Willie Stark's story because it, too, is a story of rebirth, and, although Jack does not call it that in so many words, the terms he uses to describe it are significant. Huddled over his law books, Willie is "in a room, a world, inside himself where something was swelling and growing painfully and dully and imperceptibly like a great potato in a dark, damp cellar," and "inside him something would be big and coiling and slow and clotting till he would hold his breath and the blood would beat in his head with a hollow sound as though his head were a cave as big as the dark outside. He wouldn't have any name for what was big inside him. Maybe there wasn't any name." And, like the knowledge Jack gains through rebirth, the Boss's knowledge comes to him with the shock of revelation. When Willie realizes (before he has become the Boss) that the Harrison machine is using his naïve political idealism to exploit the voters, it is—as Jack puts it—as if Willie had been on the road to Damascus and had seen a great light. When he says this of Willie at the time of Willie's great disillusionment, Jack is not aware of how apt his allusion is, and even after the years that separate his telling of the story from the event, he is not certain what name he should give Willie's "blind, inner compulsion" ("Maybe there wasn't any name."), but through his own rebirth, Jack gains an insight into the meaning of the Boss's life.

The Boss's story starts with a revelation and ends with a revelation. At the beginning of his story, it is revealed to him (through his "luck") that man must run counter to amoral nature and that man must create human good out of human bad. (Willie learns this when the crooked politicians in the state try to "run it over him like he was dirt.") But when Willie tries to spread the light among his countrymen, when he tries to awaken them to an awareness of their responsibility as human beings to separate themselves from exploitable nature, he is frustrated by their failure to understand. They roar their applause, but they do not see, actually, what is behind the bulging eyes and the forelock of hair. They are as ready for Willie to run it over them like they were dirt as they were to be exploited by the Harrison outfit. Nevertheless, the Boss's conviction, gained through a sort of revelation, impels him to persist stubbornly throughout the novel in his attempt to achieve a political state based on the assumption that men are all, potentially at least, like himself—capable of seeing the light. He becomes "the cold hand in the cold rubber glove" trying to wrest men from their submergence in brute nature. But in trying to enforce on them from without a knowledge he gained from within himself, the Boss is trying to usurp the work of the mysterious principle which brought him his knowledge. It is the same principle which operates through Jack Burden to cause his rebirth and, finally, through the Boss to kill him. But in the death of the Boss the knowledge he has tried to live by is reaffirmed; Willie realizes that what has killed him is his own failure to believe in the knowledge of his earlier revelation. So the Boss's story ends with a revelation ("It could have all happened different, Jack"), and the Boss is reborn in the sense that he regains, on his death-bed, a conviction in the validity of the knowledge which has made him the Boss.

Whereas Jack Burden's story starts out with his attempts to submerge himself in nature, the Boss's story begins with his attempt to separate himself from nature. It is as if he were trying to prove, by exploiting it as it had never been exploited before, that the human in nature will finally react to resist exploitation and prove itself capable of self-realization, just as Willie had reacted when they tried to run it over him like he was dirt. Throughout his career we have Nature standing in animal-and-plant-dumb commentary upon the Boss's actions: the stoic cows standing in the mist along the highway staring dumbly at the soaring Cadillac, the 'possum and the moccasin trying to cross the Boss's path only to be run down and churned thumpingly to death against the underside of the fender. And the domestic animals are absorbed into the symbolism: the family dog Buck in the first chapter, whose uncooperative carcass is a latent hint of the recalcitrancy of the unpredictable, uncontrollable, natural factor not only in animal but in human nature as well (Buck is equated with Old Man Stark in terms of the politically exploitable in Willie's past). Also, in many of the images, there is an equating of Willie's constituency with brute nature: "the gangs of people who looked at me with the countryman's slow, full, curious lack of shame, and didn't make room for me to pass until I was charging them down, the way a cow won't get out of your way until your radiator damn near bats her in the underslung slats." This is the nature in which Willie Stark seeks affirmation of the knowledge that isolates him.

Willie's apparently brutal and vindictive treatment of Byram B. White, erring State Auditor, reflects the Boss's grinding, probing attempt to prove to himself that man can detach himself from brute nature. It is more than a simply graphic metaphor that we get in Warren's description of Byram's bodily reaction to the Boss's verbal abuse: Byram draws himself "into a hunch as though he wanted to assume the prenatal position and be little and warm and safe in the dark." The Boss is trying to force Byram's rebirth. And when Byram has left, the Boss tells Jack:

"I gave him every chance . . . Every chance. He didn't have to say what
I told him to say. He didn't have to listen to me. He could have just
walked out the door and kept on walking. He could have just put a date
on that resignation and handed it to me. He could have done a dozen
things. But did he? Hell, no. Not Byram, and he just stands there and
his eyes blink right quick like a dog's do when he leans up against your
leg before you hit him, and, by God, you have the feeling if you don't
do it you won't be doing God's will."

The same impulse that makes him vilify Byram in an attempt to make
the man separate himself from nature drives the Boss to try to talk
Adam Stanton into a realization that he can never detach himself from
nature in an absolute sense. Adam and Byram represent opposite extremes of modern man's condition; they symbolize attitudes the Boss's
revelation has shown him to be false.

Ironically, what makes the Boss's political success possible is the fact
that his countrymen create in him a hero, an alter ego, and the Boss is
unable to get through that alter ego to them. He wants to show them the
light he has seen, to prove his knowledge (to himself as well as to them)
by changing the picture of the world they carry around in their heads.
But his downfall is a result, finally, of his inability to break down the
false conceptions of him held by the various members of his machine
and by his constituency, by his failure, in other words, to make them
understand the principle on which his actions are based. One of the
greatest ironies of the book is that the Boss thinks that among all his
men Jack Burden alone really understands him. When the others have
left them alone, the Boss confides in Jack as if Jack will understand
where others have not. But in one sense Jack is simply a more complicated and highly developed version of Byram B. White and of the people who make up the Boss's constituency, who want "the nice warm glow
of complacency, the picture that flattered him and his own fat or thin
wife standing in front of the henhouse."

Willie is a symbol of man's struggle toward integration in terms of his
whole nature. This integration is symbolized by the successful control
and cooperation he maintains in his political machine. All the Boss's
men working in harmony symbolize an integration of a sort within the
Boss. Separately, each is a symbolic correlative for an aspect of the Boss's
nature. When the Boss begins to try to operate independently of any
one of them, the integration begins to crumble. When he tries to build
his hospital without the cooperation of Tiny Duffy, he is trying to insist
upon the idealistic aspect of his nature at the expense of the animal-
gross and -predatory in his nature. And Tiny Duffy, symbol of this
aspect of the Boss's make-up, and Sadie Burke, symbol of the indivisible
bond between brute and human nature, participate with Adam Stanton,
symbol of the exclusively idealistic in the Boss's nature, to kill him. By
allowing these aspects of his nature to get out of hand, to function as

isolated impulses, the Boss kills himself. Yet in his death there is a form of salvation, for through disintegration of his personality he is reborn to a realization that man cannot violate the essential complexity of his nature with impunity.

But what Sadie and Adam are trying to kill is an image of the Boss each has created in terms of his own ego—the Boss's integration has been doomed to fall because it has rested on an unsound base. Although the Boss's own choices are responsible for his fall, his incapability of maintaining his integration in the world is a commentary on "the terrible division" of his age. After his death "all the king's men" cannot put him together again; without the principle upon which the Boss's control was based, they do not add up to the microcosm maintained by the Boss's integration. An understanding of the way in which the Boss's men stand as correlatives for aspects of his nature is a key to his characterization.

Sadie and Sugar-Boy are symbols of adjustment to nature in terms of an abstract code. When Sadie informs him of the fraud perpetrated on him by the Harrison outfit, she "made him what he is" (she is the mother of his rebirth), and it is significant that she has developed a sort of honor-among-thieves code of retaliation based on her reaction to her pock-marked face and her besotted father. And Sugar-Boy's relation to nature has been the result of his limitations, too. His stuttering and his puniness at school made the big boys try to "run it over him like he was dirt." So he has developed a code which gives him mastery over his deformity and over other men. Sugar-Boy stands for a kind of counter-predatoriness, which is in harmony with the other elements of the Boss's nature as long as it is held in check. After the Boss's death, Sugar-Boy is set adrift, has no usefulness.

If there is an affinity between the Boss and Sugar-Boy, there is no less an affinity between the Boss and another of the men upon whom he heavily depends early in his career—Hugh Miller of the "clean hands, pure heart, and no political past." There is sincere regret in the scene of their parting: "You're leaving me all alone," the Boss tells him, in semi-comic woe, "with all the sons of bitches. Mine and the other fellow's." Hugh Miller is a part of Willie's nature that he never relinquishes, just as Tiny Duffy is a symbol of "that other self of Willie Stark, and all the contempt and insult which Willie Stark was to heap on Tiny Duffy was nothing but what one self of Willie Stark did to another self of Willie Stark because of a blind, inward necessity." Adam Stanton is a symbol of the Hugh Miller aspect of Willie Stark's nature, and Willie's visit to Adam is motivated by his desire to convince himself of the truth of his self-knowledge.

Ironically, Jack Burden stands for what finally frustrates the Boss's attempt to achieve integration of his whole nature; Jack stands for a malignant skepticism that the Boss puts to work to disintegrate the other characters' conceptions of the world, and which ends in disintegrating the Boss's own conception of himself and of the people around him.

The Boss's affair with Anne Stanton symbolizes Willie's attempt to find in nature some means of achieving good through triumph over the gross and brutal in nature (the Tiny Duffy aspect of his nature). Anne's sculptured, stylized beauty, as opposed to Sadie's pock-marked, blemished face, points up the symbolic contrast between the Boss's two mistresses. It is significant that what brings the Boss and Anne together is her plea to him for assistance in her welfare work, symbol on a smaller scale of what Willie is attempting in his hospital project. Anne's disillusionment about her father and Willie's about his ability to control his son's destiny seem to determine the relationship between Anne and the Boss, as if their affair were a natural outcome of their search for a satisfactory attitude toward nature.

Tom Stark, the Boss's son, is a symbol of human incorrigibility; he is a living rebuff to his father's necessity to find proof in nature that somehow man is controllable. He is continually making not only his father, but himself too, vulnerable to exploitation. To save Tom from marriage to Sibyl Frey, Willie agrees to play ball with the opposition. In his attempt to rectify his son's blunders, the Boss is indulging a sort of parental pride that is in conflict with the code by which he is trying to live. With his eye set on the abstract political objective, the Boss is committed to give up certain of his "necessities" as a human being. But something will not allow him to relinquish his parental pride: this something is the assertion of an essential part of his nature.

The hospital scene produced by Tom Stark's injury brings Sadie, Anne and Lucy together and points up symbolic contrasts already established. Sadie, Anne and the Boss have no defense against the agony of raw grief, but Lucy, guided by her faith in human goodness and love, is able to maintain control of herself and assist her husband, unmanned by his suffering, to leave the waiting room. This is not to say that Lucy becomes the prim heroine of the novel. She does not regain her husband in the end, and we last see her clinging to a faith which makes her capable of adopting a child whose paternity is highly questionable on the long chance that it may be Tom Stark's son, and, symbolically, on the longer chance that Willie may be reborn through it. But Lucy does symbolize a faith which pronounces commentary on the Boss's faith in himself, and on Sadie's faith in her eye-for-an-eye code. Lucy's is a faith in a power before which man is helpless; and it enables her to endure the loss of her husband and of her son; ironically, it affirms the same sort of belief in the potentiality of man as that affirmed by the Boss's dying statement.

Sadie, on the other hand, has no defense against her loss of the Boss. She cannot stay away from the hospital while Tom, whom she has never liked, is suffering. Finally, when she realizes that the Boss is going to leave her permanently, she cannot discipline her attitude toward the loss in terms of her code. She kills the Boss, but, after the murder, she is unable to harden herself to the crime; Jack discovers her in a sanatorium in a state of collapse:

> So I continued to sit there for quite a while, holding Sadie's hand in the silence which she seemed to want and looking across her down toward the bayou, which coiled under the moss depending from the line of cypresses on the farther bank, the algae-mottled water heavy with the hint and odor of swamp, jungle and darkness, along the edge of the clipped lawn.

We have in the landscape a juxtaposition of the brute natural and uncontrollable and the rational and man-controlled, the elements which have gotten out of hand in Sadie's nature. But this is not to say that Sadie Burke is the villainess of the novel any more than that Lucy Stark is the heroine. Both Lucy and Sadie operate as dynamic symbols to qualify the central theme. Sadie is frustrated because she tries to live in terms of a code inappropriate to her nature. But she gains self-knowledge through her collapse, and in her letter to Jack after her recovery there is the implication that she has achieved a sort of mastery over herself in terms of this self-knowledge.

The Boss's downfall is a result of his losing sight of the relationship between man and nature. Highway 58 is a symbol of what Willie Stark achieves in terms of his knowledge that good must be built out of the bad in man. Crooked politics result in Highway 58. Throughout the novel sections describing the highway are repeated to develop a symbol of the precariousness of this relationship between man's aspirations to idealism and the inescapable, irrational, gross aspect of man's nature, an aspect he shares with the dense, uncontrolled natural world along the highway: the jungle at the edge of the clipped lawn. As long as he realizes that he is cutting across nature (Sugar-Boy realizes this with a vengeance when he swerves dexterously to run down the 'possum), he may maintain his separateness. But the "ectoplasmic fingers of the mist" reach out of the swamp, "threading out from the blackness of the cypresses" to snag them—an eerie foreshadowing of the climactic catastrophe of the novel.

For Willie Stark loses sight of nature's resistance to complete control. When his son is killed, Willie's story comes to a climax. In the face of this blow, Willie loses sight of the inseparability of good and evil; he determines to fight back and force upon nature man's ability to achieve absolute good; so he sets out to build his hospital solely out of the "good" in man (Tiny Duffy and Gummy Larson are to have no hand in it). In spite of Lucy's insistence that the hospital—"those things"—does not matter in the face of their son's death, Willie sees it as a symbol of man's undaunted march toward triumph over disease and accident; through surgery, man will control accidents of the sort which killed his son. He begins by banishing Gummy Larson, the crooked contractor, and Tiny Duffy, whom he had promised an interest in the undertaking. But he is so hypnotized by his determination to impose his will upon the nature which has taken his son that he loses sight of the fact that he is running roughshod over Tiny and Gummy and Sadie Burke, as his Cadillac has run over 'possum and moccasin; he becomes hypnotized like the driver who, in an image in the opening page of the book, loses control of his car, crashes over the shoulder of the highway into the weeds, and is killed. Gummy, Sadie and Tiny Duffy have all made him what he is, represent essential parts of his make-up. And, finally, Adam Stanton, symbol of idealism divorced from the brute natural, pulls the trigger. Willie has been struggling toward integration in terms of his whole nature, but the integration among his henchmen breaks down when he tries to divorce idealistic aspirations from their basis in his own pride and selfishness. His downfall is a symbol of the disintegration brought about by modern man's attempt to control the external world through will unguided by understanding. But the Boss's downfall is his "luck"; for through his own disintegration he gains faith in the potentiality of integration in man: he learns that something within man destroys him when he ceases to act as man.

III

Warren's point of view requires that all the imagery of the novel grow out of Jack Burden's mind, and, although it is beyond the scope of this paper to try to do more than suggest the psychological motivation for Jack's reveries, something should be said about the way in which the symbolism considered here is produced by Jack's state of mind.

At the time of the telling of the story, Jack is like a man recuperating, learning to walk again, or like a man whose mind has been liberated from the effects of a drug. He is feeling his way back over territory he had thought familiar, re-exploring it in an attempt to master the knowledge brought to him through his rebirth. Earlier, as a man sick with the "terrible division" of his age, he had seen the world through a diseased sensibility. His feeling of betrayal after the disruption of his love affair with Anne had made him turn on his sensibility as if it had betrayed him, for it had brought between them the image of Anne floating in the bay, had seemed to make him incapable of going through with the sexual act. Jack had tried, after this frustration, to develop a protection against further betrayals, had done so by seeking a "realistic" attitude toward the world. Prior to his rebirth, his speech and actions in the presence of others had shown him to be a man subordinating sentiment to the requirements of the political world in which he worked (and in this respect he had felt he was like the Boss), but in moments of inactivity, he had lapsed into reveries that took the form of ambiguous overflows of sentiment: "You see a cow standing in the water upstream near the single leaning willow. And all at once you feel like crying" After his rebirth, as he looks back on those reveries and reconstructs them, Jack can see that they were symptoms of a disease, but he cannot put a name to the sickness; and, as he tells the story in retrospect, he seems to reproduce those reveries with an almost loving and morbid relish. So what we get in the novel in Jack Burden's "style" (which cannot be equated with Warren's style) is a marked alternation between passages of straight, laconic reporting (Jack Burden describing Jack Burden the ex-reporter) and passages lyrical, rhetorical and often sentimentally ironic (Jack Burden trying to reproduce Jack Burden the ex-romanticist). By more than simple juxtaposition this alternation involves a mutual qualification; one Jack Burden qualifies the other and gives us the whole character: a man whose incorrigibly active sensibility is still resisting his attempts to subordinate it to the requirements of his adopted cynical view. In this alternation the conflict (the struggle toward and against rebirth) which is Jack's hope is dramatized. But the tension and conflict produced by this alternation do more than characterize Jack Burden. They bring to focus several meanings and implications that sharpen our perception of the total intention of the novel; these meanings and implications are brought to focus by the quality such passages possess of functioning in a number of ways simultaneously.

For example, passages produced by his unchecked flow of sensibility occur when Jack "relaxes." Lolling in a hammock while the Boss paces the yard pondering a political problem, Jack sees the leaves about his head and reflects:

> I lay there and watched the undersides of the oak leaves, dry and grayish and dusty-green, and some of them I saw had rusty-corroded-looking spots on them. Those were the ones which would turn loose their grip on the branch before long—not in any breeze, the fibers just relax, in the middle of the day maybe with the sunshine bright and the air so still it aches like the place where the tooth was on the morning after you've been to the dentist or aches like your heart when you stand on the street corner waiting for the light to change and happen to recollect how things once were and how they might have been yet if what happened had not happened.

What starts out as an apparently casual, almost languid speculation about the leaves develops into a vague, aching nostalgia. By a process of association Jack arrives at a sardonic *carpe diem* theme from which he is awakened by the crack of Sugar-Boy's automatic from behind the barn where the gunman is practicing fast draws.

We have here a reverie framed by our awareness of the Boss pacing the leaves and Sugar-Boy practicing his skill (both described in terms Jack Burden the self-styled hard-boiled henchman would use: "Well, it was his baby, and he could give it suck" and "It was Sugar-Boy off down in the lot playing with his .38 Special again"). The irony of the juxtaposition grows out of the terms in which Jack describes the three activities. He feels that he shares no responsibility for the Boss's problem: he is simply doing what he is paid to do. So he relaxes in the hammock in a sort of luxury of irresponsibility, allowing his mind to drift in a vague lack of purpose like the leaves he is contemplating; he is, in his withdrawal, trying to submerge himself in the womb of total nature, but his reflections on the leaves lead him to a contemplation of the inevitability of change. The leaves fall, the tooth deteriorates, the traffic light changes, and suddenly Sugar-Boy's automatic cracks the silence. The critical problem is this: How aware is Jack Burden, at the time of his telling of the story, of the irony of this juxtaposition—Boss pacing, Jack brooding, Sugar-Boy practicing? Certainly, at the time the events took place, Jack was unaware of any irony in the fact that while he mused on the futility of human action Sugar-Boy was diligently practicing a highly developed technique of human action. The fact that Jack forgets the leaves, listens for a while to Sugar-Boy's target practice, then dozes off in the hammock is evidence that he missed the irony completely at the time the events occurred. At the time, much later, of his report of what happened, Jack reconstructs the events in a way that suggests that he is still unable to define the irony of the scene. But the reader, through his insight into Jack's subconscious state of mind, can see how the whole sequence has functioned to point up three conflicting attitudes toward nature which produce the basic conflict in the novel.

Again, in his reverie just prior to his revealing the evidence of her father's participation in crooked politics to Anne Stanton, Jack subconsciously struggles with the conflict produced by his sensibility:

A month from now, in early April, at the time when far away, outside the city, the water hyacinths would be covering every inch of bayou, lagoon, creek, and backwater with a spiritual-mauve to obscene-purple, violent, vulgar, fleshy, solid, throttling mass of bloom over the black water, and the first heart-breaking, misty green, like girlhood dreams, on the old cypresses would have settled down to be leaf and not a damned thing else, and the arm-thick, mud-colored, slime-slick moccasins would heave out of the swamp and try to cross the highway and your front tire hitting one would give a slight bump and make a sound like *ker-whush* and a tiny thump when he slapped heavily up against the underside of the fender, and the insects would come boiling out of the swamps and day and night the whole air would vibrate with them with a sound like an electric fan, and if it was night the owls back in the swamp would be *whoo*-ing and moaning like love and death and damnation, or one would sail out of the pitch dark into the rays of your headlights and plunge against the radiator to explode like a ripped feather bolster, and the fields would be deep in that rank, hairy or slick, juicy, sticky grass which the cattle gorge on and never get flesh over their ribs for that grass is in that black soil and no matter how far down the roots could ever go, if the roots were God knows how deep, there would

never be anything but that black, grease-clotted soil and no stone down
there to put calcium into that grass—well, a month from now, in early
April, when all those things would be happening beyond the suburbs,
the husks of the old houses in the street where Anne Stanton and I were
walking would, if it were evening, crack and spill out into the stoops
and into the street all that life which was now sealed up within.

We have in such imagery a complex of references to the basic symbolism. In the water hyacinth metaphor, for example, we have the principle
of natural change and rebirth which is uncontrollable ("throttling
mass"), miraculous ("spiritual-mauve," the connotations of the ecclesiastical robe), gross and irrational (the "obscene-purple" suggests the
membrane in which the foetus huddles; "violent, vulgar, fleshy, solid,"
the bestiality of lust), and in the face of which man seems helpless. We
have the "obscene-purple" played off against the "spiritual-mauve" to
produce a tension which reflects Jack's conflicting impulse to worship
and loathe nature, to find mingled hope and despair in natural fruition
(the "misty green" of the cypress is a summons to idealism, to hope in
an ultimately "good" end toward which natural process tends; but the
"misty green" turned "leaf and not a damned thing else" seems to turn
the hope to despair, like fragile girlhood optimism frustrated in the
adult experience of womanhood). The image of the car running over
the moccasin symbolizes man running counter to brute natural process
(the passage of the highway through the dense, uncontrolled nature is
antagonistic to the passage of the moccasin impelled by the season to
cross the road): part of man's nature separates him from brute animal
nature. Yet his idealism is rooted in the mysterious, uncontrollable,
gross and irrational process which determines his environment. The un-
dernourished cows are reminders that nature is, if not inimical to man,
at least so organized that it has no regard for his welfare: the lush fruition of the season produces insects, snakes, owls, hyacinths, but it barely
supports the domestic animal upon which man depends. One could
probe the passage further and discover new connotations which function to point up the total meaning of the novel. It is enough here to
point out that the passage creates an atmosphere in which the reader's
sensibility is focused on the mystery which furnishes the basis for the
novel's theme.

It is to such passages as those just considered that critics must return
for a proper evaluation of *All the King's Men*. And those passages must
be read as the product of Jack Burden's mind. Warren's choice of his
particularly oblique point of view is an index of his rigorous and
thorough-going ontological approach to the mystery of good and evil.
We have in *All the King's Men* the story of how Willie Stark was assassi-
nated at the peak of his political career, but what we experience is that
story happening inside Jack Burden's head. The legend of political

power is brought to us through a medium which dramatizes the limits and validity of human knowledge. In fact, one might say that the whole strategy of Warren's technique thwarts any attempt to find the simplified, clear-cut answer to the question of political power; the form of the novel forces the reader to take the Willie Stark story as a mystery—a mystery thoroughly explored in the psychological terms of Jack Burden's experience.

tion. Obviously, a great many details have symbolic references, not least of which is the title itself.

If we turn to any standard encyclopedia, we discover that the Flowering Judas is a tree commonly known as the Judas tree or Red-bud. We learn further that a popular legend relates that it is from this tree that Judas Iscariot hanged himself. A second fact is that the exact title appears in a line from T. S. Eliot's poem "Gerontion":

> In the juvescence of the year
> Came Christ the tiger

> In depraved May, dogwood and chestnut, flowering judas,
> To be eaten, to be divided, to be drunk
> Among whispers.

This is scarcely a coincidence, since Eliot's passage so clearly suggests Laura's activity at the end of the story. Our first question is: what use is made of this symbol? The dividing, the eating and drinking among whispers suggests the Christian sacrament, but it is a particular kind of sacrament. "Christ the tiger" refers to the pagan ritual in which the blood of a slain tiger is drunk in order to engender in the participants the courage of the tiger heart. In a sense this is only a more primitive form a sacrament, one which presupposes a *direct* rather than symbolic transfer of virtues from the animal to man. In the Christian ritual, the symbolic blood of Christ is drunk in remembrance of atonement; that is, symbolically to engender the virtues of Christ in the participant.

If the Judas tree, then, is a symbol for the betrayer of Christ (the legend says that its buds are red because it actually became the body of Judas, who is said to have had red hair), then the sacrament in which Laura participated—the eating of the buds of the Flowering Judas—is a sacrament, not of remembrance, but of betrayal.

This leads us to other uses of the Saviour-symbol in the story. The first is Braggioni, who, at one point, is even called a "world-saviour." It is said that "his skin has been punctured in honorable warfare"; "He has a great nobility, a love of humanity raised above mere personal affection"; finally, he is depicted, like Christ, undergoing the final purification, the foot-washing. But there are important reservations in the use of this symbol: (1) the note of irony with which Braggioni is depicted and which suggests the attitude the reader should take toward him; (2) each time the Christ-like epithet is used, it is accompanied by other, non-Christian characteristics: "His skin has been *punctured* in honorable warfare, but *he is a skilled revolutionary*"; he is a *professional* lover of humanity, a *hungry* world-saviour. It is the use of the religious symbols alongside the secular which makes Braggioni the complex and interesting character that he is.*

* It is instructive to consider the implications of this statement in the light of Mark Schorer's study of metaphor in "Fiction and the 'Analogical Matrix'" in Part I of this volume.

The second use of the Christ-symbol is present in the character of Eugenio, who is seen first as one of the revolutionary workers languishing in jail, but who figures most prominently as the person in Laura's dream. His name contains the clue to his symbolic meaning—well-born. As Christ is the Son of God, he is well-born. He is, likewise, a symbol of all mankind—Man. We say he is the "Son of Man." In this respect, Eugenio is also Christ-like, for he is well-born without the reservations noted in the character of Braggioni—in the highest sense. And as Judas was the direct cause of Christ's crucifixion, so Laura becomes the murderer of Eugenio (of Man) by carrying narcotics to his prison cell, the narcotics through which he (Christ-like) surrendered himself up to death.

We can say, then, that the use of religious symbolism by Miss Porter might suggest that her story be taken as a kind of religious allegory. But there are other, complicating symbols. There is, for instance, Laura's fear of machines such as the *automobile;* there is her dislike for things made on *machines;* and finally there is the statement that *the machine is sacred* to the workers. In the last instance, we may see how the word "machine" is coupled with the religious word "sacred," thus bringing the two kinds of symbols into juxtaposition, just as the same thing is implied in the descriptions we have had of Braggioni. For instance, "His skin has been punctured in honorable warfare" suggests the act of crucifixion, but "puncture" is not a word which we would ordinarily use in describing either the nailing of Christ to the cross or the piercing of his flesh by the spear of the Roman soldier. The most common use of "puncture" now is its reference to automobile tires (of which Laura is afraid). Likewise, the word "professional" used to modify "a lover of humanity" brings the modern idea of business efficiency into conjunction with the image of Christ, as though one were to say, explicitly: "Braggioni is an impersonal, cold-blooded Christ."

A third type of symbols is composed of love-symbols (erotic, secular, and divine). The story shows Laura unable to participate in love upon any of the levels suggested: (1) as a divine lover in the Christian sense, for it is clear that she is incapable of divine passion when she occasionally sneaks into a small church to pray; (2) as a professional lover in the sense that Braggioni is one, for she cannot participate in the revolutionary fervor of the workers, which might be stated as an activity expressive of secular love for their fellow men; she cannot even feel the proper emotion for the children who scribble on their blackboards, "We lov ar ticher"; (3) as an erotic lover, for she responds to none of her three suitors, though she thoughtlessly throws one of them a rose (the symbol of erotic love), an act of profanation, since the boy wears it in his hat until it withers and dies.

Having located these symbols, it is now our problem to examine the use that is made of them. More specifically, we can say that the religious symbols represent the Christian ideology, while the secular are symbols most readily identified with the attitudes of Marxism. As philosophy, they would seem to represent the two most extreme positions possible; yet both claim as their aim the betterment of mankind. If we consider them as areas within which man may act, we might represent them as two circles.

The third field (love) is not so much an area within which man performs as it is an attitude toward his actions. The fact that we refer to "divine love" and "secular love" will illustrate this distinction. On the other hand, if we speak of a "code of love," then love comes to resemble a kind of philosophy and is similar to Christianity and Marxism. As there is evidence in the relationship of Laura to the young captain and to her suitor from the typographers' union that Miss Porter had this relationship in mind as well as the other, we might represent our third symbolic field as a circle overlapping the other two, but also existing as a separate area.

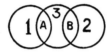

At this point, we must remember the relationship between "Flowering Judas" and Eliot's "Gerontion." The poem is concerned with a wasteland image; that is, with a view of life as a wasteland, sterile and barren as old-age, because of the absence of any fructifying element. Eliot's old man in the poem says:

> I have lost my passion: why should I need to keep it
> Since what is kept must be adulterated?
> I have lost my sight, smell, hearing, taste, and touch:
> How should I use them for your closer contact?

In "Flowering Judas" Laura has lost the use of her senses: when the children scribble their message of love, she can feel nothing for them. They are only "wise, innocent, clay-colored faces," just as the revolutionists have become "clay masks with the power of human speech." She is like the prisoners, shut off from human contact, who, when they complain to her, " 'Dear little Laura, time doesn't pass in this infernal hole, and I won't know when it is time to sleep unless I have a reminder,' she brings them their favorite narcotics, and says in a tone that does not wound them with pity, 'Tonight will be really night for you.' " Seeing the colored flowers the children have painted, she remembers the young captain who has made love to her and thinks, "I must send him a box of colored crayons." She confuses the children with the prisoners, "the poor prisoners who come every day bringing flowers to their jailor." "It is monstrous," she thinks with sudden insight, "to confuse love with revolution, night with day, life with death." Laura, like the figure in Eliot's poem, has lost her passion, she has lost her sight, smell, hearing, taste, and touch. She cannot use them for closer contact.

Now, if we return to our circles, perhaps this can be made clear. The philosophical systems represented by each circle (1. religion. 2. revolution. 3. love) represent a means of dealing with the wasteland. That is, faith in any one of the systems will provide a kind of signpost, which is the first step in transforming the wilderness of modern social living. By observing the signposts, we at least know where we are going or what we are doing there. Yet—it is still the wasteland. However, when we superimpose circle 3 upon either of the other two, the sterility disappears. In other words, either orthodox religion or socialism is a wasteland until transformed by the fructifying power of love; obversely, love is impossible without the object provided by either. In terms of our diagram, all is sterility outside the circles or at any point within the circles where 3 does not overlap either 1 or 2—that is, within the areas A or B.

Laura may be said to be outside any of the circles. Because of her early training, she is pulled away from a belief in the revolutionary cause of Braggioni. Because of her desire to accept the principles of revolution, she is unable to accept the principles of her religious education. Without either Christianity or Marxism, it is impossible for her to respond to her suitors or to the children. She cannot even feel pity for the prisoners; she can only supply them with narcotics, which likens their condition to hers, for her life seems to be a sense-less kind of existence similar to the drugged sleep of the prisoners.

Braggioni's condition is likened to Laura's ("We are more alike than you realize in some things," he tells her), but there are two important differences: (1) he has the revolutionary ideal as a guide; (2) he is capable of redemption, as the final, footwashing scene with his wife ("whose sense of reality is beyond criticism") shows. We can say, then, that Braggioni is not, as Laura is, outside the circles. He is within one of them, but it is not until he is touched with pity that he is brought wholly within the area of redemption (either A or B). Laura is not redeemed, even though she desires it, as the eating of the buds of the Judas tree suggests. Her sacrament is a devouring gesture and Eugenio calls her a cannibal, because she is devouring him (Man). She is, like Judas, the betrayer; and her betrayal, like his, consisted in an inability to believe. Without faith she is incapable of passion, thence of love, finally of life itself. Reduced to the inadequacy of statement, we might say that the theme, lacking all of the story's subtle comment, might be rendered as: Man cannot live divided by materialistic and spiritual values, nor can he live in the modern world by either without faith and love.

As the Nazi landlady in "The Leaning Tower" is made to say when overcharging the American student who wishes to cancel his lease: "Indecision is a very expensive luxury."

Laura's world, then, is as barren and sterile as the world of Eliot's "Gerontion"; it is a living death. Said another way, the living world exists only in our sensory perception of it, and any deadening of the senses (through a denial of traditional human values) constitutes a relinquishing of moral responsibility—the betrayal of mankind into the hands of the Braggionis or, as in "The Leaning Tower," into the hands of the Nazis.

This is, I suspect, what one reviewer discovered as early as 1938, when, in a review of the volume *Flowering Judas,* he wrote: "Miss Porter, I feel, is one of the most 'socially conscious' of our writers." But one might also fear that this reviewer was thinking in terms of the predominant Marxist movements of the thirties, into none of which Miss Porter could, obviously, be made to fit. "I do not mean," he continued, "simply that she is conscious of the physical suffering of her impoverished people; I mean rather that she understands the impoverishment of mind and spirit which accompanies the physical fact, and she sees too that some native goodness in these minds and spirits still lives."

But if "some native goodness" were all Miss Porter's characters had to recommend themselves to us as resolutions of our social dilemma, then every author who does not allegorize good and evil is still "socially conscious," and the reviewer's remarks represent a somewhat dubious compliment. The fact is, however, that he was right perceptually. Behind Miss Porter's elaborate structure of symbol and myth lies the psychological motivation which produces the theme. The germ which lies implicit in the grain of wheat is the central idea about which her memories cluster. An idea does not constitute her "meaning" in the usual sense of the word, but it represents a concept which makes the surface detail available to meaning. To put it another way, the very rightness of the *ideological* fact (the myth or symbol) charges the *particular* fact (the object as it exists in nature) with a meaning that is presented as an experiential whole, but which is available in all its complex relationships only when we have become aware of the entire field of reference.

PART III
THE MODE OF THE NOVELIST

THE MATERIAL of Part III has been arranged into six sections: "Experience and the Personal Element," "Naturalism," "Myth," "Vision and Sensibility," "Fantasy," and "The Novel in Our Time." It may be objected that the term "mode" is not a proper designation for all of these categories; but if "mode" is construed to mean, in the widest sense, the novelist's characteristic area of operation, including his typical subject matter and method as well as philosophical bias, its usage here may take on merit. Certainly, the novelists discussed in the essays grouped under the first heading can be distinguished from the others by their primary concern, whether conscious or unconscious, with first questions of experience and personal adjustment. That concern has been an immediate factor in their approach to the problem of their material and in their solution of it. The critics, furthermore, make use of this concern as the basis of their own approach, and indicate, with great clarity, that the personal element is of supreme importance to the total achievement which the work of these novelists represents.

Philip Rahv opens the first section with a statement of the influence of experience in the development of American literature. The distinction he makes between experience and literary material is a crucial one and sets the key for the studies which follow. Experience in the raw state is not, he suggests, successful literary material so long as writers continue to view it and present it as experience. To be successful, it must be imaginatively re-created and rendered in such a way that it will take on symbolic meaning and value. The "cult of experience" has been harmful to American literature, therefore, to the extent that it has blinded writers to the full implications of their material and led them to produce, not literature, but either a high order of journalism or a low order of self-expression.

Stephen Crane was obsessed by the native hunger for experience; yet in his best work he managed to achieve, almost in spite of himself, a dramatic and symbolic evocation of reality which was far more permanently powerful than the reality he sought, and sacrificed himself for, in life. Because of his superior strength of will and artistry, Conrad was able to translate his personal experiences, particularly his experience of moral isolation, into fictional form, "to objectify them dramatically, and thus to come into an intelligent realization of their meaning which might save him, as he expressed it, 'from the madness which, after a certain point of life is reached, awaits all those who refuse to master their sensations and bring into coherent form the mysteries of their lives.' " For Fitzgerald art represented a means to much the same personal catharsis. His fictional characters and situations were, in the final sense, symbolic resolutions of his own inner conflicts. At his best, as in *The Great Gatsby,* he expressed himself in precise, fully dramatized equivalents of his felt emotion. At his worst, as in *This Side of Paradise,* he expressed himself merely, and resorted to the device of the ghostly apparition to convey an emotion which he felt only dimly and never clearly understood. The excess of moral confidence which led James to preach of the artistic life also led him outside the sphere of the actual in which that life could be presented as a fit example of the truth of his sermon. "As his faith increased," says R. P. Blackmur, "he came less and less to make *fictions* of people and more and more to make *fables,* to draw parables, for the ulterior purposes of his faith. He came less and less to tell and more and more to merely say." In Anderson, Lionel Trilling sees a very similar problem. Anderson's philosophy made feeling an end in itself and thus rendered abstract and empty the world to which his philosophy was opposed. "In Anderson's world there are many emotions, or rather many instances of a few emotions, but there are very few sights, sounds, and smells, very little of the stuff of actuality." Lawrence, too, was the victim of his philosophy. As he found no embodiment for his religious needs in a code or faith, so he found no dramatic or symbolic embodiment for his esthetic sensibility. "His main characters, from whose point of view he writes, and whom he designs to carry the chief burden of his meaning, disappear as characters, as he dives through them in search of . . . the life stream." Huxley's early attitude of negation, coupled with his later mysticism based on a doctrine of self-denial, made for a literary condition in which the mysticism, because it was detached from the actual, could never be successfully dramatized, and the negation, because it denied the actual, could only be meaningless. Wolfe, like Eliot's Hamlet, never found an object for his emotion sufficient to justify the intensity with which he felt and wrote. His art was a prime example of the consequences of sheer creativity, uncontrolled by mind, striving not for esthetic expression, but for physical exhaustion. "The faults of the artist," John Peale Bishop concludes, "are all of them traceable to the failures of the man"; and the same might be said of the faults of all these writers. Their failure, when they do fail, is a failure of feeling or philosophy to find its proper embodiment in art.

Naturalism, because as a philosophical view it takes the form in fiction of a distinctive method and subject matter, is easily acceptable as a mode. As both a philosophy and a method, it stands to what we have come to call "realism" much as feeling stands to mere self-expression; but because, as a philosophy, it is always its own embodiment in art, we may accept it as a somewhat more successful method than self-expression. The difficulty, however, as Malcolm Cowley, H. L. Mencken, Joseph Warren Beach, and Philip Rahv take care to point out, is that it never embodies enough: the philosophy severely limits the amount and kind of reality which can be rendered through it.

Myth is used here in the same sense that Eliot uses it in his essay on *Ulysses* and that, in writing of the Elizabethan drama, he used the term "convention"—as more comparable to method than to subject (although finally indistinguishable from subject), as "a way of controlling, of ordering, of giving a shape and a significance to the immense panorama of futility and anarchy which is contemporary history." Hemingway's code of courage and forbearance and Faulkner's legend of the South are of critical interest in so far as they constitute means by which these writers have been able to give order, significance, and, especially, moral value to their material, in so far, in other words, as myth has become for them a mode of literary existence.

Vision, sensibility, and fantasy are modes in the same degree that naturalism is, and are recognized by an equally distinct form and content. The content of Virginia Woolf's novels *is* sensibility; and their form is the form of sensibility in action. Forster's philosophical vision is the framework and, finally, the substance of those arrangements of character, motive, and setting which constitute the world of his art. Fantasy, for Welty and Greene, is not only a quality engendered by their fictional atmosphere, but a highly organized method for dramatizing their view of reality. Vision, sensibility, and fantasy are the modes of these writers because they represent the conditions in which, finally, they have their being and possess their distinctive character as writers. And having come this far, one might even presume to go farther and suggest that Lionel Trilling, in his closing essay, is attempting to relate, not the novelist alone, but the novel itself to the ultimate mode— the cultural circumstances which surround it and which threaten it with destruction.

The arrangement of the sections in their present sequence is, of course, by no means the only possible one. But it does have the virtue of imposing a certain kind of order upon material for which any order must necessarily represent somewhat less than the whole truth. In the simplest terms, the arrangement is intended to illustrate a progression through the variety of methods which novelists have employed to deal dramatically with the material of art in the modern age, beginning with the expression of personal experience and philosophy in its many forms and ending with what is perhaps the most refined method of presenting the full force of the contemporary nightmare, the method of rendition through fantasy.

The arrangement of the essays in the first section is also intended to illustrate a progression, one which can be traced in the declining effectiveness with which the novelists discussed have dealt with the problem of dramatizing their experience and philosophy. Thus, the studies of Crane and Conrad, with which the section begins, have to do with successful solutions to the problem; the studies of Fitzgerald and James with the slightly less successful; and the studies of Anderson, Lawrence, Huxley, and Wolfe with the crippling effects upon art of solutions which were unsuccessful or of states of mind and heart which made a solution impossible.

The studies arranged under the subsequent headings of naturalism, myth, vision and sensibility, and fantasy illustrate more complex adjustments to the problem of literary survival; while the closing essay may be taken as a summary statement of the conditions which make these adjustments necessary and so difficult. It is fitting that in reading through the material of these sections in their present order, one should be aware of a development that is closely similar to that of Parts I and II—a development, first, from the general to the particular, and, finally, from the particularized general to the generalized particular, from the suffering man to the creative artist, the experienced feeling to the rendered emotion. As the book began with discussions of the art of rendering as principle, so it ends with discussions employing the principle as a criterion of judgment.

THE CULT OF EXPERIENCE
IN AMERICAN WRITING *

Philip Rahv

I

Every attentive reader of Henry James remembers that highly dramatic scene in *The Ambassadors*—a scene singled out by its author as giving away the "whole case" of his novel—in which Lambert Strether, the elderly New England gentleman who had come to Paris on a mission of business and duty, proclaims his conversion to the doctrine of experience. Caught in the spell of Paris, the discovery of whose grace and form is marked for him by a kind of meaning and intensity that can be likened only to the raptures of a mystic vision, Strether feels moved to renounce publicly the morality of abstention he had brought with him from Woollett, Mass. And that mellow Sunday afternoon, as he mingles with the charming guests assembled in the garden of the sculptor Gloriani, the spell of the world capital of civilization is so strong upon the sensitive old man that he trembles with happiness and zeal. It is then that he communicates to little Bilham his newly acquired piety toward life and the fruits thereof. The worst mistake one can make, he admonishes his youthful interlocutor, is not to live all one can.—"Do what you like so long as you don't make my mistake ... Live! ... It doesn't so much matter what you do in particular, so long as you have your life. If you haven't had that, what *have* you had? ... This place and these impressions ... have had their abundant message for me, have just dropped *that* into my mind. I see it now ... and more than you'd believe or I can express ... The right time is now yours. The right time is any *time* that one is still so lucky as to have ... Live, Live!"

To an imaginative European, unfamiliar with the prohibitive American past and the long-standing national habit of playing hide and seek with experience, Strether's pronouncements in favor of sheer life may well seem so commonplace as scarcely to be worth the loving concentration of a major novelist. While the idea that one should "live" one's life came to James as a revelation, to the contemporary European writers this idea had long been a thoroughly assimilated and natural

* "The Cult of Experience in American Writing" appears in *Image and Idea*, by Philip Rahv, copyright 1949 by the author. It is used here by permission of the author and the publisher, New Directions, 333 Sixth Avenue, New York, N. Y.

assumption. Experience served them as the concrete medium for the testing and creation of values, whereas in James's work it stands for something distilled or selected from the total process of living; it stands for romance, reality, civilization—a self-propelling autonomous "presence" inexhaustibly alluring in its own right. That is the "presence" which in the imagination of Hyacinth Robinson, the hero of *The Princess Casamassima,* takes on a form at once "vast, vague, and dazzling—an irradiation of light from objects undefined, mixed with the atmosphere of Paris and Venice."

The significance of this positive approach to experience and identification of it with life's "treasures, felicities, splendors and successes" is that it represents a momentous break with the then dominant American morality of abstention. The roots of this morality are to be traced on the one hand to the religion of the Puritans and, on the other, to the inescapable need of a frontier society to master its world in sober practice before appropriating it as an object of enjoyment. Such is the historical content of that native "innocence" which in James's fiction is continually being ensnared in the web of European "experience." And James's tendency is to resolve this drama of entanglement by finally accepting what Europe offers on condition that it cleanse itself of its taint of evil through an alliance with New World virtue.

James's attitude toward experience is sometimes overlooked by readers excessively impressed (or depressed) by his oblique methods and effects of remoteness and ambiguity. Actually, from the standpoint of the history of the national letters, the lesson he taught in *The Ambassadors,* as in many of his other works, must be understood as no less than a revolutionary appeal. It is a veritable declaration of the rights of man—not, to be sure, of the rights of the public, of the social man, but of the rights of the private man, of the rights of personality, whose openness to experience provides the sole effective guaranty of its development. Already in one of his earliest stories we find the observation that "in this country the people have rights but the person has none." And in so far as any artist can be said to have had a mission, his manifestly was to brace the American individual in his moral struggle to gain for his personal and subjective life that measure of freedom which, as a citizen of a prosperous and democratic community, he had long been enjoying in the sphere of material and political relations.

Strether's appeal, in curiously elaborated, varied, as well as ambivalent forms, pervades all of James's work; and for purposes of critical symbolization it might well be regarded as the compositional key to the whole modern movement in American writing. No literature, it might be said, takes on the qualities of a truly national body of expression unless it is possessed by a basic theme and unifying principle of its own. Thus the German creative mind has in the main been actuated by philosophical interests, the French by the highest ambitions of the intelligence unrestrained by system or dogma, the Russian by the passionately candid questioning and shaping of values. And since Whitman and James the American creative mind, seizing at last upon what had long been denied to it, has found the terms and objects of its activity in the urge toward and immersion in experience. It is this search for experience, conducted on diverse and often conflicting levels of consciousness, which has been the dominant, quintessential theme of the characteristic American literary productions—from *Leaves of Grass* to *Winesburg, Ohio* and beyond; and the more typically American the writer—a figure like Thomas Wolfe is a patent example—the more deeply does it engulf him.

It is through this preoccupation, it seems to me, that one can account, perhaps more adequately than through any other factor, for some of the peculiarities of American writing since the close of its classic period. A basis is thus provided for explaining the unique indifference of this literature to certain cultural aims implicit in the aesthetic rendering of experience—to ideas generally, to theories of value, to the wit of the speculative and problematical, and to that new-fashioned sense of irony which at once expresses and modulates the conflicts in modern belief. In his own way even a writer as intensely aware as James shares this indifference. He is the analyst of fine consciences, and fine minds too, but scarcely of minds capable of grasping and acting upon those ineluctable problems that enter so prominently and with such significant results into the literary art developed in Europe during the past hundred years. And the question is not whether James belonged among the "great thinkers"—very few novelists do—but whether he is "obsessed" by those universal problems, whether, in other words, his work is vitally associated with that prolonged crisis of the human spirit to which the concept of modernity is ultimately reducible. What James asks for, primarily, is the expansion of life beyond its primitive needs and elementary standards of moral and material utility; and of culture he conceives as the reward of this expansion and as its unfailing means of discrimination. Hence he searches for the whereabouts of "Life" and for the exact conditions of its enrichment. This is what makes for a fundamental difference between the inner movement of the American and that of the European novel, the novel of Tolstoy and Dostoevsky, Flaubert and Proust, Joyce, Mann, Lawrence, and Kafka, whose problem is invariably posed in terms of life's intrinsic worth and destiny.

The intellectual is the only character missing in the American novel. He may appear in it in his professional capacity—as artist, teacher, or scientist—but very rarely as a person who thinks with his entire being, that is to say, as a person who transforms ideas into actual dramatic motives instead of merely using them as ideological conventions or as theories so externally applied that they can be dispensed with at will.

Everything is contained in the American novel except ideas. But what are ideas? At best judgments of reality and at worst substitutes for it. The American novelist's conversion to reality, however, has been so belated that he cannot but be baffled by judgments and vexed by substitutes. Thus his work exhibits a singular pattern consisting, on the one hand, of a disinclination to thought and, on the other, of an intense predilection for the real: and the real appears in it as a vast phenomonology swept by waves of sensation and feeling. In this welter there is little room for the intellect, which in the unconscious belief of many imaginative Americans is naturally impervious, if not wholly inimical, to reality.

Consider the literary qualities of Ernest Hemingway, for example. There is nothing Hemingway dislikes more than experience of a make-believe, vague, or frigid nature, but in order to safeguard himself against the counterfeit he consistently avoids drawing upon the more abstract resources of the mind, he snubs the thinking man and mostly confines himself to the depiction of life on its physical levels. Of course, his rare mastery of the sensuous element largely compensates for whatever losses he may sustain in other spheres. Yet the fact remains that a good part of his writing leaves us with a sense of situations unresolved and with a picture of human beings tested by values much too simplified to do them justice. Cleanth Brooks and Robert Penn Warren have recently remarked on the interrelation between qualities of Hemingway's style and his bedazzlement by sheer experience. The following observation in particular tends to bear out the point of view expressed in this essay: "The short simple rhythms, the succession of coordinate clauses, the general lack of subordination—all suggest a dislocated and ununified world. The figures which live in this world live a sort of hand-to-mouth existence perceptually, and conceptually, they hardly live at all. Subordination implies some exercise of discrimination—the sifting of reality through the intellect. But Hemingway has a romantic anti-intellectualism which is to be associated with the premium which he places upon experience as such." [1]

But Hemingway is only a specific instance. Other writers, less gifted and not so self-sufficiently and incisively one-sided, have come to grief through this same creative psychology. Under its conditioning some of them have produced work so limited to the recording of the unmistakably and recurrently real that it can truly be said of them that their art ends exactly where it should properly begin.

"How can one make the best of one's life?" André Malraux asks in one of his novels. "By converting as wide a range of experience as possible into conscious thought." It is precisely this reply which is alien to the typical American artist, who all too often is so absorbed in experi-

[1] Cf. "The Killers," by Cleanth Brooks and Robert Penn Warren, in *American Prefaces*, Spring 1942.

ence that he is satisfied to let it "write its own ticket"—to carry him, that is, to its own chance or casual destination.

In the first part of *Faust* Goethe removes his hero, a Gothic dreamer, from the cell of scholastic devotion in order to embroil him in the passions and high-flavored joys of "real life." But in the second part of the play this hero attains a broader stage of consciousness, reconciling the perilous freedom of his newly-released personality with the enduring interests of the race, with high art, politics, and the constructive labor of curbing the chaotic forces in man and nature alike. This progress of Faust is foreshadowed in an early scene, when Mephisto promises to reveal to him "the little and then the great world."—*Wir sehen die kleine, dann die grosse Welt.*—The little world is the world of the individual bemused by his personal experience, and his sufferings, guilt-feelings, and isolation are to be understood as the penalty he pays for throwing off the traditional bonds that once linked him to God and his fellow-men. Beyond the little world, however, lies the broader world of man the inhabitant of his own history, who in truth is always losing his soul in order to gain it. Now the American drama of experience constitutes a kind of half-*Faust*, a play with the first part intact and the second part missing. And the Mephisto of this shortened version is the familiar demon of the Puritan morality-play, not at all the Goethian philosopher-sceptic driven by the nihilistic spirit of the modern epoch. Nor is the plot of this half-*Faust* consistent within itself. For its protagonist, playing Gretchen as often as he plays Faust, is evidently unclear in his own mind as to the role he is cast in—that of the seducer or the seduced?

It may be that this confusion of roles is the inner source of the famous Jamesian ambiguity and ever-recurring theme of betrayal. James's heroines—his Isabel Archers and Milly Theales and Maggie Ververs—are they not somehow always being victimized by the "great world" even as they succeed in mastering it? Gretchen-like in their innocence, they none the less enact the Faustian role in their uninterrupted pursuit of experience and in the use of the truly Mephistophelean gold of their millionaire-fathers to buy up the brains and beauty and nobility of the civilization that enchants them. And the later heroes of American fiction—Hemingway's young man, for instance, who invariably appears in each of his novels, a young man posing his virility against the background of continents and nations so old that, like Tiresias, they have seen all and suffered all—in his own way he, too, responds to experience in the schizoid fashion of the Gretchen-Faust character. For what is his virility if not at once the measure of his innocence and the measure of his aggression? And what shall we make of Steinbeck's fable of Lennie, that mindless giant who literally kills and gets killed from sheer desire for those soft and lovely things of which fate has singularly deprived him? He combines an unspeakable innocence with an unspeakable aggression.

Perhaps it is not too far-fetched to say that in this grotesque creature Steinbeck has unconsciously created a symbolic parody of a figure such as Thomas Wolfe, who likewise crushed in his huge caresses the delicate objects of the art of life.

II

The disunity of American literature, its polar division into above and below or paleface and redskin writing, I have noted elsewhere. Whitman and James, who form a kind of fatal antipodes, have served as the standard examples of this dissociation. There is one sense, however, in which the contrast between these two archetypal Americans may be said to have been overdrawn. There is, after all, a common ground on which they finally, though perhaps briefly, meet—an essential Americanism subsuming them both that is best defined by their mutual affirmation of experience. True, what one affirmed the other was apt to negate; still it is not in their attitudes toward experience as such that the difference between them becomes crucial but rather in their contradictory conceptions of what constitutes experience. One sought its ideal manifestations in America, the other in Europe. Whitman, plunging with characteristic impetuosity into the turbulent, formless life of the frontier and the big cities, accepted experience in its total ungraded state, whereas James, insisting on a precise scrutiny of its origins and conditions, was endlessly discriminatory, thus carrying forward his ascetic inheritance into the very act of reaching out for the charms and felicities of the great European world. But the important thing to keep in mind here is that this plebeian and patrician are historically associated, each in his own incomparable way, in the radical enterprise of subverting the puritan code of stark utility in the conduct of life and in releasing the long compressed springs of experience in the national letters. In this sense, Whitman and James are the true initiators of the American line of modernity.

If a positive approach to experience is the touchstone of the modern, a negative approach is the touchstone of the classic in American writing. The literature of early America is a sacred rather than a profane literature. Immaculately spiritual at the top and local and anecdotal at the bottom, it is essentially, as the genteel literary historian Barrett Wendell accurately noted, a "record of the national inexperience" marked by "instinctive disregard of actual fact." For this reason it largely left untouched the two chief experiential media—the novel and the drama. Brockden Brown, Cooper, Hawthorne, and Melville were "romancers" rather than novelists. They were incapable of apprehending the vitally new principle of realism by virtue of which the art of fiction in Europe was in their time rapidly evolving toward an hitherto inconceivable condition of objectivity and familiarity with existence. Not until James did a fiction-writer appear in America who was able to sympathise with and hence to take advantage of the methods of Thackeray, Balzac, and Turgenev. Since the principle of realism presupposes a thoroughly secularized relationship between the ego and experience, Hawthorne and Melville could not possibly have apprehended it. Though not religious men themselves, they were nevertheless held in bondage by ancestral conscience and dogma, they were still living in the afterglow of a religious faith that drove the ego, on its external side, to aggrandize itself by accumulating practical sanctions while scourging and inhibiting its intimate side. In Hawthorne the absent or suppressed experience reappears in the shape of spectral beings whose function is to warn, repel, and fascinate. And the unutterable confusion that reigns in some of Melville's narratives (*Pierre, Mardi*), and which no amount of critical labor has succeeded in clearing up, is primarily due to his inability either to come to terms with experience or else wholly and finally to reject it.

Despite the featureless innocence and moral-enthusiastic air of the old American books, there is in some of them a peculiar virulence, a feeling of discord that does not easily fit in with the general tone of the classic age. In such worthies as Irving, Cooper, Bryant, Longfellow, Whittier, and Lowell there is scarcely anything more than meets the eye, but in Poe, Hawthorne, and Melville there is an incandescent symbolism, a meaning within meaning, the vitality of which is perhaps only now being rightly appreciated. D. H. Lawrence was close to the truth when he spoke of what serpents they were, of the "inner diabolism of their underconsciousness." Hawthorne, "that blue-eyed darling," as well as Poe and Melville, insisted on a subversive vision of human nature at the same time as cultivated Americans were everywhere relishing the orations of Emerson who, as James put it, was helping them "to take a picturesque view of one's internal possibilities and to find in the landscape of the soul all sorts of fine sunrise and moonlight effects." Each of these three creative men displays a healthy resistance to the sentimentality and vague idealism of his contemporaries; and along with this resistance they display morbid qualities that, aside from any specific biographical factors, might perhaps be accounted for by the contradiction between the poverty of the experience provided by the society they lived in and the high development of their moral, intellectual, and affective natures—though in Poe's case there is no need to put any stress on his moral character. And the curious thing is that whatever faults their work shows are reversed in later American literature, the weaknesses of which are not to be traced to poverty of experience but to an inability to encompass it on a significant level.

The dilemma that confronted these early writers chiefly manifests itself in their frequent failure to integrate the inner and outer elements of their world so that they might stand witness for each other by way of the organic linkage of object and symbol, act and meaning. For that is the linkage of art without which its structure cannot stand. Lawrence thought that *Moby Dick* is profound *beyond* human feeling—which in a sense says as much against the book as for it. Its further defects are dispersion, a divided mind: its real and transcendental elements do not fully interpenetrate, the creative tension between them is more fortuitous than organic. In *The Scarlet Letter,* as in a few of his shorter fictions, and to a lesser degree in *The Blithedale Romance,* Hawthorne was able to achieve an imaginative order that otherwise eluded him. A good deal of his writing, despite his gift for precise observation, consists of phantasy unsupported by the conviction of reality.

Many changes had to take place in America before its spiritual and material levels could fuse in a work of art in a more or less satisfactory manner. Whitman was already in the position to vivify his democratic ethos by an appeal to the physical features of the country, such as the grandeur and variety of its geography, and to the infinite detail of common lives and occupations. And James too, though sometimes forced to resort to makeshift situations, was on the whole successful in setting up a lively and significant exchange between the moral and empiric elements of his subject-matter. Though he was, in a sense, implicitly bound all his life by the morality of Hawthorne, James none the less perceived what the guilt-tossed psyche of the author of *The Marble Faun* prevented him from seeing—that it is not the man trusting himself to experience but the one fleeing from it who suffers the "beast in the jungle" to rend him.

The Transcendentalist movement is peculiar in that it expresses the native tradition of inexperience in its particulars and the revolutionary urge to experience in its generalities. (Perhaps that is what Van Wyck Brooks meant when, long before prostrating himself at his shrine, he wrote that Emerson was habitually abstract where he should be concrete, and vice versa). On a purely theoretical plane. in ways curiously inverted and idealistic, the cult of experience is patently prefigured in Emerson's doctrine of the uniqueness and infinitude, as well as in Thoreau's equally steep estimate, of the private man. American culture was then unprepared for anything more drastic than an affirmation of experience in theory alone, and even the theory was modulated in a semi-clerical fashion so as not to set it in too open an opposition to the dogmatic faith that, despite the decay of its theology, still prevailed in the ethical sphere. "The love which is preached nowadays," wrote Thoreau, "is an ocean of new milk for a man to swim in. I hear no surf nor surge, but the winds coo over it." No wonder, then, that Transcendentalism declared itself most clearly and dramatically in the form of the essay—a form in which one can preach without practicing.

III

Personal liberation from social taboos and conventions was the war-cry of the group of writers that came to the fore in the second decade of the century. They employed a variety of means to formulate and press home this program. Dreiser's tough-minded though somewhat arid naturalism, Anderson's softer and spottier method articulating the protest of shut-in people, Lewis's satires of Main Street, Cabell's florid celebrations of pleasure, Edna Millay's emotional expansiveness, Mencken's worldly wisdom and assaults on the provincial pieties, the early Van Wyck Brooks's high-minded though bitter evocations of the inhibited past, his ideal of creative self-fulfillment—all these were weapons brought to bear by the party of rebellion in the struggle to gain free access to experience. And the secret of energy in that struggle seems to have been the longing for what was then called "sexual freedom"; for at the time Americans seeking emancipation were engaged in a truly elemental discovery of sex whose literary expression on some levels, as Randolph Bourne remarked, easily turned into "caricatures of desire." The novel, the poem, the play—all contributed to the development of a complete symptomatology of sexual frustration and release. In his *Memoirs,* written toward the end of his life, Sherwood Anderson recalled the writers of that period as "a little band of soldiers who were going to free life . . . from certain bonds." Not that they wanted to overplay sex, but they did want "to bring it back into real relation to the life we lived and saw others living. We wanted the flesh back in our literature, wanted directly in our literature the fact of men and women in bed together, babies being born. We wanted the terrible importance of the flesh in human relations also revealed again." In retrospect much of this writing seems but a naïve inversion of the dear old American innocence, a turning inside out of inbred fear and reticence, but the qualities one likes in it are its positiveness of statement, its zeal and pathos of the limited view.

The concept of experience was then still an undifferentiated whole. But as the desire for personal liberation, even if only from the less compulsive social pressures, was partly gratified and the tone of the literary revival changed from eagerness to disdain, the sense of totality gradually wore itself out. Since the nineteen-twenties a process of atomization of experience has forced each of its spokesmen into a separate groove from which he can step out only at the risk of utterly disorienting himself. Thus, to cite some random examples, poetic technique became the special experience of Ezra Pound, language that of Gertrude Stein, the concrete object was appropriated by W. C. Williams, super-American phenomena by Sandburg and related nationalists, Kenneth Burke experienced ideas (which is by no means the same as thinking them), Archibald MacLeish experienced public attitudes, F. Scott Fitzgerald the glamor and sadness of the very rich, Hemingway death and virile sports, and so on and so forth. Finally Thomas Wolfe plunged into a chaotic recapitulation of the cult of experience as a whole, traversing it in all directions and ending nowhere.

Though the crisis of the nineteen-thirties arrested somewhat the progress of the experiential mode, it nevertheless managed to put its stamp on the entire social-revolutionary literature of the decade. A comparison of European and American left-wing writing of the same period will at once show that whereas Europeans like Malraux and Silone enter deeply into the meaning of political ideas and beliefs, Americans touch only superficially on such matters, as actually their interest is fixed almost exclusively on the class war as an experience which, to them at least, is new and exciting. They succeed in representing incidents of oppression and revolt, as well as sentimental conversions, but conversions of the heart and mind they merely sketch in on the surface or imply in a gratuitous fashion. (What does a radical novel like *The Grapes of Wrath* contain, from an ideological point of view, that agitational journalism cannot communicate with equal heat and facility? Surely its vogue cannot be explained by its radicalism. Its real attraction for the millions who read it lies elsewhere—perhaps in its vivid recreation of "a slice of life" so horridly unfamiliar that it can be made to yield an exotic interest.) The sympathy of these ostensibly political writers with the revolutionary cause is often genuine, yet their understanding of its inner movement, intricate problems, and doctrinal and strategic motives is so deficient as to call into question their competence to deal with political material. In the complete works of the so-called "proletarian school" you will not find a single viable portrait of a Marxist intellectual or of any character in the revolutionary drama who, conscious of his historical role, is not a mere automaton of spontaneous class force or impulse.

What really happened in the nineteen-thirties is that due to certain events the public aspects of experience appeared more meaningful than its private aspects, and literature responded accordingly. But the subject of political art is *history,* which stands in the same relation to experience as fiction to biography; and just as surely as failure to generalize the biographical element thwarts the aspirant to fiction, so the ambition of the literary Left to create a political art was thwarted by its failure to lift experience to the level of history. (For the benefit of those people who habitually pause to insist on what they call "strictly literary values," I might add that by "history" in this connection I do not mean "history books" or anything resembling what is known as the "historical novel" or drama. A political art would succeed in lifting experience to the level of history if its perception of life—any life—were organized around a perspective relating the artist's sense of the *society* of the dead to his sense of the *society* of the living and the as yet unborn.)

Experience, in the sense of "felt life" rather than as life's total practice, is the main but by no means the total substance of literature. The part experience plays in the aesthetic sphere might well be compared to the part that the materialist conception of history assigns to economy. Experience, in the sense of this analogy, is the substructure of literature above which there rises a superstructure of values, ideas, and judgments —in a word, of the multiple forms of consciousness. But this base and summit are not stationary: they continually act and react upon each other.

It is precisely this superstructural level which is seldom reached by the typical American writer of the modern era. Most of the well-known reputations will bear out my point. Whether you approach a poet like Ezra Pound or novelists like Steinbeck and Faulkner, what is at once noticeable is the uneven, and at times quite distorted, development of the various elements that constitute literary talent. What is so exasperating about Pound's poetry, for example, is its peculiar combination of a finished technique (his special share in the distribution of experience) with amateurish and irresponsible ideas. It could be maintained that for sheer creative power Faulkner is hardly excelled by any living novelist, yet he cannot be compared to Proust or Joyce. The diversity and wonderful intensity of the experience represented in his narratives cannot entirely make up for their lack of order, of a self-illuminating structure, and obscurity of value and meaning. One might naturally counter this criticism by stating that though Faulkner rarely or never sets forth values directly, they none the less exist in his work by implication. Yes, but implications incoherently expressed are no better than mystifications, and nowadays it is values that we can least afford to take on faith. Moreover, in a more striking manner perhaps than any of his contemporaries, Faulkner illustrates the tendency of the experiential mode, if pursued to its utmost extreme, to turn into its opposite through unconscious self-parody. In Faulkner the excess, the systematic inflation of the horrible is such a parody of experience. In Thomas Wolfe the same effect is produced by his swollen rhetoric and compulsion to repeat himself—and repetition is an obvious form of parody. This repetition-compulsion has plagued a good many American writers. Its first and most conspicuous victim, of course, was Whitman, who occasionally slipped into unintentional parodies of himself.*

Yet there is a positive side to the primacy of experience in late American literature. For this primacy has conferred certain benefits upon it, of which none is more bracing than its relative immunity from abstraction and otherworldliness. The stream of life, unimpeded by the rocks and sands of ideology, flows through it freely. If inept in coping with the general, it particularizes not at all badly; and the assumptions of sanctity that so many European artists seem to require as a kind of guaranty of their professional standing are not readily conceded in the lighter and clearer American atmosphere. "Whatever may have been the case in years gone by," Whitman wrote in 1888, "the true use for the imaginative faculty of modern times is to give ultimate vivification to

* See Richard Chase and Malcolm Cowley on Faulkner, and Mark Schorer and John Peale Bishop on Wolfe in this volume.

facts, to science, and to common lives, endowing them with glows and glories and final illustriousness which belong to every real thing, and to real things only." As this statement was intended as a prophecy, it is worth noting that while the radiant endowments that Whitman speaks of—the "flows and glories and final illustriousness"—have not been granted, the desired and predicted vivification of facts, science, and common lives has in a measure been realized, though in the process Whitman's democratic faith has as often been belied as confirmed.

IV

It is not the mere recoil from the inhibitions of puritan and neo-puritan times that instigated the American search for experience. Behind it is the extreme individualism of a country without a long past to brood on, whose bourgeois spirit had not worn itself out and been debased in a severe struggle against an old culture so tenacious as to retain the power on occasion to fascinate and render impotent even its pre-destined enemies. Moreover, in contrast to the derangements that have continually shaken Europe, life in the United States has been relatively fortunate and prosperous. It is possible to speak of American history as "successful" history. Within the limits of the capitalist order—and until the present period the objective basis for a different social order simply did not exist here—the American people have been able to find definitive solutions for the great historical problems that faced them. Thus both the Revolutionary and the Civil War were complete actions that once and for all abolished the antagonisms which had initially caused the breakdown of national equilibrium. In Europe similar actions have usually led to festering compromises that in the end reproduced the same conflicts in other forms.

It is plain that until very recently there has really been no urgent need in America for high intellectual productivity. Indeed, the American intelligentsia developed very slowly as a semi-independent grouping; and what is equally important, for more than a century now and especially since 1865, it has been kept at a distance from the machinery of social and political power. What this means is that insofar as it has been deprived of certain opportunities, it has also been sheltered and pampered. There was no occasion or necessity for the intervention of the intellectuals—it was not mentality that society needed most in order to keep its affairs in order. On the whole the intellectuals were left free to cultivate private interests, and, once the moral and aesthetic ban on certain types of exertion had been removed, uninterruptedly to solicit individual experience. It is this lack of a sense of extremity and many-sided involvement which explains the peculiar shallowness of a good deal of American literary expression. If some conditions of insecurity have been known to retard and disarm the mind, so have some conditions of security. The question is not whether Americans have suffered less than

Europeans, but of the quality of whatever suffering and happiness have fallen to their lot.

The consequence of all this has been that American literature has tended to make too much of private life, to impose on it, to scour it for meanings that it cannot always legitimately yield. Henry James was the first to make a cause, if not a fetish, of personal relations; and the justice of his case, despite his vaunted divergence from the pioneer type, is that of a pioneer too, for while Americans generally were still engaged in "gathering in the preparations and necessities" he resolved to seek out "the amenities and consummations." Furthermore, by exploiting in a fashion altogether his own the contingencies of private life that fell within his scope, he was able to dramatize the relation of the new world to the old, thus driving the wedge of historical consciousness into the very heart of the theme of experience. Later not a few attempts were made to combine experience with consciousness, to achieve the balance of thought and being characteristic of the great traditions of European art. But except for certain narratives of James and Melville, I know of very little American fiction which can unqualifiedly be said to have attained this end.

Since the decline of the regime of gentility many admirable works have been produced, but in the main it is the quantity of felt life comprised in them that satisfies, not their quality of belief or interpretative range. In poetry there is evidence of more distinct gains, perhaps because the medium has reached that late stage in its evolution when its chance of survival depends on its capacity to absorb ideas. The modern poetic styles—metaphysical and symbolist—depend on a conjunction of feeling and idea. But, generally speaking, bare experience is still the *leitmotiv* of the American writer, though the literary depression of recent years tends to show that this theme is virtually exhausted. At bottom it was the theme of the individual transplanted from an old culture taking inventory of himself and of his new surroundings. This inventory, this initial recognition and experiencing of oneself and one's surroundings, is all but complete now, and those who persist in going on with it are doing so out of mere routine and inertia.

The creative power of the cult of experience is almost spent, but what lies beyond it is still unclear. One thing, however, is certain: whereas in the past, throughout the nineteenth and well into the twentieth century, the nature of American literary life was largely determined by national forces, now it is international forces that have begun to exert a dominant influence. And in the long run it is in the terms of this historic change that the future course of American writing will define itself.

STEPHEN CRANE: A REVALUATION * [1]

ROBERT WOOSTER STALLMAN

I

STEPHEN CRANE is frequently spoken of as the most legendary figure in American letters since Edgar Allan Poe. A whole mythology of bizarre tales (some of them not entirely untrue) surrounds his elusive and enigmatic personality, and it is difficult to distinguish the real Crane from the mythical Crane when so much of the factual is itself fantastic. The fantastic pursued him beyond the grave in the fact that when he died his wife—an extraordinary woman and a faithful wife—returned to her former trade in Jacksonville, Florida, where as the madame of a bawdy house she presided over a mansion modeled upon Brede Place, the semi-medieval residence of the Cranes in England. Crane, by nature over-generous, had an immense capacity for friendship, which he shared equally with defeated failures—Bowery bums and streetwalkers—and with the literary great, Conrad and Henry James and Ford Madox Ford. Conrad affectionately attended him during his fatal illness, and Henry James, waiting upon him with over-solicitous devotion, treated him as though he were another Keats—a pet lamb in a sentimental tragedy. He lived violently and he died young, but even while he lived the real Crane was being converted into the conventional legend of the artist—luckless, penniless, creative only when fever-ridden or drunk. There is this folk version of the wayward genius, under which Crane's myth-making personality has been likened to Poe's, and there is the more classical version of the "stricken boy," the genius who dies young—Chatterton, Keats, Schubert, Beardsley.

When we approach the work of Crane we are instantly struck by the impact of his greatness, and we marvel not only at that quite inex-

* A portion of "Stephen Crane: A Revaluation" first appeared as the Introduction to the Modern Library (College Edition) *The Red Badge of Courage,* by Stephen Crane, copyright 1951 by Random House, Inc. The complete essay appears here for the first time and is used by permission of the author and Random House, Inc.

1 I wish to thank Miss Josephine La Vecchia and Mr. Sy Kahn for assisting me in the research preparations for this essay. I am also indebted to Miss Roberta Smith, Reference Librarian at the University of Connecticut, for her constant help. This essay was finished prior to the publication of Mr. John Berryman's biography in the "American Men of Letters Series" (*Stephen Crane,* 1950). I have used most of the biographical material listed in *Stephen Crane: A Bibliography,* by Ames W. Williams and Vincent Starrett (1948), and in addition the critical material listed in my forthcoming supplement to the Williams-Starrett bibliography: "Stephen Crane: Critical and Biographical Studies 1900-1952." I have made further study of Crane's art and achievement in *The Stephen Crane Reader* (Knopf and Heinemann, 1952), a collection of Crane's best works.

plicable uniqueness of his technique and style but also that so much in so short a span as eight writing years could be produced by a mere boy who, dying at twenty-eight, left behind him more than enough perfections to place him solidly among the half-dozen major artists of American fiction in the 19th Century—not in the first rank with Hawthorne and Melville and Henry James but, counting work for work, in the second rank with Poe and Howells and Twain. Crane perfected as many works in fiction as Twain and Poe—at his best in a half-dozen stories and one novel—*The Narrative of A. Gordon Pym.* Luckless in everything else, Crane had the great luck—phenomenal among writers— to write two works of art having major importance in American letters and to write them before he was twenty-two. He first broke new ground with *Maggie: A Girl of the Streets,* the then sordid realism of that work initiating the literary trend of the next generation. *Maggie* is a tone painting rather than a realistic photograph of slum life, but it opened the door to the Norris-Dreiser-Farrell school of sociological realism. In *The Red Badge of Courage* and "The Open Boat," that flawless construct of paradox and symbol, Crane established himself among the foremost technicians in American fiction. "The Open Boat" is a perfect fusion of the impressionism of *Maggie* and the symbolism of *The Red Badge of Courage.* The two main technical movements in modern American fiction—realism and symbolism—have their beginnings here in these early achievements of Stephen Crane.

What killed Crane was not literary neglect—he died, so the popular notion has it, "tragically young"; "a boy, spiritually killed by neglect"— but rather it was his own will to burn himself out, his Byronic craving to make his body "a testing ground for all the sensations of life." He aimed not to live very long (35 at best, so he told a friend) and, knowing that his time was short—he had no time to lose! He lived in desperation against time. Like F. Scott Fitzgerald, who wrote (to quote Malcolm Cowley) "in a room full of clocks and calendars," time was what Crane feared. Dying at the same sinister hour as Fitzgerald, at three in the morning, his life was again like Fitzgerald's in this: though filled with adventure, it was neither thrilling nor romantic but actually somewhat banal. "Even his war adventures," as H. L. Mencken says, "were far less thrilling in fact than in his florid accounts of them."

Crane was intense, volatile, spontaneous—what he wrote came unwatched from his pen. He wrote as he lived, and his life was shot through with ironies. If he won any "grace" from that "cold voyage" it was, I think, the artist's gift of ironic outlook, that grace of irony which is so central to his art. Irony is Crane's chief technical instrument. It is the key to our understanding of the man and of his works. He wrote with the intensity of a poet's emotion, the compressed emotion which bursts into symbol and paradox. All his best works are built upon paradox. They are formed upon ironic contrasts between ideals or romantic illusions *and* reality.

Actually, Crane wasted his genius. Under the mistaken notion that only those who have suffered shipwreck can become its interpreters, he expended himself in a misspent search for experience. Wilfully and needlessly he risked his life—among bandits in Mexico, under shellfire in Cuba and Greece as war correspondent, and off the Florida seacoast as a filibustering seaman in the disaster which befell him when he survived shipwreck after suffering thirty hours at sea in a ten-foot dinghy. It was natural that Crane should want to see actual warfare after writing about it, and four years later as war correspondent in the Graeco-Turkish War he tested the psychological truth of his imagined picture. "My picture was all right!" he told Conrad. "I have found it as I imagined it." But at what a cost! Exposures endured in Cuba wrecked his health and impaired his art—nothing vital came from his war experience. And the pity of it all is that it could have been otherwise. He could have lived in one of his brothers' homes and done his writing there. He could have retreated from life to calculate it at a distance, as Hawthorne and James did. Instead, he deliberately chose to get as close to life as possible.

He wanted to get at the real thing and so he stood all night in a blizzard, in order to write "Men in the Storm"; to get at the real thing he spent a night in a Bowery flophouse in order to write "An Experiment in Misery"; to get at the real thing he traveled across the Western prairies, and out of it he got "The Blue Hotel" and "The Bride Comes to Yellow Sky"; out of Mexico he got "Horses—One Dash!" and other sketches; and out of Cuba and Greece impressions of war for *Wounds in the Rain,* stories like "Death and the Child" and the novel *Active Service.* But was there any need for Crane to experience a blizzard in order to write "Men in the Storm"? Wouldn't an imaginary rather than an actual blizzard have served just as well, since the germinal idea of the story is about a *symbolic* storm—the storm of social strife? Familiarizing himself with New York tenement life certainly wasn't necessary for the germinal idea of "An Auction," in which he depicts the social shame of a poor couple whose household goods are auctioned off amidst the derisive mockery of a parrot and a gaping crowd. No personal experience of Bret Harte's country was needed to write parodies of Bret Harte's Californian tales—in "Moonlight in the Snow," "Twelve O'Clock," and "A Self Made Man." Much of Crane's anecdotal material might just as well have originated in the experience of others, and in fact some of it did—for example, the incident used in "The Lone Charge of Francis B. Perkins" was taken from Ralph Paine.

Crane excels in the portrayal of mental turmoil, and for this psychological realism his creative imagination required no firsthand experience. His most directly autobiographical tales are "The Open Boat" and "Horses—One Dash!" "The Open Boat" is a direct transcript of personal experience, but it is personal experience transformed into an impersonal and symbolic representation of life: the plight of man tossed upon an indifferent sea. Crane transcribed it all from his experience, but he converted every detail into symbol, designed every image into a schemework of relationships, and manipulated the original facts and their sequence to form a patterned whole, a construct possessing a life of its own. He created his facts into patterns of contrast—the men in the dinghy *and* the people on the shore, the *white* and the *black* waves, the *sea* and the *land,* etc.—and he converted them into symbols— *viz.* the oar of the oiler, the windmill, etc. The only source that explains the calculated design and patterned significance of "The Open Boat" is the conceiving imagination of the artist.

His two greatest works represent two opposite methods of creation: art created from imagined experience and art created from actual experience. The single marvel he wrung from actual experience was "The Open Boat," and the marvel of it is that he at once transcribed life and converted it into art. Yet a paradox is here established, for the masterpiece which he salvaged from his expense of greatness (as Gorham Munson was first to point out) could have been conceived without any personal experience—as *The Red Badge of Courage* is there to testify. Crane's best works do not vindicate or support the creative principle by which they were generated.

There is thus an ironic contradiction between Crane's theory of creation and his art. His infrequent comments about art—oblique hints given out in an offhand air—amount to no more than the singlestick standard of sincerity and truth to the facts of experience. "My creed was identical with the one of Howells and Garland," he wrote in a letter of 1896. The creed of veritism which Hamlin Garland preached, the theory that art is founded upon personal experience and is copyistic of reality, Crane echoed when, not long before his death, he told a friend: "You can never do anything good aesthetically ... unless it has at one time meant something important to you." His theory was that the greater the artist the closer his contact with reality. Yet his art was at its greatest when he wrote at some distance from the reality he had experienced, or when (as in "The Upturned Face" and "An Episode of War") he wrote out of no personal experience at all.

In his quest for and immersion in experience Crane stands at the headstream of what has been defined as the dominant American theme and literary trend—exemplified in Ernest Hemingway, Sherwood Anderson, and Thomas Wolfe, who put the same premium upon personal experience. At his best Crane used not the experienced event but the event distilled for the thematic potentialities it suggested. The exception is "The Open Boat," but here—as with Conrad in his "Heart of Darkness," which is taken straight from life—the personal experience served simply as the canvas for the recreated picture. For Crane and Conrad alike, contacts with reality provided hints for characters, details of locality, themes and germinal situations. But Crane seldom presents minute descriptions of people or scenes, and details of locality are not photographically recorded. The locality of "The Blue Hotel" has symbolic import and could have been sketched without firsthand experience of it. Crane could have written it without leaving New York City. The fight which he witnessed and tried to stop during his trip west (when in Lincoln, Nebraska) became the fight which he depicted in "The Blue Hotel," but the germinal idea for the story might just as well have had a literary source instead of this personal one. "The Blue Hotel," though it has been labeled a Hemingway story, is identical in germinal conception with Robert Louis Stevenson's formula: a certain scene and atmosphere suggest the correlative action and persons for that particular locality, and they are so used as to express and symbolize it. The atmosphere of the old blue hotel, the psychic quality of its screaming blue, impels and foreshadows the action which expresses it—the murder of the Swede.

It was realism that Crane aimed at—a photographic copy of real life. But Crane is, in essence, no realist. He believed, like Chekhov, that his task was to show persons and things as they really are, yet the persons of his fiction are not persons but just Everyman—the synthetic figures of a Morality Play or a medieval tapestry, the typical representatives of a group (the young soldier from the farm, the Bowery bum, the cowboy). In "A Self Made Man," for example, we get a character called Thomas G. Somebody. Crane was always symbolizing. Henry Fleming, being a more sensitive and imaginative person than the ordinary soldier, is not solely a type (as George Wyndham, in a preface to a collection of Crane's war stories, was first to point out). One might argue that all of Crane's characters have certain marked idiosyncracies which set them apart from the type they represent, yet types they are as well as individuals. If there is any one point of common agreement among Crane's critics, it is the point that Crane in presenting a character (to quote Bushman's summing up) "was *always* at the same time dealing with generalities. . . . His characters are *representatives;* they are individuals *and* representatives of large groups."

Next to Ambrose Bierce, who despised realism (but not in his own war tales), Crane attained a reputation greater than any other American writer about war. What Crane wrote still passes as "real war literature," yet neither Crane nor Bierce rendered the actualities of recruits under fire with anything like the graphic and authentic realism of J. W. De Forest. Crane did not write our first realistic war novel (most Crane critics and historians credit him with that). De Forest's work appeared long before Crane's *Red Badge of Courage*. Nor did Crane write, as some critics have said, our first ironic novel. Neither *Maggie* nor *The Red Badge,* but Twain's *Huckleberry Finn* deserves that claim. Beside De Forest's "First Time Under Fire" and his novel *Miss Rave-nel's Conversion,* Crane's imagined account of battlefields appears somewhat synthetic and even theatrical. Crane's realism differs from the realism of Zola and Norris: it is not photographic and documentary. Crane uses the devices of realism (as Wright Morris recently remarked) "for revelatory purposes. The *charge* of the writing is always more important than the literal content." In his best works Crane uses only so much realistic detail as his symbolic intent requires, that but no more. He is commonly credited with being the forerunner of realism in America, but the truth about *The Red Badge of Courage,* as William Phillips says, is that "this novel is realistic only in a thematic sense, for its style and sensibility have little in common with the method of additive detail associated with the modern realistic school."

II

The Red Badge of Courage was the first nonromantic novel of the Civil War to attain widespread popularity and, appearing at a time when war was still treated primarily as the subject for romance, it turned the tide of the prevailing convention and established a new if not unprecedented one. In style and method Crane had no predecessors, but in viewing war from the vantage point of the unromantic and commonplace conscript he was following the line set down by Walt Whitman, whose *Specimen Days* is our first modern approach to the subject; he was anticipated by Tolstoy, whose *Sevastopol* and *War and Peace* are realistic accounts of the tragedy of the rank and file in the Napoleonic and Crimean Wars;[2] and he was indebted to Colonel Wilbur F. Hinman, whose fictionalized reminiscences of the American Civil War, in *Corporal Si Klegg and His "Pard,"* portray the everyday life of the civilian soldier.

As for Crane influences, it has been claimed that Tolstoy's *Sevastopol* exerted a powerful influence on the conception of *The Red Badge of Courage,* and, by another critic, that but for Tolstoy it would never have been written. Yet no palpable debts can be established. Other source-hunters have thought of Stendhal's battle scenes as the model for Crane's, but Crane never read *La Chartreuse de Parme* and was angered when told that he had. He is supposed to have written *The Red Badge of Courage* on the dare of a friend to do better than Zola, whose tragedy of the Franco-Prussian War is recorded in *La Débâcle,* which Crane sometime before writing his novel dipped into but never finished. Zola bored him. He disliked Zola's statistical realism, and he disliked Tolstoy's panoramic method, finding "Peace and War" (as he

[2] See V. S. Pritchett: *The Living Novel,* pp. 166. H. T. Webster identified the source of *The Red Badge* as Hinman's *Corporal Si Klegg* in an article in *American Literature* for November, 1939.

called it) tiresome: "He could have done the whole business in one third the time and made it just as wonderful. It goes on and on like Texas." Tolstoy's *Anna Karenina* and Flaubert's *Salammbô* he resented on the same grounds. Even his own *The Red Badge of Courage* he criticized for the same reason: it was too long.

Crane confessed that he had read the French realists, but it is probable that he absorbed them only through translations and from Henry James's criticism of the French novelists. Essentially uneducated, he was not a bookish man. "His reading was miscellaneous, desultory, and unguided.[3] In general he disliked the writers of his time whom it was the fashion to like—including Stevenson." He judged literature and people by the criterion of sincerity and, hating the literary dandy, he detested Stevenson—the very man he himself most nearly resembled. Both are mannered writers, addicted to the word, stylists *par excellence;* both, limited in their range, write on similar fields of experience and out of childhood reminiscences. And each personality stirred up the legend of the artist. Both men were nomadic, magnetic, charming and chivalrous, plagued by ill-health; and they resembled each other not only in temperaments but in picturesque exteriors—each wore, as it were, the same absurd mustache.

The whole question of Crane influences is very difficult to pin down. It is debatable whether Crane took over anything out of his French and Russian readings. Most of these so-called influences are in fact (I think) nothing more than parallelisms. It is true that the formula for his short stories parallels the Flaubert-Maupassant-Turgenev formulae (as F. M. Ford pointed), but this much Crane could just as readily have taken over from Ambrose Bierce. In form and theme or subject, Bierce's affinities with Maupassant are the same as Crane's. Bierce's "An Occurrence at Owl Creek Bridge" and Crane's "The Upturned Face" have the same structural design as Maupassant's bitter war story "La Mère Sauvage": They have the form of a single mood, they are patterned upon an ironic contrast, they turn upon a central paradox. Bierce casts his stories at a distance from ordinary life and he romanticizes life by employing melodramatic movie-thriller plots, but (like Crane) he invests his war pictures with a conviction of visual reality. Their short stories are alike in form, in subject (children and the untried soldier), in theme (e.g., conscience and courage), in their use of chance or coincidence, and with different emphasis, in tone and emotional tension. Not only in their fiction but in their parable poetry there is a very close kinship between Bierce and Crane.

Crane's originality had its ancestry in his readings—the Bible, Bierce, Kipling, Poe, Twain, Tolstoy, etc.—and in what he inherited from ex-

[3] From Vincent Starrett's introduction to Williams's *Bibliography*, p. 10. The contrary view is expressed by Ford Madox Ford and by Thomas Beer, who remarks that Crane "was yet a man of letters." In this matter I share Mr. Starrett's judgment.

periences on the diamond and the gridiron—"I got my sense of the rage of conflict on the football field, or else fighting is a hereditary instinct, and I wrote intuitively. . . ." As Shakespeare's *Tempest* had its source in tavern-talk about a shipwreck off the Bermudas, so Crane's *Red Badge of Courage* had its source in conversations with veterans of the Civil War: the reminiscences of his brother, William, who was an expert in the strategy of Chancellorsville, and the tactical accounts of battle which Crane got from General Van Petten, his teacher at the Claverack Academy, the Hudson River Institute where he was schooled and drilled. Crane studied, furthermore, some of the contemporary accounts of the Civil War—the four volumes of The Century's *Battles and Leaders of the Civil War,* which were written almost exclusively by veterans, Harper's *History,* and Matthew Brady's remarkable photographs. But above all these readings he drew chiefly from Colonel Hinman's *Corporal Si Klegg and His "Pard"* (1887). Colonel Hinman's book was, I think, almost certainly Crane's primary literary source. But we are still left wondering where he learned *how* to write. The answer to that question is given, I believe, in Hemingway's remark: "I learned to write looking at paintings at the Luxembourg Museum in Paris."

Crane knew Ryder personally and he knew not only Ryder's paintings but some of Monet's, and Frederic Remington's drawings, and he had Brady's poignant photographs to brood over, Coffin's illustrations to *Si Klegg,* and the apprenticeship paintings of Corwin Linson and Crane's fellow-lodgers at the "Art Students' League," where he lived during the period when he was composing his own impressionistic paintings: *Maggie* and *The Red Badge of Courage.* A recent critic contends that Crane borrowed nothing of his technique from paintings, and here again it is difficult to establish proof of positive influence. I don't think the influence of the studio on Crane can be denied. The critically relevant point, however, is that there is a close parallelism between Crane's impressionistic prose and impressionistic painting. As H. G. Wells concluded in his essay of 1900: "there is Whistler even more than there is Tolstoy in *The Red Badge of Courage.*"

Crane's style has been likened to a unique instrument which no one after his death has ever been able to play. *The Red Badge of Courage* seems unprecedented and noncomparable. But Chekhov, who was almost of an age with Crane, and a little later Katherine Mansfield, who adopted the method of Chekhov, were both masters of the same instrument. In its episodic structure and impressionistic style Chekhov's *The Cherry Orchard* suggests a legitimate parallel to *The Red Badge of Courage.* All three artists had essentially the same literary aim and method: intensity of vision and objectivity in rendering it. All three aimed at a depersonalization of art: they aimed to get outside themselves completely in order "to find the greatest truth of the idea" and "see the thing as it really is"; to keep themselves aloof from their characters, not to become emotionally involved with their subjects, and to comment on them not by statement but by evocation in picture and tone ("sentiment is the devil," said Crane, and in this he was echoing Flaubert).

Crane stands also in close kinship to Conrad and Henry James, the masters of the impressionist school. All these writers aimed to create (to use Henry James's phrase) "a direct impression of life." Their credo is voiced by Conrad in his celebrated Preface to "The Nigger of the 'Narcissus' "—it is "by the power of the written word, to make you hear, to make you feel—it is, before all, to make you *see.*" Their aim was to immerse the reader in the created experience, so that its impact on the reader would occur simultaneously with the discovery of it by the characters themselves. Instead of panoramic views of a battlefield, Crane paints not the whole scene but disconnected segments of it, which, accurately enough, is all that a participant in an action or a spectator of a scene can possibly take into his view at any one moment. "None of them knew the colour of the sky"—that famous opening sentence of "The Open Boat"—defines the restricted point of view of the four men in the wave-tossed dinghy, their line of vision being shut off by the menacing walls of angry water. Busy at the oars, they knew the color of the sky only by the color of the sea and "they knew it was broad day because the colour of the sea changed from slate to emerald-green, streaked with amber lights, and the foam was like tumbling snow." Everything is keyed in a state of tension—even their speech, which is abrupt and composed of "disjointed sentences." Crane's style is itself composed of disjointed sentences, disconnected sense-impressions, chromatic vignettes by which the reality of the adventure is evoked in all its point-present immediacy.

Crane anticipated the French Post-Impressionist painters. *His style is,* in brief, *prose pointillism.* It is composed of disconnected images which, like the blobs of color in a French Impressionist painting, coalesce one with another, every word-group having a cross-reference relationship, every seemingly disconnected detail having interrelationship to the configurated pattern of the whole. The intensity of a Crane tale is due to this patterned coalescence of disconnected things, everything at once fluid and precise.

A striking analogy is established between Crane's use of colors and the method employed by the Impressionists and the Neo-Impressionists or Divisionists, and it is as if he had known about their theory of contrasts and composed his own prose paintings by the same principle. It is the principle, as defined by the scientist Chevreul in his *Laws of Simultaneous Contrast,* that "Each plane of shade creates around itself a sort of aura of light, and each luminous plane creates around itself a zone of shade. In a similar way a coloured area communicates its 'complimentary' to the neighbouring colour, or heightens it if it is complimentary.' " [4] In almost every battle scene Crane paints in *The Red Badge of Courage,* the perspective is blurred by smoke or by the darkness of night. Here is one example of the former contrast, namely dark masses circled by light, and of the latter contrast, namely a luminous spot circled by darkness.

> The clouds were tinged an earthlike yellow in the sunrays and in the shadow were a sorry blue. The flag was sometimes eaten and lost in this mass of vapor, but more often it projected, sun-touched, resplendent. (Page 77.) *

Crane's perspectives, almost without exception, are fashioned by contrasts—black masses juxtaposed against brightness, colored light set against gray mists. At dawn the army glows with a purple hue, and "In the eastern sky there was a yellow patch like a rug laid for the feet of the coming sun; and against it, *black and pattern-like,* loomed the gigantic figure of the colonel on a gigantic horse" (pages 24-25). Black is juxtaposed against yellow (page 27), or against red (pages 31 and 149). Smoke wreathes around a square of white light and a path of yellow shade (page 5). Smoke dimly outlines a distance filled with *blue* uniforms, a *green* sward, and a *sapphire* sky (page 250). Further examples of color-contrast, particularly white *versus* black, occur throughout "The Open Boat," and blue is used symbolically in "The Blue Hotel." Crane had an extraordinary predilection for blue, which Hamlin Garland took to be the sign manual of the Impressionists. It seems likely that Crane read Garland's *Crumbling Idols,* but in any case he wrote a novel about an impressionistic painter—the hero of *The Third Violet.* And in one of his sketches he wrote:

> The flash of the impression was like light, and for this instant it illumined all the dark recesses of one's remotest idea of sacrilege, ghastly and wanton. I bring this to you merely as *an effect of mental light and shade,* something done in thought, *similar to that which the French Impressionists do in color,* something meaningless and at the same time overwhelming, crushing, monstrous. (*The Work of Stephen Crane,* vol. IX, p. 246.)

Crane paints in words exactly as the French Impressionists paint in pigments: both use pure colors and contrasts of colors. Dark clouds or dark smoke or masses of mist and vapor are surrounded by a luminous zone; or *conversely,* specks of prismatic color are enclosed by a zone of shade. Shifting gray mists open out before the splendor of the sunrays (page 160). Or *conversely,* billowing smoke is "filled with horizontal flashes" (page 57); "the mist of smoke [is] gashed by the little knives of fire . . ." (page 251). Inside the surrounding darkness the waters of the

---

[4] Cited in *Painting in France: 1895-1949,* by G. Di San Lazzaro (1949) , p. 28, fnt.

* Page references are to the Modern Library (College Editions) *The Red Badge of Courage.*

river appear wine-tinted, and campfires "shining upon the moving masses of troops, brought forth here and there sudden gleams of silver and gold. Upon the other shore a dark and mysterious range of hills was curved against the sky" (page 37; the same scene is duplicated on page 155). Cleared atmospheres, unimpeded vision of perspective, are rarely delineated, and where they occur the precision of vision is equated, symbolically, with revelation or spiritual insight. (One instance of this symbolic use of color appears on page 42.) Dark mists and vapors represent the haze of Henry's unenlightened mind ("He, the enlightened man who looks afar in the dark, had fled because of his superior perceptions and knowledge"). Darkness and smoke serve as symbols of concealment and deception, vapors masking the light of truth. Sunlight and changing colors signify spiritual insight and rebirth (as on page 1). Henry is a color-bearer, but it is not until he recognizes the truth of his self-deception that the youth keeps "the bright colors to the front." In the celebrated impression of the red sun "pasted in the sky like a wafer" Crane is at once an Impressionist painter and a symbolic artist. But more of that later. Meanwhile an important point about Crane's technique deserves mentioning in this brief discussion of Impressionism. The point is that Crane is a master craftsman in creating his illusions of reality by means of a fixed point of view, through a specifically located observer.

> *From their position* as they again faced toward the place of fighting, they could of course comprehend a greater amount of battle than when their visions had been blurred by the hurling smoke of the line. *They could see* dark stretches winding along the land, and on one cleared space there was a row of guns making *gray clouds, which were filled with large flashes of orange-colored flame* (page 198).

Crane presents his pictures from a fixed plane of vision, and his perspectives seem based upon the same principle of contrast as the Impressionists employed:—Darkness pierced by brilliant color (as in the above), or darkness tinged "with a phosphorescent glow."

III

What makes Crane of such exceptional critical interest is the great range and number of comparisons with other artists, echoes and parallelisms which suggest themselves to any critic who has studied the man and his art. The range of cross-references extends from Flaubert and Hawthorne to Mark Twain and Rudyard Kipling, or—in terms of his influence on 20th Century fiction—beyond his contemporaries Frank Norris and Theodore Dreiser to Dos Passos and Hemingway. While Crane's influence can be documented by a formidable catalogue of specific echoes in later American fiction, it persists more significantly in less subtilized form—i.e., his naturalistic outlook in modern novels of slum life, and his concept of the soldier as Everyman in modern novels of war. Maggie's brother (as other critics have pointed out) is a forebear of Studs Lonnigan, and Crane in several of his stories ("An Episode of War" is one example) foremirrors Hemingway.[5] Modern American literature has its beginnings in Mark Twain and Stephen Crane. Crane in his use of dialect and in his stories of childhood links with Twain, Kipling, and Booth Tarkington. Crane's own Tom Sawyer is Jimmie Trescott (in "Making an Orator"), and his *Sullivan County Sketches* and *Whilomville Stories* had their inspirational source in Twain's *Roughing It* and his *Life on the Mississippi* (which was Crane's favorite book). More important is the kinship they establish in the history of American literature: they each brought into fiction new subject matter and furthermore perfected the techniques for manipulating it. Technically, *The Red Badge of Courage* stands in legitimate comparison with *Huckleberry Finn*. They have the same repetitive form, namely repetitions of ironic episodes, and they deal with heroes in quest of selfhood. In *Huckleberry Finn* every episode is built upon the themes of death and deception or betrayal, and the same themes or leitmotivs are central to *The Red Badge*.

The numerous artists who collect or radiate around Crane form, as it were, a literary cartwheel. The spokes which compose it include: the legendary Poe and Robert Louis Stevenson, the adventurer and sketch-writer Robert Cunninghame Graham, the realists Howells and Garland, the naturalists Norris and Dreiser, the impressionists Chekhov and Katherine Mansfield and Conrad and Henry James, and the writers on warfare—Tolstoy, Zola, Ambrose Bierce, J. W. De Forest, Rudyard Kipling, Henri Barbusse, and others. Kipling's war tales and poems paved the way for Crane's *Red Badge* since his soldier-hero, as British reviewers detected, seemed not unrelated to Tommy Atkins. Crane's earliest style was Kiplingesque, as in some of *The Sullivan County Sketches* (e.g., "Killing His Bear"), and something of Kipling's influence infected certain later pieces such as "The Quest for Virtue," "God Rest Ye, Merry Gentlemen," and "Kim Up!"—one of his very last tales. Kipling's subject is similar to Crane's and Conrad's. The key to the

---

[5] *A Farewell to Arms* is an inverted *Red Badge of Courage*. Hemingway's hero is the idealistic Henry Fleming now turned cynic, older and already maimed. Both heroes are virtually without father and without name. Frederic Henry has a given name for a surname, and Henry Fleming has no name until halfway through the book. Through wounds both heroes come into insight and undergo change—but in opposite directions. Crane's progresses upwards toward manhood and moral triumph; Hemingway's descends toward disenchantment, withdrawal, spiritual denegation. In both novels the education of the hero ends as it began; in self-deception. Frederic Henry renounces war, society, the "comforting stench" of comrades, and he makes his "separate peace." But his farewell to arms is as illusory as Henry Fleming's farewell to vain ideals and compromising illusions. Both heroes are deluded: the one believing he can turn his back upon the battle of life, and the other believing he has triumphed in facing up to it shorn of all romantic notions. Both novels are ritualistic, mythic, symbolic, with the dominant symbolism religious.

whole work of Kipling, as Edmund Wilson defines it, is that "the great celebrant of physical courage should prove in the long run to convey his most moving and convincing effects in describing moral panic." Kipling was one of the three or four influences which Crane admitted, though not always publicly. "If I had kept to my clever Rudyard-Kipling style, the road might have been shorter but, ah, it wouldn't be the true road." Kipling's ballads read to Crane by Irving Bacheller brought forth a burst of excitement. Chance made their careers run similarly too. Both became celebrities while still but youths: Kipling in 1887, when he was twenty-two, and Crane—"a sort of American Kipling" when twenty-four. Both had been journalists before becoming authors, and both wrote about warfare they had never seen. By further coincidence, their greatest recognition came only after their books had reached England, and both suffered their greatest abuse here in America—Kipling, hurt and bewildered, fled from Vermont. Kipling might have expressed the same sad and bitter note that Crane felt, the same lament:

> Now that I have reached the goal—he wrote in a letter from England three years before he died—I suppose that I ought to be contented; but I am not. I was happier in the old days when I was always dreaming of the thing I have now attained. I am disappointed with success, and I am tired of abuse. Over here, happily, they don't treat you as if you were a dog, but give everyone an honest measure of praise or blame. There are no disgusting personalities.[6]

It was Conrad who first identified similitudes between Crane's artistic temperament and his own and who first identified *The Red Badge of Courage,* with its psychological inquiry into the moral problem of conduct, with his own "Nigger of the 'Narcissus.'" (Crane's enthusiasm for this story led him to seek out Conrad in England and thereby become his friend and later his neighbor.) Conrad might have noted further similitudes had he known Crane's "An Experiment in Misery" and *Maggie,* for the short story carries the Conradian theme of Solidarity (the theme also of "The Open Boat") and *Maggie* the Conradian theme of Fidelity—*Maggie* being a study in infidelity or betrayal. Crane and Conrad are closely akin not only in temperament, but in artistic code and in their thematic range and ironic outlook or tone. Both treat the subject of heroism ironically and both contrive for their heroes, usually weak or defeated men, unequal contests against outside forces, pitting them against the sublime obstacles of hostile or indifferent nature. "The Open Boat" epitomizes this subject for Crane, and "Typhoon" does the same for Conrad.

The Red Badge of Courage is readily identifiable with *Lord Jim,* but their differences are, I think, more instructive. Whereas *Lord Jim*

[6] Letter to John N. Hilliard, reprinted from the *New York Times, Supplement,* July 14, 1900, p. 466.

has an innate capacity for heroism, Henry Fleming has it thrust upon him by chance and at the wrong moment. For Crane, as "The End of the Battle" testifies, heroism is not a predictable possession but an impersonal gift thrust upon man with ironic consequences. The whole point of his fable "A Mystery of Heroism" is to explode the myth of heroism. The soldier Collins does a heroic deed, but as in Kipling, it's "the heroism of moral fortitude on the edge of a nervous collapse." Collins runs under shellfire to get water at a well and once there he is a hero, "an intruder in the land of fine deeds," but once there the poor hero is cut off (both literally and symbolically) from his fellow men, and the emptiness of his vainglorious triumph is symbolized by the empty bucket from which the wasted water spills as he nervously makes his way back to the men. Crane's characters are always common, insignificant, and virtually nameless persons; no Crane character is heroic, none is a leader, none is an ideal. Crane's concept of man's nature seems rather shallow, his world-view neither penetrating nor magnanimous by comparison with Conrad's.

IV

Every Crane short story worth mentioning is designed upon a single ironic incident, a crucial paradox, or an irony of opposites; all of them are built out of anecdotal material, and all are concerned with the same subject—the moral problem of conduct. Crane's method of construction is similar to the method that Chekhov employs. He constructs his stories by building up to a crucial moment of impasse and collapse. A Crane story consists of that moment when the characters confront the inescapable impasse of their situation, they are caught and boxed in by fate, and then—the moment of spiritual collapse—"nothing happens," and they are left with a sense of loss, insignificance, or defeat, futility or disillusionment.[7] Crane and Chekhov were among the first to eliminate plot.

[7] Crane's poems have the same structural design and, some of them, even the same plot and mood as his short stories. Paradox shapes them, a single turnabout. "A Youth" is a miniature copy of *The Red Badge of Courage*:

> A youth in apparel that glittered
> Went to walk in a grim forest.
> There he met an assassin
> Attired all in garb of old days;
> He, scowling through the thickets,
> And dagger poised quivering,
> Rushed upon the youth.
> 'Sir,' said the latter,
> 'I am enchanted, believe me,
> To die, thus,
> In this medieval fashion,
> According to the best legends;
> Ah, what joy!'
> Then took he the wound, smiling,
> And died, content.

Crane's best short stories, after "The Open Boat," are "The Bride Comes to Yellow Sky" and three war stories—"A Mystery of Heroism," "An Episode of War," and "The Upturned Face." A slight thing but a perfection, "The Upturned Face" is built upon a paradox. The story is a parable: the ritual of burying a dead man is exposed as a ghastly outrage, more real than riflefire itself. Crane's grotesquerie here is integral to his theme. In "The Blue Hotel" it is out there on the page, and it is misspent. The story ends with the grotesque image of the corpse of the murdered Swede whose eyes stare "upon a dreadful legend that dwelt atop of the cash-machine: 'This registers the amount of your purchase.'" Here is the legitimate ending of the story. The tone here is at odds with the off-key tone of the appended section, and the theme here is at odds with the trumped-up theme announced in the irrelevant and non-ironic conclusion. "The Blue Hotel" happens to be Hemingway's favorite among Crane's stories, Willa Cather singles it out, and one or another of Crane's critics rate it as "one of the most vivid short stories ever written by an American." But it does not stand up under critical scrutiny. I don't think it needs to be demonstrated that "The Monster," another famous anthology piece which has received undeserved acclaim, is not a unified structural whole. The opinion that "An Experiment in Misery" is "far more important than the more famous and accessible *Red Badge of Courage* or such stories of mere physical accident as 'The Open Boat'" (as Ludwig Lewisohn would have it) can be dismissed without comment.

Crane constructs his stories to effect a single mood, or a series of moods with each unit in the series composed of a contrast. *Maggie,* a sentimental melodrama that borders upon travesty, concludes with the orgy of melodramatic emotion to which Maggie's mother gives vent over the death of the daughter whom she has brutalized and driven into the streets. The final turnabout consists of her last words—a parody of pious sentiment—"Oh, yes, I'll fergive her! I'll fergive her!" The grotesque buffoonery of this mock lamentation is comic enough, but there is grim tragedy in the underlying theme that all is sham, even between mother and daughter. All Crane stories end in irony. Some of them, like *Maggie* and *George's Mother,* end in a minor note—"not

The would-be assassin of the youth meets an impasse, namely the youth's romantic illusion of wanting to die a happy heroic death in medieval fashion. Similarly in "The Bride Comes to Yellow Sky," the would-be assassin of the newly wed sheriff is disarmed by an ironic reversal of expectations. Contrast likewise shapes the parable poem "I saw a man pursuing the horizon." Henry Fleming is one of several Crane heroes who are men pursuing the horizon. Again, "A man adrift on a slim spar" reproduces the plight of the men in "The Open Boat," and the syllogistic three-line poem in *The Black Riders* (1895) states the germinal situation which developed into the short story, "The Blue Hotel" (1898):

A man feared that he might find an assassin;   20
Another that he might find a victim.
One was more wise than the other.

with a bang but a whimper." That is the characteristic ending of Chekhov's stories, as one of his critics has pointed out. Crane is a master of the contradictory effect. "The Open Boat," like Chekhov's story "The Kiss," is constructed of alternating moods, each built-up mood of hope or illusion being canceled out by contradictory moods of futility, despair, or disillusionment. This method of the double mood ("qualitative progression," as Kenneth Burke defines it) was Flaubert's major technical discovery. It is the form of *Madame Bovary*, of Joyce's *Portrait of the Artist as a Young Man* and *The Dubliners* (notably "The Dead"), and of almost all of Chekhov's and Katherine Mansfield's short stories. It is the form of Melville's masterpiece "Benito Cereno" [8] and of one of the best pieces Hawthorne wrote—that Kafka-like parable, "My Kinsman, Major Molineaux."

"The Open Boat" and *The Red Badge of Courage* are identical in form, in theme, and even in their configurated patterns of leitmotivs and imagery. The opening scene of *The Red Badge of Courage* establishes the same hope-despair pattern as the very last image of the book—"a golden ray of sun came through the hosts of leaden rain clouds." This sun-through-rain image, which epitomizes the double mood pattern that dominates every tableau in the whole sequence, is a symbol of Henry's moral triumph and it is an ironic commentary upon it. In "The Open Boat" the hope-despair mood of the men is established (and at the same time the point of view prepared for) in the opening sentence—"None of them knew the colour of the sky"—and the final scene

[8] Mr. Newton Arvin thinks that Melville's "Benito Cereno" has been "unduly celebrated," that the story "is an artistic miscarriage," and that its substance is "weak and disappointing. A greater portentousness of moral meaning is constantly suggested than is ever actually present. Of moral meaning, indeed, there is singularly little." He cannot understand why so much praise has been lavished upon the sinister atmosphere: "it is 'built up' tediously and wastefully through the accumulation of incident upon incident, detail upon detail, as if to overwhelm the dullest-witted and most resistant reader." (*Herman Melville*, pp. 238-40.) Mr. Arvin dismisses the whole thing because he can find no large significance in it, but the only way to find it is by insight into the structural principle by which the meaning is formed. Now the fact is that nothing, not a detail or incident, is wasted. Every incident and every detail function to create moods of trust or, conversely, moods of distrust and suspicion. It is not possible to apprehend what the formed meaning of the story is unless it is read in terms of this structural principle of juxtaposed contrasts.

In order to recognize the perfection of a machine it is first of all necessary to recognize the precise purpose and relationship of all its cogs. That much is elementary. Each machine has its own distinguishing kind of form, and one kind must not be mistaken for another. Not subject but form is the primary basis for establishing affinities between two literary works. In form "Benito Cereno" is identical to *The Red Badge of Courage*. Though differing in intention or over-all theme, they are formed out of similar meanings or subthemes (such as appearance *versus* reality, trust *versus* distrust); episodes in both works are patterned by the motif of deception; etc.

Burke's categories of forms have never before been applied to fiction. They provide the most illuminating key to the nature and form of fiction that I know of. Arvin's *Herman Melville* is, I should add, the best critical study of Melville that has yet appeared.

repeats the same contrast mood. At the end when the men are tossed upon "the lonely and indifferent shore," the once barbarously abrupt waves now pace "to and fro in the moonlight," and as the sea changes so, we are made to feel, the men change in heart. They experience a tranquillity of mind now, a serenity that is signified by the seemingly quieted waves. But this peacefulness is deceptive, for actually the violence of the angry sea remains unabated. Their victory over nature has cost them one of their brotherhood—the oiler lies face downward in the shallows.

When Crane began writing fiction he began, like Conrad, as a symbolic artist. One of his very earliest stories, "Men in the Storm," is an experiment in symbolism. Yet the greater number of his stories are nonsymbolic. When he does attempt symbolism all too often his potential symbols collapse. The pathetic episode of "An Auction," for one example, intends to be symbolic but remains merely pathetic. In a good number of stories he wastes what he renders, namely realistic details that could readily have been converted to symbolic use. His symbolic technique is best studied in "The Open Boat" and *The Red Badge of Courage*. In "The Open Boat," the very beginning of the story prepares for the final incident, the death of the oiler, by a symbolic detail. The oiler is represented by the thin little oar he steers: "It was a thin little oar and it seemed often ready to snap." In both these works Crane charged every realistic detail with symbolic significance.

Let us examine some of Crane's symbols here and see how they are created. One method of creating symbols is by establishing an oblique correlation (1) between the plight of the characters and their environment (i.e., the landscape or stage-setting—battlefield, sea, or forest), or (2) between the plight of the characters and juxtaposed objects, animals, or other persons whose plight parallels or stands in diametric contrast to the central one. Another method of symbolic transfer is (3) by interrupting the mental action or mood of the character with an external action or object juxtaposed at the correlative or illuminating moment. For example, in *The Red Badge of Courage* the confused mind of the hero is repeatedly objectified in the confused actions of a single object, the recurrent image of the flag. The meaning of the whole book accretes around this dominant or focal symbol. Symbols are at their most effective when they radiate multiple correspondences, or when they embody different contents (at different times or at the same time). Colors (which Crane used as pattern in early works like *The Sullivan County Sketches*, "An Experiment in Misery," and *Maggie*) become symbolically employed in *The Red Badge of Courage* with the symbolic value of any given color varying according to its location in a specific context. Symbolic patterns of life and death are established by the same color—e.g., the yellow of the sun *and* the yellow uniforms of dead soldiers.

Symbols are generated by parallelisms and repetitions. The chattering fear of a frightened squirrel who flees when Henry Fleming throws a pine cone at him (Chapter VII) parallels the plight or state of feeling of the hero when under shellfire. In "The Open Boat" an implied correlation is created between the confused mind of the men and the confused, irrational and "broken sea." Their mental state is obversely identified with the gruesome and ominous gulls who hover over them, sitting "comfortably in groups" and appearing utterly indifferent to the human plight. Again, the unconcern of the universe is symbolized in the wind-tower which stands before them as they head for the beach:

> This tower was a giant, standing with its back to the plight of the ants. It represented in a degree, to the correspondent, the serenity of nature amid the struggles of the individual—nature in the wind, and nature in the vision of the men. She did not seem cruel to him then, nor beneficient, nor treacherous, nor wise. But she was indifferent, flatly indifferent.

The death of the oiler symbolizes the treachery and indifference of nature, and it is through his death that this truth becomes revealed to them. At the end when they hear "the great sea's voice," they now understand what it says (what life means) because they have suffered. They have suffered the worst that the grim sea can exact from them —"they felt that they could *then* be interpreters." Thus the whole moral meaning of the story is focused in the death of the oiler. At the beginning (the very first image of the story), "None of them knew the colour of the sky"; but now they know it. The death of the oiler is foreshadowed and epitomized in the song recited by the correspondent during a moment of childhood reverie. He had known this verse when a child—"A soldier of the Legion lay dying in Algiers"—but then he had never regarded the death of this soldier as important or meaningful. He had never felt any sympathy for this soldier's plight because then he himself had not yet experienced it. "It was less to him than the breaking of a pencil's point." (This image of the pencil point correlates with the opening description of the delicate oar of the oiler, which seemed "often ready to snap.") The soldier's death foretells the oiler's death, the one being an analogy of the other. That Crane stands as an innovator in the technique of fiction is evidenced by his using this structural device of analogy, both in "The Open Boat" and in *The Red Badge of Courage*. It was first exploited by Flaubert, and later by James, Chekhov, and Joyce.

What is important to any artist is that he believe in his themes, not that he experience them. Crane passionately believed in the theme that no man can interpret life without first experiencing it, and he put his belief into actual practice. The result was "The Open Boat." *The Red Badge of Courage,* however, is the product of *imaginative* belief in the same theme. And that fact sums up the paradox of Crane's artistic career. "An Episode of War" contradicts Crane's personal theory. The theme that no man can interpret life without first experiencing it is here inverted. The lieutenant, because he is wounded, sees life with new insight because he is removed from the flux of life and can observe it instead of merely experiencing it. The symbol of his insight is his wound, for it is his being wounded that changes him and enables him "to see many things which as a participant in the fight were unknown to him." Now that he has no part in the battle, which is to say no part in life itself, he knows more of life than others. Life, seen now through this new point of view, appears like something in "a historical painting," or fixed and statue-like. In structure the story is formed of alternations of moods, perspectives of motion and change shifting into picture-postcard impressions where everything is felt as fixed and static. Where we get the point of view of the wounded we get *at the same time* the point of view of the unwounded, and this device of the double vision, which was later employed so expertly by Joyce in "The Dead," Crane first introduced in "The Open Boat." Things viewed by the men at sea are viewed as though they were men on land. This double vision in the point of view manifests the two-part contrast of Crane's theme, sea and land symbolizing two ways of life.

I have said that "The Open Boat" embodies the same theme as *The Red Badge of Courage*—the theme that through suffering, through immersion in experience, men become united, they undergo a change of heart, they come into spiritual insight and regeneration. In change lies salvation. This theme of immersion and regeneration is exploited in *King Lear;* it is uttered by Heyst in Conrad's *Victory;* and it is expressed as the credo of Stein in *Lord Jim.* The way is to immerse oneself in the destructive element. In *King Lear* the destructive element is represented by the storm; in *The Red Badge of Courage* by the battlefield, in "The Open Boat" by the sea. The cynic (the correspondent) becomes the believer. That the men are saved is symbolic of their spiritual salvation.

v

That Crane is incapable of architectonics has been the critical consensus that has prevailed for over half a century: "his work is a mass of fragments"; "he can only string together a series of loosely cohering incidents"; *The Red Badge of Courage* is not constructed. Edward Garnett, the first English critic to appraise Crane's work, aptly pointed out that Crane lacks the great artist's arrangement of complex effects, which is certainly true. We look to Conrad and Henry James for "exquisite grouping of devices"; Crane's figure in the carpet is a much simpler one. What it consists of is the very thing Garnett failed to detect—a schemework of striking contrasts, alternations of contradictory moods. Crane once defined a novel as a "succession of . . . sharply-outlined pictures, which pass before the reader like a panorama, leaving each its definite impression." His own novel, nonetheless, is not simply a succession of pictures. It is a sustained structural whole. Every Crane critic concurs in this mistaken notion that *The Red Badge of Courage* is nothing more than "a series of episodic scenes," but not one critic has yet undertaken an analysis of Crane's work to see *how* the sequence of tableaux is constructed. Critical analysis of Crane's unique art is practically nonexistent. Probably no American author, unless it is Mark Twain, stands today in more imperative need of critical revaluation.

The Red Badge of Courage begins with the army immobilized—with restless men waiting for orders to move—and with Henry, because the army has done nothing, disillusioned by his first days as a recruit. In the first picture we get of Henry, he is lying on his army cot—resting on an idea. Or rather, he is wrestling with the personal problem it poses. The idea is a thirdhand rumor that tomorrow, at last, the army goes into action. When the tall soldier first announced it, he waved a shirt which he had just washed in a muddy brook, waved it in banner-like fashion to summon the men around the flag of his colorful rumor. It was a call to the colors—he shook it out and spread it about for the men to admire. But Jim Conklin's prophecy of hope meets with disbelief. "It's a lie!" shouts the loud soldier. "I don't believe the derned old army's ever going to move." No disciples rally around the red and gold flag of the herald. The skeptical soldiers think the tall soldier is telling just a tall tale; a furious altercation ensues. Meanwhile Henry in his hut engages in a spiritual debate with himself; whether to believe or disbelieve the word of his friend, whom he has known since childhood. It is the gospel truth, but Henry is one of the doubting apostles.

The opening scene thus sets going the structural pattern of the whole book. Hope and faith (paragraphs 1-3) shift to despair or disbelief (4-7). The counter-movement of opposition begins in paragraph 4, in the small detail of the Negro teamster who stops his dancing, when the men desert him to wrangle over Jim Conklin's rumor. "He sat mournfully down." This image of motion and change (the motion ceasing and the joy turning to gloom) presents the dominant leitmotiv and the form of the whole book in miniature. (Another striking instance of emblematic form occurs in Chapter VI, where Crane pictures a terror-stricken lad who throws down his gun and runs: "A lad whose face had borne an expression of exalted courage, the majesty of he who dares give his life, was, at an instant, smitten abject.") In Chapter I the opening prologue ends in a coda (paragraph 7) with theme and anti-theme here interjoined. It is the picture of the corporal—his uncertainties (whether to repair his house) and his shifting attitudes of trust and distrust (whether the army is going to move) parallel the skeptical outlook of the wrangling men. The same anti-theme of distrust is dramatized in the episode which follows this coda, and every subsequent episode in the sequence is designed similarly by one contrast pattern or another.

Change and motion begin the book. The army, which lies resting upon the hills, is first revealed to us by "the retiring fogs," and as the weather changes so the landscape changes, the brown hills turning into a new green. Now as nature stirs so the army stirs too. Nature and man are in psychic affinity; even the weather changes as though in sympathetic accord with man's plight. In the final scene it is raining but the leaden rain clouds shine with "a golden ray" as though to reflect Henry's own bright serenity, his own tranquillity of mind. But now at the beginning, and throughout the book, Henry's mind is in a "tumult of agony and despair." This psychological tumult began when Henry heard the church bell announce the gospel truth that a great battle had been fought. Noise begins the whole mental melee. The clanging church bell and then the noise of rumors disorder his mind by stirring up legendary visions of heroic selfhood. The noisy world that first colored his mind with myths now clamors to Henry to become absorbed into the solidarity of self-forgetful comradeship, but Henry resists this challenge of the "mysterious fraternity born of the smoke and danger of death," and withdraws again and again from the din of the affray to indulge in self-contemplative moods and magic reveries. The walls of the forest insulate him from the noise of battle. In seeking retreat there to absolve his shame and guilt, Henry, renouncing manhood, is "seeking dark and intricate places." It is as though he were seeking return to the womb. Nature, that "woman with a deep aversion to tragedy," is Mother Nature, and the human equation for the forest is of course Henry's own mother. Henry's flight from the forest-sanctuary represents his momentary rejection of womb-like innocence; periodically he rejects Mother Nature with her sheltering arms and her "religion of peace," and his flight from Mother Nature is symbolic of his initiation into the truth of the world he must measure up to. He is the deceived youth, for death lurks even in the forest-sanctuary. In the pond a gleaming fish is killed by one of the forest creatures, and in the forest Henry meets a rotted corpse, a man whose eyes stare like a dead fish, with ants scurrying over the face. The treachery of this forest retreat, where nothing is as it seems, symbolizes the treachery of ideals—the illusions by which we are all betrayed.

Henry's mind is in constant flux. Henry's self-combat is symbolized by the conflict among the men and between the armies, their altercation being a duplication of his own. Like the regiment that marches and countermarches over the same ground, so Henry's mind traverses the same ideas over and over again. As the cheery-voiced soldier says about the battle, "It's th' most mixed up dern thing I ever see." Mental commotion, confusion, and change are externalized in the "mighty altercation" of men and guns and nature herself. Everything becomes activated, even the dead. That corpse Henry meets on the battlefield, "the *invulnerable* dead man," cannot stay still—he *"forced* a way for himself"* through the ranks. And guns throb too, "restless guns." Back and forth the stage-scenery shifts from dreams to "jolted dreams" and grim fact. Henry's illusions collapse, dreams pinpricked by reality.

Throughout the whole book *withdrawals* alternate with *engagements,* with scenes of entanglement and tumult, but the same nightmarish atmosphere of upheaval and disorder pervades both the inner and the outer realms. The paradox is that when Henry becomes activated in the "vast blue demonstration" and is thereby reduced to anonymity he is then most a man, and conversely, when he affects self-dramatizing picture-postcard poses of himself as hero he is then least a man and not at all heroic. He is then innocent as a child. When disengaged from the external tumult, Henry's mind recollects former domestic scenes. Pictures of childhood and nursery imagery of babes recur at almost every interval of withdrawal. Childhood innocence and withdrawal are thus equated. The nursery limerick which the wounded soldiers sing as they retreat from the battlefront is at once a travesty of their own plight and a mockery of Henry's mythical innocence.

> Sing a song 'a vic'try
> A pocketful 'a bullets,
> Five an' twenty dead men
> Baked in a—pie.

Everything goes awry; nothing turns out as Henry had expected. Battles turn out to be "an immense and terrible machine to him" (the awful machinery of his own mind). At his battle task Henry, we are told, "was like a carpenter who has made many boxes, making still another box, only there was furious haste in his movements." Henry, "frustrated by hateful circumstances," pictures himself as boxed in by fate, by the regiment, and by the "iron laws of tradition and law on four sides. He was in a moving box." And furthermore there are those purely theoretical boxes by which he is shut in from reality—his romantic dreams, legendary visions of heroic selfhood, illusions which the vainglorious machinery of his own mind has manufactured.

The youth who had envisioned himself in Homeric poses, the legendary hero of a Greeklike struggle, has his pretty illusion shattered as soon as he announces his enlistment to his mother. "I've knet yeh eight pair of socks, Henry. . . . " His mother is busy peeling potatoes, and, madonna-like, she kneels among the parings. They are the scraps of his romantic dreams. The youthful private imagines armies to be monsters, "redoubtable dragons," but then he sees the real thing—the colonel who strokes his mustache and shouts over his shoulder, "Don't forget that box of cigars!"

The Red Badge of Courage probes a state of mind under the incessant pinpricks and bombardments of life. The theme is that man's salvation lies in change, in spiritual growth. It is only by immersion in the flux of experience that man becomes disciplined and develops in character, conscience, or soul. Potentialities for change are at their greatest in battle—a battle represents life at its most intense flux. Crane's book is not about the combat of armies; it is about the self-combat of a youth who fears and stubbornly resists change, and the actual battle is symbolic of this spiritual warfare against change and growth. To say that the book is a study in fear is as shallow an interpretation as to say that it is a narrative of the Civil War. It is the standard reading of all Crane's writings, the reading of fear into everything he wrote, and for this misleading diagnosis Thomas Beer's biography of 1923 is almost solely responsible.[9] It is this Handbook of Fear that accounts for the neglect of all critics to attempt any other reading. Beer's thesis is that all the works from the first story to the last dissect fear and that *as* they deal exclusively with fear *so* fear was the motivating passion of Crane's life. "That newspaper feller was a nervy man," said the cook of the ill-fated *Commodore*. *"He didn't seem to know what fear was."* Yet in his art there is fear, little more than that, and in "The Blue Hotel"—so the *Literary History of the United States* tells us—the premonition of the Swede is nothing "but the manifestation of Crane's own intense fear." This equation of Crane's works with his life, however seemingly plausible, is critically fallacious, and the resultant reading is a grossly oversimplified one. Fear is only one of the many passions that comprise *The Red Badge of Courage;* they include not alone fear but rage, elation, and the equally telltale passions of pride and shame. What was Crane afraid of? If Crane was at all afraid, he was afraid of time and change. Throughout Crane's works, as in his life, there is the conflict between ideals and reality.

Our critical concern is with the plight of his hero: Henry Fleming recognizes the necessity for change and development, but he wars against it. The youth develops into the veteran—*"So it came to pass . . . his soul changed."* Significantly enough, in thus stating what his book is about Crane intones Biblical phrasing.

Spiritual change, *that* is Henry Fleming's red badge. *His red badge is his conscience reborn and purified.* Whereas Jim Conklin's red badge of courage is the literal one, the wound of which he dies, Henry's is the psychological badge, the wound of conscience. Internal wounds are more painful than external ones. It is fitting that Henry should receive a head wound, a bump that jolts him with a severe headache! But what "salve" is there to ease the pain of his internal wound of dishonor?

---

[9] "Let it be stated," says Beer, "that the mistress of this boy's mind was fear. His search in aesthetic was governed by terror as that of tamer men is governed by the desire of women." A very pretty analogy!

That is Henry's "headache"! It is the ache of his conscience that he has been honored by the regiment he has dishonored. Just as Jim runs into the fields to hide his true wound from Henry, so Henry runs into the fields to hide his false wound, his false badge of courage, from the tattered man who asks him where he is wounded. "It might be inside mostly, an' them plays thunder. Where is it located?" The men, so Henry feels, are perpetually probing his guilt-wound, "ever upraising the ghost of shame on the stick of their curiosity." The unmistakable implication here is of a flag, and the actual flag which Henry carries in battle is the symbol of his conscience. Conscience is also symbolized by the forest, the cathedral-forest where Henry retreats to nurse his guilt-wound and be consoled by the benedictions which nature sympathetically bestows upon him. Here in this forest-chapel there is a churchlike silence as insects "bow their beaks" while Henry bows his head in shame; they make a "devotional pause" while the trees chant a soft hymn to comfort him. But Henry is troubled; he cannot "conciliate the forest." Nor can he conciliate the flag. The flag registers the commotion of his mind, and it registers the restless movements of the nervous regiment—it flutters when the men expect battle. And when the regiment runs from the battle, the flag sinks down "as if dying. Its motion as it fell was a gesture of despair." Henry dishonors the flag not when he flees from battle but when he flees from himself, and he redeems it when he redeems his conscience.[10]

Redemption begins in confession, in absolution—in change of heart. Henry's wounded conscience is not healed until he confesses to himself the truth and opens his eyes to new ways; not until he strips his enemy heart of "the brass and bombast of his earlier gospels," the vainglorious illusions he had fabricated into a cloak of pride and self-vindication; not until he puts on new garments of humility and loving kindness for his fellow-men. Redemption begins in humility—Henry's example is the loud soldier who becomes the humble soldier. The loud soldier admits the folly of his former ways. Henry's spiritual change is a prolonged process, but it is signalized in moments when he loses his soul in the flux of things; *then* he courageously deserts himself instead of his fellow-men; then fearlessly plunging into battle, charging the enemy like "a pagan who defends his religion," he becomes swept up in a delirium of selflessness and feels himself "capable of profound sacrifices." The brave new Henry, "new bearer of the colors," triumphs

[10] Henry's plight is identical with the Reverend Dimmesdale's plight in Hawthorne's psychological novel, *The Scarlet Letter,* with which *The Red Badge of Courage* has bondship by the similitude of the theme of redemption through self-confession and, even more strikingly, by the symbol of the forest to signify conscience. The mythology of the scarlet letter is much the same as the mythology of the red badge: each is the emblem of moral guilt and salvation. The red badge is the scarlet letter of dishonor transferred from the bosom of Hester, the social outcast, to the mind of Henry Fleming, the "mental outcast."

over the former one. The enemy flag is wrenched from the hands of "the rival color bearer," the symbol of Henry's own other self, and as this rival color bearer dies Henry is reborn.

Henry's regeneration is brought about by the death of Jim Conklin, the friend whom Henry had known since childhood. He goes under various names. He is sometimes called the spectral soldier (his face is a pasty gray) and sometimes the tall soldier (he is taller than all other men), but there are unmistakable hints—in such descriptive details about him as his wound in the side, his torn body and his gory hand, and even in the initials of his name, Jim Conklin—that he is intended to represent Jesus Christ. We are told that there is "a resemblance in him to a devotee of a mad religion," and among his followers the doomed man stirs up "thoughts of a solemn ceremony." When he dies, the heavens signify his death—the red sun bleeds with the passion of his wounds:

The red sun was pasted in the sky like a wafer.

This grotesque image, the most notorious metaphor in American literature, has been much debated and roundly damned by Crane's critics (e.g., Pattee, Quinn, Cargill, and a dozen others) as downright bad writing, a false, melodramatic and nonfunctional figure. Joseph Hergesheimer, Willa Cather, and Conrad admired it, but no one ventured to explain it. The other camp took potshots at it without attempting to understand what it is really all about. It is, in fact, the key to the symbolism of the whole novel, particularly the religious symbolism which radiates outwards from Jim Conklin. Like any image, it has to be related to the structure of meaning in which it functions; when lifted out of its context it is bound to seem artificial and irrelevant or, on the other hand, merely "a superb piece of imagery." I do not think it can be doubted that Crane intended to suggest here the sacrificial death celebrated in communion.

Henry and the tattered soldier consecrate the death of the spectral soldier in "a solemn ceremony." Henry partakes of the sacramental blood and body of Christ, and the process of his spiritual rebirth begins at this moment when the wafer-like sun appears in the sky. It is a symbol of salvation through death. Henry, we are made to feel, recognizes in the lifeless sun his own lifeless conscience, his dead and as yet unregenerated selfhood or conscience, and that is why he blasphemes against it. His moral salvation and triumph are prepared for (1) by this ritual of purification and religious devotion and, at the very start of the book (2), by the ritual of absolution which Jim Conklin performs in the opening scene. It was the tall soldier who first "developed virtues" and showed the boys how to cleanse a flag. The way is to wash it in the muddy river. Only by experiencing life, the muddy river, can the soul be cleansed. In "The Open Boat" it is the black sea, and the whiteness of the waves as they pace to and fro in the moonlight, signifies the spiritual purification which the men win from their contest against the terrible water. The ritual of domestic comforts bestowed upon the saved men by the people on the shore, "all the remedies sacred to their minds," is a shallow thing, devoid of spiritual value. The sea offers the only true remedy, though it costs a "terrible grace." The way is to immerse oneself in the destructive element!

Kurtz, in Conrad's "Heart of Darkness," washed his soul in the Congo, and Marlow, because he had become a part of Kurtz, redeemed the heart of darkness by the same token. Conrad, like Crane, had himself experienced his own theme, but Crane was the first to produce a work based upon it. Crane's influence on Conrad is apparent in *Lord Jim,* which makes use of the same religious symbolism as *The Red Badge of Courage.* When Lord Jim goes to his death, you recall, there is an awful sunset. Conrad's "enormous sun" was suggested by Crane's grotesque symbol and paradox image of the red sun that was pasted wafer-like in the sky when Jim Conklin died. For the other Jim, "The sky over Patusan was blood-red, immense, streaming like an open vein."

Like Flaubert and James and Conrad, Crane is a great stylist. Theme and style in *The Red Badge* and in "The Open Boat" are organically conceived, the theme of change conjoined with the fluid style by which it is evoked. The deliberately disconnected and apparently disordered style is calculated to create confused impressions of change and motion. Fluidity characterizes the whole book. Crane interjects disjointed details, one nonsequitur melting into another. Scenes and objects are felt as blurred, they appear under a haze or vapor or cloud. Yet everything has relationship and is manipulated into contrapuntal patterns of color and cross-references of meaning.

Like Conrad, Crane puts language to poetic uses, which, to define it, is to use language reflexively and to use language symbolically. It is the works which employ this reflexive and symbolic use of language that constitute what is permanent of Crane.

It is the language of symbol and paradox: the wafer-like sun, in *The Red Badge;* or in "The Open Boat" the paradox of "cold, comfortable sea-water," an image which calls to mind the poetry of W. B. Yeats with its fusion of contradictory emotions. This single image evokes the sensation of the whole experience of the men in the dinghy, but it suggests furthermore another telltale significance, one that is applicable to Stephen Crane. What is readily recognizable in this paradox of "cold, comfortable sea-water" is that irony of opposites which constituted the personality of the man who wrote it. It is the subjective correlative of his own plight. The enigma of the man is symbolized in his enigmatic style.

JOSEPH CONRAD: CHANCE AND RECOGNITION * [1]

Morton Dauwen Zabel

Conrad's title-pages always taxed his scruples as severely as any part of his manuscripts, not always to his own satisfaction or to ours in the case of the titles themselves, but with notable success in the case of their epigraphs. These he employed consistently; Mrs. Conrad has said that they were always chosen with extreme care, Conrad taking pains that these "quotations had always a close and direct relation to the contents of the book itself, and that they often expressed the mood in which the work was written." Sometimes it is the mood—whether of memory, pathos, irony, or tragedy—that is emphasized. More often the epigraphs hint of the motive or attitude that directed Conrad's shaping of his material and the conception of experience it dramatizes. The quotation below the title of *Lord Jim* gives a clue not only to the narrative method which, in his long recitatives, monologues, and self-inquisitions, Conrad made his special instrument for the achievement of realism and form, but to the psychological compulsion under which his characters, caught in the moral or circumstantial prisons of their lives, are forced to speak, and by which Conrad himself, if we trace his nature in his tales and personal writings, was compelled toward his special kind of art and revelation. "It is certain my conviction gains infinitely, the moment another soul will believe in it": Novalis's sentence is the key to the method and necessity that are the source both of Conrad's originality and of his appeal to psychological realists.

Sometimes the complex of fate requires solution by something more violent than an ordeal of individual sublimation. Shakespeare's "So foul a sky clears not without a storm," at the head of *Nostromo*, suggests a prevailing symbol. When the novel is of a more exotic or melodramatic tendency, it sustains a sense of the marvelous or miraculous, of a thrilled

* "Joseph Conrad: Chance and Recognition" first appeared in the *Sewanee Review*, Winter, 1945, and later formed part of Mr. Zabel's Introduction to *The Portable Conrad* (The Viking Press, Inc., 1947). It is used here by permission of the author and the editors of the *Sewanee Review*.

1 This essay is one of a series by the present writer on Joseph Conrad, others being "Conrad: Nel Mezzo del Cammin" in the *New Republic*, December 23, 1940; "Conrad: The Secret Sharer," *ibid.*, April 21, 1941; and "Conrad in His Age," *ibid.*, November 16, 1942. See also his "Introduction" to *The Portable Conrad* (The Viking Press, Inc., 1947) and his introductions to *The Nigger of the "Narcissus"* (Harper & Brothers, 1951) and to *Under Western Eyes* (New Directions, 1951).

response to the incredible turns and hazards of life, "the strangeness of the destinies that lie in wait for the sons of men," of "marvels and mysteries acting upon our emotions and intelligence in ways so inexplicable that it would almost justify the conception of life as an enchanted state," —thus reflecting the romanticism in Conrad's temperament that involved him in the fortunes of his career and that took a lifetime of discipline to bring to terms with the critical forces of his moral intelligence. A French nursery rhyme sets the tone for *A Set of Six:* "Les petites marionnettes/Font, font, font,/Trois petits tours/Et puis s'en vont." A phrase from Boethius—". . . for this miracle or this wonder troubleth me right gretly"—stands at the head of the autobiographical *Mirror of the Sea.* Victory proceeds under the spell evoked by Milton's lines from *Comus:*

> Calling shapes and beckoning shadows dire
> And airy tongues that syllable men's names
> On sands and shores and desert wildernesses.

But there is another series of these quotations that indicates even more clearly the idea that possessed Conrad in his reading of experience. This idea originated, I believe, in a profoundly significant root-experience of his own temperament and history. He was to employ it as the incentive of his greatest tales. It is suggested repeatedly in his epigraphs from his first book to his last. The quotation on *Almayer's Folly* in 1895 is from Amiel: "Qui de nous n'a eu sa terre promise, son jour d'extase, et sa fin en exil?" Baudelaire's "D'autres fois, calme plat, grand miroir/De mon désespoir" serves as heading to *The Shadow Line* in 1917. An aphorism from La Bruyère acts as a clue to *The Arrow of Gold* in 1918: "Celui qui n'a connu que des hommes polis et raisonnables, ou ne connaît pas l'homme, ou ne le connaît qu'à demi." The motto for *The Rescue* in 1920 is from Chaucer's *Frankeleyn's Tale:*

> "Alas!" quod she, "that ever this sholde happe!
> For wende I never, by possibilitee,
> That swich a monstre or merveille mighte be!"

Most specific of all, the quotation below the title of *Chance,* in 1913, is from Sir Thomas Browne: "Those that hold that all things are governed by Fortune had not erred, had they not persisted there."

The meaning and consistency of these passages is clear. They permit us to summarize briefly, if too simply, the basic theme of Conrad's fiction. His work dramatizes a hostility of forces that exists both in the conditions of practical life and in the moral constitution of man himself. Men who show any fundamental vitality of nature, will, or imagination are not initially men of caution, tact, or prudence, "polis et raisonnables," and they are certainly unlikely to remain so. They are possessed by an enthusiasm that makes them approach life as an adven-

ture. They attack the struggle with all the impulsive force of their illusion, their pride, their idealism, their desire for fame and power, their
confidence that Chance is a friend and Fortune a guide who will lead
them to a promised goal of happiness or success, wealth or authority.
Chance, under this aspect of youthful illusion, is the ideal of expectation and generosity. She is the goddess of the ignorance we prize as sincerity before we learn that sincerity is a virtue which, like James's
cipher in arithmetic, depends for its value on the number to which it is
attached. She takes the color of her benevolence from youth's impetuosity and ardor, before those qualities have revealed their full cost in
experience and disillusionment. It sometimes happens that the illusion
we impose on our lives at their outset is not enthusiastic but cynical or
pessimistic. The cost then proves all the greater. The hero of "Youth,"
The Arrow of Gold, and *The Shadow Line* is at times supplanted by a
man like Heyst in *Victory* or Razumov in *Under Western Eyes,* whose
untested misanthropy is as fatally romantic a presumption on the conditions of the responsible life or the obligations of character as an untested optimism. ("Woe to the man whose heart has not learned while
young to hope, to love—and to put its trust in life!") An equal enemy
lies in wait for both. That enemy—"our common enemy"—leaps from
unknown coverts: sometimes from the hiding-places that fate or accident has prepared, but more often and seriously, like James's beast in
the jungle, from the unfathomed depths of our secret natures, our ignorance, our subconscious or unconscious selves.

When the moment comes, the victim is forced to commit himself to
it. It is the signal of his destiny, and there is no escape for the one who
meets it unprepared. The terms of life are reversed by it. It is the stroke
by which fate compels recognition—of one's self, of reality, of illusion,
error, mistaken expectation, and defeat. At that moment, if a man can
measure up to it, his conscious moral existence begins, an existence for
which previous intellectual or theoretical anticipation can never fully
prepare. "We begin to live when we have conceived life as tragedy."
Chance is no longer beneficent. She is a setter of traps and snares; her
opportunities have become the measure of risk and peril; and her favorites are no longer adventurers or idealists but those who can say, in
words of Yeats that are an explicit phrasing of Conrad's idea: "When I
think of life as a struggle with the Daemon who would ever set us to
the hardest work among those not impossible, I understand why there
is a deep enmity between a man and his destiny, and why a man loves
nothing but his destiny."

The crisis in almost every one of Conrad's novels—many of which
form a prolonged and exhaustive analysis or sublimation of crisis—
arrives when, by a stroke of accident or by an act of decision or error
rising from the secret necessities of temperament, a man finds himself
abruptly committed to his destiny. It is a commitment to which all men

of morally significant quality are bound. It is the test and opportunity of fundamental selfhood, and there is no escape from it. Its necessity is variously stated in Conrad's books—most memorably perhaps in *Typhoon:*

> The sea...had never put itself out to startle the silent man, who seldom looked up, and wandered innocently over the waters with the only visible purpose of getting food, raiment, and house-room for three people ashore. Dirty weather he had known, of course. He had been made wet, uncomfortable, tired in the usual way, felt at the time and presently forgotten. So that upon the whole he had been justified in reporting fine weather at home. But he had never been given a glimpse of immeasurable strength and of immoderate wrath, the wrath that passes exhausted but never appeased—the wrath and fury of the passionate sea. He knew it existed, as we know that crime and abominations exist; he had heard of it as a peaceable citizen in a town hears of battles, famines, and floods, and yet knows nothing of what these things mean—though, indeed, he may have been mixed up in a street row, have gone without his dinner once, or been soaked to the skin in a shower. Captain MacWhirr had sailed over the surface of the oceans as some men go skimming over the years of existence to sink gently into a placid grave, ignorant of life to the last, without ever having been made to see all it may contain of perfidy, of violence, and of terror. There are on sea and land such men thus fortunate—or thus disdained by destiny or by the sea.

The full implications of this final sentence extend beyond Conrad's tales and even his life; they give us his judgment on a world lapsed into the destructive violence that results from a morality of casuistry and opportunism. It was not only in political and commercial society that he saw that violence at work, with the ramifying evil he depicted in *Chance, The Secret Agent,* and *Under Western Eyes*—novels whose wholly European or English settings give little occasion for an occluding exoticism, and so bring out the full force of Conrad's critical powers. He saw it in the crisis of civilization which he witnessed in Europe, and he saw it there in terms of a question whose import he felt with personal intensity and even with guilt—the question of the fate of Poland. A few of his essays suggest his long scrutiny of this problem, but explicitly he rarely, if ever, elucidated it. It remains involved in the complex of his tales, which is what makes it memorable and dynamic. To grasp the larger significance of Conrad's vision of the violence in his age requires a special attention to what the tales contain and convey.

Conrad's temperament, like that of his characteristic heroes, was rooted in an impulse, an impetuosity, that involves the poet, as much as the man of action, in a presumption on the laws of moral responsibility. He was initially, by his emotional disposition—and perhaps inevitably, by the dramatic circumstances of his Polish youth and revolutionary heritage—an idealist whose passions were early set at a pitch of heroic resolution, committed to a struggle that called on the fullest indomitability of will and spirit. The stoic sentiment of contemporary romantics —"Nothing ever happens to the brave"—could never be the principle of such a tradition. The fiery hopes of Polish nationalism and the cause of Poland's freedom had already exacted the fullest share of bravery, suffering, and ignominy from Conrad's people, and from his own family. Yet even here the illusion of Providence was not missing. Conrad's father was a nationalist of Shelleyan tendencies, translator of Vigny's *Chatterton* and Hugo's *Hernani* and *La Légende des Siècles*. In his note to *A Personal Record* Conrad protested that his father should not be called a revolutionist, since "no epithet could be more inapplicable to a man with such a strong sense of responsibility in the region of ideas and action and so indifferent to the promptings of personal ambition," and that he was "simply a patriot in the sense of a man who, believing in the spirituality of a national existence, could not bear to see that spirit enslaved." But Danilowsky, the Polish historian, describes this father as "an honorable but too ardent patriot," who was known to the Tzarist police as an "agitator" and author of the seditious mandate which caused his arrest in October, 1861, his imprisonment in Warsaw, and his subsequent deportation to the Government Vologda for a four-year exile which brought on the death of his wife and eventually his own death as well. Apollo Korzeniowski's own poetry is passionate in its defiance of misfortune:

> May cowards tremble at lofty waves,
> To you they bring good fortune!
> You know the hidden reefs,
> And are familiar with the tempest!

This "Korzeniowski strain," as his wife's relatives called it, with its devotion to Utopian ideals and revolutionary hazards—impulsive, sarcastic, impatient—seems to have served as a warning to the members of the Bobrowski family whose daughter he courted and who considered him "an undesirable pretender." The Bobrowskis, who were, like the Korzeniowskis, of the land-owning gentry and had a brilliant record as soldiers and patriots, were of more conservative, reformist leanings. They were agricultural, closely devoted as a family, and apparently more realistic and cautious by instinct in their attitude toward the nationalist cause than the young poet whom they knew as a "Red" and who, despite his sensitive character and passionate human sympathies, was famed for his recklessness and scurrilous impatience with temporizers. The hazardous conditions of Conrad's youth (he was only five years old when his father was arrested and deported), the unsettled fortunes of the family, and his knowledge of his father's courage, must have fostered his early ambitions about his own career. When he turned away from the

East which he always feared and disliked, since it represented the national enemy Russia as well as those unfathomed conflicts that reflected his own severe doubt of himself, he looked toward the countries that promised a career of greater certainty. He looked toward France, with her marine service and political opportunities, and more particularly, in these earliest years of his travels, toward Spain of the Carlist cause, in whose service he was to take his first great chance, as a gun-runner and agitator. Conrad's celebrations of the hope and illusion of youth, of innocence, of courage and the bravery it supports in the untested nature of the immature man, of the sincerity which blesses this primitive kind of emotion—these are too well known to need rehearsal here or to be doubted as revivals, in his later memory, of the excitement with which he launched himself on life when he left Poland behind in 1874, at the age of seventeen, and boarded the west-bound Vienna express for Venice and Marseilles "as a man might get into a dream."

Once Conrad had embarked on that adventure, however, a rival strain of his inheritance asserted itself. How early we cannot tell, for the documents on this part of his life, from 1873 until the middle eighties, are few. Apparently it did not appear during his first years in Marseilles, when he circulated in the conservative *légitimiste* circle of the banker Delestang and his wife, or during his first two sea-voyages that ensued from this acquaintance—that in 1875 on the *Mont-Blanc* to Martinique and Le Havre, and that in 1876 on the *Saint-Antoine* to St. Pierre, Port-au-Prince, and the Gulf of Mexico. It apparently did not deter him during the romantic episode among the Spanish legitimists of Don Carlos' cause which involved him between October, 1876, and February, 1878, in the exploits of the gun-running tartane *Tremolino*, his love affair with the prototype of Rita de Lastaola, his duel with the American J. M. K. Blunt, and the other escapades (later to be recorded in *The Arrow of Gold*) that caused so much alarm among his relatives in Poland that his guardian uncle, Tadeusz Bobrowski, threatened to stop his allowance and compel him to come home. These experiences terminated in fiasco. Wounded in the duel, Conrad was barely on his legs when his alarmed uncle arrived in Marseilles from Kiev to find his nephew deserted by his Carlist friends, embittered by embarrassment, and ready to throw up all adventurous political schemes in favor of a job on an English coaster, the *Mavis,* carrying coal and linseed-oil cargoes between Lowestoft and Constantinople.

When Conrad arrived in Lowestoft on June 18, 1878, he stepped for the first time on English soil, knowing only as much English as he had picked up on the voyage, practically without money, without acquaintances in England, and, as his biographer tells us, "alone in the world." This is the first of two decisive dates in Conrad's life. Poland, Marseilles, Carlism, and youth were behind him. Poverty and the rigorous routine of a merchant vessel descended on him and fixed his life for the next seventeen years.

What now rose in Conrad's personality was a force more familiar to us in his books than the ecstatic emotion of youth which he often celebrates but which he was able to recapture only in moments of lyrical strain and which, as a consequence, never rings as authentically as the darker emotions which now announced themselves and persisted in his nature to the end of his life. His benevolent uncle Tadeusz began to write him in response to the letters which Conrad was sending back to Poland. Conrad's shift from youth, Poland, and France to the unsparing exactions of sea-life was one great transition in his fortunes. He was to submit to another, of even severer conditions, in 1895, when he threw up the sea and ventured on a career in literature. He did this not with convinced determination, for he tried repeatedly to get a new command even as late as 1900, when his first five books had been published. These breaks or changes have, as we now observe them, the appearance of having been undertaken with a kind of compulsion of inherent vocation, to test his strength and fortitude in the face of a long-delayed creative necessity, but conscious intention as yet played little part in his actions. Troubled, in the early eighties, by the growing melancholy and passionate introspection induced by long sea-watches, by solitary duties, and by the racking boredom which in later life he confessed to be the one sensation he remembered from his sailing days, he found welling up within him symptoms of the tragic inheritance of his race and family. His life had begun in disturbance, danger, and a great ascendant hope. It had become vividly adventurous in France, Spain, and the West Indies. Now, abruptly, it became confined, ruthlessly vigilant, curtailed to the most tyrannous necessities, calculated to the hour and moment by the charts on the captain's table, the needle of the binnacle, and the movements of the stars. His voyages to African coasts, the Americas, and the Malay and China seas brought contrasts of novelty and exotic discovery, but by the time Conrad took his journey to the Congo in 1890, reality had become unconditional. The continent of Africa and his voyage up its coiled, snake-like river figured as his descent into Hell. His journal of the trip still conveys the agony of that palpable damnation. He returned ravaged by the illness and mental disruption which undermined his health for the remaining thirty years of his life.

Between 1891 and 1895 his voyages were broken by intervals spent alone and homeless in London, with only his uncle remaining of his immediate family (and he was to die in 1894) and a distant cousin, the Polish-Belgian novelist Marguerite Poradowska, of Brussels, to serve as his confidante in Western Europe. When Conrad lay ill in London in 1891 he received a letter from his uncle Tadeusz which we may take as an account of his predicament written from the point of view of a specially privileged observer:

My dear boy:

I begin as I always do, but I ought to address you as "my dear pessimist"; for judging from your letters that description would fit you best. I cannot say that I am pleased by your state of mind, or that I am without apprehension about your future.... Thinking over the causes of your melancholy most carefully I cannot attribute it either to youth or to age. In the case of one who is thirty-four and has had as full a life as you have had, I am forced to attribute it to ill-health, to your wretched sufferings on the African adventure, to your illness which resulted from them, and to the fact that you have had lately plenty of time to give yourself up to the habit of reverie which I have observed to be part of your character. It is inherited; it has always been there, in spite of your active life.

I may be mistaken, but I think this tendency to pessimism was already in you as long ago as the days when you were at Marseilles, but it was then part of youth. I am sure that with your melancholy temperament you ought to avoid all meditations, which lead to pessimistic conclusions. I advise you to lead a more active life than ever and to cultivate cheerful habits.

Our country, as Slowacki well says (although he himself was not free from the reproach), is the "pan" of the nations, which, in plain prose, means that we are a nation who consider ourselves great and misunderstood, the possessors of a greatness which others do not recognize and will never recognize. If individuals and nations would set duty before themselves as an aim, instead of grandiose ideals, the world would be a happier place.... Perhaps you will reply that these are the sentiments of one who has always had "a place in the sun." Not at all. I have endured many ups and downs; I have suffered in my private life, in my family life, and as a Pole; and it is thanks to these mortifications that I have arrived at a calm and modest estimate of life and its duties, and that I have taken as my motto "usque ad finem"; as my guide, the love of the duty which circumstances define.

It is not to be argued that Conrad's life explains his art in its fullest dimensions, any more than his "ideas" explain his novels, or that we can use his personal documents and letters as a substitute for that explanation. Indeed, his defensive nature made it unlikely that he should write these documents as such an explanation. The reproofs he expressed to several students of his career indicate that he would have endorsed Eliot's sentence which his own preface to *The Nigger of the "Narcissus"* anticipated: "The more perfect the artist, the more completely separate in him will be the man who suffers and the mind which creates." Conrad was a dramatic genius and an artist in character; his creations are always more than the sum of his conscious motives and critical intelligence. Any comparison of his personal writings with his novels shows that he found his full voice only when writing imaginatively. Only then does he resist the charge made against him by E. M. Forster when he said that "the secret casket of his genius contains a

vapor rather than a jewel." At the same time it is impossible to neglect
the value which the events of Conrad's life and the testimony of his intimate correspondence contribute toward the interpretation of his fiction. At the least, these provide us with a comment on the problem he
dramatized in a language which almost perfectly coincides with the
spirit of his plots and situations. We know, in addition, how strongly he
protested against the purely impersonal order of art that was advocated
by the naturalists; how he considered their novels a perpetuation of the
worst vices of the old convention of arbitrary omniscience in fiction;
how lifeless he found the critical objectivity of his friend Galsworthy;
how he disagreed as vigorously as Yeats did with Stendhal's conception
of art as "un miroir qui se promène sur la grande route." Five of his
narratives were never denied as autobiographies. He said that all his
characters were "at one time or the other known by me." And although
it is inevitable that we can never prove the personal basis of his greater
novels, we cannot read them without sensing the existence of such a
basis, or observing Conrad's repeated hints of such relevance, or noting
how their motives and problems are continuously repeated, expanded,
and explored from one end of his production to the other. The letters
he wrote Mme. Poradowska between 1890 and 1900 reveal that almost
every fundamental problem of his later fiction was sketched or suggested
in that correspondence and applied there with remorseless intimacy not
to fictitious characters but to his own plight and state of mind. They
also reveal that during those critical years of his life, when he was
making a harassed transition from maritime service to the profession of
novelist, he was already groping for the means and courage to translate
these experiences into fictional form, to objectify them dramatically,
and thus to come into an intelligent realization of their meaning which
might save him, as he expresses it, "from the madness which, after a certain point of life is reached, awaits all those who refuse to master their
sensations and bring into coherent form the mysteries of their lives."

Conrad's sense of the crisis of moral isolation and responsibility in
which the individual meets his first full test of character is repeatedly
emphasized in his novels, to a degree which has put a special stamp on
his heroes. His characters are marked by a number of conditions which
have become much more familiar during the past quarter-century than
they were when he began to write, but they had even then been established by serious novelists and dramatists. James and Ibsen, to name
only two, had dramatized the plight of the man or woman upon whom
life closes down inexorably, divesting him or her of the supports and
illusory protection of friendship, social privilege, or love. By throwing
the individual violently out of an accepted relationship with family or
society, these crises suddenly make him aware of a hostile or unknown
world which must be learned anew, conquered or possibly renounced,
before survival is possible. Obviously this order of drama has a classic

ancestry, but the social and psychological analysis of modern times has given it a substance, a complex of practical moral conditions, not always apparent even in Shakespeare. It is this drama of isolation and spiritual recognition which appears in the characteristic novels of Mann, Gide, and Kafka, in Robinson's poems, and in Joyce and Hemingway; it is given social documentation in books like *Manhattan Transfer* and *Studs Lonigan;* it is carried to various extremes of symbolic extension in *Death in Venice, The Trial, Nightwood,* and ultimately in *Finnegans Wake.* Kafka, Miss Barnes, and Joyce have carried the symbolic presentation of the case to lengths of allegory not previously attempted. Joyce, in his epic elaboration of the lives of Bloom and Earwicker, has substanced the problem symbolically on a scale that leaves the normal limits of fictional realism far behind. But I doubt if any of these writers, possibly excepting Kafka, has achieved a more successful *dramatic* version of the problem than Conrad did—a more complete coincidence of the processes of psychic recognition and recovery with the dramatic necessities of the plot; and this for the reason which I believe distinguishes Conrad's contribution to modern fictional method: his imposition of the processes and structures of psychological experience (particularly the experience of recognition) on the form of the plot. Even in James, whose genius also took this direction, the ratiocinative element and structural manipulation of the drama did not permit an equal immersion in "the destructive element" of reality or an equal coincidence of sensibility with form.

The conditions that mark the plight of a Conrad character who is caught in the grip of circumstances that enforce self-discovery and its cognate, the discovery of reality or truth, are remarkably consistent in all his books. The condition of moral isolation is the first of them—the loneliness of Razumov in *Under Western Eyes,* of Heyst in *Victory,* of Flora de Barral in *Chance,* of Lord Jim, and a long series of other outcasts, exiles, or estranged souls—Willems, Lingard, Mrs. Travers, Mrs. Verloc, Peyrol, even men whom age or fame has suddenly bereft of the solid ground of security or confidence: Captain Whalley, Captain MacWhirr, the young captain on his first command in *The Shadow Line,* or Kurtz of *Heart of Darkness* in his last abandonment of soul. The isolation varies in its nature. Willems is alone because he is a banished wastrel who has made life a law to himself; Mr. George is alone because he is young and irresponsible; Lingard and Captain Whalley have accepted stoically their estrangement from the ties of normal life; Jim and Flora feel themselves excommunicated from society by disgrace and by the false confidence or idealism that has betrayed them; Razumov is isolated by an impenetrable mystery of birth and social alienation; Heyst by the disgust, induced by a fatal vein of skepticism in his nature and so tending toward a nihilism of all values, which follows a misplaced trust in his fellow men. In all these more serious cases, isolation tends to become so absolute that it can be bridged again only by some irresistible compulsion that rises out of the psychic and ethical necessities of character. Life demands justification by love or honor, as with Flora and Razumov; it exacts justice from the disillusioned, as with Mrs. Verloc; it demands, in the case of Heyst, the last and absolute testimony of honor which only suicide can give. Conrad leaves no doubt of the extreme to which he pushed this condition. Of Heyst we hear that "Not a single soul belonging to him lived anywhere on earth . . . he was alone on the bank of the stream. In his pride he determined not to enter it." And of Razumov: "He was as lonely in the world as a man swimming in the deep sea. . . . He had nothing. He had not even a moral refuge —the refuge of confidence."

But if isolation is the first condition of these lives, it is never an isolation that brings independence or liberty. Freed by choice from normal human ties and obligations, Conrad's men find themselves in the inescapable presence of conscience.

> Who knows what true loneliness is—not the conventional word, but the naked terror? To the lonely themselves it wears a mask. The most miserable outcast hugs some memory or some illusion. Now and then a fatal conjunction of events may lift the veil for an instant. For an instant only. No human being could bear a steady view of moral solitude without going mad.

"I am being crushed—and I can't even run away," cries Razumov. The solitary may take to debauchery and self-law like Willems: even that does not permit him to escape. He may rise to power and fame like Kurtz: that permits escape least of all. He may believe he has formed a world of his own like Heyst:

> Heyst was not conscious of either friends or enemies. It was the essence of his life to be a solitary achievement, accomplished not by hermit-like withdrawal with its silence and immobility, but by a system of restless wandering, by the detachment of an impermanent dweller amongst changing scenes. In this scheme he had perceived the means of passing through life without suffering and almost without care in the world—invulnerable because elusive!

But the world allows no such independence. "No decent feeling was ever scorned by Heyst" and that fact proves his undoing and finally his moral salvation. These men are all brought to discover what the oldest religious systems of the world have advocated: that the more liberty we have, the less we can use. The man who is alone in the world can never escape, for he is always with himself. Unless he is morally abandoned beyond the point of significance through profligacy or irresponsibility, he lives in the company of a ruthless inquisitor, a watcher who never sleeps, an eternally vigilant judge. A novelist who wishes to explore the full experience of the justice imposed on our faculties by conscience will be bound, like Conrad, to penetrate a world that lies below the appearances of our conscious lives. The explorations made by Conrad in that dimension have progressed, in our time, to the farthest reaches of the unconscious self. Conrad did not advance to those depths, but he pointed the way to them. *Lord Jim, Chance,* and *Under Western Eyes* stand with the most advanced experiments of Melville, Dostoievsky, James, and Joyce in indicating the matter that exists in the unconscious, and even certain of the devices by which it is to be fathomed.

Here it is that we find Conrad's work entering a dimension which is ostensibly psychological and which, for practical purposes, must be made to seem so, but which goes farther. It grapples with the problems of appearance and reality, of bringing into focus the realm of subjective intuition and the realm of social and moral fact, the values of egoism and those of moral necessity. While it treats these in terms of the relativity of appearances and sentiments as Proust exhibited it, it also insists on relating the psychic and moral contradictions of human nature to the ambivalence of reality as art embodies and struggles with it, and finally to the metaphysical condition of values itself. When Conrad enters that dimension fully he leaves his sentimental limitations and prejudices wholly behind and takes his place as one of the genuinely creative imaginations of our time—one who certainly surpasses every other English novelist of his generation.

It is interesting to turn again to Conrad's letters for confirmation of his sense of the crisis which induces the proof of selfhood to which he subjects his heroes. When Conrad passed, around 1895, out of the perfectly controlled and adjusted mechanism of sea-life, with its accurate regimen of human relations and balances, he entered into a freedom which he soon discovered to be no liberation but a prison. For him, in those middle years of the nineties, the self was doubly trapped. He found himself alone not only with his poverty and rigorous self-discipline but with his creative conscience, now struggling to express itself. His dramatizations of the trapped sensibility were preceded by that harrowing period in London in which he decided to face a kind of labor that meant daily and yearly solitude, with no give-and-take of human approval or disagreement, with no one to judge his principles or results but himself, and with a brutal aesthetic judgment— soon divested of the amateur excitement with which he wrote *Almayer's Folly*—ruling his waking and sleeping life. It is small wonder that Conrad, who was to make the trapped man the object of his special study, should have always remembered this period of his life, for it marked the beginning of anxieties and of a discipline that were not to end until his death. We find him recurring to the idea of the convict with an insistence, and with none of the defiance, that marks Rimbaud's salutations to that form of fate in the *Saison en Enfer*. Tormented all his life by the "stérilités des écrivains nerveux" which he shared with Baudelaire, Conrad began the grinding labor of his books. Years later, in 1909, he wrote to Norman Douglas that "there's neither inspiration nor hope in my work. It's mere hard labor for life—with this difference, that the life convict is at any rate out of harm's way—and may consider the account with his conscience closed; and this is not the case with me. I envy the serene fate and the comparative honesty of the gentlemen in gray who live in Dartmoor. I do really. I am not half as decent or half as useful." But earlier, in the nineties, he was already acknowledging that fate to his "cousin" in Brussels, Mme. Poradowska:

> I am not so happy to be working as you seem to think. There is nothing very exhilarating in doing disagreeable work. It is too much like penal servitude, with the difference that while rolling the stone of Sisyphus you lack the consolation of thinking of what pleasure you had in committing the crime. It is here that convicts have the advantage over your humble servant.

Again:

> I astonish and perhaps scandalize you by my joking about criminals, while you think me capable of accepting or even admitting the doctrine (or theory) of expiation through suffering ... there is no expiation. Each act of life is final and inevitably produces its consequences in spite of all the weeping and gnashing of teeth and the sorrow of weak souls who suffer as fright grips them when confronted with the results of their own actions. As for myself, I shall never need to be consoled for any act of my life, and this because I am strong enough to judge my conscience rather than be its slave, as the orthodox would like to persuade us to be.

And again:

> Remember, though, that one is never entirely alone. Why are you afraid? And of what? Is it of solitude or of death? O strange fear! The only two things that make life bearable! But cast fear aside. Solitude never comes—and death must often be waited for during long years of bitterness and anger. Do you prefer that?
> But you are afraid of yourself; of the inseparable being forever at your side—master and slave, victim and executioner—who suffers and causes suffering. That's how it is! One must drag the ball and chain of one's selfhood to the end. It is the price one pays for the devilish and divine privilege of thought; so that in this life it is only the elect who are convicts—a glorious band which comprehends and groans but which treads the earth amidst a multitude of phantoms with maniacal gestures, with idiotic grimaces. Which would you be: idiot or convict?

The *alter ego* of the conscience was an inevitable corollary—as Conrad here indicates—of his conception of inescapable selfhood. The *Doppelgänger* becomes part of the drama of character and self-determination. When Jim delivers his long monologues to Marlow; when Flora bares her soul to Marlow, Mrs. Fyne, or Captain Anthony; when Razumov writes his passionate entries in his diary and disburdens his soul to the old language-teacher and finally to Natalia Haldin herself; when Decoud or Gould ruminate their secret histories, these people are really carrying out the drama of their divided natures, objectifying under the compulsion which psychoanalysts have seized upon as therapeutic necessity their souls' dilemmas and thus saving themselves from madness. But the divided man—the face and its mask, the soul and its shadow—figures even more concretely than this in Conrad's dramatic method (though rumination and monologue were usually his own means of giving genuine substance to his realism). The rival character—sometimes a villain, sometimes a friend or lover, sometimes a fellow-fugitive like the "secret sharer" in the story of that name—serves the hero as a transferred embodiment of his other self.

Thus love, or the sense of honor, or the obligation of duty, or even the social instinct itself, enters the novels as a means by which the individual is lifted out of his isolation and morbid surrender. The inward-driving, center-fathoming obsession of the tale becomes reversed and takes a centrifugal direction toward external standards of value. It is finally the world which saves us—the world of human necessities and duty. It may be the world of a ship and its crew, as in *The Shadow Line;* it may be the world of an island and a single fellow-soul, as in *Victory;* it may be that wider world of social and political relationships which Conrad seldom explored fully but which he did build in solid form in *Nostromo, Chance,* and *Suspense.* In one of the most perfect of Conrad's tales, "The Secret Sharer," the allegory of the *alter ego* is beautifully achieved within the narrowest possible limits; in one of the finest of his novels, *Under Western Eyes,* the conception is made to embody the whole complex of Russian history: "The Secret Sharer," as Miss M. C. Bradbrook has recently pointed out, is the microcosm of the basic concept in Conrad's fiction. Leggatt, the swimmer, has committed murder and so, by a moment's blind action, has ruined his life. He escapes, but finds refuge naked under cover of night on a strange ship—"a fugitive and a vagabond on the earth, with no brand of the curse on his sane forehead to stay a slaying hand." The captain hides him in his cabin, learns his guilt, and thus becomes allied to that guilt, the refugee's secret becoming an embodiment of the captain's own secret life. The hidden self of the captain is "exactly the same" as that of the murderer, who is of necessity concealed from the world, who is dressed in a sleeping suit, the garb of the unconscious life, and who appears out of and again disappears into the sea under cover of darkness. But before he disappears at last, the captain has come to know the secret soul he lives with; his life is changed; and a new vision of humanity has broken in upon the impersonal regimen of his days. From this germinal presentation of the case, Conrad widened his drama of the individual soul until, in his most ambitious book, it came to include the larger workings of the moral law, of society and politics, and even of nations and races.

To trace fully the drama of recognition and conscience as Conrad presents it in his novels would require an analysis which cannot be given here; but until that drama is defined, neither Conrad's qualities nor his defects can be fully appreciated. The growth in his thought from an idealistic conception of life to a critical one, from his original romanticism to his later realism of values, is the pattern of his genius in its slow emergence, its self-discipline, and its eventual creative triumphs. That growth is most perfectly indicated in his three most characteristic books—*Lord Jim, Chance,* and *Under Western Eyes* (the latter of which I would almost agree with Ford Madox Ford in calling his masterpiece). But it is extended to more sheerly creative feasts of dramatization in three other books: *The Secret Agent,* his highest achievement in tragic irony, *Nostromo,* his most elaborate historical and political canvas, and *Victory,* his most concentrated dramatic narrative. The romantic element is never effaced in his work. It persists as the basis of his popularity and of those excesses of style and treatment which show in his often extravagant phraseology, in his treatment of women, in his sentimentalization of the heroic and the miraculous in human fortunes and character, in his exotic and rhetorical effects, and in the curious naïveté of fatalism which reappears in his last three books. Yet it must be noted that this inherent romanticism is a component of Conrad's kind of imagination and of his growth in moral and imaginative powers. He referred to it late in life in a passage written in defense of his work:

> The romantic feeling of reality was in me an inborn faculty. This in itself may be a curse, but when disciplined by a sense of personal responsibility and a recognition of the hard facts of existence shared with the rest of mankind becomes but a point of view from which the very shadows of life appear endowed with an internal glow. And such romanticism is not a sin. It is none the worse for the knowledge of truth. It only tries to make the best of it, hard as it may be; and in this hardness discovers a certain aspect of beauty.

His success arrives when responsibility and discipline oppose the self-indulgence which a romantic attitude toward life encouraged in his early emotions and sensibility. When these correctives make themselves felt in his pages, they provide the rigor of style and conception which stiffens and gives structure to the natural extravagance of his feelings, his impulsiveness or arrogance of sentiment, and the untested enthusiasm of his responses to scene, character and adventure. Conrad's development as an artist reproduces, on the scale of his whole career as an artist over thirty years, the ordeal of self-mastery and spiritual exoneration which he dramatized repeatedly in the lives of his heroes. "All a man can betray is his conscience," said Conrad in *Under Western Eyes*. The measure of his character and his artistry may be taken by the fact that neither his sense of honor nor his sense of realism permitted him to betray the conscience which it took him half his life to discover in himself, and the other half of his life to prove and vindicate in his books.

F. SCOTT FITZGERALD
THE POET OF BORROWED TIME *
ARTHUR MIZENER

THE COMMONPLACE about Scott Fitzgerald is that he was "the laureate of the Jazz Age." If this means anything, it means that he was a kind of eulogistic fictional historian of the half dozen years following the first World War when there was such a marked change in American manners. In fact, however, Fitzgerald never simply reported experience; every one of his books is an attempt to recreate experience imaginatively. It is true that the objects, the people, the events, and the convictions in terms of which his imagination functioned were profoundly American and of his time. Even in his worst book, as John O'Hara once remarked, "the people were right, the talk was right, the clothes, the cars were real." The substance out of which Fitzgerald constructed his stories, that is to say, was American, perhaps more completely American than that of any other writer of his time. It is possible, therefore, to read his books simply for their sensitive record of his time; but there is a great deal more to them than this.

Fitzgerald's great accomplishment is to have realized in completely American terms the developed romantic attitude, in the end at least in that most responsible form in which all the romantic's sensuous and emotional responses are disciplined by his awareness of the goodness and evilness of human experience. He had a kind of instinct for the tragic view of life and remarked himself how even at the very beginning of his career, "all the stories that came into my head had a touch of disaster in them—the lovely young creatures in my novels went to ruin, the diamond mountains of my short stories blew up, my millionaires were as beautiful and damned as Thomas Hardy's peasants." He had, moreover, with all its weakness and strength and in a time when the undivided understanding was very rare, an almost exclusively creative kind of intelligence, the kind that understands things, not abstractly, but only concretely, in terms of people and situations and events.

* "F. Scott Fitzgerald: The Poet of Borrowed Time" first appeared in a slightly different form in the *Sewanee Review,* Winter, 1946. It was later included in *The Lives of Eighteen from Princeton,* edited by Willard Thorp (Princeton University Press, 1946), from which the present version is taken. Certain sections form parts of Mr. Mizener's biography of Fitzgerald, *The Far Side of Paradise* (Houghton Mifflin Company, 1951). The essay is used here by permission of the author, Princeton University Press, and Houghton Mifflin Company.

From the very beginning he showed facility and that minute aware-ness of the qualities of times and places and persons which is sharpened to a fine point in the romantic writer by his acute consciousness of the irrevocable passage of everything into the past. "He was haunted," as Malcolm Cowley has said, "by time, as if he wrote in a room full of clocks and calendars." A romantic writer of this kind is bound to take as his characteristic subject his own past, building out of the people and places of his time fables of his own inner experience, working his way into his material by identifying himself with others as Fitzgerald, in a characteristic case, made the doctor in "Family in the Wind" an image of what he saw in himself, a talented man who had achieved great early success and then gone to pieces. As a young man he iden-tified himself imaginatively with his beautiful but less clever sister and practically lived her early social career; in middle age he entered so completely into his daughter's career that, as one of his friends re-marked, "Scott, not Scottie, went through Vassar." Thus, always, Fitz-gerald lived imaginatively the lives of those with whom, through family affection or some obscure similarity of attitude or experience, he was able to identify himself.

At its best the attitude Fitzgerald possessed produces an effect which is compounded of three clearly definable elements. There is in his mature work an almost historical objectivity, produced by his acute sense of the pastness of the past; there is also a Proustian minuteness of recollection of the feelings and attitudes which made up the experience as it was lived; and there is, finally, cast over both the historically apprehended event and the personal recollection embedded in it, a glow of pathos, the pathos of the irretrievableness of a part of oneself. "Taking things hard—" he wrote in his notebooks, "from ——— to ———: that's [the] stamp that goes into my books so that people can read it blind like braill[e]." The first of these references is to the first girl Fitzgerald was ever deeply in love with; he used his recollection of her over and over again (out of that recollection, for example, he made Josephine, who dominates a whole series of stories in *Taps at Reveille*). The second reference is to the producer who hacked to pieces his finest script. The remark thus covers the whole of Fitzgerald's career.

What develops slowly in a writer of this kind is maturity of judg-ment, for it is not easy to control what is so powerfully felt initially and is never, even in recollection, tranquil. Fitzgerald was three-fifths of the way through his career as novelist, though only five years from its start, before he produced a book in which the purpose and the form it imposes are adequate to the evoked life. With *The Great Gatsby* the "smoldering hatred" of the imaginative obtuseness, the moral vulgar-ity, and the sheer brutality of the rich—with its tangled roots in Fitz-gerald's puritanical Catholic background, in his middle-class, middle-western upbringing, and in his early poverty—had emerged enough to serve as a dramatic balance for the wonderful freedom and beauty which the life of the rich had for him. "Let me tell you about the very rich," he began in one of his finest stories; and with the establishment of this dramatically balanced view of the rich in *The Great Gatsby* he had found his theme and its fable, for wealth was Fitzgerald's central symbol; around it he eventually built a mythology which enabled him to take imaginative possession of American life.

With this view of his material he could at last give expression to his essentially tragic sense of human experience without forcing that feeling on the material so that it ceased to be probable, as it does in *The Beautiful and Damned* where the characters drift without understanding into disaster and our conviction of their suffering is undermined by the inadequacy of its causes.* Until he wrote *The Great Gatsby* Fitzgerald's ability to evoke the nightmare terror of disaster was greater than his ability to motivate the disaster. It is different at the moment in *The Great Gatsby* when we are confronted with Daisy's completely prepared betrayal, seeing her sitting with Tom at the kitchen table over a late supper with "an unmistakable air of natural intimacy," and then find Gatsby watching the house from the driveway, imagining that he is guarding Daisy from Tom. "I walked away," says Nick, "and left him standing there in the moonlight—watching over nothing." Here Fitzgerald's view of his material is completely adequate to his feeling about human experience in general, the life of the people he knows has become the fully rounded particular case for the expression of his whole understanding.

Both his admiration for the wonderful possibilities of the life of the rich and his distrust of it probably go back to Fitzgerald's childhood. He was born in St. Paul on September 24, 1896. Very early in his life he began to weave fantasies around the Hill Mansion, only a few blocks but a good many million dollars away from his home on Summit Avenue; and it was certainly Fitzgerald at Newman as well as Basil Lee at St. Regis who "writhed with shame . . . that . . . he was one of the poorest boys in a rich boys' school." But he was proud, too, of his family, which was not rich, particularly of the Francis Scott Key connection, and included his family among what he once called "the few remnants of the old American aristocracy that's managed to survive in communicable form." The Basil Lee stories, with their wonderful recreation of the emotional tensions and social conflicts of middle-class American childhood and youth, give a reasonably accurate impression of the life he lived as a boy and for two years at Newman.

In the fall of 1913 he went to Princeton, full of an intensified but otherwise normal American boy's ambition to succeed. There he plunged with characteristic energy and passion into the race for social

---

* The same weakness is evident in *This Side of Paradise* where the image of evil is presented in the trite and mechanical figure of a ghost.

prominence. But for all that he wore the right clothes, had the right manners, belonged to one of the best clubs, and was an important figure in the politically powerful Triangle Club, he neither was nor appeared to be a typical Princeton man. Of the highly competitive, socially subtle, ingrown life of Princeton he made for himself, with his gift for romance, an enormously significant world. The very imaginative intensity with which he took the normal preoccupations of a Princeton undergraduate distinguished him radically from his fellows. There was something unusual, almost flamboyant, even about his looks, which set him apart. Twenty-five years later that oddness of appearance was still before Edmund Wilson's eyes when he remembered their first meeting:

> I climbed, a quarter-century and more
> Played out, the college steps, unlatched my door,
> And, creature strange to college, found you there!
> The pale skin, hard green eyes, and yellow hair.

You can still see something of "the glitter of the hard and emerald eyes" in his pictures and, perhaps too, feel in Fitzgerald's personal history something of what Wilson meant by this figure.

Fitzgerald quickly discovered that Cottage Club was not quite the brilliant society he had dreamed of and presently turned to literature. "I want," he said to Wilson at this time, "to be one of the greatest writers who have ever lived, don't you?" But all this extracurricular activity—in addition to his social career and his writing there were the Triangle Club and a debutante in Chicago—was too much for his health and his academic standing. In November of his junior year he was forced to retire to St. Paul. He returned in 1916 to repeat this year, but his senior year lasted only a couple of months, for he left Princeton in November to join the army.

Before he left he completed the first of three versions of *This Side of Paradise*. This version appears to have contained almost nothing of what is in the final version except the early scenes of Amory's arrival at Princeton, and one of the few people who saw it has remarked that "it was actually flat, something Scott's work almost never was." One of the worst disappointments of his life was that he never got overseas but ended his military career as what he once called "the worst aide-de-camp in the army" to General A. J. Ryan at Camp Sheridan, near Montgomery, Alabama. Here he met and fell in love with Zelda Sayre, and here too, in the officers' club in the evenings, he rewrote his novel and submitted it to a publisher under the title *The Romantic Egotist*. This is the subtitle of Book I of *This Side of Paradise,* which presumably covers about the same ground. *The Romantic Egotist* was rejected.

When he was discharged in February 1919, Fitzgerald came to New York to make his fortune so that he could marry Zelda. He sold one story to *The Smart Set* for $30; for the rest he collected rejection slips and began to realize that he was not going to make a fortune as a copy-writer at $90 a month. So did Zelda, and sometime late in the spring she decided that the whole thing had been a mistake. At this Fitzgerald threw up his job, got drunk, and went back to St. Paul to write his book once more. By the end of the summer it had become *This Side of Paradise* and in the fall Scribner's accepted it. Fitzgerald hurried off to Montgomery and Zelda. The nightmare of unhappiness was over, but he never forgot it: "The man with the jingle of money in his pocket who married the girl a year later would always cherish an abiding distrust, an animosity, toward the leisure class—not the conviction of a revolutionary but the smoldering hatred of a peasant. In the years since then I have never been able to stop wondering where my friends' money came from, nor to stop thinking that at one time a sort of *droit de seigneur* might have been exercised to give one of them my girl."

II

This Side of Paradise is in many ways a very bad book. Edmund Wilson's judgment of it, made at the height of its fame, is perfectly just: "Amory Blaine is an uncertain quantity in a phantasmagoria of incident which has no dominating intention to endow it with unity and force. . . . For another thing, it is very immaturely imagined: it is always just verging on the ludicrous. And, finally, it is one of the most illiterate books of any merit ever published. . . . It is not only ornamented with bogus ideas and faked references but it is full of English words misused with the most reckless abandon."

These charges could be documented at length, and some of them were; F. P. A. devoted a number of columns to the misspellings, and the energy with which Francis Newman supported the further charge that the book was imitated in detail from Mackenzie's *Sinister Street* stung Fitzgerald to reply. Nevertheless it is obviously true that the general idea and structure of *This Side of Paradise* were suggested by *Sinister Street* and that Fitzgerald had little realization of the importance for this episodic kind of book of unity of tone. The lack of unity of tone in the book is partly due to its being made up of stories written, over a considerable period of time, before the novel was contemplated. One of the reviewers called the novel "the collected works of Mr. Scott Fitzgerald" and Fitzgerald himself once remarked, speaking of his editorship of the *Nassau Lit:* "I wrote stories about current prom girls, stories that were later incorporated into a novel."

The quality which Mr. Wilson ascribes to the book's being immaturely imagined displays itself most in the latter part and especially in the accounts of Amory's love affairs. Fitzgerald's lovers conduct their affairs by making speeches at each other, full of sentiment from Swinburne and of sweeping generalizations about "Life"; as lovers they show all the hypnotized egocentricity and intellectual immaturity of college freshmen. There is a sentence in *The Beautiful and Damned,* where Fitzgerald is describing the novels of Richard Carmel, which is an unintentionally eloquent comment on his own resources at this time. "There was," he says of Richard's novels, "a measure of vitality and a sort of instinctive technic [*sic*] in all of them."

Yet for all these faults the book is not essentially a bad one. There is in the writing something of the intensity of felt experience which is in the language of Fitzgerald's mature books. This is especially true of the first part, for the experience of Princeton life on which this part of the book was based was far enough behind Fitzgerald to have been to some extent emotionally distanced and evaluated. But even in the latter part of the book, beneath all the author's naïve earnestness about the romantic cynicism and "philosophizing" of Amory and Rosalind and Eleanor, you feel something of the real suffering of unhappiness. Fitzgerald's judgment and technique are inadequate almost everywhere in the book, but the fundamental, almost instinctive attitude toward experience which emerges, even at times through the worst of the book's surface, is serious and moving. Sixteen years later Fitzgerald himself, still remembering Edmund Wilson's remark, said of it: "A lot of people thought it was a fake, and perhaps it was, and a lot of others thought it was a lie, which it was not."

This Side of Paradise was an enormous success, and Fitzgerald, in a way very characteristic of him, responded to success with a naïve, pompous, and fundamentally good-humored vanity. He gave interviews in which he told what a great writer he was; he condoled with Heywood Broun over the latter's lost youth (Broun was thirty); he condescended to his elders and betters. He and Zelda were married in April and plunged happily into the gay and strenuous life of New York. Fitzgerald rode down Fifth Avenue on top of a taxi, dove into the Plaza fountain, and in general displayed his exuberance in the ways which were fashionable in 1920. He also worked all night again and again to pay for the fun and "riding in a taxi one afternoon between very tall buildings under a mauve and rosy sky ... I began to bawl because I had everything I wanted and knew I would never be so happy again."

For a brief period of three years following the publication of *This Side of Paradise* the Fitzgeralds were figures around New York and their house parties at Westport and Great Neck were famous. It was all very gay and light-hearted; the house guests at Great Neck were advised in a set of Rules for Guests at the Fitzgerald House that "Visitors are requested not to break down doors in search of liquor, even when authorized to do so by the host and hostess" and that "invitations to stay over Monday, issued by the host and hostess during the small hours of Sunday morning, must not be taken seriously." There was a trip to Europe in the summer of 1921 and that winter they went to St. Paul for the birth of their only child. ("It was typical of our precarious position in New York," Fitzgerald wrote later, "that when our child was to be born we played safe and went home to St. Paul.") In 1922 there was another novel, *The Beautiful and Damned,* and a second volume of stories, and in 1923 a play, *The Vegetable,* written with the rosiest expectations of profits, for they were, as usual, out of money. But the play flopped dismally in Atlantic City, and there was no attempt to bring it to New York. In 1924, in order to live more cheaply, they went abroad.

The Beautiful and Damned is an enormous improvement on *This Side of Paradise,* more than anything else because Fitzgerald, though he has not yet found out how to motivate disaster, has a much clearer sense of the precise feel of the disaster he senses in the life he knows. The book is also a great advance on its predecessor technically, much more unified, much less mixed in tone. The tendency to substitute lectures for dialogue is subdued, though as if to compensate for this restraint Fitzgerald lets himself go in a scene where Maury Noble produces an harangue which, as *The Dial's* reviewer remarked, sounds "like a *résumé* of *The Education of Henry Adams* filtered through a particularly thick page of *The Smart Set.*" The tone, too, is more evenly sustained, though Fitzgerald is still tempted by scenes in play form and once allows himself an embarrassing Shavian scene between Beauty and The Voice. There is still the curious shocked immaturity about sex. Fitzgerald obviously feels that Anthony's prep-school philandering with Geraldine is daring, and his lovers, pushing about menus on which they have written "you know I do" and describing each other as "sort of blowy clean," are childish.

Nevertheless, *The Beautiful and Damned* is much more successfully focused on a central purpose than *This Side of Paradise,* and much less often bathetic in its means. Of this central purpose Edmund Wilson wrote rather unsympathetically: "since his advent into the literary world [Fitzgerald] has discovered that there is another genre in favor: the kind which makes much of the tragedy and 'meaninglessness of life.' Hitherto, he had supposed that the thing to do was to discover a meaning in life; but he now set bravely about to produce a sufficiently desolating tragedy which should be, also, 100 percent meaningless." But the sense of tragedy is very real with Fitzgerald and his ability to realize the minutiae of humiliation and suffering seldom fails him. His difficulty is in finding a cause for this suffering sufficient to justify the importance he asks us to give it and characters of sufficient dignity to make their suffering and defeat tragic rather than merely pathetic.

Nor is it quite true that Fitzgerald did not try to give the disaster a motive and meaning. There is a fairly consistent effort to make Anthony the sensitive and intelligent man who, driven into a difficult place by his refusal to compromise with a brutal and stupid world, finds his weaknesses too strong for him. He is tempted to cowardice and drifting by his own imagination and sensitiveness; he cannot blame and fight others because of "that old quality of understanding too well to blame—that quality which was the best of him and had worked swiftly and ceaselessly toward his ruin." Over against him Fitzgerald sets Richard Carmel, too stupid to know he is compromising or that the success he has won by compromising is not worth having, and Maury Noble, cynical enough to surrender to compromise even though he knows the worthlessness of what he gets.

The trouble is that Anthony is not real as the sensitive and intelligent man; what is real is the Anthony who is weak, drifting, and full of self-pity. The Anthony who drifts into the affair with Dot under the momentary stimulus of his romantic imagination, knowing perfectly well that he does not believe in the thing; the Anthony who is continually drunk because only thus can he sustain "the old illusion that truth and beauty [are] in some way intertwined"; the partly intolerable, partly absurd, partly pathetic Anthony who seeks again and again to sustain his now fantastic vision of his own dignity and honor; this Anthony is marvelously realized. But the thing that would justify this pathos, the conviction that here is a man more sinned against than sinning, is wholly lacking. *The Beautiful and Damned* is full of precisely observed life and Fitzgerald is often able to make us feel the poignancy of his characters' suffering, but he is able to provide neither an adequate cause for their suffering nor an adequate reason within their characters for their surrender. In the end you do not believe they ever were people who wanted the opportunities for fineness that the freedom of wealth provides; you believe them only people who wanted luxury. They are pitiful, and their pathos is often brilliantly realized; but they are not tragic.

With occasional interruptions, the Fitzgeralds remained abroad from 1924 until the autumn of 1931, traveling a good deal and living in a great many hotels but usually returning for the summer to the Cap d'Antibes. They came back to America in 1927, went to California for a while, and then rented a big old house on the Delaware "to bring us a judicious tranquility." But they were soon back in Europe where they remained, except for a short trip in 1929, until their final return. Fitzgerald later described the period quite simply as "seven years of waste and tragedy," but at the time their life, particularly the summers on the Riviera, seemed the life of freedom and culture and charm. The little group which made the summer Riviera its private style for a few years before everyone else began to come there was brilliant and varied. There were the rich and cultivated like the Gerald Murphys, the writers like Charles MacArthur and Alexander Woollcott, and the musicians like Grace Moore. They led a busy, unconventional, and, as it seemed to them, somehow significant life; "whatever happened," Fitzgerald wrote later, "seemed to have something to do with art." They made private movies about such characters as "Princess Alluria, the wickedest woman in Europe," writing the unprintable subtitles on the pink walls of Grace Moore's villa and deliberately forgetting to erase them after they had been photographed; they kidnaped orchestras to play for them all night; they gave high-comedy dinners; and they drank a great deal.

But all the time Fitzgerald's almost animal sensitivity to potential disaster was at work: "By 1927, a wide-spread neurosis began to be evident, faintly signalled like a nervous beating of the feet, by the popularity of cross-word puzzles. I remember a fellow expatriate opening a letter from a mutual friend of ours, urging him to come home and be revitalized by the hardy, bracing qualities of the native soil. It was a strong letter and it affected us both deeply, until we noticed that it was headed from a nerve sanitorium in Pennsylvania." Looking back at the period afterwards he could see its weaknesses clearly without forgetting its charm. "It was borrowed time anyhow—the whole upper tenth of a nation living with the insouciance of grand ducs and the casualness of chorus girls. But moralizing is easy now and it was pleasant to be in one's twenties in such a certain and unworried time."

It was a period during which Fitzgerald produced very little serious work. *The Great Gatsby* was written during the fall and winter of 1924 and he published no other novel until *Tender Is the Night,* ten years later. This was not, however, wholly the fault of the kind of life he and Zelda were living, even indirectly; it was partly the result of the extremely ambitious plans Fitzgerald laid for himself after *The Great Gatsby's* critical success.

III

The Great Gatsby was another leap forward for Fitzgerald. He had found a situation which would allow him to exploit without loss of probability much more of his feeling about his material, and he had arrived at the point where he understood the advantage of realizing his subject dramatically. He had been reading Conrad and as a result adopted the modified first-person form which suited his purpose so well. For Fitzgerald needed a form which would at once allow him to color the scene with the feelings of an observer and yet hold the feelings within some determined limits. In earlier stories he had splashed whatever colors he wished over the scene without much regard for the structure as a whole or for the disruptive effect on the dramatic representation of the constant interference of the author's own person. But here, as later in *The Last Tycoon,* he selected a narrator sufficiently near the center of things to know all he needed to know, tied into the action by the affair with Jordan Baker which is, though muted, carefully made parallel to the affair between Gatsby and Daisy. By means of this narrator he was able to focus his story, the story of a poor boy from the Middle West who, in the social confusion of the first World War, met and fell in love with a rich girl. Daisy marries while he is in France, but he never ceases to dream of making enough money to be "worthy" of her, taking her from her husband, Tom Buchanan, and starting their life again exactly where it had stopped when he had gone to France. He therefore devotes himself to making money in whatever way he can, not because he wants money, but because he wants his dream of a life with Daisy.

Nick Carraway, the narrator, is equally carefully placed so far as his attitude is concerned. He has come East to be an Easterner and rich, but his moral roots remain in the West. In the most delicate way Fitzgerald builds up these grounds for his final judgment of the story and its people. In the book's first scene, Nick's humorous awareness of the greater sophistication of these people is marked: " 'You make me feel uncivilized, Daisy,' I confessed. . . . 'Can't you talk about crops or something?' " But only a moment later, when Daisy has confessed her unhappiness with Tom, he has an uneasy sense of what is really involved: "The instant her voice broke off, ceasing to compel my attention, my belief, I felt the basic insincerity of what she had said. . . . I waited, and sure enough, in a moment she looked at me with an absolute smirk on her lovely face, as if she had asserted her membership in a rather distinguished secret society to which she and Tom belonged."

Nick's father has told him that "Whenever you feel like criticizing anyone just remember that all the people in this world haven't had the advantages you've had." Nick does not forget; when, at the end of the book, he meets Tom, "I couldn't forgive him or like him, but I saw that what he had done was, to him, entirely justified. . . . I shook hands with him; it seemed silly not to, for I felt suddenly as though I were talking to a child. Then he went into the jewelry store to buy a pearl necklace— or perhaps only a pair of cuff buttons—rid of my provincial squeamishness forever."

Nick goes back to the West, to the country he remembered from the Christmas vacations of his childhood, to "the thrilling returning trains of my youth, and the street lamps and sleigh bells in the frosty dark and the shadows of holly wreaths thrown by lighted windows on the snow. I am part of that, a little solemn with the feeling of those long winters, a little complacent from growing up in the Carraway house in a city where dwellings are still called through decades by a family name." The East remains for him "a night scene from El Greco" in which "in the foreground four solemn men in dress suits are walking along the sidewalk with a stretcher on which lies a drunken woman in a white evening dress. Her hand, which dangles over the side, sparkles cold with jewels. Gravely the men turn in at a house—the wrong house. But no one knows the woman's name, and no one cares."

Thus, though Fitzgerald would be the last to have reasoned it out in such terms, *The Great Gatsby* becomes a kind of tragic pastoral, with the East the exemplar of urban sophistication and culture and corruption, and the West, "the bored, sprawling, swollen towns beyond the Ohio," the exemplar of simple virtue. This contrast is summed up in the book's title. In so far as Gatsby represents the simple virtue which Fitzgerald associates with the West, he is really a great man; in so far as he achieves the kind of notoriety which the East accords success of his kind, he is great about as Barnum was. Out of Gatsby's ignorance of his real greatness and his misunderstanding of his notoriety, Fitzgerald gets much of the book's irony. These terms, then, provided the occasions for all Fitzgerald's feelings, so that he was able to say everything he had to say within the terms of a single figure and to give his book the kind of focus and freedom which comes only from successful formal order.

His hero, Gatsby, is frankly romantic, a romantic, like Fitzgerald, from the West, who has missed the girl on whom he has focused all his "heightened sensitivity to the promises of life" because he had no money. He gets it, by all sorts of corrupt means, and comes back five years later to find Daisy and to fulfill "his incorruptible dream." "I wouldn't ask too much of her," Nick says to him once, "you can't repeat the past." " 'Can't repeat the past?' he cried incredulously. 'Why of course you can!' " But he could not repeat the past with Daisy, changed by her momentary passion for Tom at the time of their marriage and corrupted all her life by her dependence on the protection of wealth and the conventions of the wealthy life which have preserved and heightened her beauty, until in the end she lets Gatsby die for the murder she has committed. He dies waiting for a telephone message from Daisy, and Nick observes: "I have an idea that Gatsby himself didn't believe it would come, and perhaps he no longer cared. If that was true he must have felt that he had lost the old warm world, paid a high price for living too long with a single dream. He must have looked up at . . . a new world, material without being real, where poor ghosts, breathing dreams like air, drifted fortuitously about."

Against Nick's gradual understanding of the incorruptibility at the heart of Gatsby's corruption, Fitzgerald sets his gradual penetration of the charm and grace of Tom and Daisy's world. What he penetrates to is corruption, grossness, and cowardice. In contrast to the charm and grace of this world, Gatsby's fantastic mansion, his absurd pink suits, "his elaborate formality of speech [which] just missed being absurd" appear ludicrous; against the corruption which underlies this grace, Gatsby's essential moral incorruptibility is heroic. To the representation of this double contrast Fitzgerald brings all his now mature powers of observation, of invention, of creating for the scenes and persons the quality and tone the story requires. Because of the formal perfection of *The Great Gatsby*, this eloquence is given a concentration and intensity Fitzgerald never achieved again. The art of the book, in the narrow sense, is nearly perfect. Its limitation is the limitation of Fitzgerald's nearly complete commitment to Gatsby's romanticism. This commitment is partly concealed by Gatsby's superficial social insufficiency, and our awareness of this insufficiency is strengthened as much as Fitzgerald dares strengthen it by Nick's constant, ironic observation of it: Gatsby is, as a cultured "Oggsford man," after all a fake. But this is a romantic irony which touches only the surface; it does not cut to the heart of the matter, to the possibility that there may be some fundamental moral inadequacy in Gatsby's attitude. The world of Daisy and Tom which is set over against Gatsby's dream of a world is beautiful and appealing but in no sense justified: Tom's muddled attempts to offer a reasoned defense for it are only a proof that it is indefensible. Fitzgerald's book is a *Troilus and Cressida* with an Ajax but no Ulysses.

IV

After *The Great Gatsby* Fitzgerald set himself a task which, as Edmund Wilson once remarked, would have given Dostoevski pause. It was to be a story of matricide, and though an immense amount of work was done on it, he was never able to complete a novel on this subject. As if to mock his failure, and perhaps too his deep concern for the subject, Fitzgerald wrote a comic ballad about matricide which he used to perform with great effect as a parlor trick.

In 1930 Zelda, who had been working for several years with all her energy to become a ballet dancer, broke down, and late in 1931 the Fitzgeralds returned to America and settled in a rambling old brown house at Rodgers Forge, between Baltimore and Towson. Here they remained until Fitzgerald went to Hollywood in 1937. Meanwhile Fitzgerald had been struggling with *Tender Is the Night;* he managed, by a furious effort in the latter part of 1933, to get it into shape for publication in *Scribner's* in 1934; he revised it considerably again before book publication, and there is in existence a copy of the book with further revisions in which Fitzgerald has written: "This is the *final version* of the book as I would like it."

Much of this revision appears to have been the result of his having felt his theme everywhere in his material without always seeing a way to draw these various aspects of it together in a single whole. The war, the ducal perversion and ingrown virginity of the Chicago aristocracy which the Warrens represent—stronger and so more terrible than the corruption of the English Campions and Lady Sibley-Bierses; the hardness and lack of moral imagination of the rich in general, the anarchic nihilism represented by Tommy Barban, the self-indulgence of Abe North, destroyed, beyond even an awareness of his own destruction, as Dick will be destroyed; all these forces are beautifully realized. But, though their general bearing on the situation is clear enough, their exact incidence and precise relation to each other sometimes is not.

The result is that *Tender Is the Night,* though the most profoundly moving of all Fitzgerald's novels, is a structurally imperfect book. To this difficulty must be added the fact that its central theme is not an easy one. We believe overwhelmingly in the collapse of Dick Diver's morale because we are made to see and hear, in the most minute and subtly shaded detail, the process of that collapse. It is very like the collapse of Fitzgerald's own morale as he describes it in "The Crack-Up." But it is not easy to say in either case what, in the immediate and practical sense, happens to cause the collapse. As do many romantics with their horror of time and age, Fitzgerald tended to think of spiritual resources—of courage and generosity and kindness—as he thought of physical resources, as a sum in the bank against which a man draws. When, in his own life, he realized "with finality that in some regard [he would] never be as good a man again"; when he began to feel that "every act of life from the morning tooth-brush to the friend at dinner had become an effort . . . that my casual relations—with an editor, a tobacco seller, the child of a friend, were only what I remembered I *should* do, from other days"; then he knew the sum in the bank was nearly exhausted and that there was nothing to do but to reduce his scale of living accordingly. "In a really dark night of the soul," he wrote in "The Crack-Up," "it is always three o'clock in the morning, day after day"; and though the dazzling Mediterranean sun blazes everywhere in *Tender Is the Night,* the passage Fitzgerald chose to quote along with the title line from Keats' poem is:

> But here there is no light,
> Save what from heaven is with the breezes blown
> Through verdurous glooms and winding mossy ways.

As always, however, Fitzgerald began not with a theme but with a body of material. Describing the life portrayed in *Tender Is the Night* in an earlier essay, he had written: "Charm, notoriety, good manners, weighed more than money as a social asset. This was rather splendid, but things were getting thinner and thinner as the eternal necessary human values tried to spread over all that expanse." With this world in all its variety of corruption, hardness, sterility, and despair Fitzgerald confronts his hero and the fundamentally simple "necessary human values" which his father had given him—" 'good instincts,' honor, courtesy, and courage." At the very beginning Dick Diver has to choose between becoming a great psychologist and a fully human being when Nicole, beautiful and schizophrenic, falls in love with him.

"As you think best, Professor Dohmler," Dick conceded. "It's certainly a situation."

Professor Dohmler raised himself like a legless man mounting a pair of crutches.

"But it is a professional situation," he cried quietly.

But for Dick it is a human situation; "wanting above all to be brave and kind, he . . . wanted, even more, to be loved." So he accepted the responsibility of being loved by Nicole and, gradually, of being loved by all the others whom his life drew around him. To them he gave lavishly of his strength, of his ability to translate into their terms the necessary human values and so remind them of their best selves. "My politeness," as he says, "is a trick of the heart." But the people he worked this trick for had no energy of their own, and gradually he exhausted his supply, spun out all his strength for other people until he had none left: "If you spend your life sparing other people's feelings and feeding their vanity, you get so you can't distinguish what *should* be respected in them."

Because he is proud and sensitive, Dick deliberately breaks Nicole's psychological dependence on him, aware that Nicole's love for him is bound up with her dependence and will cease with it, has already declined with the decline of her need for him; knowing that he has exhausted even his own power to love her in the process of making her psychologically whole again. By a terrible irony it comes about that what he had refused to treat as a merely professional situation is just that. "Dick waited until she was out of sight. Then he leaned his head forward on the parapet. The case was finished. Doctor Diver was at liberty again."

"That," says Baby Warren, speaking for them all, even for Nicole, "is what he was educated for."

Whether one accepts Fitzgerald's conception of the cause of this spiritual death or not, *Tender Is the Night* remains his most brilliant book. All his powers, the microscopic observation of the life he describes, the sense of the significance and relations of every detail of it, the infallible ear, and the gift of expression, all these things are here in greater abundance than ever before. And as never before they are used for the concrete, dramatic presentation of the inner significance of human experience, so that all the people of his book lead lives of "continual allegory" and its world is a microcosm of the great world. Its scope is such as to make *The Great Gatsby* seem small and simple, for all its neatness and perfection, and its dramatic realization so complete that Fitzgerald need not ever say what is happening: we always see.

In 1935 Fitzgerald had a recurrence of the tuberculosis which had first attacked him when he was an undergraduate and he was never entirely free from it again. In August 1937 he signed a contract with Metro-Goldwyn-Mayer and settled down in Hollywood to write for them. He worked on a number of important scripts, including *Three Comrades,*

Gone with the Wind, and *Madame Curie;* he produced a large number of short stories, mostly for *Esquire;* and he began to work on a novel, *The Last Tycoon.* He said himself that he had been thinking about the subject almost from the time of his arrival in Hollywood; he certainly had a great deal of work done on it by late 1939 when he apparently began the actual writing. About half the story was written when he died, though none of it in the final form he had visualized for it.

Thanks to Edmund Wilson's brilliant unraveling of Fitzgerald's notes, it is possible to see pretty clearly what his plans for *The Last Tycoon* were, how rich its theme was to be, and how tight its structure. Of what he planned to make of the book he said: "Unlike *Tender Is the Night,* it is not a story of deterioration. . . . If one book could ever be 'like' another, I should say it is more 'like' *The Great Gatsby.* But I hope it will be entirely different—I hope it will be something new, arouse new emotions, perhaps even a new way of looking at certain phenomena."

On the evidence of what he had actually written there is every reason for supposing that, had he lived, he would have fulfilled these hopes. The material and the people he is dealing with are entirely new, yet his command of the tangled social, industrial, and creative life of Hollywood is so complete that there is no moment in what he has written which is not utterly convincing, at the same time that it exists, not for itself alone, but for what Fitzgerald wanted to say, about Hollywood, about American life, about human experience as a whole. The writing, even though none of it is final, is as subtle and flexible as anything he ever did, and so unremittingly disciplined by the book's central intention that it takes on a kind of lyric intensity, glowing with the life of Fitzgerald's feelings for everything he was trying to say. This intensity is a remarkable achievement for a man who thought—and at least on physical grounds had some reason for thinking—a year before he started to write *The Last Tycoon* that he had only enough talent left "to stretch out over two more novels" (and "I may have to stretch it a little thin"). Most remarkable of all, though less final, is the evidence that he was succeeding, as he never had before with so much to say, in holding everything within the focusing form to which he had committed his story in the beginning.

Around December 1, 1940, Fitzgerald had a serious heart attack. He went on working on his novel, however, with such persistence that on December 20 he put off a visit from his doctor in order to finish a draft of the first episode of Chapter VI. The next day he had another, fatal, heart attack. In some sense Fitzgerald's wonderful natural talent was always haunted by the exigencies of his life. This final exigency aborted what promised to be his best novel, so that it is possible to say of it only what can be said of his work as a whole, that it is very fine and that, with a little more—or a little less—help from circumstances, it might, such was his talent, have been far finer. As John Peale Bishop said in his elegy for Fitzgerald, when we think of his death we

> think of all you did
> And all you might have done, before undone
> By death, but for the undoing of despair.

V

Mr. T. S. Eliot once remarked that "art never improves, but the material of art is never quite the same." But this is a dangerous way for a writer to look at the matter, however useful it may be to the critic, because it tends to separate in his mind the material from the form and meaning; and whenever the meaning is not something that grows out of the particular circumstances which are the occasion for writing, meaning tends to become abstract, to develop independently of the circumstances, and in some sense to violate their integrity. The safest attitude for the writer seems to be a single-minded desire to realize his material, so that the meaning of the circumstances, the permanent values which emerge for the critic from the representation, are for the writer merely such a further penetration of the particular circumstances as will allow him to realize them more completely. Fitzgerald's difficulty was always of course that his characters and their circumstances were likely to be too much individuals and local habitations, too little what Dr. Johnson approvingly referred to as "general nature." But what general nature there is in Fitzgerald's books—and there is always some and sometimes a great deal—is there because he had found it a part of his knowledge of his world. Such an undistorted imaginative penetration of the particular American world Fitzgerald knew had hardly been made before. Like James, Fitzgerald saw that one of the central moral problems of American life was raised in an acute form among the rich, in the conflict between the possibilities of their life and—to give it no worse name —their insensitivity. So long, therefore, as one realizes that Mr. Eliot is not comparing the two men in stature, it is not too much to say of Fitzgerald's best work what Mr. Eliot wrote him about *The Great Gatsby:* "In fact it seems to me to be the first step that American fiction has taken since Henry James."

After *The Great Gatsby* Fitzgerald produced only two books in fifteen years, one technically less perfect than *The Great Gatsby* and one unfinished. He did, of course, produce a large number of short stories, some of them as good as anything he ever wrote, but a considerable number of them only more or less skillful hackwork. All his life he worried about the hackwork and repeated over and over again a remark he made in 1924: "I now get 2,000 a story and they grow worse and worse and my ambition is to get where I need write no more but only novels." It is easy to condemn him for not having realized this ambition; there was much extravagance in his life and, at the end, debts and unavoidable expenses. But the ambition was there to the end and, in 1939, sick, tired, and under the ceaseless pressure of tragedy, he was writing an editor to whom he proposed to sell *The Last Tycoon:* "I would infinitely rather do it, now that I am well again, than take hack jobs out here." The wonder really is, given his temperament and upbringing, the social pressures of his times and the tragic elements in his personal life, that Fitzgerald did not give in entirely to hack work, as so many of his contemporaries did, but returned again and again, to the end of his life, to the self-imposed task of writing seriously. For all its manifest faults and mistakes, it was in some ways an heroic life. But it was a life of which Fitzgerald himself, writing to an old friend, a lawyer, could only say rather sadly: "I hope you'll be a better judge than I've been a man of letters."

It is not easy at this close range to separate our opinion of the man from our opinion of the writer, particularly since circumstances combined to make the man a legendary, eponymous figure. But as the accidents of the man's life—and the lies about it—gradually fade, we may well come to feel about the writer, with his purity of imagination and his imperviousness to the abstract theories and intellectual fads which have hag-ridden our times, as Stephen Vincent Benét did when he remarked after Fitzgerald's death: "You can take off your hats, now, gentlemen, and I think perhaps you had better. This is not a legend, this is a reputation—and, seen in perspective, it may well be one of the most secure reputations of our time."

IN THE COUNTRY OF THE BLUE *

R. P. BLACKMUR

WE ARE now about to assay the deep bias, the controlling, characteristic tension in the fiction of Henry James as it erupts in those tales where the theme is that of the artist in conflict with society. To erupt is to break out irresistibly from some deep compulsion, whether of disease or disorder, into a major reaction; and that is exactly what happens to James when in the first full maturity of his fifties he began to meditate, to feel borne in upon him, the actual predicament of the artist as a man of integrity in a democratic society. He broke out, he erupted from the very center of his being, and with such violence that to save himself he had need of both that imagination which represents the actual and that which shapes the possible. James made of the theme of the artist a focus for the ultimate theme of human integrity, how it is conceived, how it is destroyed, and how, ideally, it may be regained. For James, imagination was the will of things, and as the will was inescapably moral, so the imagination could not help creating—could not fail rather to re-create— out of the evil of the artist's actual predicament the good of his possible invoked vision. As the artist is only a special case of the man, so his vision is only an emphatic image of the general human vision; that James could make so much of the special case and the emphatic image of the artist comes about because, more than any other novelist of his scope, he was himself completely the artist. By which I mean that he was free to dramatize the artist precisely because he was himself so utterly given up to his profession that he was free of the predicament of the artist the moment he began to write. He felt none of that difficulty about conviction or principle or aim in his work which troubles a lesser writer; both his experience and his values came straight and clear and unquestionable, so much so that he seems to inhabit another world, that other world which has as substance what for us is merely hoped for. James, as an artist, was above all a man of faith. As he said of one of his characters in another connection, he was copious with faith.

But there is a disadvantage in too complete a faith, as well for an artist as for a saint. Complete faith runs to fanaticism or narrowness. The act of faith tends to substitute for understanding of the thing believed in. If your values come to you unquestioned, you risk taking them on principle and of course. Only the steady supplication of doubt, the

* "In the Country of the Blue" first appeared in the *Kenyon Review*, Autumn, 1943. It is used here by permission of the author and the magazine editors.

constant resolution of infirmity, can exercise your values and your principles enough to give them, together, that stretch and scope which is
their life. If you dismiss doubt and ignore infirmity, you will restrict the
scope that goes with the equivocal and reduce the vitality that goes with
richness of texture. So it was with Henry James. His very faith in his
powers kept him from using them to their utmost and caused him to
emphasize only his chosen, his convicted view. That is why he is not of
the very greatest writers, though he is one of the indubitably great artists, and especially in our present focus, the portrait of the artist. That
is why, too, as his faith increased he came less and less to make *fictions*
of people and more and more to make *fables,* to draw parables, for the
ulterior purposes of his faith. He came less and less to tell and more and
more to merely say. But—and this is what saves him to us for reading—
the habit of the novelist was so pervasive in him that he could no more
than breathing help dramatizing his fables or actualizing, to the possible limit of his frame, the story of his parables. Indeed, in his old age,
which for him constituted a continuing rebirth, he made of the frame
of his fables a new frame for the novel or tale only less than the greatest
frames. I refer to *The Ambassadors, The Wings of the Dove, The
Golden Bowl,* perhaps to *The Sense of the Past* and *The Ivory Tower,*
and certainly to the tales in *The Finer Grain;* for in these works the
form of the fable, the point of the parable, are brought to extreme use
precisely by being embedded in the sensibility of fiction. These take rise
I think in *The Sacred Fount,* which, not a novel at all but a vast shadowy disintegrating parable, disturbing, distressing, distrait, indeed dis-
traught, remains in the degree of its fascination quite ineluctable. It is
the nightmare nexus, in James's literary life, between the struggle to
portray the integrity of the artist and the struggle to portray, to discover, the integrity of the self.

This is another way of saying that the tales which exhibit the artist
occupy an intermediate position in James's work; and we shall see that
they look both ways, to the social novels that preceded them and to
the fiction of fate that came after them. They look back to the conditions of life in general and forward to the prophecy of life beyond and
under, or at any rate in spite of, the mutilating conditions. I think of
Isabelle Archer, in *The Portrait of a Lady,* how the conditions of life,
particularly the conditions of money and marriage and their miring in
manners, slowly dawned on her. You feel that if Isabelle can only acknowledge the conditions, if she can see for once what life is like, she
will be free to go on, where to go on means to meet more and more conditions. We know that in the process of going on she will lose—indeed
she has already lost them—the freshness and promise and candor of
youth, which are taken as the ordinary expenses laid out for the general
look, whether dimmed or sharpened always somehow maimed and
marked, of maturity. So for Isabelle Archer and most of the early fiction.

On the other hand I think of Milly Theale in *The Wings of the Dove,* whom we see actually killed by the conditions of life, acknowledge them how she will, but who yet so transcends them that her image—the image of the lost dead—brings to Kate Croy and Merton Densher, who had betrayed her in life, an unalterable, unutterable knowledge of what life is under its mutilated likeness. Things could, as Kate told Merton at the end, never again be the same between them; all because of the freshness and candor which had not perished but been discovered in the death of Milly Theale, and the unbroken, unbreakable promise of life which merely for *them,* as they had failed Milly, could not be kept but was to hover over them unavailingly ever afterwards. Milly had her triumph in death; but in *The Ambassadors,* Lambert Strether had his triumph in life, and so Maggie Verver in *The Golden Bowl,* both triumphing precisely over the most mutilating conditions of life that could well have come their way. So again, perhaps with the most beautiful lucidity of all, there is the shabby little bookseller Herbert Dodd in "The Bench of Desolation," whom we see deprived of the last resource of outward dignity—as a character he is all scar-tissue—till he has nothing left but his lonely hours upon his seaside bench of desolation. The bench of desolation is where you sit still with your fate—that of which you cannot be deprived. For Herbert Dodd that bench has these many years turned out to be enough, when the return of the lost love of his youth, who he thought had betrayed him, makes it a bench of triumph as well. The triumph consists for him, as for the others, in the gradual inward mastery of the outward experience, a poetic mastery which makes of the experience conviction.

Between the earlier persons who master life by submitting to its conditions and the later persons who master what lies under the conditions by achieving a conviction of the self—for surely a man's convictions may be said to be the very shape of his self—comes the little, the slightly anomalous race of artists. Why they come between rather than either as a culmination or a beginning is plain when we look at their characteristic fate. The man who is completely an artist is incompletely a man, though in his art he may envisage man completely. The meaning of the artist in history, that is in life as he lives it, in the conditions under which he works, is like the meaning of history itself. History, as Niebuhr says, is meaningful, but the meaning is not yet. The history of the artist is prophetic, but the meaning of the prophecy cannot now be known. What happens to the artist apart from his meaning, is common enough knowledge. If we look at the fables Henry James offers us, we see at once that all these artists are doomed men, as doomed as the characters in Hemingway, but not as in Hemingway by the coming common death. They are doomed either because they cannot meet the conditions of life imposed upon them by society or because society will have none of them no matter how hard they try. That, for James, was the drama of the artist, and he put it in the simple white and black terms of the fable and the fairy story. The artist either gave in to the evil and corruption of society, or society refused a living to the good and incorruptible artist. But let us ask why James chose the artist for the living focus of his drama, when it might as well have been the queen or the kitchen maid as in the fairy tales, or the men and women next door who provide us, unadulterated with any self-interest, such excellent views of our selves. Why, that is, did not James begin with the persons he came to?

We may say that he did not know enough, that he had not matured enough, and perhaps it would be better so to beg the question. But there is a kind of logic which we can apply after the event, which is where logic works best. The artist is *given* as in death-struggle with society, as much so as the thief or the murderer but with the advantage of heroism and nobility as a luminous character in the mere murk of the struggle. That every man and woman, and perhaps more so every child, is also engaged in a death-struggle with society, or at least with his neighbor's society, is not so clear; you would not think of *yourself* as struggling with society, but the artist and his critics have I regret to say vied with each other at every opportunity to see which could say so louder, especially since the spread of literacy and education has multiplied artists of all sorts at the same time that changing institutions took away the function of the artist in society. The artist became thus a natural puppet, ready-made, completely understandable, to represent the great central struggle of man as an individual, which is not often, when you consider the stakes, an understandable struggle at all, and to make a drama of which the novelist has to work from the ground up. It is no wonder then that James should consider the struggle of the artist as one of the great primary themes, especially when you add to the picture that he might incidentally dramatize himself a little—a temptation not beyond the purest artist—and do his trade a good turn.

But the evidence is not limited to the writings of artists and critics. There comes particularly pat to the kind of artist of whom James wrote a passage in de Tocqueville's classic work on The Republic of The United States of America. It was not quite going to be, he foresaw long before Henry James began writing novels, a model republic of letters. There is a little chapter in the first book of the second part called "The Trade of Literature" from which I extract the following passage. "Democracy not only infuses a taste for letters among the trading classes, but introduces a trading spirit into literature. . . . Among democratic nations, a writer may flatter himself that he will obtain at a cheap rate a meager reputation and a large fortune. For this purpose he need not be admired, it is enough that he is liked. . . . In democratic periods the public frequently treat authors as kings do their courtiers; they enrich and they despise them. . . . Democratic literature is always infested by a tribe of writers who look upon letters as a mere trade; and for some few great authors who adorn it, you may reckon thousands of idea-mongers." The picture is fresh enough for our own day, and we take it with the more authority because it was frankly prophetic on the part of a man more than generously disposed towards democracy. It is a description that James could have made for himself, and which in fact he did largely make, both in his life of Hawthorne and in the fiction which we are about to engage. De Tocqueville only reminds us of what James well knew, that an author can expect his readers to know that the race of literary artists is itself composed of good and bad, of very black and very white practitioners; so that the nobility of the good writer will go as granted once it is mentioned, as will the flunkeyism of the bad writer. Thus the author of a fiction about an artist has all the advantages of coarse melodrama without losing any of the advantages of high tragedy. He can merely impute unto his chosen character what virtues or vices he likes without being under any necessity to show them. In fiction, the stated intent of goodness, of high seriousness, is worthless in every realm of life except that of artist; elsewhere the character must be shown as actual, in the artist the stated intention is enough. We shall see that James fully availed himself of this freedom, redeeming himself only by the eloquence of his statement and the lesson of his parable. These, the eloquence and the lesson, will be what we bring away with us. For it goes without saying that James was never taken in, in his created characters, by the meretricious, and was always deliberately sold by the high serious. In this respect, as perhaps nowhere else in James, the reader always knows exactly where he is at. What happens to the literary personages will vary with the incident and the conditions recorded; but nothing can happen to their characters once they are stated, for their characters are articulated ready made as soon after their first appearance as possible, like puppets or like gods as you may choose to think.

This is no accident nor any part of James's idiosyncrasy; it is a limiting condition of the artist as a character in fiction to the extent that he is represented in the rôle of artist. If he drops the rôle, anything within the power of the author to represent may happen to him as a person; as artist he is only a shrunken and empty simulacrum of himself in his other rôles; he may know the meaning, but he cannot share the motion.

This is one of the lessons that if James's fables are taken literally they best attest; and literally is very near how James meant his lessons to be taken. But we do not need to stick to James. The character of Stephen Dedalus, both in *The Portrait of the Artist as a Young Man* and in *Ulysses*, certainly works of the greatest richness and scope, comes to us very fully as a young man, but as an artist he comes to us only by the eloquence of Joyce's mere statement. The poem he writes and the diary he keeps, the lecture he gives on Hamlet, come to us quite independent of the created figure of Stephen. Even the great declaration that ends the earlier book, where Stephen resolves that he will "forge in the smithy of his soul the uncreated conscience of his race," must be taken either as a free lyric spoken by an actor, where something else might have done as well, or as an image in which the whole boy shrinks suddenly into an agonized intention that can never be realized in life or act but only in art itself. It is much the same thing with Herr Aschenbach, the old novelist in Thomas Mann's *Death in Venice,* who is never given to us as a novelist except by imputation. The rôle of artist is indeed called on for other purposes, to give quickly a background against which the reader will find credible and dramatic the image of old Aschenbach, the famous and dignified novelist, as an outsider, a figure so isolated by his profession of artist that he fairly aches to corrupt himself, to debase himself, both as a man and as an artist. It might almost be put that to the degree that he had become an artist he had ceased existing—as it were, ceased living—so that the desire for life becomes identified with the temptation to corruption. And so it turns out. The only possible resumption of life for him is tainted with corruption, with effeminate infatuation, with deliberate indignity and self-humiliation. But it is too late in the season, the season of his life and the season in Venice, both of which are struck down by pestilence. His adored and beautiful Tadzio is taken away to safety, and Herr Aschenbach resumes his profession, in the act of dying, by in his delirium reenacting the Phaedo of Plato. Aschenbach the artist could have no life except in that terrible privation of life which is art.

It is only the obverse of the same coin that André Gide shows us in *The Counterfeiters* where the novelist reaches life only by a driven and deliberate corruption, a personal disintegration as great as the formal disintegration of the work of art in which it is represented. That Mann and Gide show us corruption as the necessary predilection of the artist, where James and Joyce show us art—that is, integrity of spirit—as the redemption of life, is perhaps due to the seeming fact that neither the German nor the Frenchman has as full and fanatic a conviction of his profession of artist as that suffered at an equal maximum by both James and Joyce.

To get back a little nearer to our particular problem of the portrait of the artist in Henry James—though indeed we have never been far from it—there is another way of expressing the predicament of the artist as a character in fiction. He comes to life only as he ceases to be an artist; he comes to life, in a word, only as he *fails* to be an artist, and he fails when the conditions of life overcome him at the expense of his art. This becomes a very pretty problem indeed when the novelist reflects that all this amounts to saying that the actual source of art, the life of which it is the meaning, is the artist's undoing. Gide solves the problem, and so does Mann, by disintegrating the art as well as the life. Joyce, with no greater honesty but with greater moral insight, represents the struggle of the man *in society,* not as an outsider but as one very much at the heart of things, to become an artist. It was not for nothing that Joyce defined the sentimentalist as he who "is unwilling to incur the enormous responsibility for a thing done." Stephen Dedalus is shown to us in the very process of realizing, for the sake of his art, responsibility for every deed of his life. In Joyce, the artist, like God, dies every day. He dies into man and is reborn; the death is necessary to the birth. Henry James had neither the catholicism of Joyce, the bitter protestant-ism of Gide, nor the faustian spirit of Mann at his back; he had rather —and only—his unquestioned faith in the adequacy of the free intelli-gence in life and the freed imagination in art. He had thus less equip-ment, or at any rate a less articulated philosophy, than the others, and it is perhaps for that reason that he produced his ideal artists who failed only in life and succeeded only in art, and his other artists, equally ideal, who failed in art only because they insisted on success, financial or social success, in life. The realm of the ideal is often nearest to those who have nearest to no philosophy; but so is the realm of the actual, which is the artist's realm, and James may have been nearer right in what he did with his facts than the others.

At least we have James's own abundantly eloquent answer to the charge that he ought never to have exhibited in art creatures who never existed in life. I give part of the answer as he made it in the preface to "The Lesson of the Master." "What does your contention of non-existent conscious *exposures,* in the midst of all the stupidity and vul-garity and hypocrisy, imply but that we have been, nationally, so to speak, graced with no instance of recorded sensibility fine enough to react against these things?—an admission too distressing. What one would accordingly fain do is to baffle any such calamity, to *create* the record, in default of any other enjoyment of it; to imagine, in a word, the honourable, the producible case. What better example than this of the high and helpful public and, as it were, civic use of the imagina-tion?—a faculty for the possible fine employments of which in the interest of morality my esteem grows every hour that I live. How can one consent to make a picture of the preponderant futilities and vul-garities and miseries of life without the impulse to exhibit as well from time to time, in its place, some fine example of the reaction, the opposition or the escape?"

In this passage, and in the whole preface from which it is taken, I think James reaches the pinnacle of principle to which he was able to expose the idealism with which he worked; and I have planted my quo-tations here in the center of this discussion of the portrait of the artist because they raise—especially just after our references to the practice of Joyce and Gide and Mann—considerations of great importance not only to the criticism, the appreciation, of James's fictions but also to the whole general theory of fiction itself—if you like, to the whole theory of art. There are several theories of the value of art which are tenable until you begin to apply them in the interpretation of particular works of art, when as a rule the value of the art shrinks at once to nothing and there is *nothing but* moral value left. No artist and hardly any user of art whose eyes are open can take the slightest interest in any *nothing but* theory of art's value. James's theory is very tempting because, if adopted, it shows how moral value gets into a work of art without leaving you to shudder for the fate of the art. The artist, he says with all the rush and eloquence of immediate experience, the artist *creates* the moral value out of the same material and by the same means with which he creates his other values—out of the actual and by means of imagination. The values are, though distinguishable, inextricable. Some works may show aesthetic values without moral values, and other works very clearly have no aesthetic values and yet shriek to heaven with their moral values, but where you have both orders of value as they are created, together, so they must be felt together, at least so long as the work being enjoyed is enjoyed as art.

Among the consequences which flow from James's statement, if I understand it right, there are two which deserve emphasis for the freedom and the privation they impose on the artist. One has to do with the inclusive nature of moral value in art. As the experience in art must be somehow of the actual and as the record must be somehow of the imaginative, then the artist is free to create evil as well as good without risk of police interference. It is not that his vision of evil may overcome his vision of good, but that, if he is to be an artist of any scope, he must create both, and if the emphasis is on the one in a given work it must have the other as its under or supporting side. It is truly the devil who minds God's business as it is God who gives the devil something to do. But, and this is the second consequence kept for emphasis from James's statement, to have validity whether moral or aesthetic, whatever the artist *creates* (though not what he merely puts in by the way) must show its source in the actual; for it is otherwise either immoral or vapid, and likely both. If the architecture of even the noblest cathedral were not based on the actual it would fall apart, but without a vision beyond the actual it could have never been built at all. Art, on this view, tends toward the ideal but without ever quite transcending the actual from which it sprang. The ideal, in fact, in this restricted sense of the word, is what the artist creates; but the ideal, to have any significant worth, must approach the actual, with the striking effect which needs every meditation we can give it, that the nearer it approaches the actual the more greatly ideal the creation will seem. There is the force of Dante's ideal hell, that it approaches so close to the actual of this life; and there is the relative weakness of James's tales of the literary life, and despite his plea of moral necessity, that though they spring from hints in the actual world the "super-subtle fry" of his authors do not approach near enough to the actual. The fable is always frailer than the image, how-ever more cogent. Thus Joyce's Dubliners who translated the initials IHS of *In Hoc Signo* over the cross, as I Have Suffered, were not blas-phemers but better believers for so doing.

The examples are endless; but to our present interest it is the prin-ciple that counts, and its relation to the artist, and if we turn to our chosen tales of Henry James we shall find that though as dramas they do not show us very much of the actual, as fables they illuminate the principles by which James was later to anchor his most difficult and pre-carious ideals safe and firm—poetically valid—in flesh and blood. That is, as these tales occupy an intermediate position in the general develop-ment of James as works of art, so they represent for us an intermediate state of knowledge, that critical and fascinating state when principles fairly itch for action but have not yet run down into the skill of the hand that acts, that in this case writes. As stories they are stories about stories, and the most fascinating kind of stories, those that for both aesthetic and moral reasons can never quite be written. All the moral value is in the possibility not lived up to, and all the aesthetic value is in the possibility not lived down to. It is the same possibility, looking either way, the possibility of the really superior artist triumphing over society by cutting himself off from every aspect of it except the expres-sive, or the possibility of this same superior fellow—and I hardly know which version is more tragic—coming to failure and ruin, expressive failure and personal ruin, by hands whose caresses are their most bru-talizing blows, the hands of society itself, the society that, in de Tocque-ville's phrases, would like an author rather than admire him, or, worse, would enrich and despise him.

The possibilities are indeed wonderful, and furnish half the conversa-tion at literary parties, where the most enriched authors always turn out the most despised, very often justly. James does not deal with the liter-ary party, whether because the institution had not grown much in his day or because it was open only to satire, which was not his purpose. He deals rather with the English house party and the English dinner party where there is a reputable author present for demolition. The effect is not too different, and affords the advantages of an outwardly more de-corous set of conventions and even for a welcome shift of scenes from lawn to church, dinner-table to parlor, or parlor to smoking room, smoking room to bedroom; which taken together, as even a novice at fiction should know, makes the problem of moving people from place to place and so of setting up new relations or modifying old ones, relatively easy. So it is that all but one of the fables we are dealing with make use of the machinery of entertainment for the mechanics of the plot. That is, the artifices that in actual society do most to prevent communication and obscure situations, James uses to promote intimacy and to clarify situations. He mastered the means which because of his life—in one

London year he dined out three hundred times—were almost alone at his disposal; the lesson of which may be that it explains why so many of James's people are never able to meet each other openly and yet contrive to put everything between them that is necessary.

That is exactly the situation in "The Figure in the Carpet" where I think we may put it that we know what the puzzle is precisely to the extent we realize it is insoluble, like the breath of life. The narrator who is himself a writer and nameless (the narrators of all these tales are writers and most of them are nameless) reviews the latest novel of Hugh Vereker in a magazine called *The Middle,* and shortly afterwards attends a houseparty where Vereker is a guest, as is his book, both unopened by any of the company, though both are the principal subjects of attention. Some one shows Vereker the review and Vereker says it is very bad; he has not realized the reviewer is present. When he does so, he apologises to the narrator but insists that, nevertheless, like everybody else, he has missed the Figure in the Carpet: the general intention, the string to his pearls, the passion of his passion. The narrator tries his best to make up, both by reading Vereker's works and by tackling him personally. On his failure he passes the puzzle along to his friend George Corvick, who shares the problem with his fiancée. They in their turn grow futile and frenzied—so frenzied that their marriage comes to hang upon their success. Corvick goes off to Bombay as a correspondent, and while there wires: Eureka. The narrator and Corvick's fiancée, Gwendolyn Erme, try to guess what it must be. Corvick stops off on Vereker at Rapallo during his return journey, and writes that Vereker has verified his discovery. Gwendolyn marries George on condition that he reveal his secret; he dies on his honeymoon before writing it down. Gwen refuses to tell the narrator what it is, because, says she, it is her life. Vereker dies. Then Gwen, who has re-married to Drayton Deane a critic, herself dies on the birth of a second child. After a decent but excruciated interval—for in James decency most of all is subject to excruciation—the narrator does his best to discover from Deane what the secret of Vereker's work had been. But Gwendolyn had never told him; and the figure in the carpet is safe. Nobody knows or can know what it can be. What then was the puzzle? It may be that there was none, or none except to those who wrote—or read—for the passion of the passion; which was certainly not how the narrator, nor any of his friends, either wrote or read. A frenzied curiosity is not passion. Or it may be that the figure in the carpet is necessarily ineluctable. Perhaps it only ought to be there; that much, acuteness can discover. In his prefatory remarks, James does nothing to help; but says only that "the question that accordingly comes up, the issue of the affair, can be but whether the very secret of perception hasn't been lost. That is the situation, and 'The Figure in the Carpet' exhibits a small group of well-meaning persons engaged in a test."

We can only note that well-meaning persons are notoriously unpercep-
tive, and add that the secret of perception in readers comes very near
the secret of creation in artists.

"The Figure in the Carpet" is perhaps a tea-time and tepid whiskey
fable, for it is over these beverages that it largely occurs; and so represents, I think, no more than at most can be made out of obsessed gossip.
James may have meant more for it—his preface suggests that he did—but
it would seem actually, as written, to mean no more than that there is
a figure in the carpet if you can imagine it for yourself; it is not there
to discover. It is rather like Kafka, manqué, the exasperation of the mystery without the presence of the mystery, or a troubled conscience without any evidence of guilt.

Rather similar but carried further, further for actuality, by the very
conventionality of its fantasy—its *glaring* incredibility—is the fable of
"The Private Life." Here again the narrator is a writer unnamed, this
time on vacation in the Alps in a house full of people connected with
the arts. Among the guests are Clare Vawdrey, a writer of genius but
a second-rate man; Lord Mellfont, a magnificent public figure but
nothing much when not in public; and Blanche Adney, a great actress,
for whom Vawdrey is writing a play, and who is quite friendly with the
narrator. The second-rateness of Vawdrey and the magnificent public
presence of Mellfont gradually become suspect to Blanche and the narrator. Pursuing their curiosity, the narrator sneaks into Vawdrey's room
in the evening, while Vawdrey is outside talking to Blanche; there the
narrator discovers Vawdrey's other self writing industriously in the dark.
Later, by plan, Blanche gets her chance, and while the narrator keeps
Vawdrey outside herself makes the acquaintance of the other or "ghost"
self and falls in love with him. Meantime the narrator finds the outer
self even duller than he had thought: "the world," he reflects, "was
vulgar and stupid, and the real man would have been a fool to come out
for it when he could gossip and dine by deputy." Lord Mellfont, on the
other hand, must be himself an apparition, called into being by a public relation only; by himself he must be nothing, literally nothing.
Blanche and the narrator go looking for him on that assumption, and
of necessity he appears in front of them; if they had not looked for him,
he would have been unable to materialize. "He was all public and had
no corresponding private life, just as Clare Vawdrey was all private and
had no corresponding public." Of this little piece what does one say but
that the ghost story is the most plausible form of the fairy tale; it makes
psychological penetration ominous because not verifiable. Who would
care to verify a ghost, especially two ghosts who have the unity only of
opposites? Life, the actuality, lies somewhere between; and it is a relief
to think that your dull man of genius keeps a brilliant ghost in his work-
room, just as it is a malicious delight to figure that your brilliant public
man is utterly resourceless without a public.

"The Private Life," is a fantastic statement, so far as it has a serious side, of the inviolable privacy of the man of genius. "The Death of the Lion" makes a plea for the protection of that privacy, and for much more, on the ground that if you successfully violate it your genius, if he have no deputy self to gossip and dine, perishes from exposure. The narrator is again a young, detached writer and journalist with a strong sense of allegiance to the great, is sent to write up Neil Paraday at the moment he achieves, at the age of fifty, after a long illness, with his new book, the public success of being made a subject of a leader in *The Empire*. An interviewer for 37 syndicated papers arrives just after Paraday has read the narrator the manuscript plan—a plan finished and perfect in itself—of his next and greatest book. The narrator takes over the interviewer, and goes on to take over as much protective custody of Paraday as possible. But Paraday, with his success, is nevertheless taken up by the unreading, by those who hate literature in the guise of adoring writers, especially by a Mrs. Wimbush who has the fortune of a great brewery. Paraday a little excuses his not throwing Mrs. Wimbush out of doors on the ground that he can get material for his writing out of her. The narrator, however, has a single success in keeping off an American girl with an autograph album to fill, but who really loves Paraday's work, understands that reading is greater than personality, and agrees to seek the author, as the narrator tells her to, "in his works even as God in Nature." Neil Paraday had been made, as the narrator says, a contemporary. "That was what had happened: the poor man was to be squeezed into his horrible age. I felt as if he had been overtaken on the crest of the hill and brought back to the city. A little more and he would have dipped down the short cut to posterity and escaped." To be a contemporary was to be a lion and lions of the contemporary necessarily die soon. Thus Paraday soon *wants* to become ill again; he knew what was happening to him, but he could not help surrendering to it. "He filled his lungs, for the most part, with the comedy of his queer fate: the tragedy was in the spectacles through which I chose to look. He was conscious of inconvenience, and above all of a great renouncement; but how could he have heard a mere dirge in the bells of his accession?"

What happens is inevitable from the title and from what has already been said. Paraday is seduced into going to a house-party at Mrs. Wimbush's country place which is called Prestidge—a surface quality obtained, if you remember your etymology, by sleight of hand. There is to be a great foreign Princess there, and many others, all to hear him read his precious manuscript plan. He falls sick and, dying, instructs the narrator to print it as his last work, small but perfect. However, Mrs. Wimbush has lent it to a guest who in turn has lent it to another, and so on, none of them by any chance reading it; so that it is lost. Before our Lion actually dies he has become a burden, for the next two in Mrs. Wimbush's series of Lions come before he is out of the way; and it is in the identity of the new beasts that we see the true estimation in which Mrs. Wimbush—in which society—holds literature. The new beasts are two popular successes, Guy Walsingham, who is a woman, and Dora Forbes, who is a man with red moustaches. Their publishers think it necessary that they take opposite sexes in their pen names. But the narrator says rather that they are writers of some third sex: the success-sex, no doubt, which can alone cope with the assaults of an adulating society.

Here we see the figure of a great writer preyed upon; the Lion is brought down by the brutality of a society which could have no use for him except as quarry. In "The Next Time" we have the contrary fable, that of the writer who struggles desperately to make society his prey, but fails because he cannot help remaining the harmless, the isolated monarch of his extreme imaginative ardent self. Society, seen as his prey, has no trouble at all in keeping out of his way. Ray Limbert's only successful step was the initial step of a "bad" marriage to a good wife, who has a mother and bears children who require support. He has a sister-in-law who is a successful popular novelist, where he himself is incontestably a great writer. He gave the narrator (again a literary man) "one of the rarest emotions of the literary life, the sense of an activity in which I could critically rest." However, it was necessary for him to earn his living, and after failing at journalism, he manages to get the post of editor with a year's contract at complete liberty. As an editor, Ray Limbert resolves to contribute serially a deliberately bad novel in the hope of achieving success, and requires of his friends that they do not read the instalments for shame. His difficulty there was that he was one of those "people who can't be vulgar for trying." He loses his post as editor, partly because of the authors whom he had printed but mostly because of his own novel, which so far from being popular or obvious was "charming with all his charm and powerful with all his power: it was an unscrupulous, an unsparing, a shameless merciless masterpiece. . . . The perversity of the effort, even though heroic, had been frustrated by the purity of the gift." As the narrator finished his reading he looked out the window for a sight of the summer dawn, his eyes "compassionately and admiringly filled. The eastern sky, over the London housetops, had a wonderful tragic crimson. That was the colour of his magnificent mistake." It was a mistake which Ray Limbert—by the terms of the fable—repeated, always believing that the next time he would do the trick. All the narrator could say was "that genius was a fatal disturber or that the unhappy man had no effectual *flair*. When he went abroad to gather garlic he came home with heliotrope." Finally he forgot "the next time." "He had merely waked up one morning again in the country of the blue and had stayed there with a good conscience and a great idea," and died, writing.

"In the country of the blue" is a very lonely place to be, for it is very nearly empty except for the self, and is gained only by something like a religious retreat, by an approximation of birth or death or birth-in-death. James tried for it in fiction I think but once, in "The Great Good Place," here mentioned but in passing, where there is an adumbration rather than an account given of the retreat of the author George Doane, made for the recovery of genius, "which he had been in danger of losing"; he had returned to himself after eight hours to find his room "disencumbered, different, twice as large. It was all right." Yet there was some constant recourse for James to the country of the blue; it was where he would have had his projected great authors live, and it was where, as we shall see he reported, he sometimes lived himself.

But before we look at that sight, let us look at the tale which of all that James wrote best prepares us for it, "The Lesson of the Master." This is probably the finest, surely the clearest, most brilliant, and most eloquent of all James's pleading fables of the literary life. It has greater scope than the others, itself rings with greatness, and is more nearly dramatic in character, more nearly joins the issue of the ideal and the actual. Unlike the other tales in our present list it is related in the third person from the point of view of the most implicated person in it, Paul Overt. The relations between that distinguished young talent and the Master, Henry St. George, who has for years done less than his best work, are exhibited in terms of Marian Fancourt, of an interest and an intelligence in the arts hardly less than her beauty, as a nexus for the conflict of loyalties between the master and the disciple. All three meet for the first time on a country weekend at Summersoft. Both men are taken with Marian Fancourt. Overt respects St. George vastly, and when St. George tells him that he is good and must be better, referring to his own inadequacy, he responds by a kind of preliminary submission. In London Overt falls in love with Marian, St. George more or less making way for him. For each the two others are the poles of attraction. Overt visits St. George in his study after a party, and for most of thirteen pages St. George exhorts him magnificently to give up everything, marriage, money, children, social position—all the things to which St. George himself had succumbed—for the sake of his art. Overt takes the master pretty much at his word and goes abroad for two years writing his best thing yet under great privation of all personal life. While he is abroad St. George's wife dies, and Overt returns to find St. George and Marian on the verge of marriage, and so feels brutally cheated. It turns out that St. George has married Marian partly to save Overt from succumbing to the false gods, to save him from having everything but the great thing.

The great thing is "The sense of having done the best—the sense which is the real life of the artist and the absence of which is his death, of having drawn from his intellectual instrument the finest music that nature had hidden in it, of having played it as it should be played."

When Overt complains that he is not to be allowed the common pas
sions and affections of men, St. George answers that art is passion
enough. The whole ascetic position—for it is no less than ascetic
in that it draws the artist as mostly not a man—Overt sums up for
him by crying that it leaves the artist condemned to be "a mere dis-
franchised monk" who "can produce his effect only by giving up personal happiness. What an arraignment of art!" And St. George takes
him up: "Ah, you don't imagine that I'm defending art? 'Arraignment'
—I should think so! Happy the societies in which it hasn't made its
appearance, for from the moment it comes they have a consuming ache,
they have an uncurable corruption, in their breast. Most assuredly is
the artist in a false position! But I thought we were taking him for
granted." It was when Overt found Marian married to St. George that
he realized *what* he had been taking for granted. One *hardly* knows
whether society or the artist is worse flayed here; but one knows, and
there is only the need one feels for a grace note in James's concluding
remark that "the Master was essentially right and that Nature had
dedicated him to intellectual, not to personal passion."

The portrait of the artist in Henry James is now almost complete:
the man fully an artist is the man, short of the saint, most wholly
deprived. This is the picture natural to the man still in revolt, to the
man who still identifies the central struggle of life in society as the
mere struggle of that aspect of his life of which he makes his profession,
and who has not yet realized, but is on the verge of doing so, that all
the professions possible in life are mutually inclusive. One's own profession is but the looking glass and the image of the others; and the
artist is he who being by nature best fitted to see the image clear is
damned only if he does not. If he sees, his vision disappears in his work,
which is the country of the blue. That is why the only possible portrait
to paint of the artist will be a portrait of him as a failure. Otherwise
there will be only the portrait of the man. That is why James portrayed
the artist chiefly during his intermediate dubious period, and why in
his full maturity, like St. George, but in a different richer sense, he took
the artist for granted and portrayed men and women bent not on a
privation but a fullness of being.

There remains still to record only James's portrait of himself as the
artist in the man mature, and for that there are two passages to quote,
of which one is from a letter written when James was seventy to Henry
Adams urging him to cultivate the interest of his consciousness. "You
see I still, in the presence of life (or of what you deny to be such,) have
reactions—as many as possible—and the book I sent you is proof of
them. It's, I suppose, because I am that queer monster, the artist, an
obstinate finality, an inexhaustible sensibility. Hence the reactions—
appearances, memories, many things, go on playing upon it with con-

sequences that I note and 'enjoy' (grim word!) noting. It all takes doing—and I *do*. I believe I shall do yet again—it is still an act of life."

That is the man in life as artist. The other passage, with which we
end the chapter, is taken from some pencilled notes written some time
in his last years on a New Year's eve, near midnight during a time of
inspiration. Lubbock prints the whole of the notes in the Introduction
to his edition of the Letters, saying that "There is no moment of all
his days in which it is now possible to approach him more clearly." I
quote only the last paragraph. The shape, the life, the being of a novel
having shown itself clear, the exaltation is so great that James is left
once again with just the story of a story to tell, this time of himself.

> Thus just these first little wavings of the oh so tremulously passionate
> little old wand (now!) make for me, I feel, a sort of promise of richness
> and beauty and variety; a sort of portent of the happy presence of the
> elements. The good days of last August and even my broken September
> and my better October come back to me with their gage of divine pos-
> sibilities, and I welcome these to my arms, I press them with unutter-
> able tenderness. I seem to emerge from these recent bad days—the fruit
> of blind accident—and the prospect clears and flushes, and my poor
> blest old Genius pats me so admirably and lovingly on the back that I
> turn, I screw round, and bend my lips to passionately, in my gratitude,
> kiss its hands.

The feeling in this passage is not uncommon; most of us have been
terrified at its counterpart; but the ability to surrender to the expression of it is rare, and is what brought James himself, for the moment
of expression, into the blue.

SHERWOOD ANDERSON *

LIONEL TRILLING

I FIND it hard, and I think it would be false, to write about Sherwood Anderson without speaking of him personally and even emotionally. I did not know him; I was in his company only twice and on neither occasion did I talk with him. The first time I saw him was when he was at the height of his fame; I had, I recall, just been reading *A Story-Teller's Story* and *Tar,* and these autobiographical works had made me fully aware of the change that had taken place in my feelings since a few years before when almost anything that Anderson wrote had seemed a sort of revelation. The second time was about two years before his death; he had by then not figured in my own thought about literature for many years, and I believe that most people were no longer aware of him as an immediate force in their lives. His last two novels (*Beyond Desire* in 1932 and *Kit Brandon* in 1936) had not been good; they were all too clearly an attempt to catch up with the world, but the world had moved too fast; it was not that Anderson was not aware of the state of things but rather that he had suffered the fate of the writer who at one short past moment has had a success with a simple idea which he allowed to remain simple and to become fixed. On both occasions—the first being a gathering, after one of Anderson's lectures, of eager Wisconsin graduate students and of young instructors who were a little worried that they would be thought stuffy and academic by this Odysseus, the first famous man of letters most of us had ever seen; the second being a crowded New York party—I was much taken by Anderson's human quality, by a certain serious interest he would have in the person he was shaking hands with or talking to for a brief, formal moment, by a certain graciousness or gracefulness which seemed to arise from an innocence of heart.

I mention this very tenuous personal impression because it must really have arisen not at all from my observation of the moment but rather have been projected from some unconscious residue of admiration I had for Anderson's books even after I had made all my adverse judgments upon them. It existed when I undertook this notice of Anderson on the occasion of his death, or else I should not have undertaken it. And now that I have gone back to his books again and have found that I like them even less than I remembered, I find too that the residue of admiration still remains; it is quite vague, yet it requires to be articulated with the clearer feelings of dissatisfaction; and it needs to be spoken of, as it has been, first.

There is a special poignancy in the failure of Anderson's later career. According to the artistic morality to which he and his friends sub-scribed—Robert Browning seems to have played a large if anonymous part in shaping it—Anderson should have been forever protected against artistic failure by the facts of his biography. At the age of forty-five, as everyone knows, he found himself the manager of a small paint factory in Elyria, Ohio; one day, in the very middle of a sentence he was dictating, he walked out of the factory and gave himself to litera-ture and truth. From the wonder of that escape he seems never to have recovered, and his continued pleasure in it did him harm, for it seems to have made him feel that the problem of the artist was defined wholly by the struggle between sincerity on the one hand and commercialism and gentility on the other. He did indeed say that the artist needed not only courage but craft, yet it was surely the courage by which he set the most store. And we must sometimes feel that he had dared too much for his art and therefore expected too much merely from his boldness, believing that right opinion must necessarily result from it. Anderson was deeply concerned with the idea of justification; there was an odd, quirky, undisciplined religious strain in him that took this form; and he expected that although Philistia might condemn him, he would have an eventual justification in the way of art and truth. He was justified in some personal way, as I have tried to say, and no doubt his great escape had something to do with this, but it also had the effect of fatally fixing the character of his artistic life.

Anderson's greatest influence was probably upon those who read him in adolescence, the age when we find the books we give up but do not get over. And it now needs a little fortitude to pick up again, as many must have done upon the news of his death, the one book of his we are all sure to have read, for *Winesburg, Ohio* is not just a book, it is a personal souvenir. It is commonly owned in the Modern Library edi-tion, very likely in the most primitive format of that series, even before it was tricked out with its vulgar little ballet-Prometheus; and the brown oilcloth binding, the coarse paper, the bold type crooked on the page, are dreadfully evocative. Even the introduction by Ernest Boyd is rank with the odor of the past, of the day when criticism existed in heroic practical simplicity, when it was all truth against hypocrisy, idealism against philistinism, and the opposite of "romanticism" was not "classicism" but "realism," which—it now seems odd—negated both. As for the Winesburg stories themselves, they are as dangerous to read again, as paining and as puzzling, as if they were old letters we had written or received.

It is not surprising that Anderson should have made his strongest appeal, although by no means his only one, to adolescents. For one thing, he wrote of young people with a special tenderness; one of his best-known stories is called "I Want To Know Why": it is the great adolescent question, and the world Anderson saw is essentially, and even when it is inhabited by adults, the world of the sensitive young person. It is a world that does not "understand," a world of solitude, of running away from home, of present dullness and far-off joy and eventual fulfillment; it is a world seen as suffused by one's own personality and yet—and therefore—felt as indifferent to one's own personality. And Anderson used what seems to a young person the very language to penetrate to the heart of the world's mystery, what with its rural or primeval willingness to say things thrice over, its reiterated "Well..." which suggests the groping of boyhood, its "Eh?" which implies the inward-turning wisdom of old age.

Most of us will feel now that this world of Anderson's is a pretty inadequate representation of reality and probably always was. But we cannot be sure that it was not a necessary event in our history, like adolescence itself; and no one has the adolescence he would have liked to have had. But an adolescence must not continue beyond its natural term, and as we read through Anderson's canon what exasperates us is his stubborn, satisfied continuance in his earliest attitudes.* There is something undeniably impressive about the period of Anderson's work in which he was formulating his characteristic notions. We can take, especially if we have a modifying consciousness of its historical moment, *Windy MacPherson's Son*, despite its last part which is so curiously like a commercial magazine story of the time; *Marching Men* has power even though its political mysticism is repellent; *Winesburg, Ohio* has its touch of greatness; *Poor White* is heavy-handed but not without its force; and some of the stories in *The Triumph of the Egg* have the kind of grim quaintness which is, I think, Anderson's most successful mood, the mood that he occasionally achieves now and then in his later short pieces, such as "Death in the Woods." But after 1921, in *Dark Laughter* and *Many Marriages*, the books that made the greatest critical stir, there emerges in Anderson's work the compulsive, obsessive, repetitive quality which finally impresses itself on us as his characteristic quality.

Anderson is connected with the tradition of the men who maintain a standing quarrel with respectable society and have a perpetual bone to pick with the rational intellect. It is a very old tradition, for the Essenes, the early Franciscans, as well as the early Hasidim, may be said to belong to it. In modern times it has been continued by Blake and Whitman and D. H. Lawrence. Those who belong to the tradition usually do something more about the wrong way the world goes than

* The parallel to Hemingway here is striking and highly suggestive.

merely to denounce it—they *act out* their denunciations and assume a role and a way of life. Typically they take up their packs and leave the doomed respectable city, just as Anderson did. But Anderson lacked what his spiritual colleagues have always notably had. We may call it *mind,* but *energy* and *spiritedness,* in their relation to mind, will serve just as well. Anderson never understood that the moment of enlightenment and conversion—the walking out—cannot be merely celebrated but must be developed, so that what begins as an act of will grows to be an act of intelligence. The men of the anti-rationalist tradition mock the mind's pretensions and denounce its restrictiveness; but they are themselves the agents of the most powerful thought. They do not of course really reject mind at all, but only mind as it is conceived by respectable society. "I learned the Torah from all the limbs of my teacher," said one of the Hasidim. They think with their sensations, their emotions, and, some of them, with their sex. While denouncing intellect, they shine forth in a mental blaze of energy which manifests itself in syntax, epigram, and true discovery.

Anderson is not like them in this regard. He did not become a "wise" man. He did not have the gift of being able to throw out a sentence or a metaphor which suddenly illuminates some dark corner of life—his role implied that he should be full of "sayings" and specific insights, yet he never was. But in the preface to *Winesburg, Ohio* he utters one of the few really "wise" things in his work, and, by a kind of irony, it explains something of his own inadequacy. The preface consists of a little story about an old man who is writing what he calls "The Book of the Grotesque." This is the old man's ruling idea:

> That in the beginning when the world was young there were a great many thoughts but no such thing as a truth. Man made the truths himself and each truth was a composite of a great many vague thoughts. All about in the world were truths and they were all beautiful.
>
> The old man listed hundreds of the truths in his book. I will not try to tell you all of them. There was the truth of virginity and the truth of passion, the truth of wealth and of poverty, of thrift and of profligacy, of carelessness and abandon. Hundreds and hundreds were the truths and they were all beautiful.
>
> And then the people came along. Each as he appeared snatched up one of the truths and some who were quite strong snatched up a dozen of them.
>
> It was the truths that made the people grotesques. The old man had quite an elaborate theory concerning the matter. It was his notion that the moment one of the people took one of the truths to himself, called it his truth, and tried to live his life by it, he became a grotesque and the truth he embraced became a falsehood.

Anderson snatched but a single one of the truths and it made him, in his own gentle and affectionate meaning of the word, a "grotesque";

eventually the truth itself became a kind of falsehood. It was the truth—
or perhaps we must call it a simple complex of truths—of love-passion-
freedom, and it was made up of these "vague thoughts": that each
individual is a precious secret essence, often discordant with all other
essences; that society, and more particularly the industrial society,
threatens these essences; that the old good values of life have been
destroyed by the industrial dispensation; that people have been cut
off from each other and even from themselves. That these thoughts
make a truth is certain; and its importance is equally certain. In what
way could it have become a falsehood and its possessor a "grotesque"?

The nature of the falsehood seems to lie in this—that Anderson's
affirmation of life by love, passion, and freedom had, paradoxically
enough, the effect of quite negating life, making it gray, empty, and
devoid of meaning. We are quite used to hearing that this is what excessive intellection can do; we are not so often warned that emotion, if
it is of a certain kind, can be similarly destructive. Yet when feeling is
understood as an answer, a therapeutic, when it becomes a sort of
critical tool and is conceived of as excluding other activities of life, it
can indeed make the world abstract and empty. Love and passion,
when considered as they are by Anderson as a means of attack upon the
order of the respectable world, can contrive a world which is actually
without love and passion and not worth being "free" in.[1]

In Anderson's world there are many emotions, or rather many instances of a few emotions, but there are very few sights, sounds, and
smells, very little of the stuff of actuality. The very things to which he
gives moral value because they are living and real and opposed in their
organic nature to the insensate abstractness of an industrial culture
become, as he writes about them, themselves abstract and without life.
His praise of the racehorses he said he loved gives us no sense of a
horse; his Mississippi does not flow; his tall corn grows out of the soil
of his dominating subjectivity. The beautiful organic things of the
world are made to be admirable not for themselves but only for their
moral superiority to men and machines. There are many similarities
of theme between Anderson and D. H. Lawrence, but Lawrence's far

[1] In the preface of *The Sherwood Anderson Reader,* Paul Rosenfeld, Anderson's
friend and admirer, has summarized in a remarkable way the vision of life which
Anderson's work suggests: "Almost, it seems, we touch an absolute existence, a
curious semi-animal, semi-divine life. Its chronic state is banality, prostration,
dismemberment, unconsciousness; tensity with indefinite yearning and infinitely
stretching desire. Its manifestation: the non-community of cranky or otherwise
asocial solitaries, dispersed, impotent and imprisoned. . . . Its wonders—the wonders
of its chaos—are fugitive heroes and heroines, mutilated like the dismembered Osiris,
the dismembered Dionysius. . . . Painfully the absolute comes to itself in consciousness of universal feeling and helplessness. . . . It realizes itself as feeling, sincerity,
understanding, as connection and unity; sometimes at the cost of the death of its
creatures. It triumphs in anyone aware of its existence even in its sullen state. The
moment of realization is tragically brief. Feeling, understanding, unity pass. The
divine life sinks back again, dismembered and unconscious."

stronger and more sensitive mind kept his faculty of vision fresh and true; Lawrence had eyes for the substantial and even at his most doctrinaire he knew the world of appearance.

And just as there is no real sensory experience in Anderson's writing, there is also no real social experience. His people do not really go to church or vote or work for money, although it is often said of them that they do these things. In his desire for better social relationships Anderson could never quite see the social relationships that do in fact exist, however inadequate they may be. He often spoke, for example, of unhappy, desperate marriages and seemed to suggest that they ought to be quickly dissolved, but he never understood that marriages are often unsatisfactory for the very reasons that make it impossible to dissolve them.

His people have passion without body, and sexuality without gaiety and joy, although it is often through sex that they are supposed to find their salvation. John Jay Chapman said of Emerson that, great as he was, a visitor from Mars would learn less about life on earth from him than from Italian opera, for the opera at least suggested that there were two sexes. When Anderson was at the height of his reputation, it seemed that his report on the existence of two sexes was the great thing about him, the thing that made his work an advance over the literature of New England. But although the visitor from Mars might be instructed by Anderson in the mere fact of bisexuality, he would still be advised to go to the Italian opera if he seeks fuller information. For from the opera, as never from Anderson, he will acquire some of the knowledge which is normally in the possession of natives of the planet, such as that sex has certain manifestations which are socially quite complex, that it is involved with religion, politics, and the fate of nations, above all that it is frequently marked by the liveliest sort of energy.

In their speech his people have not only no wit, but no idiom. To say that they are not "real" would be to introduce all sorts of useless quibbles about the art of character creation; they are simply not *there*. This is not a failure of art; rather, it would seem to have been part of Anderson's intention that they should be not there. His narrative prose is contrived to that end; it is not really a colloquial idiom, although it has certain colloquial tricks; it approaches in effect the inadequate use of a foreign language; old slang persists in it and elegant archaisms are consciously used, so that people are constantly having the "fantods," girls are frequently referred to as "maidens," and things are "like unto" other things. These mannerisms, although they remind us of some of Dreiser's, are not the result, as Dreiser's are, of an effort to be literary and impressive. Anderson's prose has a purpose to which these mannerisms are essential—it has the intention of making us doubt our familiarity with our own world, and not, we must note, in order to make things fresher for us but only in order to make them seem puzzling to us and remote from us. When a man whose name we know is frequently referred to as "the plowmaker," when we hear again and again of "a kind of candy called Milky Way" long after we have learned, if we did not already know, that Milky Way is a candy, when we are told of someone that "He became a radical. He had radical thoughts," it becomes clear that we are being asked by this false naïveté to give up our usual and on the whole useful conceptual grasp of the world we get around in.

Anderson liked to catch people with their single human secret, their essence, but the more he looks for their essence the more his characters vanish into the vast limbo of meaningless life, the less they are human beings. His great American heroes were Mark Twain and Lincoln, but when he writes of these two shrewd, enduring men, he robs them of all their savor and masculinity, of all their bitter resisting mind; they become little more than a pair of sensitive, suffering happy-go-luckies. The more Anderson says about people, the less alive they become—and the less lovable. Is it strange that, with all Anderson's expressed affection for them, we ourselves can never love the people he writes about? But of course we do not love people for their essence or their souls, but for their having a certain body, or wit, or idiom, certain specific relationships with things and other people, and for a dependable continuity of existence: we love them for being there.

We can even for a moment entertain the thought that Anderson himself did not love his characters, else he would not have so thoroughly robbed them of substance and hustled them so quickly off the stage after their small essential moments of crisis. Anderson's love, however, was real enough; it is only that he loves under the aspect of his "truth"; it is love indeed but love become wholly abstract. Another way of putting it is that Anderson sees with the eyes of a religiosity of a very limited sort. No one, I think, has commented on the amount and quality of the mysticism that entered the thought of the writers of the twenties. We may leave Willa Cather aside, for her notion of Catholic order differentiates her; but in addition to Anderson himself, Dreiser, Waldo Frank, and Eugene O'Neill come to mind as men who had recourse to a strong but undeveloped sense of supernal powers.

It is easy enough to understand this crude mysticism as a protest against philosophical and moral materialism; easy enough, too, to forgive it, even when, as in Anderson, the second births and the large revelations seem often to point only to the bosom of a solemn bohemia, and almost always to a lowering rather than a heightening of energy. We forgive it because some part of the blame for its crudity must be borne by the culture of the time. In Europe a century before, Stendhal could execrate a bourgeois materialism and yet remain untempted by the dim religiosity which in America in the twenties seemed one of the likeliest of the few ways by which one might affirm the value of spirit; but then Stendhal could utter his denunciation of philistinism in the name of Mozart's music, the pictures of Cimabue, Masaccio, Giotto, Leonardo, and Michelangelo, the plays of Corneille, Racine, and Shakespeare. Of what is implied by these things Anderson seems never to have had a real intimation. His awareness of the past was limited, perhaps by his fighting faith in the "modern," and this, in a modern, is always a danger. His heroes in art and morality were few: Joyce, Lawrence, Dreiser, and Gertrude Stein, as fellow moderns; Cellini, Turgeniev; there is a long piece in praise of George Borrow; he spoke of Hawthorne with contempt, for he could not understand Hawthorne except as genteel, and he said of Henry James that he was "the novelist of those who hate," for mind seemed to him always a sort of malice. And he saw but faintly even those colleagues in art whom he did admire. His real heroes were the simple and unassuming, a few anony-mous Negroes, a few craftsmen, for he gave to the idea of craftsmanship a value beyond the value which it actually does have—it is this as much as anything else that reminds us of Hemingway's relation to Anderson—and a few racing drivers of whom Pop Geers was chief. It is a charming hero worship, but it does not make an adequate antagonism to the culture which Anderson opposed, and in order to make it compelling and effective Anderson reinforced it with what is in effect the high language of religion, speaking of salvation, of the voice that will not be denied, of dropping the heavy burden of this world.

The salvation that Anderson was talking about was no doubt a real salvation, but it was small, and he used for it the language of the most strenuous religious experience. He spoke in visions and mysteries and raptures, but what he was speaking about after all was only the salva-tion of a small legitimate existence, of a quiet place in the sun and moments of leisurely peace, of not being nagged and shrew-ridden, nor deprived of one's due share of affection. What he wanted for himself and others was perhaps no more than what he got in his last years: a home, neighbors, a small daily work to do, and the right to say his say carelessly and loosely and without the sense of being strictly judged. But between this small, good life and the language which he used about it there is a discrepancy which may be thought of as a willful failure of taste, an intended lapse of the sense of how things fit. Wynd-ham Lewis, in his attack in *Paleface* on the early triumphant Anderson, speaks of Anderson's work as an assault on responsibility and thought-ful maturity, on the pleasures and uses of the mind, on decent human pride, on Socratic clarity and precision; and certainly when we think of the "marching men" of Anderson's second novel, their minds lost in their marching and singing, leaving to their leader the definitions of their aims, we have what might indeed be the political consequences of Anderson's attitudes if these were carried out to their ultimate implications. Certainly the precious essence of personality to which Anderson was so much committed could not be preserved by any of the people or any of the deeds his own books delight in.

But what hostile critics forget about Anderson is that the cultural situation from which his writing sprang was actually much as he described it. Anderson's truth may have become a falsehood in his hands by reason of limitations in himself or in the tradition of easy populism he chose as his own, but one has only to take it out of his hands to see again that it is indeed a truth. The small legitimate existence, so necessary for the majority of men to achieve, is in our age so very hard, so nearly impossible, for them to achieve. The language Anderson used was certainly not commensurate with the traditional value which literature gives to the things he wanted, but it is not incommensurate with the modern difficulty of attaining these things. And it is his unending consciousness of this difficulty that constitutes for me the residue of admiration for him that I find I still have.

D. H. LAWRENCE'S SENSIBILITY *

FRANCIS FERGUSSON

I

THE difficulty in studying Lawrence is not exactly to determine what he was. He put himself down with such candor that even his bewilderments and his gradually overcome self-deception are transparent. Those who read his letters, especially, come to know him like an old friend. The difficulty is to know what to accept from Lawrence, what to reject, what to believe and how to believe it—what to make of him, in a word. There is no use trying to derive any consistent doctrine from his works, for he was not a system builder, and there is no use trying to appreciate him solely as an artist; he was himself too often impatient of the demands of art, which seemed to him trivial compared with the quest he followed. He was the kind of romantic poet whose writings are seldom self-subsistent creations, but rather signs of his inspiration, which is itself the important thing. If you think only of his personality, of what he was with people, you reduce him to the dimensions of the people he was with. If you try to judge his soul, you usurp the functions that belong to Saint Peter, and you risk making a terrible mistake. You will probably be demanding of Lawrence something he never tried to give, and was by nature unfitted to give; and so you fail to see what his contribution really was, in itself.

Mrs. Mable Dodge Luhan tries [1] the first method. She tells us about Lawrence's visits to Taos as honestly and completely as she can, not sparing herself in the process, and showing us everything that she herself can see. Her book is so vivid and earnest that we get an impression of Lawrence's personality out of it almost better than we do out of his letters. We can see how exciting he was as an individual, how generous, how full of hope, how subject to petty fits of anger, how willing to try anything once. And Mrs. Luhan makes it clear that he did not find what he was looking for in Taos. The little colony of highbrows between the Pueblo and the Mexican town fluttered to its rather shallow depths when he approached; but Lawrence himself presently rushed off to Mexico, having had an experience of some sort, but as unrealized in Taos as he had been everywhere else. It is no doubt the pattern of Lawrence's periodic efforts to belong to some community. In the semi-

* "D. H. Lawrence's Sensibility" first appeared in *Hound and Horn*, April-June, 1933. It is used here by permission of the author.
[1] *Lorenzo in Taos*

autobiographical work *Kangaroo* Lawrence tells a rather similar story which confirms and amplifies this impression.

Mr. Middleton Murry [2] tries the far more difficult and dubious method. He speaks of Lawrence and Jesus in the same breath; but what he gives with one hand he takes away with the other: "We needed a leader and a prophet," he says, addressing Lawrence's ghost; "you were marked by destiny to be the man, and you failed us." His interpretation of Lawrence is that he was a deeply believing Christian (as Mr. Murry understands the word) without the strength to live up to or even recognize his belief; and he gives us to understand that Lawrence ended in the most horrible disintegration. He quotes chapter and verse at every point, and as you read his book you are likely to feel that it is full of suggestive half-truths, at least. But then, one could quote chapter and verse for almost any interpretation of Lawrence, and Mrs. Catherine Carswell [3] disputes not only Mr. Murry's thesis but many of his facts. Mr. Murry relies very heavily on evidence from Lawrence's gloomiest period, which was in England, during the War; the period when Lawrence was forced by the persecution of the military authorities to be inactive; when he was finishing *Women in Love,* and trying to digest his first acute vision of chaos on all sides. Mr. Murry would have us believe that Lawrence never recovered from this experience, but declined, with a few partial recoveries, into some sort of sensual degeneration. Mrs. Carswell's idea is that his flight to the joyous Mediterranean was simply a healthy rejection of too much horror. Mr. Murry seems to think of Lawrence as a saint and theologian combined, who fell into a temptation which he really understood, though he wouldn't quite admit it, in more or less Christian terms; Mrs. Carswell makes him out a poetic nature turning instinctively from gloom and decay toward the sunshine and happiness he required.

Mrs. Carswell's different conception of Lawrence makes her write a study which is entirely different in method and intention. "I believe that there not only may, but must be, a new way of life, and that Lawrence was on the track of it," she writes. So from the very beginning she gives him credit for his avowed intentions. Mr. Murry is more often compelled to disregard, in the interests of his thesis, what Lawrence himself said he was trying to do. While Mrs. Carswell sticks very close to the letter of Lawrence, the Lawrence whose voice we hear in every word he wrote, Mr. Murry tends to replace the man with a religio-psychoanalytic map of his subconscious—an exercise which is easy enough nowadays and not very satisfactory. Mr. Murry says, "It is absolutely necessary to distinguish what Lawrence, as a living person, is demanding, from what Lawrence, as a man of profound impersonal vision, declares to be necessary." This distinction

2 *Son of Woman*
3 *The Savage Pilgrimage*

is a good one, very fair and cautious; but one gradually comes to see that the "impersonal vision" Mr. Murry really uses is not so much a vision Lawrence recognized as it is Mr. Murry's own notion of what Lawrence's vision should have been. Lawrence had many visions, but no consistent doctrine. Mrs. Carswell draws a different distinction: between Lawrence the man and Lawrence's poetic or prophetic voice. Mr. Aldous Huxley [4] separates the man from the *daimon* that possessed him. It is this primary gift, call it voice, *daimon,* inspiration, sensibility, or what you will, a gift that Lawrence never lost, but exploited to the end of his life, that makes him important—and neither his personal salvation, about which we can hardly judge, nor his systematic theology, which was for him as unimportant as his art.

Perhaps one reason Mrs. Carswell's book is so good is that it is by a woman. Women seem to be able to be disciples of Lawrence's without losing their bearings: they apparently do not have the same need to codify that men do. "Le grand effort de l'homme, s'il est sincère, c'est d'ériger en lois ses impressions personelles." This is not a woman's effort, and it was not Lawrence's effort. His effort was to accept every moment of life as true in itself; to respect the reality of the feeling rather than the reality of the impersonal ideal. Those who were too absorbed in their ideals struck him as unbearably false, and women are grateful to him for this feeling. A couple of years before his death he writes as follows to Aldous Huxley: "Your idea of the grand perverts is excellent. You might begin with a Roman—and go on to Saint Francis—Michael Angelo and Leonardo—Goethe or Kant—Jean-Jacques Rousseau or Louis Quatorze. . . . They all did the same thing, or tried to: to kick off or to intellectualize, and so utterly falsify the phallic consciousness, which is the basic consciousness, and the thing we mean, in the best sense, by common sense. . . . Goethe began millions of intimacies, and never got beyond the how-do-you-do stage, then fell off into his own boundless ego. . . . Back of them all is ineffable conceit." Mr. Hyatt Mayor has remarked that Lawrence writes as women ought to write, and don't; and I think one feels that this passage should have been written by a woman, but obviously wasn't. Mrs. Carswell quotes Lawrence's wife to the effect that life with him was always worth while. This humility before the feeling, this complete emotional availability, is a very difficult thing for a man to give, perhaps even for Lawrence; but in return for it a man may maintain, as Lawrence knew, his contact with the earth, with common sense. Mr. Murry does not see in the least this important fact about Lawrence.

II. "GOD IN ME IS MY DESIRE."—LETTER TO CATHERINE CARSWELL

All those who write about Lawrence try to make him out as some sort of religious teacher. For Mr. Murry he is a spectacular Dostoevsky

[4] *The Letters of D. H. Lawrence,* with an Introduction by Aldous Huxley.

saint and sinner; for Mrs. Carswell he is the prophet of a new life, and Mr. Huxley, in the very thoughtful introduction to the Letters, compares him with Pascal, and draws a suggestive analogy between his feeling of "otherness" and mystery in the universe, and his insistence that in the love relation a man and woman shall feel each other as mysterious and different, instead of mere extensions of their own "boundless egos." Lawrence was always announcing that the age was corrupt, and that he rejected it; and he was continually haunted by the notion of a pure terrestrial paradise. While he sits in England trying to last out the dreary war years, he plans a colony in Florida. As soon as the war is over, and he is free to move, he seeks in Italy, then in the Orient, Australia, Taos, and Mexico, in that order. His geographical wanderings were accompanied by a quest of a different kind. The *Fantasia of the Unconscious,* for example, is a search for the "dark gods" of the belly, an attempt, which would be ridiculous if it were not so suggestive, to write a mythology of the bowels and nervous system. When he is in the grip of this spirit his prose can sound like Apocalypse, or at other times like a revivalist preacher in Harlem.

It seems to me that his sense of the eternal quest for Eden on earth was connected even more closely than his sense of mystery and "otherness" with his picture of what the love relation should be. In *The Plumed Serpent* we read,

> That which he brought to marriage was something flamy and un-abashed, fresh and virginal. Not, as she had always known in men, yearning and seeking their own ends. Naïvely bringing his flame to her flame.

Certainly this is not a traditionally Christian religious sentiment. In Dante the earthly paradise is empty, and it is only a moment in a vast scheme. Lawrence not only craves a strictly terrestrial paradise, he seems to crave nothing beyond it. Hence his peculiar and profound understanding of America. Lawrence would have tried to join the Shakers, or the Mormons, or any of the religious societies in early nineteenth century America, which, reacting against Calvinism and the doctrine of original sin, announced that the age of innocence was at hand, and that the proper thing to do was retire from the world and live like Adam before the Fall with one's wife or wives. It is a centrifugal, rebellious spirit, which Lawrence, from the Non-Conformist strain in England, was legitimately heir to.

Studies in Classic American Literature, many other essays and several short stories, *The Boy in the Bush,* and much of *The Plumed Serpent* and *Mornings in Mexico* owe their existence very directly to Lawrence's sympathy with the America of Promised Lands. *The Boy in the Bush,* which Lawrence rewrote from a story by Skinner, is laid in Australia, but it might have been laid in the American West and it might have been called *The Mormon*. But *Classic American Literature* is the great monument of this part of Lawrence's sensibility. His gift worked best when it could work directly on real objects, instead of having to construct or invent. His travel books are extraordinarily successful for this reason; and in this book of literary history he has the American authors to react to directly—to interview, to praise, and to abuse. He is fascinated with them all: with Cooper and Crèvecoeur, who had romantic and rather European cults of the Indian; with Poe, and his sinister or transcendental loves; with Melville, and his metaphysical and geographical wanderings. He lives over vicariously and in retrospect each of their careers. He seems to survey them enviously, yet at the same time with a terrible sense of their futility. Their succession gives him a myth: the myth of the breaking-up of the European tradition into many eccentric quests. There have been theses about American literature and American culture, but probably no other study on a large scale so deep and many-sided and suggestive as Lawrence's. You may say that it is only a myth, a fiction, after all; but the myth is still one of the few ways we have of understanding our fundamental desires, the psychoanalysts to the contrary notwithstanding. You may say the book is nervous and personal, only a projection of Lawrence's sense of his own destiny. But no one had a better right than he, both by temperament and background, to appropriate our authors. And his ultimate justification is the fine, tragic ordering he gives them.

Lawrence wrote *Classic American Literature* during the gloomy war years in England, while toying from time to time with the idea of a colony in Florida. It is characteristic of him that he should have been planning a promised land and celebrating the failure of promised lands at one and the same moment. The reason his books on America are so good is that he knew more than the founders of Oneida Communities. He not only had their experience to instruct him, but everywhere he looked he discerned examples of the same *hubris* in different forms. The sophisticated people among whom he lived much of his life, with their various efforts to escape by way of sex, consistently attracted and repelled him. He says somewhere that such people were important, not in themselves, but as sensitive indicators of the trends of the times. There is no doubt that he knew, in a way, what they were; yet his sense of life lay close to theirs:

> Beneath the stars, upon yon meteor
> Ever hung my fate, 'mongst things corruptible.
> ... My loathing
> Was prophet to the rest, but ne'er believed.

In short, Lawrence knew more about the need for Paradise than the need itself; he knew something of its destiny on earth. Much of what is sometimes called his religious sense could equally well be called a tragic sense. His sympathy was really with the Aristotelian hero of tragedy, the passionate man, not the saint, the man who lives by his desires and illusions. His piety is a sense of the human lot and the human limitation; some female voice is always in his ear, like the voice of Kate in *The Plumed Serpent:*

> "Oh!" she cried to herself, stifling. "For heaven's sake let me get out of this, and back to simple human people. I loathe the very sound of Quetzalcoatl and Huitzilopochtli. . . . And they want to put it over me, with their high-flown bunk and their Malintzi. . . ."

In the continual effort to find a religious system he could believe in, Lawrence was much influenced by anthropological studies of classic and primitive cultures. In his happy moments what he worships is very much like Priapus, the garden god, who keeps the boundaries of a man's fields, the hearth and home, and whose enormous phallus, as Catullus says, the householder will sometimes use to club marauders over the head with. When he tries to think out in detail how he would like to have his religion embodied, he thinks of some patriarchal or tribal organization with church and state in one. For him a human society was nothing unless it embodied in its structure some of the spiritual and emotional life of the people that composed it. The United States was in his opinion not a human society at all, but a nest of one hundred and ten million china eggs. In *Kangaroo* he tells us how the foreigners of Australia made him feel the pull of the tribe *he* belonged to: the English tribe, with its aristocratic tradition.[5] Even the big country houses which he sometimes hated made him homesick for this tribal past. Shakespeare was in his bones; and loyalty to Coolidge Republicanism or Greenwich Village Technocracy would have seemed to him a very weak substitute indeed for the loyalty that attached Shakespeare's Romans to Coriolanus or Anthony. So that at the same time that his religious sense connected him with the centrifugal, romantic, individualistic spirit of the modern world, it connects him with that more pagan, more Catholic tradition which England inherited from the ancient European cultures.

These multiple awarenesses in Lawrence made him a most rich and exciting spirit, and an almost unbearably stimulating companion or guide. But as he found no embodiments of his belief, he never

---

[5] In *Lady Chatterley's Lover,* which contains Lawrence's final word on his native Midlands, he sees as it were *through* the dreary, restless industrial population to a more or less fictitious time when a peasant population preserved its pagan tradition, its seasonal festivals and dances, and its ancient, sensuous, earthy way of life, beneath a superimposed Catholicism. As for Christianity, he says here, it will do for a minority, perhaps, never for the sensual mass.

finally attached or committed himself. He makes us feel the richness of the modern intellectual world, with its learning, its memories, and its emotional facility; and at the same time he makes us feel how barren it is of accomplishment, and at last how frivolously arbitrary its faiths are. His sober muse, who was always starting out to imitate the tragedy of life, as in the magnificent opening chapters of *The Plumed Serpent,* was always being interrupted by his *daimon* yelling that only the quest for innocence on earth was worth while. And his *daimon* could never finish a sermon without being interrupted by his muse, grown ironic and disgusted. He can be as tragic as he likes, there is nearly always a certain agony left over, unfulfilled, disembodied, and destructive of him, of us, and of his art. Yet on the other hand he never makes the traditionally saintly effort to renounce and transcend human life, but clings to the fate of unregenerate humanity.

III. "THE STYLE IS THE MAN."

It is tempting to assert that Lawrence would have been an artist pure and simple if he had been able to find a traditional belief, of the kind which in the past has given both content and stability to what an artist had to say. His sufferings may be regarded as those of a frustrated artist rather than those of a seer, if these distinctions have any meaning when applied to so Protean a spirit as Lawrence's. These points may be illustrated by a consideration of the order of his works.

He still considered himself a novelist while writing *Sons and Lovers.* He accepted the large, loose form of the Nineteenth Century novel, as it was still being turned out in England by Arnold Bennett and others. For theme and subject matter he had his own history and the history of his family to write—all he had to say for the moment: the prophet is not yet born. But *The Rainbow* is already more ambitious. The form begins to seem stale to him, and he becomes bored with his characters, which come to seem so numerous and monotonous as to lose all meaning. "Human beings ultimately bore me, and you can't have fiction without human beings," he says in one of his war-time letters. By the time he reached *Women in Love* he was sure that he was through with the traditional novel, that he no longer cared for individual character and circumstance. Mrs. Carswell writes as follows about this development of Lawrence's: "Those who say 'What a pity he did not care!' have a point of view with which it is difficult not to sympathize at times. With Lawrence, and perhaps with Lawrence alone, the dumb cottagers and inexpressive 'workers' of industrial England might for the first time have found a voice. Even as it is, we now see them *because* of Lawrence, as they have not been seen before. We are pierced by a passional knowledge of them never even suggested by any other writer. But he has given us, practically speaking, no characters."

This is a very good description of *Women in Love*. He will give you his people's feelings for the earth, the sky, and the ruins of industry, so sharply that it is like living in the Midlands yourself. He will render the essence of the emotional relations between them so well that you almost forget the parties to the relation are not realized. As for his minor characters, whom he studies more externally, he makes you feel their presence, their emotional effect, so surely, that if you happen to have known any of the real people that suggested them you can identify them with certainty, even after a period of years. But his main characters, from whose point of view he writes, and whom he designs to carry the chief burden of his meaning, disappear as characters, as he dives through them in search of what Mrs. Carswell calls the life stream. He was simply not interested in what they were in the objective world; he was interested only in the inner world of their emotional and spiritual life. And his trouble was that the people he found to study were not interested in it, or not aware of it, as he was.

Lawrence was not the first novelist to encounter this problem. Henry James met it in his way, by suggesting a vast structure of scruples and heroisms behind and above the little destinies he knew. Joyce elaborates a point-to-point correspondence between the spiritual movements of a little Dublin city-dweller and the mythical wanderings of Ulysses. The effect is all the stronger for Bloom's unconsciousness of the antique pattern he fits into. But Lawrence rejected both the moral nature of man as Henry James knew it and the mythical and cultural heritage of the race, searching, as he proclaimed, for new values and new symbols. Yet he was far too much of an artist to try to do without symbols; he knew better than anyone that our emotional or moral or religious sensibility is shared only by means of "objective equivalents." You might almost say that his imagination was so concrete that he failed to distinguish between the reality and the metaphor or symbol which makes it plain to us. Certainly he is always improvising with his metaphors, laying about him informally for things to body forth his meanings: endowing a landscape with human emotions, or seeing his agony in the wobblings of the moon's reflection in troubled water.

If you go to Lawrence with a great deal of free and undefined emotion, he will orchestrate it for you; he will provide sensuous molds for your emotion to flow into. Birkin's continual smashing of the moon's reflection in the pond is a good example of this. The scattering and the regathering of the sparkles of light will do to embody any sort of struggle for control, for the very reason that the image itself has no exact reference and the context does not provide it. It is like romantic music: it might be about anything, and only if you ask what it *is* all about do you feel that something has been put over on you.

Why not simply call Lawrence a pantheist and be done with it? He seems to perceive the "objective equivalents" at one glance, inextricably mixed with the reality they are to convey. It seems that they are themselves the new territory he is exploring. Certainly they are always part of his initial inspiration, never conscious technical devices. He can never see anything without feeling it as part of his own spiritual life. Besides, his most characteristic metaphors are interwoven with the whole sweep of his longer works, and receive their full development only as the whole work develops, so that it is very hard to quote examples with any fairness. In *Women in Love* Gerald is likened to the white moon, to the Alps, to the Arctic snow-wilderness. His place in history, his human relations, and his class, are gradually involved in this figure. Even Lawrence's poems, especially the later ones in *Birds, Beasts and Flowers,* are developed figures of this kind, too long to quote in their entirety. The object and the symbol or figure of the object are built up side by side, together.

Mr. Eliot's distinction between Shakespeare's use of simile and Dante's gives us, I think, the clue. "Whereas the simile of Dante is merely to make you see how the people looked, and is explanatory, the figure of Shakespeare is expansive rather than intensive; its purpose is to *add* to what you see." In Lawrence's poem "Figs" we read,

> Folded upon itself, enclosed like any Mohammedan woman,
> Its nakedness all within walls, its flowering forever unseen....

Lawrence is not trying to make you see the fig more closely, but through the fig to see something different and larger. When Lawrence's style is successful it is because he has found something which can stand exactly for some particular meaning; and he lets the image stand in all its roundness and suggestiveness.

But in "Figs" he puts as it were an intolerable burden on the poor fig. When his style fails it is because he himself feels—sooner than the reader, usually—that the image will not do for the meaning. Sometimes he has not quite found the meaning itself, but is only feeling for it with images. Sometimes the correspondence is not clear, and he will break off the fiction entirely and write a long explanatory philosophical essay. Sometimes, as in *Kangaroo,* he will introduce a frankly personal narrative, as though to say that the work of art is only an improvisation, a makeshift, for some more direct means of communication. Dante takes the inner world for granted, and writes only for those who accept it as he does, and have some experience of it. All he expects his style to do is to record his impression of what is, was and ever shall be. Even Hamlet, who was struggling with the archetype of Lawrence's problem, contents himself with telling Horatio that there are more things in heaven and earth than are dreamt of in his philosophy. But Lawrence in his longer works was trying to force a new experience upon us.

In Lawrence's case it is peculiarly true to say that the style is the man. True because of his unique candor, because of his life-long effort to respect the reality of every moment's feeling. He had not one style, but several voices. In *The Plumed Serpent,* when the naturalistic narrative fades away, he speaks out through Ramon Carrasco in parables and apothegms, with a voice like that of Nietzsche's Zarathustra. It is a kind of synthetic modern biblical style. He has the voice of a bewildered, angry, and repetitious man when he loses his bearings; yet when he records his visits to Sicily or Mexico, or his interviews with the Classic American authors, he speaks crisply, nimbly and neatly. And when his other voices are exhausted, or disgusted, or have fallen silent for some other reason, his muse creeps out.

Lawrence's moments of pure artistry are scattered through all his works, and they dominate certain short stories, including "Smile," "Two Bluebirds," and "The Captain's Doll." It is not that his vision of reality is different at these times, it is rather as though he had accepted a vision that was there all the time, and as though with the acceptance had come the ability to render it objectively. For the moment he lets the fiction stand. Take "The Captain's Doll." It is laid in Germany and Austria after the War. Its subject is as usual the relation between a man and a woman, and as usual the characters interest him far less than the emotional states they share. The unity of the whole includes the geographical and historical setting, the crowds of pleasure-seekers, like weary Tristans and unbelieving Isoldes, and the end of the old Austrian Empire. The doll itself is an extraordinarily suggestive symbol; and though he explains it in various ways he never explains it away. The two lovers' mountain climbing, the Captain's scrambling absurdly up over the slippery ice while sceptical Hannele eyes him from below, is a dramatic or scenic device comparable to Paolo and Francesca's restless wind.

When Lawrence is in possession of his subject his style achieves another kind of triumph which is extremely rare, and very characteristic of Lawrence: it seems entirely limpid, natural, and effortless. This quality is the reward of serving always one's own sensibility, and Lawrence sought it very consciously. He never polished or fixed his writings: if he thought they needed polishing he rewrote them entire. So he stayed as close as possible to his source. When this source is impure it is Lawrence's own voice we hear yelling in its agony; when it is pure, the prose which flows from it is as clear and living as a trout-stream.*

* See Mark Schorer's "Technique as Discovery" essay in Part I of this volume.

IV. "ART IS A QUESTION OF BEING ALIVE. GO IN PEACE."—*him.*

Lawrence has been likened to Keats, Blake, Burns, and with less aptness to Dostoevsky. Toward the end of his life especially he is very comparable to Nietzsche. Certainly he is in the tradition of romantic writers whose sensibility is more important than their works. Professor Borgese has said (in his lectures at the New School) that romantic writers identify art with its source or root in inspiration, while classical writers identify it with its realization or flowering in achieved form. Lawrence's sensibility, whether religious, moral, or poetic, was a root sensibility. The distinction is very good, because it does not attempt to say whether *root* in this sense is to mean rudimentary and primitive, or basic and profound. Was Lawrence religious?—Yes; but whether Greek, Christian, or Hopi it would be hard to say. He was a moralist, but sometimes his ethics seem hardly more than a psychological therapy analogous to M. Fernandez' training of the personality, while at other times he gives us to understand that nothing matters but faith. And he was an artist who seldom produced a work of art. Yet with his very live, very acute and very courageous sensibility he performed for our day the root function of the poet or the seer, at a level where the two functions are hardly distinguishable. One might say that "the conscience of a blackened street impatient to assume the world" could never quite assume the world while Lawrence was in it.

For some readers, perhaps especially women, this sensibility is enough. They find Lawrence a touchstone for vitality, integrity, or faith, and are satisfied. His influence on other writers is different. Whether they agree with him or not, they find him a source or a beginning, fertile in problems and nearly devoid of solutions; and they tend to try to elaborate or crystallize the raw materials of pure perception he gives them. Mr. Wyndham Lewis and Mr. Aldous Huxley are examples. Most of the important contemporary writers live in the same world as Lawrence did, a world which he did as much as anyone to make us aware of. So in *The Rainbow,* when Ursula is struggling with her first experience of love in the industrial chaos of the Midlands, she has the following reverie:

> . . . It was a place of Kings for her—Richard and Henry and Wolsey and Queen Elizabeth. She divined great lawns with noble trees, and terraces whose steps the water washed softly, where the swans sometimes came to earth. Still she must see the stately, gorgeous barge of the Queen float down, the crimson carpet put upon the landing stairs, the gentlemen in their purple velvet cloaks, bare-headed, standing in the sunshine grouped on either side waiting.
>
> "Sweet Thames run softly till I end my song."

And in *The Waste Land* the following passages occur:

> ... The nymphs are departed.
> And their friends, the loitering heirs of city directors,
> Departed, have left no addresses.
> By the waters of Leman I sat down and wept....
> Sweet Thames run softly till I end my song....
>
> Elizabeth and Leicester
> Beating oars
> The stern was formed
> A gilded shell
> The brisk swell
> Rippled both shores....

It is evident that the inspiration or primary poetic idea is similar in the two episodes, with their startling juxtapositions of images from the past with an awareness of the present, and the quotation from Spenser to bring it home to us. It is not necessary to my point to assume that Mr. Eliot had been reading *The Rainbow;* it is enough to point out that in their feeling of where we are, nowadays, the two writers are very close together. And a study of *The Waste Land* would reveal the difference between Lawrence's inspirations and a poetic idea realized. What Lawrence gets partially, as a flash of intuition, Eliot is able to see as part of a much larger and more highly developed pattern —as round, solid, and independent of the observer or recorder. Lawrence's works are all invitations to try to realize something. That is why it is so difficult to write about him without trying to realize him, in necessarily alien terms, better than he bothered to realize himself.

ALDOUS HUXLEY AND THE DISSOCIATION OF PERSONALITY *

D. S. Savage

THE reputation of Aldous Huxley—that initial reputation, through which his claim upon popular esteem still persists—was made, it should be recollected, in the era of post-Great War "disillusionment," whose predominant mood was faithfully reflected in the bright and bitter humour, the sardonic portrayal of human futility, which marked the early novels and tales. In his earlier days Huxley was read with enthusiasm by many of his contemporaries, not only in England, who felt that, in sophisticated hedonism, his freedom from outworn loyalties, and even in his licence, he spoke for a generation. He was detached, ironical, and he knew how to be amusing with that wryness which revealed an awareness of the corruption at the bottom of the glass of pleasure.

Huxley's work as a whole has taken the form of a thinly disguised autobiographical sequence. Its shape has been determined by its author's changing attitude to life, which has always found its corresponding intellectual expression (reviewers were wont, as a matter of course, to prostrate themselves before his overwhelming "intellect"). The problem for the critic therefore lies in the difficulty of keeping a just balance between Huxley's changing responses to life, the artistic productions which have arisen from and been shaped by those responses, and the resultant ideas which the novelist has abstracted, as it were, from the creative process, and which he now arrays formidably and somewhat menacingly before his public.

For, as it happens, that early entertainer ("that different person," Huxley writes in a recent new preface to one of his old novels, "who was oneself in youth . . .") is a figure from whom the later, and at first glance strangely altered Huxley, would wish rather pointedly to dissociate himself. Today there confronts us, not the sardonic portrayer of futility, but the prophet and the philosopher of Enlightenment, of Liberation, through a species of mystical contemplation. And this

* "Aldous Huxley and the Dissociation of Personality" appeared in Great Britain in *The Withered Branch*, by D. S. Savage (Eyre and Spottiswoode, 1950). It was first published in this country in the *Sewanee Review*, Autumn, 1947, and is used here by permission of the author, the magazine editors, and Paul R. Reynolds & Son, 599 Fifth Avenue, New York, N. Y.

prophet, or teacher, quite overshadows, if he has not finally eliminated, the artist.

What in fact is the nature of the teaching which emerges? It is rather a simple doctrine. Man's final end, according to Huxley's most recent work, a compendium entitled *The Perennial Philosophy* (1946), is nothing less than "unitive love-knowledge of the Divine Ground," a knowledge which one must attain by "making oneself loving, pure in heart and poor in spirit," through "a discipline more arduous and unremitting than any imposed by ecclesiastical authority"—a discipline which involves, indeed, a "total dying to self."

Salvation, deliverance, enlightenment are apostrophized; but always the emphasis, in this version of mysticism, is upon self-obliteration; and self-obliteration, it appears, in an impassive, non-personal, not-God (as with strange candour the "Divine Ground" is here described). Time and all its works, being evil, must be annihilated: the goal is *Nirvana,* complete cessation of the pain which comes through individuation, separation from the abysmal One.

> Man must live in time in order to be able to advance into eternity, no longer on the animal, but on the spiritual level; he must be conscious of himself as a separate ego in order to be able consciously to transcend separate selfhood; he must do battle with the lower self in order that he may become identified with that higher Self within him, which is akin to the divine Not-Self; and finally he must make use of his cleverness in order to pass beyond cleverness to the intellectual vision of Truth, the immediate, unitive knowledge of the Divine Ground.

The mystics—Catholic, Quaker, Hindu, Buddhist, Taoist, Sufi, and the rest—have pointed out the way; Huxley annotates it: we refuse to follow at our peril.

Whether in fact the new doctrine can be so completely dissociated from its literary antecedents is something which we owe it to truth and to ourselves to investigate rather than to take on trust. A hundred years ago Sören Kierkegaard in a masterly essay categorically described the fundamental disorientation which afflicts all human existence not lived under the rubric, Faith, as the "sickness unto death"; the sickness unto death being—despair. To designate Aldous Huxley as the novelist of despair—if despair is the emotional potentiation of futility, the central theme of his work—will seem unquestionably fitting to the earlier "Pyrrhonic aesthete," and if it should arouse some surprise, here and there, when applied with even greater emphasis to the later Huxley, in his "Perennial" avatar, that surprise will, I trust, be modified in the light of what is said below.

That there is, in reality, more than a marked affinity between Huxley's earlier and his later work and ideas we shall discover if, disregarding whatever overt attitudes the abstract theorist would have us accept, we scrutinize the underlying structure of the novelist's and the thinker's world. The fictional universe which he creates and populates possesses certain well-defined features which might all be said to be explicable in the light of a fundamental *discontinuity*. If we say of Huxley's characters that they are static and isolated, that a certain impersonal detachment shows itself in their creator's attitude towards them, and that at the same time their existence presumes a context of pointlessness, we shall have sketched a readily recognizable picture of Huxley's constant frame of reference. For, by a curious irony, while Huxley himself would claim a radical discontinuity between the divergent attitudes to life—"Pyrrhonic hedonism" and contemplative mysticism—which in turn grow out of and condition his earlier and his later work, in fact the two originate in a common dislocation of being; the one exaggeration of attitude finds its balancing counterpart in the other; and the irony is pointed in the fact that discontinuity itself can even be said to be the only continuous factor in decisive operation throughout Huxley's artistic career. Huxley's development follows not a spiral but an hour-glass pattern. The psychological structure underlying *Crome Yellow, Antic Hay,* and *Those Barren Leaves* becomes modified as the novelist's dissatisfaction with his non-committal relationship to life draws him towards a closer engagement, only to reassert itself with finality as he crosses over into a yet further detachment which is the obverse of the earlier attitude, and which reinforces its pronounced bias towards the impersonal, the non-human.

I

The mental structure upon which Huxley was to raise his successive fictional edifices is discoverable with little difficulty in his first novel, *Crome Yellow* (1921). A dualism of mind and matter, of the ideal and the actual, is fundamental to it, and is the source at once of Huxley's pessimism, of the purely static and episodic quality of his work, and of his humour. Futility and frustration, humorously presented, the disparity between intention and accomplishment, are the themes of this slight, episodic narrative which tells of a short holiday spent by a young poet, Denis, at the country house of Crome, during the course of which he encounters a succession of interestingly odd characters, is pursued by a young female while himself unsuccessfully pursuing another, and eventually allows himself to be bundled off for home just as he seems to be within reach of amorous success. The appropriate note is struck in the opening paragraph:

> Oh, this journey! It was two hours cut clean out of his life; two hours in which he might have done so much, so much—written the perfect poem, for example, or read the one illuminating book. Instead of which —his gorge rose at the smell of the dusty cushions against which he was leaning. . . .

And it is maintained with fair consistency throughout.

The character of Denis is indeterminate. He is young and very un-certain of his own feelings and beliefs, and is moreover somewhat isolated from human contacts. Denis's response to living is involuntarily moralistic; theoretically he is a hedonist:

> "I've always taken things as they come," said Anne. "It seems so obvious. One enjoys the pleasant things, avoids the nasty ones. There's nothing more to be said."
> "Nothing—for you. But, then, you were born a pagan. I am trying laboriously to make myself one. I can take nothing for granted, I can enjoy nothing as it comes along. Beauty, pleasure, art, women—I have to invent an excuse, a justification for everything that's delightful. Otherwise I can't enjoy it with an easy conscience. . . . Pleasure is one of the mystical roads to union with the infinite—the ecstasies of drinking, dancing, love-making. As for women, I am perpetually assuring myself that they're the broad highway to divinity. And to think that I'm only just beginning to see through the silliness of the whole thing!"

Of Huxley's two themes, the first, the disparity of the ideal and the actual, is expressed characteristically in the account from Mr. Wim-bush's "History of Crome," of the Elizabethan baronet's sanitary ar-rangements; "the necessities of nature are so base and brutish that in obeying them we are apt to forget that we are the noblest creatures of the universe," so that accordingly the privy must be a book-lined room at the top of the house, commanding "an extensive and noble pros-pect." It finds expression also in the interpolated anecdote of the three lovely sisters who in public maintained a pretence of wan, ethereal spirituality, while surreptitiously gorging themselves at elabo-rate private repasts in their chamber. Huxley's second theme, his coupling of a deliberate hedonism with an underlying sense of personal futility, is asserted in this novel by Mr. Scogan:

> "Worried about the cosmos, eh?" Mr. Scogan patted him on the arm. "I know the feeling," he said. "It's a most distressing symptom. What's the good of continuing to function if one's doomed to be snuffed out at last along with everything else? Yes, yes, I know exactly how you feel. It's most distressing if one allows oneself to be distressed. But then why allow oneself to be distressed? After all, we all know that there's no ultimate point. But what difference does that make?"

We shall see that throughout his successive works Huxley has never departed from these foundations.

Antic Hay (1923) is at once more serious and more farcical, a mordant blaze of characters and incidents against a starker background of futility. Yet there is a pronounced thread of morality running through the tale's desperate gaiety. When we are introduced first to Theodore Gumbril we find him "speculating, in his rapid and rambling way, about the existence and the nature of God," and then, a little later, disturbed by a pricking conscience over his "first serious and deliberate lie"—in childhood.

The element of broad farce enters with Gumbril's invention and marketing of trousers with pneumatic seats. On the strength of his hopes from this venture he leaves his job as schoolmaster and embarks upon a random course of dissipation, during which he encounters such exponents of depravity as Myra Viveash, whose voice "seemed always on the point of expiring, as though each word were the last, uttered faintly and breakingly from a death-bed . . ."; Coleman, whose career of debauchery is carried out on principle and is accompanied by blasphemy; and Mr. Mercaptan, whose speciality is seduction according to the precepts of Crebillon *fils,* upon a white satin sofa in his taste-fully decorated apartment. The thread of quasi-moral narrative—that which concerns Gumbril's relations of simple, genuine affection with the girl Emily, whom he is led to abandon at a whim of Mrs. Viveash's —is slight in proportion to the whole novel, which concerns the erratic futilities of Gumbril and the others as they are whirled around in the dry wind of boredom, vanity, and despair.

Beneath the amusing surface there is a clear enunciation of the theme of futility:

> "It's appalling, it's horrible," said Gumbril at last, after a long, long silence, during which he had, indeed, been relishing to the full the horror of it all. "Life, don't you know . . ."

And when, after his betrayal of Emily, he goes, with Mrs. Viveash, the dreary, anguished, pleasure-hunting round of night clubs in an episode which palely reflects the Walpurgisnacht scenes of *Ulysses,* the night perpetuates itself with yet further revelations of human depravity and the farcical pointlessness of things, until finally:

> "To-morrow," said Gumbril at last, meditatively.
> "To-morrow," Mrs. Viveash interrupted him, "will be as awful as to-day." She breathed it like a truth from beyond the grave prematurely revealed, expiringly from her death-bed within.

Those Barren Leaves (1925), the novel following, is the first to be written from a serious questioning of life. The three major characters among the company assembled at the wealthy Mrs. Aldwinkle's Italian villa are Cardan, Chelifer, and Calamy, the disenchanted man of the world, whose temper provides a point of location for the mood of the book. All three share a common disillusionment with the human state. But whereas Cardan has pursued to the end a course of genial parasit-ical pleasure-seeking, Chelifer is a self-torturing romantic who takes a perverse delight in seeking out and identifying himself with life's most dingy aspects, while Calamy himself has simply wearied of the amorous round of the idle, affluent set, and is on the verge of a vaguely envisioned quest for the "way."

"...It seems to me," says Calamy, when Mr. Cardan, true to character, is praising "love" as the most enjoyable of indoor sports, "...that I'm beginning to have had enough of sports, whether indoor or out-of-door. I'd like to find some more serious occupation." And he continues, in response to Mr. Cardan's profession of amorality, in this vein:

> "You're fortunate.... It's not all of us whose personalities have such a natural odour of sanctity that they can disinfect our septic actions and render them morally harmless. When I do something stupid or dirty I can't help feeling that it is stupid or dirty. My soul lacks virtues to make it wise or clean. And I can't dissociate myself from what I do. I wish I could. One does such a devilish number of stupid things. Things one doesn't want to do. If only one could be a hedonist and only do what was pleasant! But to be a hedonist one must be wholly rational; there's no such thing as a genuine hedonist, there never has been. Instead of doing what one wants to do or what would give one pleasure, one drifts through existence doing exactly the opposite, most of the time—doing what one has no desire to do, following insane promptings that lead one, fully conscious, into every sort of discomfort, misery, boredom and remorse.... I don't like running after women, I don't like wasting my time in futile social intercourse, or in the pursuit of what is technically known as pleasure. And yet for some reason and quite against my will I find myself passing the greater part of my time immersed in precisely these occupations. It's an obscure kind of insanity. ...And what's the most depressing of all...is the feeling that one will go on like this forever, in the teeth of every effort to stop. I sometimes wish I weren't externally free. For then at any rate I should have something to curse at, for getting in my way, other than my own self. Yes, positively, I sometimes wish I were a navvy."

Mr. Cardan, for his part, remains the advocate of the hedonism criticized by Calamy. But he is forced continually to realize that he is in a blind alley, finding, towards the end of his career of pleasure, only bodily decrepitude and death. Alone, his reflections tend to take on a morbid tinge:

> It would be tiresome to end one's days with recurrent fever and an enlarged spleen. It would be tiresome, for that matter, to end one's days anyhow, in one's bed or out, naturally or unnaturally, by the act of God or of the King's enemies. Mr. Cardan's thoughts took on, all at once, a dismal complexion. Old age, sickness, decrepitude; the bath-chair, the doctor, the bright efficient nurse; and the long agony, the struggle for breath, the thickening darkness, the end, and then—how did that merry little song go?

> More work for the undertaker,
> 'Nother little job for the coffin-maker.
> At the local cemetery they are
> Very, very busy with a brand new grave.
> He'll keep warm next winter.

Mr. Cardan hummed the tune to himself cheerfully enough. But his tough, knobbly face became so hard, so strangely still, an expression of such bitterness, such a profound melancholy, appeared in his winking and his supercilious eye, that it would have frightened a man to look at him.

The tone then is markedly more serious. And for the first time we find the disparity fundamental to Huxley's outlook emphasized as a cleavage between "the flesh" and "the spirit." Thus, while Chelifer derives a mordant satisfaction from the ironic contrast which he delights to point between man's aspirations and the brute facts of his animal existence, the elderly Mr. Cardan's ruminations take a melancholy turn, and the disparity is seen like this:

> Only the tragedy of the spirit can liberate and uplift. But the greatest tragedy of the spirit is that sooner or later it succumbs to the flesh. Sooner or later every soul is stifled by the sick body; sooner or later there are no more thoughts, but only pain and vomitings and stupor. The tragedies of the spirit are mere struttings and posturings on the margin of life, and the spirit itself is only an accidental exuberance, the products of spare vital energy, like the feathers on the head of a hoopoe or the innumerable populations of useless and foredoomed spermatozoa. The spirit has no significance; there is only the body. When it is young, the body is beautiful and strong. It grows old, its joints creak, it becomes dry and smelly; it breaks down, the life goes out of it and it rots away. However lovely the feathers on a bird's head, they perish with it; and the spirit, which is a lovelier ornament than any, perishes too. The farce is hideous, thought Mr. Cardan, and in the worst of bad taste.

But at this point we must pause to collect the threads which have so far been taken up, in order to trace them to their common centre in that basic disjunction of personality which is the psychological source of all disjunctions in the Huxley world-picture. Let us begin with the two principal obsessions which have so clearly emerged this far— "hedonism" and "futility."

Huxley's central character, whichever of his books we take up, is remarkable primarily for placing so little value upon his existence as a man that he is implicitly prepared to forgo his claim to personal destiny and meaning, albeit with an uneasy conscience, for the immediate gain of a random succession of disrelated sensations. Inwardly inert, led this way and that by mere appetite, he becomes immersed consequently in a world which is deprived of value. Unaware that meaning and purpose do not reside as objective facts in the world of things but are interior realities which await for their realization upon interior dynamic movement, oblivious to the truth that personality is not a substance with which we are endowed by nature, but an inward integration which may be achieved only by the decisive choice of one-self, he arbitrarily attributes his own purposelessness to the universe as a whole. "Hedonism" and "futility" thus complement each other.

In *Crome Yellow* the chief character, Denis, is young, his hedonism an aspect of the common bewilderment of youth. Gumbril, in the second novel, is an older man, and hedonism takes on a cynical tinge, while futility is emphasized. Calamy, in the present novel, represents a further stage still—he is the disillusioned hedonist; and now the disparity of the Huxley world is presented from a new aspect. As a disillusioned hedonist Calamy has wearied of a life without *meaning,* he is beginning to look for another path, and hence the concept "spirit" for the first time makes its appearance; but "spirit" itself, superimposed upon the existing psychological pattern, takes the impress of the fundamental duality of mind, and appears as directly antithetical to "matter," or "the flesh," as something in some way beyond the limits of the sensual plane upon which human life is actually lived. Thus we find that Calamy unquestioningly assumes that the "way" of which he is in quest must lie somewhere beyond the region of ordinary human experience, and that it is to be found in opposition to the path of sensual indulgence from which that experience is inseparable.

He speaks in this manner to Chelifer and Mr. Cardan just prior to his departure for the mountain retreat:

> ". . . there is a whole universe within me, unknown and waiting to be explored; a whole universe that can only be approached by way of introspection and patient uninterrupted thought. Merely to satisfy curiosity it would surely be worth exploring. But there are motives more impelling than curiosity to persuade me. What one may find there is so important that it's almost a matter of life and death to undertake the search."
>
> "H'm," said Mr. Cardan. "And what will happen at the end of three months' chaste meditation when some lovely young temptation comes toddling down this road, 'balancing her haunches,' as Zola would say, and rolling the large black eye? What will happen to your explorations of the inward universe then, may I ask?"
>
> "Well," said Calamy, "I hope they'll proceed uninterrupted."
>
> "You hope? Piously?"
>
> "And I shall certainly do my best to see that they do," Calamy added.
>
> "It won't be easy," Mr. Cardan assured him.
>
> "I know."
>
> "Perhaps you'll find that you can explore simultaneously both the temptation and the interior universe."

Calamy shook his head. "Alas, I'm afraid that's not practicable. It would be delightful if it were. But for some reason it isn't. Even in moderation it won't do. I know that, more or less, by experience. And the authorities are all agreed about it."

This brings us at last to the structure of Huxley's novels, all of which—it is one of their principal defects—are remarkable for their lack of total dramatic movement and impetus. And this is precisely explicable as a consequence of the absence of dynamic movement in the mind of the novelist himself, a defect which is naturally communicated to his creatures, whose intercourse with each other, prepared and sustained by the accidents of social life, is virtually confined, as we have often heard it remarked, to sexuality and cerebration. No character in the course of this novel undergoes any modifications of outlook or temperament; each remains immobile within the limits marked out for it from the first. We know nothing of the particular events and motives which move Calamy towards the tentative renunciation which begins to take effect at the novel's close. Mr. Cardan is a lay figure as rigid as any in a morality play, and Chelifer is a study only in deliberate self-stultification. And such figures as the doctrinaire socialist, Mr. Falx, and the preposterous Mrs. Aldwinkle herself, are merely caricatures sardonically sketched by the satirist of social types. Only with the immature—in this case with Irene and the young Lord Hovingden, in their naïvely innocent courtship—does the novelist show any movement of human sympathy. Between such inwardly static characters, it is clear, there can be no dramatic interplay and thus no movement of the novel as an entity. Hence, instead of the movement of life, we are presented with episodes, blocks of incident and conversation broken up peremptorily by external change.

But this is something which deserves further exploration, for it is evidently bound up with the whole question of movement and purpose. Movement in a work of fiction is required, of course, to be significant—to bear some purposeful relation to an end. In that vivid portrayal of purposeless activity, *Antic Hay,* the dance of futility is necessarily non-dramatic and presupposes the stasis of character—which in turn is static just because, according to the context, the possibility of purposeful movement is non-existent; life itself is purposeless. In the succeeding novel there is some endeavour to move beyond this static condition dictated by life's total futility. Yet all that the novel succeeds in doing in this respect is to lay bare at great length the absolute cleavage between "matter" and "spirit" which underlies the idea of pointlessness. Nowhere in it is there any questioning of the reality and the appropriateness of this dualism.

The novel ends inconclusively. Calamy retires to his mountain retreat, but it is uncertain whither his lonely quest will lead him;

whether, indeed, it will lead anywhere. All we are told is that, looking at the distant skyline, he feels "somehow reassured."

II

That there is a progression of a sort within the first three novels is clear. And while *Point Counter Point* (1928) seems to show a divergence from what was later to appear as Huxley's main line of development, it nevertheless derives from the same basic pattern (though with a different emphasis) while continuing the movement towards human responsibility already hinted at in the portrait of Calamy.

That *Point Counter Point* represents a movement away from the detached manipulation of puppet-characters towards a sympathetic approach to human life is a fact not entirely contradicted by the novel's ill success in this aim, which is most signally exhibited by the emergence in its pages, for the first time, of a patently deliberate autobiographical character, the novelist Philip Quarles, whose personal views and problems, identical with Huxley's own, are placed directly before us.

The central problem in Philip Quarles's life is his personal isolation; "All his life long he had walked in a solitude, in a private void, into which nobody, not his mother, not his friends, not his lovers had ever been permitted to enter."

Although, we are given to understand, he is a man of exceptional intellectual endowments, his convictions are fluid, his response to life indeterminate:

> If there was any single way of life he could lastingly believe in, it was that mixture of pyrrhonism and stoicism which had struck him, an enquiring schoolboy among the philosophers, as the height of human wisdom and into whose mould of sceptical indifference he had poured his unimpassioned adolescence. Against the pyrrhonian suspense of judgment and the stoical imperturbability he had often rebelled. But had the rebellion ever been really serious? Pascal had made him a Catholic—but only so long as the volume of *Pensées* was open before him. There were moments when, in the company of Carlyle or Whitman or bouncing Browning, he had believed in strenuousness for strenuousness' sake. And then there was Mark Rampion. After a few hours in Mark Rampion's company he really believed in noble savagery; he felt convinced that the proudly conscious intellect ought to humble itself a little and admit the claims of the heart, aye and the bowels, the loins, the bones and skin and muscles, to a fair share of life.

This last sentence provides the clue to the book's central "idea"— a variation on the spirit-flesh duality, but with the scales weighted this time towards the "flesh"—not now in the name of an irresponsible hedonism but of a biological vitalism obviously borrowed, in large measure, from D. H. Lawrence, who is here caricatured admiringly in the painter, Mark Rampion. The following is a sample of Rampion's remarks:

> "This damned soul," he went on, "this damned abstract soul—it's like a kind of cancer, eating up the real, human, natural reality, spreading and spreading at its expense. Why can't he be content with reality, your stupid old Beethoven? Why should he find it necessary to replace the real, warm, natural thing by this abstract cancer of a soul? The cancer may have a beautiful shape; but, damn it all, the body's more beautiful. I don't want your spiritual cancer."

The spirit-matter dualism has not been resolved, but instead of an orientation towards the spirit à la Calamy, we have, not indeed a despairing acceptance of the futility of sensual-human life, but an attempt at its justification in terms of nature, vitality, health. Thus, to take but one typical example:

> John Bidlake a [sexagenarian philanderer] made no apologies for the kind of love he had to offer. So far as it went, it entirely justified itself. A healthy sensualist, he made his love straightforwardly, naturally, with the good animal gusto of a child of nature.
> ... It was a love without pretensions, but warm, natural, and, being natural, good so far as it went—a decent, good-humoured, happy sensuality.

This novel, however, shows Huxley at his most inept. Badly constructed, incoherent, puerile in conception and presentation, and written in shoddy journalese, it reveals the fatal juvenility which, beneath the sophisticated surface, vitiates his understanding of life. Huxley's attempt to extend his inherently limited range of characterization results in his crowding these pages with flat caricatures of living personages, whose characters and activities are interpreted in terms no more searching than their relationship, "wholesome" or "perverted," to sex and physical life. With the conclusion of the novelette called *Brave New World* (1932)—a satirical projection into the future of the way of life implicit in a deliberate hedonism, which need not concern us here—the shadow of D. H. Lawrence lifts from Huxley's pages, and with his next work we are back to the main line of his development: to the haunting preoccupation with the futility of life and the possibility of finding a way of escape from its pointlessness and tedium.

III

Four years after *Brave New World* and eight after *Point Counter Point* there appeared Huxley's crucial novel, *Eyeless in Gaza* (1936); crucial, because it represents a direct attempt to deal with the problems raised by his earlier works, and because it stands at the mid-point of his career as a novelist. Here the characters, previously formalized to excess, gain in definition and humanity, and genuine drama begins to emerge, centring around the autobiographical figure of the writer, Anthony Beavis, and his movement from a self-indulgent, cynical detachment towards personal regeneration and the acceptance of human responsibility.

The autobiographical novelist-character in *Point Counter Point*, we have seen, was signally isolated from the world, from other persons. The following extract from his notebook links him indubitably with Anthony Beavis, who has come to precisely the same realization, and who, moreover, takes at last the hazardous step of implementing it in action:

> "Till quite recently, I must confess [Philip Quarles writes], I took learning and philosophy and science—all the activities that are magniloquently lumped under the title of 'The Search for Truth'— very seriously. I regarded the Search for Truth as the highest of human tasks and the Searchers as the noblest of men. But in the last year or so I have begun to see that this famous Search for Truth is just an amusement, a distraction like any other, a rather refined and elaborate substitute for genuine living; and that Truth-Searchers become just as silly, infantile and corrupt in their way as the boozers, the pure aesthetes, the business men, the Good-Timers in theirs. . . . Shall I ever have the strength of mind to break myself of these indolent habits of intellectualism and devote my energies to the more serious and difficult task of living integrally?"

The personal theme of *Eyeless in Gaza* is Anthony's realization of the fatal error which has distorted and vitiated his life as a human being; but there is also an impersonal theme—that of the process of time. Once more the opening paragraph sets the key:

> The snapshots had become almost as dim as memories. This young woman who had stood in a garden at the turn of the century was like a ghost at cock-crow. His mother, Anthony Beavis recognized. A year or two, perhaps only a month or two, before she died. . . .

And the structure of the novel, the erratic alternation of pages from the remote past, the near past and the present of Anthony's history, while it reveals the temporal preoccupation, at the same time perfectly expresses the essential discontinuity of Anthony's existence as a result of his crucial, though always unacknowledged, refusal to go forward to claim his personal destiny as a human being, to "become himself."

Anthony has chosen not to be humanly responsible, chosen not only "the part of the detached philosopher" but of the detached sensualist, desiring neither to love nor to be loved. The crisis in his life occurs on his forty-second birthday when, with his mistress of the moment, Helen—who happens to be the daughter of a former mistress, Mary Amberley—he is lying on the roof of his retreat in southern France,

"in a golden stupor of sunlight and fulfilled desire." Despite his volition, his wish to sever himself from his past and to live only in the
immediate enjoyment of the present, perspectives of memory, invoked
by this and that apparently trivial sense-association, persistently open
up before him:

> Even the seemingly solid fragments of present reality are riddled with
> pitfalls. What could be more uncompromisingly *there*, in the present,
> than a woman's body in the sunshine? And yet it had betrayed him. The
> firm ground of its sensual immediacy and of his own physical tenderness
> had opened beneath his feet and precipitated him into another time and
> place. Nothing was safe. Even this skin had the scent of smoke under
> the sea. This living skin, this present skin; but it was nearly twenty years
> since Brian's death. . . . What if that picture gallery had been recorded
> and stored away in the cellars of his mind for the sole and express pur-
> pose of being brought up into consciousness at this present moment?
> Brought up, to-day, when he was forty-two and secure, forty-two and
> fixed, unchangeably himself, brought up along with those critical years
> of his adolescence, along with the woman who had been his teacher, his
> first mistress, and was now a hardly human creature festering to death,
> alone, in a dirty burrow? And what if that absurd childish game with
> the flints had had a point, a profound purpose, which was simply to be
> recollected here on this blazing roof, now as his lips made contact with
> Helen's sun-warmed flesh? In order that he might be forced, in the midst
> of this act of detached and irresponsible sensuality, to think of Brian
> and of the things that Brian had lived for; yes, and had died for—died
> for, another image suddenly reminded him, at the foot of just such a cliff
> as that beneath which they had played as children in the chalk pit. Yes,
> even Brian's suicide, he now realized with horror, even the poor huddled
> body on the rocks, was mysteriously implicit in this hot skin.

Anthony's spiritual crisis, its antecedents and outcome, has been
subterraneously prepared out of his unwilling but inescapable realization of the treacherous quality of time, with its accompaniments, age
and death; and this is reproduced in the narrative, which takes us
consecutively through various stages of Anthony's history, always returning to the point of departure—the sunlit roof. It is precipitated
by the shock of an unexpected and startling incident. Out of an aero-
plane flying immediately above there falls a yelping dog, to drop like a
missile on to the roof, spattering the reclining lovers with its blood.
Recovering from the shock, Anthony feebly passes it off as a joke, but
"For all answer, Helen covered her face with her hands and began to
sob."

> For a moment Anthony stood quite still, looking at her crouched
> there, in the hopeless abjection of her blood-stained nakedness, listen-
> ing to the painful sound of her weeping. "Like seccotine": his own
> words re-echoed disgracefully in his ears. Pity stirred within him, and
> then an almost violent movement of love for this hurt and suffering

woman, this *person,* yes, this person whom he had ignored, deliberately, as though she had no existence except in the context of pleasure. Now, as she knelt there sobbing, all the tenderness he had ever felt for her body, all the affection implicit in their sensualities and never expressed, seemed suddenly to discharge themselves, in a kind of lightning flash of accumulated feeling, upon this person, this embodied spirit, weeping in solitude behind concealing hands.

He knelt down beside her on the mattress, and, with a gesture that was meant to express all that he now felt, put an arm round her shoulder.

But at his touch she winced away as if from a defilement. With a violent, shuddering movement she shook her head.

This is the crisis which jerks Anthony into an abrupt awareness of his mistaken path. The rest of the novel conducts us through the corridors of Anthony's past history, his long, mistaken path being traced to its primal root in his early liaison with Mary Amberley, by whom he is idly prompted to betray his friend's trust and ultimately to cause Brian's suicide, by wantonly seducing the girl to whom he is betrothed; while concurrently, we are shown his later progress towards responsible participation in human affairs and the eventual acceptance of an ascetic, neo-Buddhist "spirituality."

The story, written with manifest sincerity, is a serious attempt to state a genuine human predicament and to find a way around it. Yet the statement, and the solution, when all is allowed, leave one with a disturbed feeling that all is not well, that somewhere there is a hiatus, a dislocation and a spiritual failure.

Anthony's conversion takes place at the point where he is abruptly made to realize that he has denied the inwardness of another person; that he has denied love for the sake of a detached sensuality. But as the narrative proceeds, we become aware that his personal discovery of love is turning from its proper object and becoming generalized, at first into hypothetical beneficence for humanity and at last into a cold moralism which derives its sanctions from a peculiarly impersonal metaphysic.

Returning to the antecedents of his conversion, we find that the tentative emotion of love (for Helen) becomes confused and finally submerged in the emotion of disgust (for Helen's mother, his once charming mistress, now a drunkard, a dope-addict, a squalid wreck). Simultaneously, this disgust fuses with the horror of time, of the accumulation of moments which leads inexorably to decay and death. The horror of time, as it accumulates in human life as age, is in turn associated with disgust for the physical body which experiences and expresses this accumulation. So that we are back at the position stated so clearly, eleven years before, in *Those Barren Leaves.* When, in his thirties, Anthony re-encounters Mary Amberley after an estrangement of more than ten years' duration, his predominant emotion is not pity but horror:

> "Doing what one doesn't want," she repeated, as though to herself. "Always doing what one doesn't want." She released his hand, and, clasping her own behind her head, leaned back against the pillows in the attitude, the known and familiar attitude, that in the Hôtel des Saints-Pères had been so delicious in its graceful indolence, so wildly exciting because of that white round throat stretched back like a victim's, those proffered breasts, lifted and taut beneath the lace. But to-day the lace was soiled and torn, the breasts hung tired under their own weight, the victim throat was no more a smooth column of white flesh, but withered, wrinkled, hollow between starting tendons.
>
> She opened her eyes, and, with a start, he recognized the look she gave him as the same, identically the same look, at once swooning and cynical, humorous and languidly abandoned, as had invited him, irresistibly then, in Paris fifteen years ago. It was the look of 1913 in the face of 1928—painfully out of its context. He stared at her for a second or two, appalled; then managed to break the silence.

It becomes clear that Anthony's conversion is merely negatively and passively motivated. He has not sought reality and truth, but evaded them, until at last reality has found him and chased him—the analogy is his own—from his bolt-hole:

> Even in the deepest sensual burrow, Anthony reflected as he walked back to his rooms, even in the snuggest of intellectual other-worlds, fate could find one out. And suddenly he perceived that, having spent all his life trying to react away from the standards of his father's universe, he had succeeded only in becoming precisely what his father was—a man in a burrow. With this small difference, that in his case the burrow happened to be intermittently adulterous instead of connubial all the time; and that the ideas were about societies and not words. For the moment, he was out of his burrow—had been chased out, as though by ferrets. But it would be easy and was already a temptation to return.

Anthony is in fact seeking some way of *escape* from the conditions of human life rather than some way of positively transforming those conditions. And the spirituality which he is indicated as making his own towards the end of the book does actually fortify him, though with a shift of emphasis, in that very detachment and impersonality from which the incident of the dog and his emotional crisis have momentarily jolted him.

"God may or may not exist," he writes in his diary, "But there is the empirical fact that contemplation of the divinity—of goodness in its most unqualified form—is a method of realizing that goodness to some slight degree in one's life. . . ." His form of belief seems quite unashamedly chosen to conform to his own ingrained life-attitude:

God—a person or not a person? *Quien sabe?* Only revelation can decide such metaphysical questions. And revelation isn't playing the game —is equivalent to pulling three aces of trumps from up your sleeve.

Of more significance is the practical question. Which gives a man more power to realize goodness—belief in a personal or an impersonal God? Answer: it depends. Some minds work one way, some another.

Mine, as it happens, finds no need, indeed, finds it impossible to think of the world in terms of personality. . . .

And, appropriate to this central laxity, his new-found "spirituality," so far from attending upon the wind that blows where it lists, resolves into the cataloguing of technicalities:

The fundamental problem is practical—to work out systems of psychological exercises for all types of men and women. Catholicism has many systems of mental prayer—Ignatian, Franciscan, Liguorian, Carmelite, and so on. Hinduism, Northern, Southern and Zen Buddhism also have a variety of practices. There is a great work to be done here. Collecting and collating information from all these sources. Consulting books and, more important, people who have actually practised what is in the books, have had the experience of teaching novices. In time it might be possible to establish a complete and definite *Ars Contemplativa*. A series of techniques, adapted to every type of mind. Techniques for meditating on, communicating with and contemplating goodness. Ends in themselves and at the same time means for realizing some of that goodness in practice. . . .

What better comment could be made on this than that which Anthony himself commits to his diary at one candid stage of his reflections:

Reflect that we all have our Poonas, bolt-holes from unpleasant reality. The danger, as Miller is always insisting, of meditation becoming such a bolt-hole. Quietism can be mere self-indulgence. Charismata like masturbations. Masturbations, however, that are dignified, by the amateur mystics who practise them, with all the most sacred names of religion and philosophy. "The contemplative life." It can be made a kind of high-brow substitute for Marlene Dietrich: a subject for erotic musings in the twilight.

IV

"Man," wrote Sören Kierkegaard in a famous definition, "is spirit. But what is spirit? Spirit is the self"; and, further, "eternity is essential continuity." "Selfness or personality," according to Aldous Huxley in his last, mystical-didactic phase, is a "stinking lump" . . . which has to be passionately repented of and completely died to before there can be any "true knowing of God in purity of spirit."

The mind-body carries with it the ineradicable smell of all that has been thought and done, desired and felt, throughout its racial and personal past. . . . The world is what (in our eyes) it is, because of all the consciously or unconsciously and physiologically remembered habits formed by our ancestors or by ourselves, either in our present life or in previous existences. These remembered bad habits cause us to believe that multiplicity is the sole reality and that the idea of "I," "me," "mine," represents the ultimate truth. *Nirvana* consists in "seeing into the abode of reality as it is," and not reality *quoad nos,* as it seems to us. Obviously, this cannot be achieved so long as there is an "us," to which reality can be relative. Hence the need, stressed by every exponent of the Perennial Philosophy, for mortification, for dying to self. And this must be a mortification not only of the appetites, the feelings and the will, but also of the reasoning powers, of consciousness itself and of that which makes our consciousness what it is—our personal memory and our inherited habit-energies. To achieve complete deliverance, conversion from sin is not enough; there must also be a conversion of the mind, a *paravritti,* as the Mahayanists call it, or revulsion in the very depths of consciousness. As the result of this revulsion, the habit-energies of accumulated memory are destroyed, and, along with them, the sense of being a separate ego. Reality is no longer perceived *quoad nos* (for the good reason that there is no longer a *nos* to perceive it), but as it is in itself.

Sin, for Huxley, is selfness. For Kierkegaard, as a Christian believer, sin is despair, and despair is precisely the dissociation, the dislocation of the self in its refusal to "choose itself"—to put itself into inward motion and go forward to claim its unique destiny as a messenger of meaning to the world.

"When did the ego begin to stink?" asks a recent aesthetic sage, in a phrase which seems to have captured the public ear. Answer: *When it began to decompose.*

The later work of Aldous Huxley must be interpreted as a bitter diatribe against personality, which he sees as synonymous with selfness —selfness *when it begins to decompose.*

The word "personality" is derived from the Latin, and its upper partials are in the highest degree respectable. For some odd philological reason, the Saxon equivalent of "personality" is hardly ever used. Which is a pity. For if it were used—used as currently as "belch" is used for "eructation"—would people make such a reverential fuss about the thing connoted as certain English-speaking philosophers, moralists and theologians have recently done? For "selfness," though it means precisely the same, carries none of the high-class overtones that go with "personality." On the contrary its primary meaning comes to us embedded, as it were, in discords, like the note of a cracked bell. For, as all exponents of the Perennial Philosophy have constantly insisted, man's obsessive consciousness of, and insistence on being a separate self is the final and most formidable obstacle to the unitive knowledge of God. To be a self is, for them, the original sin, and to die to self, in feeling, will and intellect, is the final and all-inclusive virtue. . . .

That this God-eclipsing and anti-spiritual selfness should have been given the same name as is applied to the God who is a Spirit, is, to say the least of it, unfortunate. Like all such mistakes, it is probably, in some obscure and subconscious way, voluntary and purposeful. We love our selfness; we want to be justified in our love; therefore we christen it with the same name as is applied by theologians to Father, Son and Holy Spirit.

A man who has never gone forward to claim his self and achieve personality can obviously never comprehend the meaning of personality, just as he can never understand the nature of communion and love. For him, personality *is* selfness, that dissolute conglomeration of appetites, volitions, perceptions which are functions of the body he is given by nature. And when the natural ego begins to disintegrate and to "stink" beyond endurance there is only one course left—to get rid of it.

Not only must the sufferer withdraw from his offending self—he must withdraw from the world, from other persons, and finally from God. Huxley's mysticism is therefore a-historical, anti-personal and atheistic. The whole cosmic order is, in its eyes, a pointless and inexplicable escapade of an inert and irresponsible deity, or non-deity—an escapade from which we are called to "liberate" ourselves with all possible speed, in order to turn to "the pure One, the absolute not-God in whom we must sink from nothingness to nothingness [and who] is called in Mahayana Buddhism the clear light of the Void." (*The Perennial Philosophy*.)

How is the novelist, the portrayer of human life and character, to work within this scheme? ". . . On the strictly human level, there was nothing that deserved to be taken seriously except the suffering men inflicted upon themselves by their crimes and follies . . ." reflects Huxley's Mr. Propter in the next novel, *After Many a Summer* (1939). "No, a good satire was much more deeply truthful and, of course, much more profitable than a good tragedy. The trouble was that so few good satires existed, because so few satirists were prepared to carry their criticism of human values far enough." A defect Huxley undertakes to remedy, for here criticism of human values is carried to the point of their complete abolition.

Huxley's basic dualism is here made unconditional. As a result we have on the one hand the group of puppet-characters—Jo Stoyte, the millionaire, whose palatial Californian residence is the scene of the novel, Dr. Obispo, the ruthless, scientific-minded sensualist, Jeremy Pordage, the ineffectual flute-voiced litterateur from Oxford, Virginia Maunciple, the innocent-depraved little chorus-girl—puppets whose thoughts and actions bespeak their utter worthlessness and futility—and on the other the more than human, withdrawn, contemplative-practical sage, Mr. Propter, the essentially static mouthpiece of Huxley's teachings on the futility of life on the "strictly human level" and the necessity

for a withdrawal from human life to "the level of eternity." Between the
two poles significant movement is quite precluded. Life is a dance of
puppets, grimly, savagely pointless.

The anti-personal bias of the novel is pronounced; thus Mr. Propter:

> Bondage is the life of personality, and for bondage the personal self
> will fight with tireless resourcefulness and the most stubborn cunning.
> ... The spirit is always willing; but the person, who is a mind as well as
> a body, is always unwilling—and the person, incidentally, is not weak
> but extremely strong.

This strange hatred of "the stinking slough of our personality" is carried
to the point of absurdity—

> 'Turn round, please.'
> Mr. Stoyte obeyed. The back, Dr. Obispo reflected, was perceptibly
> less revolting than the front. Perhaps because it was less personal.

The dislocation of being is expressed by setting a neutral, arid and
abstract 'mysticism' against a grossly material sensualism: life is separated into two mutually exclusive compartments. On the one hand—

> "What is man?" he whispered to himself.... "A nothingness sur-
> rounded by God, indigent and capable of God, filled with God if he so
> desires." And what is this God of which men are capable?
> Mr. Propter answered with the definition given by John Tauler in the
> first paragraph of his *Following of Christ*. "God is a being withdrawn
> from creatures, a free power, a pure working." Man, then, is a nothing-
> ness surrounded by, and indigent of, a being withdrawn from creatures,
> a nothingness capable of free power, filled with a pure working if he
> so desires.

And on the other:

> Through his dark glasses, Mr. Stoyte looked up at her with an expres-
> sion of possessiveness at once gluttonous and paternal. Virginia was his
> baby, not only figuratively and colloquially, but also in the literal sense
> of the word. His sentiments were simultaneously those of the purest
> father-love and the most violent eroticism. ...
> Delicious creature! The hand that had lain inert, hitherto, upon her
> knee, slowly contracted. Between the broad spatulate thumb and the
> strong fingers, what smoothness, what a sumptuous and substantial
> resilience!
> "Jinny," he said. "My Baby!" ...

Mr. Propter's peculiarly arid and abstract mysticism has its end in "a
non-personal experience of timeless peace. Accordingly, non-personal-
ity, timelessness and peace are what it means ..." And it involves,
centrally, a repudiation of, and an escape from, time:

"... potential evil is *in* time; potential good isn't. The longer you live, the more evil you automatically come into contact with. Nobody comes automatically into contact with good. Men don't find more good by merely existing longer.... The solution is very simple and profoundly unacceptable. Actual good is outside time.... Time is potential evil, and craving converts the potentiality into actual evil. Whereas a temporal act can never be more than potentially good, with a potentiality, what's more, that can't be actualized except out of time."

Time as evil, once more, manifests in human life as age, physical decrepitude, death. Thus the thread of narrative depends primarily from Jo Stoyte's haunting fear of the grave, which causes him to employ Dr. Obispo upon researches into the possibilities of artificial longevity. Wound with this principal thread is the intermittent commentary on the human characters provided by the baboons in their enclosure outside the Stoyte mansion:

To the right, on another shelf of rock, a formidable old male, leather-snouted, with the grey bobbed hair of a seventeenth-century Anglican divine, stood guard over his submissive female.... The coast was clear. The young male who had been looking for dandruff suddenly saw his opportunity. Chattering with excitement, he bounded down to the shelf on which, too frightened to follow her master, the little female was still squatting. Within ten seconds they had begun to copulate.

Virginia clapped her hands with pleasure. "Aren't they cute!" she cried. "Aren't they *human!*"

These threads wind together as the researches of Dr. Obispo coincide with Jeremy Pordage's discovery, among the ancient papers he is cataloguing for Jo Stoyte, that the eighteenth-century fifth earl of the all-but extinct line of Gonister has in his old age been similarly experimenting with a diet of raw carps' guts, and has mysteriously arranged for his own counterfeit funeral. On the insistence of the millionaire, in his terror of death, the fifth Earl is eventually located in his stinking underground cave:

Beyond the bars, the light of the lanterns had scooped out of the darkness a narrow world of forms and colours. On the edge of a low bed, at the centre of this world, a man was sitting, staring, as though fascinated, into the light. His legs, thickly covered with coarse reddish hair, were bare. The shirt, which was his only garment, was torn and filthy. Knotted diagonally across the powerful chest was a broad silk ribbon that had evidently once been blue. From a piece of string tied round his neck was suspended a little image of St. George and the Dragon in gold and enamel. He sat hunched up, his head thrust forward and at the same time sunk between his shoulders. With one of his huge and strangely clumsy hands he was scratching a sore place that showed red between the hairs of his left leg.

"A foetal ape that's had time to grow up," Dr. Obispo managed at last to say. "It's *too* good!" Laughter overtook him again. "Just look at his face!" he gasped, and pointed through the bars. Above the matted hair that concealed the jaws and cheeks, blue eyes stared out of cavernous sockets. There were no eyebrows; but under the dirty, wrinkled skin of the forehead a great ridge of bone projected like a shelf. . . .

. . . "But what's happened to them?"

"Just time," said Dr. Obispo airily.

"Time?"

"I don't know how old the female is," Dr. Obispo went on. "But the Earl there—let me see, he was two hundred and one last January."

The novel closes, bitingly acidulous, with Jo Stoyte's mentally preparing himself to accept the identical regime undergone by the fifth Earl.

That Huxley, driven by self-hatred and disgust with life has reached a dead-end, is finally demonstrated by his last, most tasteless production, *Time Must Have a Stop* (1945). Here the puppets, fixed in their unbreakable abstracts of human qualities, and offset by the static and detached figure of a pharisaical "saint," exist at a remove from reality which gives the novel an air of complete falsity to human experience. The "saved" Bruno Rontini, like Mr. Propter a mere mouthpiece for Huxley's renunciatory gospel, is deprived of inward movement no less than the "damned" puppet-characters immobilized in their habit of selfhood. In the previous novel, the only character not quite immune from "the contagion of goodness" is the naïve and inarticulate Pete. It is no accident that for his hero this time Huxley should have chosen an adolescent (Sebastian Barnack is seventeen), that he should have involved him to his undoing for twenty-nine chapters in the depraved realm of "the flesh" and then, by means of an abrupt hiatus, presented us, with the briefest of explanations, in the final chapter with a reformed and "saintly" character, complete with copious extracts from those now alltoo-familiar notebooks. For Huxley, as we have seen before, is for some reason at which one can only guess—we might label it "arrested development"—at ease only with the immature. Incapable as he is of revealing the inner processes by which human beings come to inward maturity, even his supposedly adult characters remain adolescents upon whose juvenile responses has been superimposed arbitrarily the veneer of a quasi-adult sophistication and intellectuality.

Sensual depravity or an unreal "spirituality"—down goes one scale heavily weighted with "the flesh," and up goes the other with its insubstantial featherweight of spirit. The falsity to human experience of this naïve dislocation of being is paralleled in the novel both by the failure of its action to carry conviction and the air of unreality in which that action takes place. We cannot believe in the authenticity of Uncle Eustace's Italian villa, located in accordance with Huxley's now pronounced retreat from history, in a dream-like version of the nineteen-twenties, any more than we can accept the authenticity of Uncle Eustace himself or for that matter any of the book's characters. The vision, distorted for the satire of *After Many a Summer,* is here quite out of focus. The adult reader is utterly unable to make the required connection between Uncle Eustace's trivial sensualities—his cheerful over-indulgence in wine, women, and cigars—and the bathetic solemnities of his postmortem experiences in the spirit world when, after an evening of luxury, he dies on the seat of the toilet. And the anti-climax of the disembodied Uncle Eustace's eventual choice of reincarnation out of the "living uterine darkness," the "vegetative heaven" of Mme. Weyle, should serve, at least, in the mind of no uncommonly penetrating reader, to put Huxley's "mysticism" in its proper, very humble place.

With this final novel, we may safely conclude, Huxley's career as a significant novelist of the modern plight has come to an end. It is an end implicit, like so many, in its beginning. The novelist of futility, undergoing in mid-career a period in which the potentiality of meaning seemed for a time to offer itself—a potentiality accompanied by a realization of love and the value of human personality—has crossed over into a positive accentuation of futility accompanied by a positive doctrine of non-attachment and impersonality. No hope of development here! And, necessarily, this positive acceptance of the meaninglessness of human life, the worthlessness of personality, has its implications for art. When human life is seen as intrinsically meaningless and evil, then the work of the novelist, whose task is to present a picture of that life in terms of its significance and value, is deprived of all justification. Art and life must be thrown overboard together.

THE SORROWS OF THOMAS WOLFE *

JOHN PEALE BISHOP

I

THOMAS WOLFE is dead. And that big work which he was prepared to write, which was to have gone to six long volumes and covered in the course of its narrative the years between 1781 and 1933, with a cast of characters whose numbers would have run into the hundreds, will never be finished. The title which he had chosen for it, *Of Time and the River,* had already been allowed to appear on the second volume. There its application is not altogether clear; how appropriate it would have been to the work as a whole we can only conjecture. No work of such magnitude has been projected by another of his generation in America; Wolfe's imagination, it appears, could conceive on no smaller scale. He was, he confesses, devoted to chance; he had no constant control over his faculties; but his fecundity was nothing less than prodigious. He had, moreover, a tenacity which must, but for his dying, have carried him through to the end.

Dying, he left behind him a mass of manuscript; how much of it can be published there is now no knowing. Wolfe was the most wasteful of writers.

His aim was to set down America as far as it can belong to the experience of one man. Wolfe came early on what was for him the one available truth about this continent—that it was contained in himself. There was no America which could not be made out—mountains, rivers, trains, cities, people—in the memory of an American. If the contours were misty, then they must be made clear. It was in flight from a certain experience of America, as unhappy as it had been apparently sterile—it was in Paris, in an alien land, that Wolfe first understood with hate and with love the horror and the wonder of his native country. He had crossed the seas from the West to East only to come upon the North Carolina hills where he had been born. "I found out," he says, "during those years that the way to discover one's own country was to leave it; that the way to find America was to find it in one's own heart, one's memory and one's spirit, and in a foreign land. I think I may say that

* "The Sorrows of Thomas Wolfe" first appeared in the *Kenyon Review,* Winter, 1939, and was later included in *The Collected Essays of John Peale Bishop,* copyright 1948 by Charles Scribner's Sons. It is used here by permission of the publishers. The reader should remember that the essay was written shortly after Wolfe's death and prior to the publication of his posthumous works.

I discovered America during those years abroad out of my very need of her."

This is not an uncommon experience, but what made it rewarding in Wolfe's case was that his memory was anything but common. He could —and it is the source of what is most authentic in his talents—displace the present so completely by the past that its sights and sounds all but destroyed surrounding circumstance. He then lost the sense of time. For Wolfe, sitting at a table on a terrace in Paris, contained within himself not only the America he had known; he also held, within his body, both his parents. They were there, not only in his memory, but more portentously in the make-up of his mind. They loomed so enormous to him that their shadows fell across the Atlantic, their shade was on the café table under which he stretched his long American legs.

"The quality of my memory," he said in his little book, *The Story of a Novel,* "is characterized, I believe, in a more than ordinary degree by the intensity of its sense impressions, its power to evoke and bring back the odors, sounds, colors, shapes and feel of things with concrete vividness." That is true. But readers of Wolfe will remember that the mother of Eugene Gant was afflicted with what is known as total recall. Her interminable narratives were the despair of her family. Wolfe could no more than Eliza Gant suppress any detail, no matter how irrelevant; indeed, it was impossible for him to feel that any detail was irrelevant to his purpose. The readers of *Look Homeward, Angel* will also remember that Eugene's father had a gift, unrivalled among his associates, of vigorous utterance. Nobody, they said, can tie a knot in the tail of the English language like old W. O. But the elder Gant's speech, for all that it can on occasion sputter into fiery intensity, more often than not runs off into a homespun rhetoric. It sounds strong, but it has very little connection with any outer reality and is meaningless, except in so far as it serves to convey his rage and frustration. We cannot avoid supposing that Wolfe drew these two characters after his own parents. At the time he began writing *Look Homeward, Angel,* he stood far enough apart from them to use the endlessness of Eliza's unheard discourses, the exaggerated violence of old Gant's objurgations, for comic effect. He makes father and mother into something at once larger and less than human. But in his own case, he could not, at least so long as he was at his writing, restrain either the course of his recollections or their outcome in words. He wrote as a man possessed. Whatever was in his memory must be set down—not merely because he was Eliza's son, but because the secret end of all his writing was expiation—and it must be set down in words to which he constantly seems to be attaching more meaning than they can properly own. It was as though he were aware that his novel would have no meaning that could not be found in the words. The meaning of a novel should be in its structure. But in Wolfe's novel, as far as it has gone, it is impossible to discover any structure at all.

II

It is impossible to say what Wolfe's position in American letters would have been had he lived to bring his work to completion. At the moment he stands very high in the estimation both of the critics and of the common reader. From the time of *Look Homeward, Angel,* he was regarded, and rightly, as a young man of incomparable promise. *Of Time and the River* seemed to many to have borne out that promise and, since its faults were taken as due merely to an excess of fecundity, it was met with praise as though it were the consummation of all Wolfe's talents. Yet the faults are fundamental. The force of Wolfe's talents is indubitable; yet he did not find for that novel, nor do I believe he could ever have found, a structure of form which would have been capable of giving shape and meaning to his emotional experience. He was not without intelligence; but he could not trust his intelligence, since for him to do so would have been to succumb to conscience. And it was conscience, with its convictions of guilt, that he was continually trying to elude.

His position as an artist is very like that of Hart Crane. Crane was born in 1899, Wolfe in 1900, so that they were almost of an age. Both had what we must call genius; both conceived that genius had been given them that they might celebrate, the one in poetry, the other in prose, the greatness of their country. But Wolfe no more than Crane was able to give any other coherence to his work than that which comes from the personal quality of his writing. And he found, as Crane did before him, that the America he longed to celebrate did not exist. He could record, and none better, its sights, its sounds and its odors, as they can be caught in a moment of time; he could try, as the poet of *The Bridge* did, to absorb that moment and endow it with the permanence of a myth. But he could not create a continuous America. He could not, for all that he was prepared to cover one hundred and fifty of its years, conceive its history. He can record what comes to his sensibility, but he cannot give us the continuity of experience. Everything for Wolfe is in the moment; he can so try to impress us with the immensity of the moment that it will take on some sort of transcendental meaning. But what that meaning is escapes him, as it does us. And once it has passed from his mind, he can do nothing but recall another moment, which as it descends into his memory seems always about to deliver itself, by a miracle, of some tremendous import.

Both Crane and Wolfe belonged to a world that is indeed living from moment to moment. And it is because they voice its breakdown in the consciousness of continuity that they have significance for it.

Of the two, Wolfe, I should say, was the more aware of his plight. He was, he tells us, while writing *Of Time and the River,* tormented by a dream in which the sense of guilt was associated with the forgetting of time. "I was unable to sleep, unable to subdue the tumult of these creative energies, and, as a result of this condition, for three years I prowled the streets, explored the swarming web of the million-footed city and came to know it as I had never done before. . . . Moreover, in this endless quest and prowling of the night through the great web and jungle of the city, I saw, lived, felt and experienced the full weight of that horrible human calamity. [The time was that of the bottom of the depression, when Wolfe was living in Brooklyn.] And from it all has come, as a final deposit, a burning memory, a certain evidence of the fortitude of man, his ability to suffer and somehow survive. And it is for this reason now that I think I shall always remember this black period with a kind of joy that I could not at that time have believed possible, for it was during this time that I lived my life through to a first completion, and through the suffering and labor of my own life came to share those qualities in the lives of the people around me."

This passage is one of extreme interest, not only for what it tells us of Wolfe at this time, but for the promise it contains of an emotional maturity. For as far as Wolfe had carried the history of Eugene Gant, he was dealing with a young man whose isolation from his fellow men was almost complete. Eugene, and we must suppose the young Wolfe, was incarcerated in his own sensibility. Locked in his cell, he awaits the coming of every moment, as though it would bring the turning of a releasing key. He waits like Ugolino, when he woke uncertain because of his dream and heard not the opening but the closing of the lock. There is no release. And the place of Wolfe's confinement, no less than that of Ugolino, deserves to be called Famine.

It can be said of Wolfe, as Allen Tate has said of Hart Crane, that he was playing a game in which any move was possible, because none was compulsory. There is no idea which would serve as discipline to the event. For what Wolfe tells us was the idea that furiously pursued him during the composition of *Of Time and the River,* the search for a father, can scarcely be said to appear in the novel, or else it is so incidentally that it seems to no purpose. It does not certainly, as the same search on the part of Stephen Dedalus does in *Ulysses,* prepare a point toward which the whole narrative moves. There was nothing indeed in Wolfe's upbringing to make discipline acceptable to him. He acts always as though his own capacity for feeling, for anguished hope and continual frustration, was what made him superior, as no doubt, along with his romantic propensity for expression, it was. But he was wrong in assuming that those who accept any form of discipline are therefore lacking in vigor. He apparently did not understand that there are those who might say with Yeats, "I could recover if I shrieked my heart's agony," and yet like him are dumb "from human dignity." And his failure to understand was due to no fault of the intelligence, but to lack of love. The Gant family always strikes us, with its howls of rage, its loud hah-hahs of hate and derision, as something less than human. And Eugene is a Gant. While in his case we are ready to admit that genius is a law unto itself, we have every right to demand that it discover its own law.

Again like Crane, Wolfe failed to see that at the present time so extreme a manifestation of individualism could not but be morbid. Both came too late into a world too mechanic; they lacked a wilderness and constantly tried to create one as wild as their hearts. It was all very well for them, since both were in the way of being poets, to start out to proclaim the grandeur of America. Such a task seemed superb. But both were led at last, on proud romantic feet, to Brooklyn. And what they found there they abhorred.

They represent, each in his way, a culmination of the romantic spirit in America. There was in both a tremendous desire to impose the will on experience. Wolfe had no uncommon will. And Crane's was strong enough to lead him deliberately to death by drowning. For Wolfe the rewards of experience were always such that he was turned back upon himself. Isolated in his sensations, there was no way out. He continually sought for a door, and there was really none, or only one, the door of death.

III

The intellectual labor of the artist is properly confined to the perception of relations. The conscience of the craftsman must see that these relations are so presented that, in spite of all complications, they are ultimately clear. It is one of the conditions of art that they cannot be abstractly stated, but must be presented to the senses.

What we have at the center of all Wolfe's writing is a single character, and it was certainly the aim of that writing to present this character in all his manifold contacts with the world of our time. Eugene has, we are told, the craving of a Faust to know all experience, to be able to record all the races and all the social classes which may be said to exist in America. Actually, Eugene's experience is not confined to America.

But when we actually come to consider Eugene closely, we see that, once he is beyond the overwhelming presence of his family, his contacts with other people are all casual. The perfect experience for Eugene is to see someone in the throes of an emotion which he can imagine, but in which he has no responsible part. From one train, he sees people passing in another train, which is moving at a faster speed than his own.

> And they looked at one another for a moment, they passed and vanished and were gone forever, yet it seemed to him that he had known these people, that he knew them far better than the people in his own train, and that, having met them for an instant under immense and timeless skies, as they were hurled across the continent to a thousand destina-

tions, they had met, passed, vanished, yet would remember this forever. And he thought the people in the two trains felt this, also; slowly they passed each other now, and their mouths smiled and their eyes grew friendly, but he thought there was some sorrow and regret in what they felt. For having lived together as strangers in the immense and swarming city, they had now met upon the everlasting earth, hurled past each other for a moment between two points of time upon the shining rails; never to meet, to speak, to know each other any more, and the briefness of their days, the destiny of man, was in that instant greeting and farewell.

He sees from a train a boy trying to decide to go after a girl; wandering the streets of New York, he sees death come to four men; through one of his students at the university, he comes in contact with an old Jewess wailing a son dead for a year. Each of these moments is completely done; most of them, indeed, overwrought. From the country seen from a train he derives "a wild and solemn joy—the sense of nameless hope, impossible desire, and man's tragic brevity." He reacts to most circumstances, it must seem to us, excessively. But to men and women he does not really answer. The old Jewess's grief fills him "with horror, anger, a sense of cruelty, disgust, and pity." The passion aroused returns to himself. And it is precisely because his passions cannot attain their object, and in one person know peace, that he turns in rage and desire toward the millions. There is in Eugene every emotion you wish but one; there is no love.

The most striking passages in Wolfe's novels always represent these moments of comprehension. For a moment, but a moment only, there is a sudden release of compassion, when some aspect of suffering and bewildered humanity is seized, when the other's emotion is in a timeless completion known. Then the moment passes, and compassion fails. For Eugene Gant, the only satisfactory relationship with another human creature is one which can have no continuity. For the boy at the street corner, seen in the indecision of youthful lust, he has only understanding and pity; the train from which he looks moves on and nothing more is required of Eugene. But if he should approach that same boy on the street, if he should come close enough to overhear him, he would hear only the defilement of language, words which would awaken in him only hate and disgust. He would himself become lonely, strange and cruel. For emotions such as these, unless they can be used with the responsibility of the artist, must remain a torment to the man.

The only human relationship which endures is that of the child to his family. And that is inescapable: once having been, it cannot cease to be. His father is still his father, though dying; and his brother Ben, though dead, remains his brother. He loves and he hates and knows why no more than the poet he quotes. What he does know is that love has been forbidden him.

The only contemporary literary influence on Wolfe which was at all strong was that of Joyce. I shall consider it here only to note that while we know that Joyce could only have created Stephen Dedalus out of the conflicts of his own youth, we never think of Stephen simply as the young Joyce, any more than we think of Hamlet as Shakespeare. He is a creation. But in Wolfe's novels it is impossible to feel that the central figure has any existence apart from the author. He is called Eugene Gant, but that does not deceive any one for a moment; he is, beyond all doubt, Thomas Wolfe. There is, however, one important distinction to be made between them, and one which we should not allow ourselves to forget: Eugene Gant is always younger, by at least ten years, than Thomas Wolfe.

Wolfe described *Of Time and the River* as being devoted to "the period of wandering and hunger in a man's youth." And in it we are meant to take Eugene as every young man. The following volume would, Wolfe said, declare "a period of greater certitude, which would be dominated by a single passion." That, however, still remains to be seen. So far, Eugene has shown no capacity as a lover, except in casual contact with whores. When for a moment he convinces himself that he is in love with Ann, who is a nice simple conventional girl from Boston, he can only shriek at her and call her a bitch and a whore, which she certainly is not. The one contact which lasts for any time—leaving aside the blood ties which bind him to the Pentlands, his mother's people, and the Gants —is that with Starwick. Starwick is the only friend he makes in his two years at Harvard, and in Paris, some years later, he still regards his friendship with Starwick as the most valuable he has ever known.

It ends when he discovers that Starwick is a homosexual. And it has usually been assumed that the violence and bitterness with which it ends are due to disillusionment; the sudden turn in Eugene's affections for the young man may well be taken as a natural reaction to his learning, first that Ann is in love with Starwick, and only a little later how hopelessly deep is Starwick's infatuation with the young tough he has picked up, by apparent chance, one night in a Paris bar. But that is, I think, to take too simple a view of the affair. There is more to it than that. What we have been told about Starwick from his first appearance in the book is that, despite a certain affectation and oddity of manner, he is, as Eugene is not, a person capable of loving and being loved. What is suddenly revealed in Paris is that for him, too, love is a thing the world has forbidden. In Starwick's face Eugene sees his own fate. Just as in his brother Ben's complaint at his neglect, he had looked back through another's sight at his own neglected childhood and in his brother's death fore-mourned his own, so now, when he beats Starwick's head against the wall, he is but raging against his own frustration and despair.

In his father's yard, among the tombstones, has stood for years a marble angel. Old Gant curses it, all hope he thinks lost that he will ever get his money back for it. It stands a magnificent reminder of the time when as a boy, with winged ambition, he had wanted to be not merely a stonecutter but a sculptor. Then, unexpectedly a customer comes for it. The one symbol of the divine in the workshop is sold to adorn the grave of a prostitute; what the boy might have been the man lets go for such a purpose. It cannot be said that Thomas Wolfe ever sold his angel. But the faults of the artist are all of them traceable to the failures of the man. He achieved probably the utmost intensity of which incoherent writing is capable; he proved that an art founded solely on the individual, however strong his will, however vivid his sensations, cannot be sound, or whole, or even passionate, in a world such as ours, in which "the integrity of the individual consciousness has been broken down." How far it has broken down, I do not believe he ever knew, yet all that he did is made of its fragments.

A NATURAL HISTORY OF AMERICAN NATURALISM *

Malcolm Cowley

THERE have been too many unfruitful arguments over naturalism in American fiction. Now that the movement has flourished for half a century, we can forget to attack or defend it and instead can look back in an objective or naturalistic spirit at the work of the many authors it has inspired. We can note that their line extends from Norris and the early Dreiser through Farrell and Steinbeck. We can describe their principles, note how these were modified in practice, and finally try to reach some judgment of their literary remains.

Naturalism has been defined in two words as pessimistic determinism and the definition is true so far as it goes. The naturalistic writers were all determinists in that they believed in the omnipotence of abstract forces. They were pessimists so far as they believed that men and women were absolutely incapable of shaping their own destinies. They regarded the individual as "a pawn on a chessboard"; the phrase recurs time and again in their novels. They felt that he could not achieve happiness by any conscious decision and that he received no earthly or heavenly reward for acting morally; man was, in Dreiser's words, "the victim of forces over which he has no control."

In some of his moods, Frank Norris carried this magnification of forces and minification of persons to an even greater extreme. "Men were nothings, mere animalculae, mere ephemerides that fluttered and fell and were forgotten between dawn and dusk," he said in the next-to-last chapter of *The Octopus*. "Men were naught, life was naught; FORCE only existed—FORCE that brought men into the world, FORCE that made the wheat grow, FORCE that garnered it from the soil to give place to the succeeding crop." But Norris, like several other naturalists, was able to combine this romantic pessimism about individuals with romantic optimism about the future of mankind. "The individual suffers, but the race goes on," he said at the very end of the novel. "Annixter dies, but in a far distant corner of the world a thousand lives are saved. The larger view always and through all shams, all wicked-

* "A Natural History of American Naturalism" first appeared in the *Kenyon Review*, Summer, 1947. It was later reprinted, in somewhat expanded form, in *Evolutionary Thought in America*, edited by Stow Persons (Yale University Press, 1950), and is used here by permission of the author and the Yale University Press.

nesses, discovers the Truth that will, in the end, prevail, and all things, surely, inevitably, resistlessly work together for good." This was, in its magniloquent way, a form of the belief in universal progress announced by Herbert Spencer, but it was also mingled with native or Emersonian idealism, and it helped to make naturalism more palatable to Norris' first American readers.

Zola had also declared his belief in human perfectibility, in what he called "a constant march toward truth"; and it was from Zola rather than Spencer or any native sources that Norris had borrowed most of his literary doctrines. Zola described himself as "a positivist, an evolutionist, a materialist." In his working notes, which Norris of course had never seen, but which one might say that he divined from the published text of the novels, Zola had indicated some of his aims as a writer. He would march through the world observing human behavior as if he were observing the forms of animal life. "Study men as simple elements and note the reactions," he said. And again, "What matters most to me is to be purely naturalistic, purely physiological. Instead of having principles (royalism, Catholicism) I shall have laws (heredity, atavism)." And yet again, "Balzac says that he wishes to paint men, women and things. I count men and women as the same, while admitting their natural differences, and *subject men and women to things.*" In that last phrase, which Zola underlined, he expressed the central naturalistic doctrine: that men and women are part of nature and subject to the same indifferent laws.

The principal laws, for Zola, were those of heredity, which he assumed to be as universal and unchanging as the second law of thermodynamics. He fixed upon the hereditary weakness of the Rougon-Macquart family as a theme that would bind together his vast series of novels. Suicide, alcoholism, prostitution, and insanity were all to be explained as the result of the same hereditary taint. "Vice and virtue," he said, "are products like vitriol and sugar." Norris offered the same explanation for the brutality of McTeague. "Below the fine fabric of all that was good in him," Norris said, "ran the foul stream of hereditary evil, like a sewer. The vices and sins of his father and of his father's father, to the third and fourth and five hundredth generation, tainted him. The evil of an entire race flowed in his veins. Why should it be? He did not desire it. Was he to blame?" Others of the naturalistic school, and Norris himself in his later novels, placed more emphasis on environmental forces. When Stephen Crane sent a copy of *Maggie* to the Reverend Thomas Dixon, he wrote on the flyleaf: "It is inevitable that this book will greatly shock you, but continue, pray, with great courage to the end, for it tries to show that environment is a tremendous thing and often shapes lives regardlessly. If I could prove that theory, I would make room in Heaven for all sorts of souls (notably an occasional street girl) who are not confidently expected to be there by many excellent people." Maggie, the victim of environment, was no more to blame for her transgressions than McTeague, the victim of hereditary evil. Nobody was to blame in this world where men and women are subject to the laws of things.

A favorite theme in naturalistic fiction is that of the beast within. As the result of some crisis—usually a fight, a shipwreck, or an expedition into the Arctic—the veneer of civilization drops or is stripped away and we are faced with "the primal instinct of the brute struggling for its life and for the life of its young." The phrase is Norris', but it might have been written by any of the early naturalists. When evolution is treated in their novels, it almost always takes the opposite form of devolution or degeneration. It is seldom that the hero evolves toward a superhuman nature, as in Nietzsche's dream; instead he sinks backward toward the beasts. Zola set the fashion in *L'Assommoir* and *La Bête humaine* and Norris followed him closely in the novel he wrote during his year at Harvard, *Vandover and the Brute*. Through yielding to his lower instincts, Vandover loses his humanity; he tears off his clothes, paddles up and down the room on his hands and feet and snarls like a dog.

A still earlier story, *Lauth,* was written at the University of California after Norris had listened to the lectures of Professor Joseph Le Conte, the famous evolutionist. The action takes place in medieval Paris, where Lauth, a student at the Sorbonne, is mortally wounded in a brawl. A doctor brings him back to life by pumping blood into his veins, but the soul had left the body and does not return. Without it, Lauth sinks back rapidly through the various stages of evolution: he is an ape, then a dog, then finally "a horrible shapeless mass lying upon the floor. It lived, but lived not as do the animals or the trees, but as the protozoa, the jellyfish, and those strange lowest forms of existence wherein the line between vegetable and animal cannot be drawn." That might have been taken as a logical limit to the process of devolution; but Jack London, who was two parts naturalist, if he was also one part socialist and three parts hack journalist, tried to carry the process even further, into the realm of inanimate nature. Here, for example, is the description of a fight in *Martin Eden:*

> Then they fell upon each other, like young bulls, in all the glory of youth, with naked fists, with hatred, with desire to hurt, to maim, to destroy. All the painful, thousand years' gains of man in his upward climb through creation were lost. Only the electric light remained, a milestone on the path of the great human adventure. Martin and Cheese-Face were two savages, of the stone age, of the squatting place and the tree refuge. They sank lower and lower into the muddy abyss, back into the dregs of the raw beginnings of life, striving blindly and chemically, as atoms strive, as the star-dust of the heavens strives, colliding, recoiling and colliding again and eternally again.

It was more than a metaphor when London said that men were atoms and star dust; it was the central drift of his philosophy. Instead of moving from the simple to the complex, as Herbert Spencer tells us that everything does in this world, the naturalists kept moving from the complex to the simple, by a continual process of reduction. They spoke of the nation as "the tribe," and a moment later the tribe became a pack. Civilized man became a barbarian or a savage, the savage became a brute and the brute was reduced to its chemical elements. "Study men as simple elements," Zola had said; and many years later Dreiser followed his advice by presenting love as a form of electromagnetism and success in life as a question of chemical compounds; thus he said of his brother Paul that he was "one of those great Falstaffian souls who, for lack of a little iron or sodium or carbon dioxide in his chemical compost, was not able to bestride the world like a Colossus."

There was a tendency in almost all the naturalistic writers to identify social laws with biological or physical laws. For Jack London, the driving force behind human events was always biology—"I mean," says his autobiographical hero, Martin Eden, "the real interpretative biology, from the ground up, from the laboratory and the test tube and the vitalized inorganic right on up to the widest esthetic and social generalizations." London believed that such biological principles as natural selection and the survival of the fittest were also the laws of human society. Thomas Hardy often spoke as if men's destinies were shaped by the physical sciences. He liked to say that his characters were doomed by the stars in their courses; but actually they were doomed by human conflicts or by the still Puritan conventions of middle-class England. Norris fell into the same confusion between the physical and the social world when he pictured the wheat as "a huge Niagara . . . flowing from West to East." In his novels wheat was not a grain improved by men from various wild grasses and grown by men to meet human needs; it was an abstract and elemental force like gravity. "I corner the wheat!" says Jadwin, the hero of *The Pit*. "Great heavens, it is the wheat that has cornered me." Later, when he is ruined by the new grain that floods the market, Jadwin thinks to himself,

> The Wheat had grown itself: demand and supply, these were the two great laws that the Wheat obeyed. Almost blasphemous in his effrontery, he had tampered with these laws, and roused a Titan. He had laid his puny human grasp upon Creation and the very earth herself, the great mother, feeling the touch of the cobweb that the human insect had spun, had stirred at last in her sleep and sent her omnipotence moving through the grooves of the world, to find and crush the disturber of her appointed courses.

Just as the wheat itself had grown, so, in the first volume of Norris' trilogy, the Pacific and Southwestern Railroad had built itself. This octopus that held a state in its tentacles was beyond human control. Even Shelgrim, the president of the railroad, was merely the agent of a superhuman force. At the end of the novel he gives a lecture to Presley which overwhelms the poet and leaves him feeling that it rang "with the clear reverberation of truth." "You are dealing with forces," Shelgrim says, "when you speak of Wheat and the Railroads, not with men. There is the Wheat, the supply. It must be carried to the People. There is the demand. The Wheat is one force, the Railroad, another, and there is the law that governs them—supply and demand. Men have little to do with the whole business." If the two forces came into conflict—if the employees of the railroad massacred the wheat ranchers and robbed them of their land—then Presley should "blame conditions, not men."

The effect of naturalism as a doctrine is to subtract from literature the whole notion of human responsibility. "Not men" is its constant echo. If naturalistic stories had tragic endings, these were not to be explained by human wills in conflict with each other or with fate; they were the blind result of conditions, forces, physical laws, or nature herself. "There was no malevolence in Nature," Presley reflects after meeting the railroad president. "Colossal indifference only, a vast trend toward appointed goals. Nature was, then, a gigantic engine, a vast, cyclopean power, huge, terrible, a leviathan with a heart of steel, knowing no compunction, no forgiveness, no tolerance; crushing out the human atom standing in its way, with nirvanic calm." Stephen Crane had already expressed the same attitude toward nature in a sharper image and in cleaner prose. When the four shipwrecked men in *The Open Boat* are drifting close to the beach but are unable to land because of the breakers, they stare at a windmill that is like "a giant standing with its back to the plight of the ants. It represented in a degree, to the correspondent, the serenity of nature amid the struggles of the individual—nature in the wind, and nature in the visions of men. She did not seem cruel to him, then, nor beneficent, nor treacherous, nor wise. But she was indifferent, flatly indifferent."

These ideas about nature, science, and destiny led to the recurrent use of words and phrases by which early naturalistic fiction can be identified. "The irony of fate" and "the pity of it" are two of the phrases; "pawns of circumstance" is another. The words that appear time and again are "primitive," "primordial" (often coupled with "slime"), "prehensile," "apelike," "wolflike," "brute" and "brutal," "savage," "driving," "conquering," "blood" (often as an adjective), "master" and "slave" (also as adjectives), "instinct" (which is usually "blind"), "ancestor," "huge," "cyclopean," "shapeless," "abyss," "biological," "chemic" and "chemism," "hypocrisy," "taboo," "unmoral." Time and again we read that "The race is to the swift and the battle to the strong." Time and again we are told about "the law of claw and fang," "the struggle for existence," "the blood of his Viking ancestors," and "the foul stream of hereditary evil." "The veneer of civilization" is always being "stripped away," or else it "drops away in an instant." The characters in early naturalistic novels "lose all resemblance to humanity," reverting to "the abysmal brute." But when they "clash together like naked savages," or even like atoms and star dust, it is always the hero who "proves himself the stronger"; and spurning his prostrate adversary he strides forward to seize "his mate, his female." "Was he to blame?" the author asks his readers; and always he answers, "Conditions, not men, were at fault."

All these characteristics of the earlier American naturalists might have been deduced from their original faith in Darwinian evolution and in the need for applying biological and physical laws to human affairs. But they had other characteristics that were more closely connected with American life in their own day.

The last decade of the nineteenth century, when they started their literary careers, was an age of contrasts and sudden changes. In spite of financial panics, the country was growing richer, but not at a uniform rate for all sections: the South was hopelessly impoverished and rural New England was returning to wilderness. Cities were gaining in population, partly at the expense of the Eastern farms, industry was thriving at the expense of agriculture, and independent factories were being combined into or destroyed by the trusts. It was an age of high interest rates, high but uncertain profits, low wages and widespread unemployment. It was an age when labor unions were being broken, when immigrants were pouring through Ellis Island to people the new slums and when the new American baronage was building its magnificently ugly chateaux. "America," to quote again from Dreiser's memoirs, "was just entering upon the most lurid phase of that vast, splendid, most lawless and most savage period in which the great financiers were plotting and conniving at the enslavement of the people and belaboring each other." Meanwhile the ordinary citizen found it difficult to plan his future and even began to suspect that he was, in a favorite naturalistic phrase, "the plaything of forces beyond human control."

The American faith that was preached in the pulpits and daily reasserted on editorial pages had lost its connection with American life. It was not only an intolerable limitation on American writing, as all the rebel authors had learned; it also had to be disregarded by anyone who hoped to rise in the business world and by anyone who, having failed to rise, wanted to understand the reasons for his failure. In its simplest terms, the American faith was that things were getting better year by year, that the individual could solve his problems by moving, usually westward, and that virtue was rewarded with wealth, the greatest virtue with the greatest wealth. Those were the doctrines of the editorial page; but reporters who worked for the same newspaper looked around them and decided that wealth was more often the fruit of selfishness and fraud, whereas the admirable persons in their world—the kind, the philosophic, the honest, and the open-eyed—were usually failures by business standards. Most of the early naturalistic writers, including Stephen Crane, Harold Frederic, David Graham Phillips, and Dreiser, were professional newspaper men; while the others either worked for short periods as reporters or wrote series of newspaper articles. All were more or less affected by the moral atmosphere of the city room; and the fact is important, since the newspaper men of the 1890's and 1900's were a special class or type. "Never," says Dreiser, speaking of his colleagues on the Pittsburgh *Dispatch,* "had I encountered more intelligent or helpful or companionable albeit more cynical men than I met here"; and the observation leads to general remarks about the reporters he had known:

> One can always talk to a newspaper man, I think, with the full confidence that one is talking to a man who is at least free of moralistic mush. Nearly everything in connection with those trashy romances of justice, truth, mercy, patriotism, public profession of all sorts, is already and forever gone if they have been in the business for any length of time. The religionist is seen by them for what he is: a swallower of romance or a masquerader looking to profit and preferment. Of the politician, they know or believe but one thing: that he is out for himself.

Essentially the attitude forced upon newspaper men as they interviewed politicians, evangelists, and convicted criminals was the same as the attitude they derived or might have derived from popular books on evolution. Reading and experience led to the same convictions: that Christianity was a sham, that all moral professions were false, that there was nothing real in the world but force and, for themselves, no respectable role to play except that of detached observers gathering the facts and printing as many of them as their publishers would permit. They drank, whored, talked shop, and dreamed about writing cynical books. "Most of these young men," Dreiser says, "looked upon life as a fierce, grim struggle in which no quarter was either given or taken, and in which all men laid traps, lied, squandered, erred through illusion: a conclusion with which I now most heartily agree." His novels one after another would be based on what he had learned in his newspaper days.

In writing their novels, most of the naturalists pictured themselves as expressing a judgment of life that was scientific, dispassionate, and, to borrow one of their phrases, completely unmoral; but a better word for their attitude would be "rebellious." Try as they would, they could not remain merely observers. They had to revolt against the moral standards of their time; and the revolt involved them more or less unconsciously in the effort to impose new standards that would be closer to what they regarded as natural laws. Their books are full of little essays or sermons addressed to the reader; in fact they suggest a naturalistic system of ethics complete with its vices and virtues. Among the vices those most often mentioned are hypocrisy, intolerance, conventionality, and unwillingness to acknowledge the truth. Among the virtues perhaps the first is strength, which is presented as both a physiological and a moral quality; it implies the courage to be strong in spite of social restraints. A second virtue is naturalness, that is, the quality of acting in accordance with one's nature and physical instincts. Dreiser's Jennie Gerhardt was among the first of the purely natural heroines in American literature, but she had many descendants. A third virtue is complete candor about the world and oneself; a fourth is pity for others; and a fifth is tolerance, especially of moral rebellion and economic failure. Most of the characters presented sympathetically in naturalistic novels are either the victors over moral codes which they defy (like Cowperwood in *The Financier* and Susan Lenox in the novel by David Graham Phillips about her fall and rise) or else victims of the economic struggle, paupers and drunkards with infinitely more wisdom than the respectable citizens who avoid them. A great deal of naturalistic writing, including the early poems of Edwin Arlington Robinson, is an eloquent hymn to loneliness and failure as the destiny, in America, of most superior men.

There are other qualities of American naturalism that are derived not so much from historical conditions as from the example of the two novelists whom the younger men regarded as leaders or precursors. Norris first and Dreiser after him fixed the patterns that the others would follow.

Both men were romantic by taste and temperament. Although Norris was a disciple of Zola's, his other favorite authors belonged in one way or another to the romantic school; they included Froissart, Scott, Dickens, Dumas, Hugo, Kipling, and Stevenson. Zola was no stranger in that company, Norris said; on one occasion he called him "the very head of the Romanticists."

> Terrible things must happen [he wrote], to the characters of the naturalistic tale. They must be twisted from the ordinary, wrenched from the quiet, uneventful round of everyday life and flung into the throes of a vast and terrible drama that works itself out in unleashed passions, in blood and sudden death. . . . Everything is extraordinary, imaginative, grotesque even, with a vague note of terror quivering throughout like the vibration of an ominous and low-pitched diapason.

Norris himself wished to practice naturalism as a form of romance, instead of taking up what he described as the "harsh, loveless, colorless, blunt tool called Realism." Dreiser in his autobiographical writings often refers to his own romantic temper. "For all my modest repute as a realist," he says, "I seem, to my self-analyzing eyes, somewhat more of a romanticist." He speaks of himself in his youth as "a creature of slow and uncertain response to anything practical, having an eye to color, romance, beauty. I was but a half-baked poet, romancer, dreamer." The other American naturalists were also romancers and dreamers in their fashion, groping among facts for the extraordinary and even the grotesque. They believed that men were subject to natural forces, but they felt those forces were best displayed when they led to unlimited wealth, utter squalor, collective orgies, blood, and sudden death.

Among the romantic qualities they tried to achieve was "bigness" in its double reference to size and intensity. They wanted to display "big" —that is, intense—emotions against a physically large background. Bigness was the virtue that Norris most admired in Zola's novels. "The world of M. Zola," he said, "is a world of big things; the enormous, the formidable, the terrible, is what counts; no teacup tragedies here." In his own novels, Norris looked for big themes; after his trilogy on Wheat, he planned to write a still bigger trilogy on the three days' battle of Gettysburg, with one novel devoted to the events of each day. The whole notion of writing trilogies instead of separate novels came to be connected with the naturalistic movement, although it was also adopted by the historical romancers. Before Norris there had been only one planned trilogy in serious American fiction: *The Littlepage Manuscripts,* written by James Fenimore Cooper a few years before his death; it traces the story of a New York state landowning family through a hundred years and three generations. After Norris there were dozens of trilogies, with a few tetralogies and pentalogies: to mention some of the better known, there were Dreiser's trilogy on the career of a financier, T. S. Stribling's trilogy on the rise of a poor-white family, Dos Passos' trilogy on the United States from 1900 to 1930, James T. Farrell's trilogy on Studs Lonigan and Eugene O'Neill's trilogy of plays, *Mourning Becomes Electra.* Later O'Neill set to work on a trilogy of trilogies, a drama to be complete in nine full-length plays. Farrell wrote a pentalogy about the boyhood of Danny O'Neill and then attacked another theme that would require several volumes, the young manhood of Bernard Clare. Trilogies expanded into whole cycles of novels somehow related in theme. Thus, after the success of *The Jungle,* which had dealt with the meat-packing industry in Chicago, Upton Sinclair wrote novels on other cities (Denver, Boston) and other industries (oil, coal, whisky, automobiles); finally he settled on a character, Lanny Budd, whose adventures were as endless as those of Tarzan or Superman. Sinclair Lewis dealt one after another with various trades and professions: real estate, medicine, divinity, social service, hotel management, and the stage; there was no limit to the subjects he could treat, so long as his readers' patience was equal to his own.

With their eyes continually on vast projects, the American naturalists were careless about the details of their work and indifferent to the materials they were using; often their trilogies resembled great steel-structural buildings faced with cinder blocks and covered with cracked stucco ornaments. Sometimes the buildings remained unfinished. Norris set this pattern, too, when he died before he could start his third novel on the Wheat. Dreiser worked for years on *The Stoic,* which was to be the sequel to *The Financier* and *The Titan;* but he was never satisfied with the various endings he tried, and the book had to be completed by others after his death. Lewis never wrote his novel on labor unions, although he spent months or years gathering material for it and spoke of it as his most ambitious work. In their effort to achieve bigness at any cost, the naturalists were likely to undertake projects that went beyond their physical or imaginative powers, or in which they discovered too late that they weren't interested.

Meanwhile they worked ahead in a delirium of production, like factories trying to set new records. To understand their achievements in speed and bulk one has to compare their output with that of an average novelist. There is of course no average novelist, but there are scores of men and women who earn their livings by writing novels, and many of them try to publish one book each year. If they spend four months planning and gathering material for the book, another four months writing the first draft (at the rate of about a thousand words a day), and the last four months in revision, they are at least not unusual. Very few of the naturalists would have been satisfied with that modest rate of production. Harold Frederic wrote as much as 4,000 words a day and often sent his manuscripts to the printer without corrections. At least he paused between novels to carry on his work as a foreign correspondent; but Jack London, who wrote only 1,000 words a day, tried to fulfill that quota six days a week and fifty-two weeks a year; he allowed himself no extra time for planning or revision. He wrote fifty books in seventeen years, and didn't pretend that all of them were his best writing. "I have no unfinished stories," he told an interviewer five years before his death. "Invariably I complete every one I start. If it's good, I sign it and send it out. If it isn't good, I sign it and send it out." David Graham Phillips finished his first novel in 1901 and published sixteen others before his death in 1911, in addition to the articles he wrote for muckraking magazines. He left behind him the manuscripts of six novels (including the two-volume *Susan Lenox*) that were published posthumously. Upton Sinclair set a record in the early days when he was writing half-dime novels for boys. He kept three secretaries busy; two of them would be transcribing their notes while the third was taking dictation. By this method he once wrote 18,000 words in a day. He gained a fluency that helped him later when he was writing serious books, but he also acquired a contempt for style that made them painful to read, except in their French translations. Almost all the naturalists read better in translation; that is one of the reasons for their international popularity as compared with the smaller audience that some of them found at home.

The naturalistic writers of all countries preferred an objective or scientific approach to their material. As early as 1864 the brothers Goncourt had written in their journal, "The novel of today is made with documents narrated or selected from nature, just as history is based on written documents." A few years later Zola defined the novel as a scientific experiment; its purpose, he said in rather involved language, was to demonstrate the behavior of given characters in a given situation. Still later Norris advanced the doctrine "that no one could be a writer until he could regard life and people, and the world in general, from the objective point of view—until he could remain detached, outside, maintain the unswerving attitude of the observer." The naturalists as a group not only based their work on current scientific theories, but tried to copy scientific methods in planning their novels. They were writers who believed, or claimed to believe, that they could deliberately choose a subject for their work instead of being chosen by a subject; that they could go about collecting characters as a biologist collected specimens; and that their fictional account of such characters could be as accurate and true to the facts as the report of an experiment in the laboratory.

It was largely this faith in objectivity that led them to write about penniless people in the slums, whom they regarded as "outside" or alien subjects for observation. Some of them began with a feeling of contempt for the masses. Norris during his college years used to speak of "the canaille" and often wished for the day when all radicals could be "drowned on one raft." Later this pure contempt developed into a contemptuous interest, and he began to spend his afternoons on Polk Street, in San Francisco, observing with a detached eye the actions of what he now called "the people." The minds of the people, he thought, were simpler than those of persons in his own world; essentially these human beings were animals, "the creatures of habit, the playthings of forces," and therefore they were ideal subjects for a naturalistic novel. Some of the other naturalists revealed the same rather godlike attitude toward workingmen. Nevertheless they wrote about them, a bold step at a time when most novels dealt only with ladies, gentlemen, and faithful retainers; and often their contemptuous interest was gradually transformed into sympathy.

Their objective point of view toward their material was sometimes a pretense that deceived themselves before it deceived others. From the outside world they chose the subjects that mirrored their own conflicts and obsessions. Crane, we remember, said his purpose in writing *Maggie* was to show "that environment is a tremendous thing and often shapes lives regardlessly." Yet, on the subjective level, the novel also revealed an obsessive notion about the blamelessness of prostitutes that affected his career from beginning to end; it caused a series of scandals, involved him in a feud with the vice squad in Manhattan and finally led him to marry the madam of bawdy house in Jacksonville. Norris's first novel, *Vandover and the Brute,* is an apparently objective study of degeneration, but it also mirrors the struggles of the author with his intensely Puritan conscience; Vandover is Norris himself. He had drifted into some mild dissipations and pictured them as leading to failure and insanity. Dreiser in *Sister Carrie* was telling a story based on the adventures of one of his sisters; that explains why Carrie Meeber in the novel is "Sister" Carrie, even though her relatives disappear after the first few pages. "My mind was a blank except for the name," Dreiser said when explaining how he came to write the novel. "I had no idea who or what she was to be. I have often thought that there was something mystic about it, as if I were being used, like a medium." In a sense he was being used by his own memories, which had become subconscious. There was nothing mystic to Upton Sinclair about his fierce emotion in writing *The Jungle;* he knew from the beginning that he was telling his own story. "I wrote with tears and anguish," he says in his memoirs,

> pouring into the pages all that pain which life had meant to me. Externally, the story had to do with a family of stockyards workers, but internally it was the story of my own family. Did I wish to know how the poor suffered in Chicago? I had only to recall the previous winter in a cabin, when we had only cotton blankets, and cowered shivering in our separate beds.... Our little boy was down with pneumonia that winter, and nearly died, and the grief of that went into the book.

Indeed, there is personal grief and fury and bewilderment in all the most impressive naturalistic novels. They are at their best, not when they are scientific or objective, in accordance with their own theories, but when they are least naturalistic, most personal and lyrical.

If we follow William James and divide writers into the two categories of the tough and the tender-minded, then most of the naturalists are tender-minded. The sense of moral fitness is strong in them; they believe in their hearts that nature *should* be kind, that virtue *should* be rewarded on earth, that men *should* control their own destinies. More than other writers, they are wounded by ugliness and injustice, but they will not close their eyes to either; indeed, they often give the impression of seeking out ugliness and injustice in order to be wounded again and again. They have hardly a trace of the cynicism that is often charged against them. It is the quietly realistic or classical writers who are likely to be cynics, in the sense of holding a low opinion of life and human beings; that low estimate is so deeply ingrained in them that they never bother to insist on it—for why should they try to make converts in such a hopeless world? The naturalists are always trying to convert others and themselves, and sometimes they build up new illusions simply to enjoy the pain of stripping them away. It is their feeling of fascinated revulsion toward their subject matter that makes some of the naturalists hard to read; they seem to be flogging themselves and their audience like a band of penitentes.

So far I have been trying to present the positive characteristics of a movement in American letters, but naturalism can also be defined in terms of what it is not. Thus, to begin a list of negations, it is not journalism in the bad sense, merely sensational or entertaining or written merely to sell. It has to be honest by definition, and honesty in literature is a hard quality to achieve, one that requires more courage and concentration than journalists can profitably devote to writing a novel. Even when an author holds all the naturalistic doctrines, his books have to reach a certain level of observation and intensity before they deserve to be called naturalistic. Jack London held the doctrines and wrote fifty books, but only three or four of them reached the required level. David Graham Phillips reached it only once, in *Susan Lenox,* if he reached it then.

Literary naturalism is not the sort of doctrine that can be officially sponsored and taught in the public schools. It depends for too many of its effects on shocking the sensibilities of its readers and smashing their illusions. It always becomes a threat to the self-esteem of the propertied classes. *Babbitt,* for example, is naturalistic in its hostile treatment of American businessmen. When Sinclair Lewis defended Babbittry in a later novel, *The Prodigal Parents,* his work had ceased to be naturalistic.

For a third negative statement, naturalism is not what we have learned to call literature "in depth." It is concerned with human behavior and with explanations for that behavior in terms of heredity or environment. It presents the exterior world, often in striking visual images; but unlike the work of Henry James or Sherwood Anderson or William Faulkner—to mention only three writers in other traditions —it does not try to explore the world within. Faulkner's method is sometimes described as "subjective naturalism," but the phrase is self-contradictory, almost as if one spoke of "subjective biology" or "subjective physics."

Naturalism does not deal primarily with individuals in themselves, but rather with social groups or settings or movements, or with individuals like Babbitt and Studs Lonigan who are regarded as being typical of a group. The naturalistic writer tries not to identify himself with any of his characters, although he doesn't always succeed; in general his aim is to present them almost as if they were laboratory specimens. They are seldom depicted as being capable of moral decisions. This fact makes it easy to distinguish between the early naturalists and some of their contemporaries like Robert Herrick and Edith Wharton who also tried to write without optimistic illusions. Herrick and Wharton, however, dealt with individuals who possessed some degree of moral freedom; and often the plots of their novels hinge on a conscious decision by one of the characters. Hemingway, another author whose work is wrongly described as naturalistic, writes stories that reveal some moral quality, usually stoicism or the courage of a frightened man.

Many naturalistic works are valuable historical documents, but the authors in general have little sense of history. They present each situation as if it had no historical antecedents, and their characters might be men and women created yesterday morning, so few signs do they show of having roots in the past. "Science" for naturalistic writers usually means laboratory science, and not the study of human institutions or patterns of thoughts that persist through generations.

With a few exceptions they have no faith in reform, whether it be the reform of an individual by his own decision or the reform of society by reasoned courses of action. The changes they depict are the result of laws and forces and tendencies beyond human control. That is the great difference between the naturalists and the proletarian or Marxian novelists of the 1930's. The proletarian writers—who were seldom proletarians in private life—believed that men acting together could make a new world. But they borrowed the objective and exterior technique of the naturalists, which was unsuited to their essentially religious purpose. In the beginning of each book they portrayed a group of factory workers as the slaves of economic conditions, "the creatures of habit, the playthings of forces"; then later they portrayed the conversion of one or more workers to Communism. But conversion is a psychological, not a biological, phenomenon, and it could not be explained purely in terms of conditions or forces. When the conversion took place, there was a shift from the outer to the inner world, and the novel broke in two.

It was not at all extraordinary for naturalism to change into religious Marxism in the middle of a novel, since it has always shown a tendency to dissolve into something else. On the record, literary naturalism does not seem to be a doctrine or attitude to which men are likely to cling through their whole lives. It is always being transformed into satire, symbolism, lyrical autobiography, utopian socialism, Communism, Catholicism, Buddhism, Freudian psychology, hack journalism or the mere assembling of facts. So far there is not in American literature a single instance in which a writer has remained a naturalist from beginning to end of a long career; even Dreiser before his death became a strange mixture of Communist and mystic. There are, however, a great many works that are predominantly naturalistic; and the time has come to list them in order to give the basis for my generalities.

I should say that those works, in fiction, were *Maggie* and *George's Mother* by Stephen Crane, with many of his short stories; *The Damnation of Theron Ware* by Harold Frederic; *Vandover, McTeague* and *The Octopus* (but not *The Pit*) by Frank Norris; *The Call of the Wild*, which is a sort of naturalistic Aesop's fable, besides *The Sea Wolf* and *Martin Eden* by Jack London; *The Jungle* by Upton Sinclair, as far as the page where Jurgis is converted to socialism; *Susan Lenox* by David Graham Phillips; all of Dreiser's novels except *The Bulwark* which has a religious ending written at the close of his life; all the serious novels of Sinclair Lewis between *Main Street* (1920) and *Dodsworth* (1929), but none he wrote afterward; Dos Passos' *Manhattan Transfer* and *U.S.A.;* James T. Farrell's work in general, but especially *Studs Lonigan;* Richard Wright's *Native Son;* and most of John Steinbeck's novels, including *In Dubious Battle* and all but the hortatory passages in *The Grapes of Wrath*. In poetry there is Robinson's early verse (*The Children of the Night*) and there is Edgar Lee Masters' *Spoon River Anthology*. In the drama there are the early plays of Eugene O'Neill, from *Beyond the Horizon* to *Desire under the Elms*. Among essays there are H. L. Mencken's *Prejudices* and Joseph Wood Krutch's *The Modern Temper,* which is the most coherent statement of the naturalistic position. There are other naturalists in all fields, especially fiction, and other naturalistic books by several of the authors I have mentioned; but these are the works by which the school is likely to be remembered and judged.

And what shall we say in judgment?—since judge we must, after this long essay in definition. Is naturalism true or false in its premises and good or bad in its effect on American literature? Its results have been good, I think, in so far as it has forced its adherents to stand in opposition to American orthodoxy. Honest writing in this country, the only sort worth bothering about, has almost always been the work of an opposition, chiefly because the leveling and unifying elements in our culture have been so strong that a man who accepts orthodox judgments is in danger of losing his literary personality. Catullus and Villon might be able to write their poems here; with their irregular lives they wouldn't run the risk of being corrupted by the standards of right-thinking people. But Virgil, the friend of Augustus, the official writer who shaped the myth of the Roman state—Virgil would be a dubious figure as an American poet. He would be tempted to soften his values in order to become a prophet for the masses. The American myth of universal cheap luxuries, tiled bathrooms, and service with a smile would not serve him as the basis for an epic poem.

The naturalists, standing in opposition, have been writers of independent and strongly marked personalities. They have fought for the right to speak their minds and have won a measure of freedom for themselves and others. Yet it has to be charged against them that their opposition often takes the form of cheapening what they write about; of always looking for the lowdown or the payoff, that is, for the meanest explanation of everything they describe. There is a tendency in literary naturalism—as distinguished from philosophical naturalism, which is not my subject—always to explain the complex in terms of the simple: society in terms of self, man in terms of his animal inheritance, and the organic in terms of the inorganic. The result is that something is omitted at each stage in this process of reduction. To say that man is a beast of prey or a collection of chemical compounds omits most of man's special nature; it is a metaphor, not a scientific statement.

This scientific weakness of naturalism involves a still greater literary weakness, for it leads to a conception of man that makes it impossible for naturalistic authors to write in the tragic spirit. They can write about crimes, suicides, disasters, the terrifying, and the grotesque; but even the most powerful of their novels and plays are case histories rather than tragedies in the classical sense. Tragedy is an affirmation of man's importance; it is "the imitation of noble action," in Aristotle's phrase; and the naturalists are unable to believe in human nobility. "We write no tragedies today," said Joseph Wood Krutch in his early book, *The Modern Temper*, which might better have been called "The Naturalistic Temper." "If the plays and novels of today deal with littler people and less mighty emotions it is not because we have become interested in commonplace souls and their unglamorous adventures but because we have come, willy-nilly, to see the soul of man as commonplace and its emotions as mean." But Krutch was speaking only for those who shared the naturalistic point of view. There are other doctrines held by modern writers that make it possible to endow their characters with human dignity. Tragic novels and plays have been written in these years by Christians, Communists, humanists, and even by existentialists, all of whom believe in different fashions and degrees that men can shape their own fates.

For the naturalists, however, men are "human insects" whose brief lives are completely determined by society or nature. The individual is crushed in a moment if he resists; and his struggle, instead of being tragic, is merely pitiful or ironic, as if we had seen a mountain stir itself to overwhelm a fly. Irony is a literary effect used time and again by all the naturalistic writers. For Stephen Crane it is the central effect on which almost all his plots depend: thus, in *The Red Badge of Courage* the boy makes himself a hero by running away. In *A Mystery of Heroism* a soldier risks his life to bring a bucket of water to his comrades, and the water is spilled. In *The Monster* a Negro stableman is so badly burned in rescuing a child that he becomes a faceless horror; and the child's father, a physician, loses his practice as a reward for sheltering the stableman. The irony in Dreiser's novels depends on the contrast between conventional morality and the situations he describes: Carrie Meeber loses her virtue and succeeds in her career; Jennie Gerhardt is a kept woman with higher principles than any respectable wife. In Sinclair Lewis the irony is reduced to an obsessive and irritating trick of style; if he wants to say that a speech was dull and stupid, he has to call it "the culminating glory of the dinner" and then, to make sure that we catch the point, explain that it was delivered by

Mrs. Adelaide Tarr Gimmitch, "known throughout the country as 'the Unkies' Girl." The reader, seeing the name of Gimmitch, is supposed to smile a superior smile. There is something superior and ultimately tiresome in the attitude of many naturalists toward the events they describe. Irony—like pity, its companion—is a spectator's emotion, and it sets a space between ourselves and the characters in the novel. They suffer, but their cries reach us faintly, like those of dying strangers we cannot hope to save.

There is nothing in the fundamental principles of naturalism that requires a novel to be written in hasty or hackneyed prose. Flaubert, the most careful stylist of his age, was the predecessor and guide of the French naturalists. Among the naturalistic writers of all countries who wrote with a feeling for language were the brothers Goncourt, Ibsen, Hardy, and Stephen Crane. But it was Norris, not Crane, who set the standards for naturalistic fiction in the United States, and Norris had no respect for style. "What pleased me most in your review of 'McTeague,' " he said in a letter to Isaac Marcosson, "was 'disdaining all pretensions to style.' It is precisely what I try most to avoid. I detest 'fine writing,' 'rhetoric,' 'elegant English'—tommyrot. Who cares for fine style! Tell your yarn and let your style go to the devil. We don't want literature, we want life." Yet the truth was that Norris' novels were full of fine writing and lace-curtain English. "Untouched, unassailable, undefiled," he said of the wheat, "that mighty world force, that nourisher of nations, wrapped in Nirvanic calm, indifferent to the human swarm, gigantic, resistless, moved onward in its appointed grooves." He never learned to present his ideas in their own clothes or none at all; it was easier to dress them in borrowed plush; easier to make all his calms Nirvanic and all his grooves appointed.

Yet Norris wrote better prose than most of his successors among the American naturalists. With a few exceptions like Dos Passos and Steinbeck, they have all used language as a blunt instrument; they write as if they were swinging shillelaghs. O'Neill is a great dramatist, but he has never had an ear for the speech of living persons. Lewis used to have an ear, but now listens only to himself. He keeps being arch and ironical about his characters until we want to snarl at him, "Quit patronizing those people! Maybe they'd have something to say if you'd only let them talk." Farrell writes well when he is excited or angry, but most of the time he makes his readers trudge through vacant lots in a South Chicago smog. Dreiser is the worst writer of all, but in some ways the least objectionable; there is something native to himself in his misuse of the language, so that we come to cherish it as a sign of authenticity, like the tool marks on Shaker furniture. Most of the others simply use the oldest and easiest phrase.

But although the naturalists as a group are men of defective hearing, they almost all have keen eyes for new material. Their interest in themes that others regarded as too unpleasant or ill-bred has immensely broadened the scope of American fiction. Moreover, they have had enough vitality and courage to be exhilarated by the American life of their own times. From the beginning they have exulted in the wealth and ugliness of American cities, the splendor of the mansions and the squalor of the tenements. They compared Pittsburgh to Paris and New York to imperial Rome. Frank Norris thought that his own San Francisco was the ideal city for storytellers; "Things happen in San Francisco," he said. Dreiser remarked of Chicago, "It is given to some cities, as to some lands, to suggest romance, and to me Chicago did that hourly. . . . Florence in its best days must have been something like this to young Florentines, or Venice to the young Venetians." The naturalists for all their faults were embarked on a bolder venture than those other writers whose imaginations can absorb nothing but legends already treated in other books, prepared and predigested food. They tried to seize the life around them, and at their best they transformed it into new archetypes of human experience. Just as Cooper had shaped the legend of the frontier and Mark Twain the legend of the Mississippi, so the naturalists have been shaping the harsher legends of an urban and industrial age.

THEODORE DREISER *

H. L. MENCKEN

I

OUT OF the desert of American fictioneering, so populous and yet so drear, Dreiser stands up—a phenomenon unescapably visible, but disconcertingly hard to explain. What forces combined to produce him in the first place, and how has he managed to hold out so long against the prevailing blasts—of disheartening misunderstanding and misrepresentation, of Puritan suspicion and opposition, of artistic isolation, of commercial seduction? There is something downright heroic in the way the man has held his narrow and perilous ground, disdaining all compromise, unmoved by the cheap success that lies so inviting around the corner. He has faced, in his day, almost every form of attack that a serious artist can conceivably encounter, and yet all of them together have scarcely budged him an inch. He still plods along in the laborious, cheerless way he first marked out for himself; he is quite as undaunted by baited praise as by bludgeoning, malignant abuse; his later novels are, if anything, more unyieldingly dreiserian than his earliest. As one who has long sought to entice him in this direction or that, fatuously presuming to instruct him in what would improve him and profit him, I may well bear a reluctant and resigned sort of testimony to his gigantic steadfastness. It is almost as if any change in his manner, any concession to what is usual and esteemed, any amelioration of his blind, relentless exercises of *force majeure,* were a physical impossibility. One feels him at last to be authentically no more than a helpless instrument (or victim) of that inchoate flow of forces which he himself is so fond of depicting as at once the answer to the riddle of life, and a riddle ten times more vexing and accursed.

And his origins, as I say, are quite as mysterious as his motive power. To fit him into the unrolling chart of American or even of English fiction is extremely difficult. Save one thinks of H. B. Fuller (whose *With the Procession* and *The Cliff-Dwellers* are still remembered by Huneker, but by whom else? [1]) he seems to have had no forerunner among

* "Theodore Dreiser" first appeared in *A Book of Prefaces,* by H. L. Mencken, copyright 1917 by Alfred A. Knopf, Inc. Sections I, II, III of the original essay are used here by permission of the author and the publishers.

[1] Fuller's disappearance is one of the strangest phenomena of American letters. I was astonished some time ago to discover that he was still alive. Back in 1899 he was already so far forgotten that William Archer mistook his name, calling him Henry Y. Fuller. *Vide* Archer's pamphlet, *The American Language,* New York, 1899. H.L.M.

us, and for all the discussion of him that goes on, he has few avowed disciples, and none of them gets within miles of him. One catches echoes of him, perhaps, in Willa Sibert Cather, in Mary S. Watts, in David Graham Phillips, in Sherwood Anderson, and in Joseph Medill Patterson, but, after all, they are no more than echoes. In Robert Herrick the thing descends to a feeble parody; in imitators further removed to sheer burlesque. All the latter-day American novelists of consideration are vastly more facile than Dreiser in their philosophy, as they are in their style. In the fact, perhaps, lies the measure of their difference. What they lack, great and small, is the gesture of pity, the note of awe, the profound sense of wonder—in a phrase, that "soberness of mind" which William Lyon Phelps sees as the hallmark of Conrad and Hardy, and which even the most stupid cannot escape in Dreiser. The normal American novel, even in its most serious forms, takes color from the national cocksureness and superficiality. It runs monotonously to ready explanations, a somewhat infantile smugness and hopefulness, a habit of reducing the unknowable to terms of the not worth knowing. What it cannot explain away with ready formulae, as in the later Winston Churchill, it snickers over as scarcely worth explaining at all, as in the later Howells. Such a brave and tragic book as *Ethan Frome* is so rare as to be almost singular, even with Mrs. Wharton. There is, I daresay, not much market for that sort of thing. In the arts, as in the concerns of everyday, the American seeks escape from the insoluble by pretending that it is solved. A comfortable phrase is what he craves beyond all things—and comfortable phrases are surely not to be sought in Dreiser's stock.

I have heard argument that he is a follower of Frank Norris, and two or three facts lend it a specious probability. *McTeague* was printed in 1899; *Sister Carrie* a year later. Moreover, Norris was the first to see the merit of the latter book, and he fought a gallant fight, as literary advisor to Doubleday, Page & Co., against its suppression after it was in type. But this theory runs aground upon two circumstances, the first being that Dreiser did not actually read *McTeague,* nor, indeed, grow aware of Norris, until after *Sister Carrie* was completed, and the other being that his development, once he began to write other books, was along paths far distant from those pursued by Norris himself. Dreiser, in truth, was a bigger man than Norris from the start; it is to the latter's unending honor that he recognized the fact instanter, and yet did all he could to help his rival. It is imaginable, of course, that Norris, living fifteen years longer, might have overtaken Dreiser, and even surpassed him; one finds an arrow pointing that way in *Vandover and the Brute* (not printed until 1914). But it swings sharply around in *The Epic of the Wheat.* In the second volume of that incomplete trilogy, *The Pit,* there is an obvious concession to the popular taste in romance; the thing is so frankly written down, indeed, that a play has been made of it, and Broadway has applauded it. And in *The Octopus*, despite some excellent writing, there is a descent to a mysticism so fantastic and preposterous that it quickly passes beyond serious consideration. Norris, in his day, swung even lower—for example, in *A Man's Woman* and in some of his short stories. He was a pioneer, perhaps only half sure of the way he wanted to go, and the evil lures of popular success lay all about him. It is no wonder that he sometimes seemed to lose his direction.

Emile Zola is another literary father whose paternity grows dubious on examination. I once printed an article exposing what seemed to me to be a Zolaesque attitude of mind, and even some trace of the actual Zola manner, in *Jennie Gerhardt;* there came from Dreiser the news that he had never read a line of Zola, and knew nothing about his novels. Not a complete answer, of course; the influence might have been exerted at second hand. But through whom? I confess that I am unable to name a likely medium. The effects of Zola upon Anglo-Saxon fiction have been almost *nil;* his only avowed disciple, George Moore, has long since recanted and reformed; he has scarcely rippled the prevailing romanticism. . . . Thomas Hardy? Here, I daresay, we strike a better scent. There are many obvious likenesses between *Tess of the D'Urbervilles* and *Jennie Gerhardt* and again between *Jude the Obscure* and *Sister Carrie*. All four stories deal penetratingly and poignantly with the essential tragedy of women; all disdain the petty, specious explanations of popular fiction; in each one finds a poetical and melancholy beauty. Moreover, Dreiser himself confesses to an enchanted discovery of Hardy in 1896, three years before *Sister Carrie* was begun. But it is easy to push such a fact too hard, and to search for likenesses and parallels that are really not there. The truth is that Dreiser's points of contact with Hardy might be easily matched by many striking points of difference, and that the fundamental ideas in their novels, despite a common sympathy, are anything but identical. Nor does one apprehend any ponderable result of Dreiser's youthful enthusiasm for Balzac, which antedated his discovery of Hardy by two years. He got from both men a sense of the scope and dignity of the novel; they taught him that a story might be a good one, and yet considerably more than a story; they showed him the essential drama of the commonplace. But that they had more influence in forming his point of view, or even in shaping his technique, than any one of half-a-dozen other gods of those young days—this I scarcely find. In the structure of his novels, and in their manner of approach to life no less, they call up the work of Dostoevsky and Turgenev far more than the work of either of these men—but of all the Russians save Tolstoy (as of Flaubert) Dreiser himself tells us that he was ignorant until ten years after *Sister Carrie*. In his days of preparation, indeed, his reading was so copious and so disorderly that antagonistic influences must have well-nigh neutralized one another, and so left the curious youngster to work out his own method and his own philosophy. Stevenson went down with Balzac, Poe and Hardy, Dumas *fils* with Tolstoy. There were even months of delight in Sienkiewicz, Lew Wallace, and E. P. Roe! The whole repertory of the pedagogues had been fought through in school and college: Dickens, Thackeray, Hawthorne, Washington Irving, Kingsley, Scott. Only Irving and Hawthorne seem to have made deep impressions. "I used to lie under a tree," says Dreiser, "and read *Twice-Told Tales* by the hour. I thought *The Alhambra* was a perfect creation, and I still have a lingering affection for it." Add Bret Harte, George Ebers, William Dean Howells, Oliver Wendell Holmes, and you have a literary stew indeed! . . . But for all its bubbling I see a far more potent influence in the chance discovery of Spencer and Huxley at twenty-three —the year of choosing! Who, indeed, will ever measure the effect of those two giants upon the young men of that era—Spencer with his inordinate meticulousness, his relentless pursuit of facts, his overpowering syllogisms, and Huxley with his devastating agnosticism, his insatiable questionings of the old axioms, above all, his brilliant style? Huxley, it would appear, has been condemned to the scientific hulks, along with bores innumerable and unspeakable; one looks in vain for any appreciation of him in treatises on beautiful letters.[2] And yet the man was a superb artist in works, a master-writer even more than a master-biologist, one of the few truly great stylists that England has produced since the time of Anne. One can easily imagine the effect of two such vigorous and intriguing minds upon a youth groping about for self-understanding and self-expression. They swept him clean, he tells us, of the lingering faith of his boyhood—a mediaeval, Rhenish Catholicism;—more, they filled him with a new and eager curiosity, an intense interest in the life that lay about him, a desire to seek out its hidden workings and underlying causes. A young man set afire by Huxley might perhaps make a very bad novelist, but it is a certainty that he could never make a sentimental and superficial one. There is no need to go further than this single moving adventure to find the genesis of Dreiser's disdain of the current platitudes, his sense of life as a complex biological phenomenon, only dimly comprehended, and his tenacious way of thinking things out, and of holding to what he finds good. Ah, that he had learned from Huxley, not only how to inquire, but also how to report! That he had picked up a talent for that dazzling style, so sweet to the ear, so damnably persuasive, so crystal-clear!

But the more one examines Dreiser, either as writer or as theorist of man, the more his essential isolation becomes apparent. He got a habit

[2] For example, in *The Cambridge History of English Literature,* which runs to fourteen large volumes and a total of nearly 10,000 pages, Huxley receives but a page and a quarter of notice, and his remarkable mastery of English is barely mentioned in passing. His two debates with Gladstone, in which he did some of the best writing of the century, are not noticed at all. H.L.M.

of mind from Huxley, but he completely missed Huxley's habit of writing. He got a view of woman from Hardy, but he soon changed it out of all resemblance. He got a certain fine ambition and gusto out of Balzac, but all that was French and characteristic he left behind. So with Zola, Howells, Tolstoy, and the rest. The tracing of likenesses quickly becomes rabbinism, almost cabalism. The differences are huge and sprout up in all directions. Nor do I see anything save a flaming up of colonial passion in the current efforts to fit him into a German frame, and make him an agent of Prussian frightfulness in letters. Such bosh one looks for in the *Nation* and the Boston *Transcript,* and there is where one actually finds it. Even the *New Republic* has stood clear of it; it is important only as material for that treatise upon the Anglo-Saxon under the terror which remains to be written. The name of the man, true enough, is obviously Germanic; he has told us himself, in *A Traveler at Forty,* how he sought out and found the tombs of his ancestors in some little town of the Rhine country. There are more of these genealogical revelations in *A Hoosier Holiday,* but they show a Rhenish strain that was already running thin in boyhood. No one, indeed, who reads a Dreiser novel can fail to see the gap separating the author from these half-forgotten forbears. He shows even less of German influence than of English influence.

There is, as a matter of fact, little in modern German fiction that is intelligibly comparable to *Jennie Gerhardt* and *The Titan,* either as a study of man or as a work of art. The naturalistic movement of the eighties was launched by men whose eyes were upon the theater, and it is in that field that nine-tenths of its force has been spent. "German naturalism," says George Madison Priest, quoting Gotthold Klee's *Grunzüge der deutschen Literaturgeschichte,* "created a new type only in the drama." [3] True enough, it has also produced occasional novels, and some of them are respectable. Gustav Frenssen's *Jörn Uhl* is a specimen: it has been done into English. Another is Clara Viebig's *Das tägliche Brot,* which Ludwig Lewisohn compares to George Moore's *Esther Waters.* Yet another is Thomas Mann's *Buddenbrooks.* But it would be absurd to cite these works as evidences of a national quality, and doubly absurd to think of them as inspiring such books as *Jennie Gerhardt* and *The Titan,* which excel them in everything save workmanship. The case of Mann reveals a tendency that is visible in nearly all of his contemporaries. Starting out as an agnostic realist not unlike the Arnold Bennett of *The Old Wives' Tale,* he has gradually taken on a hesitating sort of romanticism, and in one of his later books, *Königliche Hoheit* (in English, *Royal Highness*), he ends upon a note of sentimentalism borrowed from Wagner's *Ring.* Fräulein Viebig has also succumbed to banal and extra-artistic purposes. Her *Die Wacht am Rhein,*

[3] *A Brief History of German Literature;* New York, Charles Scribner's Sons, 1909. H.L.M.

for all its merits in detail, is, at bottom, no more than an eloquent hymn
to patriotism—the most doggish and dubious of all the virtues. As for
Frenssen, he is a parson by trade, and carries over into the novel a good
deal of the windy moralizing of the pulpit. All of these German naturalists—and they are the only German novelists worth considering—share
the weakness of Zola, their *Stammvater*. They, too, fall into the morass
that engulfed *Fécondité,* and make sentimental propaganda.

I go into this matter in detail, not because it is intrinsically of any
moment, but because the effort to depict Dreiser as a secret agent of the
Wilhelmstrasse, told off to inject subtle doses of *Kultur* into a naïf and
pious people, has taken on the proportions of an organized movement.
The same critical imbecility which detects naught save a tom-cat in
Frank Cowperwood can find naught save an abhorrent foreigner in
Cowperwood's creator. The truth is that the trembling patriots of letters, male and female, are simply at their old game of seeing a man
under the bed. Dreiser, in fact, is densely ignorant of German literature,
as he is of the better part of French literature, and of much of English
literature. He did not even read Hauptmann until after *Jennie Gerhardt* had been written, and such typical German moderns as Ludwig
Thoma, Otto Julius Bierbaum, and Richard Dehmel remain as strange
to him as Heliogabalus.

II

In his manner, as opposed to his matter, he is more the Teuton, for he
shows all of the racial patience and pertinacity and all of the racial lack
of humor. Writing a novel is as solemn a business to him as trimming
a beard is to a German barber. He blasts his way through his interminable stories by something not unlike main strength; his writing, one feels,
often takes on the character of an actual siege operation, with tunnel-
ings, drum-fire, assaults in close order, and hand-to-hand fighting. Once,
seeking an analogy, I called him the Hindenburg of the novel. If it
holds, then *The "Genius"* is his Poland. The field of action bears the
aspect, at the end, of a hostile province meticulously brought under the
yoke, with every road and lane explored to its beginning, and every
crossroads village laboriously taken, inventoried, and policed. Here is
the very negation of Gallic lightness and intuition, and of all other
forms of impressionism as well. Here is no series of illuminating flashes,
but a gradual bathing of the whole scene with white light, so that every
detail stands out.

And many of those details, of course, are trivial; even irritating. They
do not help the picture; they muddle and obscure it; one wonders im-
patiently what their meaning is, and what the purpose may be of revealing them with such a precise, portentous air.... Turn to page 703 of
The "Genius." By the time one gets there, one has hewn and hacked
one's way through 702 large pages of fine print—97 long chapters, more

than 250,000 words. And yet, at this hurried and impatient point, with the *coda* already begun, Dreiser halts the whole narrative to explain the origin, nature, and inner meaning of Christian Science, and to make us privy to a lot of chatty stuff about Mrs. Althea Jones, a professional healer, and to supply us with detailed plans and specifications of the apartment house in which she lives, works her tawdry miracles, and has her being. Here, in sober summary, are the particulars:

1. That the house is "of conventional design."
2. That there is "a spacious areaway" between its two wings.
3. That these wings are "of cream-colored pressed brick."
4. That the entrance between them is "protected by a handsome wrought-iron door."
5. That to either side of this door is "an electric lamp support of handsome design."
6. That in each of these lamp supports there are "lovely cream-colored globes, shedding a soft luster."
7. That inside is "the usual lobby."
8. That in the lobby is "the usual elevator."
9. That in the elevator is the usual "uniformed Negro elevator man."
10. That this Negro elevator man (name not given) is "indifferent and impertinent."
11. That a telephone switchboard is also in the lobby.
12. That the building is seven stories in height.

In *The Financier* there is the same exasperating rolling up of irrelevant facts. The court proceedings in the trial of Cowperwood are given with all the exactness of a parliamentary report in the London *Times*. The speeches of the opposing counsel are set down nearly in full, and with them the remarks of the judge, and after that the opinion of the Appellate Court on appeal, with the dissenting opinions as a sort of appendix. In *Sister Carrie* the thing is less savagely carried out, but that is not Dreiser's fault, for the manuscript was revised by some anonymous hand, and the printed version is but little more than half the length of the original. In *The Titan* and *Jennie Gerhardt* no such brake upon exuberance is visible; both books are crammed with details that serve no purpose, and are as flat as ditchwater. Even in the two volumes of personal record, *A Traveler at Forty* and *A Hoosier Holiday*, there is the same furious accumulation of trivialities. Consider the former. It is without structure, without selection, without reticence. One arises from it as from a great babbling, half drunken. On the one hand the author fills a long and gloomy chapter with the story of the Borgias, apparently under the impression that it is news, and on the other hand he enters into intimate and inconsequential confidences about all the persons he meets en route, sparing neither the innocent nor the obscure. The children of his English host at Bridgely Level strike him as fantastic little creatures, even as a bit uncanny—and he duly sets it down. He meets an Englishman on a French train who pleases him much, and the two become good friends and see Rome together, but the fellow's wife is "obstreperous" and "haughty in her manner" and so "loud-spoken in her opinions" that she is "really offensive"—and down it goes. He makes an impression on a Mlle. Marcelle in Paris, and she accompanies him from Monte Carlo to Ventimiglia, and there gives him a parting kiss and whispers, *"Avril-Fontainebleau"*—and lo, this sweet one is duly spread upon the minutes. He permits himself to be arrested by a fair privateer in Piccadilly, and goes with her to one of the dens of sin that suffragettes see in their nightmares, and cross-examines her at length regarding her ancestry, her professional ethics and ideals, and her earnings at her dismal craft—and into the book goes a full report of the proceedings. He is entertained by an eminent Dutch jurist in Amsterdam—and upon the pages of the chronicle it appears that the gentleman is "waxy" and "a little pedantic," and that he is probably the sort of "thin, delicate, well-barbered" professor that Ibsen had in mind when he cast about for a husband for the daughter of General Gabler.

Such is the art of writing as Dreiser understands it and practices it—an endless piling up of minutiae, an almost ferocious tracking down of ions, electrons, and molecules, an unshakable determination to tell it all. One is amazed by the molelike diligence of the man, and no less by his exasperating disregard for the ease of his readers. A Dreiser novel, at least of the later canon, cannot be read as other novels are read—on a winter evening or summer afternoon, between meal and meal, traveling from New York to Boston. It demands the attention for almost a week, and uses up the faculties for a month. If, reading *The "Genius,"* one were to become engrossed in the fabulous manner described in the publishers' advertisements, and so find oneself unable to put it down and go to bed before the end, one would get no sleep for three days and three nights.

Worse, there are no charms of style to mitigate the rigors of these vast steppes and pampas of narration. Joseph Joubert's saying that "words should stand out well from the paper" is quite incomprehensible to Dreiser; he never imitates Flaubert by writing for *"la respiration et l'oreille."* There is no painful groping for the inevitable word, or for what Walter Pater called "the gipsy phrase"; the common, even the commonplace, coin of speech is good enough. On the first page of *Jennie Gerhardt* one encounters "frank, open countenance," "diffident manner," "helpless poor," "untutored mind," "honest necessity," and half a dozen other stand-bys of the second-rate newspaper reporter. In *Sister Carrie* one finds "high noon," "hurrying throng," "unassuming restaurant," "dainty slippers," "high-strung nature," and "cool, calculating world"—all on a few pages. Carrie's sister, Minnie Hanson, "gets" the supper. Hanson himself is "wrapped up" in his child. Carrie decides to

enter Storm and King's office, "no matter what." In *The Titan* the word
"trig" is worked to death; it takes on, toward the end, the character of
a banal and preposterous refrain. In the other books one encounters
mates for it—words made to do duty in as many senses as the American
verb "to fix" or the journalistic "to secure." . . .

I often wonder if Dreiser gets anything properly describable as pleasure out of this dogged accumulation of threadbare, undistinguished,
uninspiring nouns, adjectives, verbs, adverbs, pronouns, participles, and
conjunctions. To the man with an ear for verbal delicacies—the man
who searches painfully for the perfect word, and puts the way of saying
a thing above the thing said—there is in writing the constant joy of
sudden discovery, of happy accident. A phrase springs up full blown,
sweet and caressing. But what joy can there be in rolling up sentences
that have no more life and beauty in them, intrinsically, than so many
election bulletins? Where is the thrill in the manufacture of such a
paragraph as that in which Mrs. Althea Jones's sordid habitat is described with such inexorable particularity? Or in the laborious confection of such stuff as this, from Book I, Chapter IV, of *The "Genius"*:

> The city of Chicago—who shall portray it! This vast ruck of life that
> has sprung suddenly into existence upon the dank marshes of a lake
> shore!

Or this from the epilogue to *The Financier:*

> There is a certain fish whose scientific name is *Mycteroperca Bonaci,*
> and whose common name is Black Grouper, which is of considerable
> value as an afterthought in this connection, and which deserves much
> to be better known. It is a healthy creature, growing quite regularly to
> a weight of two hundred and fifty pounds, and living a comfortable,
> lengthy existence because of its very remarkable ability to adapt itself to
> conditions. . . .

Or this from his pamphlet, *Life, Art and America:* [4]

> Alas, alas! for art in America. It has a hard stubby row to hoe.

But I offer no more examples. Every reader of the Dreiser novels must
cherish astounding specimens—of awkward, platitudinous marginalia,
of whole scenes spoiled by bad writing, of phrases as brackish as so many
lumps of sodium hyposulphite. Here and there, as in parts of *The Titan*
and again in parts of *A Hoosier Holiday,* an evil conscience seems to
haunt him and he gives hard striving to his manner, and more than
once there emerges something that is almost graceful. But a backsliding
always follows this phosphorescence of reform. *The "Genius,"* coming
after *The Titan,* marks the high tide of his bad writing. There are passages in it so clumsy, so inept, so irritating that they seem almost un-

4 New York, 1917; reprinted from *The Seven Arts* for February, 1917. H.L.M.

believable; nothing worse is to be found in the newspapers. Nor is there any compensatory deftness in structure, or solidity of design, to make up for this carelessness in detail. The well-made novel, of course, can be as hollow as the well-made play of Scribe—but let us at least have a beginning, a middle, and an end! Such a story as *The "Genius"* is as gross and shapeless as Brünnhilde. It billows and bulges out like a cloud of smoke, and its internal organization is almost as vague. There are episodes that, with a few chapters added, would make very respectable novels. There are chapters that need but a touch or two to be excellent short stories. The thing rambles, staggers, trips, heaves, pitches, struggles, totters, wavers, halts, turns aside, trembles on the edge of collapse. More than once it seems to be foundering, both in the equine and in the maritime senses. The tale has been heard of a tree so tall that it took two men to see the top of it. Here is a novel so brobdingnagian that a single reader can scarcely read his way through it. . . .

III

Of the general ideas which lie at the bottom of all of Dreiser's work it is impossible to be in ignorance, for he has exposed them at length in *A Hoosier Holiday* and summarized them in *Life, Art and America*. In their main outlines they are not unlike the fundamental assumptions of Joseph Conrad. Both novelists see human existence as a seeking without a finding; both reject the prevailing interpretations of its meaning and mechanism; both take refuge in "I do not know." Put *A Hoosier Holiday* beside Conrad's *A Personal Record,* and you will come upon parallels from end to end. Or better still, put it beside Hugh Walpole's *Joseph Conrad,* in which the Conradean metaphysic is condensed from the novels even better than Conrad has done it himself: at once you will see how the two novelists, each a worker in the elemental emotions, each a rebel against the current assurance and superficiality, each an alien to his place and time, touch each other in a hundred ways.

"Conrad," says Walpole, "is of the firm and resolute conviction that life is too strong, too clever, and too remorseless for the sons of men." And then, in amplification: "It is as though, from some high window, looking down, he were able to watch some shore, from whose security men were forever launching little cockleshell boats upon a limitless and angry sea. . . . From his height he can follow their fortunes, their brave struggles, their fortitude to the very end. He admires their courage, the simplicity of their faith, but his irony springs from his knowledge of the inevitable end." . . .

Substitute the name of Dreiser for that of Conrad, and you will have to change scarcely a word. Perhaps one, to wit, "clever." I suspect that Dreiser, writing so of his own creed, would be tempted to make it "stupid," or, at all events, "unintelligible." The struggle of man, as he sees it, is more than impotent; it is gratuitous and purposeless. There is, to his eye, no grand ingenuity, no skillful adaptation of means to end, no moral (or even dramatic) plan in the order of the universe. He can get out of it only a sense of profound and inexplicable *dis*order. The waves which batter the cockleshells change their direction at every instant. Their navigation is a vast adventure, but intolerably fortuitous and inept—a voyage without chart, compass, sun, or stars. . . .

So at bottom. But to look into the blackness steadily, of course, is almost beyond the endurance of man. In the very moment that its impenetrability is grasped the imagination begins attacking it with pale beams of false light. All religions, I daresay, are thus projected from the questioning soul of man, and not only all religions, but also all great agnosticisms. Nietzsche, shrinking from the horror of that abyss of negation, revived the Pythagorean concept of *der ewigen Wiederkunft*—a vain and blood-curdling sort of comfort. To it, after a while, he added explanations almost Christian—a whole repertoire of whys and wherefores, aims and goals, aspirations and significances. The late Mark Twain, in an unpublished work, toyed with an equally daring idea: that men are to some unimaginably vast and incomprehensible Being what the unicellular organisms of his body are to man, and so on *ad infinitum*. Dreiser occasionally inclines to much the same hypothesis; he likens the endless reactions going on in the world we know, the myriadal creation, collision, and destruction of entities, to the slow accumulation and organization of cells *in utero*. He would make us specks in the insentient embryo of some gigantic Presence whose form is still unimaginable and whose birth must wait for Eons and Eons. Again, he turns to something not easily distinguishable from philosophical idealism, whether out of Berkeley or Fichte it is hard to make out—that is, he would interpret the whole phenomenon of life as no more than an appearance, a nightmare of some unseen sleeper or of men themselves, an "uncanny blur of nothingness"—in Euripides' phrase, "a song sung by an idiot, dancing down the wind." Yet again, he talks vaguely of the intricate polyphony of a cosmic orchestra, cacophonous to our dull ears. Finally, he puts the observed into the ordered, reading a purpose in the displayed event: "life was intended to sting and hurt" . . . But these are only gropings, and not to be read too critically. From speculations and explanations he always returns, Conrad-like, to the bald fact: to "the spectacle and stress of life." All he can make out clearly is "a vast compulsion which has nothing to do with the individual desires or tastes or impulses of individuals." That compulsion springs "from the settling processes of forces which we do not in the least understand, over which we have no control, and in whose grip we are as grains of dust or sand, blown hither and thither, for what purpose we cannot even suspect." [5] Man is not only doomed to defeat, but denied any glimpse or understanding of his antagonist. Here we come upon an agnosticism that has almost got be-

[5] *Life, Art and America*, p. 5. H.L.M.

yond curiosity. What good would it do us, asks Dreiser, to know? In our
ignorance and helplessness, we may at least get a slave's consolation out
of cursing the unknown gods. Suppose we saw them striving blindly, too,
and pitied them? . . .

But, as I say, this skepticism is often tempered by guesses at a possibly
hidden truth, and the confession that this truth may exist reveals the
practical unworkableness of the unconditioned system, at least for
Dreiser. Conrad is far more resolute, and it is easy to see why. He is, by
birth and training, an aristocrat. He has the gift of emotional detachment. The lures of facile doctrine do not move him. In his irony there
is a disdain which plays about even the ironist himself. Dreiser is a
product of far different forces and traditions, and is capable of no such
escapement. Struggle as he may, and fume and protest as he may, he can
no more shake off the chains of his intellectual and cultural heritage
than he can change the shape of his nose. What that heritage is you may
find out in detail by reading *A Hoosier Holiday,* or in summary by
glancing at the first few pages of *Life, Art and America.* Briefly described, it is the burden of a believing mind, a moral attitude, a lingering superstition. One half of the man's brain, so to speak, wars with the
other half. He is intelligent, he is thoughtful, he is a sound artist—but
there come moments when a dead hand falls upon him, and he is once
more the Indiana peasant, snuffling absurdly over imbecile sentimental-
ities, giving a grave ear to quackeries, snorting and eye-rolling with the
best of them. One generation spans too short a time to free the soul of
man. Nietzsche, to the end of his days, remained a Prussian pastor's son,
and hence two-thirds a Puritan; he erected his war upon holiness, toward the end, into a sort of holy war. Kipling, the grandson of a Methodist preacher, reveals the tin-pot evangelist with increasing clarity as
youth and its ribaldries pass away and he falls back upon his fundamen-
tals. And that other English novelist who springs from the servants' hall
—let us not be surprised or blame him if he sometimes writes like a
bounder.

The truth about Dreiser is that he is still in the transition stage between Christian Endeavor and civilization, between Warsaw, Indiana,
and the Socratic grove, between being a good American and being a free
man, and so he sometimes vacillates perilously between a moral sentimentalism and a somewhat extravagant revolt. *The "Genius,"* on the
one hand, is almost a tract for rectitude, a Warning to the Young; its
motto might be *Scheut die Dirnen!* And on the other hand, it is full of
a laborious truculence that can only be explained by imagining the author as heroically determined to prove that he is a plain-spoken fellow
and his own man, let the chips fall where they may. So, in spots, in *The
Financier* and *The Titan,* both of them far better books. There is an
almost moral frenzy to expose and riddle what passes for morality among
the stupid. The isolation of irony is never reached; the man is still evan-

gelical; his ideas are still novelties to him; he is as solemnly absurd in some of his floutings of the Code American as he is in his respect for Bouguereau, or in his flirtings with the New Thought, or in his naïf belief in the importance of novel-writing. Somewhere or other I have called all this the Greenwich Village complex. It is not genuine artists, serving beauty reverently and proudly, who herd in those cockroached cellars and bawl for art; it is a mob of half-educated yokels and cockneys to whom the very idea of art is still novel, and intoxicating—and more than a little bawdy.

Not that Dreiser actually belongs to this ragamuffin company. Far from it, indeed. There is in him, hidden deep-down, a great instinctive artist, and hence the makings of an aristocrat. In his muddled way, held back by the manacles of his race and time, and his steps made uncertain by a guiding theory which too often eludes his own comprehension, he yet manages to produce works of art of unquestionable beauty and authority, and to interpret life in a manner that is poignant and illuminating. There is vastly more intuition in him than intellectualism; his talent is essentially feminine, as Conrad's is masculine; his ideas always seem to be deduced from his feelings. The view of life that got into *Sister Carrie,* his first book, was not the product of a conscious thinking out of Carrie's problems. It simply got itself there by the force of the artistic passion behind it; its coherent statement had to wait for other and more reflective days. The thing began as a vision, not as a syllogism. Here the name of Franz Schubert inevitably comes up. Schubert was an ignoramus, even in music; he knew less about polyphony, which is the mother of harmony, which is the mother of music, than the average conservatory professor. But nevertheless he had such a vast instinctive sensitiveness to musical values, such a profound and accurate feeling for beauty in tone, that he not only arrived at the truth in tonal relations, but even went beyond what, in his day, was known to be the truth, and so led an advance. Likewise, Giorgione da Castelfranco and Masaccio come to mind: painters of the first rank, but untutored, unsophisticated, uncouth. Dreiser, within his limits, belongs to this sabot-shod company of the elect. One thinks of Conrad, not as artist first, but as savant. There is something of the icy aloofness of the laboratory in him, even when the images he conjures up pulsate with the very glow of life. He is almost as self-conscious as the Beethoven of the last quartets. In Dreiser the thing is more intimate, more disorderly, more a matter of pure feeling. He gets his effects, one might almost say, not by designing them, but by living them.

But whatever the process, the power of the image evoked is not to be gainsaid. It is not only brilliant on the surface, but mysterious and appealing in its depths. One swiftly forgets his intolerable writing, his mirthless, sedulous, repellent manner, in the face of the Athenian tragedy he instills into his seduced and soul-sick servant-girls, his barbaric pirates of finances, his conquered and hamstrung supermen, his wives who sit and wait. He has, like Conrad, a sure talent for depicting the spirit in disintegration. Old Gerhardt, in *Jennie Gerhardt,* is alone worth all the *dramatis personae* of popular American fiction since the days of *Rob o' the Bowl;* Howells could no more have created him, in his Rodinesque impudence of outline, than he could have created Tartuffe or Gargantua. Such a novel as *Sister Carrie* stands quite outside the brief traffic of the customary stage. It leaves behind it an unescapable impression of bigness, of epic sweep and dignity. It is not a mere story, not a novel in the customary American meaning of the word; it is at once a psalm of life and a criticism of life—and that criticism loses nothing by the fact that its burden is despair. Here, precisely, is the point of Dreiser's departure from his fellows. He puts into his novels a touch of the eternal *Weltschmerz.* They get below the drama that is of the moment and reveal the greater drama that is without end. They arouse those deep and lasting emotions which grow out of the recognition of elemental and universal tragedy. His aim is not merely to tell a tale; his aim is to show the vast ebb and flow of forces which sway and condition human destiny. One cannot imagine him consenting to Conan Doyle's statement of the purpose of fiction, quoted with characteristic approval by the New York *Times:* "to amuse mankind, to help the sick and the dull and the weary." Nor is his purpose to instruct; if he is a pedagogue it is only incidentally and as a weakness. The thing he seeks to do is to stir, to awaken, to move. One does not arise from such a book as *Sister Carrie* with a smirk of satisfaction; one leaves it infinitely touched.

JAMES T. FARRELL: THE PLIGHT
OF THE CHILDREN *

Joseph Warren Beach

THE three books of the *Studs Lonigan* series amount to less than half of Farrell's output so far in the novel. Before the completion of the trilogy, he had already published *Gas-House McGinty* (1933), and since its completion he has brought out the first three volumes of a series of four—*A World I Never Made* (1936), *No Star Is Lost* (1939), and *Father and Son* (1940). These books deal with much the same class of people as *Studs Lonigan,* but in somewhat different aspects and more comprehensively, so that we have a greatly enlarged view of the social conditions of which Studs was a product. In *Studs Lonigan* it is the life of the young man on the streets that is featured; in *Gas-House McGinty* it is the working life of the adult; in the beginning novels of the new tetralogy it is, more broadly, family life. Many of the same basic motives of action are present in all the novels; but in *Studs Lonigan* they are shown leading a young man into gross and dreary dissipation; in *Gas-House McGinty* we see how they are affected by conditions of employment and display themselves under those conditions; in the later series we see them working in the larger theater of family life, with the effect on parents at home and on their families of growing children.

Gas-House McGinty has for its special subject the men who drive the express wagons and the men who take the calls and route the wagons for the "Continental Express Co." in Chicago. Most of the action takes place in the office, where the men fill in the time between taking calls wisecracking and playing practical jokes. The central character is Ambrose J. McGinty, who is boss in the call office until he is transferred and put on the street as the result of a shindy in the office. The narrative is almost entirely made up of what the men say to one another, together with some sprinkling of their thoughts, their daydreams, and their dreams at night. But out of this unplotted pandemonium we gather a very adequate notion of the ways of life, and above all of the dominant preoccupations, ideals and motives in this little industrial microcosm.

These men are of course concerned with keeping their jobs, supporting their families, and bringing up their children. And they are also bent on finding entertainment and relaxation in their leisure time. But all this would seem to be secondary to the more essential compulsion to maintain their self-esteem, to keep up, each one, a sense of his personal importance or build up defenses against the realization that he is a "mutt." The work is hard and leads nowhere; employment is precarious, subject to the whim of a boss or to the accident of ill-health or crippling injury. They work not in their own vineyards but are constantly subject to command and abuse from patrons and superiors. They live meanly, and enjoy only the social prestige which attaches to having fairly steady jobs. In spite of this they are men, and they have the ineradicable need to demonstrate to themselves and to all the world their force and worth as men. No Epictetus has taught them how dignity is won through stoicism. Of Christianity they comprehend little but hell-fire. They must find means less elusive than those of religion and philosophy for salving a self-esteem which is hourly bruised and lacerated and trampled in the dust.

For some of them—and notably for Ambrose McGinty (Mac)—the chief of such means is the satisfaction he takes in his work, his personal efficiency, and the importance he derives from his connection with the Continental—great and powerful organization indispensable to the carrying on of the world's work. Mac has in the business a position of responsibility and command. He can be proud of the order which he puts into things; he has even worked out the percentage of reduction in overhead which he has brought about.

But he has his troubles too. His wife is a despotic, suspicious woman, a mountain of flesh, and he has not the satisfaction of being master in his own house. He has no children to make him proud of his manhood. And for some reason which he cannot comprehend, he is the object of constant razzing on the part of the other men, who regard him, in spite of his efficiency, as a "fat slob." It is impossible for the reader to make out whether or not to like Mac, he is such an assorted bundle of natural impulses, the mean and generous all mixed up together. Which means, I suppose, that he is all too human, or, as the French say, *l'homme moyen sensuel.*

He certainly has his provocations. His friends humiliate him by getting a "fairy" to make up to him and then joking him in the office on his Oscar Wildean propensities. When in a fit of showy generosity he gives his last dime to a beggar, expecting his friends to pay his street car fare, they decline to acknowledge his acquaintance until he is on the point of being put off by the conductor. When he brings pillows to the office to lighten his suffering from the piles, they hide the pillows and provoke the hullabaloo that results in his being demoted. And, dirtiest trick of all, they telephone his wife that back pay has been distributed, so that she thinks he is keeping his pay envelope from her. This results in a period of sourness and alienation under which he suffers acutely.

He tries to be friendly to his little stepdaughter Josephine, of whom he is very fond; but Mame breaks this up with her sarcasm. He is denied the restorative consolations of sexual intercourse. His self-esteem is flattened out completely. He has urgent need of psychological compensations, and the mechanism works automatically. He falls asleep and dreams.

The account of his dream, which fills one of the longest chapters, is a perfect primer in the ways of the unconscious—at least in the more direct and obvious ways. The dream takes its start from his bodily condition, and the "manifest content" is much of it derived from the experiences of the day. But the dreaming mind ranges widely among images and symbols that free him from the restrictions of commonplace reality and morality. Long passages of anxiety, shame, fear, and baffled seeking resolve themselves in a burst of triumph and liberation. The dream begins with naked girls inviting him to join them. But shame and confusion come upon him when a girl he is chasing turns out to be Josephine, his little stepdaughter. He finds himself in hell, but even Satan cannot abide him and he is thrown out and told to go dig his own hole in the bottom of the sea. All through there is much made of this theme, derived from Mac's dream-identification with the hero of the popular song. McGinty jumps from towers, defies lions, and lands in a dreary Nowhere. Then begins his process of recovery. He is soothed by a sweet girl-voice (the voice of Josephine) bidding him arise and fight. The man in him asserts himself. "McGinty arose, brandishing a sword with monkey-glands tied to the handle, faced the blankly forward-marching Legions of Death, and declaimed: McGinty never, never dies!" There are many relapses into fear and humiliation; there is long searching for a woman whom he cannot identify or visualize. But at length the notes of victory prevail. McGinty is crowned King of all Ireland, and St. Patrick himself says a nuptial mass and inaugurates "the marital ceremonies of McGinty, first King of all Ireland, to My Irish Molly-O, Rosie O'Grady, My Wild Irish Rose, Peggy O'Neill, the Colleen of the River Shannon, Ellen May Mahoney the girl of his youthful dreams, Little Annie Rooney, and Sweet Sue, the fairy from the Jew's cigar store, who stood with sprouting wings and an orange tie about his long hair." But McGinty has not reached the zenith in his dream-flight until he has slain God and freed himself from the last constraint and mastership under which mortal man must labor.

Thus by the fantasy of dreams McGinty has raised himself above the humiliations to which he has been subject and set his manhood above all question. A similar process is shown in the daydreaming of Danny O'Neill, the office boy, who is supposed to be more or less modeled after the author; in the boastful lies of Dusty Anderson, who pretends that he keeps his driver's job merely for exercise and to relieve his mind, that his main earnings are from his tony gambling house, or that he has turned down lucrative offers from big league baseball teams; and in the vicarious adventures indulged in by men at the moving pictures. In all of this, as well as in McGinty's dreams, we are often reminded of the fantasies of Leopold Bloom and other characters in Joyce's *Ulysses*.

In many cases the men support their sense of manhood in more socially constructive ways. They are concerned for the coming child; they take satisfaction in the thought of educating their little girls, sending a sick boy to a farm out West to restore his health, or putting their mother in steam heat. The most touching case is Jim O'Neill, Danny's father, a poor teamster with a large family, who has served the company for many years, and now has an office job, with some prospect of a raise if he can stand the gaff. But he has much to suffer from the insolence of his bosses, and he has had a stroke and is in fear that his health will not hold out. As he looks at himself in the washroom mirror his heart rises up in desperate prayers. "If God would only give him ten more years. God, please! God, please give the kids a chance." He was nothing but a workman; but he had been honest. He had done his share of drinking, but a man had a right to some diversion, and he had provided for his wife and kids with his hands and his back. He prays God to make his kids tough and give them guts. "God, they'll be workingmen, and they'll have to fight like workingmen. Give them fight, God, and two big fists."

More prominent, at least as a subject of conversation, are the pleasures of the bed, which are rightly understood by Farrell as having far more than a sensual character—as constituting, quite as much, a means of gratifying the vanity and restoring a man's sense of his own dignity and importance. Indeed, I cannot think of an author who has shown a better understanding of the psychological importance—we might almost say the spiritual importance—of the sexual act. These teamsters and route inspectors are often embarrassingly frank on this theme, and sometimes foul enough; but there is occasionally a simple eloquence in reference to the subject on the part of married men that should not be mistaken for obscenity. And the author is clearly aware of the unique value of this common experience for relieving nervous tensions and delivering poor devils from the indignities of life and from the burden of themselves.

With unmarried men the whole business has a more unsavory cast, because of its casual, promiscuous and hugger-mugger nature, the social irresponsibility, and the mainly commercial and mechanical character of the transaction. There is nothing very appetizing about the atmosphere of the Elite Hotel where the expressmen assuage their carnal hungers. But it is clear how large a part is played in the whole affair by the ideal or psychical element in these men's make-up—the need they have to satisfy the demands of the "persona" or ideal image a man has of himself, including the view of himself as a virile being. Even the diseases incident to purchased love are invested with some of the glamour attaching to the whole subject. The risk of disease adds to the adventurous nature of the enterprise; a man shows himself more manly by recklessness in the face of danger, and "you ain't a man till you get a dose."

But an even more constant and unattractive way for men to raise themselves is by lowering others. It is not that these men are by nature unfriendly or disinclined to do a good turn to one who needs it. But they are constantly eaten up with a gnawing sense of their being nobodies. There is so little chance to establish their worth by skill and knowledge; of doing so by goodness of heart or urbanity of manner the idea has not occurred to them. Where someone rises above the common level the impulse of the rest is to bring him down with ridicule. The language of these men is racy and vivid within a narrow range; but the use of any words from beyond that range, however exact or expressive, is universally frowned upon as affectation and show-off. These men would profit materially by a little education, but they make no end of fun of those among them who take pains to acquire it. This is no conspiracy, but the automatic working of an instinct to depreciate whatever you do not have. These men have a natural gift for conversation, but it takes the form of wisecracking and scurrility. You salve your own wounds by getting under the skin of another; and when he retaliates, it is a question of who can be most insulting. Your wife and in-laws are subject to abuse, and nothing is too intimate to be dragged in the mud.

If you have authority, however humble, you use it to humiliate those beneath you. You bawl them out on the slightest occasion. You make them toe the line. The blackest mark against McGinty was his procuring the discharge of Jimmy Horan, who was a good workman and had nothing against him except that he was sick of his job and had expressed the usual grudge against the boss. The report of this came to McGinty at a time when he was peculiarly down in the mouth. There is no indication that he understood the reasons for his action. His superior had told him that the call department needed jacking up. His vanity demanded a victim, and he persuaded himself that the firing of Horan was necessary for the good of the service. When the other men protested that Horan was a good workman, it was too late to reverse his decision without losing face. He had to go through with his injustice in order not to fall into lower depths of self-depreciation. McGinty was not a bad sort as human nature goes, but the strongest urge of his nature was to establish his own superiority.

The same mechanism is shown at work in his meeting with Jim O'Neill. Jim is a sad and dreary figure since he has had his stroke and goes limping about. And Mac is really sorry for him. But his dominant sentiment is self-congratulation over his own good health. "Mac strode away, feeling sorry for Jim. Jim was through. Well, it hadn't gotten him yet, he thought with a pride that he immediately regretted. It was lousy for a healthy man to feel proud when he sees a sick friend. But he couldn't help feeling that it hadn't gotten McGinty yet."

Self-maximation is the word applied by some psychologists to the motive here at work. It is the clue to nearly every aspect of human nature displayed in this novel. It is a motive that may work for good or ill; and here, through lack of enlightenment, it comes out almost altogether in cheap and ugly ways. These lives are like pictures painted in a mean tradition through want of knowledge or through bad instruction. The fine energies of the ego are turned into foul channels. It is a pitiful want of economy of spiritual forces from which there was so much to be hoped. Instead of fair and goodly lives we are left to mourn "the expense of spirit in a waste of shame." [1]

A broadly similar motivation is much in evidence in the later novels, *A World I Never Made, No Star Is Lost,* and *Father and Son.* Only, here the scene is transferred from the office to the home, and we have the more tragic spectacle of young children subjected to the same blighting and deforming influences. The central character here is Danny O'Neill as a young boy. The series is not completed. We know that in the end this boy was destined to break the evil spell and make his way out of the foul labyrinth, though it is not yet clear by just what turn of fortune he was granted light and strength to perform this feat.

The scenes are laid in two households, those of the O'Flahertys and the O'Neills. Mrs. O'Flaherty is Danny's grandmother, who is kept in steam heat and electricity by her son Al, a traveling salesman in shoes. She lives with her daughter Margaret, a cashier in a hotel. Lizz O'Neill is Danny's mother. She is supported by his father Jim, the teamster, whose aquaintance we have made in *Gas-House McGinty.* In the period covered by the first two books, he has not had his stroke; he is strong and hard-working. But he has too many children, and they must live in

---

[1] A special instance of this sort of motivation is given by Farrell in *Tommy Gallagher's Crusade* (1939), a brand of self-motivation which is capable of having disastrous effects in the political life of a nation. Tommy Gallagher is not content with the ordinary steady jobs held by his father and brothers. He is the kind who thinks the boss is against him, that he has always been a football to be kicked around. His brothers consider him lazy; for instead of working, he prefers to stand about all day trying to sell a few copies of Father Moylan's *Christian Justice* (anti-Semitic). He thinks himself that he is making sacrifices for the noble cause of Americanism. His craving for excitement leads him to join with other hoodlums in attacking Jews and breaking up "radical" meetings ... where the risks are not too great; and by such activities, too, he drugs the consciousness of his own cowardice. Like so many of Farrell's characters, Tommy Gallagher is long on fantasy, making up in his imagination for what he wants in fact. Scorned by his family and baffled in his craving for a girl, "He lay awake, pitying himself, telling himself that he was brave, vowing over and over again that his day was coming, and assuring himself that when it did come, it would be a day of bitter vengeance. Look at Hitler in Germany! Hitler had known days like this, too!" Farrell, in this slight work, makes no pretense of describing political phenomena. But he does make an illuminating psychological study of one of the types that have played a major part in the Nazi movement.

squalid quarters, without even gas or water-closet, and in neighborhoods
infested with negroes and other undesirables.

The O'Flahertys have come to the rescue, taking Danny and later his
little sister Margaret to live with them. The old woman is "shanty Irish"
—completely illiterate, vain, boastful, foul-mouthed, violent, supersti-
tious, stingy, and as hard as nails. But she is fond of her children and
grandchildren. She claims Danny for her son, does her best to spoil him,
and centers on him her hopes for the future honor of the family. She is
proud of her son Al and grateful to him for making her comfortable.
She is ashamed of the poverty of Lizz and Jim, and on public occasions
dissociates herself from them as persons beneath her notice. She never
admits being Irish, since in the old country only landlords and the English had social caste. And yet in her cups she often speaks of the time
when she was "a wisp of a girl running the bush in the old country, bare-
footed and with her backside showing through her dress." Jim O'Neill
is deeply resentful of her vulgar toploftiness and of having his son
brought up to scorn his father; and this is the occasion of many quarrels
between him and Lizz. At bottom they are tenderly devoted to each
other and to their children; but poverty puts a heavy strain upon them.
It has turned Lizz into a slattern and brought out in her the gutter
strain she had from her mother.

The other O'Flahertys are all in reaction against this gutter strain.
Ned has married someone who passes for a lady. Al has remained a
bachelor, his heart set on lifting the family out of the bog of vulgar in-
digence. He reads the letters of Lord Chesterfield; he shuns the drinking and obscene storytelling of his comrades of the road, their boasting
and fighting; he strives to improve the speech of his relatives, and
recommends to his drummer friends "the touch delicate and the retort
adroit." He takes seriously his obligations to Danny O'Neill, teaches
him to walk properly, plays baseball with him, disciplines him consid-
erately. In the family circle he strives for harmony, good feeling, urbane
manners, and "constructive" ideals. He dreams of a happy fireside, with
the "Rosary" sung by self-respecting wives or "Kathleen Mavourneen"
played on the victrola while children sport about the Christmas tree. It
is only the dread of vice in the home that rouses his temper and leads
him to violence and brutality. Altogether, Al O'Flaherty is one of the
great creations of modern fiction—a slightly ridiculous old bachelor,
priggish and limited, but a man of genuine character and goodwill,
struggling valiantly with circumstances that make of him a profoundly
pathetic figure.

His sister Margaret is a tragic figure. She is by endowment the richest
and finest of all the family. She is warmly affectionate and generous by
nature, an Irish heart of gold, full of romantic sentiment. She should
have been a devoted wife and the life-giving mother of a family of chil-

dren. Her fine nature has been warped by unhappy experiences—dreary meanness and quarrelsomeness in the home, cruel beatings as a child, the cynical construction placed by Irish puritanism on her association with boys. Her romantic nature has found satisfaction not in marriage and home but in a secret liaison with a married man—a Protestant lumber tycoon—who after a few years of furtive meetings ceases to answer her letters and leaves her to blank misery and despair. She tries to console herself with other men and with gin; she falls into terrible fits of drunkenness culminating in attempts at suicide and fearful visions of snakes and devils. There are dreadful scenes where her mother calls her a whore, puts upon her the curse of a parent, or exorcises the devils with prayer and holy water. And the worst of it all is the presence of terrified young children, who must stay up all night to keep their aunt from turning on the gas, or sit by helpless while aunt and grandmother engage in foul exchanges of insult and recrimination.

The real subject of the whole study is the plight of children reading in such a book their first lessons in the art of living. One hardly knows which of the children are the more unfortunate—Danny and little Margaret, who pay for cleanly surroundings and steam heat with subjection to spectacles like these, or the children who remain in the slums with their mother, or the one who passes back and forth between the two infernos and picks up on the way the criminal inspirations of the street. This one is Bill, Danny's older brother (an incipient Studs Lonigan), who comes to play with Danny and teach him the facts of life as observed in his home.

As for the younger children, we see them in their sordid home playing the games of children, sedulously copying their parents in every detail of speech and behavior, especially in the scolding exercise of authority and in the use of foul and abusive language. As babies they are adorable little animals; their parents sincerely love them and fiercely defend them against all comers. But it is alarming to see how fast they take on the less attractive features of adulthood; and one looks forward dolefully to a new generation repeating the errors and imbecilities of the last.

It is the moral blight that is most distressing to contemplate. But more immediate is the physical peril. They live in filth and ignorance, with no defense against disease but prayers and holy water. *No Star Is Lost* concludes with a series of scenes in which the baby of the family is struck down with diphtheria and dies before a doctor or priest can be had, and all the other children are bundled off in the police wagon to a hospital for contagious diseases. Meantime, at the O'Flahertys', little Margaret has been taken down with the same malady. But the O'Flahertys have better standing with the doctor, and he comes promptly to their call. What is most bitter for Jim O'Neill is the thought that his poverty is so great he cannot even command a doctor for his dying child. No doubt, with a little more enterprise or imagination, he could have had free medical care; but enterprise and imagination do not thrive in the midst of so much ignorance.

Perhaps I have laid too much stress on the unfavorable influences brought to bear on these children. After all, their father and mother were honest, religious, well-intentioned people; the father wrought manfully to support his family; and they and all the other relatives duly preached the gospel of industry, sobriety and Christian goodness. In *Father and Son,* Farrell shows the O'Neills in a period of greater prosperity, with Jim now in the supervision end of the express business and Bill, too, settled down and bringing home his pay envelope from the express company. It is not quite clear what turn of heart has brought Bill to a sense of responsibility. But there is every prospect of his marrying and setting out on a way of life that is an exact duplication of his father's.

Danny is destined to emerge upon another cultural level, but the process of his emancipation is distressingly protracted. The psychologist would doubtless find in this record plentiful indications of how the character of Danny O'Neill was beaten into shape and given its bent by his childhood experience. And the discerning psychologist could even make clear how the most apparently unfavorable influences were working, by some logic of reaction, to free him from the dark web which circumstance was weaving about him. We see him playing the games and thinking the long, long thoughts of youth. Every defeat begets daydreams of success and triumph. His older brother leads him into various mischief, which fails to take strong hold upon him. He labors with the problems of theology and suffers from a sense of guilt and the consciousness of making bad confessions. He engages in bloody fights with bullies, and he does not always tell the truth. He witnesses scenes of hatefulness and violence. It is perhaps a congenital defect which proves in the end his great advantage. From early years he has had to wear glasses and be nicknamed Four Eyes. He suffers from the imputation of being tied to his grandmother's apron strings, and then from the social stigma of having a drunkard for an aunt and a beer-guzzling grandmother.

The most poignant scenes in *No Star Is Lost* are those of his birthday party. Danny has managed to secure the attendance of several of the most attractive girls from school, and the refreshments are of the best. His great dread is that Aunt Peg will get drunk and cause a scandal; but she is persuaded to stay in her room and babble tearfully of her innocence as a child. Danny hopes by this party to make himself popular with the kids and get pretty Virginia Doyle for his girl. But the kids resent his choosing the prettiest girl for his partner, and the girls do not take to the game of postoffice. The net result is that the girls avoid him and the boys kid him more than ever. He is greatly relieved when the family moves to a new neighborhood. He hopes that Aunt Margaret will give up drinking and he may make a fresh start in his social life. One of the first acquaintances he makes in the new street is young Studs Lonigan. Ominous portent! But Danny O'Neill has not the making of a tough guy. His very deficiencies will drive him into the larger life of the mind, the liberator.

But that is a long process, which will take more than the four years at St. Stanislaus high school, recorded in *Father and Son*. This is one of the most frank and convincing studies of adolescence ever made in fiction. It is a most uncomfortable affair for all concerned. Young O'Neill is determined to make himself respected by the boys and admired by the girls, and this he achieves in some degree by dint of thoughtful application to the arts of pugilism, baseball, football and basketball. But he never succeeds in getting himself accepted by the other boys as quite one of them, in spite of being an athletic star, dressing like a dude, and spending all his money on fraternity dances. As a ladies' man he is a flop, and the harder he tries the less he enjoys himself. He cannot seem to strike the right tone with boys or girls, and is censured by his fraternity brothers for wisecracking and want of dignity. Everybody insists on treating him as a goof, and he is more and more impressed with his ineptness and his difference from other boys. For a time, under the suggestions of Sister Magdalen, he thinks he has a call to the priesthood; perhaps his awkwardness with the girls is an indication that way. But he is glad enough to have the support of father and uncles in giving up that idea. In the final year at high school he does a good deal of heavy drinking, but that satisfies nothing but his social vanity. Altogether it is a painful and obstinate case of growing pains—a disease common enough at Danny's age, but likely to be most severe and protracted under conditions that do nothing to feed the mind or employ the faculties of the growing organism, and hardest of all perhaps on the boy whose faculties are the greatest, since he is likely to suffer most from an obscure sense of frustration, boredom and bewilderment, and beat his wings most wildly against the invisible bars.

Dramatically, the most interesting and moving theme in the last book is Danny's relation to his father—Jim crippled, dying and anxious over the fate of his family, Danny all absorbed in the crude desires and ambitions of adolescence. It is the familiar tale of a father angered and dismayed at the sight of a son precariously entrenched on the top of "Tom Fool's Hill" (to use the term most often on my own father's lips) and a son too much preoccupied by his own urgencies to appreciate his father's merits or understand his point of view. There are many beautiful and poignant touches in the account of Jim's decline. As for the blind egotism and crudity of the boy, they were a measure of his inexperience and the desperation of his spirit, starved and bewildered in a world that had so little to offer for its satisfaction. In his conscientious portrayal of Danny's relation to his father, Farrell has done bitter penance for us all.

On his father's death, Danny came down to earth. He went to work dutifully for the support of the family and gave up his dreams of life as a college man. Work in the wagon call department was anything but congenial, and leaden skies closed down upon him.

But there is a lightening on the horizon in one direction. Danny has sometimes thought that he might be a writer. He has read much in a battered volume of poetry cherished by his father, and in the little blue books of his Uncle Al. The men at the express office make fun of him for reading Shakespeare between calls. But the reader knows better. The reader knows that the written word is the key for which he is seeking, the key to all the doors of the mind and imagination, freeing him from the prison house of Ambrose McGinty and admitting him to the open world of Plato and Dewey, of Housman and Tolstoy. The reader knows that what Danny is seeking is just the magic word that makes the difference between a Studs Lonigan and a Robert Burns.

Farrell's writing is perhaps the plainest, soberest, most straightforward of any living novelist. There is nothing commonplace about it, for there is none of the prosing self-consciousness of an author displaying his skill or his wisdom. The acts and thoughts of the characters are stated in the simplest terms, and the rest is their very speech, with the edge and tang of what is said in deadly earnest. It is, in Wordsworth's phrase, a "selection from the real language of men." Selection because the author eliminates everything trivial and superfluous, leaving only what will illuminate the primary concerns of his people. Real language of men; for it has an unmistakable ring of authenticity. There is no attempt to point up the dialect, exaggerate the slanginess, or give phonetic representation to the local accent. Nor, on the other hand, is there any prudish toning down of the grossness of language. There is nothing facetious, nothing smartly satirical in the author's tone. These are linguistic documents, as they are social documents, of high seriousness and value, but not slavishly photographic. Farrell is obviously more concerned with the spirit than the letter of truth.

The fictional method is purest naturalism, unrelieved by the traditional interest of plot and drama, mystery and suspense, unalloyed with "idealism," with theory, moralizing, sentimentality, or humorous comment. The pathos is the pathos of human suffering; the tragedy is the tragedy of act and fact. The naturalism is not that of elaborate documentation; there is no suggestion of the notebook and the subject worked up for literary use. Nor is there any suggestion of data collected and forced into the frame of theory. The documentation is really prodigious, but it did not require the author's going beyond the limits of experience and memory. Scene crowds on scene with suffocating profusion, till the reader cries out for mercy. But no scene has the air of being made up; none is forced, not many can be spared. They spring like geysers from the seething burdened depths of the author's being. They are not the cold and labeled cases of the sociologist. Each one is presented in the concrete terms of story; the appeal is first to the imagination, and only in retrospect to the mind and conscience.

In so far as anything is lacking it is some principle of relief. And this is felt most in the third volume of the Danny O'Neill series. Too many of the episodes are on the same level of interest. This is the price paid for fullness and sobriety in the recording. One is conscious of something like monotony of effect. When the series is completed this may seem a frivolous objection. The level stretches of *Father and Son* may fit in perfectly in the planned perspective of the whole. Let it be stated then not as criticism but as simple matter of fact that one grows a little tired of the delays and repetitions of Danny O'Neill. One is impatient to see him get his toes and fingers in the clefts and make a start at scaling the cliff that towers above him.

The best single test for a writer of fiction is the creation of characters that live in the imagination. Farrell has brought to life an unusual number of such living characters. Studs Lonigan, Ambrose McGinty, Jim O'Neill, Al O'Flaherty, Aunt Margaret, and grandmother O'Flaherty are among the memorable people in English fiction. I have not been able to do justice to any of them, and above all to Mary O'Flaherty.

There is one scene that must not be passed without mention—that in which the old woman visits the grave of her dead husband. It will remind us that Farrell is not unprovided with that type of imagination which we associate with poetry and with the most famous of the Irish dramatists. The old woman sits on a bench in a well-tended plot, nibbling her sandwiches, and looks toward the weed-grown sandy lot where her husband and daughter Louise are buried. She thinks of the hard days they led together in the past and of the evil life of her daughter Margaret, of the grievous sorrow which her Tom has been spared by death. Her indignation is roused at the thought of how her daughter has neglected the father's grave. And as she sits there in the gentle breeze from the lake, with the sounds of the city distant and dreamlike, the limits between real and imaginary fade away. She sees her husband rise from the grave in his habit as he was; and she finds herself talking with him, complaining of her daughter, recalling their days together as children in the old country—their first communion— and exchanging views at last on his character and hers, and the obligations laid upon her as the spiritual head of the house. He asks her if she "do be missing" him. "Indeed, I do," she answers. "You were a good man, but I had to make you toe the mark." "You're a good woman yourself, Mary, but, ah, you're a hard woman, you are," he seemed to say. And to this she agrees, taking it as a compliment. "Hard I am, and hard I'll be till they'll be carrying me sorry old bones out here to be laid at rest beside you, Tom," she said. And almost the last thing he has to say to her is to bid her make the children all toe the mark—"Be hard on them, Mary," he seemed to say.

It is a ticklish undertaking for anyone to record the visions of an old woman communing with the spirits of the departed, and doubly ticklish in the context of hard facts provided by Farrell. But this whole scene is managed with a simple naturalness (born of a grudging tenderness) which is a signal triumph of literary tact. To any reader who thinks that in Farrell he has to do with a commonplace or insensitive spirit, I heartily recommend this eighth chapter of *No Star Is Lost.*

Farrell's type of naturalism is not of a kind to appeal to the common run of readers. It has little to offer those who go to fiction for light entertainment, the glamour of the stage, or the gratification of their bent for wishful thinking. There is no reason why the squeamish or tender-minded should put themselves through the ordeal of trying to like his work. But there will always be a sufficient number of those whom life and thought have ripened and disciplined, who have a taste for truth however unvarnished provided it be honestly viewed, deeply pondered, and imaginatively rendered. For many such it may well turn out that James T. Farrell is the most significant of American novelists writing in 1940.

NOTES ON THE DECLINE OF
NATURALISM *

Philip Rahv

Quite a few protests have been aired in recent years against the sway of the naturalist method in fiction. It is charged that this method treats material in a manner so flat and external as to inhibit the search for value and meaning, and that in any case, whatever its past record, it is now exhausted. Dissimilar as they are, both the work of Franz Kafka and the works of the surrealist school are frequently cited as examples of release from the routines of naturalist realism, from its endless book-keeping of existence. Supporting this indictment are mostly those writers of the younger group who are devoted to experimentation and who look to symbolism, the fable, and the myth.

The younger writers are stirred by the ambition to create a new type of imaginative prose into which the recognizably real enters as one component rather than as the total substance. They want to break the novel of its objective habits; some want to introduce into it philo-sophical ideas; others are not so much drawn to expressing ideas as to expressing the motley strivings of the inner self—dreams, visions, and fantasies. Manifestly the failure of the political movement in the litera-ture of the past decade has resulted in a revival of religio-esthetic atti-tudes. The young men of letters are once again watching their own image in the mirror and listening to inner promptings. Theirs is a program calling for the adoption of techniques of planned derange-ment as a means of cracking open the certified structure of reality and turning loose its latent energies. And surely one cannot dispose of such a program merely by uncovering the element of mystification in it. For the truth is that the artist of the avant-garde has never hesitated to lay hold of the instruments of mystification when it suited his purpose, especially in an age such as ours, when the life about him belies more and more the rational ideals of the cultural tradition.

It has been remarked that in the long run the issue between natural-ism and its opponents resolves itself into a philosophical dispute con-cerning the nature of reality. Obviously those who reject naturalism in philosophy will also object to its namesake in literature. But it seems to me that when faced with a problem such as that of naturalist fiction,

* "Notes on the Decline of Naturalism" appears in *Image and Idea,* by Philip Rahv, copyright 1949 by the author. It is used here by permission of the author and the publisher, New Directions, 333 Sixth Avenue, New York City.

the critic will do well not to mix in ontological maneuvres. From the standpoint of critical method it is impermissible to replace a concrete literary analysis with arguments derived from some general theory of the real. For it is plainly a case of the critic not being able to afford metaphysical commitments if he is to apply himself without preconceived ideas to the works of art that constitute his material. The art-object is from first to last the one certain datum at his disposal; and in succumbing to metaphysical leanings—either of the spiritualist or materialist variety—he runs the risk of freezing his insights in some kind of ideational schema, the relevance of which to the task in hand is hardly more than speculative. The act of critical evaluation is best performed in a state of *ideal aloofness* from abstract systems. Its practitioner is not concerned with making up his mind about the ultimate character of reality but with observing and measuring its actual proportions and combinations within a given form. The presence of the real affects him directly, with an immediate force contingent upon the degree of interest, concreteness, and intensity in the impression of life conveyed by the literary artist. The philosopher can take such impressions or leave them, but luckily the critic has no such choice.

Imaginative writing cannot include fixed and systematic definitions of reality without violating its own existential character. Yet in any imaginative effort that which we mean by the real remains the basic criterion of viability, the crucial test of relevance, even if its specific features can hardly be determined in advance but must be *felt anew* in each given instance. And so far as the medium of fiction is concerned, one cannot but agree with Henry James that it gains its "air of reality" —which he considers to be its "supreme virtue"—through "its immense and exquisite correspondence with life." Note that James's formulation allows both for analogical and realistic techniques of representation. He speaks not of copies or reports or transcripts of life but of relations of equivalence, of a "correspondence" which he identifies with the "illusion of life." The ability to produce this illusion he regards as the storyteller's inalienable gift, "the merit on which all other merits . . . helplessly and submissively depend." This insight is of an elementary nature and scarcely peculiar to James alone, but it seems that its truth has been lost on some of our recent catch-as-catch-can innovators in the writing of fiction.

It is intrinsically from this point of view that one can criticise the imitations of Kafka that have been turning up of late as being one-sided and even inept. Perhaps Kafka is too idiosyncratic a genius to serve as a model for others, but still it is easy to see where his imitators go wrong. It is necessary to say to them: To know how to take apart the recognizable world is not enough, is in fact merely a way of letting oneself go and of striving for originality at all costs. But originality of this sort is nothing more than a professional mannerism of the avant-garde.

The genuine innovator is always trying to make us actually experience his creative contradictions. He therefore employs means that are subtler and more complex: *at the very same time that he takes the world apart he puts it together again.* For to proceed otherwise is to dissipate rather than alter our sense of reality, to weaken and compromise rather than change in any significant fashion our feeling of relatedness to the world. After all, what impressed us most in Kafka is precisely this power of his to achieve a simultaneity of contrary effects, to fit the known into the unknown, the actual into the mythic and vice versa, to combine within one framework a conscientiously empirical account of the visibly real with a dreamlike and magical dissolution of it. In this paradox lies the pathos of his approach to human existence.

A modern poetess has written that the power of the visible derives from the invisible; but the reverse of this formula is also true. Thus the visible and the invisible might be said to stand to each other in an ironic relation of inner dependence and of mutual skepticism mixed with solicitude. It is a superb form of doubletalk; and if we are accustomed to its exclusion from naturalistic writing, it is all the more disappointing to find that the newly-evolved "fantastic" style of the experimentalists likewise excludes it. But there is another consideration, of a more formal nature. It seems to be a profound error to conceive of reality as merely a species of material that the fiction-writer can either use or dispense with as he sees fit. It is a species of material, of course, and something else besides: it also functions as the *discipline of fiction,* much in the same sense that syllabic structure functions as the discipline of verse. This seeming identity of the formal and substantial means of narrative-prose is due, I think, to the altogether free and open character of the medium, which prevents it from developing such distinctly technical controls as poetry has acquired. Hence even the dream, when told in a story, must partake of some of the qualities of the real.

Whereas the surrealist represents man as immured in dreams, the naturalist represents him in a continuous waking state of prosaic daily living, in effect as never dreaming. But both the surrealist and the naturalist go to extremes in simplifying the human condition. J. M. Synge once said that the artist displays at once the difficulty and the triumph of his art when picturing the dreamer leaning out to reality or the man of real life lifted out of it. "In all the poets," he wrote, and this test is by no means limited to poetry alone, "the greatest have both these elements, that is they are supremely engrossed with life, and yet with the wildness of their fancy they are always passing out of what is simple and plain."

The old egocentric formula, "Man's fate is his character," has been altered by the novelists of the naturalist school to read, "Man's fate is his environment." (Zola, the organizer and champion of the school, drew his ideas from physiology and medicine, but in later years his disciples cast the natural sciences aside in favor of the social sciences.) To the naturalist, human behavior is a function of its social environment; the individual is the live register of its qualities; he exists in it as animals exist in nature.[1] Due to this emphasis the naturalist mode has evolved historically in two main directions. On the one hand it has tended towards passive documentation (milieu-panoramas, local-color stories, reportorial studies of a given region or industry, etc.), and on the other towards the exposure of socio-economic conditions (muckraking). American fiction of the past decade teems with examples of both tendencies, usually in combination. The work of James T. Farrell, for instance, is mostly a genre-record, the material of which is in its very nature operative in producing social feeling, while such novels as *The Grapes of Wrath* and *Native Son* are exposure-literature, as is the greater part of the fiction of social protest. Dos Passos' triology, *U. S. A.*, is thoroughly political in intention but has the tone and gloss of the methodical genre-painter in the page by page texture of its prose.

I know of no hard and fast rules that can be used to distinguish the naturalist method from the methods of realism generally. It is certainly incorrect to say that the difference is marked by the relative density of detail. Henry James observes in his essay *The Art of Fiction* that it is above all "solidity of specification" that makes for the illusion of life—the air of reality—in a novel; and the truth of this dictum is borne out by the practice of the foremost modern innovators in this medium, such as Proust, Joyce, and Kafka. It is not, then, primarily the means employed to establish verisimilitude that fix the naturalist imprint upon a work of fiction. A more conclusive test, to my mind, is its treatment of the relation of character to background. I would classify as naturalistic that type of realism in which the individual is portrayed not merely as subordinate to his background but as wholly determined by it—that type of realism, in other words, in which the environment displaces its inhabitants in the role of the hero. Theodore Dreiser, for example, comes as close as any American writer to plotting the careers

---

[1] Balzac, to whom naturalism is enormously indebted, explains in his preface to the *Comédie Humaine* that the idea of that work came to him in consequence of a "comparison between the human and animal kingdoms." "Does not society," he asks, "make of man, in accordance with the environment in which he lives and moves, as many different kinds of man as there are different zoological species? ... There have, therefore, existed and always will exist social species, just as there are zoological species."
Zola argues along the same lines: "All things hang together: it is necessary to start from the determination of inanimate bodies in order to arrive at the determination of living beings; and since savants like Claude Bernard demonstrate now that fixed laws govern the human body, we can easily proclaim ... the hour in which the laws of thought and passion will be formulated in their turn. A like determination will govern the stones of the roadway and the brain of man.... We have experimental chemistry and medicine and physiology, and later on an experimental novel. It is an inevitable evolution." (*The Experimental Novel*)

of his characters strictly within a determinative process. The financier Frank Cowperwood masters his world and emerges as its hero, while the "little man" Clyde Griffiths is the victim whom it grinds to pieces; yet hero and victim alike are essentially implements of environmental force, the carriers of its contradictions upon whom it stamps success or failure—not entirely at will, to be sure, for people are marked biologically from birth—but with sufficient autonomy to shape their fate.

In such a closed world there is patently no room for the singular, the unique, for anything in fact which cannot be represented plausibly as the product of a particular social and historical complex. Of necessity the naturalist must deal with experience almost exclusively in terms of the broadly typical. He analyses characters in such a way as to reduce them to standard types. His method of construction is that of accretion and enumeration rather than of analysis or storytelling; and this is so because the quantitative development of themes, the massing of detail and specification, serves his purpose best. He builds his structures out of literal fact and precisely documented circumstance, thus severely limiting the variety of creative means at the disposal of the artist.

This quasi-scientific approach not only permits but, in theory at least, actually prescribes a neutral attitude in the sphere of values. In practice, however, most naturalists are not sufficiently detached or logical to stay put in such an ultra-objective position. Their detractors are wrong in denying them a moral content; the most that can be said is that theirs is strictly functional morality, bare of any elements of gratuity or transcendence and devoid of the sense of personal freedom.[2] Clearly such a perspective allows for very little self-awareness on the part of characters. It also removes the possibility of a tragic resolution of experience. The world of naturalist fiction is much too big, too inert, too hardened by social habit and material necessity, to allow for that tenacious self-assertion of the human by means of which tragedy justifies and ennobles its protagonists. The only grandeur naturalism knows is the grandeur of its own methodological achievement in making available a vast inventory of minutely described phenomena, in assembling an enormous quantity of data and arranging them in a rough figuration of reality. *Les Rougon-Macquart* stands to this day as the most imposing monument to this achievement.

But in the main it is the pure naturalist—that monstrous offspring of the logic of a method—that I have been describing here. Actually no such literary animal exists. Life always triumphs over methods, over formulas and theories. There is scarcely a single novelist of any importance wearing the badge of naturalism who is all of a piece, who fails to compensate in some way for what we miss in his fundamental con-

---

2 Chekhov remarks in one of his stories that "the sense of personal freedom is the chief constituent of creative genius."

ception. Let us call the roll of the leading names among the French and American naturalists and see wherein each is saved.

The Goncourts, it is true, come off rather badly, but even so, to quote a French critic, they manage "to escape from the crude painting of the naked truth by their impressionistic mobility" and, one might add, by their mobile intelligence. Zola's case does not rest solely on our judgment of his naturalist dogmas. There are entire volumes by him—the best, I think, is *Germinal*—and parts of volumes besides, in which his naturalism, fed by an epic imagination, takes on a mythic cast. Thomas Mann associates him with Wagner in a common drive toward an epic mythicism:

> They belong together. The kinship of spirit, method, and aims is most striking. This lies not only in the ambition to achieve size, the propensity to the grandiose and the lavish; nor is it the Homeric leitmotiv alone that is common to them; it is first and foremost a special kind of naturalism, which develops into the mythical. . . . In Zola's epic . . . the characters themselves are raised up to a plane above that of every day. And is that Astarte of the Second Empire, called Nana, not symbol and myth? (*The Sufferings and Greatness of Richard Wagner*).

Zola's prose, though not controlled by an artistic conscience, overcomes our resistance through sheer positiveness and expressive energy—qualities engendered by his novelistic ardor and avidity for recreating life in all its multiple forms.[3] As for Huysmans, even in his naturalist period he was more concerned with style than with subject-matter. Maupassant is a naturalist mainly by alliance, i.e. by virtue of his official membership in the School of Médan; actually he follows a line of his own, which takes off from naturalism never to return to it. There are few militant naturalists among latter-day French writers. Jules Romains is sometimes spoken of as one, but the truth is that he is an epigone of all literary doctrines, including his own. Dreiser is still unsurpassed so far as American naturalism goes, though just at present he may well be the least readable. He has traits that make for survival—a Balzacian grip on the machinery of money and power; a prosiness so primary in texture that if taken in bulk it affects us as a kind of poetry of the commonplace and ill-favored; and an emphatic eroticism which is the real climate of existence in his fictions—Eros hovering over the shambles. Sinclair Lewis was never a novelist in the proper sense that Zola and Dreiser are novelists, and, given his gift for exhaustive reporting, naturalism did him more good than harm by providing him with a ready literary technique. In Farrell's chronicles there is an underlying moral code which, despite his explicit rejection of the Church, seems to me indisputably orthodox and Catholic; and his Studs Lonigan—a product

---

[3] Moreover, it should be evident that Zola's many faults are not rectified but merely inverted in much of the writing—so languidly allusive and decorative—of the literary generations that turned their backs on him.

of those unsightly urban neighborhoods where youth prowls and fights to live up to the folk-ideal of the "regular guy"—is no mere character but an archetype, an eponymous hero of the street-myths that prevail in our big cities. The naturalism of Dos Passos is most completely manifested in *U. S. A.*, tagged by the critics as a "collective" novel recording the "decline of our business civilization." But what distinguishes Dos Passos from other novelists of the same political animus is a sense of justice so pure as to be almost instinctive, as well as a deeply elegiac feeling for the intimate features of American life and for its precipitant moments. Also, *U. S. A.* is one of the very few naturalist novels in which there is a controlled use of language, in which a major effect is produced by the interplay between story and style. It is necessary to add, however, that the faults of Dos Passos' work have been obscured by its vivid contemporaneity and vital political appeal. In the future, I think, it will be seen more clearly than now that it dramatizes social symptoms rather than lives and that it fails to preserve the integrity of personal experience. As for Faulkner, Hemingway, and Caldwell, I do not quite see on what grounds some critics and literary historians include them in the naturalist school. I should think that Faulkner is exempted by his prodigious inventiveness and fantastic humor. Hemingway is a realist on one level, in his attempts to catch the "real thing, the sequence of motion and fact which made the emotion"; but he is also subjective, given to self-portraiture and to playing games with his ego; there is very little study of background in his work, a minimum of documentation. In his best novels Caldwell is a writer of rural abandon—and comedy. His *Tobacco Road* is a sociological area only in patches; most of it is exotic landscape.

It is not hard to demonstrate the weakness of the naturalist method by abstracting it, first, from the uses to which individual authors put it and, second, from its function in the history of modern literature. The traditionalist critics judge it much too one-sidedly in professing to see in its rise nothing but spiritual loss—an invasion of the arcanum of art by arid scientific ideas. The point is that this scientific bias of naturalism was historically productive of contradictory results. Its effect was certainly depressive in so far as it brought mechanistic notions and procedures into writing. But it should be kept in mind that it also enlivened and, in fact, revolutionized writing by liquidating the last assets of "romance" in fiction and by purging it once and for all of the idealism of the "beautiful lie"—of the long-standing inhibitions against dealing with the underside of life, with those inescapable day-by-day actualities traditionally regarded as too "sordid" and "ugly" for inclusion within an aesthetic framework. If it were not for the service thus rendered in vastly increasing the store of literary material, it is doubtful whether such works as *Ulysses* and even *Remembrance of Things Past* could have been written. This is not clearly understood in the English-speaking countries, where naturalism, never quite forming itself into a "movement," was at most only an extreme emphasis in the general onset of realistic fiction and drama. One must study, rather, the Continental writers of the last quarter of the 19th century in order to grasp its historical role. In discussing the German naturalist school of the 1880's, the historian Hans Naumann has this to say, for instance:

> Generally it can be said that to its early exponents the doctrine of naturalism held quite as many diverse and confusing meanings as the doctrine of expressionism seemed to hold in the period just past. Imaginative writers who at bottom were pure idealists united with the dry-as-dust advocates of a philistine natural-scientific program on the one hand and with the shameless exploiters of erotic themes on the other. All met under the banner of naturalism—friends today and enemies tomorrow. ... But there was an element of historical necessity in all this. The fact is that the time had come for an assault, executed with glowing enthusiasm, against the epigones ... that it was finally possible to fling aside with disdain and anger the pretty falsehoods of life and art (*Die Deutsche Dichtung der Gegenwart*, Stuttgart, 1930, p. 144).

And he adds that the naturalism of certain writers consisted simply in their "speaking honestly of things that had heretofore been suppressed."

But to establish the historical credit of naturalism is not to refute the charges that have been brought against it in recent years. For whatever its past accomplishments, it cannot be denied that its present condition is one of utter debility. What was once a means of treating material truthfully has been turned, through a long process of depreciation, into a mere convention of truthfulness, devoid of any significant or even clearly definable literary purpose or design. The spirit of discovery has withdrawn from naturalism; it has now become the common denominator of realism, available in like measure to the producers of literature and to the producers of kitsch. One might sum up the objections to it simply by saying that it is no longer possible to use this method *without taking reality for granted*. This means that it has lost the power to cope with the ever-growing element of the problematical in modern life, which is precisely the element that is magnetizing the imagination of the true artists of our epoch. Such artists are no longer content merely to question particular habits or situations or even institutions; it is reality itself which they bring into question. Reality to them is like that "open wound" of which Kierkegaard speaks in his *Journals:* "A healthy open wound; sometimes it is healthier to keep a wound open; sometimes it is worse when it closes."

There are also certain long-range factors that make for the decline of naturalism. One such factor is the growth of psychological science and, particularly, of psychoanalysis. Through the influence of psychology literature recovers its inwardness, devising such forms as the interior monologue, which combines the naturalistic in its minute description of the mental process with the anti-naturalistic in its disclosure of the subjective and the irrational. Still another factor is the tendency of naturalism, as Thomas Mann observes in his remarks on Zola, to turn into the mythic through sheer immersion in the typical. This dialectical negation of the typical is apparent in a work like *Ulysses,* where "the myth of the *Odyssey,*" to quote from Harry Levin's study of Joyce, "is superimposed upon the map of Dublin" because only a myth could "lend shape or meaning to a slice of life so broad and banal." And from a social-historical point of view this much can be said, that naturalism cannot hope to survive the world of 19th-century science and industry of which it is the product. For what is the crisis of reality in contemporary art if not at bottom the crisis of the dissolution of this familiar world? Naturalism, which exhausted itself in taking an inventory of this world while it was still relatively stable, cannot possibly do justice to the phenomena of its disruption.

One must protest, however, against the easy assumption of some avant-gardist writers that to finish with naturalism is the same as finishing with the principle of realism generally. It is one thing to dissect the real, to penetrate beneath its faceless surface and transpose it into terms of symbol and image; but the attempt to be done with it altogether is sheer regression or escape. Of the principle of realism it can be said that it is the most valuable acquisition of the modern mind. It has taught literature how to take in, how to grasp and encompass, the ordinary facts of human existence; and I mean this in the simplest sense conceivable. Least of all can the novelist dispense with it, as his medium knows of no other principle of coherence. In Gide's *Les Faux-Monnayeurs* there is a famous passage in which the novelist Edouard enumerates the faults of the naturalist school. "The great defect of that school is that it always cuts a slice of life in the same direction: in time, lengthwise. Why not in breadth? Or in depth? As for me, I should like not to cut at all. Please understand: I should like to put everything into my novel." "But I thought," his interlocutor remarks, "that you want to abandon reality." Yes, replies Edouard, "my novelist wants to abandon it; but I shall continually bring him back to it. In fact that will be the subject; the struggle between the facts presented by reality and the ideal reality."

ULYSSES, ORDER, AND MYTH *

T. S. Eliot

Mr. Joyce's book has been out long enough for no more general expression of praise, or expostulation with its detractors, to be necessary; and it has not been out long enough for any attempt at a complete measurement of its place and significance to be possible. All that one can usefully do at this time, and it is a great deal to do, for such a book, is to elucidate any aspect of the book—and the number of aspects is indefinite—which has not yet been fixed. I hold this book to be the most important expression which the present age has found; it is a book to which we are all indebted, and from which none of us can escape. These are postulates for anything that I have to say about it, and I have no wish to waste the reader's time by elaborating my eulogies; it has given me all the surprise, delight, and terror that I can require, and I will leave it at that.

Amongst all the criticisms I have seen of the book, I have seen nothing—unless we except, in its way, M. Valery Larbaud's valuable paper which is rather an Introduction than a criticism—which seemed to me to appreciate the significance of the method employed—the parallel to the Odyssey, and the use of appropriate styles and symbols to each division. Yet one might expect this to be the first peculiarity to attract attention; but it has been treated as an amusing dodge, or scaffolding erected by the author for the purpose of disposing his realistic tale, of no interest in the completed structure. The criticism which Mr. Aldington directed upon *Ulysses* several years ago seems to me to fail by this oversight—but, as Mr. Aldington wrote before the complete work had appeared, fails more honourably than the attempts of those who had the whole book before them. Mr. Aldington treated Mr. Joyce as a prophet of chaos; and wailed at the flood of Dadaism which his prescient eye saw bursting forth at the tap of the magician's rod. Of course, the influence which Mr. Joyce's book may have is from my point of view an irrelevance. A very great book may have a very bad influence indeed; and a mediocre book may be in the event most salutary. The next generation is responsible for its own soul; a man of genius is responsible to his peers, not to a studio-full of uneducated and undisciplined coxcombs. Still, Mr. Aldington's apathetic solicitude for the half-witted seems to me to carry certain implications about the nature

* "*Ulysses*, Order, and Myth" first appeared in the *Dial*, November, 1923, and is used here by permission of the author.

of the book itself to which I cannot assent; and this is the important issue. He finds the book, if I understand him, to be an invitation to chaos, and an expression of feelings which are perverse, partial, and a distortion of reality. But unless I quote Mr. Aldington's words I am likely to falsify. "I say, moreover," he says,[1] "that when Mr. Joyce, with his marvellous gifts, uses them to disgust us with mankind, he is doing something which is false and a libel on humanity." It is somewhat similar to the opinion of the urbane Thackeray upon Swift. "As for the moral, I think it horrible, shameful, unmanly, blasphemous; and giant and great as this Dean is, I say we should hoot him." (This, of the conclusion of the Voyage to the Houyhnhnms—which seems to me one of the greatest triumphs that the human soul has ever achieved.)—It is true that Thackeray later pays Swift one of the finest tributes that a man has ever given or received: "So great a man he seems to me that thinking of him is like thinking of an empire falling." (And Mr. Aldington, in his time, is almost equally generous.)

Whether it is possible to libel humanity (in distinction to libel in the usual sense, which is libelling an individual or a group in contrast with the rest of humanity) is a question for philosophical societies to discuss; but of course if *Ulysses* were a "libel" it would simply be a forged document, a powerless fraud, which would never have extracted from Mr. Aldington a moment's attention. I do not wish to linger over this point: the interesting question is that begged by Mr. Aldington when he refers to Mr. Joyce's "great *undisciplined* talent."

I think that Mr. Aldington and I are more or less agreed as to what we want in principle, and agreed to call it classicism. It is because of this agreement that I have chosen Mr. Aldington to attack on the present issue. We are agreed as to what we want, but not as to how to get it, or as to what contemporary writing exhibits a tendency in that direction. We agree, I hope, that "classicism" is not an alternative to "romanticism," as of political parties, Conservative and Liberal, Republican and Democrat, on a "turn-the-rascals-out" platform. It is a goal toward which all good literature strives, so far as it is good, according to the possibilities of its place and time. One can be "classical," in a sense, by turning away from nine-tenths of the material which lies at hand, and selecting only mummified stuff from a museum—like some contemporary writers, about whom one could say some nasty things in this connexion, if it were worth while (Mr. Aldington is not one of them). Or one can be classical in tendency by doing the best one can with the material at hand. The confusion springs from the fact that the term is applied to literature and to the whole complex of interests and modes of behaviour and society of which literature is a part; and it has not the same bearing in both applications. It is much easier to be a classicist in literary criticism than in creative art—because in criti-

[1] *English Review,* April, 1921.

cism you are responsible only for what you want, and in creation you are responsible for what you can do with material which you must simply accept. And in this material I include the emotions and feelings of the writer himself, which, for that writer, are simply material which he must accept—not virtues to be enlarged or vices to be diminished. The question, then, about Mr. Joyce, is: how much living material does he deal with, and how does he deal with it: deal with, not as a legislator or exhorter, but as an artist?

It is here that Mr. Joyce's parallel use of the Odyssey has a great importance. It has the importance of a scientific discovery. No one else has built a novel upon such a foundation before: it has never before been necessary. I am not begging the question in calling *Ulysses* a "novel"; and if you call it an epic it will not matter. If it is not a novel, that is simply because the novel is a form which will no longer serve; it is because the novel, instead of being a form, was simply the expression of an age which had not sufficiently lost all form to feel the need of something stricter. Mr. Joyce has written one novel—*The Portrait;* Mr. Wyndham Lewis has written one novel—*Tarr.* I do not suppose that either of them will ever write another "novel." The novel ended with Flaubert and with James. It is, I think, because Mr. Joyce and Mr. Lewis, being "in advance" of their time, felt a conscious or probably unconscious dissatisfaction with the form, that their novels are more formless than those of a dozen clever writers who are unaware of its obsolescence.

In using the myth, in manipulating a continuous parallel between contemporaneity and antiquity, Mr. Joyce is pursuing a method which others must pursue after him. They will not be imitators, any more than the scientist who uses the discoveries of an Einstein in pursuing his own, independent, further investigations. It is simply a way of controlling, of ordering, of giving a shape and a significance to the immense panorama of futility and anarchy which is contemporary history. It is a method already adumbrated by Mr. Yeats, and of the need for which I believe Mr. Yeats to have been the first contemporary to be conscious. It is a method for which the horoscope is auspicious. Psychology (such as it is, and whether our reaction to it be comic or serious), ethnology, and *The Golden Bough* have concurred to make possible what was impossible even a few years ago. Instead of narrative method, we may now use the mythical method. It is, I seriously believe, a step toward making the modern world possible for art, toward that order and form which Mr. Aldington so earnestly desires. And only those who have won their own discipline in secret and without aid, in a world which offers very little assistance to that end, can be of any use in furthering this advance.

AN INTRODUCTION TO
WILLIAM FAULKNER *

MALCOLM COWLEY

WHEN the war was over—the other war—William Faulkner went back
to Oxford, Mississippi. He had been trained as a flyer in Canada, and
had served at the front in the Royal Air Force. Now he was home again
and not at home, or at least not able to accept the postwar world. He
was writing poems, most of them worthless, and dozens of immature
but violent and effective stories, while at the same time he was brooding over his own situation and the decline of the South. Slowly the
brooding thoughts arranged themselves into the whole interconnected
pattern that would form the substance of his later novels.

This pattern was based on what he saw in Oxford or remembered
from his childhood; on scraps of family tradition (the Falkners, as they
spelled the name, had played their part in the history of the state); on
kitchen dialogues between the black cook and her amiable husband;
on Saturday-afternoon gossip in Courthouse Square; on stories told
by men in overalls squatting on their heels while they passed around a
fruit-jar full of white corn liquor; on all the sources familiar to a small-
town Mississippi boy—but the whole of it was elaborated, transformed,
given conclusive life by his emotions; until, by the simple intensity of
feeling, the figures in it became a little more than human, became
heroic or diabolical, became symbols of the old South, of war and reconstruction, of commerce and machinery destroying the standards of
the past. There in Oxford, Faulkner performed a labor of imagination
that has not been equaled in our time, and a double labor; first, to
invent a Mississippi county that was like a mythical kingdom, but was
complete and living in all its details; second, to make his story of
Yoknapatawpha County stand as a parable or legend of all the Deep
South.

For this double task, Faulkner was better equipped by talent and
background than he was by schooling. He had never been graduated
from Oxford High School. For a year after the war, he was a student

* "An Introduction to William Faulkner" is printed here for the first time in
complete form. A considerable portion of it was used as the Introduction to *The
Portable Faulkner* (The Viking Press, Inc., 1946), and another long portion was
published as a separate essay, "William Faulkner's Legend of the South," first in
the *Sewanee Review*, Summer, 1945, and later in *A Southern Vanguard*, edited by
Allen Tate (Prentice-Hall, 1947). The essay is used here by permission of the author
and The Viking Press, Inc.

at the University of Mississippi, in Oxford, where veterans could then matriculate without a high-school diploma; but he neglected his class-room work and left without taking a degree. He had less of a formal education than any other good writer of his time, except Hart Crane—less even than Hemingway, who never went to college but learned to speak three foreign languages and studied writing in Paris from the best masters. Faulkner taught himself, largely, as he says, by "undi-rected and uncorrelated reading." Among the authors either mentioned or echoed in his early stories and poems are Keats, Balzac, Flaubert, Swinburne, Mallarmé, Wilde, Housman, Joyce, Eliot, Sherwood Anderson, and E. E. Cummings, with fainter suggestions of Hemingway (in a fishing scene), Dos Passos (in the spelling of compound words), and Scott Fitzgerald. The poems he wrote in those days were wholly derivative, but his prose from the beginning was a form of poetry; and in spite of the echoes it was always his own. He traveled less than any of his writing contemporaries. After a succession of odd jobs in Oxford, there was a brief period when he lived in New Orleans with Sherwood Anderson and met the literary crowd—he even satirized them in a bad early novel, *Mosquitoes;* he went to New York, where for a few months he clerked in a bookstore; in 1925 he took a long walking trip in Europe without settling on the Left Bank. Except for recent visits to Hollywood, the rest of his life has been spent in the town where he grew up, less than forty miles from his birthplace.

Although Oxford, Mississippi, is the seat of a university, it is even less of a literary center than was Salem, Massachusetts, during Haw-thorne's early years as a writer; and Faulkner himself has shown an even greater dislike than Hawthorne for literary society. His novels are the books of a man who broods about literature but doesn't often discuss it with his friends; there is no ease about them, no feeling that they come from a background of taste refined by argument and of opinion held in common. They make me think of a passage from Henry James's little book on Hawthorne:

> The best things come, as a general thing, from the talents that are members of a group; every man works better when he has companions working in the same line, and yielding to the stimulus of suggestion, comparison, emulation. Great things of course have been done by soli-tary workers; but they have usually been done with double the pains they would have cost if they had been produced in more genial circum-stances. The solitary worker loses the profit of example and discussion; he is apt to make awkward experiments; he is in the nature of the case more or less of an empiric. The empiric may, as I say, be treated by the world as an expert; but the drawbacks and discomforts of empiricism remain to him, and are in fact increased by the suspicion that is mingled with his gratitude, of a want in the public taste of a sense of the propor-tion of things.

Like Hawthorne, Faulkner is a solitary worker by choice; and he has done great things not only with double the pains to himself that they might have cost if produced in more genial circumstances, but sometimes also with double the pains to the reader. Two or three of his books as a whole and many of them in part are awkward experiments. All of them are full of overblown words like "imponderable," "immortal," "immutable," and "immemorial" that he would have used with more discretion, or not at all, if he had followed Hemingway's example and served an apprenticeship to an older writer. He is a most uncertain judge of his own work, and he has no reason to believe that the world's judgment of it is any more to be trusted; indeed, there is no American author who would be justified in feeling more suspicion of "a want in the public taste of a sense of the proportion of things." His early novels were overpraised, usually for the wrong reasons; his later and in many ways better novels were obstinately condemned or simply neglected; and in 1945—before the recent revival of interest in his work—all his seventeen books were out of print, with some of them unobtainable in the secondhand bookshops.

Even his warm admirers, of whom there are many—no author has a higher standing among his fellow novelists—have sometimes shown a rather vague idea of what he is trying to do; and Faulkner himself has never explained. He holds a curious attitude toward the public that appeared to be lofty indifference (in the one preface he wrote, for the Modern Library edition of *Sanctuary*), but really comes closer to being a mixture of skittery distrust and pure unconsciousness that the public exists. He doesn't furnish information or correct misstatements about himself (most of the biographical sketches that deal with him are full of preposterous errors). He doesn't care which way his name is spelled in the records, with or without the "u"—"Either way suits me," he said. Once he has finished a book, he is apparently not concerned with the question how it will be presented, to what sort of audience; and sometimes he doesn't bother to keep a private copy of it. He said in a letter, "I think I have written a lot and sent it off to print before I actually realized strangers might read it." Others might say that Faulkner, at least in those early days, was not so much composing stories for the public as he was telling them to himself—like a lonely child in his imaginary world, but also like a writer of genius.

II

Faulkner's mythical kingdom is a county in northern Mississippi, on the border between the sand hills covered with scrubby pine and the black earth of the river bottoms. Except for the storekeepers, mechanics, and professional men who live in Jefferson, the county seat, all the inhabitants are farmers or woodsmen. Except for a little lumber, their only product is baled cotton for the Memphis market. A few of them live in big plantation houses, the relics of another age, and more of them in substantial wooden farmhouses; but most of them are tenants, no better housed than slaves on good plantations before the Civil War. Yoknapatawpha County—"William Faulkner, sole owner and proprietor," as he inscribed on one of the maps he drew—has a population of 15,611 persons scattered over 2,400 square miles. It sometimes seems to me that every house or hovel has been described in one of Faulkner's novels; and that all the people of the county, black and white, townsmen, farmers, and housewives, have played their parts in one connected story.

He has so far written eleven books wholly concerned with Yoknapatawpha County and its people, who also appear in parts of three others and in thirty or more uncollected stories. *Sartoris* was the first of the books to be published, in the spring of 1929; it is a romantic and partly unconvincing novel, but with many fine scenes in it, like the hero's visit to a family of independent pine-hill farmers; and it states most of the themes that the author would later develop at length. *The Sound and the Fury* was written before *Sartoris,* but wasn't published until six months later; it describes the fall of the Compson family, and it was the first of Faulkner's novels to be widely discussed. The books that followed, in the Yoknapatawpha series, are *As I Lay Dying* (1930), about the death and burial of Addie Bundren; *Sanctuary* (1931), always the most popular of his novels; *Light in August* (1932), in many ways the best; *Absalom, Absalom!* (1936), about Colonel Sutpen and his ambition to found a family; *The Unvanquished* (1938), a book of interrelated stories about the Sartoris dynasty; *The Wild Palms* (1939), half of which deals with a convict from back in the pine hills; *The Hamlet* (1940), a novel about the Snopes clan; *Go Down, Moses* (1942), in which Faulkner's theme is the Negroes; and *Intruder in the Dust* (1948), in which he is talking about civil rights and the relation between nation and region. There are also many Yoknapatawpha stories in *These Thirteen* (1931) and *Dr. Martino* (1934) besides other stories privately printed (like "Miss Zilphia Gant") or published in magazines and still to be reprinted or used as episodes in novels.

Just as Balzac, who seems to have inspired the series, divided his *Comédie Humaine* into "Scenes of Parisian Life," "Scenes of Provincial Life," "Scenes of Private Life," so Faulkner might divide his work into a number of cycles: one about the planters and their descendants, one about the townspeople of Jefferson, one about the poor whites, one about the Indians (consisting of stories already written but never brought together), and one about the Negroes. Or again, if he adopted a division of families, there would be the Compson-Sartoris saga, the still unfinished Snopes saga, the McCaslin saga, dealing with the white and black descendants of Carothers McCaslin, and the Ratliff-Bundren saga, devoted to the backwoods farmers of Frenchman's Bend. All the cycles or sagas are closely interconnected; it is as if each new book was a chord or segment of a total situation always existing in the author's mind. Sometimes a short story is the sequel to an earlier novel. For example, we read in *Sartoris* that Byron Snopes stole a packet of letters from Narcissa Benbow; and in "There Was a Queen," a story published five years later, we learn how Narcissa got the letters back again. Sometimes, on the other hand, a novel contains the sequel to a story; and we discover from an incidental reference in *The Sound and the Fury* that the Negro woman whose terror of death was described in "That Evening Sun" had later been murdered by her husband, who left her body in a ditch for the vultures. Sometimes an episode has a more complicated history. Thus, in the first chapter of *Sanctuary*, we hear about the old Frenchman place, a ruined mansion near which the people of the neighborhood had been "digging with secret and sporadic optimism for gold which the builder was reputed to have buried somewhere about the place when Grant came through the country on his Vicksburg campaign." Later this digging for gold served as the subject of a story published in the *Saturday Evening Post:* "Lizards in Jamshyd's Courtyard." Still later the story was completely rewritten and became the last chapter of *The Hamlet*.

As one book leads into another, Faulkner sometimes falls into inconsistencies of detail. There is a sewing-machine agent named V. K. Suratt who appears in *Sartoris* and some of the later stories. By the time we reach *The Hamlet,* his name has changed to Ratliff, although his character remains the same (and his age, too, for all the twenty years that separate the backgrounds of the two novels). Henry Armstid is a likable figure in *As I Lay Dying* and *Light in August;* in *The Hamlet* he is mean and half-demented. His wife, whose character remains consistent, is called Lula in one book and Martha in another; in the third she is nameless. There is an Indian chief named Doom who appears in several stories; he starts as the father of Issetibeha and ends as his grandson. The mansion called Sutpen's Hundred was built of brick at the beginning of *Absalom, Absalom!* but at the end of the novel it is all wood and inflammable except for the chimneys. But the errors are comparatively few and inconsequential, considering the scope of Faulkner's series; and I should judge that most of them are the result of afterthoughts rather than oversights.

All his books in the Yoknapatawpha series are part of the same living pattern. It is this pattern, and not the printed volumes in which part of it is recorded, that is Faulkner's real achievement. Its existence helps to explain one feature of his work: that each novel, each long or short story, seems to reveal more than it states explicitly and to have a subject bigger than itself. All the separate works are like blocks of marble from the same quarry: they show the veins and faults of the mother rock. Or else—to use a rather strained figure—they are like wooden planks that were cut, not from a log, but from a still living tree. The planks are planed and chiseled into their final shapes, but the tree itself heals over the wound and continues to grow.

Faulkner is incapable of telling the same story twice without adding new details. In the *Portable Faulkner* I wanted to use part of *The Sound and the Fury,* the novel that deals with the fall of the Compson family. I thought that the last part of the book would be most effective as a separate episode, but still it depended too much on what had gone before. Faulkner offered to write a very brief introduction that would explain the relations of the characters. What he finally sent me was the much longer passage printed as an appendix: a genealogy of the Compsons from their first arrival in this country. Whereas the novel is confined to a period of eighteen years ending in 1928, the genealogy goes back to the battle of Culloden in 1745, and forward to the year 1945, when Jason, last of the Compson males, has sold the family mansion, and Sister Caddy has last been heard of as the mistress of a German general. The novel that Faulkner wrote about the Compsons had long ago been given its final shape; but the pattern or body of legend behind the novel—and behind all his other books—was still developing.

Although the pattern is presented in terms of a single Mississippi county, it can be extended to the Deep South as a whole; and Faulkner always seems conscious of its wider application. He might have been thinking of his own novels when he described the ledgers in the commissary of the McCaslin plantation, in *Go Down, Moses.* They recorded, he said, "that slow trickle of molasses and meal and meat, of shoes and straw hats and overalls, of plowlines and collars and heelbolts and clevises, which returned each fall as cotton"—in a sense they were local and limited; but they were also "the continuation of that record which two hundred years had not been enough to complete and another hundred would not be enough to discharge; that chronicle which was a whole land in miniature, which multiplied and compounded was the entire South."

III

"Tell about the South," says Quentin Compson's roommate at Harvard, a Canadian named Shreve McCannon who is curious about the unknown region beyond the Ohio. "What's it like there," he asks. "What do they do there? Why do they live there? Why do they live at all?" And Quentin, whose background is a little like that of Faulkner himself and who sometimes seems to speak for him—Quentin answers, "You can't understand it. You would have to be born there." Nevertheless, he tells a long and violent story that he regards as the essence of the Deep South, which is not so much a mere region as it is, in Quentin's mind, an incomplete and frustrated nation trying to relive its legendary past.

There was a boy, Quentin says—I am trying to summarize the plot of *Absalom, Absalom!*—a mountain boy named Thomas Sutpen whose family drifted into the Virginia lowlands, where his father found odd jobs on a plantation. One day the father sent him with a message to the big house, but he was turned away at the door by a black man in livery. Puzzled and humiliated, the mountain boy was seized upon by the lifelong ambition to which he would afterwards refer as "the design." He would own a plantation, with slaves and a liveried butler; he would build a mansion as big as any in the Tidewater; and he would have a son to inherit his wealth.

A dozen years later Sutpen appeared in the frontier town of Jefferson, Mississippi, and, by some transaction the nature of which was never explained—though it certainly wasn't by honest purchase—he obtained a hundred square miles of land from the Chickasaws. He disappeared again, and this time he returned with twenty wild Negroes from the jungle and a French architect. On the day of his appearance, he set about building the largest house in northern Mississippi, with timbers from the forest and bricks that his Negroes molded and baked on the spot; it was as if his mansion, Sutpen's Hundred, had been literally torn from the soil. Only one man in Jefferson—he was Quentin's grandfather, General Compson—ever learned how and where Sutpen had acquired his slaves. He had shipped to Haiti from Virginia, worked as an overseer on a sugar plantation and married the rich planter's daughter, who had borne him a son. Then, finding that his wife had Negro blood, he had simply put her away, with her child and her fortune, while keeping the twenty slaves as a sort of indemnity. He explained to General Compson in the stilted speech he had taught himself that she could not be "adjunctive to the forwarding of the design."

"Jesus, the South is fine, isn't it," says Shreve McCannon. "It's better than the theatre, isn't it. It's better than Ben Hur, isn't it. No wonder you have to come away now and then, isn't it."

In Jefferson, he married again, Quentin continues. This time his wife belonged to a pious family of the neighborhood and she bore him two children, Henry and Judith. He became the biggest landowner and cotton planter in the county, and it seemed that his "design" had already been fulfilled. At this moment, however—it was Christmas in 1859—Henry came home from the University of Mississippi with an older and worldlier new friend, Charles Bon, who was in reality Sutpen's son by his first marriage. Charles became engaged to Judith. Sutpen learned his identity and, without making a sign of recognition, ordered him from the house. Henry, who refused to believe that Charles was his half-brother, renounced his birthright and followed him to New Orleans. In 1861 all the male Sutpens went off to war, and all of them survived four years of fighting. Then, in the spring of 1865,

Charles suddenly decided to marry Judith, even though he was certain by now that she was his half-sister. Henry rode beside him all the way back to Sutpen's Hundred, but tried to stop him at the gate, killed him when he insisted on going ahead with his plan, told Judith what he had done, and disappeared.

"The South," Shreve McCannon says as he listens to the story. "The South. Jesus. No wonder you folks all outlive yourselves by years and years." And Quentin says, remembering his own sister with whom he was in love—just as Charles Bon, and Henry too, were in love with Judith—"I am older at twenty than a lot of people who have died."

But Quentin's story of the Deep South does not end with the war. Colonel Sutpen came home, he says, to find his wife dead, his son a fugitive, his slaves dispersed (they had run away before they were freed by the Union army) and most of his land about to be seized for debt. Still determined to carry out "the design," he did not even pause for breath before undertaking to restore his house and plantation as nearly as possible to what they had been. The effort failed; Sutpen lost most of his land and was reduced to keeping a crossroads store. Now in his sixties, he tried again to beget a son; but his wife's younger sister, Miss Rosa Coldfield, was outraged by his proposal ("Let's try it," he had said, "and if it's a boy we'll get married"); and later poor Milly Jones, whom he seduced, gave birth to a baby girl. At that Sutpen abandoned hope and provoked Milly's grandfather into killing him. Judith survived her father for a time, as did the half-caste son of Charles Bon by a New Orleans octoroon. After the death of these two by yellow fever, the great house was haunted rather than inhabited by an ancient mulatto woman, Sutpen's daughter by one of his slaves. The fugitive Henry Sutpen came home to die; the townspeople heard of his illness and sent an ambulance after him; but old Clytie thought they were arresting him for murder and set fire to Sutpen's Hundred. The only survivor of the conflagration was Jim Bond, a half-witted, saddle-colored creature who was Charles Bon's grandson.

"Do you know what I think?" says the Canadian Shreve McCannon after the story has ended. "I think that in time the Jim Bonds are going to conquer the western hemisphere. Of course it won't be quite in our time and of course as they spread toward the poles they will bleach out again like the rabbits and the birds do, so they won't show up so sharp against the snow. But it will still be Jim Bond; and so in a few thousand years, I who regard you will also have sprung from the loins of African kings. Now I want you to tell me just one thing more. Why do you hate the South?"

"I don't hate it," Quentin says quickly, at once. "I don't hate it," he repeats, speaking for the author as well as himself. *I don't hate it,* he thinks, panting in the cold air, the iron New England dark; *I don't. I don't! I don't hate it! I don't hate it!*

The reader cannot help wondering why this sombre and, at moments, plainly incredible story had so seized upon Quentin's mind that he trembled with excitement when telling it and felt that it revealed the essence of the Deep South. It seems to belong in the realm of Gothic romances, with Sutpen's Hundred taking the place of the haunted castle on the Rhine, with Colonel Sutpen as Faust and Charles Bon as Manfred. Then slowly it dawns on you that most of the characters and incidents have a double meaning; that besides their place in the story, they also serve as symbols or metaphors with a general application.

Sutpen's great design, the land he stole from the Indians, the French architect who built his house with the help of wild Negroes from the jungle, the woman of mixed blood whom he married and disowned, the unacknowledged son who ruined him, the poor white whom he wronged and who killed him in anger, the final destruction of the mansion like the downfall of a social order: all these might belong to a tragic fable of Southern history. With a little cleverness, the whole novel might be explained as a connected and logical allegory, but this, I think, would be going far beyond the author's intention. First of all he was writing a story, and one that affected him deeply, but he was also brooding over a social situation. More or less unconsciously, the incidents in the story came to represent the forces and elements in the social situation, since the mind naturally works in terms of symbols and parallels. In Faulkner's case, this form of parallelism is not confined to *Absalom, Absalom!* It can be found in the whole fictional framework that he has been elaborating in novel after novel, until his work has become a myth or legend of the South.

I call it a legend because it is obviously no more intended as a historical account of the country south of the Ohio that *The Scarlet Letter* was intended as a history of Massachusetts or *Paradise Lost* as a factual description of the Fall. Briefly stated, the legend might run something like this: The Deep South was settled partly by aristocrats like the Sartoris clan and partly by new men like Colonel Sutpen. Both types of planters were determined to establish a lasting social order on the land they had seized from the Indians (that is, to leave sons behind them). They had the virtue of living single-mindedly by a fixed code; but there was also an inherent guilt in their "design," their way of life; it was slavery that put a curse on the land and brought about the Civil War.

After the War was lost, partly as a result of their own mad heroism (for who else but men as brave as Jackson and Stuart could have frightened the Yankees into standing together and fighting back?) they tried to restore "the design" by other methods. But they no longer had the strength to achieve more than a partial success, even after they had freed their land from the carpetbaggers who followed the Northern armies. As time passed, moreover, the men of the old order found that they had Southern enemies too: they had to fight against a new exploiting class descended from the landless whites of slavery days. In this struggle between the clan of Sartoris and the unscrupulous tribe of Snopes, the Sartorises were defeated in advance by a traditional code that kept them from using the weapons of the enemy. As a price of victory, however, the Snopeses had to serve the mechanized civilization of the North, which was morally impotent in itself, but which, with the aid of its Southern retainers, ended by corrupting the Southern nation. In our own day, the problems of the South are still unsolved, the racial conflict is becoming more acute; and Faulkner's characters in their despairing moments foresee or forebode some catastrophe of which Jim Bond and his like will be the only survivors.

This legend of Faulkner's, if I have stated it correctly, is clearly not the plantation legend that has been embodied in hundreds of romantic novels. Faulkner presents the virtues of the old order as being moral rather than material. There is no baronial pomp in his novels; no profusion of silk and silver, mahogany and moonlight and champagne. The big house on Mr. Hubert Beauchamp's plantation (in "Was") had a rotted floorboard in the back gallery that Mr. Hubert never got round to having fixed. Visitors used to find him sitting in the springhouse with his boots off and his feet in the water while he sipped his morning toddy, which he invited them to share. Visitors to Sutpen's Hundred were offered champagne: it was the best, doubtless, and yet it was "crudely dispensed out of the burlesqued pantomime elegance of Negro butlers who (and likewise the drinkers who gulped it down like neat whiskey between flowery and unsubtle toasts) would have treated lemonade the same way." All the planters lived comfortably, with plenty of servants, but Faulkner never lets us forget that they were living on what had recently been the frontier. What he admires about them is not their wealth or their manners or their fine horses, but rather their unquestioning acceptance of a moral code that taught them "courage and honor and pride, and pity and love of justice and of liberty." Living with single hearts, they were, says Quentin Compson's father:

> ... people too as we are, and victims too as we are, but victims of a different circumstance, simpler and therefore, integer for integer, larger, more heroic and the figures therefore more heroic too, not dwarfed and involved but distinct, uncomplex, who had the gift of living once or dying once instead of being diffused and scattered creatures drawn blindly limb from limb from a grab bag and assembled, author and victim too of a thousand homicides and a thousand copulations and divorcements.

The old order was a moral order: briefly that was its strength and the secret lost by its heirs. But also—and here is another respect in which Faulkner's legend differs from the Southern story more commonly presented—it bore the moral burden of a guilt so great that the war and even reconstruction were in some sense a merited punishment. There is madness, but there is metaphorical meaning too, in Miss Rosa Coldfield's belief that Sutpen was a demon and that his sins were the real reason " . . . why God let us lose the War: that only through the blood of our men and the tears of our women could He stay this demon and efface his name and lineage from the earth." Colonel Sutpen himself has a feeling, not exactly of guilt, since he has never questioned the rightness of his design, but rather of amazement that so many misfortunes have fallen on him. Sitting in General Compson's office, he goes back over his career, trying to see where he had made his "mistake," for that is what he calls it. Sometimes the author seems to be implying that the sin for which Sutpen and his class are being punished is simply the act of cohabiting with Negroes. But before the end of *Absalom, Absalom!* we learn that miscegenation is only part of it. When Charles Bon's curious actions are explained, we find that he was taking revenge on his father for having refused to recognize him by so much as a single glance. Thus, heartlessness was the "mistake" that ruined Sutpen, not the taking of a partly Negro wife and Negro concubines.

The point becomes clearer in a long story called "The Bear" (in *Go Down, Moses*), possibly the best single piece that Faulkner has written. When Isaac McCaslin is twenty-one, he insists on relinquishing the big plantation that is his by inheritance; he thinks that the land is cursed. It is cursed in his eyes by the deeds of his grandfather: "that evil and unregenerate old man who could summon, because she was his property, a human being because she was old enough and female, to his widower's house and get a child on her and then dismiss her because she was of an inferior race, and then bequeath a thousand dollars to the infant because he would be dead then and wouldn't have to pay it." The lesson is that the land was cursed—and the Civil War was part of the curse—because its owners had treated human beings as instruments; in a word, it was cursed by slavery.

IV

All through his boyhood, Faulkner must have dreamed of fighting in the Civil War. It was a Sartoris war and not a Snopes war, like the one in which he afterwards risked his life in a foreign army. And yet his sympathies did not wholly lie with the slaveholding clan of Sartoris, even though it was his own clan. The men he most admired and must have pictured himself as resembling were the Southern soldiers—after all, they were the vast majority—who owned no slaves themselves and suffered from the institution of slavery. The men he would praise in his novels were those "who had fought for four years and lost . . . not because they were opposed to freedom as freedom, but for the old reasons for which man (not the generals and politicians but man) has always fought and died in wars: to preserve a status quo or to establish a better future one to endure for his children." You might define his position as that of anti-slavery Southern nationalist.

Just what do I mean by calling Faulkner a nationalist instead of a regionalist? The point is important in relation to his Southern legend. Obviously he belongs in a different category from writers like Ruth Suckow of Iowa or Mary Ellen Chase of Maine or Elsie Singmaster of Pennsylvania. The Corn Belt as described by Miss Suckow, northern New England as described by Miss Chase and the Pennsylvania Dutch counties as described by Miss Singmaster are all of them regions properly speaking—with a feeling of local particularity, but also with a feeling of incompleteness, of existing in relation to the country as a whole. The South contains many such regions, and Faulkner's Mississippi is one of them. The South has also produced its share of strictly regional writers, among whom might be mentioned Marjorie Kinnan Rawlings of the Florida scrub country and Jesse Stuart of the Kentucky hills.

Faulkner is something broader than a regionalist. With a stronger sense of history than the writers I have mentioned, he tries to speak for all the South; and the South is more than a region. For the space of four years it was an independent country; for a dozen years more it was a conquered and occupied country, with its white inhabitants united in defeat. To an observer from north of the Potomac, it seems like nothing so much as an incomplete or frustrated nation trying to maintain or revive a national consciousness.

There is more to be said on this subject. Nationality is not an absolute quality, but is something that exists in varying degrees. In the contemporary world there are dozens of half-nations and three-quarter nations; there are—to mention a few examples—Scotland, Wales, French Canada, the Boers in South Africa, the Flemings in Belgium— and other half-nations, too—Catalonia, Croatia, Macedonia, White Russia, the Ukraine. Sometimes they become politically independent, as Ireland has recently done, and try to revive their own language. Sometimes they create their own language out of peasant dialects, as was done in Slovakia and Norway. Often they create their own literature, like the Flemings and the Catalans and the Ukrainians. They move up and down the scale of nationality. Some of them lose their independence, like the three Baltic states in 1939. Some of them disappear completely, not only from political maps, as happened long ago with the great Burgundian kingdom, but even from the consciousness of their own people—so that a courtly language, like that of Languedoc, may be reduced to a group of dialects spoken with different accents by people of different villages and revived from time to time by poets of an antiquarian bent. On the other hand, the sense of being a nation can survive without a special language, as in the case of Scotland and Croatia (to mention only two examples), without political independence, and sometimes without a serious desire for independence. It can be based simply on a common history, a common culture, and standards of value that differ from those prevailing north or south of an imaginary border.

What I am trying to say is simply that Southern nationalism or sectionalism—as it is usually called—takes on a different aspect when it is viewed against the background of all the other incomplete nations that exist in the world. For something more than a hundred years the South has been trying first to create and then to maintain its own identity. It has adopted various means toward this end, sometimes successively and sometimes all at the same time. It has tried to achieve its identity by politics, economics, mythology, open warfare, secret resistance—and of late years increasingly by stories, poems, plays, essays, novels. Since 1930 we are justified in speaking of a Southern renaissance, and we are justified in saying that Faulkner has played a leading part in it, by supplying what is in effect a mythology of the Southern nation, from its beginning in the early 1800's down to the present day.

Faulkner's novels of contemporary Southern life continue the legend into a period that he regards as one of moral confusion and social decay. He is continually seeking in them for violent images to convey his sense of despair. *Sanctuary* is the most violent of all his novels; it is also the most popular and by no means the least important (in spite of Faulkner's comment that it was "a cheap idea . . . deliberately conceived to make money"). The story of Popeye and Temple Drake has more meaning than appears on a first hasty reading—the only reading that most of the critics have been willing to grant it. Popeye himself is one of several characters in Faulkner's novels who represent the mechanical civilization that has invaded and partly conquered the South. He is always described in mechanical terms: his eyes "looked like rubber knobs"; his face "just went awry, like the face of a wax doll set too near a hot fire and forgotten"; his tight suit and stiff hat were "all angles, like a modernistic lampshade"; and in general he had "that vicious depthless quality of stamped tin." Popeye was the son of a professional strikebreaker, from whom he had inherited syphilis, and the grandson of a pyromaniac. Like two other villains in Faulkner's novels, Joe Christmas and Januarius Jones, he had spent most of his childhood in an institution. He was the man "who made money and had nothing he could do with it, spend it for, since he knew that alcohol would kill him like poison, who had no friends and had never known a woman"—in other words, he was the compendium of all the hateful qualities that Faulkner assigns to finance capitalism. *Sanctuary* is not a connected allegory, as one critic explained it, but neither is it a mere accumulation of pointless horrors. It is an example of the Freudian method turned backwards, being full of sexual nightmares that are in reality social symbols. It is somehow connected in the author's mind with what he regards as the rape and corruption of the South.

In all his novels dealing with the present, Faulkner makes it clear that the descendants of the old ruling caste have the wish but not the courage or the strength to prevent this new disaster. They are defeated by Popeye (like Horace Benbow), or they run away from him (like Gowan Stevens, who had gone to school at Virginia and learned to drink like a gentleman, but hadn't learned to fight for his principles), or they are robbed and replaced in their positions of influence by the Snopeses (like old Bayard Sartoris, the president of the bank), or they drug themselves with eloquence and alcohol (like Quentin Compson's father), or they retire into the illusion of being inviolable Southern ladies (like Mrs. Compson, who says, "It can't be simply to flout and hurt me. Whoever God is, He would not permit that. I'm a lady"), or they dwell so much on the past that they are incapable of facing the present (like Reverend Hightower of *Light in August*), or they run from danger to danger (like young Bayard Sartoris) frantically seeking their own destruction. Faulkner's novels are full of well-meaning and even admirable persons, not only the grandsons of the cotton aristocracy, but also pine-hill farmers and storekeepers and sewing-machine agents and Negro cooks and sharecroppers; but they are almost all of them defeated by circumstances and they carry with them a sense of their own doom.

They also carry, whether heroes or villains, a curious sense of submission to their fate. "There is not one of Faulkner's characters," says André Gide in his dialogue on "The New American Novelists," "who properly speaking, has a soul"; and I think he means that not one of them exercises the faculty of conscious choice between good and evil. They are haunted, obsessed, driven forward by some inner necessity. Like Miss Rosa Coldfield, in *Absalom, Absalom!* they exist in "that dream state in which you run without moving from a terror in which you cannot believe, toward a safety in which you have no faith." Or, like the slaves freed by General Sherman's army, in *The Unvanquished,* they blindly follow the roads toward any river, believing that it will be their Jordan:

> They were singing, walking along the road singing, not even looking to either side. The dust didn't even settle for two days, because all that night they still passed; we sat up listening to them, and the next morning every few yards along the road would be the old ones who couldn't keep up any more, sitting or lying down and even crawling along, calling to the others to help them; and the others—the young ones—not stopping, not even looking at them. "Going to Jordan," they told me. "Going to cross Jordan."

All Faulkner's characters, black and white, are a little like that. They dig for gold frenziedly after they have lost their hope of finding it (like

Henry Armstid in *The Hamlet* and Lucas Beauchamp in *Go Down, Moses*); or they battle against and survive a Mississippi flood for the one privilege of returning to the state prison farm (like the tall convict in "Old Man"); or, as a whole family together, they carry a body through flood and fire and corruption to bury it in the cemetery at Jefferson (like the Bundrens in *As I Lay Dying*); or they tramp the roads week after week in search of men who had promised but never intended to marry them (like Lena Grove, the pregnant woman of *Light in August*); or, pursued by a mob, they turn at the end to meet and accept death (like Joe Christmas in the same novel). Even when they seem to be guided by a conscious purpose, like Colonel Sutpen, it is not something they have chosen by an act of will, but something that has taken possession of them: Sutpen's great design was "not what he wanted to do but what he just had to do, had to do it whether he wanted to or not, because if he did not do it he knew that he could never live with himself for the rest of his life." In the same way, Faulkner himself writes, not what he wants to, but what he just has to write whether he wants to or not.

In addition to being a fatalist he is also an idealist, more strongly so than any other American writer of our time. The idealism disguises itself as its own opposite, but that is because he is deeply impressed by and tends to exaggerate the contrast between the life around him and the ideal picture in his mind. No other American writer makes such a use of negative turns of speech: his stories abound in words like "paintless," "lightless," "windowless," "not-feeling," "unvisioned." He speaks of "that *roadless* and even *pathless* waste of *unfenced* fallow and wilderness jungle—*no* barn, *no* stable, *not so much as* a hen-coop; just a log cabin built by hand and *no* clever hand either, a meagre pile of clumsily cut firewood sufficient for about one day and *not even* a gaunt hound to come bellowing out from under the house when he rode up." In the same story ("The Bear"), he speaks of ". . . the empty fields without plow or seed to work them, fenceless against the stock which did not exist within or without the walled stable which likewise was not there." He speaks of faces watching "without alarm, without recognition, without hope," and he speaks of the South under Reconstruction as "a lightless and gutted and empty land." Always in his mind he has an ideal picture of how the land and the people should be—a picture of painted, many-windowed houses, fenced fields, overflowing barns, eyes lighting up with recognition; and always, being honest, he measures that picture against the land and people he has seen. And both pictures are not only physical but moral; for always in the background of his novels is a sense of moral standards and a feeling of outrage at their being violated or simply pushed aside. Seeing little hope in the future, he turns to the past, where he hopes to discover a legendary and recurrent pattern that will illuminate and lend dignity to the world about him. So it is that Reverend Hightower of *Light in August,* dying in the dingy ruin of his plans, sees a vision of Bedford Forrest's troopers, who lived without question by a single and universally accepted code:

> He hears above his heart the thunder increase, myriad and drumming. Like a long sighing of wind in trees it begins, then they sweep into sight, borne now upon a cloud of phantom dust. They rush past, forwardleaning in the saddles, with brandished arms, beneath whipping ribbons from slanted and eager lances; with tumult and soundless yelling they sweep past like a tide whose crest is jagged with the wild heads of horses and the brandished arms of men like the crater of the world in explosion. They rush past, are gone; the dust swirls skyward sucking, fades away into the night which has fully come. Yet, leaning forward in the window . . . it seems to him that he still hears them: the wild bugles and the clashing sabres and the dying thunder of hooves.

v

He is not primarily a novelist: that is, his stories do not occur to him in book-length units of 70,000 to 150,000 words. Almost all of his novels have some weakness in structure. Some of them combine two or more themes having little relation to each other, like *Light in August,* while others, like *The Hamlet,* tend to resolve themselves into a series of episodes resembling beads on a string. In *The Sound and the Fury,* which is superb as a whole, we can't be sure that the four sections of the novel are presented in the most effective order; at any rate, we can't fully understand and perhaps can't even read the first section until we have read the other three. *Absalom, Absalom!* though pitched in too high a key, is structurally the soundest of all the novels in the Yoknapatawpha series; but even here the author's attention shifts halfway through the book from the principal theme of Colonel Sutpen's ambition to the secondary and overemphasized theme of incest and miscegenation.

Faulkner is best and most nearly himself either in long stories like "The Bear," in *Go Down, Moses,* and "Old Man," which was published as half of *The Wild Palms,* and "Spotted Horses," which was first printed separately, then greatly expanded and fitted into the loose framework of *The Hamlet*—or else in the Yoknapatawpha series as a whole. That is, he is most effective in dealing with the total situation that is always present in his mind as a pattern of the South; or else in shorter units that can be conceived and written in a single burst of creative effort. It is by his best that we should judge him, like every other author; and Faulkner at his best—even sometimes at his worst—has a power, a richness of life, an intensity to be found in no other American novelist of our time. He has—once more I am quoting from

Henry James's essay on Hawthorne—"the element of simple genius, the quality of imagination."

Moreover, he has a brooding love for the land where he was born and reared and where, unlike other writers of his generation, he has chosen to spend his life. It is ". . . this land, this South, for which God has done so much, with woods for game and streams for fish and deep rich soil for seed and lush springs to sprout it and long summers to mature it and serene falls to harvest it and short mild winters for men and animals." So far as Faulkner's country includes the Delta, it is also (in the words of old Ike McCaslin)—

> . . . this land which man has deswamped and denuded and deriverred in two generations so that white men can own plantations and commute every night to Memphis and black men own plantations and ride in jim-crow cars to Chicago and live in millionaires' mansions on Lake Shore Drive, where white men rent farms and live like niggers and niggers crop on shares and live like animals, where cotton is planted and grows man-tall in the very cracks of the sidewalks, and usury and mortgage and bankruptcy and measureless wealth, Chinese and African and Aryan and Jew, all breed and spawn together.

Here are the two sides of Faulkner's feeling for the South: on the one side, an admiring and possessive love; on the other, a compulsive fear lest what he loves should be destroyed by the ignorance of its native serfs and the greed of traders and absentee landlords.

No other American writer takes such delight in the weather. He speaks in various novels of "the hot still pinewiney silence of the August afternoon"; of "the moonless September dust, the trees along the road not rising soaring as trees should but squatting like huge fowl"; on "the tranquil sunset of October mazy with windless wood-smoke"; of the "slow drizzle of November rain just above the ice point"; of "those windless Mississippi December days which are a sort of Indian summer's Indian summer"; of January and February when there is "no movement anywhere save the low constant smoke . . . and no sound save the chopping of axes and the lonely whistle of the daily trains." Spring in Faulkner's country is a hurried season, "all coming at once, pell mell and disordered, fruit and bloom and leaf, pied meadow and blossoming wood and the long fields shearing dark out of winter's slumber, to the shearing plow." Summer is dust-choked and blazing, and it lasts far into what should be autumn. "That's the one trouble with this country," he says in *As I Lay Dying*. "Everything, weather, all, hangs on too long. Like our rivers, our land: opaque, slow, violent; shaping and creating the life of man in its implacable and brooding image."

Shaped as it has always been by land and weather, rural life in the South is presented in Faulkner's novels as being essentially the same for the two races that inhabit the countryside, even though whites and

Negroes move on different levels. Thus, he says in *Absalom, Absalom!*
that the young planters were

> ... only in the surface matter of food and clothing and daily occupation
> any different from the Negro slaves who supported them—the same
> sweat, the only difference being that on the one hand it went for labor
> in fields where on the other it went as the price of the spartan and
> meagre pleasures which were available to them because they did not
> have to sweat in the fields: the hard violent hunting and riding; the
> same pleasures: the one, gambling for worn knives and brass jewelry and
> twists of tobacco and buttons and garments because they happened to
> be easiest and quickest to hand; on the other for the money and horses,
> the guns and watches, and for the same reason; the same parties: the
> identical music from identical instruments, rude fiddles and guitars, now
> in the big house with candles and silk dresses and champagne, now in
> dirt-floored cabins with smoking pine knots and calico and water
> sweetened with molasses.

"They will endure. They are better than we are," Ike McCaslin says
of the Negroes, although he finds it more painful to utter this heresy
than it is to surrender his plantation. "Stronger than we are," he continues. "Their vices are vices aped from white men or that white men
and bondage have taught them: improvidence and intemperance and
evasion—not laziness . . . and their virtues are their own: endurance
and pity and tolerance and forbearance and fidelity and love of children, whether their own or not or black or not." In Faulkner's novels,
the Negroes are an element of stability and endurance, just as the
octoroons (like Charles Bon and Joe Christmas) are an element of
tragic instability. His favorite characters are the old Negro cooks who
hold a white family together: Elnora and Dilsey and Clytie and Aunt
Mollie Beauchamp. After the Compson family has gone to pieces (in
The Sound and the Fury), it is Dilsey the cook who endures and is left
behind to mourn. Looking up at the square, unpainted house with its
rotting portico, she thinks, "Ise seed de first and de last"; and later in
the kitchen, looking at the cold stove, "I seed de first en de last."

He has other favorites besides the Negro matriarchs. After a second
reading of his novels you continue to be impressed by his villains,
Popeye and Jason and Joe Christmas and Flem Snopes; but this time
you find more place in your memory for other figures standing a
little in the background yet presented by the author with quiet
affection: old ladies like Miss Jenny Du Pre, with their sharp-tongued
benevolence; shrewd but kindly bargainers like Ratliff, the sewing-
machine agent, and Will Varner, with his cotton gin and general store;
long suffering farm wives like Mrs. Henry Armstid (whether her name
be Lula or Martha), and backwoods patriarchs like Pappy MacCallum,
with his six middle-aged but unmarried sons named after the generals
of Lee's army. You remember the big plantation houses that collapse

in flames as if a whole civilization was dying, but you also remember men in patched and faded but quite clean overalls sitting on the gallery—in the North we should call it the porch—of a crossroads store that is covered with posters advertising soft drinks and patent medicines; and you remember the stories they tell while chewing tobacco until the suption is out of it (everything in their world is reduced to anecdote, and every anecdote is based on character). You remember Quentin Compson, not in his despairing moments, but riding with his father behind the dogs as they quarter a sedge-grown hillside after quail; and not listening to his father's story, but still knowing every word of it, because, as he thought to himself, "You had learned, absorbed it already without the medium of speech somehow from having been born and living beside it, with it, as children will and do: so that what your father was saying did not tell you anything so much as it struck, word by word, the resonant strings of remembering."

Faulkner's novels have the quality of being lived, absorbed, remembered, rather than merely observed. And they have what is rare in the novels of our time, a warmth of family affection, brother for brother and sister, the father for his children—a love so warm and proud that it tries to shut out the rest of the world. Compared with that affection, married love is presented as something calculating, and illicit love as a consuming fire. And because the blood relationship is central in his novels, Faulkner finds it hard to create sympathetic characters between the ages of twenty and forty. He is better with children, Negro and white, and incomparably good with older people who preserve the standards that have come down to them "out of the old time, the old days."

In some of his later books there is a quality not exactly new to Faulkner—it had appeared already in passages of *Sartoris* and *Sanctuary*—but now much stronger and no longer overshadowed by violence and horror. It is a sort of homely and sober-sided frontier humor that is seldom achieved in contemporary writing (except by Erskine Caldwell, another Southerner). The horse-trading episodes in *The Hamlet*, and especially the long story of the spotted ponies from Texas, might have been inspired by the Davy Crockett almanacs. "Old Man," the story of the convict who surmounted the greatest of all the Mississippi floods, might almost be a continuation of *Huckleberry Finn*. It is as if some older friend of Huck's had taken the raft and drifted on from Aunt Sally Phelps's farm into wilder adventures, described in a wilder style among Chinese and Cayjuns and bayous crawling with alligators. In a curious way, Faulkner combines two of the principal traditions in American letters: the tradition of psychological horror, often close to symbolism, that begins with Charles Brockden Brown, our first professional novelist, and extends through Poe, Melville, Henry James (in his later stories), Stephen Crane, and Hemingway; and the other tradition of frontier humor and realism beginning with Davy Crockett and having Mark Twain as its best example.

But the American author he most resembles is Hawthorne, for all their polar differences. They stand to each other as July to December, as heat to cold, as swamp to mountain, as the luxuriant to the meagre but perfect, as planter to Puritan; and yet Hawthorne had much the same attitude toward New England that Faulkner has toward the South, together with a strong sense of regional particularity. The Civil War made Hawthorne feel that "the North and the South were two distinct nations in opinions and habits, and had better not try to live under the same institutions." In the spring of 1861, he wrote to his Bowdoin classmate, Horatio Bridge, "We were never one people and never really had a country."—"New England," he said a little later, "is quite as large a lump of earth as my heart can really take in." But it was more than a lump of earth for him; it was a lump of history and a permanent state of consciousness. Like Faulkner in the South, he applied himself to creating its moral fables and elaborating its legends, which existed, as it were, in his solitary heart. Pacing the hillside behind his house in Concord, he listened for a voice; you might say that he lay in wait for it, passively but expectantly, like a hunter behind a rock; then, when it had spoken, he transcribed its words—more slowly and carefully than Faulkner, it is true; with more form and less fire, but with the same essential fidelity. If the voice was silent, he had nothing to write. "I have an instinct that I had better keep quiet," he said in a letter to his publisher. "Perhaps I shall have a new spirit of vigor if I wait quietly for it; perhaps not." Faulkner is another author who has to wait for the spirit and the voice. Essentially he is not a novelist, in the sense of not being a writer who sets out to observe actions and characters, then fits them into the architectural framework of a story. For all the weakness of his own poems, he is an epic or bardic in prose, a creator of myths that he weaves together into a legend of the South.

ERNEST HEMINGWAY *

ROBERT PENN WARREN

I

IN MAY, 1929, in *Scribner's Magazine,* the first installment of *A Farewell to Arms* appeared. The novel was completed in the issue of October, and was published in book form the same year. Ernest Hemingway was already regarded, by a limited literary public, as a writer of extraordinary freshness and power, as one of the makers, indeed, of a new American fiction. *A Farewell to Arms* more than justified the early enthusiasm of the connoisseurs for Hemingway, and extended his reputation from them to the public at large. Its great importance was at once acknowledged, and its reputation has survived through the changing fashions and interests of twenty years.

What was the immediate cause of its appeal? It told a truth about the first world war, and a truth about the generation who had fought the war and whose lives, because of the war, had been wrenched from the expected pattern and the old values. Other writers had told or were to tell similar truths about this war. John Dos Passos in *Three Soldiers,* E. E. Cummings in *The Enormous Room,* William Faulkner in *Soldier's Pay,* Maxwell Anderson and Laurence Stallings in *What Price Glory?* All these writers had presented the pathos and endurance and gallantry of the individual caught and mangled in the great anonymous mechanism of a modern war fought for reasons that the individual could not understand, found insufficient to justify the event, or believed to be no reasons at all. And *A Farewell to Arms* was not the first book to record the plight of the men and women who, because of the war, had been unable to come to terms with life in the old way. Hemingway himself in *The Sun Also Rises,* of 1926, had given the picture of the dislocated life of young English and American expatriates in the bars of Paris, the "lost generation," as the phrase from Gertrude Stein defined them. But before that F. Scott Fitzgerald, who had been no nearer to the war than an officers' training camp, had written of the lost generation. For the young people about whom Fitzgerald wrote, even when they were not veterans and even when their love stories were enacted in parked cars, fraternity houses, and country clubs and not in

* "Ernest Hemingway" first appeared, in a slightly different form, in the *Kenyon Review,* Winter, 1947, and was later used in the present version as the Introduction to the Modern Standard Authors edition of *A Farewell to Arms,* by Ernest Hemingway, copyright 1949 by Charles Scribner's Sons. It is reprinted here by permission of the author and the publishers.

the cafés and hotels of Paris, were like Hemingway's expatriates under the shadow of the war and were groping to find some satisfaction in a world from which the old values had been withdrawn. Hemingway's expatriates had turned their backs on the glitter of the Great Boom of the 1920's, and Fitzgerald's young men were usually drawn to the romance of wealth and indulgence, but this difference is superficial. If Hemingway's young men begin by repudiating the Great Boom, Fitzgerald's young men end with disappointment in what even success has to offer. "All the sad young men" of Fitzgerald—to take the title of one of his collections of stories—and the "lost generation" of Hemingway are seekers for landmarks and bearings in a terrain for which the maps have been mislaid.

A Farewell to Arms, which appeared ten years after the first world war and on the eve of the collapse of the Great Boom, seemed to sum up and bring to focus an inner meaning of the decade being finished. It worked thus, not because it disclosed the end results that the life of the decade was producing—the discontents and disasters that were beginning to be noticed even by unreflective people—but because it cut back to the beginning of the process, to the moment that had held within itself the explanation of the subsequent process. Those who had grown up in the war, or in the shadow of the war, could look back nostalgically, as it were, to the lost moment of innocence of motive and purity of emotion. If those things had been tarnished or manhandled by the later business of living, they had, at least, existed, and on a grand scale. If they had been tarnished or manhandled, it was not through the fault of the individual who looked back to see the image of the old simple and heroic self in Frederic or Catherine, but through the impersonal grindings of the great machine of the universe. *A Farewell to Arms* served, in a way, as the great romantic alibi for a generation, and for those who aped and emulated that generation. It showed how cynicism or disillusionment, failure of spirit or the worship of material success, debauchery or despair, might have been grounded in heroism, simplicity, and fidelity that had met unmerited defeat. The early tragedy could cast a kind of flattering and extenuating afterglow over what had come later. The battlefields of *A Farewell to Arms* explained the bars of *The Sun Also Rises* —and explained the young Krebs, of the story "Soldier's Home," who came back home to a Middle-Western town to accept his own slow disintegration.

This is not said in disparagement of *A Farewell to Arms.* It is, after all, a compliment to the hypnotic force of the book. For the hypnotic force of the book was felt from the first, and it is not unusual for such a book to be relished by its first readers for superficial reasons and not for the essential virtues that may engage those who come to it later.

In accounting for the immediate appeal of *A Farewell to Arms,* the history of the author himself is of some importance. In so far as the reader knew about Ernest Hemingway in 1929, he knew about a young man who seemed to typify in his own experience the central experience of his generation. Behind the story of *A Farewell to Arms* and his other books there was the shadow of his own story that could stamp his fiction with the authenticity of a document and, for the more impressionable, with the value of a revelation. He could give an ethic and a technique for living, even in the face of defeat or frustration, and yet his own story was the story that we have always loved: the American success story.

He was born in Oak Park, Illinois, in the Middle West, that region that it was fashionable to condemn (after Mencken and Sinclair Lewis) as romanceless, but, with its Main Streets and Winesburg, Ohio's, became endowed, paradoxically enough, with the romance of the American average. His father was a physician. There were two boys and four girls in the family. In the summers the family lived in northern Michigan, where there were Indians, and where lake, streams, and forests gave boyhood pursuits their appropriate setting. In the winters he went to school in Oak Park. He played football in high school, ran away from home, returned and, in 1917, graduated. After graduation he was for a short time a reporter on the *Kansas City Star,* but the war was on and he went to Italy as a volunteer ambulance driver. He was wounded and decorated, and after his recovery served in the Italian army as a soldier. For a time after the war he was a foreign correspondent for the *Toronto Star,* in the Near East.

In the years after the war Hemingway set about learning, quite consciously and with rigorous self-discipline, the craft and art of writing. During most of his apprenticeship he lived in Paris, one of the great number of expatriates who were drawn to the artistic capital of the world to learn to be writers, painters, sculptors, or dancers, or simply to enjoy on a low monetary exchange the freedom of life away from American or British conventions. "Young America," writes Ford Madox Ford, the eminent English novelist and then editor of the *transatlantic review,* "from the limitless prairies leapt, released, on Paris. They stampeded with the madness of colts when you let down the slip-rails between dried pasture and green. The noise of their advancing drowned all sounds. Their innumerable forms hid the very trees on the boulevards. Their perpetual motion made you dizzy." And of Hemingway himself: "He was presented to me by Ezra [1] and Bill Bird and had rather the aspect of an Eton-Oxford, huskyish young captain of a midland regiment of His Britannic Majesty. . . . Into that animated din would drift Hemingway, balancing on the point of his toes, feinting at my head with hands as large as hams and relating sinister stories of Paris landlords. He told them with singularly choice words in a slow voice." [2]

[1] Ezra Pound, the American poet. William Bird published in Paris, in 1924, Hemingway's second book, the original version of *In Our Time.*
[2] Introduction to the Modern Library edition of *A Farewell to Arms.*

The originality and force of Hemingway's early stories, published in little magazines, and in limited editions in France, were recognized from the first by many who made their acquaintance. The seeds of his later work were in those stories of *In Our Time,* concerned chiefly with scenes of inland American life and a boy's growing awareness of that life in contrast to vivid flashes of the disorder and brutality of the war years and the immediate post-war years in Europe. There are both contrast and continuity between the two elements of *In Our Time.* There is the contrast between the lyric rendering of one aspect of the boyhood world and the realistic rendering of the world at war, but there is also a continuity because in the boyhood world there are recurring intimations of the blackness into which experience can lead even in the peaceful setting of Michigan.

With the publication of *The Sun Also Rises,* in 1926, Hemingway's work reached a wider audience, and at the same time defined more clearly the line his genius was to follow and his role as one of the spokesmen for a generation. But *A Farewll to Arms* gave him his first substantial popular success and established his reputation. It was a brilliant and compelling novel; it provided the great alibi; it crowned the success story of the American boy from the Middle West, who had hunted and fished, played football in high school, been a newspaper reporter, gone to war and been wounded and decorated, wandered exotic lands as a foreign correspondent, lived the free life of the Latin Quarter of Paris, and, at the age of thirty, written a best seller—athlete, sportsman, correspondent, soldier, adventurer, and author.

II

It would be possible and even profitable to discuss *A Farewell to Arms* in isolation from Hemingway's other work. But Hemingway is a peculiarly personal writer, and for all the apparent objectivity and self-suppression in his method as a writer, his work forms a continuous whole to an uncommon degree. One part explains and interprets another part. It is true that there have been changes between early and late work, that there has been an increasing self-consciousness, that attitudes and methods that in the beginning were instinctive and simple have become calculated and elaborated. But the best way to understand one of his books is, nevertheless, to compare it with both earlier and later pieces and seek to discern motives and methods that underlie all of his work.

Perhaps the simplest way into the whole question is to consider what kind of world Hemingway writes about. A writer may write about his special world merely because he happens to know that world, but he may also write about that special world because it best dramatizes for him the issues and questions that are his fundamental concerns—because, in other words, that special world has a kind of symbolic significance for him. There is often—if we discount mere literary fashion and imitation—an inner and necessary reason for the writer's choice of his characters and situations. What situations and characters does Hemingway write about?

They are usually violent. There is the hard-drinking and sexually promiscuous world of *The Sun Also Rises;* the chaotic and brutal world of war as in *A Farewell to Arms, For Whom the Bell Tolls,* many of the inserted sketches of *In Our Time,* the play *The Fifth Column,* and some of the stories; the world of sport, as in "Fifty Grand," "My Old Man," "The Undefeated," "The Snows of Kilimanjaro"; the world of crime as in "The Killers," "The Gambler, the Nun, and the Radio," and *To Have and Have Not.* Even when the situation of a story does not fall into one of these categories, it usually involves a desperate risk, and behind it is the shadow of ruin, physical or spiritual. As for the typical characters, they are usually tough men, experienced in the hard worlds they inhabit, and not obviously given to emotional display or sensitive shrinking, men like Rinaldi or Frederic Henry of *A Farewell to Arms,* Robert Jordan of *For Whom the Bell Tolls,* Harry Morgan of *To Have and Have Not,* the big-game hunter of "The Snows of Kilimanjaro," the old bull-fighter of "The Undefeated," or the pugilist of "Fifty Grand." Or if the typical character is not of this seasoned order, he is a very young man, or boy, first entering the violent world and learning his first adjustment to it.

We have said that the shadow of ruin is behind the typical Hemingway situation. The typical character faces defeat or death. But out of defeat or death the character usually manages to salvage something. And here we discover Hemingway's special interest in such situations and such characters. His heroes are not defeated except upon their own terms. They are not squealers, welchers, compromisers, or cowards, and when they confront defeat they realize that the stance they take, the stoic endurance, the stiff upper lip mean a kind of victory. If they are to be defeated they are defeated upon their own terms; some of them have even courted their defeat; and certainly they have maintained, even in the practical defeat, an ideal of themselves, some definition of how a man should behave, formulated or unformulated, by which they have lived. They represent some notion of a code, some notion of honor, that makes a man a man, and that distinguishes him from people who merely follow their random impulses and who are, by consequence, "messy."

In case after case, we can illustrate this "principle of sportsmanship," as one critic has called it,[3] at the center of a story or novel. Robert Jordan, in *For Whom the Bell Tolls,* is somehow happy as he lies, wounded, behind the machine gun that is to cover the escape of his friends and his sweetheart from Franco's Fascists. The old bullfighter, in "The Un-

[3] Edmund Wilson, "Hemingway: Gauge of Morale," in *The Wound and the Bow,* Houghton Mifflin Co.

defeated," continues his incompetent fight even under the jeers and hoots of the crowd until the bull is dead and he himself is mortally hurt. Francis Macomber, the rich young sportsman who goes lion-hunting in "The Short, Happy Life of Francis Macomber," and who has funked it and bolted before a wounded lion, at last learns the lesson that the code of the hunter demands that he go into the bush after an animal he has wounded. Brett, the heroine of *The Sun Also Rises,* gives up Romero, the young bullfighter with whom she is in love, because she knows she will ruin him, and her tight-lipped remark to Jake, the newspaper man who is the narrator of the novel, might almost serve as the motto of Hemingway's work: "You know it makes one feel rather good deciding not to be a bitch." *

It is the discipline of the code that makes man human, a sense of style or good form. This applies not only in isolated, dramatic cases such as those listed above, but is a more pervasive thing that can give meaning, partially at least, to the confusions of living. The discipline of the soldier, the form of the athlete, the gameness of the sportsman, the technique of an artist can give some sense of the human order, and can achieve a moral significance. And here we see how Hemingway's concern with war and sport crosses his concern with literary style. If a writer can get the kind of style at which Hemingway professes, in *Green Hills of Africa,* to aim, then "nothing else matters. It is more important than anything else he can do." It is more important because, ultimately, it is a moral achievement. And no doubt for this reason, as well as for the reason of Henry James's concern with cruxes of a moral code, he is, as he says in *Green Hills of Africa,* an admirer of the work of Henry James, the devoted stylist.

But to return to the subject of Hemingway's world: the code and the discipline are important because they can give meaning to life that otherwise seems to have no meaning or justification. In other words, in a world without supernatural sanctions, in the God-abandoned world of modernity, man can realize an ideal meaning only in so far as he can define and maintain the code. The effort to define and maintain the code, however limited and imperfect it may be, is the characteristically human effort and provides the tragic or pitiful human story. Hemingway's attitude on this point is much like that of Robert Louis Stevenson as Stevenson states it in one of his essays, "Pulvis et Umbra":

* It is possible to take issue with Mr. Warren's interpretation of Brett's statement. One might argue that at this point in the novel the discipline of the code has been destroyed by Cohn's bad behavior and that it is Brett's discovery that the code will no longer serve that causes her to give up Romero. If, in the earlier stages of the novel, Brett has acted in accordance with the code, then the code has dictated that she *should* be a bitch. She has managed to hold herself together by practicing a continuous bitchery. Thus, her statement may be taken as an outburst of astonishment at discovering how pleasant it feels to act for once according to a conventional moral standard. For with the old code destroyed she suddenly finds herself left with no other recourse.

Poor soul, here for so little, cast among so many hardships, filled with desires so incommensurate and so inconsistent, savagely surrounded, savagely descended, irremediably condemned to prey upon his fellow lives: who should have blamed him had he been of a piece with his destiny and a being merely barbarous? And we look and behold him instead, filled with imperfect virtues ... an ideal of decency, to which he would rise if it were possible; a limit of shame, below which, if it be possible, he will not stoop. ... Man is indeed marked for failure in his effort to do right. But where the best consistently miscarry how tenfold more remarkable that all should continue to strive; and surely we should find it both touching and inspiriting, that in a field from which success is banished, our race should not cease to labor. ... It matters not where we look, under what climate we observe him, in what stage of society, in what depth of ignorance, burthened with what erroneous morality; by campfires in Assiniboia, the snow powdering his shoulders, the wind plucking his blanket, as he sits, passing the ceremonial calumet and uttering his grave opinions like a Roman senator; on ships at sea, a man inured to hardship and vile pleasures, his brightest hope a fiddle in a tavern and a bedizened trull who sells herself to rob him, and he for all that, simple, innocent, cheerful, kindly like a child, constant to toil, brave to drown, for others; ... in the brothel, the discard of society, living mainly on strong drink, fed with affronts, a fool, a thief, the comrade of thieves, and even here keeping the point of honor and the touch of pity, often repaying the world's scorn with service, often standing firm upon a scruple, and at a certain cost, rejecting riches:—everywhere some virtue cherished or affected, everywhere some decency of thought or carriage, everywhere the ensign of man's ineffectual goodness! ... under every circumstance of failure, without hope, without help, without thanks, still obscurely fighting the lost fight of virtue, still clinging, in the brothel or on the scaffold, to some rag of honor, the poor jewel of their souls! They may seek to escape, and yet they cannot; it is not alone their privilege and glory, but their doom; they are condemned to some nobility. ...

Hemingway's code is more rigorous than Stevenson's and perhaps he finds fewer devoted to it, but like Stevenson he can find his characteristic hero and characteristic story among the discards of society, and like Stevenson is aware of the touching irony of that fact. But for the moment the important thing in the parallel is that, for Stevenson, the world in which this drama of pitiful aspiration and stoic endurance is played out, is apparently a violent and meaningless world—"our rotary island loaded with predatory life and more drenched with blood ... than ever mutinied ship, scuds through space."

Neither Hemingway nor Stevenson invented this world. It had already appeared in literature before their time, and that is a way of saying that this cheerless vision had already begun to trouble men. It is the world we find pictured (and denied) in Tennyson's "In Memoriam"—the world in which human conduct is a product of "dying Nature's earth and

lime." It is the world pictured (and not denied) in Hardy and Housman, a world that seems to be presided over by blind Doomsters (if by
anybody), as Hardy put it in his poem "Hap," or made by some brute
and blackguard (if by anybody), as Housman put it in his poem "The
Chestnut Casts Its Flambeaux." It is the world of Zola or Dreiser or
Conrad or Faulkner. It is the world of, to use Bertrand Russell's phrase,
"secular hurryings through space." It is the God-abandoned world, the
world of Nature-as-all. We know where the literary men got this picture.
They got it from the scientists of the nineteenth century. This is Hemingway's world, too, the world with nothing at center.

Over against this particular version of the naturalistic view of the
world, there was, of course, an argument for Divine Intelligence and a
Divine purpose, an argument that based itself on the beautiful system
of nature, on natural law. The closely knit order of the natural world,
so the argument ran, implies a Divine Intelligence. But if one calls
Hemingway's attention to the fact that the natural world is a world of
order, his reply is on record in a story called "A Natural History of the
Dead." There he quotes from the traveller Mungo Park, who, naked
and starving in an African desert, observed a beautiful little moss-flower
and meditated thus:

> Can the Being who planted, watered, and brought to perfection, in
> this obscure part of the world, a thing which appears of so small im-
> portance, look with unconcern upon the situation and suffering of
> creatures formed after his own image? Surely not. Reflections like these
> would not allow me to despair: I started up and, disregarding both
> hunger and fatigue, travelled forward, assured that relief was at hand;
> and I was not disappointed.

And Hemingway continues:

> With a disposition to wonder and adore in like manner, as Bishop
> Stanley says [the author of *A Familiar History of Birds*], can any branch
> of Natural History be studied without increasing that faith, love and
> hope which we also, everyone of us, need in our journey through the
> wilderness of life? Let us therefore see what inspiration we may derive
> from the dead.

Then Hemingway presents the picture of a modern battlefield, where
the bloated and decaying bodies give a perfect example of the natural
order of chemistry—but scarcely an argument for faith, hope, and love.
That picture is his answer to the argument that the order of nature
implies meaning in the world.

In one of the stories, "A Clean, Well-Lighted Place," we find the best
description of this world that underlies Hemingway's world of violent
action. In the early stages of the story we see an old man sitting late in
a Spanish café. Two waiters are speaking of him.

"Last week he tried to commit suicide," one waiter said.
"Why?"
"He was in despair."
"What about?"
"Nothing."
"How do you know it was nothing?"
"He has plenty of money."

The despair beyond plenty of money—or beyond all the other gifts of the world: its nature becomes a little clearer at the end of the story when the older of the two waiters is left alone, reluctant too to leave the clean, well-lighted place:

> Turning off the electric light he continued the conversation with himself. It is the light of course but it is necessary that the place be clean and pleasant. You do not want music. Certainly you do not want music. Nor can you stand before a bar with dignity although that is all that is provided for these hours. What did he fear? It was not fear or dread. It was a nothing that he knew too well. It was all a nothing and a man was nothing too. It was only that and light was all it needed and a certain cleanness and order. Some lived in it and never felt it but he knew it all was nada y pues nada y nada y pues nada.[4] Our nada who art in nada, nada be thy name thy kingdom nada thy will be nada in nada as it is in nada. Give us this nada our daily nada and nada us our nada as we nada our nadas and nada us not into nada but deliver us from nada; pues nada. Hail nothing full of nothing, nothing is with thee. He smiled and stood before a bar with a shining steam pressure coffee machine.
> "What's yours?" asked the barman.
> "Nada."

At the end the old waiter is ready to go home:

> Now, without thinking further, he would go home to his room. He would lie in bed and finally, with daylight, he would go to sleep. After all, he said to himself, it is probably only insomnia. Many must have it.

And the sleepless man—the man obsessed by death, by the meaninglessness of the world, by nothingness, by nada—is one of the recurring symbols in the work of Hemingway. In this phase Hemingway is a religious writer. The despair beyond plenty of money, the despair that makes a sleeplessness beyond insomnia, is the despair felt by a man who hungers for the sense of order and assurance that men seem to find in religious faith, but who cannot find grounds for his faith.

Another recurring symbol, we have said, is the violent man. But the sleepless man and the violent man are not contradictory but complementary symbols. They represent phases of the same question, the same hungering for meaning in the world. The sleepless man is the man brooding upon nada, upon chaos, upon Nature-as-all. (For Nature-as-all equals

4 nada y pues nada, etc.: nothing and after that nothing, etc.

moral chaos; even its bulls and lions and kudu are not admired by Hemingway as creatures of conscious self-discipline; their courage has a meaning only in so far as it symbolizes human courage.) The violent man is the man taking an action appropriate to the realization of the fact of nada. He is, in other words, engaged in the effort to discover human values in a naturalistic world.

Before we proceed with this line of discussion, it might be asked, "Why does Hemingway feel that the quest necessarily involves violence?" Now, at one level, the answer to this question would involve the whole matter of the bias toward violence in modern literature. But let us take it in its more immediate reference. The typical Hemingway hero is the man aware, or in the process of becoming aware, of nada. Death is the great nada. Therefore whatever code or creed the hero gets must, to be good, stick even in the face of death. It has to be good in the bull-ring or on the battlefield and not merely in the study or lecture room. In fact, Hemingway is anti-intellectual, and has a great contempt for any type of solution arrived at without the testings of immediate experience.

So aside from the question of a dramatic sense that would favor violence, and aside from the mere matter of personal temperament (for Hemingway describes himself on more than one occasion as obsessed by death), the presentation of violence is appropriate in his work because death is the great nada. In taking violent risks man confronts in dramatic terms the issue of nada that is implicit in all of Hemingway's world.

But to return to our general line of discussion. There are two aspects to this violence that is involved in the quest of the Hemingway hero, two aspects that seem to represent an ambivalent attitude toward nature.

First, there is the conscious sinking into nature, as we may call it. On this line of reasoning we would find something like this: if there is at center only nada, then the only sure compensation in life, the only reality, is gratification of appetite, the relish of sensation.

Continually in the stories and novels one finds such sentences as this from *Green Hills of Africa:* "... drinking this, the first one of the day, the finest one there is, and looking at the thick bush we passed in the dark, feeling the cool wind of the night and smelling the good smell of Africa, I was altogether happy." What is constantly interesting in such sentences is the fact that happiness, a notion that we traditionally connect with a complicated state of being, with notions of virtue, of achievement, etc., is here equated with a set of merely agreeable sensations. For instance, in "Cross-Country Snow," one of the boys, George, says to the other, Nick, who in story after story is a sort of shadow of Hemingway himself, "Maybe we'll never go skiing again, Nick." And Nick replies, "We've got to. It isn't worth while if you can't." The sensations of skiing are the end of life. Or in another story, "Big Two-Hearted River: Part II," a story that is full of the sensation-as-happiness theme, we find this remark about Nick, who has been wading in a trout stream: "Nick climbed out onto the meadow and stood, water running down his trousers and out of his shoes, his shoes squelchy. He went over and sat on the logs. He did not want to rush his sensations any." The careful relish of sensation—that is what counts, always.

This intense awareness of the world of the senses is, of course, one of the things that made the early work of Hemingway seem, upon its first impact, so fresh and pure. Physical nature is nowhere rendered with greater vividness than in his work, and probably his only competitors in this department of literature are William Faulkner, among the modern, and Henry David Thoreau, among the older American writers. The meadows, forests, lakes, and trout streams of America, and the arid, sculpturesque mountains of Spain, appear with astonishing immediacy, an immediacy not dependent upon descriptive flourishes. But not only the appearance of landscape is important; a great deal of the freshness comes from the discrimination of sensation, the coldness of water in the "squelchy" shoes after wading, the tangy smell of dry sagebrush, the "cleanly" smell of grease and oil on a field piece.[5] Hemingway's appreciation of the aesthetic qualities of the physical world is important, but a peculiar poignancy is implicit in the rendering of those qualities; the beauty of the physical world is a background for the human predicament, and the very relishing of the beauty is merely a kind of desperate and momentary compensation possible in the midst of the predicament.

This careful relishing of the world of the senses comes to a climax in drinking and sex. Drink is the "giant-killer," the weapon against man's thought of nada. And so is sex, for that matter, though when sexual attraction achieves the status of love, the process is one that attempts to achieve a meaning rather than to forget meaninglessness in the world. In terms of drinking and sex, the typical Hemingway hero is a man of monel-metal stomach and Homeric prowess in the arts of love. And the typical situation is love, with some drinking, against the background of nada—of civilization gone to pot, or war, or death—as we get it in all of the novels in one form or another, and in many of the stories.

It is important to remember, however, that the sinking into nature, even at the level of drinking and mere sexuality, is a self-conscious act. It is not the random gratification of appetite. We see this quite clearly in *The Sun Also Rises* in the contrast between Cohn, who is merely a random dabbler in the world of sensation, who is merely trying to amuse himself, and the initiates like Jake and Brett, who are aware of the nada at the center of things and whose dissipations, therefore, have a philosophical significance. The initiate in Hemingway's world raises the gratification of appetite to the level of a cult and a discipline.

5 Commented on by Ford Madox Ford in his introduction to the Modern Library edition of *A Farewell to Arms*.

The cult of sensation, as we have already indicated, passes over very readily into the cult of true love, for the typical love story is presented primarily in terms of the cult of sensation. (*A Farewell to Arms,* as we shall see when we come to a detailed study of that novel, is closely concerned with this transition.) Even in the cult of true love it is the moment that counts, and the individual. There is never any past or future to the love stories and the lovers are always isolated, not moving in an ordinary human society within its framework of obligations. The notion of the cult—a secret cult composed of those who have been initiated into the secret of nada—is constantly played up. In *A Farewell to Arms,* for instance, Catherine and Frederic are, quite consciously, two against the world, a world that is, literally as well as figuratively, an alien world. The peculiar relationship between Frederic and the priest takes on a new significance if viewed in terms of the secret cult. We shall come to this topic later, but for the moment we can say that the priest is a priest of Divine Love, the subject about which he and Frederic converse in the hospital, and that Frederic himself is a kind of priest, one of the initiate in the end, of the cult of profane love. This same pattern of two against the world with an understanding confidante or interpreter, reappears in *For Whom the Bell Tolls*—with Pilar, the gipsy woman who understands "love," substituting for the priest of *A Farewell to Arms.*

The initiates of the cult of love are those who are aware of nada, but their effort, as members of the cult, is to find a meaning to put in place of the nada. That is, there is an attempt to make the relationship of love take on a religious significance in so far as it can give meaning to life. This general topic is not new with the work of Hemingway. It is one of the literary themes of the nineteenth century—and has, as a matter of fact, a longer history than that.

If the cult of love arises from and states itself in the language of the cult of sensation, it is an extension of the sinking-into-nature aspect of the typical Hemingway violence; but in so far as it involves a discipline and a search for a "faith," it leads us to the second aspect of the typical violence.

The violence, although in its first aspect it represents a sinking into nature, at the same time, in its second aspect, represents a conquest of nature, and of nada in man. It represents such a conquest, not because of the fact of violence, but because the violence appears in terms of a discipline, a style, and a code. It is, as we have already seen, in terms of a self-imposed discipline that the heroes make one gallant, though limited, effort to redeem the incoherence of the world: they attempt to impose some form upon the disorder of their lives, the technique of the bullfighter or sportsman, the discipline of the soldier, the fidelity of the lover, or even the code of the gangster, which, though brutal and apparently dehumanizing, has its own ethic. (Ole Anderson, in "The Killers," is willing to take his medicine without whining, and even recognizes some necessity and justice in his plight. Or the dying Mexican, in "The Gambler, the Nun, and the Radio," refuses to squeal despite the detective's argument: "One can, with honor, denounce one's assailant.")

If it is said that Frederic in *A Farewell to Arms* does not, when he deserts, exhibit the discipline of the soldier, the answer is simple: his obligation has been constantly presented as an obligation to the men in his immediate command, and he and the men in his command have never recognized an obligation to the total war—they recognize no meaning in the war and are bound together only by a squad sense and by their immediate respect for one another; when Frederic is separated from his men his obligation is gone. His true obligation then becomes the fidelity to Catherine.

The discipline, the form, is never quite capable of subduing the world, but fidelity to it is part of the gallantry of defeat. By fidelity to it the hero manages to keep one small place "clean" and "well-lighted," and manages to retain, or achieve for one last moment, his dignity. As the old Spanish waiter muses, there should be a "clean, well-lighted place" where one could keep one's dignity at the late hour.

We have said earlier that the typical Hemingway character is tough and, apparently, insensitive. But only apparently, for the fidelity to a code, to the discipline, may be the index to a sensitivity that allows the characters to see, at moments, their true plight. At times, and usually at times of stress, it is the tough man in the Hemingway world, the disciplined man, who is actually aware of pathos or tragedy. The individual toughness (which may be taken to be the private discipline demanded by the world) may find itself in conflict with the natural human reaction; but the Hemingway hero, though he may be aware of the claims of the natural reaction, the spontaneous human emotion, cannot surrender to it because he knows that the only way to hold on to the definition of himself, to "honor" or "dignity," is to maintain the discipline, the code. For example, when pity appears in the Hemingway world—as in "The Pursuit Race"—it does not appear in its maximum but in its minimum manifestation.

What this means in terms of style and method is the use of understatement. This understatement, stemming from the contrast between the sensitivity and the superimposed discipline, is a constant aspect of the work, an aspect that was caught in a cartoon in the *New Yorker*. The cartoon showed a brawny, muscle-knotted forearm and a hairy hand that clutched a rose. It was entitled "The Soul of Ernest Hemingway." Just as there is a margin of victory in the defeat of the Hemingway characters, so there is a little margin of sensitivity in their brutal and apparently insensitive world. Hence we have the ironical circumstance—a central circumstance in creating the pervasive irony of Hemingway's work—that the revelation of the values characteristic of his work arises from the most unpromising people and the most unpromising situations —the little streak of poetry or pathos in "The Pursuit Race," "The Killers," "My Old Man," "A Clean, Well-Lighted Place," or "The Undefeated." We have a perfect example of it in the last-named story. After the defeat of the old bullfighter, who is lying wounded on an operating table, Zurito, the picador, is about to cut off the old fellow's pigtail, the mark of his profession. But when the wounded man starts up, despite his pain, and says, "You couldn't do a thing like that," Zurito says, "I was joking." Zurito becomes aware that, after all, the old bullfighter is, in a way, undefeated, and deserves to die with his coleta on.

This locating of the poetic, the pathetic, or the tragic in the unpromising person or situation is not unique with Hemingway. It is something with which we are acquainted in a great deal of our literature since the Romantic Movement. The sensibility is played down, and an anti-romantic surface sheathes the work; the point is in the contrast. The impulse that led Hemingway to the simple character is akin to the one that drew Wordsworth to the same choice. Wordsworth felt that his unsophisticated peasants were more honest in their responses than the cultivated man, and were therefore more poetic. Instead of Wordsworth's peasant we have in Hemingway's work the bullfighter, the soldier, the revolutionist, the sportsman, and the gangster; instead of Wordsworth's children we have the young men like Nick, the person just on the verge of being initiated into the world. There are, of course, differences between the approach of Wordsworth and that of Hemingway, but there is little difference on the point of marginal sensibility. In one sense, both are anti-intellectual, and in such poems as "Resolution and Independence" or "Michael" one finds even closer ties.

I have just indicated a similarity between Wordsworth and Hemingway on the grounds of a romantic anti-intellectualism. But with Hemingway it is far more profound and radical than with Wordsworth. All we have to do to see the difference is to put Wordsworth's Preface to the *Lyrical Ballads* over against any number of passages from Hemingway. The intellectualism of the eighteenth century had merely put a veil of stereotyped language over the world and a veil of snobbism over a large area of human experience. That is Wordsworth's indictment. But Hemingway's indictment of the intellectualism of the past is that it wound up in the mire and blood of 1914 to 1918; that it was a pack of lies leading to death. We can put over against the Preface of Wordsworth, a passage from *A Farewell to Arms:*

> I was always embarrassed by the words sacred, glorious, and sacrifice and the expression in vain. We had heard them, sometimes standing in the rain almost out of earshot, so that only the shouted words came through, and had read them, on proclamations that were slapped up by billposters over other proclamations, now for a long time, and I had seen nothing sacred, and the things that were glorious had no glory and the

sacrifices were like the stockyards at Chicago if nothing was done with
the meat except to bury it. There were many words that you could not
stand to hear and finally only the names of places had dignity....
Abstract words such as glory, honor, courage, or hallow were obscene
beside the concrete names of villages, the numbers of roads, the names
of rivers, the numbers of regiments and the dates.

I do not mean to say that the general revolution in style, and the revolt
against the particular intellectualism of the nineteenth century was a
result of the first world war. As a matter of fact, that revolt was going
on long before the war, but for Hemingway, and for many others, the
war gave the situation a peculiar depth and urgency.

Perhaps we might scale the matter thus: Wordsworth was a revolutionist—he truly had a new view of the world—but his revolutionary
view left great tracts of the world untouched; the Church of England,
for instance. Arnold and Tennyson, a generation or so later, though not
revolutionists themselves, are much more profoundly stirred by the revolutionary situation than ever Wordsworth was; that is, the area of the
world involved in the debate was for them greater. Institutions are called
into question in a more fundamental way. But they managed to hang
on to their English God and their English institutions. With Hardy, the
area of disturbance has grown greater, and what can be salvaged is much
less. He, like the earlier Victorians, had a strong sense of community to
sustain him in the face of the universe that was for him, as not finally
for Arnold and Tennyson, unfriendly, or at least neutral and Godless.
But his community underlay institutions. It was a human communion
that, as a matter of fact, was constantly being violated by institutions.
Their violation of it is, in fact, a constant source of subject matter and
a constant spring of irony. Nevertheless Hardy could refer to himself as
a meliorist. He could not keep company with Wordsworth or Tennyson
or Arnold; and when Hardy, having been elected an Honorary Fellow
of Magdalene College, Cambridge, was to be formally admitted, the
Master, Doctor Donaldson (as we know from A. C. Benson's *Diary*)
was much afraid that Hardy might dislike the religious service. The occasion, however, went off very well, even though Hardy, after impressing
the Master with his knowledge of ecclesiastical music, did remark, "Of
course it's only a sentiment to me now." Hardy listened to a sermon by
the Archdeacon of Zanzibar, who declared that God was "a God of
desire—who both hated and loved—not a mild or impersonal force." But
even though Hardy could not accept the God of the Bishop of Zanzibar,
he still had faith in the constructive power of the secret community.

Now in Hemingway we see something very like Hardy's secret community, but one much smaller, one whose definition has become much
more specialized. Its members are those who know the code. They recognize each other, they know the password and the secret grip, but they are
few in number, and each is set off against the world like a wounded lion

ringed round by waiting hyenas (*Green Hills of Africa* gives us the hyena symbol—the animal whose death is comic because it is all hideously "appetite": wounded, it eats its own intestines). Furthermore, this secret community is not constructive; Hemingway is no meliorist. In fact, there are hints that somewhere in the back of his mind, and in behind his work, there is a kind of Spenglerian view of history: our civilization is running down. We get this most explicitly in *Green Hills of Africa:*

> A continent ages quickly once we come. The natives live in harmony with it. But the foreigner destroys, cuts down the trees, drains the water, so that the water supply is altered and in a short time the soil, once the sod is turned under, is cropped out and, next, it starts to blow away as it has blown away in every old country and as I had seen it start to blow in Canada. The earth gets tired of being exploited. A country wears out quickly unless man puts back in it all his residue and that of all his beasts. When he quits using beasts and uses machines, the earth defeats him quickly. The machine can't reproduce, nor does it fertilize the soil, and it eats what he cannot raise. A country was made to be as we found it. We are the intruders and after we are dead we may have ruined it but it will still be there and we don't know what the next changes are. I suppose they all end up like Mongolia.
>
> I would come back to Africa but not to make a living from it. . . . But I would come back to where it pleased me to live; to really live. Not just let my life pass. Our people went to America because that was the place for them to go then. It had been a good country and we had made a bloody mess of it and I would go, now, somewhere else as we had always had the right to go somewhere else and as we had always gone. You could always come back. Let the others come to America who did not know that they had come too late. Our people had seen it at its best and fought for it when it was well worth fighting for. Now I would go somewhere else.

This is the most explicit statement, but the view is implicit in case after case. The general human community, the general human project, has gone to pot. There is only the little secret community of, paradoxically enough, individualists who have resigned from the general community, and who are strong enough to live without any of the illusions, lies, and big words of the herd. At least, this is the case up to the novel *To Have and Have Not,* which appeared in 1937. In that novel and in *For Whom the Bell Tolls* Hemingway attempts to bring his individualistic hero back to society, to give him a common stake with the fate of other men.

But to return to the matter of Wordsworth and Hemingway. What in Wordsworth is merely simple or innocent is in Hemingway violent: the gangster or bullfighter replaces the leech-gatherer or the child. Hemingway's world is a more disordered world, and the sensibility of his characters is more ironically in contrast with their world. The most immediate consideration here is the playing down of the sensibility as such, the sheathing of it in the code of toughness. Gertrude Stein's tribute is here relevant: "Hemingway is the shyest and proudest and sweetest-smelling storyteller of my reading." But this shyness manifests itself in the irony. In this, of course, Hemingway's irony corresponds to the Byronic irony. But the relation to Byron is even more fundamental. The pity is only valid when it is wrung from the man who has been seasoned by experience. Therefore a premium is placed on the fact of violent experience. The "dumb ox" character, commented on by Wyndham Lewis,[6] represents the Wordsworthian peasant; the character with the code of the tough guy, the initiate, the man cultivating honor, gallantry, and recklessness, represents the Byronic aristocrat.

The failures of Hemingway, like his successes, are rooted in this situation. The successes occur in those instances where Hemingway accepts the essential limitations of his premises, that is, when there is an equilibrium between the dramatization and the characteristic Hemingway "point," when the system of ironies and understatements is coherent. On the other hand, the failures occur when we feel that Hemingway has not respected the limitations of his premises; that is, when the dramatization seems to be "rigged" and the violence, therefore, merely theatrical. The characteristic irony, or understatement, in such cases, seems to be too self-conscious. For example, let us glance at Hemingway's most spectacular failure, *To Have and Have Not*. The point of the novel is based on the contrast between the smuggler and the rich owners of the yachts along the quay. But the irony is essentially an irony without any center of reference. It is superficial, for, as a critic in the *Partisan Review* [7] indicated, the only difference between the smuggler and the rich is that the rich were successful in their buccaneering. The revelation that comes to the smuggler dying in his launch—"a man alone ain't got no . . . chance" —is a meaningless revelation, for it has no reference to the actual dramatization. It is, finally, a failure in intellectual analysis of the situation.

There is, I believe, a good chance that *For Whom the Bell Tolls* will turn out to be not Hemingway's best novel—an honor I should reserve for *A Farewell to Arms*—primarily because in this most ambitious of the novels Hemingway does not accept the limitations of his premises. I do not mean to imply that it is on a level with *To Have and Have Not*. There is a subtler irony in the later novel. I have pointed out that the irony in *To Have and Have Not* is that of the contrast between the smuggler and the rich in the yachts along the pier; that is, it is a simple irony, in direct line with the ostensible surface direction of the story. But the irony in *For Whom the Bell Tolls* runs counter to the ostensible surface direction of the story. As surface, we have a conflict between the forces of light and the forces of darkness, freedom versus fascism, etc.

[6] "The Dumb Ox, A Study of Ernest Hemingway," *American Review*, June, 1934.
[7] "The Social Muse and the Great Kudu," by Philip Rahv, *Partisan Review*, December, 1937.

Hero and heroine are clearly and completely and romantically aligned on the side of light. We are prepared to see the fascist atrocities and the general human kindness of the Loyalists. It happens to work out the other way. The scene of horror is the massacre by the Loyalists, not by the Fascists. Again, in the attack on El Sordo's hill by the Fascists, we are introduced to a young Fascist lieutenant, whose bosom friend is killed in the attack. We are suddenly given this little human glimpse— against the grain of the surface. But this incident, we discover later, is preparation for the very end of the novel. We leave the hero lying wounded, preparing to cover the retreat of his friends. The man who is over the sights of the machine gun as the book ends is the Fascist lieutenant, whom we have been made to know as a man not as a monster. This general ironical conditioning of the overt story line is reflected also in the attitude of Anselmo, who kills but cannot believe in killing. In other words, the irony here is much more functional, and more complicated, than that of the other novel mentioned; the irony affirms that the human values may transcend the party lines.

Much has been said to the effect that *To Have and Have Not* and *For Whom the Bell Tolls* represent a basic change of point of view, an enlargement of what I have called the secret community. Now no doubt that is the intention behind both books, but the temper of both books, the good one and the bad one, is the old temper, the cast of characters is the old cast, and the assumptions lying far below the explicit intention are the old assumptions.

The monotony and self-imitation, into which Hemingway's work sometimes falls, are again effects of a failure in dramatization. Hemingway, apparently, can dramatize his "point" in only one basic situation and with only one set of characters. He has, as we have seen, only two key characters, with certain variations from them by way of contrast or counterpoint. His best women characters, by the way, are those who most nearly approximate the men; that is, they embody the masculine virtues and point of view characteristic of Hemingway's work.

But the monotony is not merely a monotony deriving from the characters as types; it derives, rather, from the limitations of the author's sensibility, which seems to come alive in only one issue. A more flexible sensibility, one capable of making nicer discriminations, might discover great variety in such key characters and situations. But Hemingway's successes are due, in part at least, to the close coordination that he sometimes achieves between the character and situation, on the one hand, and the sensibility as it reflects itself in the style, on the other hand.

The style characteristically is simple, even to the point of monotony. The characteristic sentence is simple, or compound; and if compound, there is no implied subtlety in the coordination of the clauses. The paragraph structure is, characteristically, based on simple sequence. There is an obvious relation between this style and the characters and situations with which the author is concerned—a relation of dramatic decorum. (There are, on the other hand, examples, especially in the novels, of other, more fluent, lyrical effects, but even here this fluency is founded on the conjunction *and;* it is a rhythmical and not a logical fluency. And the lyrical quality is simply a manifestation of that marginal sensibility, as can be demonstrated by an analysis of the occasions on which it appears.)

But there is a more fundamental aspect of the question, an aspect that involves not the sensibility of the characters but the sensibility of the author. The short, simple rhythms, the succession of coordinate clauses, the general lack of subordination—all suggest a dislocated and ununified world. The figures who live in this world live a sort of hand-to-mouth existence perceptually, and conceptually they hardly live at all. Subordination implies some exercise of discrimination—the sifting of reality through the intellect. But in Hemingway we see a Romantic anti-intellectualism.

In Wordsworth, too, we see this strain of anti-intellectualism. He too wishes to clear away the distorting sophistications of the intellect, and to keep his eye on the object. The formulations of the intellect create the "veil of familiarity" that he would clear away. His mode, too, was to take unpromising material and reveal in it the lyric potentiality. He, too, was interested in the margin of sensibility. He, too, wished to respect the facts, and could have understood Hemingway's rejection of the big abstract words in favor of "the concrete names of villages, the numbers of roads, the names of rivers, the numbers of regiments and the dates."

The passage from *A Farewell to Arms* from which the above quotation comes is, of course, the passage most commonly used to explain the attitude behind Hemingway's style. But we can put with it other passages of a similar import, and best of all a sentence from the story "Soldier's Home." Krebs, the boy who has been through the war and who comes back home to find himself cut off from life, had "acquired the nausea in regard to experience that is the result of untruth or exaggeration." He is a casualty, not of bullet or bayonet, but of the big, abstract words. Hemingway's style is, in a way, an attempt to provide an antidote for that "nausea."

III

A Farewell to Arms is a love story. It is a compelling story at the merely personal level, but it is much more compelling and significant when we see the figures of the lovers silhouetted against the flame-streaked blackness of war, of a collapsing world, of nada. For there is a story behind the love story. That story is the quest for meaning and certitude in a world that seems to offer nothing of the sort. It is, in a sense, a religious book; if it does not offer a religious solution it is nevertheless conditioned by the religious problem.

The very first scene of the book, though seemingly casual, is important if we are to understand the deeper motivations of the story. It is the scene at the officers' mess where the captain baits the priest. "Priest every night five against one," the captain explains to Frederic. But Frederic, we see in this and later scenes, takes no part in the baiting. There is a bond between him and the priest, a bond that they both recognize. This becomes clear when, after the officers have advised Frederic where he should go on his leave to find the best girls, the priest turns to him and says that he would like to have him to go to Abruzzi, his own province:

> "There is good hunting. You would like the people and though it is cold it is clear and dry. You could stay with my family. My father is a famous hunter."
> "Come on," said the captain. "We go whorehouse before it shuts."
> "Goodnight," I said to the priest.
> "Goodnight," he said.

In this preliminary contrast between the officers, who invite the hero to go to the brothel, and the priest, who invites him to go to the cold, clear, dry country, we have in its simplest form the issue of the novel.

Frederic does go with the officers that night, and on his leave he does go to the cities, "to the smoke of cafés and nights when the room whirled and you needed to look at the wall to make it stop, nights in bed, drunk, when you knew that that was all there was, and the strange excitement of waking and not knowing who it was with you, and the world all unreal in the dark and so exciting that you must resume again unknowing and not caring in the night, sure that this was all and all and all and not caring." Frederic, at the opening of the novel, lives in the world of random and meaningless appetite, knowing that it is all and all and all, or thinking that he knows that. But behind that there is a dissatisfaction and disgust. Upon his return from his leave, sitting in the officers' mess, he tries to tell the priest how he is sorry that he had not gone to the clear, cold, dry country—the priest's home, which takes on the shadowy symbolic significance of another kind of life, another view of the world. The priest had always known that other country.

> He had always known what I did not know and what, when I learned it, I was always able to forget. But I did not know that then, although I learned it later.

What Frederic learns later is the story behind the love story of the book.

But this theme is not merely stated at the opening of the novel and then absorbed into the action. It appears later, at crucial points, to de-

fine the line of meaning in the action. When, for example, Frederic is
wounded, the priest visits him in the hospital. Their conversation makes
even plainer the religious background of the novel. The priest has said
that he would like to go back after the war to Abruzzi. He continues:

> "It does not matter. But there in my country it is understood that a
> man may love God. It is not a dirty joke."
> "I understand."
> He looked at me and smiled.
> "You understand but you do not love God."
> "No."
> "You do not love Him at all?" he asked.
> "I am afraid of him in the night sometimes."
> "You should love Him."
> "I don't love much."
> "Yes," he said. "You do. What you tell me about in the nights. That
> is not love. That is only passion and lust. When you love you wish to do
> things for. You wish to sacrifice for. You wish to serve."
> "I don't love."
> "You will. I know you will. Then you will be happy."

We have here two important items. First, there is the definition of
Frederic as the sleepless man, the man haunted by nada. Second, at
this stage in the novel, the end of Book I, the true meaning of the love
story with Catherine has not yet been defined. It is still at the level of
appetite. The priest's role is to indicate the next stage of the story, the
discovery of the true nature of love, the "wish to do things for." And
he accomplishes this by indicating a parallel between secular love and
Divine love, a parallel which implies Frederic's quest for meaning and
certitude. And to emphasize further this idea, Frederic, after the priest
leaves, muses on the high, clean country of Abruzzi, the priest's home
that has already been endowed with the symbolic significance of the religious view of the world.

In the middle of Book II (Chapter xviii), in which the love story begins to take on the significance that the priest had predicted, the point
is indicated by a bit of dialogue between the lovers.

> "Couldn't we be married privately some way? Then if anything hap-
> pened to me or if you had a child."
> "There's no way to be married except by church or state. We are
> married privately. You see, darling, it would mean everything to me if I
> had any religion. But I haven't any religion."
> "You gave me the Saint Anthony."
> "That was for luck. Some one gave it to me."
> "Then nothing worries you?"
> "Only being sent away from you. You're my religion. You're all I've
> got."

Again, toward the end of Book IV (chapter xxxv), just before Frederic and Catherine make their escape into Switzerland, Frederic is talking with a friend, the old Count Greffi, who has just said that he thought H. G. Wells's novel *Mr. Britling Sees It Through* a very good study of the English middle-class soul. But Frederic twists the word *soul* into another meaning.

> "I don't know about the soul."
> "Poor boy. We none of us know about the soul. Are you *Croyant?*"
> "At night."

Later in the same conversation the Count returns to the topic:

> "And if you ever become devout pray for me if I am dead. I am ask-ing several of my friends to do that. I had expected to become devout myself but it has not come." I thought he smiled sadly but I could not tell. He was so old and his face was very wrinkled, so that a smile used so many lines that all gradations were lost.
> "I might become very devout," I said. "Anyway, I will pray for you."
> "I had always expected to become devout. All my family died very devout. But somehow it does not come."
> "It's too early."
> "Maybe it is too late. Perhaps I have outlived my religious feeling."
> "My own comes only at night."
> "Then too you are in love. Do not forget that is a religious feeling."

So here we find, again, Frederic defined as the sleepless man, and the relation established between secular love and Divine love.

In the end, with the death of Catherine, Frederic discovers that the attempt to find a substitute for universal meaning in the limited mean-ing of the personal relationship is doomed to failure. It is doomed be-cause it is liable to all the accidents of a world in which human beings are like the ants running back and forth on a log burning in a campfire and in which death is, as Catherine says just before her own death, "just a dirty trick." But this is not to deny the value of the effort, or to deny the value of the discipline, the code, the stoic endurance, the things that make it true—or half true—that "nothing ever happens to the brave."

The question of the characteristic discipline takes us back to the be-ginning of the book, and to the context from which Frederic's effort arises. We have already mentioned the contrast between the officers of the mess and the priest. It is a contrast based on the man who is aware of the issue of meaning in life and those who are unaware of it, who give themselves over to the mere flow of accident, the contrast between the disciplined and the undisciplined. But the contrast is not merely be-tween the priest and the officers. Frederic's friend, the surgeon Rinaldi, is another who is on the same "side" of the contrast as the priest. He may go to the brothel with his brother officers, he may even bait the priest a little, but his personal relationship with Frederic indicates his affiliations; he is one of the initiate. Furthermore, he has the discipline of his profession, and, as we have seen, in the Hemingway world, the discipline that seems to be merely technical, the style of the artist or the form of the athlete or bullfighter, may be an index to a moral value. "Already," Rinaldi says, "I am only happy when I am working." (Already the seeking of pleasure in sensation is inadequate for Rinaldi.) This point appears more sharply in the remarks about the doctor who first attends to Frederic's wounded leg. He is incompetent and does not wish to take the responsibility for a decision.

> Before he came back three doctors came into the room. I have noticed that doctors who fail in the practice of medicine have a tendency to seek one another's company and aid in consultation. A doctor who cannot take out your appendix properly will recommend to you a doctor who will be unable to remove your tonsils with success. These were three such doctors.

In contrast with them there is Doctor Valentini, who is competent, who is willing to take responsibility, and who, as a kind of mark of his role, speaks the same lingo, with the same bantering, ironical tone, as Rinaldi —the tone that is the mark of the initiate.

So we have the world of the novel divided into two groups, the initiate and the uninitiate, the aware and the unaware, the disciplined and the undisciplined. In the first group are Frederic, Catherine, Rinaldi, Valentini, Count Greffi, the old man who cut the paper silhouettes "for pleasure," and Passini, Manera, and the other ambulance men in Frederic's command. In the second group are the officers of the mess, the incompetent doctors, the "legitimate hero" Ettore, and the "patriots"— all the people who do not know what is really at stake, who are deluded by the big words, who do not have the discipline. They are the messy people, the people who surrender to the flow and illusion of things. It is this second group who provide the context of the novel, and more especially the context from which Frederic moves toward his final complete awareness.

The final awareness means, as we have said, that the individual is thrown back upon his private discipline and his private capacity to endure. The hero cuts himself off from the herd, the confused world, which symbolically appears as the routed army at Caporetto. And, as Malcolm Cowley has pointed out,[8] the plunge into the flooded Tagliamento,

---

[8] Introduction to the *Portable Hemingway*, The Viking Press. In this general connection one may consider the strategic advantage that Hemingway has in that it is the Italian army from which his hero deserts. If his hero had, for instance, deserted from the American army, the American reader's resistance to accepting the act would have been much greater—the reader's own immediate loyalties, etc., would have been betrayed by Frederic's act. And by the same token the resistance to the symbolic meaning of the act—the resigning from society—would have been much greater. The reader is led to accept the act because the desertion is from a "foreign" army. The point is indicated in a passage of dialogue between Frederic

when Frederic escapes from the battle police, has the significance of a rite. By this "baptism" Frederic is reborn into another world; he comes out into the world of the man alone, no longer supported by and involved in society.

> Anger was washed away in the river along with my obligation. Although that ceased when the carabiniere put his hands on my collar. I would like to have had the uniform off although I did not care much about the outward forms. I had taken off the stars, but that was for convenience. It was no point of honor. I was not against them. I was through. I wished them all the luck. There were the good ones, and the brave ones, and the calm ones and the sensible ones, and they deserved it. But it was not my show any more and I wished this bloody train would get to Maestre and I would eat and stop thinking.

So Frederic, by a decision, does what the boy [9] Nick does as the result of the accident of a wound. He makes a "separate peace." And from the waters of the flooded Tagliamento arises the Hemingway hero in his purest form, with human history and obligation washed away, ready to enact the last phase of his appropriate drama, and learn from his inevitable defeat the lesson of lonely fortitude.

IV

This is not the time to attempt to give a final appraisal of Hemingway's work as a whole or even of his particular novel—if there is ever a time for a "final" appraisal. But we may touch on some of the objections which have been brought against his work.

First, there is the objection that his work is immoral or dirty or disgusting. This objection appeared in various quarters against *A Farewell to Arms* at the time of its first publication. For instance, Robert Herrick, himself a respected novelist, wrote that if suppression were to be justified at all it would be justified in this case. He said that the book had no significance, was merely a "lustful indulgence," and smelled of the "boudoir," and summarized his view by calling it "garbage." [10] That objection has, for the most part, died out, but its echoes can still be occasionally heard, and now and then at rare intervals some bigot or

---

and Catherine. Frederic complains that he doesn't want them to have to live in secret and on the run like criminals.

"I feel like a criminal. I've deserted from the army."

"Darling, *please* be sensible. It's not deserting from the army. It's only the Italian army."

It may be objected that since Hemingway himself saw service on the Italian front it is only natural that his story should be laid there and that by consequence the fact has no symbolic significance and no significance as fictional strategy. But the fact that circumstances of personal history dictated the setting of the story does not prevent the author from seizing on and using the advantages inherent in the situation.

[9] *In Our Time,* chap. vi.

[10] "What Is Dirt?" *Bookman,* November, 1929.

high-minded but uninstructed moralist will object to the inclusion of *A Farewell to Arms* in a college course. The answer to such an objection is fundamentally an answer to the charge that the book has no meaning. The answer would seek to establish the fact that the book does deal seriously with a moral and philosophical issue, which, for better or worse, does exist in the modern world in substantially the terms presented by Hemingway. This means that the book, even if it does not end with a solution that is generally acceptable, still embodies a moral effort and is another document of the human effort to achieve ideal values. As for the bad effect it may have on some readers, the best answer is perhaps to be found in a quotation from Thomas Hardy, who is now sanctified but whose most famous novels, *Tess of the D'Urbervilles* and *Jude the Obscure*, once suffered the attacks of the dogmatic moralists, and one of whose books was burned by a bishop:

> Of the effects of such sincere presentation on weak minds, when the courses of the characters are not exemplary and the rewards and punishments ill adjusted to deserts, it is not our duty to consider too closely. A novel which does moral injury to a dozen imbeciles, and has bracing results upon intellects of normal vigor, can justify its existence; and probably a novel was never written by the purest-minded author for which there could not be found some moral invalid or other whom it was capable of harming.[11]

Second, there is the objection that Hemingway's work, especially of the period before *To Have and Have Not*, has no social relevance, that it is off the main stream of modern life, and that it has no concern with the economic structure of society. Critics who hold this general view regard Hemingway, like Joseph Conrad and perhaps like Henry James, as an exotic. There are several possible lines of retort to this objection. One line is well stated in the following passage if we substitute the name of Hemingway for Conrad:

> Thus it is no reproach to Conrad that he does not concern himself at all with the economic and social background underlying human relationships in modern civilization, for he never sets out to study those relationships. The Marxists cannot accuse him of cowardice or falsification, because in this case the charge is not relevant [though it might be relevant to *To Have and Have Not* or to *For Whom the Bell Tolls*]. That, from the point of view of the man with a theory, there are accidents in history, no one can deny. And if a writer chooses to discuss those accidents rather than the events which follow the main stream of historical causation, the economic, or other, determinist can only shrug his shoulder and maintain that these events are less instructive to the students than are the major events which he chooses to study; but he cannot accuse the writer of falsehood or distortion.[12]

[11] "The Profitable Reading of Fiction," in *Life and Art, Essays, Notes and Letters*.
[12] David Daiches, "Joseph Conrad," in *The Novel and the Modern World*.

That much is granted by one of the ablest critics of the group who would find Hemingway an exotic. But a second line of retort would fix on the word *instructive* in the foregoing passage, and would ask what kind of instruction, if any, is to be expected of fiction, as fiction. Is the kind of instruction expected of fiction in direct competition, at the same level, with the kind of instruction offered in Political Science I or Economics II? If that is the case, then out with Shakespeare and Keats and in with Upton Sinclair.

Perhaps *instruction* is not a relevant word, after all, for this case. This is a very thorny and debatable question, but it can be ventured that what good fiction gives us is the stimulation of a powerful image of human nature trying to fulfill itself, and not instruction in an abstract sense. The economic and political man are important aspects of human nature and may well constitute part of the *materials* of fiction. But the economic and political man are not the complete man and other concerns may still be important enough to engage worthily the attention of a writer—such concerns as love, death, courage, the point of honor, and the moral scruple. A man does not only have to live with other men in terms of economic and political arrangements; he has to live with them in terms of moral arrangements, he has to live with himself, he has to define himself. It can truly be said that these concerns are all interrelated in fact, but it might be dangerously dogmatic to insist that a writer should not bring one aspect into sharp, dramatic focus.

And it might be dangerously dogmatic to insist that Hemingway's ideas are not relevant to modern life. The mere fact that they exist and have stirred a great many people is a testimony to their relevance. Or to introduce a variation on that theme, it might be dogmatic to object to his work on the ground that he has few basic ideas. The history of literature seems to show that good artists may have very few *basic* ideas. They may have many ideas, but the ideas do not lead a life of democratic give-and-take, of genial camaraderie. No, there are usually one or two basic, obsessive ones. Like the religious reformer Savonarola, the artist may say: *"Le mie cose erano poche e grandi"*—my ideas were few and grand. And the ideas of the artist are grand because they are intensely felt, intensely realized—not because, by objective standards, by public, statistical standards, "important." No, that kind of public, statistical importance may be a condition of their being grand but is not of the special essence of their grandeur. (Perhaps not even the condition—perhaps the grandeur inheres in the fact that the artistic work shows us a parable of meaning—how idea is felt and how passion becomes idea through order.)

An artist may need few basic ideas, but in assessing his work we must introduce another criterion in addition to that of intensity. We must introduce the criterion of area. An artist's basic ideas do not operate in splendid isolation; to a greater or lesser degree, they prove them- selves by their conquest of other ideas. Or again differently, the focus is a focus of experience, and the area of experience involved gives us another criterion of condition, the criterion of area. Perhaps an ex- ample would be helpful here. We have said that Hemingway is con- cerned with the scruple of honor, that this is a basic idea in his work. But we find that he applies this idea to a relatively small area of experi- ence. In fact, we never see a story in which the issue involves the prob- lem of definition of the scruple, nor do we ever see a story in which honor calls for a slow, grinding, day-to-day conquest of nagging difficul- ties. In other words, the idea is submitted to the test of a relatively small area of experience, to experience of a hand-picked sort, and to characters of a limited range.

But within that range, within the area in which he finds congenial material and in which competing ideas do not intrude themselves too strongly, Hemingway's expressive capacity is very powerful and the degree of intensity is very great. He is concerned not to report variety of human nature or human situation, or to analyze the forces operating in society, but to communicate a certain feeling about, a certain atti- tude toward, a special issue. That is, he is essentially a lyric rather than a dramatic writer, and for the lyric writer virtue depends upon the intensity with which the personal vision is rendered rather than upon the creation of a variety of characters whose visions are in conflict among themselves. And though Hemingway has not given—and never intended to give—a documented diagnosis of our age, he has given us one of the most compelling symbols of a personal response to our age.

E. M. FORSTER *

Austin Warren

THE ENGLISH novel has traditionally admitted of no exact definition, no generic purity. Written by all sorts and conditions of men, as was the poetic drama of the Elizabethans, it has been designed for as many kinds of readers. The responsibility of the nineteenth-century novelist was to offer his readers a "story"; apart from that, and within the bounds of Victorian taste, he might provide what *extras* he would— sociological, psychological, moral. Sweeping his puppets aside, he might preach the new ethics, expound the nature of things, prophesy the future actions of his characters or the future of human character; returning again to his puppets, he was free to pass in and out of their minds, now seeing through this pair of subsidiary eyes, now through that, now exerting the omniscience of his own sight.

At the end of the century the popular novelists continued the practice; but George Moore and Henry James, both aliens to England, both trained in France, felt dissatisfaction at such looseness. A genre so readily susceptible of illustrated homily on prison reform or the loss of clerical faith lacked minimal aesthetic dignity. They busied themselves—James in particular—in devising an "art of fiction." Of this gospel the chief dogma was that of the "point of view." The novelist, James held, must preliminarily decide through whose eyes the proposed narration may, most profitably, be viewed. Or he may, instead, decide to use a series of instruments in turn: the ten books of *The Awkward Age* utilize the vision of as many persons. But there must be no mere convenient, unpremeditated transit. Further, the author must rigorously exclude himself as public commentator or "chorus." The only point of view inadmissible is that of the author.

James's technical experiments have, properly, commanded the respect of subsequent artists; and his influence upon them has been impressive. Consciousness of form has marked the work of authors otherwise so various as Gide, Joyce, Hemingway, Mrs. Woolf. *Les Faux-Monnayeurs* is a novel analyzing the composition of a novel; each section of *Ulysses* employs a different method and a different style; Hemingway has removed from the novel all save its public or behavioristic

---

* "E. M. Forster" originally appeared in the *American Review*, Summer, 1937, and later formed chap. viii of *Rage For Order*, by Austin Warren (The University of Chicago Press, 1948). It is used here by permission of the author and the publishers.

device, its dialogue.* Mrs. Woolf has subtracted almost all the banks which define the stream of consciousness; she has practiced the limited vision, successive instruments of vision; in *The Waves* she has offered in place of dialogue a series, symphonically arranged, of interior soliloquies. Like Proust's, like Huxley's *Point Counterpoint,* her work seems to aim at musical form—a pattern of recurrent and recurrently enriched motifs.

E. M. Forster has full and appreciative acquaintance with the work of Gide, Proust, Joyce, and Mrs. Woolf; but his personal masters are, rather, Jane Austen, Samuel Butler, and Dostoevski. In his *Aspects of the Novel* (1927) he expounds the Jamesian theory only to reject, or to minimize it. It is dangerous, he thinks, for the writer to take the reader into his confidence about his characters; but "to take your reader into your confidence about the universe is a different thing. It is not dangerous for a novelist to draw back from his characters, as Hardy and Conrad do, and to generalize about the conditions under which he thinks life is carried on." To be sure, the novelist must not anticipate, publicly, that future end of his characters which he must, out of elementary artistic decency, foresee. As the characters develop, the author interprets, concomitantly, their states of sensibility; he must keep his dramatic or factual surprises until they reach, and take on or off their guard, his persons. But it can impair no proper aesthetic faith that the novelist should articulate such observations and insights upon humanity at large as the conduct of his personae may suggest. Indeed, if the novelist be a man of wisdom as well as mimetic power, his imaginative self can assuredly, only with loss, be spared from the dramatis personae. He should move among his characters, though certainly not as man among dolls; he is to be cast as the most deeply seeing member of a company.

Both in theory and in practice Forster declines to restrict the novelist's ancient liberties. The richness of the novel, for him, lies in its range of levels. There is the "story"; then there are the persons of the story who act and speak; then there is the "inner life" of the characters, to be overheard and translated by the author; and, finally, there is the philosophic commentary of the author.

Plot, characters, philosophy: each has a life of its own and threatens to expand until it menaces its competitors. If the novel restrict itself to action and speech, it does no more than reduplicate—and with the subtraction of mimes present "in person"—the drama or even the biography. To avoid being less, the novel must be more. "A memoir," says Forster, "is history, it is based on evidence. . . . And it is the function of the novelist to reveal the hidden life at its source: to tell us more than could be known. In daily life we never understand each

---

* Those readers of Hemingway who see his portraits of background and landscape as symbolically functional will not agree with Mr. Warren here.

other; neither complete clairvoyance nor complete confessional exists. ... But people in a novel can be understood completely by the reader, if the novelist wishes; their inner vision as well as their outer life can be exposed."

If, on the other hand, the "inner life" become all, then, like some parts of Proust's *A la Recherche,* the novel turns into a psychological treatise and the persons decompose into their constituent moods and "intermittences." The too intense self-consciousness, the self-consciousness divorced from action, dissolving its object, discovers no residual self.

In *Howard's End* the Wilcoxes are characterized as people incomplete because they eliminate the personal, cannot say "I"; but Helen Schlegel, overconcerned with the subconscious self, speaking of mankind as puppets whom an invisible showman twitches into love and war, herself risks, though by an opposite method, the elimination of the personal.

To Forster, then, the novel has its own function, that of a persuasive equilibrism; it must balance the claims of the existence and the essence, of personalities and ideas. To Forster, values are more important than facts; and the real values are friendship, intellectual exploration, insight and imagination, the values of the "inner life." But observation and interpretation, though terminal values, are, biologically, parasitic upon the body and the life of action. Forster's own work very satisfyingly preserves the equilibrium both in its repertory of characters and in its narrative method.

Even more than the drama, the novel suits the mind which pushes beyond gossip and news but is unable or unwilling to accept a creed. Such a mind habitually generalizes its insights but, through indolence, self-distrust, or skepticism of absolutes, attempts no thoroughgoing system. It goes beyond judgments of John and John's attitude toward Jane to the conception of types—men like John and men who have such attitudes toward women like Jane; its propositions are not universals about men and women but linger halfway between John and "all men." Forster's essays, assembled in *Abinger Harvest* (1936),[1] document the conclusion that he has ideas but no "idea."

In *Howard's End* he expresses the view that the complexity of the modern world offers to the best-prepared and best-intentioned but an

---

[1] Like the *Dickinson,* the book of essays is disappointing to a Forsterian. Its eighty constituent parts should, if their author deemed them all worth reprinting, have been collected in five or six thinnish volumes addressed rather to pockets than library shelves. The two sketches of Howard Sturgis and Ronald Firbank are deft and discerning; "My Wood," a parable on the effects of owning property, is a little masterpiece; "Liberty in England," Forster's address before the International Congress of Writers at Paris, has a finely simple candor and dignity. But too many of the pieces, though stylistically meticulous, produce the impression of a coy sprightliness alien to the novels. Without a mask, pushed to the front of the stage to make his speech, Forster grows self-conscious.

option of alternative visions: seeing life steadily *or* seeing it whole. His own choice is clearly the latter; like Santayana, he has the excellent manners, the freedom from exaggerated emphases and extravagant exclusions, which traditionally have been the marks of the humanist.

Santayana's *Last Puritan* showed unexpected lapses in comprehension. Though it saw value in man as animal (Lord Jim), as epicure (Peter Alden), as social creature (Mario), as high-minded spectator (Oliver), his catholicity failed to see any "life of reason" in New England Brahminism. Forster's range of "partial sympathies" is even greater. Though his cardinal virtues are courage, candor, sympathy, insight, disinterestedness, he can find worth in almost every quality except humbug and muddledom. People are "far more different than is pretended," says wise Margaret Schlegel, who loves her Philistine husband, to her sister Helen, an unmarried mother. "All over the world men and women are worrying because they cannot develop as they are supposed to develop. Here and there they have the matter out, and it comforts them. . . . Develop what you have; love your child. I do not love children. I am thankful to have none. . . . And others—others go further still and move outside humanity altogether. . . . It is part of the battle against sameness. Differences—external differences, planted by God in a single family, so that there may always be color; sorrow perhaps, but color in the daily grey." Only, different as human beings are, they have the common obligation of self-knowledge. Those who "follow neither the heart nor the brain, and march to their destiny by catch-words" are the truly benighted. "The armies are full of pleasant and pious folk. But they have yielded to the only enemy that matters—the enemy within. They have sinned against passion and truth, and vain will be their strife after virtue."

Forster's England is chiefly that of the upper middle classes and the intelligentsia of the universities and London, an England exempt alike from Lady Catherine de Bourgh and from the sadistic peasants of T. F. Powys, a world set on "gold islands." From this world, cruelty and lust are almost absent. The vice of the bourgeois, as Arnold and Carlyle never wearied of pointing out, is self-complacent, unimaginative respectability; the vice of the intelligentsia is another form of Phariseeism: the snobbery of "culture."

Poor culture! We recall, as one of its exemplars, Miss Austen's Mary Bennett, who, "being the only plain one in the family, worked hard for knowledge and accomplishments, [and] was always impatient for display." In Forster's novels, "culture" appears as the Rev. Cuthbert Eager at Santa Croce, lecturing to English lady tourists with "prayer books as well as guide-books in their hands"; as Cecil Vyse, who acknowledges the truth of Lucy's impassioned analysis: "You may understand beautiful things, but you don't know how to see them; and you wrap yourself up in art and books and music, and would try to wrap me up"; as poor lower-class Leonard Bast, who read Mr. Ruskin, spouted R.L.S., tinkled a little Grieg, and "hoped to come to Culture suddenly, much as the Revivalist hopes to come to Jesus."

One of Forster's short fantasies concerns the "Celestial Omnibus," driven now by Sir Thomas Browne, now by Jane Austen, now by Dante, and conducting the candidly imaginative to the land of vicarious experience, where Achilles and Mrs. Gamp and Hamlet and Tom Jones disport themselves companionably. A "boy" makes the journey in innocence, because he is too ignorant and wise to attribute the experience to his personal "merit." Not so Mr. Bons, Surbiton councilman who owns seven copies of Shelley. Rich in his spiritual possessions and conscious of how they set him above his fellows, Mr. Bons invokes the great Dante: "I have honored you. I have quoted you. I have bound you in vellum." But in vain; for poetry is means and not end. Poetry is a spirit, not to be won like a degree but to be cherished like a flame. And those who, like Mr. Bons, do not *connect* their conduct with their "culture," will, like Mr. Bons, topple from the precipice of heaven into a junk-heap of glittering fragments.

Elementary "culture," the pathos of isolated aspirants, lists, with an epithet or two apiece, the books it has read. "Give me a list of books, worth-while ones," it bids the professor; "I want to improve myself." "How whimsical Lamb is." "Henry James, how subtle." "Should I read Thackeray next, or Tolstoi?" Culture is a list of books.

Then there is that more rarefied culture which keeps up with the newest ideas and the latest names, which is allusive and light of touch, which, in order to play dexterously about the peripheral, takes the central for granted—the "clever" culture of people who live for books, concerts, art shows, and chatter about them. "In spite of the season, Mrs. Vyse managed to scrape together a dinner-party consisting entirely of the grandchildren of famous people. The food was poor, but the talk had a witty weariness. . . . One was tired of everything, it seemed. One launched into enthusiasm only to collapse gracefully, and pick oneself up amid sympathetic laughter."

The "real thing" of which "culture" is the parody or the pastiche appears in Forster's novels also. It is represented by Cecil and Tibby, more completely by Philip, Ricky Elliott, and Mr. Beebe. These men are all ascetics, scholars, aesthetes; are all, in varying degrees, detached observers, contemplatives. They are not, Forster makes clear, capable of passion for women or indeed, perhaps, for persons at all. Tibby is a scholar for whom the human is tiresome and crude, who desires the the passionless air of knowledge. Ansell is a professional philosopher, who believes it "worth while to grow old and dusty seeking for truth though truth is unattainable, restating questions that have been stated at the beginning of the world."

Cecil, the comic hero of *A Room with a View*, is a born curator. Wrong in seeking to pervert the nature of others, wrong in being so ignorant of his own nature as to "make love," in himself he is a genuine, if restricted and indoor, person. The Middle Ages would have understood Cecil and have made a place for him. "He was mediaeval. ... well educated, well endowed, and not deficient physically, he remained in the grip of a certain devil whom the modern world knows as self-consciousness, and whom the mediaeval, with dimmer vision, worshipped as asceticism. A Gothic statue implies celibacy, just as a Greek statue implies fruition." Cecil does not fit "Nature": he is a muff at sports; he is to be imagined, thinks Lucy, as in a drawing-room, one with drawn draperies. His one attempt at love-making turns into high, rueful comedy. "As he approached her, he found time to wish that he could recoil. As he touched her, his gold pince-nez became dislodged and was flattened between them." Cecil's pince-nez was genuine; his passion, secondhand and temporary.

Yet, ludicrous as this scene displays him, Cecil is absurd only as he pretends a range of feelings denied him. Forster's books house few "flat" characters, to be summarized in a gesture or a recurrent phrase; for as we are just about to catalogue them, they turn toward us another side, a side which surprises us but surprises us in a way which is compatible with the sides' being sides of the same person. When Lucy eventually rebels against Cecil's attempt to mold a Vyse out of a Honeychurch, she treats him to a ruthless portrait of himself. He is unexpectedly, convincingly, honest and grateful. He cannot change his character; but, for the first time, he recognizes it.

Where Angels Fear to Tread offers Philip, a contemplative of larger stature. The short book is yet long enough to show Philip's growth from a culture-snob, vain of his taste for art and Italy, vain of his emancipation from British provincialism, into a man of insight and good will. Philip becomes capable of imaginative sympathy with persons as alien as the son of an Italian dentist; he grows in humanity. But his final triumph is self-awareness; and to this recognition he, like Cecil, is helped by a woman whom, in his ignorance, he fancies he desires. He sees all, "appreciates" all, but cannot act. To Caroline Abbott he confesses: "You would be surprised to know what my great events are. Going to the theatre yesterday, talking to you now—I don't suppose I shall ever meet anything greater. I seem fated to pass through the world without colliding with it or moving it—and I'm sure I can't tell you whether the fate's good or evil. I don't die—I don't fall in love ... you are quite right; life to me is just a spectacle."

This is perhaps the best which "culture" singlehanded can achieve. To know "the best that has been said and thought in the world"; to know with any fulness, to make one's own, the thought and experience of Aristotle, Lucretius, Racine, Montaigne, Bossuet, Goethe, Sophocles,

Plotinus, Confucius, Aristophanes, Dante: that would be a formidable "task." The outlines of the knower's personality would grow vague; he would have no appetite left for life, no capacity for action, no energy for creation; he would be infected with a sense of personal futility. "Tout est dit: et l'on vient trop tard depuis plus de sept mille ans qu'il y a des hommes, et qui pensent."

There are times when, by reaction, Forster turns, temporarily, to primitivism—as Philip turns to Gino, as Rickey turns to that child of nature, his half-brother, Stephen. An animal is better than a prig, that parody of the saint; a child is better than a prude. But then Forster sees, too, the virtues of downright, unashamed, healthy extroverts like Henry Wilcox and Son, men devoid of intellectual curiosity and extra-domestic sympathy who can "do" and build. Himself a habituate of the "inner life," Forster feels, as must all half-men aware of their incompleteness, the attraction of his opposites; the child, the animal, the Philistine. Himself English, he has felt the fascination not only of Italy but of Italians—warm, spontaneous Italians, untroubled by scrupulosity or the miasma of introspection, affectionate by impulse not duty.

But Forster's humanity will know all: the earth, passion and friendship, thirst for the truth, and hunger for the Absolute. For him, the "Greek view of life" is the right one; and the problem of morality is not to set mind against body or soul against either, not to antithesize but to reconcile, by proportion and subordination to effect a harmony. In the language of metaphysics, Forster must be described as a "naturalist"; but, he is a "naturalist" with wings and humanistic manners and balancing perceptions, one who, like Santayana, believes that everything ideal has a natural basis and that nothing in nature is incapable of an ideal fulfilment.

Is this balance attainable by the individual? That is to ask whether the individual can exemplify the universal man; and the answer seems clear: never completely; often not at all. Yet it is the undeniable nisus of large natures. Forster's character who most closely approaches universality is Margaret Schlegel: though she possesses her own personal mark and stamp, she can comprehend natures as diverse from her own as Mrs. Wilcox, Helen, and Henry; and she achieves the triumph not only of marrying a Philistine but of achieving with him a marriage of spiritual union. Then there is Forster's friend and hero, Lowes Dickinson, who admired the versatility of Goethe, who himself longed to be a poet, a scientist, and a dominating figure in European politics, yet who, doomed to dondom, expanded his vision through his friendships with men of affairs and philosophers and painters. "He solved his particular problem in later life by developing the power of entering into other people's positions while he retained his own. . . ."

Forster's "humanist," Mr. Jackson, warns Ricky that the Greeks were not broad church clergymen, that Sophocles was not a kind of enlightened bishop. If there is a "golden mean," it is not what so often passes for it—tepidity or compromise or apathetic good humor. "The business man who assumes that this life is everything, and the mystic who asserts that it is nothing, fail, on this side and on that, to hit the truth. 'Yes, I see, dear; it's about halfway between,' [the Schlegels'] Aunt Juley had hazarded in earlier years. No; truth, being alive, was not halfway between anything. It was only to be found by continuous excursions into either realm, and though proportion is the final secret, to espouse it at the outset is to insure sterility."

Much which passes for "the mean" is not virtue, one must agree. There is no virtue in low vitality, intellectual or moral indolence, unwillingness to think one's thought to its end, cowardice in failing to take one's stand. To be moderate is not glibly to utter, "It takes all sorts to make a world" and forthwith to give up definition and distinction. Moderation is an achievement, not an endowment. Its pursuit necessitates the exercise of the will, checking this excessive impulse and that disorderly propensity; and the really central man must have a passion for proportion.

The doctrine of the mean needs a modern re-examination. G. K. Chesterton used to argue that equilibrium was the character of a sound society, like that of the Middle Ages, when the monk was bidden to be as pacific as possible and the knight to be as warlike as he could; and such a conception finds support in Plato's *Republic*. Shall we say, rather, that every man must seek to be the "balanced" man? This was undoubtedly the doctrine of the *honnête homme;* but, outside the confines of a leisure class, it is almost impossible to apply.

One might, of course, chart out his day so that all the chief values received representation; one might do his "daily dozen" at calisthenics and dialectics and social intercourse and prayer. Gamaliel Bradford's meticulous regimen gave a half-hour to French, another to Greek, another to the piano, and so on through a half-prescribed horarium. But this seems somewhat mechanical as well as meticulous; and it seems doubtful whether such precision is advisable outside of a monastic community. A week of solitude and hard thinking or writing, followed by a week of society (with a capital letter or a small) might be a kind of balance more appropriate to the life of a man in the "world." "The great rule," says von Hügel, "is, Variety up to the verge of dissipation: Recollection up to the verge of emptiness: each alternating with the other and making a rich, fruitful tension."

Is proportion to be thought of in terms of the day, the year, or the lifetime? Forster votes for the last of these conceptions; and, by his passage from mysticism to politics and back again, his youthful thrusts into many directions, his subsequent mellow maturity, Lowes Dickinson, who said, "I shall be at my best in old age," best illustrates Forster's thesis that "proportion is the final secret."

Common to Dickinson and Forster is the belief that reason is neither the foundation of knowledge (which is animal faith) nor its spire (which is intuition). "It is difficult for most of us to realize both the importance and unimportance of reason. But it is a difficulty which the profounder humanists have managed to solve." Complete rationalism, like glaring sunlight, dries up the vegetation. Complete credulity produces so lush, so rank a growth of vegetation that the human way is lost, the human stature dwarfed. The lamplit table is surrounded by darkness, an unknown to be neither apostasized nor denied. What science and intellect can tell us can be said; the rest, which, too, must be articulated, can be uttered only in myth and poetry. Dickinson and Forster are equilibrists and mediators. As the human or the historical context seems to require, they affirm the achieved known or the limits of "exact knowledge" and final function of the imagination.

Forster's earlier novels, *Where Angels Fear To Tread* (1905), *The Longest Journey* (1907), and *A Room with a View* (1908), of which the first and the third are high comedy, keep to the sunlight of realism. With *Howard's End* (1910), however, Forster introduces what his friend Dickinson called the "double vision," the sense of this world and a world or worlds behind. *A Passage to India* (1924) came between two volumes of fantasies, *The Celestial Omnibus* (1923) and *The Eternal Moment* (1928). In all these works there is an element which might loosely be called mystical, the brooding presence of worlds unreachable by the ordinary processes of the mind. Yet these "intimations" are not to be thought of as breakings-in of a supernatural "Other," and no theology is adumbrated. Sometimes the tales suggest abnormal psychology, psychic powers rarely possessed; sometimes they are fanciful, symbolical expositions of the nature of things. In several of them, a myth of the "future life" envisions the real values attainable now.

In none of his tales does Forster attempt to suggest a diabolic supernatural; and, in all save the frankly parabolic sketches of the "future life," he restricts himself to what, in action, belongs to the normal. He has written no *Lady into Fox,* that fantasy at the end of which no reverse metamorphosis occurs. Nor has he used Hawthorne's sometimes routine supplying of alternatives, natural and magical: Donatello had, or had not, the ears of a faun; there was, or was not, an actual scarlet letter visibly incised on Dimmesdale's breast or visible as portent in the heaven. The element of fantasy, with Forster, is conveyed not through a mechanism but through a coloring: ordinary existence is illuminated by the white light of eternity or the blue light of "value," so that the familiar landscape gains an arresting strangeness.

Two tales, "The Eternal Moment" and "The Road from Colonus," contrast existence and reality: all that matters in life may happen in a day or an hour; and even the experiencer may afterwards forget this normative moment. Sometimes the tale presents, in heightened contrast, the opposition between sense and sensibility, between the Philistine, even of the kind which teaches Virgil or quotes Dante, and the impractical romantic, who may not have read the poets but who can see into the life of things. Mr. Worters, the Englishman of great possessions, of "public school" culture and conventional churchmanship, owns a copse of beeches which he equips with fences and neat paths and a bridge, all the accouterments for destroying its small wildness, so cherished by his fiancée and an inefficient young man. Disillusioned by "culture," the girl runs off into the woods. "On the Other Side of the Hedge" from the world of unanalyzed efficiency and uncritical belief in "progress," she discovers the world of happy leisure. "Where does this place lead to?" "Nowhere, thank the Lord." Though frequently they contain a flight, it would be crass to bear down on these tales as so many escapes. Escape is a form of criticism in these tales; and the goal of the flight and its starting-point offer an opposition and a contrast in values. In essence, the tales are all parables addressed to the Philistine who, like Mr. Wilcox, fails to "connect" prose and poetry, who has never seen that art and religion cannot be assigned to museums and churches but must be apprehended through participation in the same spirit which prompted the painter and the saint.

In both *Howard's End* and *A Passage to India* the central figure is that of an old woman without cleverness or articulateness who appears but briefly yet whose presence attends and pervades the book. Mrs. Wilcox and Mrs. Moore are studies of the same type. Both have, intermittently, telepathic and clairvoyant power. Recognizing in Margaret Schlegel a spiritual heir to her own feelings for her country home, Mrs. Wilcox bequeaths it on an unsigned scrap of paper; the sensible Wilcoxes, knowing the testament to possess no legal validity and thinking the act was of momentary aberration, pay no heed to it. But, without design, Margaret becomes the second Mrs. Wilcox, comes (in spite of obstacles) to live at Howard's End, and on the last page of the novel, learns by chance, from her husband, that the house had been left her. Says Margaret to her sister: "I feel that you and I and Henry are only fragments of that woman's mind. She knows everything. She is everything. She is the house, and the tree that leans over it. People have their own deaths as well as their own lives, and even if there is nothing beyond death, we shall differ in our nothingness. I cannot believe that knowledge such as hers will perish with knowledge such as mine. She knew about realities."

Mrs. Moore visits India, where her son is a British official. Shortly after her arrival, she goes into a mosque to feel God's presence, falls into conversation with a young Moslem physician, journeys to the Marabar Hills on an excursion which he arranges. While within the caves, she is made ill by the echoes, and her son's fiancée has the hallucination of having been assaulted by the Moslem host. Mrs. Moore refuses to testify at the momentous trial of the Indian, and leaves the country, dying on the journey; but she has massively impressed the perceptive, whether Western or Eastern, who knew her. No presence is so real at the trial as hers; her name becomes Indianized into Esmiss Esmoor and reverberates, like that of a Hindu goddess, through the crowd; votive tombs spring up; she is accepted as one Westerner who comprehended the East, who was indeed an Oriental; the goodness of Mrs. Moore, which had amounted to nothing more tangible than her good will, survived, in the heart of the Moslem Aziz, his bitter abandonment of further traffic with the English. Like Mrs. Wilcox, Mrs. Moore "knew."

How did these women know, and what did they know? The answers are left vague. Mrs. Wilcox loved the soil and the garden and her house; she was a goddess of place, a local spirit in whom, apparently, the personal was transcended. There is (Forster seems to say) the level of consciousness and selfhood, to which some human beings never ascend; and there is a level above the personal which looks down upon it with loving impersonality. Without any practical knowledge of how to unite, politically, the many contending, contentious sects of Indians, or how to reconcile the Indians and their imperial masters, Mrs. Moore affirms the oneness of all humanity.

In both women there are elements of what Forster, in his *Aspects of the Novel,* calls the "prophetic." The center of *A Passage,* structurally and psychologically, is the excursion to the Marabar Caves. The drama of the novel, the trial, springs from it; but what happened there affected, permanently, the lives of all the excursionists. Dickinson, as well as others, asked Forster: What really happened in the caves? The author does not say—not, I think, for the reasons which led Hawthorne to leave vague so much in *The Marble Faun,* but because he has made it sufficiently clear that no assault on Adela took place. What happened, to Adela and to Mrs. Moore, was the hysterical experience of the caves, bare, dark, echoing. The echo is that of eternity, infinity, the Absolute, which for optimistic Shaftesbury and Pope might seem to say:

> All Nature is but Art unknown to thee;
> All Chance, Direction, which thou canst not see;
> All Discord, Harmony not understood;
> All partial Evil, universal Good....

To fatigued Mrs. Moore, on the contrary, it murmured: "Pathos, piety, courage—they exist, but are identical, and so is filth. Everything exists; nothing has value." "If one had spoken vileness in that place, or quoted lofty poetry, the comment would have been the same—*ou-boum....* Religion appeared, poor little talkative Christianity, and she knew that all its divine words from 'Let there be Light' to 'It is finished' only amounted to 'boum.' " "She had come to that state where the horror of the universe and its smallness are both visible at the same time—the twilight of the double vision in which so many elderly people are involved. If this world is not to our taste, well, at all events there is Heaven, Hell, Annihilation.... All heroic endeavor, and all that is known as art, assumes that there is such a background, just as all practical endeavor, when the world is to our taste, assumes that the world is all. But in the twilight of the double vision, a spiritual muddledom is set up for which no high-sounding words can be found; we can neither act nor refrain from action, we can neither ignore nor respect Infinity." "Visions are supposed to entail profundity but—Wait till you get one, dear reader! The abyss also may be petty, the serpent of eternity made of maggots...." The Absolute may be a demon.

The skeptical blight which descended, as infernal vision, upon Mrs. Moore is possible, doubtless, only to one reared in the Christian tradition. This skepticism insinuates that human values have no basis in the nature of things; that our moral distinctions are factitious; that the universe mocks sinner and saint alike; that both our aspirations and our intellections are folly in the presence of the blind if not malevolent destiny which begat us.

Mrs. Moore's first sentiment in India was to feel the unity of all religions; her second, to feel the futility of all. Upon all save the steadiest and soundest minds, the effect of sojourn *in partibus infidelium* must be a bland tolerance, or an insular bigotry, or the reduction of all morality to mores. The older generation of missionaries to India were, like the English civil officials, too little given to distinguishing between what was British and what was Christian, too contemptuously intolerant of alien faiths; the newest generation suffers from the opposite danger of making too few discriminations. The echoes from the caves of cosmopolitanism say, with sentimentality or with cynicism, that all moralities and all religions stand on the same footing of priest-craft, ruler-craft, traditions, and custom. The serpent of eternity whispers, Ye shall be like gods, knowing not good from evil.

In his life of Dickinson, Forster declares that his two visits to India were "wonderful" by reason of the happiness and peacefulness he found, and he disagrees with his friend's judgment that "There is no solution to the problem of governing India. Our presence is a curse both to them and to us. Our going will be worse." Yet, in his candor, the novelist has offered testimony to this painful conclusion. Even such English "liberals" as Fielding and Adela and such a well-intentioned Indian as Aziz fail of mutual understanding. Between the masses of rulers and ruled, only hostility and suspicion exist. And, divided by their religions, Moslem, Hindu, Sikh, Jain, the Indians cannot achieve a national unity. On this note, the novel ends.

Leaving India, Fielding lands at Venice. He doubtless speaks for Forster when he contrasts romantic India with classical Europe, "the civilization that has escaped muddle." "The Mediterranean is the human norm. When men leave that exquisite lake, whether through the Bosphorus or the Pillars of Hercules, they approach the monstrous and extraordinary. . . ."

Yet the novel offers a chastened hopefulness. Mrs. Moore and her younger children, who share something of her nature, do "reach" this alien world even if they do not intellectually comprehend it. Personal relationships are precious; and, though nation misconceives nation, individuals can pass the boundaries into intuitive communion.

In *The Passage,* as in his two high comedies, Forster shows an extraordinary capacity for disinterested observation which plays alike over Indians, Italians, and English. His "Notes on English Character," the inaugural essay in *Abinger Harvest* (1936), shows the same capacity. The English, he says, are essentially middle class and "public school," not unfeeling but afraid to feel, not unemotional but slow of emotional response, moral rather than religious, self-complacent, muddle-headed. The English character is not vicious and not really cold, but it is incomplete. But then, "No national character is complete. We have to look for some qualities in one part of the world and others in another." This perception gives Forster the basis for the amiable satire with which he treats the more ludicrous of international misunderstandings. The position from which the satire is urged is that of a complete and balanced human nature which has never been incarnated in race nor even in individual, but which the critic, like the novelist, can imaginatively conceive.

Without bigotry or bitterness, Forster has endeavored to attain wholeness and steadiness of vision; his passion is for dispassionate comprehension.

Neither at wholeness nor at steadiness do his novels completely succeed. There are wide and deep *lacunae:* except for the Basts, there are no poor. From poverty, hunger, lust, and hate, his people are exempt. Love between the sexes, though recognized with sympathy, is never explored and is central to none of his novels. Except in *A Passage to India,* the individual is not portrayed in relation to society: Church and State, institutions, communal causes which engage men and draw them out of themselves, do not engage and draw his self-aware individuals.

Forster's "double vision" allows him that modulation from crisp comedy to a delicate pathos, the passage from prose to poetry and back again, which is his prime quality. But the gift has its perils; and he does not always succeed in keeping the two worlds in proper focus. *Howard's End,* in many respects his most mellow and mature performance, fails centrally, just here. The titular theme of *genius loci* is too vague, too "mystical," to bear the weight placed upon it, just as Mrs. Wilcox, who embodies it and is intended to pervade the novel, does not succeed in doing so. Sometimes Forster's forays into the land behind reason bring him only to the "misty mid-region of Weir," the realm of romantic fantasy. In *A Passage to India,* on the other hand, the "double vision" gives depth and perspective. The two worlds need not, however, appear explicitly. In the earlier novels, prose and comedy hold the stage; the "poetry" is in the imaginative lighting of the action. Forster's adjustments are various and varyingly successful; but his constant consciousness of levels, levels of experience and of knowledge, gives the vibration of life to his work.

His production has been sparse—five novels in a lifetime; it is unlikely that there will be others. Except for *A Passage to India,* the ostensible theme of which attracted attention, his work has had no wide popularity; yet he is not a proper object for the peculiar devotion of a cult. Witty, sensitive, epigrammatic and metaphorical, he never becomes precious. He rather conceals than obtrudes his defects and mild perversities; conscious eccentricities he is without. Though he lacks power, the deficiency is felt only upon retrospect; for his subtleties, instead of springing apart as separate perceptions, reticulate into substance. Aided as he is by the preservative of style, it is probable that his fine distinction will survive some more strident originalities of our day.

VIRGINIA WOOLF *

David Daiches

Virginia Woolf, perhaps more than any other novelist of her time, achieved at least a temporary success in coming to terms with the conflicting values of the age. For her the problem may have been simpler than for many others, for she consistently refused to implicate herself in the twentieth-century bourgeois world. And she was able to make that refusal with naturalness and grace because she was born into an intellectual aristocratic tradition in the midst of which the lot of very few English novelists has been cast. Leslie Stephen, her father, was as good an example of the intellectual aristocracy of the nineteenth century as England has produced. The activities of a person belonging to such a class consist largely in using the world of actuality as a source of data, which data are brought carefully home to the study and there refined and refined into a system which may be logical or metaphysical or poetical or something of all three. It is perhaps the most respectable way of avoiding the conflict. The civilization of your time begins to show signs of confusion and disintegration; you can avoid being involved in the disintegration either by abstracting yourself from that world from the very beginning or by postulating a new (or a revived) civilization and writing in terms of its values. There are perhaps other ways, but none that are honest.

A refining intelligence is a highly desirable quality. But some materials are more subject to refinement than others, and in spite of itself the refining intelligence will tend to seize on those materials. If the social life of your time is of such a character as readily to admit of such treatment, the result will be more than an expression of your sensibility; it will also be a convincing and significant picture of that life. But if the life of your time is of a different character, such treatment will be unable to do justice to it and will result in a kind of rarification which is something between lyrical poetry and fiction; something which provides insights and illuminations to the reader, yet too fleeting, too insubstantial, unballasted; something which vanishes when one tries to grasp it, yet not before one thinks one has seen some tenuous body. Such is the work of Virginia Woolf.

* "Virginia Woolf" appears as chap. x of *The Novel and the Modern World,* by David Daiches (The University of Chicago Press, 1939) . It is used here by permission of the author and the publishers.

If Mrs. Dalloway had lived in the first part of the eighteenth century she might have been refined into a symbol without fading in the process, for a stable and well-anchored society can allow its representatives to be carried off into the upper air with a certain amount of confidence. But Mrs. Dalloway lived in the post-war world; she was deliberately set in the heart of London, with the seething emotions of men, as well as the traffic, swirling around her. The refining intelligence in spite of itself seizes on what is most refinable, and the society woman of immediate post-war London becomes a problem of time and space. The artist's mind ignores history and its implications at its peril. *Mrs. Dalloway,* Mrs. Woolf herself has told us, was constructed in order to house an idea. Ideas, speculations, meditations, always come first with this novelist, and the lives of her characters are molded to fit. But this is to risk missing certain objective facts about the characters and their world through a presentation of which alone the particular can become most adequately universal. It is no rule of the critics which separates lyrical from narrative writing, but something in the nature of things. If you do not speak in your own person, but create characters whom you desire to live, you have a responsibility to those characters: they must submit to the conditions of the world in which you place them; they must pay the individual's debt to his environment. You may refine their emotions into tenuous meditation once or twice, but if you let it settle like a covering mist over all your characters alike, and in all circumstances alike, people will not believe you. And for a novelist not to be believed is a hard penalty. Very wisely Mrs. Woolf removed the Ramsays and their friends to the western islands of Scotland, where the refining intelligence and the lyrical, meditative faculty can operate without doing violence to the natural world. The Ramsays we see only on holiday, in a remote and misty isle, and the rest of their life we see only through this atmosphere. But Mrs. Dalloway and the unfortunate Septimus are in workaday London, and need to be more careful. This is one reason why *To the Lighthouse* is a better novel than *Mrs. Dalloway*—indeed, the most successful of all Virginia's Woolf's novels. This is the temporary success that she achieved in coming to terms with the conflicting values of her time: she did this by taking her characters on holiday. But no novelist can keep his characters on holiday throughout his whole career as a writer.

Fantasy is a legitimate enough literary form, but we can be fairly certain that none of Mrs. Woolf's novels, with the possible exception of *Orlando,* was written as fantasy. Mrs. Woolf is interested in the life and problems of her time; she has given sufficient evidence of this in her nonfictional writing. In her novels she is endeavoring to present some essential truth about experience through the presentation of the contents of individual minds. She is not guilty of the heresy that by expressing herself she necessarily produces something of universal significance. She reaches out after life consciously, deliberately. "Perhaps without life nothing else is worth while," she has said herself in her essay on modern fiction. When we read many technically accomplished modern novels, she says, we recognize the craftsmanship: "but sometimes, more and more often as time goes by, we suspect a momentary doubt, a spasm of rebellion, as the pages fill themselves in the customary way. Is life like this? Must novels be like this?" [1] "Is life like this?" This is her criterion. There is no "art for art's sake" nonsense about Virginia Woolf; she recognizes the function of literature as that of illuminating experience for its readers. But where does one find experience? And how is it to be illuminated?

It is not only in the questions she poses but also in the manner in which she answers them that Mrs. Woolf displays the refining qualities of an aristocratic intellect. This is her answer:

> Examine for a moment an ordinary mind on an ordinary day. The mind receives a myriad impressions—trivial, fantastic, evanescent, or engraved with the sharpness of steel. From all sides they come, an incessant shower of innumerable atoms; and as they fall, as they shape themselves into the life of Monday or Tuesday, the accent falls differently from of old; the moment of importance came not here but there; so that, if a writer were a free man and not a slave, if he could write what he chose, not what he must, if he could base his work upon his own feeling and not upon convention, there would be no plot, no comedy, no tragedy, no love interest or catastrophe in the accepted style, and perhaps not a single button sewn on as the Bond Street tailors would have it. Life is not a series of gig lamps symmetrically arranged; life is a luminous halo, a semi-transparent envelope surrounding us from the beginning of consciousness to the end. Is it not the task of the novelist to convey this varying, this unknown and uncircumscribed spirit, whatever aberration or complexity it may display, with as little mixture of the alien and external as possible? [2]

We have seen how Katherine Mansfield, in her search for a more complete objectivity, came to equate the fact with her own personal sense of fact.* Here we see Virginia Woolf tending in the same direction. "Life is a luminous halo, a semi-transparent envelope surrounding us from the beginning of consciousness to the end." Life as it is objectively, that is to say, consists of that particular vision of life which certain sensitive beholders are blessed with. It is interesting that when faced with the problem of defining "real life" Mrs. Woolf asks her readers to look within. Katherine Mansfield asked rather for a clearer vision with which to look out. Yet the two procedures are not dia-

[1] Essay on "Modern Fiction," *The Common Reader* (1st ser., 1923).
[2] *Ibid.*
* See chap. v, *The Novel and the Modern World.*

metrically opposite, but tend rather to amount to very much the same thing. In practice, what it came to was this: Katherine Mansfield refined herself before looking out on life, while Virginia Woolf refined life before looking out on it. Katherine Mansfield regarded her preliminary personal refinement as a clarification of her vision; Virginia Woolf regarded her preliminary refinement of life as guaranteeing that she would concern herself only with what is important, true, or enduring. About the novels of Wells, Bennett, and Galsworthy, she says:

> If we fasten . . . . one label on all these books, on which is one word materialists, we mean by it that they write of unimportant things; that they spend immense skill and immense industry making the trivial and the transitory appear the true and the enduring.[3]

But under what conditions can one man's sensibility judge between two rival views of truth and permanence in experience? A question we should like Mrs. Woolf to have answered for us.

So in Virginia Woolf we have one more novelist in whom a purely personal sense of significance replaces the sense of significance supplied by a tradition. The disintegration of the background of belief manifests itself in many interesting ways. To accept the traditional schematization was unartistic to Joyce, meant the lack of objective truth to Katherine Mansfield, and meant the presentation of the unimportant and the trivial to Virginia Woolf.

It is rarely that an artist is conscious of the forces in civilization that are compelling him to write as he does. The artistic mind tends to think in terms of absolutes and universal laws: there have been few if any leaders of new movements in art who were aware of what conditioned their view or who regarded their movement only as a temporary expedient for meeting a transient situation. But Mrs. Woolf has laid her finger on one of the main conditioning factors of her attitude and technique:

> To believe that your impressions hold good for others is to be released from the cramp and confinement of personality. It is to be free, as Scott was free, to explore with a vigour which still holds us spell-bound the whole world of adventure and romance. It is also the first step in that mysterious process in which Jane Austen was so great an adept. The little grain of experience once selected, believed in, and set outside herself, could be put precisely in its place, and she was then free to make it . . . . into that complete statement which is literature.
>
> So then our contemporaries afflict us because they have ceased to believe. The most sincere of them will only tell us what it is that happens to himself. They cannot make a world, because they are not free of other human beings.[4]

[3] *Ibid.*
[4] "How It Strikes a Contemporary," *ibid.*

It is a matter of belief. Your own impressions hold good for others if both you and your public accept automatically a common schematization of reality, but not otherwise. That was why Scott and Jane Austen enjoyed the freedom Mrs. Woolf describes. That is why "our contemporaries afflict us because they have ceased to believe." This is precisely the problem of a transition period. Mrs. Woolf's attitude and technique represent one attempt to solve that problem: it is understandable that she should think it the only possible one.

Mrs. Woolf's particular kind of refinement of life led eventually to the emergence of one theme which dominates all her fiction, from *Mrs. Dalloway* to *The Years*. This is a theme characteristically abstract, characteristically philosophical, to which action, character, and commentary are alike subordinated; the theme of time, death, and personality and the relations of these three to each other and to some ultimate which includes them all. Significance in events is increasingly judged in terms of these three factors. It is not so much the quality of the observation of life (as it is in Katherine Mansfield) which makes her points, but reflection after observation. A twofold process of rarification goes on. First, life is refined before it is observed with the artist's eye; second, the results of observation are meditatively chewed on as they are being presented to the reader. A certain lack of body in her work is the result.

Mrs. Woolf began her career as a novelist with the publication of *The Voyage Out* in 1915. It is a slow and rather dull piece of work, traditional in style and conventionally ambitious in scope. It is, in fact, the promising first novel—but with a difference. The plot is quiet, with no complications and no moments of high tension, no usual feature of the promising first novel. There is a quiet impressionism in the telling of the story which deals with the development of Rachel Vinrace from the time when she sails on the voyage out with the other characters on the "Euphrosyne" up to her peaceful death in the hospital at Santa Marina just after she has acquired the ability to take a grip on life. Already we see what is to be a characteristic theme of the author's—death as a part of life, an incident in life, and a means to its interpretation. Throughout the book a highly rarified life flows gently on, the individuals merging gracefully into the stream. Death is an incident, and the stream flows on. There is a suggestion that reality is, in a sense, outside time—a suggestion that we are to meet with again and again in Virginia Woolf's work. The escape from chronology is a common and significant feature of modern fiction: when life as a series of chronological events ceases to have meaning, every possible new way of re-creating value is explored.

Night and Day (1919) demonstrated to Mrs. Woolf herself that the disparity between her matter and her manner was threatening her with inhibition as a novelist altogether. You cannot distil refined essences of time and personality while employing the traditional technique of the novel. The kind of novel form Mrs. Woolf had up till now been using had been evolved over a period of well over a century as the best means of presenting a pattern of significant events. But Mrs. Woolf wanted to present a distillation of significant ideas about events, which was a very different thing, and required a much less rigid form. This is not the "novel of ideas," which is a very much older form, but a much more tenuous thing—the novel of refined lyrical speculation. In *Night and Day* Mrs. Woolf makes her last attempt to use the traditional novel form for her increasingly untraditional purposes. But she is caught in its toils. And the more she struggles the more she becomes enmeshed, until the novel becomes the very opposite, we suspect, of what it was intended to be—a heavy protracted piece of work with a quite glaring disparity between form and content. As though to compensate, the characters are made to indulge desperately in long monologues, trying to break down the restricting barriers of fact and event, trying to win through to the freer realms of meditative lyricism which Mrs. Woolf achieved in *Mrs. Dalloway* and, most successfully of all, in parts of *To the Lighthouse*. Katherine, the heroine, with her fierce desire to be honest with herself and her many intellectual qualities (we catch many glimpses of her creator) drags her way slowly through the book, proceeding from action to speculation and from speculation to action in a manner which finally wearies the reader. We can see now that what Virginia Woolf required was a technique which would unite action and speculation in one "semi-transparent envelope."

Night and Day has many impressive qualities. The individual characters are carefully studied and presented; the psychological aspect of the novel is seriously and thoughtfully done; many of the critical incidents are presented with vividness and power. But the traditional form of patterned external action illustrating or corresponding to the relevant ideas of the author is too rigid to contain successfully what Mrs. Woolf had to say. When fiction is part of a stable and confident civilization, such a technique becomes the natural one; but a sensitive and original artist of Mrs. Woolf's generation, with her heredity, her problems, her desire to emancipate herself from a background which she believed to be far more rigid than the nature of things warranted— such a writer would soon be forced to realize the inadequacy of that technique and to search for a new one.

It was not a long search. It is represented in a little volume published in 1921 under the title *Monday or Tuesday*. Here the no man's land between prose and poetry, between fiction and lyricism, is carefully explored. Here all the traditional features of prose narrative— plot, characterization, description, etc.—are deliberately blurred into a new unity, into a "luminous halo, a semi-transparent envelope." Sensibility is sent wandering to and fro, noting this, lingering on that, collecting facts, impressions, moods, ideas, uniting them all into that diaphanous whole which for Mrs. Woolf is the true symbol of life. Some of the sketches in this volume are simply studies in impressionism. "The String Quartet" and "The Haunted House" are little more than this. But even here it is not impressionism for its own sake that Mrs. Woolf is giving us, but an exploration of the possibilities of certain types of impressionist approach—their possibilities for novel-writing, for helping to create the feel of life as she understood it. Sketches like "The Mark on the Wall" and "Kew Gardens" explore the subtler aspects of the relation between the senses and the emotions, between physical and mental experience; we see, for example, a certain color effect suggesting certain ideas which in turn suggest certain effects in terms of one of the other senses. The mind, or perhaps more accurately the sensibility, is a kind of general junction; something enters as a sense perception and emerges as a thought or a mood or another kind of sense perception. And around the whole lies the semi-transparent envelope. The whole purpose of these experiments is most adequately illustrated by the title sketch, "Monday or Tuesday," where we see clearly the attempt to create a distilled essence of reality by combining in a unity, whose context is more poetical or lyrical than fictional, a host of sense impressions, records of fact, and speculations. What larger purpose this new technique is to serve is not altogether clear from *Monday or Tuesday,* although in the light of her subsequent work it is not difficult to find its microcosm in this book of sketches. One thing, however, could have been predicted with certainty by the first reviewer of the book: henceforth, Mrs. Woolf had cast the traditional technique behind her and was to use it no more.

In her essay on "Modern Fiction," from which we have already quoted, Virginia Woolf referred with approval to Joyce's *Ulysses,* then (1919) appearing in the *Little Review.* There were many aspects of the technique of *Ulysses* that must have appealed to her. The "stream of consciousness" method, so useful in breaking down the distinction between subject and object and in suggesting rather than describing states of mind, must have impressed her in Joyce and in Dorothy Richardson (five parts of whose *Pilgrimage* had already appeared). For breaking down distinctions and suggesting rather than stating were two important ways of creating the "luminous halo, [the] semi-transparent envelope surrounding us from the beginning of consciousness to the end." Already in 1919 Virginia Woolf was contrasting Joyce with the other English novelists of her time:

> In contrast with those whom we have called materialists Mr. Joyce is spiritual; he is concerned at all costs to reveal the flickerings of that in-nermost flame which flashes its messages through the brain, and in order to preserve it he disregards with complete courage whatever seems to him adventitious, whether it be probability, or coherence or any other

of these signposts which for generations have served to support the imagination of a reader when called upon to imagine what he can neither touch nor see.[5]

It is interesting to see Mrs. Woolf discussing Joyce's technique in terms of her own purpose. Their purposes were in fact very different. Joyce's aim was to isolate reality from all human attitudes—an attempt to remove the normative element from fiction completely, to create a self-contained world independent of all values in the observer, independent even (as though this were possible) of all values in the creator. But Virginia Woolf refines on values rather than eliminates them. Her reaction to crumbling norms is not agnosticism but sophistication. It might be argued that a meditative refinement of experience, of the kind that Mrs. Woolf gives us in *To the Lighthouse* or *Mrs. Dalloway,* is halfway to the vacuum world of Joyce, because the ultimate point of refinement comes when we refine out of existence. From the rarified atmosphere of *To the Lighthouse* to the completely neutral atmosphere of *Ulysses* is perhaps but a step. Such an argument would at least have the merit of recognizing a common object in the work of these two writers, namely, escape from the necessity of utilizing a value framework which they both recognized, consciously or unconsciously, to have crumbled. A sufficiently rarified philosophy is, for all practical purposes, very close to complete unbelief. But it is not complete unbelief, and therefore Mrs. Woolf does not have Joyce's problem, which is to present to the reader a world for contemplation without believing, or implying any belief, that that world is worth contemplating. Joyce's colossal technical virtuosity is a way of hiding that problem from himself, just as the slogan "art for art's sake" is a way of disguising a belief in the worthlessness of art which, if expressed bluntly, would be too discouraging for the artist. So if the immediate purposes of James Joyce and Virginia Woolf were very different, their ultimate purposes were perhaps the same—to find a solution to the all-important value problem. Joyce went the whole way in rejecting the normative and involved himself in an immense paradox; Virginia Woolf went only halfway (probably without being conscious that she was going in that direction at all) and stopped at subtilization. When she calls Wells, Bennett, and Galsworthy materialists, what she really means is that they accept the old, traditional criteria in describing events, while she is conscious of the dissolution of those criteria. The issue does not really lie between materialists and idealists, but between those who accept and those who reject the traditional norms in discussing experience. When Virginia Woolf said that "Mr. Joyce is spiritual," she meant that Mr. Joyce had shown himself, by his method of writing, to be unsatisfied with those norms. If in her own case such dissatisfaction

[5] "Modern Fiction," *ibid.*

was to result in spiritualization of experience, in meditative refinement of events, that did not mean that spiritualization was the only way out.

But whatever the precise relation of Joyce's work to that of Mrs. Woolf, the fact remains that after *Monday or Tuesday* Mrs. Woolf was committed to the search for a new method in the organization and presentation of narrative which arose from the necessity of finding a method of treating experience which, while normative, was yet liberated from the traditional schematization. To seek for such liberation and yet desire to retain value criteria is a very delicate task, and perhaps this explains why Mrs. Woolf achieved her state of unstable equilibrium only twice in her career as a novelist. It is, however, a task which does not raise the even greater problems which await those who, like Joyce, profess to believe in experience without distinguishing values within it.

Jacob's Room appeared in 1922, and here we see Virginia Woolf deliberately experimental both in theme and in technique. The theme is to become her favorite one: the nature of personality and its relation to time and death. Jacob, the hero, is presented, not directly through description, but through the impressions which are relevant to his personality. Thus we are shown what he sees and what is to be seen in his environment; the reflection of him in other persons' minds; what he himself thinks, feels, does (but little of the last); what is felt and thought by others who move in his world; and finally what impressions which originally took their origin in his personality remain with others after his death. Jacob's character emanates, as it were, from the book; Virginia Woolf's technique is deliberately by indirections to find directions out. Jacob's room is used as an integrating factor, though not so consistently as the title might lead us to believe. The atmosphere of the whole book is tenuous, largely because the author's aim is speculative rather than descriptive. The question implicitly posed by the story—if story it can be called—is in essence a metaphysical rather than a psychological one; and the answer is not stated but suggested. What is personality? How does it impinge on its environment? What is its relation to events in time? What is the nature of reality in so far as it is related to the mental and emotional world of men? It is to answer these questions that Virginia Woolf selects and refines on data abstracted with care and delicacy from human experience.

The aeration of her style which was one of the many ways in which Mrs. Woolf tried to free herself from the inhibiting features of the traditional novel—an aeration which *Night and Day* showed her to be much in need of, and which is shown in process in *Monday or Tuesday*—was perhaps carried a little too far in *Jacob's Room,* and in her following novel, *Mrs. Dalloway* (1925), there is a successful attempt to redress the balance. By this time the "stream of consciousness" technique had become almost a commonplace in fiction, and the problem was not so much to win freedom to employ it as to find a way of disciplining it. It is one thing to have the relation between your characters' impressions clear in your own mind and quite another to have them objectively clear in the form of the work itself. Virginia Woolf seems to have grappled carefully with the latter problem in *Mrs. Dalloway:* she limits its scope in time and place; her characters are few and their relations to each other clear-cut; impressions and thought processes are assigned clearly to those to whom they belong, even at the risk of losing some immediacy of effect; the time scheme is patterned with extraordinary care; and altogether the novel represents as neat a piece of construction as she has ever achieved. It is therefore an excellent example to take for a more detailed technical analysis.

Just as Joyce in *Ulysses* takes one day in the life of Leopold Bloom and enlarges its implications by patterning its events with sufficient care, so Virginia Woolf takes from morning to evening in the life of Mrs. Dalloway and builds her story through the events of this short

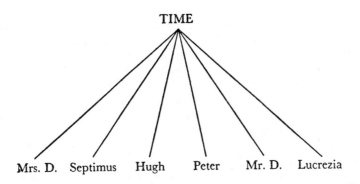

TIME

Mrs. D.   Septimus   Hugh   Peter   Mr. D.   Lucrezia

time. (Events, of course, include psychological as well as physical happenings.) Being a far shorter and less ambitious work than *Ulysses,* *Mrs. Dalloway* employs a simpler and more easily analyzable technique. The whole novel is constructed in terms of the two dimensions of space and time. We either stand still in time and are led to contemplate diverse but contemporaneous events in space or we stand still in space and are allowed to move up and down temporarily in the consciousness of one individual. If it would not be extravagant to consider personality rather than space as one dimension, with time as the other, we might divide the book quite easily into those sections where time is fluid and time is stable, and regard this as a careful alternation of the dimensions. So that at one point we are halted at a London street to take a peep into the consciousness of a variety of people who are all on the spot at the same moment in the same place, and at another we are halted within the consciousness of one individual moving up and down in time within the limits of one individual's memory. The two methods might be represented diagrammatically as shown on page 497 and below.

In the first case time is the unifying factor, making, without the knowledge of anyone except the omniscient author, significant patterns out of chance. (But, Is it chance? and What is chance? Mrs. Woolf would ask.)

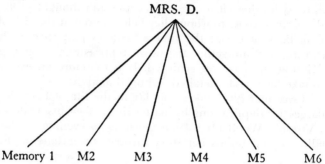

Here personality is the unifying factor, seeking a pattern in time by means of memory. Taking A, B, C, etc., to represent characters, T to represent the present moment (in terms of the action of the novel) and T_1, T_2, T_3, etc., to represent past moments, we might diagrammatically represent the movement of the novel as a whole as shown on page 499.

The groups of T's are, of course, different, as being presented through the consciousness of different characters. And the book does not proceed in the straightforward mathematical way indicated by the diagrams; but that is its general movement. The plot is carried forward through the line ATFTATBTA, beginning and ending with the principal character on the day whose action is described. Of course, T in the diagram is not a unique moment of time, but simply any moment of the day in question; actually, T progresses from morning to night through each stage in the diagram. The fact that the line ATFTAT-BTA, though it represents the carrying-forward of the chronological action (the plot, in the vulgar sense), represents only discrete fragments of thought and action and gives no adequate view of the real story is partly the measure of Mrs. Woolf's deviation from traditional methods in her construction of the story.

It would be simple to go through *Mrs. Dalloway* to show how first we get the "stream of consciousness" of a particular character; then we pause to look over the character's environment and take a glance inside the minds of other characters who are in or relevant to that environment; then we come to rest within the mind of one of those other characters and investigate his consciousness for a while; and then again we emerge to contemplate the environment, etc. And each time we pause to investigate the mind of any one character in some detail, that mind takes us into the past, and we escape altogether from the chronological time sequence of the story. As in *Ulysses,* though on a much smaller scale, the past figures more than the present, even though the action covers one single day.

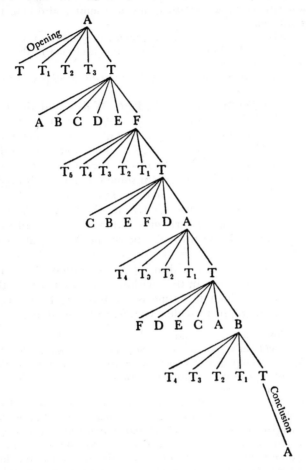

Mrs. Woolf, although her scope is much more limited than Joyce's, takes much more care than Joyce does to put up signposts. When we are staying still in time and moving rapidly through the minds of various characters, Mrs. Woolf is very careful to mark those points of time, to see to it that the unifying factor which is holding these quite disparate consciousnesses together is made clear to the reader. That is why the clocks of London chime right through the book, from start to finish. When we wander through different personalities, we are kept from straying by the time indications, and, conversely, when we go up and down in time through the memory of one of the characters, we are kept from straying by the constant reminder of the speaker's identity. There is nothing haphazard about the striking of the clocks:

> "The time, Septimus," Rezia repeated. "What is the time?"
> He was talking, he was starting, this man must notice him. He was looking at them.
> "I will tell you the time," said Septimus, very slowly, very drowsily, smiling mysteriously. As he sat smiling at the dead man in the grey suit the quarter struck—the quarter to twelve.
> And that is being young, Peter Walsh thought as he passed them.

We pass from Septimus Smith to Peter Walsh, and the striking of the hour marks the transition. If we are not to lose our way among the various consciousnesses, we must understand why we are taken from one to another: because they impinge in time, and that impingement is symbolized by the striking of the clock. Almost every fifteen minutes is indicated by a clock chiming, or in some other way, throughout the book. We can always find out, at most by looking a page ahead or consulting the previous page, just what time of day it is. And these indications of time are most clearly given when we are about to go from personality to personality—through one of the ABCD rather than the $T_1 T_2 T_3$ lines.

Similarly, when we pause within the consciousness of one character only to move up and down in time within that consciousness, the identity of the thinker, which this time is the unifying factor, is stressed. The opening paragraphs provide a characteristic example:

> Mrs. Dalloway said she would buy the flowers herself.
> For Lucy had her work cut out for her. The doors would be taken off their hinges; Rumpelmayer's men were coming. And then, thought Clarissa Dalloway, what a morning—fresh as if issued to children on a beach.
> What a lark! What a plunge! For so it had always seemed to her, when, with a little squeak of the hinges, which she could hear now, she had burst open the French windows and plunged at Bourton into the open air. How fresh, how calm, stiller than this of course, the air was in the early morning; like the flap of a wave; the kiss of a wave; chill and sharp and yet (for a girl of eighteen as she then was) solemn, feeling as she did, standing there at the open window, that something awful was about to happen. . . . .

The compromise between reported and direct thought here seems to be due to Mrs. Woolf's desire to keep the unifying factor always present to the reader's mind, but it has some interesting results. The "I" of the reverie becomes an indeterminate kind of pronoun midway between "she" (which it would have been had Mrs. Woolf used the straight objective reporting of the traditional novel) and the first personal pronoun employed naturally by the real "stream of consciousness" writer. It is not surprising to find Mrs. Woolf frequently taking refuge in "one," as in the following very characteristic sentence: "For having lived in Westminster—how many years now? over twenty—one feels even in the midst of the traffic, or waking at night, Clarissa was positive, a particular hush, or solemnity...."

Here the movement is from a suppressed "I" (in the parenthetical clause) to a "one" and then, on account of the necessity of stressing the unifying factor, namely the identity of Clarissa Dalloway, to a straight third-person use of "Clarissa." We might note, too, the frequent use of the present participle ("....she cried to herself, pushing through the swing doors"; "she thought, waiting to cross," "....she asked herself, walking towards Bond Street"), which enables her to identify the thinker and carry her into a new action without interrupting the even flow of the thought stream; and the frequent commencement of a paragraph with "for," the author's conjunction (not the thinker's), whose purpose is to indicate the vague, pseudo-logical connection between the different sections of a reverie.

It is through a technique of this kind that Virginia Woolf in *Mrs. Dalloway* endeavors to present the results of her refined speculation. There is no doubt that the technique is, in itself, successful, even masterly; but whether she has really achieved the end to which the technique is a means is another question. A highly abstract pattern of life is meant to be distilled out of certain fairly commonplace events which happen at the same time to be a slice of life chosen from the activity of men and women in a big city. Is that pattern convincing or even intelligible? And, if it is, do we feel it to be true, to correspond to facts about human experience that matter (which is one of the ultimate criteria of all art)? In the introduction to the Modern Library edition of *Mrs. Dalloway,* the author has this to say:

> Books are the flowers or fruit stuck here and there on a tree which has its roots deep down in the earth of our earliest life, of our first experiences. But here again to tell the reader anything that his own imagination and insight have not already discovered would need not a page or two of preface but a volume or two of autobiography. Slowly and cautiously one would have to go to work, uncovering, laying bare, and even so when everything had been brought to the surface, it would still be for the reader to decide what was relevant and what not. Of *Mrs. Dalloway* then one can only bring to light at the moment a few scraps, of little importance or none perhaps; as that in the first version Septimus, who later is intended to be her double, had no existence; and that Mrs. Dalloway was originally to kill herself, or perhaps merely to die at the end of the party.

The present writer must confess that he received a considerable shock on first reading this. The casual remark about the part meant to be played by Septimus seemed to be a refinement on the events described, so utterly unwarranted by the events themselves, and seemed to indicate so remote an attitude on the part of the author to the relation between fact and its interpretation, that for the moment the book ceased to have such meaning as it had possessed before and became a fantastic abstract allegory, which might mean anything and therefore meant nothing. This was but a momentary reaction, but it did seem to have reference to some inherent defect in the book. Is it simply that the relation between the real and the symbolic aspects of the characters was not made sufficiently clear? Or is it that the symbolic aspects are out of proportion to the real aspects? Perhaps the latter question gets nearer the truth. The refining intellect seems to have "o'er-leapt itself and fallen on the other side."

The author must be a freeborn citizen of the world he is describing and interpreting if his description and interpretation are to result in a permanently valid pattern of experience. One can become a freeborn citizen through imagination—though imagination working always on a minimum of knowledge. If, however, you live both imaginatively and—might one say?—epistemologically in a world other than the one you are describing, somewhere in your work there will be something that does not fit. The themes of time, death, and personality that run through *Mrs. Dalloway* as through so many of Mrs. Woolf's novels are not in themselves unreal or insignificant; but when a twentieth-century novelist tries to present these themes through a picture, however refined, of post-war London society, they may become insignificant or unreal. True, a work of art, once accomplished, stands on its own legs and is not good in one century and bad in another; but that does not mean that the artist is free to ignore the intellectual climate of his time in creating a work. You can bring your world into your study and deal with it in complete abstraction or you can go out to meet it and surrender freedom for substance. There are unfortunate extremes in both procedures, but the latter is the safer (and harder) way. One wonders if Mrs. Woolf's conception of fiction in terms of poetry is not an excuse for remaining in her study. The lyrical mood has many disguises, but its basis, like that of the metaphysical mood, is egotism. Egotism can be one of the greatest virtues in art, but that depends on the author's right to speak for others: that right only history can decide, not the individual.

Mrs. Dalloway is an impressive work; it shows a brilliance and finesse in execution that no critic can forbear to admire. But somehow there is a crack that shows the light between form and substance. To take what is perhaps an overcurious analogy: it is (or was) a noble thing to be a suffragette, and nothing else. But who would be a suffragette and nothing else in a world menaced by fascism?

To the Lighthouse, published in 1927, represents what one may call the Virginian compromise to perfection. Virginia Woolf has taken into her study aspects of experience which suffer least in that environment; she has compromised between her refining intellect and the real world by limiting her definition of the real to its refinable aspects and at the same time recognizing the definition as a limited one. The setting, in northwest Scotland, is not only appropriate to the half-lyrical mood in which the book is written, but it is also an adequate symbol of those aspects of action and emotion in which she is most interested and which she is best able to handle. The time-death-personality theme is handled much more explicitly than in the earlier novels, and with real success. The rarified atmosphere for the first time is right; it corresponds adequately to the situation. This is minor fiction at its most triumphant— minor, because after all it does deal with a backwater of human experience; triumphant, because it is done so perfectly. In terms of diurnal reviewing, to call a work minor might imply the height of abuse, but it is not in that sense that the term is here used. A first-rate minor work is worth many second-rate major ones.

There are some interesting differences in technique between *Mrs. Dalloway* and *To the Lighthouse.* In the latter book the time scheme is wider and mood and retrospect are shown against a background of actual change, not only remembered change as in the former. In the first part of *To the Lighthouse* the reader is presented with what the characters look back on in the last part, and this leaves the author freer than she was in *Mrs. Dalloway* in her weaving of musing and recollection. There is no need to be so careful about signposts. The wider freedom in *To the Lighthouse* is the direct result of the greater limitation of the world presented. If you limit your world to a circumscribed area within which everything is relevant to the pattern you wish to weave, you are freer to move where you will in that world than you would be if you chose a larger world and wove your pattern by means of rigid selection and abstraction. That is the difference between the two novels.

To the Lighthouse represents that state of unstable equilibrium which most really good minor artists achieve but once in their careers. Everything conspires to minimize the author's characteristic defects. Virginia Woolf's fatal gift for making everything transparent, including the most solid things of life, is not recognized as fatal when it works on a collection of intellectuals set down at holiday time in the Isle of Skye. Perhaps the author realized this, for her next work, *Orlando,* published in 1928, is a deliberate attempt to express some of her main themes through fantasy. It is a threefold stage: First, there is the attempt to create an abstract pattern by unduly refining on the events of the real world; then comes a restriction of the real world to those aspects which can stand such refinement with least distortion; finally, the real world is left behind, to be drawn on or ignored at will, and the abstract pattern has no responsibility to life at all.

Orlando is a brilliant *jeu d'esprit* rather than a serious novel. Tracing the physical and literary ancestors of her friend, Victoria Sackville West, from late Elizabethan times to the present, through the adventures of a hero who changes sex en route, and treating that hero as nevertheless a single personality, Mrs. Woolf manages to collect on her way some highly effective descriptions of scenes partly historical and partly imaginary, displaying a colorfulness and a vivacity that the rest of her fiction conspicuously lacks. It is perhaps illuminating that the most vivacious of her books should be the most fantastic and in many ways the least serious. In spite of the element of fantasy, in spite of the irresponsible hero who marches through time from one impossible situation to another, the book has tremendous vigor and pulses with life. The earlier portions particularly, when the hero is still in the seventeenth century, have a reality that poor Mrs. Dalloway never attained. Probably no two novelists were ever more dissimilar than Virginia Woolf and Eric Linklater, but there is a smack of Linklater in *Orlando,* which certainly adds to the book's qualities. It would be a weary task to disentangle the profoundly symbolic from the deliberately irresponsible in *Orlando:* it is a book to be read with the surface of the mind and enjoyed for its surface brilliance. It would be unfair to its author and to its readers to treat it as a great novel.

So ended the second round. *The Waves,* published in 1931, ushers in the third. In this final section of Mrs. Woolf's work, which so far includes *The Waves* and *The Years,* her refining and abstracting tendencies are given full scope, and the result is an exhibition of unconvincing virtuosity which depresses as much as it impresses. The former of the two is almost wholly symbolic; time divisions in the lives of the six characters are marked by set descriptions of seascapes at different periods of the day, and the characters speak throughout in stylized monologues through which their natures, their attitudes, and the story of their lives from infancy to death are presented. Again, time, death, and personality, and their interrelations, provide the main theme; here, the emphasis being on time. The book is more artificial than anything else Mrs. Woolf has written, owing to the continuous use of the formal interior monologue. It contains some beautiful prose, some sensitive and suggestive writing, but there is nothing to warm the book into vitality. *The Years,* a ponderous and overambitious novel, is equally obviously the product of the study. In its scope and tone it reminds us of one of the very early novels, such as *Night and Day;* it has the same defect of appearing to fall into heaviness through excessive abstraction. There are no startling innovations of technique; we are led with every sign of intelligence and even profundity through the life-histories of the main characters; nothing is too obscure or too unusual. But somehow life does not respond to this intelligent bullying, and the book never lights up. Having gone all the way to fantasy in *Orlando,* it seems that Mrs. Woolf has not been able to come back into serious fiction and to bring with her that lightness of touch and delicacy of treatment that distinguished her middle novels. That side of her art was left permanently behind with *Orlando*.

The Years was a best seller both in Britain and America, but that represented a belated tribute to her genius as manifested in her earlier work rather than a spontaneous outburst of enthusiasm for this particular novel. Critics praised *The Years* more or less out of a sense of duty. The reviews were more important as an indication of the position Virginia Woolf had attained in popular estimation than as indicating the quality of the book. And her reputation is high, and deservedly so. For she tried honestly and sincerely to solve by compromise a problem which Joyce tried to solve by a "revolution of the word" (to use Eugene Jolas' favorite phrase) but which most contemporary novelists did not try to solve at all. Her own training and mental habits led her to see the problem as one of finding a new technique to fit a vision, while the problem was really much wider and much more fundamental. But her attempts have by no means been in vain. They have led her to produce at least one excellent minor novel and to make an important contribution to the technique of fiction. Contributions to technique, whatever their origin, are never made in vain.

The history of the twentieth-century novel will always have added interest because of the cultural transition which is taking place in our time—the gap in the background of belief and the paving of the way toward a new background. Joyce met the problem by retreating into a realm without values; Katherine Mansfield met it by endeavoring to cultivate an impossible purity of vision; Aldous Huxley met it by denunciation followed by romantic compensation; Virginia Woolf met it by trying to refine all life into a problem for the meditative intellect. There were very many worse ways.

FANTASY IN THE FICTION OF
EUDORA WELTY *

Eunice Glenn

Somewhere between the prose fiction regarded as "realism" and that, on the other hand, which purports to deal only with the inner life of the mind, is the fiction of Eudora Welty; in its method implicating both tendencies and yet, somehow, transcending each. The kind of reality which is not immediately apparent to the senses is described by the late Virginia Woolf as "what remains over when the skin of the day has been cast into the hedge." Miss Welty takes full account of the "skin of the day," even withholding it from the hedge; it is a vital element in her work, for she is not afraid to face and report the harsh, even the brutal reality of everyday life. But at the same time she is fully sensitive to "what remains over." The kernel, with all its richness and germinative power, is there, well preserved; but it is covered by the husk, coarse and substantial.

It is in the inter-relationship of the external and the internal—reality and the imagination—that the particular significance of Miss Welty's method would seem to be. Logic is her background, the logic in the relationship of ideas. The dream, reflecting the irrational world in which we live, goes out to meet it. Sometimes near the beginning of a story, sometimes at intervals throughout it, and again perhaps only at the end, these two worlds become fused; and usually a reconciliation is produced, for both are concurring toward the same end. Instead of serving as an escape from ordinary experience, fantasy brings it into a fuller light and contributes to its interpretation. It is as though the author brought actual events up under a microscopic lens and threw the force of an illuminating mirror upon them. What she shows us could not be seen with the naked human eye; therefore, it appears as improbable. Reality, thus magnified, becomes fantasy.

A microscopic vision such as this, naturally, involves careful focusing; and within the limits of the short story, which is Miss Welty's chief medium, it is understandable that much exclusion is necessary. Her characters, representing ideas as they do, cannot be fully realized as individuals *per se.* She leaves that to the novelist, whose scope is larger, and to the writer of short stories who is concerned primarily with the portrayal of

* "Fantasy in the Fiction of Eudora Welty" originally appeared in *A Southern Vanguard,* edited by Allen Tate (Prentice-Hall, 1947), and is here reprinted for the first time by permission of the author.

character. She is not interested, in her short pieces, in telling us everything about a character; instead, she selects only such material as will
suit her needs. Deliberately fixing her boundaries, like those of a picture
frame, she arranges the elements within a particular area of experience
that will fit into the frame and produce a harmonious result.

In her concern with theme, however, Miss Welty does not succumb to
a mere manipulation of her characters, like puppets, for the representation of ideas. Her people are real individuals, even when they may seem
to be only caricatures. They are never oversimplified, though, from the
standpoint of art, they may exist in the smallest sphere. This remarkable
achievement is undoubtedly due to the author's power of discrimination; her keen psychological insight—her understanding of the subtleties
of human behavior.

Miss Welty is very much interested in abnormal behavior and treats
it with deep discernment. But her mentally deficient and particularly
her mentally ill individuals consistently show traits that are commonly
regarded as normal. Thus they symbolize insane persons living in an
insane modern world. Out of their crazed brains, however, there always
emerges some rationality, some sanity: the backfire of the inner life
against prevailing disorder. Many other types of "unfortunates," as well,
in Miss Welty's stories exemplify this tendency to assume individual dignity, from an inner direction. There are members of racial minorities,
the economically oppressed, shut-ins, and various individuals in the grip
of social forces. Little Lee Roy, a Negro man in the story, "Keela, The
Outcast Indian Maid," does not wish or need the reparation offered him
for a terrible wrong. Partly because of their utter lack of comprehension
of the intricate reason for this, those who have done him the wrong are
the ones who suffer; they are their own victims. In the beautiful story,
"A Worn Path," the nurse at the clinic becomes aware of a barrier, the
nature of which she is unable to explain, between herself and Grandma,
an old Negro woman. Similarly, "A Visit of Charity" reveals a Campfire
Girl's helplessness on the occasion of a dutiful visit to an Old Ladies'
Home. Then there is the half-witted girl, in "Lyly Daw and the Three
Ladies," who is superior to misdirected efforts to help her. The well-
meaning but patronizing ladies are pathetically unable to cross the imponderable distance between themselves and the girl; to grasp her real
needs.

In all of these and in many other stories of Miss Welty the conventional pattern is rearranged and the people appear in new positions.
Those who are seemingly defenseless become superior; while those who
are tangibly superior become the really unfortunate, because of a more
important deficiency within themselves. They are inevitably turned
back upon their feelings of guilt.

Thus, Miss Welty shows us the individual pitted against modern society—a diseased society, which finds its reflection in distorted minds and

lives. But the individual's conscious, or perhaps more often unconscious reaction to a mad world is one of defiance. At the most unexpected moments those who would seem to be in total despair manage somehow to rise out of it. The pathos of the heroine in "Why I Live at the Post Office," who is a victim of painful self-consciousness and the will to be imposed upon, is balanced by something in her that exults; she strikes back. So does Little Lee Roy, and Lyly Daw, and Grandma; the frustrated old maid in "Clytie," who walks upon the street looking at faces and for beauty, and finds it in the face of a child; and the heroine in the story, "Livvie," who has her own way of ascendancy.

The neuroses that result from the individual's inability to reconcile himself with society are thoroughly realized in Miss Welty's characters. She writes of those whose lives are circumscribed by corruption, many forms of it—triviality, malignity, vulgarity, snobbery, self-pity, bitterness, power mania, and human cruelty that cuts deep. But her superior technique relieves her work from many of the faults common to fiction which attempts to deal with bare reality. She escapes the mere spreading of grossness and evil before your eyes, and asking you to weep, or approve, or to conclude that human nature is hopeless. Nor is there in her work the slightest hint of collusion with characters who exemplify symptomatic wrongs; an impression which is so often obtained from realistic fiction, in spite of the intentions of the author. Miss Welty is, indeed, far removed from any trace of such slackness or negativism; or tender indulgence, so easily resolving into soft sentimentality. Her tolerance is one that is more magnanimous, superseding that which is remiss. For it is apparent that Miss Welty believes that there is such a thing as individual responsibility; and also that conscious volition is a quality to be taken into account, if not the core of human existence—a sane human existence.

Miss Welty's knowledge and attitudes can only be realized, however, in terms of her art. Her transcendence of bold sensationalism and of slackness, on the one hand, and hardness and restricted moral teaching, on the other, is inherent in the structure of her stories. Tone is controlled with sureness and delicacy. Her diverse shadings in tone, the shifts, the blending of two or more tones together, and the complexity—all do wonders with the material. It would be simplifying the matter to say only that she has a qualifying irony; but that lies over it all: toughness continuously controls, where otherwise pathos would get out of hand, and bring ruin. Her blade of satire cuts through human evil with unfailing sharpness; and she adds her scalding humor; as well as an enviable compound of compassion and just condemnation. The result is a totality, that refuses to be restricted to any one conventional attitude.

Miss Welty often employs the grotesque for evoking a sense of the horror of evil. Intensified, magnified into unreasonable proportions, the baseness of the everyday world confronts the reader, whose first impulse is to revolt: at the humiliation of Little Lee Roy when he is forced to eat live chickens and drink their blood, for the amusement of spectators; at the highly symbolical jeweled hat pin as it enters the ribs and pierces the heart of its victim, in "The Purple Hat"; at the spectacle of the old maid drowning herself in a barrel of rain water, her feet sticking up ludicrously, in "Clytie"; at the morbid river-dragging party in "The Wide Net"; and at the stone man, pygmies and twins in a bottle, of the traveling freak show, in "Petrified Man." Unlike Poe, Miss Welty is far removed from conjuring scenes of horror for its own sake. She uses it for a specific purpose: to make everyday life appear as it often does, without the use of a magnifying glass, to the person with extraordinary acuteness of feeling. Her fantastical characters become actual persons; her incongruous events those that are taking place every day. As in Thomas Mann's novel of the grotesque, *The Transposed Heads,* gruesomeness sharpens the sense of social and individual distortion.

Symbols achieve much of the meaning in such stories. In "Petrified Man" the little stone man symbolizes the pettiness, hypocrisy, all the shallowness in the lives of the beauty parlor women in the story. Formidable and hard, the stone is their obdurateness, their death-in-life. The jeweled hat pin is the flashing, steely substance that represents lurking, criminal passions. Symbols like these are strongly reminiscent of some of those used by Nathaniel Hawthorne: in "Ethan Brand," for example, where the leaping flames of the lime-kiln, the fiendlike facial expression, the fearful peals of laughter, and the snow white skeleton crumbling into fragments, characterize Ethan's "Unpardonable Sin."

The story, "Old Mr. Marblehall," is one of the best examples of Miss Welty's unique device in interweaving fantasy and surface reality. Each world, the real and the imagined, impinges upon the other, without obtruding in the actual sense. Both are so real to Mr. Marblehall that he has lost the power to distinguish them, one from the other. And in terms of the story, they are not to be distinguished: at certain points they become one and the same thing, even while maintaining their separate identities, because their end is the same. This coalescence takes place in Mr. Marblehall's mind, particularly when he catches on, "... he thinks, to what people are supposed to do. That is it: they endure something inwardly—for a time secretly; they establish a past, a memory; thus they store up life. ..." His is a soul obsessed with terror (he even reads *Terror Tales*), to be treated with the ironical indulgence, or pity that one might bestow upon a crazy world. But out of his chaotic mind streams some logic that gives him hope. He speculates upon the future, "... upon some glorious finish, a great explosion of revelations." Roderick Usher, in Poe's story, is without such an outlook; he is *completely* enveloped in fear; he realizes his terror, but, unlike Mr. Marblehall, lacks the vision that would give him relief. Mr. Marblehall's "castle in the air," like that of Dickens's character in "The Poor Relation's Story," is his *only secure* "castle."

"Death of a Traveling Salesman," a more powerful and subtle story, demonstrates the same technique, with some variances, and a slightly different resolution. Mr. Bowman comes to terms with reality in an incident which reveals a whole lifetime of experience to him, the sort of which he feels that he has been cheated. The realization in him of his estrangement from humanity is enormous. It comes with such violence of impact that he is stunned—to death. The story is a superb study in autosuggestion, that resulting from an individual's inability to clear his complexes, to cope with the real world. In the story, "Powerhouse," also, a privately constructed world clashes with reality and brings it into focus. "A Piece of News," though a slighter story, illustrates a similar method. The method is general in Miss Welty's stories—that is, reality inevitably collides with the imagination—but these are mentioned merely because of a very noticeable closeness in the technique employed.

All of the stories that have been referred to, with the exception of "The Wide Net" and "The Purple Hat," are to be found in the volume entitled *A Curtain of Green*.[1] In a later volume, *The Wide Net*,[2] Miss Welty moves, for the most part, in a slightly different realm. The imagination has fuller play; there is less of the actual world, except by implication; more of the dream. In no sense are these stories farther from life; on the contrary, they seem to be closer to the very heart of life. But in almost all of them the setting is strange and unearthly. "A Still Moment," the most poetic of them all, has a distinctly legendary flavor. It concerns three persons who at the same moment come across a snow-white heron in the woods: the evangelist, Lorenzo, riding in the wilderness, crying for souls to save; Murrel, the bandit, who too wishes to solve the mystery of life, but by laying hold of men and murdering them; and Audubon, the student, who seeks only radiance and beauty for his art. For one brief moment the snowy shy bird lays quiet over them and unburdens them of their furious desires.

There is a marked similarity in the theme of this story and that of Hawthorne's "The Minister's Black Veil"; there is also a likeness in method, particularly in the conjunction of fantasy with actuality, and the use of symbols. The veil is Hawthorne's symbol of mystery. By hiding his visage the minister hides the secret from the world. In trembling at the sight of the veil, the people tremble at the manifold mystery of their own lives. But Miss Welty's story finds a really remarkable parallel in method in Hawthorne's "The Artist of the Beautiful." In "A Still Moment" the three characters, like Virgil at the moment of his death, discover the meaning of life; with the disintegration of their separate

[1] Doubleday, Doran and Company, 1941.
[2] Harcourt, Brace and Company, 1943.

purposes (which, after all, were the same, with different methods of pursuit) they gain a common insight into the mystery they sought. "As he [Audubon] had seen the bird most purely at its moment of death, in some fatal way, in his care for looking outward, he saw his long labor most revealingly *at the point where it met its limit.*" (Italics mine) This is the experience of Hawthorne's artist, Owen Warland, "... who leaves half his conception on the canvas to sadden us with its imperfect beauty, and goes forth to picture the whole ... in the hues of heaven." Also Lorenzo, fearing death more than anything, and yet managing to escape it by "... turning half-beast and half-divine, dividing himself like a Centaur ...," finds a counterpart in Warland, who felt "... an anxiety lest death should surprise him in the midst of his labors"; whose "anxiety," as Hawthorne adds in a generalization, "is common to all men who set their hearts upon anything so high, in their own view of it, that life becomes of importance only as conditioned to its accomplishment. So long as we love life for itself," he adds, "we seldom dread losing it." Hawthorne could have said this concerning Miss Welty's theme, so identical is it to his. (Miss Welty would not have made the generalization.)

Most striking is the resemblance in the use of symbols in the two stories: the heron in Miss Welty's and the butterfly in Hawthorne's. "It was as if three whirlwinds had drawn together at some center, to find there feeding in peace a snowy heron. Its own slow spiral of flight could take it away in its own time, but for a little it held them still ..." So, the butterfly "had there been no obstruction ... might have soared into the sky and grown immortal." The various effects of the heron and the butterfly upon those who observe them are also interesting in comparison. In Lorenzo the bird incites awe and reverence: "... nothing could really take away what had happened to him ... its beauty had been greater than he could account for ..." As to Murrel, his faith in the innocence of travelers and the knowledge of ruin is shaken; he knows now that there is something outside his grasp. Audubon, because of his quest for beauty, comes nearer than they to appreciating it; but he knows that it has not "... been all his belonging ..." The butterfly causes Robert Danforth to say: "That goes beyond me, I confess. There is more real use in one downright blow of my sledge hammer than in the whole five years' labor that ... Owen has wasted on this butterfly"; and the butterfly droops its wings at his touch. The child who looks at it knows more of its mystery than any of the others, besides its creator. Yet he compresses it in his hands and the mystery of beauty flees forever from the "small heap of glittering fragments." Owen, knowing all of its mystery, can look placidly at what to the others is ruin; the symbol means nothing to him, now that he has achieved the beautiful and made it perceptible to mortals. There are some apparent differences in the way the symbols are used, and in their intended meaning. But at this point Hawthorne and Miss Welty seem to come closer together in specific meaning *and* method than they do elsewhere.

The accident of similar theme and method in particular stories of Hawthorne and Miss Welty, however, seems worthy of attention only for what it indicates: a more general resemblance, which goes much deeper. Throughout the work of the two is a startling similarity, which can come only from related caliber of mind. You feel them striving toward expression of the same values, and finding methods of achievement that are closely kin; Hawthorne, to be sure, more explicit, using more care to make his meaning unmistakable, sometimes intruding in such a way as to damage the structure; Miss Welty leaving more to the discernment of the reader, accomplishing meaning so completely *through* structure that there is little possibility of reducing it to a simple statement, or to any statement at all. But the same preoccupation with the deepening of the ego is there, in both of them; the same effort to discover an equilibrium between inner and outer experience; the same concern with a full recognition of self and the consequent integration with the Universe; the same consciousness of the unutterable loneliness of man: although in the latter Miss Welty comes nearer being a twin of Melville. The Hawthorne who created Ethan Brand would have felt completely at home while reading Miss Welty's story, "At the Landing," which in its characters effects a realization of the mystery of love that seeks wisdom, but finds that the complete vision is always hidden; that one must remain lost in wonder, because of the lack of ability ever to penetrate another's complete being. Hawthorne's story is concerned with wisdom without love; but the same prevailing kinship of theme is there.

However, Hawthorne would probably have liked "The Robber Bridegroom" [3] best of all of Miss Welty's work, because of its greater supernaturalism, closer approximating of idea with image, its more faithful use of material objects as tokens. In *The House of the Seven Gables,* as Miss Welty does in this tale, Hawthorne varies the key, going from realism to supernaturalism, and back again; although *The Robber Bridegroom* better succeeds in reconciling the two. Hawthorne's novel also vacillates from tragedy to comedy; while Miss Welty's shows less variation but more complexity in this sense. In the latter, serious meaning *comes through* wit. The tone is one of mock irony: you see the characters as ridiculous, while at the same time you are appalled at their evil. This skillful control of tone relieves the tale from the somberness of *The Scarlet Letter,* where only one tone is maintained.

It is in *The Robber Bridegroom* that Miss Welty's fantasy has its fullest reach. Whereas many of her short stories are in the nature of parables, some partaking of the nature of allegory, this longer tale is more purely allegory, in its greater consistency in the representation of ideas by characters. Yet it goes beyond an allegory like *Pilgrim's Progress,* where the

[3] Doubleday, Doran and Company, 1942.

pattern is more obvious, the meaning cut in straighter, sharper and simpler lines. Structure in *The Robber Bridegroom* is infinitely more complicated: ideas and characters are interwoven in a system that ingeniously reveals meaning. In its satire, as well as its subtlety and complexity, it is much closer to *Gulliver's Travels*.

Yet the characters in *The Robber Bridegroom,* as in Miss Welty's short stories, could never be said to exist *only* for the conveyance of ideas. Indeed, they are thoroughly realized as individuals; for in the larger expanse that is here, there is more room for a complete presentation of characters. In fact, the story may be said to possess three distinct levels. First, the mere surface, which itself comprises an entertaining and interesting tale that could be read (and probably has been by many) as a story of horror and mystery. There is the strange and exciting wilderness setting, and the romantic and gruesome happenings, in the medieval manner. Bandits capture young maidens and whisk them away on their horses to huts in the woods, where they engage in idyllic and sometimes strange lovemaking. People wrestle with ghosts, who suddenly appear on pathways in the forest, and sometimes turn out to be willow trees! Someone is hidden in a trunk for days, and cries to be let out. And they slice off one another's heads at the slightest provocation. A second level is the story of the characters as such, and much value could be obtained by the reader who never got beyond that level.

The real significance of the work would be lost, however, by the reader who failed to get to what we shall call the third level; for that is where the richest meaning lies, and where the power of Miss Welty's artistry shows to greatest advantage. Each of the characters, some to a larger extent than others, tends to embody certain general traits of humanity at large. Jamie Lockhart, the chief protagonist, has a double role in life —one as a bad, ruthless bandit, the other as a respectable, prosperous merchant. His purposes are many and complex; as are his deeds. He has the "power to look both ways and to see a thing from all sides." The mixture of good and evil in him—the cunning, the treachery, brutality counterbalancing the kindliness, the wisdom, the humaneness—is, without saying, universal. But, more particularly, the dualistic nature of his character symbolizes the conflict between idealism and realism, the neuroses that result from modern man's inability to attain his ideals. Interestingly enough, Jamie manages to free himself, by refusing to feel any guilt: he will not discriminate between right and wrong. He permits no one to ask of him *what* he is; *who* he is becomes all that is important to him. He determines not to recognize evil as a part of himself; it is, to him, merely something that he has been caught up into, and over which he has no control. In his imagination he keeps his personal *self* inviolable, and in that manner comes to terms with reality. Clement, one of his victims, is a sort of Don Quixote, caught in his own trap. Clement's wife, Salome, a catlike creature, having suffered great loss and cruelty, has nothing left in her destroyed heart but ambition, which she exerts in her domineering treatment of Clement and Rosamond (whom she hates but also seems to love). She even commands the sun to stand still and dances in order to make it obey her. The convincing force of the story is in the juxtaposition of the rough-and-tumble and grotesque life in the wilderness with the conventional, the real; and the harmonizing of the two. The beginning is in the realm of the actual; there is reversion to it at intervals: and at the end the sense of reality is restored, when Jamie and Rosamond settle in New Orleans, and there is a shift of scene to the streets of that city. Yet the magic and dreamlike quality of those surroundings, where "beauty and vice and every delight" are hospitable to one another, repeats the nature of the wilderness, and ties the actual world with the dream world.

Miss Welty's exploration of the adult mind is closely allied to her extraordinary penetration of the mind of childhood. Like Franz Kafka, she seems to regard the relationship of childhood and the dream as very near; since the dream has childlike qualities. Her reproduction of the sensibilities of childhood has a decidedly Proustian quality. In the little but exceedingly dimensional story, "A Memory," she brings the whole world of impressionable childhood up against the adult world, with all of its sordidness. The child, estranged from adults, can look upon them only as observer and dreamer. Out of the wisdom she possesses, intensified by love, she constructs her own vision of it. A story entitled "The Winds" also is an illustration of the author's acute insight into the perceptions of children, with all of the implications. Nothing seems omitted that would illuminate their inner minds.

This skill in getting inside the minds of her characters, in establishing motivation from within, is a very essential part of Miss Welty's technique. In this connection, she is a master in implying inner states of mind by physical description. In "Death of a Traveling Salesman" there are such subtle strokes as these, which transfer the intangible to the tangible: "People standing in the fields now and then, or on top of the haystacks, had been too far away, looking like leaning sticks or weeds . . . the stares of these distant people had followed him solidly like a wall, impenetrable, behind which they turned back after he had passed." And, ". . . When that was done she lit the lamp. It showed its dark and light. The whole room turned golden-yellow like some sort of flower, and the walls smelled of it and seemed to tremble with the quiet rushing of the fire and the waving of the burning lampwick in its funnel of light." In such a way as this the portrait of the salesman's mind comes through; description has a definite function, and is not just tacked on for purposes of decoration. And in the same story one comes across such arresting similes as this: "He could not hear his heart—it was as quiet as ashes falling." Or a metaphysical figure like this one: "In docility he held his eyes stiffly wide; they fixed themselves on the woman's clasped hands as though she held the cord they were strung on." Miss Welty's work is liberally sprinkled with such striking poetry; and the poetizing in each instance is identified with the characters; it assists in revealing the state of their thoughts and feelings.

Miss Welty's primary interest in theme is easily confused with moral intention; and there an important distinction should be made. Only by a consideration of her method does it become apparent that she is not interested in enforcing any moral "truth"; or in exhortation—far from it—to any particular line of conduct. True enough, her characters are clear symbols for basic ideas. But by means of the attitudes that are taken toward the characters any moral purpose is subdued. The reader is required to take full stock of the context; in this way the resolution cannot appear as simple. The moral conviction, when and if it comes, does so through the process of the story; which is to say that it is realized in the experiences of the characters, and the reader draws his own conclusions, without direct assistance from the author. In the story, "Asphodel," for example, the reader, while he is horrified at Miss Sabine's domineering cruelty to innocent people, feels also the tragedy of her life and the necessity within her for wreaking vengeance upon others. In Salome, as well, is a demonstration of the same psychologically basic truth. This—and, as we have seen, it is representative of the ideas in Miss Welty's stories—is not really a moral, but a truth upon which there is no necessity for the reader to agree or disagree. It is generally recognized among mature and thoughtful readers that any inflicting of wrong is due to an inadequacy within the wrongdoer, and that he is likely to suffer more than his victims; so, without disputing it, the reader will concede that it is a question that is worthy of serious reflection. He may judge that his own reflection, or someone else's, is more fruitful than the author's; but in this case the author would have no objection; Miss Welty, like any other of like caliber, would be ready to admit that she is only a fellow explorer.

But the fiction writer has more opportunity than those using other writing mediums, to make his idea convincing and alive. Tension, a necessary device for this accomplishment, in Miss Welty's fiction takes the form of conflict between the real and the imagined. Fantasy, therefore, serves as an agent in making the conflict more dramatic, in *rendering* the idea. The same device is recognizable in much of the work of Hawthorne, who works out his ideas in terms of structure, although not with the craftsmanship that in every instance comes up to Miss Welty's. "The Birthmark," among others of his stories, comes to mind as an illustration of his method of presenting a basic truth, not a moral. For, though Hawthorne is closer to Puritanism as an institution, and perhaps in spirit, almost the same could be said of him in answer to a charge of moral intention as can be said of Miss Welty. Both are sensitive to a distinction between right and wrong—not, of course, the conventional or puritanical standards, even though Hawthorne in some instances does come nearer the latter. Although we are more concerned with their similarity in method, a conclusion of Henry James seems applicable to a clarification of the moral purpose of both: "There is, I think, no more nutritive or suggestive truth than that of the perfect dependence of the 'moral' sense of a work of art on the amount of felt life concerned in producing it." The reader of Eudora Welty can entertain no doubt concerning the amount of "felt life" that is in her work.

It is her profound search of human consciousness and her illumination of the underlying causes of the compulsions and fears of modern man that would seem to comprise the principal value of Miss Welty's work. She, like other best writers of this century, implies that the confusion of our age tends to force individuals back upon conscience, as they have not been since the seventeenth century; for in the intervening centuries, values were more clearly defined, behavior was more outwardly controlled. Miss Welty's prose fiction, like much of the poetry and fiction of this era that seeks to explore the possibilities of the imagination, is comparable to the rich prose of Sir Thomas Browne; and reminiscent of the poetry of the seventeenth century.

Franz Kafka precedes Miss Welty in an analysis of the backgrounds of abnormal human behavior and an understanding of the psychology of the feeling of guilt. He, too, was concerned with modern man's ambivalence, with the potentialities that are within him of dispensing with the rationalizations, the impotence of will, and the laxness that grow out of a diseased society. And a general impression gained from his work, as from that of Miss Welty, is that it is the world that we regard as actual that is irrational; that the positions are reversed—the actual world becoming a dream and the one created by the imagination the only reality.

Miss Welty's distinction, then, is rather in her method: one that, as we have observed, effects a reconciliation of the inner and outer worlds in a particular way. Kafka, too, uses fantasy, but not in detail as does Miss Welty. The contrast in the style of the two is another matter; suffice it to say here that Miss Welty relies more upon fantasy, by it implying much of the factual; while Kafka, at least in his short stories, does the opposite. Miss Welty employs fantasy to reveal the heightened consciousness of man, and relates it to surface reality. The individual, even in his irrational state, becomes rational and capable of choice. The effect is one that is compelling, and rare in modern literature.

For all her strange and dreamlike settings, Miss Welty never strays far from the Natchez Trace, in Mississippi, her home state. This in itself is evidence of the sense of reality that she conveys. She observes a Bird Festival in a Negro church in her home town, Jackson, and describes it in non-fiction.[4] Yet the piece is as steeped in fantasy as some of her fiction. She has caught the tendency of man to dream, to build a world of

---

[4] "Pageant of Birds," *New Republic*, October 25, 1943.

his own, and, without violating reality greatly, used it as a device in fiction. Actuality is placed on the plane of the dream; and thereby a more perfect realism is attained.

Her characters are thoroughly Southern—in temperament, customs and speech. Yet they transcend any geographical limitation. She is concerned with Southern traditionalism only in respect to the values which it seeks to conserve; and only, apparently, as those values relate to people anywhere, in any society.

It would be presumptuous to attempt to place a final evaluation on the work that Miss Welty has done thus far (incidentally, she is still young and is still writing); as though that could be done for any individual reader, except by himself. But a key to some of its treasures may have been furnished by Schopenhauer in these sentences: ... "This is worth noticing, and indeed wonderful, how, besides his life in the concrete, man always lives another life in the abstract. In the former he is given as a prey to all the storms of life, and to the influence of the present; he must struggle, suffer, and die like the brute. But his life in the abstract, as it lies before his rational consciousness, is the still reflection of the former, and of the world in which he lives ..."

GRAHAM GREENE *

MORTON DAUWEN ZABEL

"THERE WAS something about a fête which drew Arthur Rowe irre-sistibly, bound him a helpless victim to the distant blare of a band ... called him like innocence: it was entangled in childhood, with vicarage gardens, and girls in white summer frocks, and the smell of herbaceous borders, and security." We meet him in blitzed and gutted London, stumbling on a charity bazaar in a Bloomsbury square, a man alone and a murderer, but fearless because he has made a friend of his guilt: when he gave his wife the poison that released her from the suffering he pitied, he had not asked her consent; "he could never tell whether she might not have preferred any sort of life to death." A fortune-teller slips him, mistakenly, the password by which he wins a cake in the bazaar's raffle. But there are others who want it and the thing concealed in its heart. Visited that night in his shabby room by a cripple, Rowe has barely tasted the hyoscine in his tea when out of a droning sky a bomb drops, explodes the house, and blows him and us into a dream of horrors—man-hunt, spies, sabotage, amnesia, murders, and suicide: an "entertainment" by Graham Greene.

We enter once more the familiar phantasm of our age, and Greene's remarkable evocation of it through thirteen novels—of which *The Ministry of Fear* is the most recent of those he calls "entertainments" [1] —has justly won him the title of "the Auden of the modern thriller." Here again is the haunted England of *l'entre deux guerres,* the European nightmare of corruption and doom, a *Blick ins Chaos* where

> taut with apprehensive dreads
> The sleepless guests of Europe lay
> Wishing the centuries away,
> And the low mutter of their vows
> Went echoing through her haunted house,
> As on the verge of happening
> There crouched the presence of The Thing.
> All formulas were tried to still
> The scratching on the window-sill,
> All bolts of custom made secure

---

* Reprinted from the *Nation,* July 3, 1943, by permission of the author and the editors. The essay appears here in revised and amplified form.

[1] *The Ministry of Fear: An Entertainment,* by Graham Greene (New York: The Viking Press, 1943). Mr. Greene's latest novel, *The Heart of the Matter,* appeared in 1948, but it was not sub-titled "an entertainment." [1951.]

Against the pressure on the door,
But up the staircase of events
Carrying his special instruments,
To every bedside all the same
The dreadful figure swiftly came.[2]

The fustian stage sets of Oppenheim, Chambers, and Edgar Wallace are gone with their earlier innocent day. We are in a world whose fabulous realities have condensed terribly out of contemporary legend and prophecy—out of the portentous journalism of Tabouis, Thompson, Sheean, Gunther, and the apotheosis of foreign correspondence; the films of Lang, Murnau, Renoir, and Hitchcock; the Gothic fables of Ambler, Hammett, and Simenon; the putsches, pogroms, marches, and mobilizations that have mounted to catastrophe in the present moment of our lives. Its synthetic thrills and anarchic brutality are ruses of melodrama no longer. Guilt pervades all life. All of us are trying to discover how we entered the nightmare, by what treachery we were betrayed to the howling storm of history. "Mother, please listen to me," cries Rowe to a mother who is dead; "I've killed my wife and the police want me." —"My little boy couldn't kill anyone":

> His mother smiled at him in a scared way but let him talk: he was the master of the dream now. He said, "I'm wanted for a murder I didn't do. People want to kill me because I know too much. I'm hiding underground, and up above the Germans are methodically smashing London to bits all round me. You remember St. Clements—the bells of St. Clements. They've smashed that—St. James's Piccadilly, the Burlington Arcade, Garland's Hotel where we stayed for the pantomime, Maples, and John Lewis. It sounds like a thriller, doesn't it?—but the thrillers are like life—more like life than you are, this lawn, your sandwiches, that pine . . . it's what we've all made of the world since you died. I'm your little Arthur who wouldn't hurt a beetle and I'm a murderer too. The world has been remade by William LeQueux.

Every age has its aesthetic of crime and horror, its attempt to give form to its special psychic or neurotic climate. No age has imposed greater handicaps on the effort than ours. Crime has gone beyond Addison's "chink in the chain armour of civilized communities." It has become the symptom of a radical lesion in the stamina of humanity. The hot violence of the Elizabethans is as different from the cold brutality of Hitlerian or Communist Europe, the heroic sin in Aeschylus or Webster from the squalid and endemic degeneracy in Céline or Henry Miller, the universal proportions of Greek or Shakespearean wrong from the gratuitous calculation and *inconséquences* of Gide's aesthetic murderers, as the worth at which the individual life was held in those times from its worthlessness in ours. A criminal takes his dignity from his de-

2 W. H. Auden, "New Year Letter" (1940), ll. 15-29, in *The Double Man* (1941).

fiance of the intelligence or merit that surrounds him, from the test his act imposes on the human community. He becomes trivial when that measure is denied him. So the modern thriller is permitted its prodigies of contrivance and holocausts of death at the cost of becoming a bore. So film audiences fidget restlessly through the news reel, waiting to be overwhelmed by the edifying bilge of Hollywood. The thrill-habit, fed by novels, headlines, and events, has competed successfully with gin, drugs, and aspirin, and doped the moral nerve of a generation.

The hardship this imposes on the artist is obvious. When felony, by becoming political, becomes impersonal; when the *acte gratuit* elicits not only secret but public approval, its dramatist faces the desperate task of restoring to his readers their lost instinct of values, the sense of human worth. It is not enough that the thriller become psychic: Freudian behavior patterns have become as much an open commodity and stock property as spy rings and torture chambers were fifty years ago. It must become moral as well.

The Victorian *frisson* of crime was all the choicer for the rigor of propriety and sentiment that hedged it in. Dickens's terrors are enhanced less by his rhetoric than by his coziness. The reversion to criminality in Dostoevski takes place in a ramifying hierarchy of authority—family life, social caste, political and religious bureaucracy, czarist militarism and repression. The horror of *The Turn of the Screw* is framed by the severest decorum, taste, and inhibition. James—like Conrad, Gide, and Mann—knew the enchantment of crime, but he also knew its artistic conditions. "Everything you may further do will be grist to my imaginative mill," he once wrote William Roughead of Edinburgh in thanks for a book of the latter's criminal histories: "I'm not sure I enter into such matters best when they are very archaic or remote from our familiarities, for then the testimony to manners and morals is rather blurred for me by the *whole* barbarism. . . . The thrilling in the comparatively modern much appeals to me—for there the special manners and morals become queerly disclosed. . . . Then do go back to the dear old human and sociable murders and adulteries and forgeries in which we are so agreeably at home." The admonition might have served as the cue for Graham Greene's talent.[3]

³ The titles and dates of Greene's book-length tales are: *The Man Within* (1929), *The Name of Action* (1930), *Rumour at Nightfall* (1932), *Orient Express* (titled in England *Stamboul Train*, 1932), *It's a Battlefield* (1934), *England Made Me* (1935), *This Gun for Hire* (English title *A Gun for Sale*, 1936), *Brighton Rock* (1938), *The Confidential Agent* (1939), *The Labyrinthine Ways* (1940; titled in England *The Power and the Glory* and reissued under this title in America, 1947), *The Ministry of Fear* (1943), *The Heart of the Matter* (1948). Some of these are sub-titled "Entertainments" (*Orient Express, The Confidential Agent, The Ministry of Fear*), others being submitted as novels (*The Man Within, It's a Battlefield, The Labyrinthine Ways*), but since *Brighton Rock* is called an "Entertainment" the force of Greene's discrimination is not always clear. There are also four books of shorter tales, two books of travel (*Journey Without Maps*, 1936, and *Another Mexico*, 1939, the latter titled in England *The Lawless Roads*), and a short study of *British Dramatists*

Greene, dealing in a "whole barbarism" equalling or surpassing any-thing in history, has undertaken to redeem that dilapidation from the stupefying mechanism and inconsequence to which modern terrorism has reduced it. Arthur Calder-Marshall has rightly said, in an article in *Horizon*,[4] that "few living English novelists derive more material from the daily newspaper than Graham Greene." His *mise-en-scène* includes the Nazi underground and fifth column (in *The Confidential Agent* and *The Ministry of Fear*), organized Marxism riddled by schisms and be-trayals (*It's a Battlefield*), Kruger and his swindles (*England Made Me*), Zaharoff and the alliance between munitions-making and *Machtpolitik* (*This Gun For Hire*), the English racetrack gang warfare (*Brighton Rock*), the Mexican church suppression (*The Labyrinthine Ways*); and his *Orient Express* is the same train we've traveled on all the way from *Shanghai Express* to *Night Train* and *The Lady Vanishes*. But where once—in James, Conrad, Dostoevski, in Dickens, Defoe, and the Eliza-bethans—it was society, state, kingdom, world, or the universe itself that supplied the presiding order of law or justice, it is now the isolated, betrayed, and finally indestructible integrity of the individual life that must furnish that measure. Humanity, having contrived a world of mindless and psychotic brutality, reverts for survival to the atom of the single man. Marked, hunted, Ishmaelite, or condemned, he may work for evil or for good, but it is his passion for a moral identity of his own that provides the nexus of values in a world that has reverted to an-archy. His lineage is familiar—Raskolnikov, Stavrogin, Kirilov; Conrad's Jim, Razumov, and Heyst; Mann's Felix Krull and Gide's Lafcadio; Hesse's Steppenwolf and Demian, and, more immediately, Kafka's K. He appears in every Greene novel—as hero or victim in Drover, Dr. Czinner, the nameless D., and Major Scobie; as pariah or renegade in Raven, Farrant, Rowe, and the whisky priest of *The Labyrinthine Ways;* as the incarnation of pure malevolence in Pinkie, the boy gangster of *Brighton Rock.*

The plot that involves him is fairly constant. *Brighton Rock* presents it in archetype. Its conflict rests on a basic dualism of forces, saved from the prevalent danger of becoming crude mechanism by Greene's skill in suggestion and insight, yet radical in its antithesis of elements. Pinkie is a believing Catholic, knows Hell as a reality, and accepts his damna-tion. *Corruptio optimi pessima* is the last faith left him to live or die by. Ida Arnold, the full-blown, life-loving tart whose casual lover the gang has killed, sets out to track him down: "unregenerate, a specimen of the 'natural man,' coarsely amiable, bestially kind, the most danger-

---

(1942); also a number of films, among them *The Fallen Idol* and *The Third Man*. Greene has also written much criticism of books, plays, and films for *The Spectator* and *The New Statesman and Nation;* has gone on wartime missions to western Africa; and has visited the United States and Mexico.

[4] *Horizon*, May, 1940, pp. 367-375: "The Works of Graham Greene."

ous enemy to religion." She pursues him with ruthless and deadly intention, corners him, sees him killed. The boy is sped to his damnation and
Ida triumphs ("God doesn't mind a bit of human nature. . . . I know
the difference between Right and Wrong"). The hostility is crucial. It
appears in all of Greene's mature books—Mather the detective against
Ravin the assassin in *This Gun For Hire;* the Inspector against Drover
in *It's a Battlefield;* the Communist lieutenant of police, accompanied
by the *mestizo* who acts as nemesis, against the hunted, shameless, renegade priest in *The Labyrinthine Ways,* trailing his desecrated sanctity through the hovels and jungles of the Mexican state yet persisting
in his office of grace and so embracing the doom that pursues him. It
reappears in the hunting down of Major Scobie by the agent Wilson
in *The Heart of the Matter.* A recent critic in *The New Statesman* put
the case concisely: "Mr. Greene is a Catholic, and his novel *Brighton
Rock* betrays a misanthropic, almost Jansenist, contempt for the virtues
that do not spring from grace." [5]

It is this grace that operates as the instrument which makes palpable
its necessary enemy, Evil. And it is the evil that materializes out of vice,
crime, nightmare, and moral stupefaction in his books that bring
Greene to join a notable company. The same evil works behind the
dramatic mystery and psychic riddle in *The Turn of the Screw* and
behind the squalid violence in Conrad's *The Secret Agent,* that parent
classic in this field of fiction which appeared in 1907 and established
the kind of novel that Greene and his generation have carried to such
exorbitant lengths. To fix and objectify it, to extricate it from the
relativity of values and abstractions—abstract justice, impersonal hu-
manitarianism, pity, right and wrong, good and bad—is the ultimate
motive of Greene's work. His pursuit of it has carried him among the
totems and horrors of coastal Africa which he conjures in *Journey
Without Maps*—his descent to the heart of darkness:

> It isn't a gain to have turned the witch or the masked secret dancer,
> the sense of supernatural evil, into the small human viciousness of the
> thin distinguished military gray head in Kensington Gardens with the
> soft lips and the eye which dwelt with dull luster on girls and boys of a
> certain age. . . . They are not, after all, so far from the central darkness.
> . . . When one sees to what unhappiness, to what peril of extinction,
> centuries of cerebration have brought us, one sometimes has a curiosity
> to discover if one can from what we have come, to recall at which point
> we went astray.

(An echo sounds here from Eliot on Baudelaire:

> So far as we are human, what we do must be either evil or good; so
> far as we do evil or good we are human; and it is better, in a paradoxical

5 *The New Statesman and Nation* (London), March 20, 1943, page 188. The critic
is not named; he is discussing a dramatic production, made at that time in London,
of *Brighton Rock.*

way, to do evil than to do nothing: at least, we exist. It is true to say that the glory of man is his capacity for salvation; it is also true to say that his glory is his capacity for damnation. The worst that can be said of most of our malefactors, from statesmen to thieves, is that they are not men enough to be damned.)

Greene's progress in his task has not escaped the pitfalls of his compromise with popularity, or of the insistence with which he applies his theological thesis to material that often refuses to submit to it. His expert contrivance frequently descends to sleight of hand; the surrealism of his action and atmosphere too often results in efflorescences of sheer conjuring; the machinery of the thriller—chases, coincidences, convenient accidents, and exploding surprises—can collapse into demented catastrophe. His superiority in these matters to the general tradition in which he works is clear, but on the other hand it tends to run uncomfortably close to the kind of jig-saw puzzle manipulation which Ambler, Hammett, and Chandler have made so readable and so trivial. And Greene drives his philosophical ambition hard.

His plots are made to enforce absolutes of moral judgment—a kind of metaphysical *vis inertiae*—which result in the stock humors to which his characters and their psychic pathology, as well as the social and emotional realities they stand for, tend to reduce. The "sanctified sinner" who appears in most of Greene's books is the most prominent of these. The type has become a feature of a good share of the modern literature of religious or metaphysical motivation; Baudelaire, Rimbaud, and Leon Bloy probably combined to give it its characteristic stamp and utility in modern literary mysticism, and since their day it has become a virtual cliché of contemporary drama and symbolism. George Orwell's point, in reviewing Greene's *Heart of the Matter* in 1948,[6] deserves critical attention. It was not only the frivolity of the cult he found distasteful: its suggestion that "there is something rather distingué in being damned" and its hint of a "weakening of belief" ("when people really believed in Hell, they were not so fond of striking graceful attitudes on its brink"). It was also its results in dramatic artistry: "by trying to clothe theological speculations in flesh and blood, it produces psychological absurdities." The cases both of Pinkie in *Brighton Rock* and of Major Scobie in *The Heart of the Matter* are illustrative of its dangers: that of Pinkie presupposing "that the most brutishly stupid person can, merely by having been brought up a Catholic, be capable of great intellectual subtlety," and that of Scobie becoming incredible "because the two halves of him do not fit together" ("If he were capable of getting into the kind of mess that is described, he would have got into it earlier. If he really felt that adultery is mortal sin, he would stop committing it; if he persisted in it, his sense of sin would

6 *The New Yorker,* July 17, 1948, pp. 61-63.

weaken. If he believed in Hell, he would not risk going there merely to spare the feelings of a couple of neurotic women.") Just as Greene's great gifts in dialogue, invention, marginal commentary, and halluinated scenery run the risk of ending in exorbitance through the uncanny facility which is the danger of his special kind of brilliance, so his moral seriousness—one cannot deny him the faculty—produces a determinism, a begging of the dramatic and psychological question, which dissipates the moral realism in which every novelist, no matter how poetic or visionary his purpose, must find his real basis.

Greene owns, at his best, a genuine poetry of vision and invention. It appears at its best in a book like *The Labyrinthine Ways* (i.e., *The Power and the Glory*), where the tale and milieu are not only invested with a really convincing atmosphere of legend, but where the legend itself, and the truth it poetically evokes, is believably enacted by the two central characters—the priest with his inescapable vocation, the lieutenant with his—who are not made to represent more than their primitive and rudimentary functions in the drama. *The Heart of the Matter* is probably Greene's most ambitious book, but it is not, in spite of its commendable advance beyond the formula that dominated too many of its predecessors, his most serious or inspired one.

But Greene remains interesting because of the conviction that works behind even his popular and cinematic effects. He uses horror for what it has signified in every age, Elizabethan, Gothic, Romantic, or Victorian: as a medium for exploring the evasions, fears, and panic that drag us back from the dignity of pride or reason to infantilism and brutality but which must, in any age, be met and faced if salvation is to escape the curse of presumption, the fatal condition of moral ignorance. "The abyss destroys; the abyss exalts; descend that you may be saved. The enemy we conquer is the enemy we embrace and love." The identity Greene's heroes seek is the selfhood, the self-knowledge, of the conscience that admits its share in the mystery and terror of human nature. If the "destructive element" engulfs them, it is the passion of their resistance to it that sustains them. And it is because he manages to convey the rival forces of experience and conscience, a kind of dialectic between the moral oblivion with which nature threatens man and the absolute tests of moral selfhood, that Greene has brought about one of the most stimulating collaborations between realism and poetry that have appeared in the dull wastes of recent English fiction. His skill in this line gives him a distinction shared by only a few other practitioners of the novel among his countrymen—Isherwood, Elizabeth Bowen, Henry Green; and it saves his best work as much from the squashy hocus-pocus of the common thriller as from the didactic sanctimony of conventional religious writing.

In three of his books—*It's a Battlefield, Brighton Rock,* and *The Power and the Glory*—he may claim the ancestry, however distant, of

James, Conrad, and Joyce, and a critical comparison, however rigorous, with men like Kafka, Auden, Faulkner, and Mauriac. For a decade or more he has stood at the threshold of major fiction; twice at least he has promised to step across it; even while something—a hesitation or a facility in temporizing which seems to be the affliction of many talents, fictional and otherwise, in this unsettled time—keeps him from crossing it decisively, he remains an exceptional talent, a skilled magician in the words and spells of symbolic drama. He has found an instrument for probing the temper and tragedy of his age, the perversions and fears that have betrayed it, and the stricken weathers of its soul. It still remains for him to surmount not only its distractions and negative appeals but also the inflexible judgments by which these are too often opposed and to which the real work of the honest imagination is too often sacrificed, in order to become a fully responsible novelist in his English generation. It is a role to which his acute sense of history and his remarkable gift of consciousness have committed him.

ART AND FORTUNE *

LIONEL TRILLING

I

IT IS impossible to talk about the novel nowadays without having in our minds the question of whether or not the novel is still a living form. Twenty-five years ago T. S. Eliot said that the novel came to an end with Flaubert and James,** and at about the same time Señor Ortega said much the same thing. This opinion is now heard on all sides. It is heard in conversation rather than read in formal discourse, for to insist on the death or moribundity of a great genre is an unhappy task which the critic will naturally avoid if he can, yet the opinion is now an established one and has a very considerable authority. Do we not see its influence in, for example, V. S. Pritchett's recent book, *The Living Novel*? Although Mr. Pritchett is himself a novelist and writes about the novel with the perception that comes of love, and even by the name he gives his book disputes the fact of the novel's death, yet still, despite these tokens of his faith, he deals with the subject under a kind of constraint, as if he had won the right to claim life for the novel only upon condition of not claiming for it much power.

I do not believe that the novel is dead. And yet particular forms of the creative imagination may indeed die—English poetic drama stands as the great witness of the possibility—and there might at this time be an advantage in accepting the proposition as an hypothesis which will lead us to understand under what conditions the novel may live.

If we consent to speak of the novel as dead, three possible explanations of the fact spring at once to mind. The first is simply that the genre has been exhausted, worked out in the way that a lode of ore is worked out—it can no longer yield a valuable supply of its natural matter. The second explanation is that the novel was developed in response to certain cultural circumstances which now no longer exist but have given way to other circumstances which must be met by other forms of the imagination. The third explanation is that although the circumstances to which the novel was a response do still exist we either lack the power to use the form,[1] or no longer find value in the answers that

* "Art and Fortune" appears in *The Liberal Imagination*, by Lionel Trilling, copyright 1941, 1947, 1948, 1950 by Lionel Trilling, and is used here by permission of the author and the publishers.

** See Eliot's *"Ulysses*, Order, and Myth" in this volume.

[1] This might seem to beg the cultural question; yet certain technical abilities do deteriorate or disappear for reasons which although theoretically ascertainable are almost beyond practical determination.

the novel provides, because the continuing circumstances have entered a phase of increased intensity.

The first theory was put forward by Ortega in his essay "Notes on the Novel." It is an explanation which has its clear limitations, but it is certainly not without its cogency. We have all had the experience of feeling that some individual work of art, or some canon of art, or a whole idiom of art, has lost, temporarily or permanently, its charm and power. Sometimes we weary of the habitual or half-mechanical devices by which the artist warms up for his ideas or by which he bridges the gap between his ideas; this can happen even with Mozart. Sometimes it is the very essence of the man's thought that fatigues; we feel that his characteristic insights can too easily be foreseen and we become too much aware of how they exist at the expense of blindness to other truths; this can happen even with Dostoevski. And so with an entire genre of art—there may come a moment when it cannot satisfy one of our legitimate demands, which is that it shall surprise us. This demand, and the liability of our artistic interests to wear out, do not show us to be light-minded. Without them our use of art would be only ritualistic, or commemorative of our past experiences; and although there is nothing wrong in using art for ritual and commemoration, still these are not the largest uses to which it can be put. Curiosity is as much an instinct as hunger and love, and curiosity about any particular thing may be satisfied.

Then we must consider that technique has its autonomy and that it dictates the laws of its own growth. Aristotle speaks of Athenian tragedy as seeking and finding its fulfillment, its entelechy, and it may be that we are interested in any art only just so long as it is in process of search; that what moves us is the mysterious energy of quest. At a certain point in the development of a genre, the practitioner looks back and sees all that has been done by others before him and knows that no ordinary effort can surpass or even match it; ordinary effort can only repeat. It is at this point that, as Ortega says, we get the isolated extraordinary effort which transcends the tradition and brings it to an end. This, no doubt, is what people mean when they speak of Joyce and Proust bringing the novel to its grave.

Here is the case, as strongly as I can put it, for the idea that a genre can exhaust itself simply by following the laws of its own development. As an explanation of the death of the novel it does not sufficiently exfoliate or sufficiently connect with the world. It can by no means be ignored, but of itself it cannot give an adequate answer to our question.

II

So we must now regard the novel as an art form contrived to do a certain kind of work, its existence conditioned by the nature of that work. In another essay [2] I undertook to say what the work of the novel was—I said that it was the investigation of reality and illusion. Of course the novel does not differ in this from all other highly developed literary forms; it differs, however, in at least one significant respect, that it deals with reality and illusion in relation to questions of social class, which in relatively recent times are bound up with money.

In Western civilization the idea of money exercises a great fascination—it is the fascination of an actual thing which has attained a metaphysical ideality or of a metaphysical entity which has attained actual existence. Spirits and ghosts are beings in such a middling state of existence; and money is both real and not real, like a spook. We invented money and we use it, yet we cannot either understand its laws or control its actions. It has a life of its own which it properly should not have; Karl Marx speaks with a kind of horror of its indecent power to reproduce, as if, he says, love were working in its body. It is impious, being critical of existent social realities, and it has the effect of lessening their degree of reality. The social reality upon which it has its most devastating effect is of course that of class. And class itself is a social fact which, whenever it is brought into question, has like money a remarkable intimacy with metaphysics and the theory of knowledge—I have suggested how for Shakespeare any derangement of social classes seems always to imply a derangement of the senses in madness or dream, some elaborate joke about the nature of reality. This great joke is the matter of the book which we acknowledge as the ancestor of the modern novel, *Don Quixote;* and indeed no great novel exists which does not have the joke at its very heart.

In the essay to which I refer I also said that, in dealing with the questions of illusion and reality which were raised by the ideas of money and class, the novel characteristically relied upon an exhaustive exploitation of manners. Although I tried to give a sufficiently strong and complicated meaning to the word *manners,* I gather that my merely having used the word, or perhaps my having used it in a context that questioned certain political assumptions of a pious sort, has led to the belief that I am interested in establishing a new genteel tradition in criticism and fiction. Where misunderstanding serves others as an advantage, one is helpless to make oneself understood; yet to guard as well as I can against this imputation, I will say not only that the greatest exploitation of manners ever made is the *Iliad,* but also that *The Possessed* and *Studs Lonigan* are works whose concern with manners is of their very essence.

To these characteristics of the novel—the interest in illusion and reality as generated by class and money, this interest expressed by the observation of manners—we must add the unabashed interest in ideas. From its very beginning the novel made books the objects of its regard.

[2] "Manners, Morals, and the Novel."

Nowadays we are inclined to see the appearance of a literary fact in a novel as the sign of its "intellectuality" and specialness of appeal, and even as a sign of decadence. But Joyce's solemn literary discussions in *A Portrait of the Artist as a Young Man,* or his elaborate literary play in the later works, or Proust's critical excursions, are in the direct line of *Don Quixote* and *Tom Jones,* which are works of literary criticism before they are anything else. The Germans had a useful name for a certain kind of novel which they called a *Kulturroman;* actually every great novel deserves that name, for it is hard to think of one that is not precisely a romance of culture. By culture we must mean not merely the general social condition to which the novel responds but also a particular congeries of formulated ideas. The great novels, far more often than we remember, deal explicitly with developed ideas, and although they vary greatly in the degree of their explicitness they tend to be more explicit rather than less—in addition to the works already mentioned one can adduce such diverse examples as *Lost Illusions, The Sentimental Education, War and Peace, Jude the Obscure,* and *The Brothers Karamazov.* Nowadays the criticism which descends from Eliot puts explicit ideas in literature at a discount, which is one reason why it is exactly this criticism that is most certain of the death of the novel, and it has led many of us to forget how in the novel ideas may be as important as character and as essential to the given dramatic situation.

This then as I understand it is the nature of the novel as defined by the work it does. Of these defining conditions how many are in force today?

I think it is true to say that money and class do not have the same place in our social and mental life that they once had. They have certainly not ceased to exist, but certainly they do not exist as they did in the nineteenth century or even in our own youth. Money of itself no longer can engage the imagination as it once did; it has lost some of its impulse, and certainly it is on the defensive; it must compete on the one hand with the ideal of security and on the other hand with the ideal of a kind of power which may be more directly applied. And for many to whom the ideal of mere security is too low and to whom the ideal of direct political power is beyond the reach of their imagination, money, in order to be justified, must be involved with virtue and with the virtuous cultivation of good taste in politics, culture, and the appointments of the home—money is terribly ashamed of itself. As for class, in Europe the bourgeoisie together with its foil the aristocracy has been weakening for decades. It ceased some time ago to be the chief source of political leaders; its nineteenth-century position as ideologue of the world has vanished before the ideological strength of totalitarian communism; the wars have brought it to the point of economic ruin. In England the middle class is in process of liquidating itself. In this country the real basis of the novel has never existed—that is, the tension between a middle class and an aristocracy which brings manners into observable relief as the living representation of ideals and the living comment on ideas. Our class structure has been extraordinarily fluid; our various upper classes have seldom been able or stable enough to establish their culture as authoritative. With the single exception of the Civil War, our political struggles have not had the kind of cultural implications which catch the imagination, and the extent to which this one conflict has engaged the American mind suggests how profoundly interesting conflicts of culture may be. (It is possible to say that the Cromwellian revolution appears in every English novel.) For the rest, the opposition between rural and urban ideals has always been rather factitious; and despite a brief attempt to insist on the opposite view, the conflict of capital and labor is at present a contest for the possession of the goods of a single way of life, and not a cultural struggle. Our most fervent interest in manners has been linguistic, and our pleasure in drawing distinctions between a presumably normal way of speech and an "accent" or "dialect" may suggest how simple is our national notion of social difference.[3] And of recent years, although we grow more passionately desirous of status and are bitterly haunted by the ghost of every status-conferring ideal, including that of social class, we more and more incline to show our status-lust not by affirming but by denying the reality of social difference.

I think that if American novels of the past, whatever their merits of intensity and beauty, have given us very few substantial or memorable people, this is because one of the things which makes for substantiality of character in the novel is precisely the notation of manners, that is to say, of class traits modified by personality. It is impossible to imagine a Silas Wegg or a Smerdyakov or a Félicité (of *A Simple Heart*) or a Mrs. Proudie without the full documentation of their behavior in relation to their own class and to other classes. All great characters exist in part by reason of the ideas they represent. The great characters of American fiction, such, say, as Captain Ahab and Natty Bumppo, tend to be mythic because of the rare fineness and abstractness of the

---

[3] Lately our official egalitarianism has barred the exploitation of this interest by our official arts, the movies and the radio; there may be some social wisdom in this, yet it ignores the fact that at least certain forms and tones of the mockery of their speech habits are a means by which "extraneous" groups are accepted. Mention of this naturally leads to the question of whether the American attitude toward "minority" groups, particularly Negroes and Jews, is not the equivalent of differentiation. I think it is not, except in a highly modified way. And for the purposes of the novel it is not the same thing at all, for two reasons: it involves no real cultural struggle, no significant conflict of ideals, for the excluded group has the same notion of life and the same aspirations as the excluding group, although the novelist who attempts the subject naturally uses the tactic of showing that the excluded group has a different and better ethos; and it is impossible to suppose that the novelist who chooses this particular subject will be able to muster the satirical ambivalence toward both groups which marks the good novel even when it has a social *parti pris*.

ideas they represent; and their very freedom from class gives them a
large and glowing generality; for what I have called *substantiality* is
not the only quality that makes a character great. They are few in
number and special in kind; and American fiction has nothing to show
like the huge, swarming, substantial population of the European novel,
the substantiality of which is precisely a product of a class existence. In
fiction, as perhaps in life, the conscious realization of social class, which
is an idea of great power and complexity, easily and quickly produces
intention, passion, thought, and what I am calling substantiality. The
diminution of the reality of class, however socially desirable in many
respects, seems to have the practical effect of diminishing our ability to
see people in their difference and specialness.

Then we must be aware of how great has been the falling-off in the
energy of ideas that once animated fiction. In the nineteenth century
the novel followed the great lines of political thought, both the conservative and the radical, and it documented politics with an original
and brilliant sociology. In addition, it developed its own line of psychological discovery, which had its issue in the monumental work of
Freud. But now there is no conservative tradition and no radical tradition of political thought, and not even an eclecticism which is in the
slightest degree touched by the imagination; we are in the hands of the
commentator. On the continent of Europe political choice may be possible but political thought is not, and in a far more benign context the
same may be said of England. And in the United States, although for
different reasons, there is a similar lack of political intelligence: all
over the world the political mind lies passive before action and the
event. In psychological thought we find a strange concerted effort of
regression from psychoanalysis, such as the reformulations of the analytical psychology which Dr. Horney and Dr. Sullivan make in the name
of reason and society and progress, which are marked by the most
astonishing weakness of mind, and which appeal to the liberal intellectual by an exploitation of the liberal intellectual's fond belief that he
suspects "orthodoxy." Nor really can it be said that Freudian psychology itself has of late made any significant advances.

This weakness of our general intellectual life is reflected in our
novels. So far as the novel touches social and political questions it
permits itself to choose only between a cheery or a sour democratism;
it is questionable whether any American novel since *Babbitt* has told
us a new thing about our social life. In psychology the novel relies
either on a mechanical or a clinical use of psychiatry or on the insights
that were established by the novelists of fifty years ago.*

It is not then unreasonable to suppose that we are at the close of a
cultural cycle, that the historical circumstances which called forth the

* One wonders if this is because our social life has not changed basically since
Babbitt was written or our psychiatry advanced significantly in the last fifty years.

particular intellectual effort in which we once lived and moved and had our being is now at an end, and that the novel as part of that effort is as deciduous as the rest.

III

But there is an explanation of the death of the novel which is both corollary and alternative to this. Consider a main intellectual preoccupation of the period that ends with Freud and begins with Swift or with Shakespeare's middle period or with Montaigne—it does not matter just where we set the beginning so long as we start with some typical and impressive representation, secular and not religious, of man's depravity and weakness. Freud said of his own theories that they appealed to him as acting, like the theories of Darwin and Copernicus, to diminish man's pride, and this intention, carried out by means of the discovery and demonstration of man's depravity, has been one of the chief works of the human mind for some four hundred years. What the mind was likely to discover in this period was by and large much the same thing, yet mind was always active in the enterprise of discovery; discovery itself was a kind of joy and sometimes a hope, no matter how great the depravity that was turned up; the activity of the mind was a kind of fortitude. Then too there was reassurance in the resistance that was offered to the assaults of mind upon the strong texture of the social façade of humanity. That part of the mind which delights in discovery was permitted its delight by the margin that existed between speculation and proof; had the mind been able fully to prove what it believed, it would have fainted and failed before its own demonstration, but so strongly entrenched were the forces of respectable optimism and the belief in human and social goodness that the demonstration could never be finally established but had to be attempted over and over again. Now, however, the old margin no longer exists; the façade is down; society's resistance to the discovery of depravity has ceased; now everyone knows that Thackeray was wrong, Swift right. The world and the soul have split open of themselves and are all agape for our revolted inspection. The simple eye of the camera shows us, at Belsen and Buchenwald, horrors that quite surpass Swift's powers, a vision of life turned back to its corrupted elements which is more disgusting than any that Shakespeare could contrive, a cannibalism more literal and fantastic than that which Montaigne ascribed to organized society. A characteristic activity of mind is therefore no longer needed. Indeed, before what we now know the mind stops; the great psychological fact of our time which we all observe with baffled wonder and shame is that there is no possible way of responding to Belsen and Buchenwald. The activity of mind fails before the incommunicability of man's suffering.

This may help to explain the general deterioration of our intellectual life. It may also help to explain an attitude to our life in general.

Twenty-five years ago Ortega spoke of the "dehumanization" of modern art. Much of what he said about the nature of modern art has, by modern art, been proved wrong, or was wrong even when he said it. But Ortega was right in observing of modern art that it expresses a dislike of holding in the mind the human fact and the human condition, that it shows "a real loathing of living forms and living beings," a disgust with the "rounded and soft forms of living bodies"; and that together with this revulsion, or expressed by it, we find a disgust with history and society and the state. Human life as an aesthetic object can perhaps no longer command our best attention; the day seems to have gone when the artist who dealt in representation could catch our interest almost by the mere listing of the ordinary details of human existence; and the most extreme and complex of human dilemmas now surely seem to many to have lost their power to engage us. This seems to be supported by evidence from those arts for which a conscious exaltation of humanistic values is stock-in-trade—I mean advertising and our middling novels, which, almost in the degree that they celebrate the human, falsify and abstract it; in the very business of expressing adoration of the rounded and soft forms of living bodies they expose the disgust which they really feel.

IV

At this point we are in the full tide of those desperate perceptions of our life which are current nowadays among thinking and talking people, which even when we are not thinking and talking haunt and control our minds with visions of losses worse than that of existence—losses of civilization, personality, humanness. They sink our spirits not merely because they are terrible and possible but because they have become so obvious and cliché that they seem to close for us the possibility of thought and imagination.

And at this point too we must see that if the novel is dead or dying, it is not alone in its mortality. The novel is a kind of summary and paradigm of our cultural life, which is perhaps why we speak sooner of its death than of the death of any other form of thought. It has been of all literary forms the most devoted to the celebration and investigation of the human will; and the will of our society is dying of its own excess. The religious will, the political will, the sexual will, the artistic will— each is dying of its own excess. The novel at its greatest is the record of the will acting under the direction of an idea, often an idea of will itself. All else in the novel is but secondary, and those examples which do not deal with the will in action are but secondary in their genre. Sensibility in the novel is but notation and documentation of the will in action. Again *Don Quixote* gives us our first instance. In its hero we have the modern conception of the will in a kind of wry ideality. Flaubert said that Emma Bovary was Quixote's sister, and in her we have the modern will in a kind of corruption. Elizabeth Bennett and Emma Woodhouse and Jane Eyre are similarly related to all the Karamazovs, to Stavrogin, and to that Kirillov who was led by awareness of the will to assert it ultimately by destroying it in himself with a pistol shot.

Surely the great work of our time is the restoration and the reconstitution of the will. I know that with some the opinion prevails that, apart from what very well *may* happen by way of Apocalypse, what *should* happen is that we advance farther and farther into the darkness, seeing to it that the will finally exhausts and expends itself to the end that we purge our minds of all the old ways of thought and feeling, giving up all hope of ever reconstituting the great former will of humanism, which, as they imply, has brought us to this pass. One must always listen when this opinion is offered in true passion. But for the vision and ideal of apocalyptic renovation one must be either a particular kind of moral genius with an attachment to life that goes beyond attachment to any particular form of life—D. H. Lawrence was such a genius—or a person deficient in attachment to life in any of its forms. Most of us are neither one nor the other, and our notions of renovation and reconstitution are social and pragmatic and in the literal sense of the word conservative. To the restoration and reconstitution of the will thus understood the novelistic intelligence is most apt.

When I try to say on what grounds I hold this belief, my mind turns to a passage in Henry James's preface to *The American*. James has raised the question of "reality" and "romance," and he remarks that "of the men of largest resounding imagination before the human scene, of Scott, of Balzac, even of the coarse, comprehensive, prodigious Zola, we feel, I think, that the reflexion toward either quarter has never taken place"; they have never, that is, exclusively committed themselves either to "reality" or to "romance" but have maintained an equal commerce with both. And this, James goes on to say, is the secret of their power with us. Then follows an attempt to distinguish between "reality" and "romance," which defines "reality" as "the things we cannot possibly not know," and then gives us this sentence: "The romantic stands . . . for the things that, with all the facilities in the world, all the wealth and all the courage and all the wit and all the adventure, we never *can* directly know; the things that can reach us only through the beautiful circuit of thought and desire."

The sentence is perhaps not wholly perspicuous, yet, if I understand it at all, it points to the essential moral nature of the novel. Julien Sorel eventually acquired all the facilities in the world; he used "all the wealth and all the courage and all the wit and all the adventure" to gain the things that are to be gained by their means; what he gained was ashes in his mouth. But what in the end he gained came to him in prison not by means of the "facilities" but through the beautiful circuit of thought and desire, and it impelled him to make his great speech to the Besançon jury in which he threw away his life; his happiness and his heroism came, I think, from his will having exhausted all that part of itself which naturally turns to the inferior objects offered by the social world and from its having learned to exist in the strength of its own knowledge of its thought and desire. I have said that awareness of the will in its beautiful circuit of thought and desire was the peculiar property of the novel, yet in point of fact we find it long before the novel came into existence and in a place where it always surprises us, in the *Inferno,* at the meetings of Dante with Paolo and Francesca, with Brunetto Latini and with Ulysses, the souls who keep the energy of thought and desire alive and who are therefore forever loved however damned. For James the objects of this peculiarly human energy go by the name of "romance." The word is a risky one and therefore it is necessary to say that it does not stand for the unknowable, for what is vulgarly called "the ideal," let alone for that which is pleasant and charming because far off. It stands for the world of unfolding possibility, for that which, when brought to actuality, is powerfully operative. It is thus a synonym for the will in its creative aspect, especially in its aspect of *moral* creativeness, as it subjects itself to criticism and conceives for itself new states of being. The novel has had a long dream of virtue in which the will, while never abating its strength and activity, learns to refuse to exercise itself upon the unworthy objects with which the social world tempts it, and either conceives its own right objects or becomes content with its own sense of its potential force—which is why so many novels give us, before their end, some representation, often crude enough, of the will unbroken but in stasis.

It is the element of what James calls "romance," this operative reality of thought and desire, which, in the novel, exists side by side with the things "we cannot possibly not know," that suggests to me the novel's reconstitutive and renovating power.

V

If there is any ground for my belief that the novel can, by reason of one of its traditional elements, do something in the work of reconstituting and renovating the will, there may be some point in trying to say under what particular circumstances of its own nature and action it may best succeed.

I think it will not succeed if it accepts the latest-advanced theory of the novel, Jean-Paul Sartre's theory of "dogmatic realism." According to the method of this theory, the novel is to be written as if without an author and without a personal voice and "without the foolish business of storytelling." The reader is to be subjected to situations as nearly equivalent as possible to those of life itself; he is to be prevented from falling out of the book, kept as strictly as possible within its confines and power by every possible means, even by so literal a means as the

closest approximation of fictional to historical time, for the introduction of large periods of time would permit the reader to remember that
he is involved in an illusion; he is, in short, to be made to forget that
he is reading a book. We all know the devices by which the sensations
of actual life, such as claustrophobia and fatigue, are generated in the
reader; and although the novels which succeed in the use of these
devices have had certain good effects, they have had bad effects too. By
good and bad effects I mean, as Sartre means, good and bad social
effects. The banishment of the author from his books, the stilling of his
voice, have but reinforced the faceless hostility of the world and have
tended to teach us that we ourselves are not creative agents and that
we have no voice, no tone, no style, no significant existence. Surely
what we need is the opposite of this, the opportunity to identify ourselves with a mind that willingly admits that it is a mind and does not
pretend that it is History or Events or the World but only a mind
thinking and planning—possibly planning our escape.

There is not very much that is actually original in Sartre's theory,
which seems to derive from Flaubert at a not very great remove. Flaubert himself never could, despite his own theory, keep himself out of
his books; we always know who is there by guessing who it is that is
kept out—it makes a great difference just which author is kept out of a
novel, and Flaubert's absence occupies more room than Sartre's, and is
a much more various and impressive thing. And Flaubert's mind, in or
out of his novels, presents itself to us as an ally—although, as I more
and more come to think, the alliance it offers is dangerous.

As for what Sartre calls "the foolish business of storytelling," I believe that, so far from giving it up, the novel will have to insist on it
more and more. It is exactly the story that carries what James calls
"romance," which is what the theologians call "faith," and in the
engaged and working literature which Sartre rightly asks for this is an
essential element. To know a story when we see one, to know it *for* a
story, to know that it is not reality itself but that it has clear and effective relations with reality—this is one of the great disciplines of the
mind.

In speaking against the ideal of the authorless novel I am not, of
course, speaking in behalf of the "personality" of the author consciously displayed—nothing could be more frivolous—but only in behalf
of the liberating effects that may be achieved when literature understands itself to be literature and does not identify itself with what it
surveys. (This is as intellectually necessary as for science not to represent itself as a literal picture of the universe.) The authorial minds
that in *Tom Jones* and *Tristram Shandy* play with events and the
reader in so nearly divine a way become the great and strangely effective symbols of liberty operating in the world of necessity, and this is
more or less true of all the novelists who *contrive* and *invent*.

Yet when I speak in defense of the salutary play of the mind in the controlled fantasy of storytelling I am not defending the works of consciously literary, elaborately styled fantasy in the manner of, let us say, *Nightwood*, which in their own way subscribe to the principles of Sartre's dogmatic realism, for although the conscious literary intention of the author is always before us, yet style itself achieves the claustral effect which Sartre would manage by the representation of events.

Mr. Eliot praises the prose of *Nightwood* for having so much affinity with poetry. This is not a virtue, and I believe that it will not be mistaken for a virtue by any novel of the near future which will interest us. The loss of a natural prose, one which has at least a seeming affinity with good common speech, has often been noted. It seems to me that the observation of the loss has been too complacently made and that its explanations, while ingenious, have had the intention of preventing it from being repaired in kind. A prose which approaches poetry has no doubt its own value, but it cannot serve to repair the loss of a straightforward prose, rapid, masculine, and committed to events, making its effects not by the single word or by the phrase but by words properly and naturally massed. I conceive that the creation of such a prose should be one of the conscious intentions of any novelist.[4]

And as a corollary to my rejection of poetic prose for the novel, I would suggest that the novelist of the next decades will not occupy himself with questions of form. The admitted weakness of the contemporary novel, the far greater strength of poetry, the current strong interest in the theory of poetry, have created a situation in which the canons of poetical perfection are quite naturally but too literally applied to the novel. These canons have not so much reinforced as displaced the formal considerations of Flaubert and James, which have their own dangers but which were at least conceived for the novel itself. I make every expectable disclaimer of wishing to depreciate form and then go on to say that a conscious preoccupation with form at the present time is almost certain to lead the novelist, particularly the young novelist, into limitation. The notions of form which are at present current among even those who are highly trained in literature— let alone among the semi-literary, who are always very strict about

[4] The question of prose is as important as that of prosody and we never pay enough attention to it in criticism. I am far from thinking that my brief paragraph even opens the subject adequately. The example of Joyce has been urged against the little I have just said. It seems to me that whenever the prose of *A Portrait of the Artist* becomes what we call poetic, it is in a very false taste; this has been defended as being a dramatic device, an irony against the hero. *Ulysses* may be taken as making a strong case against my own preference, yet I think that its basic prose, which is variously manipulated, is not without its affinities with the prose I ask for. The medium of *Finnegans Wake* may, without prejudice, be said to be something other than prose in any traditional sense; if it should establish a tradition it will also establish new criteria and problems.

enforcing the advanced ideas of forty years ago—are all too simple and often seem to come down to nothing more than the form of the sonata, the return on the circle with appropriate repetitions of theme. For the modern highly trained literary sensibility, form suggests completeness and the ends tucked in; resolution is seen only as all contradictions equated, and although form thus understood has its manifest charm, it will not adequately serve the modern experience. A story, like the natural course of an emotion, has its own form, and I take it as the sign of our inadequate trust of story and of our exaggerated interest in sensibility that we have begun to insist on the precise ordering of the novel.

Then I venture the prediction that the novel of the next decades will deal in a very explicit way with ideas. The objections to this will be immediate. Everybody quotes Mr. Eliot's remark about Henry James having a mind so fine that no idea could violate it, which suggests an odd, violent notion of the relation of minds and ideas, not at all the notion that James himself held; and everybody knows the passage in which Mr. Eliot insists on the indifferent connection which Dante and Shakespeare had with the intellectual formulations of their respective times. I think I can understand—and sympathetically as well as sociologically—Mr. Eliot's feeling for a mode of being in which the act and tone of ideation are not dominant, just as I can understand something of the admiration which may be felt for a society such as Yeats celebrated, which expresses its sense of life not by means of words but by means of houses and horses and by means of violence, manners, courage, and death. But I do not understand what Mr. Eliot means when he makes a sharp distinction between ideas and emotions in literature; I think that Plato was right when in *The Symposium* he represented ideas as continuous with emotions, both springing from the appetites.

It is a prevailing notion that a novel which contains or deals with ideas is bound to be pallid and abstract and intellectual. As against this belief here is an opinion from the great day of the novel: "There are active souls who like rapidity, movement, conciseness, sudden shocks, action, drama, who avoid discussion, who have little fondness for meditation and take pleasure in results. From such people comes what I should call the Literature of Ideas." This odd definition, whose seeming contradictions we will not pause over, was made by Balzac in the course of his long review of *The Charterhouse of Parma,* and it is Stendhal whom Balzac mentions as the great exemplar of the literature of ideas. And we know what ideas are at work in *The Charterhouse* and *The Red and the Black:* they are the ideas of Rousseau and they are named as such. These ideas are not to be separated from the passions of Julien and Fabrice; they are reciprocally expressive of each other. To us it is strange that ideas should be expressed so, and also in terms of prisons and rope ladders, pistols and daggers. It should not seem strange, for it is in the nature of ideas to be so expressed.

Yet although these two great examples support much of my view of the place of ideas in the novel, they do not support all of it. They make for me the point of the continuity of ideas and emotions, which in our literary context is forgotten. And they remind us forcibly of the ideological nature of institutions and classes. But in Stendahl's novels the ideas, although precisely identified, are chiefly represented by character and dramatic action, and although this form of representation has of course very high aesthetic advantages, yet I would claim for the novel the right and the necessity to deal with ideas by means other than that of the "objective correlative," to deal with them as directly as it deals with people or terrain or social setting.

There is an obvious social fact which supports this claim. No one who is in the least aware of our social life today can miss seeing that ideas have acquired a new kind of place in society. Nowadays everyone is involved in ideas—or, to be more accurate, in ideology. The impulse of novelists, which has been much decried, to make their heroes intellectuals of some sort was, however dull it became, perfectly sound: they wanted people of whom it was clear that ideas were an important condition of their lives. But this limitation to avowed intellectuals is no longer needed; in our society the simplest person is involved with ideas. Every person we meet in the course of our daily life, no matter how unlettered he may be, is groping with sentences toward a sense of his life and his position in it; and he has what almost always goes with an impulse to ideology, a good deal of animus and anger. What would so much have pleased the social philosophers of an earlier time has come to pass—ideological organization has cut across class organization, generating loyalties and animosities which are perhaps even more intense than those of class. The increase of conscious formulation, the increase of a certain kind of consciousness by formulation, makes a fact of modern life which is never sufficiently estimated. This is a condition which has been long in developing, for it began with the movements of religious separatism; now politics, and not only politics but the requirements of a whole culture, make verbal and articulate the motive of every human act: we eat by reason, copulate by statistics, rear children by rule, and the one impulse we do not regard with critical caution is that toward ideation, which increasingly becomes a basis of prestige.

This presents the novel with both an opportunity and a duty. The opportunity is a subject matter. Social class and the conflicts it produces may not be any longer a compelling subject to the novelist, but the organization of society into ideological groups presents a subject scarcely less absorbing. Ideological society has, it seems to me, nearly as full a range of passion and nearly as complex a system of manners as a society based on social class. Its promise of comedy and tragedy is enormous; its assurance of relevance is perfect. Dostoevski adequately demonstrated this for us, but we never had in this country a sufficiently complex ideological situation to support it in our own practice of the novel. We have it now.

This opportunity of the novel clearly leads to its duty. Ideology is not ideas; ideology is not acquired by thought but by breathing the haunted air. The life in ideology, from which none of us can wholly escape, is a strange submerged life of habit and semihabit in which we attach strong passions to ideas, but have no very clear awareness of the concrete reality of their consequences. To live the life of ideology with its special form of unconsciousness is to expose oneself to the risk of becoming an agent of what Kant called "the Radical Evil," which is "man's inclination to corrupt the imperatives of morality so that they may become a screen for the expression of self-love." [5] But the novel is a genre with a very close and really a very simple relation to actuality, to the things we cannot possibly not know—not if they are pointed out to us; it is the form in which the things we cannot possibly not know live side by side with thought and desire, both in their true and beautiful state and in their corrupt state; it is the form which provides the perfect criticism of ideas by attaching them to their appropriate actuality. No less than in its infancy, and now perhaps with a greater urgency and relevance, the novel passionately concerns itself with reality, with appearance and reality.

VI

But I must not end on a note so high—it would falsify my present intention and my whole feeling about the novel. To speak now of "duty" and, as I earlier did, of the work the novel may do in the reconstitution and renovation of the will, to formulate a function and a destiny for the novel, is to put it into a compromised position where it has been far too long already. The novel was better off when it was more humbly conceived than it is now; the novelist was in a far more advantageous position when his occupation was misprized, or when it was estimated by simpler minds than his own, when he was nearly alone in his sense of wonder at the possibilities of his genre, at the great effects it might be made to yield. The novel was luckier when it had to compete with the sermon, with works of history, with philosophy and poetry and with the ancient classics, when its social position was in question and like one of its own poor or foundling or simple heroes it had to make its way against odds. Whatever high intentions it may have had, it was permit-

---

[5] Reinhold Niebuhr, *The Nature and Destiny of Man*, vol. 1, p. 120: " 'This evil is radical,' [Kant] declares, 'because it corrupts the very basis of all maxims.' In analyzing the human capacity for self-deception and its ability to make the worse appear the better reason for the sake of providing a moral façade for selfish actions, Kant penetrates into spiritual intricacies and mysteries to which he seems to remain completely blind in his *Critique of Practical Reason*."

ted to stay close to its own primitive elements from which it drew power. Believing this, I do not wish to join in the concerted effort of contemporary criticism to increase the superego of the novel, to conspire with our sense of cultural crisis to heap responsibilities upon it, to hedge it about with prescribed functions and spiked criteria; as things are, the novel feels quite guilty enough.

A sentence in Aristotle's *Ethics* has always been memorable, perhaps because I have never wholly understood it. Aristotle says, "There is a sense in which Chance and Art have the same sphere; as Agathon says, 'Art fosters Fortune; Fortune fosters Art.'" Taken out of its context, and merely as a gnomic sentence, this says much. It says something about the reciprocation which in the act of composition exists between form and free invention, each making the other, which even the most considerate criticism can never really be aware of and often belies. *Fortune fosters Art:* there is indeed something fortuitous in all art, and in the novel the element of the fortuitous is especially large. The novel achieves its best effects of art often when it has no concern with them, when it is fixed upon effects in morality, or when it is simply reporting what it conceives to be objective fact. The converse is of course also true, that the novel makes some of its best moral discoveries or presentations of fact when it is concerned with form, when it manipulates its material merely in accordance with some notion of order or beauty, although it must be stipulated that this is likely to occur only when what is manipulated resists enough, the novel being the form whose aesthetic must pay an unusually large and simple respect to its chosen material. This predominance of fortuitousness in the novel accounts for the roughness of grain, even the coarseness of grain as compared with other arts, that runs through it. The novel is, as many have said of it, the least "artistic" of genres. For this it pays its penalty and it has become in part the grave as well as the monument of many great spirits who too carelessly have entrusted their talents to it. Yet the headlong, profuse, often careless quality of the novel, though no doubt wasteful, is an aspect of its bold and immediate grasp on life.

But from this very sense of its immediacy to life we have come to overvalue the novel. We have, for example, out of awareness of its power, demanded that it change the world; no genre has ever had so great a burden of social requirement put upon it (which, incidentally, it has very effectively discharged), or has been so strictly ordered to give up, in the fulfillment of its assigned function, all that was unconscious and ambivalent and playful in itself. Our sense of its comprehensiveness and effectiveness has led us to make a legend of it: one of the dreams of a younger America, continuing until recently, was of *the* Great American Novel, which was always imagined to be as solitary and omniseminous as the Great White Whale. Then we have subjected it to criteria which are irrelevant to its nature—how many of us happily share the horror which John Gould Fletcher expressed at the discovery that Trollope thought of novel-writing as a trade. The overvaluation of love is the beginning of the end of love; the overvaluation of art is the beginning of the end of art.

What I have called the roughness of grain of the novel, and praised as such, corresponds with something in the nature of the novelists themselves. Of all practitioners of literature, novelists as a class have made the most aggressive assault upon the world, the most personal demand upon it, and no matter how obediently they have listened to their daemons they have kept an ear cocked at the crowd and have denounced its dullness in not responding with gifts of power and fame. This personal demand the haughtiest reserve of Flaubert and James did not try to hide. The novelists have wanted much and very openly; and with great simplicity and naïveté they have mixed what they personally desired with what they desired for the world and have mingled their mundane needs with their largest judgments. Then, great as their mental force has been, they have been touched with something like stupidity, resembling the holy stupidity which Pascal recommends: its effects appear in their ability to maintain ambivalence toward their society, which is not an acquired attitude of mind, or a weakness of mind, but rather the translation of a biological datum, an extension of the pleasure-pain with which, in a healthy state, we respond to tension, and effort; the novelist expresses this in his coexistent hatred and love of the life he observes. His inconsistency of intellectual judgment is biological wisdom.

It is at this point that I must deal with a lapse in my argument of which I am aware. My statement of belief that the novel is not dead, together with what I have said about what the novel should or should not do, very likely does not weigh against those circumstances in our civilization which I have adduced as accounting for the hypothetical death of the novel. To me certainly these circumstances are very real. And as I describe the character of the novelist they inevitably occur to me again. For it is exactly that character and what it suggests in a culture that the terrible circumstances of our time destroy. The novelist's assertion of personal demand and his frank mingling of the mundane and personal with the high and general, his holy stupidity, or as Keats called it, "negative capability," which is his animal faith—can these persist against the assaults which the world now makes on them? If the novel cannot indeed survive without ambivalence, does what the world presents us with any longer permit ambivalence? The novelist could once speak of the beautiful circuit of thought and desire which exists beside the daily reality, but the question is now whether thought and desire have any longer a field of possibility. No answer can soon be forthcoming. Yet, "as Agathon says, 'Art fosters Fortune; Fortune fosters Art.'" There is both an affirmation and an abdication in that sentence; the abdication is as courageous as the affirmation, and the two together make up a good deal of wisdom. If anything of the old novelistic character survives into our day, the novelist will be sufficiently aware of Fortune, of Conditions, of History, for he is, as Fielding said, the historian's heir; but he will also be indifferent to History, sharing the vital stupidity of the World-Historical Figure, who of course is not in the least interested in History but only in his own demands upon life and thus does not succumb to History's most malign and subtle trick, which is to fix and fascinate the mind of men with the pride of their foreknowledge of doom. There are times when, as the method of Perseus with the Medusa suggests, you do well not to look straight at what you are dealing with but rather to see it in the mirror-shield that the hero carries. Which is to say, "Art fosters Fortune."

But the shrug which is implied by the other half of the sentence is no less courageous. It does not suggest that we compare our position with what appears to be the more favored situation of the past, or keep in mind how History has robbed the novelist of a great role. What a demand upon the guarantees of History this would imply! What an overvaluation of security, and of success and the career, and of art, and of life itself, which must always be a little undervalued if it is to be lived. Rather should the phrase suggest both the fortuitous and the gratuitous nature of art, how it exists beyond the reach of the will alone, how it is freely given and not always for good reason, and for as little reason taken away. It is not to be demanded or prescribed or provided for. The understanding of this cannot of itself assure the existence of the novel but it helps toward establishing the state of the soul in which the novel becomes possible.

BIOGRAPHICAL NOTES

JOSEPH WARREN BEACH, born in Gloversville, New York, January 14, 1880, was educated at the University of Minnesota and at Harvard (Ph.D., 1907). He has taught at Harvard and at the Universities of Washington, Chicago, Illinois, and Minnesota, where, for the past eight years, he has been Professor and Chairman of the Department of English. One of the pioneer critics of the modern novel, he is the author of *The Outlook for American Prose* (1926), *The Twentieth Century Novel* (1932), and *American Fiction 1920-1940* (1941), as well as of two volumes of poetry, *Beginning with Plato* (1944) and *Involuntary Witness* (1950), a novel, and several other works of literary scholarship. In the summer of 1950 he taught at the Salzburg Seminar in American Studies, and in 1951-52, was a Fulbright lecturer at the Universities of Paris and Strasbourg. At present he is at work on a study of modern poetry.

JOHN PEALE BISHOP was born in Charles Town, West Virginia, on May 21, 1892. He attended Mercersburg Academy and graduated from Princeton in 1917. In 1922 he succeeded Edmund Wilson as managing editor of *Vanity Fair,* and in the same year collaborated with Wilson on *The Undertaker's Garland,* a collection of verse and prose. For most of the next ten years he lived with his family in France and worked on his two books of southern fiction, *Many Thousands Gone* (1932) and *Act of Darkness* (1935). Returning to this country in 1933 he settled on Cape Cod, where he lived with only occasional absences—in 1941-42, to serve on the Council of National Defense, and, in 1943, to take a job as Consultant in Comparative Literature at the Library of Congress—until his death in 1944. Although best known during his lifetime for his works of poetry, *Now with His Love* (1932), *Minute Particulars* (1936), and *Selected Poems* (1941), Bishop was a critic of rare sensitivity and insight. The simultaneous publication, in 1948, of his *Collected Poems* and *Collected Essays,* edited by his friends Allen Tate and Edmund Wilson, served to establish his contemporary reputation in both fields.

R. P. BLACKMUR was born in Springfield, Massachusetts, on January 21, 1904. One of the editors of *Hound and Horn* (1927-34), he held a Guggenheim Fellowship in 1936 and 1937. He has published two influential volumes of criticism—*The Double Agent* (1935) and *The Expense of Greatness* (1940)—and two books of poems—*From Jor-*

544

dan's Delight (1937) and *The Second World* (1942). His poetry and essays have appeared in several books and in most of the leading literary periodicals. Formerly a Resident Fellow in Creative Writing at Princeton University (1940-43; 1946-48) and a staff member of the Institute for Advanced Study (1944-45; 1945-46), he is now Professor of English at Princeton and a Fellow of the Indiana School of Letters. He is currently at work on studies of Henry Adams, Dostoevsky, and the European novel, and will shortly publish *Language as Gesture*.

RICHARD CHASE, born in Lakeport, New Hampshire, October 12, 1914, was educated at Dartmouth College and Columbia University (Ph.D., 1946). Holder of a Guggenheim Fellowship in 1947 and 1948, he has taught at Connecticut College (1945-49) and at Columbia, where he is now Assistant Professor of English. His critical articles and reviews have appeared in the *Nation* and the *Partisan* and *Kenyon Reviews;* and he is the author of three volumes of criticism and critical biography, *Quest For Myth* (1949), *Herman Melville* (1949), and *Emily Dickinson* (1951).

MALCOLM COWLEY was born in Belsano, Pennsylvania, on August 24, 1898. He was graduated from Harvard in 1920 and, in 1921, was awarded an American Field Service Fellowship for further study at the Université de Montpellier. One of our foremost literary historians and critics as well as a poet of considerable sensitivity, he is the author of *Exile's Return* (1934; 1951), a personalized account of the literary 1920's; two books of poems, *Blue Juniata* (1929) and *The Dry Season* (1941); and of many critical articles for the *New Republic,* the *New Yorker, Kenyon Review,* and other magazines. He has also contributed three chapters to the *Literary History of the United States* (1948), edited two volumes of essays, *After the Genteel Tradition* (1937) and *Books That Changed Our Minds* (1939), and translated into English works by Valéry, Barrès, and Gide. His most definitive recent criticism has appeared in the form of introductions to the *Portable Hemingway* (1944), the *Portable Faulkner* (1946), the *Portable Hawthorne* (1948), and the *Complete Whitman* (1948). In 1951 he edited *The Short Stories of F. Scott Fitzgerald* and a revised *Tender Is the Night.* Formerly literary editor of the *New Republic* (1929-44), Cowley is now a literary adviser to the Viking Press. He is currently at work on a critical study of American literature since 1900.

DAVID DAICHES was born in Scotland in 1912 and educated at the Universities of Edinburgh and Oxford. In 1937 he came to the United States and joined the English faculty of the University of Chicago. Until 1951, when he returned to England to accept the position of University Lecturer in English at Cambridge, he was, for a number of years, Professor of English and Chairman of the Division of Literature at Cornell. Before he was thirty, Daiches had written five books of criticism, *The Place of Meaning in Poetry* (1935); *New Literary Values* (1936); *Literature and Society* (1938); *The Novel and the Modern World* (1939), an indispensable study of the works of Conrad, Galsworthy, Huxley, Joyce, Mansfield, and Woolf; and a companion volume, *Poetry and the Modern World* (1941). His more recent works include *Virginia Woolf* (1942), *Robert Louis Stevenson* (1947), *A Study of Literature* (1948), *Robert Burns* (1951), and *Willa Cather* (1951).

T. S. ELIOT was born in St. Louis, Missouri, on September 26, 1888. He was educated at Harvard, the Sorbonne, and Merton College, Oxford. He has worked in London as teacher, bank clerk, as an editor of the *Egoist* (1917-19), as editor of the *Criterion,* which he founded in 1922, and more recently as a member of the editorial board of Faber & Faber, Ltd. He became a British subject in 1927. Holder of the Norton Professorship of Poetry at Harvard (1932-33), Eliot was awarded the Nobel Prize for Literature in 1948. His most important works in criticism are *The Sacred Wood* (1920), which, together with I. A. Richards' *The Principles of Literary Criticism* (1924), initiated the modern critical movement in poetry, and *Selected Essays* (1932). His poetry, beginning with *The Waste Land* (1922) and culminating in *The Four Quartets* (1943), represents one of the finest and most influential creative achievements of our time. Among his other works in poetry are *Prufrock* (1917), *Ash Wednesday* (1930), and *Poems 1909-1935* (1936). In poetic drama Eliot has been a bold and persistent experimenter. His *Murder in the Cathedral* (1935), *Family Reunion* (1939), and *The Cocktail Party* (1950), which was a brilliant Broadway success, have opened new possibilities for the use of poetry in the modern theatre.

FRANCIS FERGUSSON, one of our finest scholars and critics of the drama, began his career as associate director of the Laboratory Theatre in New York (1927-29), and as drama critic for the *Bookman* (1930-32). He has lectured at the New School for Social Research (1932-34), taught drama and creative writing at Bennington College (1934-47), and served as a member of the Institute for Advanced Study (1948–49). He has published essays and reviews in *Hound and Horn,* the *Bookman,* the *Kenyon, Sewanee,* and *Partisan Reviews,* and other magazines, poetry in *New Directions, Partisan Review,* and *Poetry,* a translation of Sophocles' *Electra* (1937), a critical introduction to Joyce's *Exiles* (1947), and an introduction to a recent edition of *Molière* (1950). He is also the author of a distinguished book of dramatic criticism, *The Idea of a Theatre* (1949). Director, during the summers, of the Cummington School of the Arts, Fergusson is regularly Director of the Princeton Seminars in Literary Criticism. At present he is at work on studies of Dante's *Purgatorio*.

JOSEPH FRANK was born on October 6, 1918, in New York City. He has published critical essays on poetry and fiction in the *Sewanee, Hudson, Partisan,* and *Southern Reviews* and in *La Revista Belga*. A member of the editorial staff of the Bureau of National Affairs in Washington, D. C., he is currently in Europe on a Fulbright Fellowship. His present critical project is a study of Flaubert.

NORTON R. GIRAULT was born in New Orleans, Louisiana, on March 29, 1918. He has studied at Louisiana State University (1934-39) and at the University of North Carolina (1939-40), and has been a teaching fellow and instructor in English at North Carolina and Minnesota. At present he is a Lieutenant Commander in the United States Navy.

EUNICE GLENN, a native of Georgia, was educated at Louisiana State and Vanderbilt Universities and the University of Chicago. She has published criticism in the *Sewanee Review* and Allen Tate's *A Southern Vanguard* (1947). Her poems and stories have appeared in *New Mexico Quarterly Review* and *Prairie Schooner*. She has done editorial work in New York City and now lives in Tennessee.

IRENE HENDRY, born in Rye, New York, April 9, 1918, was educated at Columbia and New York Universities and the University of Illinois. She has taught at George Washington University and has done editorial work in Washington, D. C. Her essays, reviews, and poems have appeared in the *Sewanee* and *Kenyon Reviews;* and she is at work on a book-length study of symbol and theme in Melville.

F. R. LEAVIS, born in Cambridge, England, July 16, 1895, was educated at Emmanuel College, Cambridge University (Ph.D., 1926). Since 1931 he has been Director of English Studies at Downing College, Cambridge, and, since 1937, University Lecturer in the Faculty of English. For the past twenty years he has edited *Scrutiny,* one of the most influential critical journals in Great Britain. Author of *Mass Civilization and Minority Culture* (1930), *D. H. Lawrence* (1930), *How to Teach Reading* (1932), *New Bearings in English Poetry* (1932), *For Continuity* (1933), *Revaluation* (1936) and *Education and the University* (1943), he has edited two anthologies of critical essays—*Towards Standards of Criticism: Selections from the Calendar of Modern Letters, 1925-27* (1933) and *Determinations* (1934)—and has published in *Scrutiny* a great many reviews and essays on poetry and fiction. His most recent books are *The Great Tradition* (1948) and *The Common Pursuit* (1951). He is currently at work on a study of critics and criticism, an evaluation of D. H. Lawrence, and a volume to be called *Judgment and Analysis*.

HARRY LEVIN, born in Minneapolis, Minnesota, July 18, 1912, was educated at Harvard and the University of Paris. A Junior Fellow at Harvard from 1934 to 1939 and a Guggenheim Fellow in 1943, he was made Faculty Instructor at Harvard in 1939 and Professor of English in 1948. He is the author of *The Broken Column: A Study in Romantic Hellenism* (1931), *James Joyce: A Critical Introduction* (1941), *Toward Stendhal* (1945), and *Toward Balzac* (1947), and the editor of *The Selected Works of Ben Jonson* (1938), *A Satire Against Mankind and Other Poems* by the Earl of Rochester (1942), *Three Tales* by Flaubert (1944), *The Portable James Joyce* (1947), and *Perspectives of Criticism* (1950). He is currently at work on *The Gates of Horn: A Study of Five French Realists* and *The Overreacher: A Study of Christopher Marlowe.*

PERCY LUBBOCK, born on June 4, 1879, was educated at Eton and at King's College, Cambridge. One of the first formalist critics of fiction, he is the author of the distinguished volume, *The Craft of Fiction* (1921), as well as of *The Region Cloud* (1925) and other novels. He has edited *The Middle Years* by Henry James (1917) and *The Letters of Henry James* (1920).

H. L. MENCKEN was born in Baltimore, Maryland, on September 12, 1880. He began his career as a member of the staff of the Baltimore *Sun* (1906) and was a regular contributor until 1941. He has been literary critic (1908-23) and editor (1914-23) of *Smart Set* and editor of *American Mercury* (1924-33). An accomplished rhetorician, polemicist, and etymologist, and a remorseless critic of the American scene, he is the author of *A Book of Prefaces* (1917), *Prejudices* (1919, 1920, 1922, 1924, 1926, 1927), *Selected Prejudices* (1930), *The American Language* (1936), and many other works.

ARTHUR MIZENER was born in Erie, Pennsylvania, on September 3, 1907. He was educated at Harvard and Princeton Universities and has taught at Yale (1934-40), Wells College (1940-45), Carleton College (1945-51), and Cornell University where he is now Professor of English. A frequent contributor of reviews and essays to the *Sewanee, Kenyon,* and *Partisan Reviews,* he is the author of the well-known biography of F. Scott Fitzgerald, *The Far Side of Paradise* (1951).

PHILIP RAHV was born in Russia on March 10, 1908. He is an editor of *Partisan Review,* an instructor at New York University, and a Fellow of the Indiana School of Letters. A contributor to the *Kenyon* and *Southern Reviews, Commentary, Nation, New Republic,* and other magazines, he is the author of *Discovery of Europe* (1947) and *Image and Idea* (1949). At present he holds a Guggenheim Fellowship for work on the greater novels of Dostoevsky.

D. S. Savage was born in Harlow, Essex, England, on March 6, 1917. Holder of an Atlantic Award in Literature in 1947, he has contributed critical essays and poems to *The Adelphi, The Spectator,* and the *Sewanee* and *Western Reviews.* Author of *The Personal Principle: Studies in Modern Poetry* (1944), *Hamlet and the Pirates: An Exercise in Literary Detection* (1950), *The Withered Branch: Six Studies in the Modern Novel* (1950) and two books of poems, *The Autumn Wood* (1938) and *A Time to Mourn: Poems 1934-43* (1943), he is at present at work on a study of Hamlet to be entitled *The Underground Man.*

Mark Schorer was born in Sauk City, Wisconsin, May 17, 1908, and educated at Harvard and the University of Wisconsin (Ph.D., 1936). He has taught at the University of Wisconsin (1931-35), Dartmouth College (1936-37), Harvard (1937-45), and, since 1945, at the University of California at Berkeley where he is a Professor of English. A Fellow of the Indiana School of Letters, he has participated in the Princeton Seminars in Literary Criticism (1950) and has been a Visiting Lecturer in English at Harvard (1952). He has contributed to the *Kenyon, Sewanee,* and *Hudson Reviews, The New Yorker,* and other magazines, and is the author of two novels—*A House Too Old* (1935) and *The Hermit Place* (1941)—and a collection of short stories, *The State of Mind* (1948). His critical works include *William Blake: The Politics of Vision* (1947) and introductions to *Moll Flanders* (1950), *Wuthering Heights* (1950), *The Good Soldier* (1951), and *Sons and Lovers* (1951). He has edited *The Story: A Critical Anthology* (1950) and, with Josephine Miles and Gordon McKenzie, *Criticism: The Foundations of Modern Literary Judgment* (1948). At present he is at work on a novel, a critical evaluation of D. H. Lawrence, and a study of the novel as genre.

Delmore Schwartz, born on December 8, 1913, was educated at Columbia, Harvard, and New York University and the University of Wisconsin. He has taught at Harvard (1940-47), New York University (1947), and the Indiana School of Letters (1951). Since 1943 he has been an associate editor of *Partisan Review.* A Guggenheim Fellow in 1940-41, he has contributed poems and essays to *Nation* and the *Southern, Kenyon,* and *Partisan Reviews,* and has published *In Dreams Begin Responsibilities* (1938), *Shenandoah* (1941), *Genesis* (1943), *The World is a Wedding* (1948), and *Vaudeville for a Princess* (1950). He is currently at work on critical studies of T. S. Eliot and F. Scott Fitzgerald.

Robert Wooster Stallman, born on September 27, 1911, in Milwaukee, Wisconsin, was educated at the University of Wisconsin (Ph.D., 1942). He has taught at Wisconsin (1939-42, 1946), Yale (1944-45), the University of Kansas (1946-49), the University of Minnesota (1947), and, since 1949, at the University of Connecticut where he is an Associate Professor of English. An associate editor (1946-49) and contributing editor (1949-   ) of *Western Review,* he has published essays and critical checklists in *Accent, Sewanee Review, College English,* and other magazines. He has edited *Critiques and Essays in Criticism* (1949), *The Critics' Notebook* (1949), *The Art of Modern Fiction*—with Ray B. West, Jr.—(1949), and *The Stephen Crane Reader* (1952).

ALLEN TATE was born in Winchester, Kentucky, November 19, 1899, and was graduated from Vanderbilt University in 1922. A founder and editor of *The Fugitive* (1922-25), the Southern editor of the *Hound and Horn* (1931-34), an advisory editor of the *Kenyon Review* (1939-42), and the editor of the *Sewanee Review* (1944-46), he has done free-lance writing in New York (1924-28) and, on a Guggenheim Fellowship, lived in France from 1928 to 1930. He has taught at the University of North Carolina, Princeton, New York University, and the University of Minnesota where he is now a Professor of English. He is the author of four distinguished volumes of criticism, *Reactionary Essays* (1936), *Reason in Madness* (1941), *On the Limits of Poetry* (1948), and *The Hovering Fly* (1948); two biographies, *Stonewall Jackson* (1928) and *Jefferson Davis* (1929); a novel, *The Fathers* (1938); and five books of poetry, *Mr. Pope* (1928), *Poems: 1928-1931* (1932), *The Mediterranean* (1936), *Selected Poems* (1937), and *Poems: 1922-1947* (1948). He has also edited *A Southern Vanguard* (1947), *The Collected Poems of John Peale Bishop* (1948), and, with his wife Caroline Gordon, *The House of Fiction* (1950). At present he is at work on a critical biography of Edgar Allan Poe and a study of Dante and Poe, to be entitled *The Angelic Imagination.*

LIONEL TRILLING was born in New York City on July 4, 1905, and educated at Columbia University (Ph.D., 1938). He was a University Fellow at Columbia in 1931-32 and a Guggenheim Fellow in 1947-48. He has taught at the University of Wisconsin (1926-27), Hunter College (1927-31), and Columbia (1932-   ) where he is now a Professor of English. A frequent contributor to the *Nation,* the *Partisan* and *Kenyon Reviews,* and other magazines, he is the author of *Matthew Arnold* (1939), *E. M. Forster* (1943), a novel, *The Middle of the Journey* (1947), and a volume of critical essays, *The Liberal Imagination* (1950).

AUSTIN WARREN was born in Waltham, Massachusetts, on July 4, 1899, and attended Wesleyan, Harvard, and Princeton Universities. A Professor of English at the University of Michigan and a Senior Fellow of the Indiana School of Letters, he has taught previously at Boston University (1926-39) and the University of Iowa (1939-48).

His essays and reviews have appeared in the *American, Kenyon, Sewanee,* and *Southern Reviews;* and his works in criticism include *Pope as Critic* (1929), *The Elder Henry James* (1934), *Hawthorne* (1934), *Crashaw: A Study in Baroque Sensibility* (1939), *Rage For Order: Essays in Criticism* (1948), and *Theory of Literature*—with René Wellek— (1949). At present he is engaged on a critical study of Donne, a book of essays on New England philosophical writers, and an intellectual autobiography, to be entitled *Becoming What One Is.*

ROBERT PENN WARREN, born in Kentucky in 1905, was educated at Vanderbilt University, the University of California, Yale University, and Oxford University (Rhodes Scholar). He has taught at Southwestern College (1930), Vanderbilt University (1931-34), Louisiana State University (1934-42), the University of Minnesota (1942-50), and Yale University where, since 1950, he has been a member of the drama faculty. In 1945, succeeding Allen Tate, he held the Chair of Poetry in the Library of Congress. A member of the Southern Agrarian group, he was joint editor, with Cleanth Brooks, of the *Southern Review* (1935-42) and since 1942 an advisory editor of *Kenyon Review.* He has published a biography, *John Brown* (1929), and, in joint authorship with Cleanth Brooks, three textbooks, two of which have won wide recognition: *Understanding Poetry* (1938) and *Understanding Fiction* (1943). Author of four novels and three books of poetry, he was awarded the Pulitzer Prize for *All the King's Men* (1945) and the American Academy Prize for his *Selected Poems: 1923-1943* (1944). His previous novels were *Night Rider* (1939) and *At Heaven's Gate* (1943), and his other poetic works were *Thirty-Six Poems* (1935) and *Eleven Poems on the Same Theme* (1942). While on his second Guggenheim Fellowship, Warren lived in Italy and there wrote his fourth novel, *World Enough and Time* (1950).

RAY B. WEST, JR., born in Logan, Utah, on July 30, 1908, was educated at Utah State College, the University of Utah, and the University of Iowa, where he took his doctorate in 1945. He has taught at Utah State College and the Universities of Kansas and Iowa, and has directed writers' conferences at each of these institutions. Now an Associate Professor of English at Iowa and editor of the *Western Review,* he has contributed reviews and articles to the *Sewanee* and *University of Kansas City Reviews* and has edited *Writing in the Rocky Mountains* (1947) and *The Art of Modern Fiction*—with Robert W. Stallman—(1949).

EDMUND WILSON was born on May 8, 1895, in Red Bank, New Jersey, and was graduated from Princeton in 1916. Before serving in World War I, he worked as a reporter for the *New York Evening Sun*

(1916-17), was managing editor of *Vanity Fair* (1920-21), an associate editor of the *New Republic* (1926-31), and, for a number of years, literary critic for the *New Yorker*. He has published two books of fiction—*I Thought of Daisy* (1929) and *Memoirs of Hecate County* (1946)—and a book of poems, *Poets Farewell!* (1929); four books of social reporting—*The American Jitters* (1932), *Travels in Two Democracies* (1936), *To the Finland Station* (1940), *Europe Without Baedeker* (1947); and several books of criticism including: *Axel's Castle* (1931), *The Triple Thinkers* (1938, 1948), and *The Wound and the Bow* (1941, 1947). He has edited *The Collected Essays of John Peale Bishop* (1948).

MORTON DAUWEN ZABEL, born at Minnesota Lake, Minnesota, August 10, 1901, was educated at St. Thomas Military College, the University of Minnesota, and the University of Chicago (Ph.D., 1933). An associate editor (1928-36) and editor (1936-37) of *Poetry*, he has taught at Loyola University (1922-46), held visiting professorships at Notre Dame (1930), the University of Chicago (1934, 1947), Northwestern University (1939), the University of California (1942), at various South American universities, and, since 1947, has been a Professor of English at Chicago. He has contributed articles and reviews to many periodicals including *Poetry*, the *New Republic*, *Nation*, and the *Southern, Sewanee,* and *Partisan Reviews*, and is the author of *The Romantic Idealism of Art in England, 1800-1848* (1933), *The Critical and Popular Background of Art in England, 1800-1848* (1937), *Shakespeare's Imagery: A Criticism* (1936), *Two Years of Poetry: 1937-1939* (1939), *The Situation in American Criticism: 1939* (1939), and other works of scholarship and criticism. He has edited *Literary Opinion in America* (1937, 1951), *The Portable Conrad* (1947), and *The Portable Henry James* (1951), and written definitive critical introductions to novels by Conrad and Butler. At present Zabel is at work on a biographical and critical study of Conrad and a study of Victorian poetry from Landor to Yeats.

A SELECTED BIBLIOGRAPHY OF CRITICISM
OF MODERN FICTION *

Compiled by ROBERT WOOSTER STALLMAN

I. GENERAL FICTION CHECKLIST: BOOKS AND ESSAYS.

II. TOPIC CHECKLISTS.

III. AUTHOR CHECKLISTS.

I. GENERAL FICTION CHECKLIST: BOOKS AND ESSAYS

ADAMS, J. D. *The Shape of Books to Come.* Viking, 1945. Reprinted as *The Writer's Responsibility.* Secker & Warburg, 1946.

ALDRIDGE, JOHN W. *After the Lost Generation.* McGraw-Hill, 1951.

—— "America's Young Novelists." *Sat. Rev. Lit.,* 32 (Feb. 12, 1949), 6-8, 36-37, 42. Repr. in a condensed form in *Neue Auslese* (Sept., 1949), 79-83.

—— "The New Generation of Writers." *Harper's,* 195 (Nov., 1947), 423-432. Repr. with a "Postscript" in *The Penguin New Writing,* No. 35, 1948. Pp. 101-122.

ALLEN, FREDERICK LEWIS. *Paul Revere Reynolds.* Privately printed, 1944.

ALLEN, WALTER. *Reading a Novel.* Alan Swallow Pr., 1949.

ALTICK, RICHARD. *The Scholar Adventurers.* Macmillan, 1950.

AMES, VAN METER. *Aesthetics of the Novel.* Univ. of Chicago Pr., 1928.

—— "Enjoying the Novel," in *The Enjoyment of the Arts,* edited by Max Schoen. Philosophical Library, 1944.

—— "The Novel: Between Art and Science," *Kenyon Rev.,* 5 (Winter, 1943), 34-47.

BADER, A. L. "The Structure of the Modern Short Story," *College English,* 7 (Nov., 1945), 86-92.

BAKER, DENYS VAL, editor. *Writers of Today. Sidgwick,* 1946.

BAKER, ERNEST A. *The History of the English Novel.* H. F. & G. Witherby, 1937.

BAKER, HOWARD. "The Contemporary Short Story," *Southern Rev.,* 2 (Winter, 1938), 576-596.

—— "An Essay on Fiction With Examples," *Southern Rev.,* 7 (Autumn, 1941), 385-406.

—— "In Praise of the Novel," *Southern Rev.,* 5 (Spring, 1940), 793 ff.

—— "Some Notes on New Fiction," *Southern Rev.,* 1 (July, 1935), 178-191.

BALDWIN, C. C. *The Men Who Make Our Novels.* Moffat, Yard & Co., 1914. Rev. ed., 1924.

* I am grateful to the members of English 380 (University of Connecticut, Spring 1950) who contributed to this bibliography, and for assistance in preparing the manuscript I wish to thank Mr. Gregory Polletta. My debts are for additions to my listings in Part III contributed by Mr. Ben Collins and Mr. Gregory Polletta on Joyce, Mr. Herbert Martey and Ted Sinitsky on James, Mr. Paul Obler on Lawrence, Mr. B. T. Perry on Faulkner, and Mary Lynch Thatcher on Virginia Woolf. For use of Mr. Perry's checklist on Faulkner acknowledgement is also due to the Editors of the *University of Kansas City Review.* Mr. Ben Collins has in preparation a bibliography of James Joyce. Mr. Polletta typed most of the manuscript and helped in proofreading it. I also wish to thank Miss Roberta Smith, Reference Librarian at the University of Connecticut, for her constant help.

This bibliography is limited to British and American fiction.

BARZUN, JACQUES. "Our Non-Fiction Novelists," *Atlantic,* 178 (1946) , 129-132.

BATES, H. E. *The Modern Short Story, A Survey.* The Writer, Inc., 1950.

BEACH, J. W. *American Fiction: 1920-1940.* Macmillan, 1941, 1948. (See pages 402-414 of this book for chap. xiv.)

—— *The Outlook for American Prose.* Univ. of Chicago Pr., 1926.

—— *The Twentieth Century Novel: Studies in Technique.* Appleton Century, 1932.

BECK, WARREN. "Art and Formula in the Short Story," *College English,* 5 (Nov., 1943) , 55-62.

BELGION, MONTGOMERY. "The Testimony of Fiction," *Southern Rev.,* 4 (Summer, 1938) , 143-155.

BENTLEY, ERIC, editor. *The Importance of Scrutiny.* Stewart, 1948.

BISHOP, J. P. *The Collected Essays,* edited by Edmund Wilson. Scribner's, 1948.

BJORKMAN, EDWIN. "Fiction and Life," *Virginia Quar. Rev.,* 7 (1931) , 271-280.

BLACKMUR, R. P. "Notes on the Novel: 1936," *The Expense of Greatness.* Arrow Editions, 1940. Pp. 176-198, 277-305.

BLANKENSHIP, RUSSELL. *American Literature As an Expression of the National Mind.* Routledge, 1931; Holt, 1931, 1949.

BLIVEN, BRUCE, editor. *Twentieth Century Unlimited.* Lippincott, 1950.

BOURNE, R. S. *History of a Literary Radical.* Huebsch, 1920.

BOWEN, ELIZABETH. *Collected Impressions.* Knopf, 1950.

BOYD, ERNEST. *Portraits: Real and Imaginary.* George H. Doran, 1924.

BOYNTON, PERCY H. *Some Contemporary Americans.* Univ. of Chicago Pr., 1924.

—— *More Contemporary Americans.* Univ. of Chicago Pr., 1927.

—— *Literature and American Life.* Ginn & Co., 1936.

—— *America in Contemporary Fiction.* Univ. of Chicago Pr., 1940.

BRACE, MARJORIE. "Thematic Problems of the American Novelist," *Accent,* 6 (Autumn, 1945) , 44-54.

BREWSTER, DOROTHY, AND BURRELL, ANGUS. *Modern Fiction.* Columbia Univ. Pr., 1934. (Revised and extended edition of *Dead Reckonings in Fiction.*)

BRADLEY, SCULLEY, editor. *The Arts in Renewal.* Univ. of Pennsylvania Pr., 1951.

BROOKS, CLEANTH, AND WARREN, R. P. *Understanding Fiction.* Crofts, 1943.

BROOKS, VAN WYCK. *New England: Indian Summer, 1865-1915.* Dutton, 1940.

—— *Sketches in Criticism.* Dutton, 1932.

BROWN, CURTIS. *Contact.* Harper, 1935.

BROWN, ROLLO, editor. *The Writer's Art.* Harvard Univ. Pr., 1921.

BURGUM, E. B. *The Novel and the World's Dilemma.* Oxford Univ. Pr., 1947.

BURKE, KENNETH. "A Decade of American Fiction," *Bookman,* 69 (Aug., 1929) , 561-567.

—— *The Philosophy of Literary Form.* Louisiana State Univ. Pr., 1941.

CABELL, J. B. *Some of Us.* McBride, 1930.

CALVERTON, V. F. *The Liberation of American Literature.* Scribner's, 1932.

Cambridge Bibliography of English Literature. Macmillan, 1940.

The Cambridge History of American Literature, edited by William Trent, John Erskine, S. P. Sherman. Putnam's, 1927.

CANBY, HENRY SEIDEL. *American Estimates.* Harcourt, 1929.

—— *Definitions.* Harcourt, 1922. Second Series, 1924.

—— *Designed for Reading.* Macmillan, 1934.

—— "Fiction Tells All." *Harper's,* 171 (Aug., 1935), 308-315.

—— *Seven Years' Harvest.* Farrar & Rinehart, 1936.

CARGILL, OSCAR. *Intellectual America: Ideas on the March.* Macmillan, 1941.

CATHER, WILLA. "The Novel Démeublé," *New Rep.,* 30 (Apr. 12, 1922) , Supplement.

CECIL, DAVID. *Poets and Story-Tellers: A Book of Critical Essays.* Macmillan, 1948.

—— *Reading as One of the Fine Arts.* Clarendon Pr., 1949.

CHAMBERLAIN, JOHN. "American Writers," *Life,* 23 (Sept. 1, 1949) , 82-84, 86, 89, 91-92.

—— *Farewell to Reform.* John Day Co., 1932.

CHURCH, RICHARD. *The Growth of the English Novel.* Methuen, 1951.
COBLENTZ, STANTON A. *The Literary Revolution.* Frank-Maurice, 1927.
COLLINS, JOSEPH. *Taking the Literary Pulse.* George H. Doran, 1924.
COLUM, MARY M. *From These Roots.* Columbia Univ. Pr., 1937.
COMFORT, ALEX. *The Novel & Our Time.* Dent; Alan Swallow Pr., 1948.
CONNOLLY, CYRIL. *The Condemned Playground: Essays 1927-1944.* Routledge & Kegan Paul, 1945; Macmillan, 1946.
—— *Enemies of Promise.* Routledge, 1938; Macmillan, 1948.
CONRAD, JOSEPH. *Last Essays.* Dent, 1926.
—— *Notes on Life and Letters.* Dent, 1921.
COWIE, ALEXANDER. *The Rise of the American Novel.* American Book, 1948.
COWLEY, MALCOLM, editor. *After the Genteel Tradition: American Writers Since 1910.* Norton, 1937.
—— "The Alger Story," *New Republic,* 113 (Sept. 10, 1945), 319-320.
—— *Exile's Return.* Norton, 1934; rev. ed., Viking, 1951.
—— "Reviewers on Parade." *New Rep.,* 93 (Feb. 2, 9, 1938), 23-24, 371-372.
CUNLIFFE, J. W. *English Novelists in the Twentieth Century.* Macmillan, 1933.
DAICHES, DAVID. "The Nature of Fiction," *A Study of Literature.* Cornell Univ. Pr., 1948.
—— *The Novel and the Modern World.* Univ. of Chicago Pr., 1939.
DAVIS, ROBERT G. "Fiction and Thinking." *Epoch,* 1 (Spring, 1948), 87-96.
DEVOTO, BERNARD. *The Literary Fallacy.* Little Brown, 1944.
—— *Minority Report.* Little Brown, 1940.
—— *The World of Fiction.* Houghton, 1950.
DOBRÉE, BONAMY. *The Lamp and the Lute.* Clarendon Pr., 1929.
DREW, ELIZABETH. *The Modern Novel: Some Aspects of Contemporary Fiction.* Harcourt, 1926; Cape, 1926.
DU BREVIL, ALICE. *The Novel of Democracy in America.* Johns Hopkins Univ. Pr., 1923.
EASTMAN, MAX. *Art and the Life of Action.* Knopf, 1934.
—— "Is the Novel at a Dead End?" *The Literary Mind.* Scribner's, 1935. Pp. 225-237.
EDGAR, PELHAM. *The Art of the Novel.* Macmillan, 1933.
ELIOT, T. S. *After Strange Gods.* Faber & Faber; Harcourt, 1934.
FARBER, MARJORIE. "Subjectivity in Modern Fiction," *Kenyon Rev.,* 7 (Autumn, 1945), 645-652.
FARRAR, JOHN, editor. *The Literary Spotlight.* George H. Doran, 1924.
FARRELL, JAMES T. *Literature and Morality.* Vanguard Pr., 1947.
FERNÁNDEZ, RAMÓN. *Messages.* Harcourt, 1927.
FLINT, F. C. "Remarks on the Novel," *Symposium,* 1 (Jan., 1930), 84-96.
FLORES, ANGEL, editor. *The Kafka Problem.* New Directions Pr., 1946.
FOERSTER, NORMAN, editor. *Humanism and America.* Farrar & Rinehart, 1930.
FOLLETT, WILSON. *The Modern Novel: A Study of the Purpose and Meaning of Fiction.* Knopf, 1918. Rev. ed., 1923.
FORD, F. M. *The March of Literature.* Dial Pr., 1938.
—— *Return to Yesterday.* Liveright, 1932.
—— *Thus to Revisit.* Chapman & Hall; Dutton, 1921. (Reminiscences).
—— *Portraits from Life.* Houghton, 1937.
FORSTER, E. M. *Aspects of the Novel.* Harcourt, 1927, 1947.
FOX, RALPH. *The Novel and the People.* Lawrence & Wishart, 1937; International Publishers, 1945.
—— *Writers in Arms.* Lawrence & Wishart, 1937.
FRAENKEL, MICHAEL. *Death is not Enough.* Daniel, 1936.
FRANK, WALDO. *In the American Jungle.* Farrar & Rinehart, 1937.
—— *Time Exposures.* Boni & Liveright, 1926.
FREEMAN, JOSEPH. *An American Testament.* Farrar & Rinehart, 1936.

FRIERSON, WILLIAM. *The English Novel in Transition.* Univ. of Oklahoma Pr., 1942.

FROHOCK, W. M. *The Novel of Violence in America, 1920-1950.* Southern Methodist Univ. Pr., 1950.

FRYE, NORTHROP. "Levels of Meaning in Literature," *Kenyon Rev.*, 12 (Spring, 1950), 246-273.

"The Future of the Novel: Towards a New Classicism," *Times Lit. Suppl.*, Sept. 6, 1941 (Leading article).

GALE, ZONA. "The Novel and the Spirit," *Yale Rev.*, 12 (Oct., 1922), 41-55.

GARNETT, DAVID. "Some Tendencies of the Novel," *Symposium*, 1 (Jan., 1930), 96-105.

GARNETT, EDWARD. *Friday Nights.* Knopf, 1922.

GEISMAR, MAXWELL. "A Cycle of Fiction," in *Literary History of the United States*, edited by Robert Spiller and others. Vol. II. Macmillan, 1948.

—— *Writers in Crisis: 1925-1940.* Houghton, 1942.

—— *The Last of the Provincials: The American Novel 1915-1925.* Houghton, 1948.

GOULD, GERALD. *The English Novel of Today.* Castle, 1924.

GRABO, CARL. *The Art of the Short Story.* Scribner's, 1913.

—— *The Techniques of the Novel.* Scribner's, 1928.

GRAY, JAMES. *On Second Thought.* Univ. of Minnesota Pr., 1948.

GREGORY, HORACE. *The Shield of Achilles.* Harcourt, 1944.

HAINES, HELEN. *What's in a Novel.* Columbia Univ. Pr., 1942.

HAMILL, ELIZABETH. *These Modern Writers: An Introduction for Modern Readers.* Georgian House (Melbourne), 1946.

HANSEN, AGNES. *Twentieth Century Forces in European Fiction.* American Library Association, 1934.

HANSEN, HARRY. *Midwest Portraits.* Harcourt, 1923.

HART, HARRY. *Writers in a Changing World.* Equinox Pr., 1937.

HART, J. D., editor. *The Oxford Companion to American Literature.* Oxford Univ. Pr., 1948. 2nd ed.

HARTWICK, HARRY. *The Foreground of American Fiction.* American Book, 1934. Bibliography, pp. 410-430.

HASTINGS, W. T. *A Syllabus of American Literature.* Univ. of Chicago Pr., 1923.

HATCHER, HARLAN. *Creating the Modern American Novel.* Farrar & Rinehart, 1935; Williams & Norgate, 1936.

HEARN, LAFCADIO. *Life and Literature*, edited by John Erskine. Dodd Mead, 1917.

HENDERSON, PHILIP. *The Novel Today.* Lane (Bodley Head), 1936.

HENDRY, IRENE. "The Regional Novel," *Sewanee Rev.*, 53 (Jan., 1945), 84-102.

HERRON, IMA HONEKER. *The Small Town and American Literature.* Duke Univ. Pr., 1939.

HERTZ, RICHARD. *Chance and Symbol: A Study in Aesthetic and Ethical Consistency.* Univ. of Chicago Pr., 1948.

HICKS, GRANVILLE. *The Great Tradition: An Interpretation of American Literature Since the Civil War.* Macmillan, 1933.

HIND, C. L. *Authors and I.* John Lane, 1921.

HOARE, DOROTHY M. *Some Studies in the Modern Novel.* Chatto & Windus, 1938.

HOFFMAN, F. J. *Freudianism and the Literary Mind.* Louisiana State Univ. Pr., 1945.

—— *The Modern Novel in America.* Henry Regnery Co., 1951.

HOFFMAN, FREDERICK, ALLEN, CHARLES, AND ULRICH, C. F. *The Little Magazine: A History and a Bibliography.* Princeton Univ. Pr., 1946. *See also:* Malcolm Cowley, "The Little Magazines Grow Up," New York Times Book Rev., Sept. 14, 1945, pp. 5, 35; Malcolm Cowley, "Ten Little Magazines," *New Rep.* 116 (Mar. 31, 1947), 30-33.

Hogarth Essays. Doubleday Doran, 1928.

HOWE, IRVING. "The Future of the Novel: The Political Novel (1)," *Tomorrow*, 10 (May, 1951), 51-58.

Howe, Irving. "The Future of the Novel: The Political Novel (2)," *Tomorrow,* 10 (June, 1951), 49-53.

Huxley, Aldous. *Music at Night, and Other Essays.* Fountain Pr., 1931.

—— *The Olive Tree.* Harper, 1937.

—— *On the Margin, Notes and Essays.* George H. Doran, 1923.

Index to Little Magazines, 1950. Alan Swallow Pr., 1951.

Isherwood, Christopher. *Lions and Shadows: An Education in the Twenties.* Hogarth Pr., 1938.

James, Henry. *The Art of Fiction and Other Essays,* edited by Morris Roberts. Oxford Univ. Pr., 1948.

Johnson, R. B. *Some Contemporary Novelists: Women.* Parsons, 1920.

Jolas, Eugene, editor. *Transition Workshop.* Vanguard Pr., 1949.

Jones, Howard Mumford. *The Theory of American Literature.* Cornell Univ. Pr., 1948.

Josephson, Matthew. *Portrait of the Artist as American.* Harcourt, 1930.

Kazin, Alfred. *On Native Grounds: An Interpretation of Modern American Prose Literature.* Reynal & Hitchcock, 1942.

Kerr, Elizabeth. *Bibliography of the Sequence Novel.* Univ. of Minnesota Pr., 1950.

Knight, Grant C. *American Literature and Culture.* Ray Long & Richard R. Smith, 1932.

—— *The Novel in English.* Farrar & Rinehart, 1931; R. R. Smith, 1935.

Kohler, Dayton. "Time in the Modern Novel," *College English,* 10 (Oct., 1948), 15-24.

Krutch, J. W. *The Modern Temper.* Harcourt, 1929.

Kunitz, Stanley, and Haycraft, H. *Twentieth Century Authors: A Bibliographical Dictionary.* Wilson, 1942.

Lawrence, D. H. *Studies in Classic American Literature.* Boni, 1923. Reprinted in *The Shock of Recognition,* edited by Edmund Wilson. Doubleday, 1943.

—— *Phoenix.* Heinemann, Viking, 1936.

Leavis, F. R. *The Great Tradition.* Chatto & Windus, 1948; George W. Stewart, 1949.

Levin, Harry. "The Novel," *Dictionary of World Literature,* edited by Joseph Shipley. Philosophical Library, 1943. Pp. 405-407.

Lewis, Wyndham. *Men Without Art.* Cassell, Harcourt, 1934.

—— *Paleface.* Chatto & Windus, 1929.

—— *Time and Western Man.* Harcourt, 1928.

Lewisohn, Ludwig. "The Crisis of the Novel," *Yale Rev.,* 20 (Mar., 1933), 533-544.

—— *Expression in America.* Harper, 1932.

Liddell, Robert. *Treatise on the Novel.* Cape, 1947.

Linn, J. W., and Taylor, H. W. *A Foreword to Fiction.* Appleton Century, 1935.

Literary History of the United States, edited by Robert Spiller, Willard Thorp, Thomas H. Johnson, Henry Seidel Canby. Vol. II. Macmillan, 1948. Bibliography, Vol. III.

Loggins, Vernon. *I Hear America: Literature in the United States Since 1900.* Crowell, 1937.

Lubbock, Percy. *The Craft of Fiction.* Cape; Scribner's, 1921, 1929; Peter Smith, 1947. (See pages 9-30 of this book for chaps. xi, xiii, xvii.)

Lukács, George. "Essay on the Novel," *International Literature,* No. 5 (May, 1936), 68-74.

—— "The Intellectual Physiognomy of Literary Characters," *International Literature,* No. 8 (Aug., 1936), 55-83.

MacCarthy, Desmond. *Portraits.* Putnam, 1931.

—— *Criticism.* Putnam, 1932.

Mann, Thomas. *Past Masters and Other Essays.* Secker, 1933.

Marble, Annie Russell. *A Study of the Modern Novel.* Appleton, 1930.

MARTIN, ERNEST W. L., editor. *New Spirit*. Dobson, 1946.

MATTHIESSEN, F. O. *The American Renaissance*. Oxford Univ. Pr., 1941.

MAUGHAM, W. SOMERSET. *Great Novelists and Their Novels*. John C. Winston Co., 1948.

—— "What Makes a Good Novel Great?" *New York Times Book Rev.*, Nov. 30, 1947, pp. 1, 48-49.

McCOLE, CAMILLE. *Lucifer at Large*. Longmans Green, 1937.

McCULLOUGH, BRUCE. *Representative British Novelists*. Harper, 1946.

McHUGH, VINCENT. *Primer of the Novel*. Random House, 1950.

MEGROZ, R. L. *Five Novelist Poets of To-day*. Joiner, 1933.

MENCKEN, H. L. "The American Novel," *Prejudices: Fourth Series*. Knopf, 1924. Pp. 278-293.

—— *A Mencken Chrestomathy*. Knopf, 1949.

MICHAUD, REGIS. *The American Novel To-day: A Social and Psychological Study*. Little Brown, 1931.

MILLETT, FRED. *Contemporary American Authors*. Harcourt, 1943.

—— *Contemporary British Literature*. Harcourt, 1943.

MITCHELL, E. V. *The Art of Authorship*. Loring & Mussey, 1935.

MIZENER, ARTHUR. "The Novel of Manners in America," *Kenyon Rev.*, 12 (Winter, 1950), 1-19.

MONROE, N. E. *The Novel and Society: A Critical Study of the Modern Novel*. Univ. of North Carolina Pr., 1941.

MOORE, GEORGE. *Conversations in Ebury Street*. Boni & Liveright, 1924.

MOORE, VIRGINIA. *Distinguished Women Writers*. Dutton, 1934.

MORGAN, CHARLES. *Reflections in a Mirror*. First Series, 1944. Second Series, 1946. Macmillan, 1944, 1946.

MORRIS, L. R. *Postscript to Yesterday, America: The Last Fifty Years*. Random House, 1947.

MORRIS, RUTH. "The Novel as Catharsis," *Psychoan. Rev.*, 31 (1944), 88-104.

MORTIMER, R. *Channel Packet*. Hogarth Pr., 1942.

MUIR, EDWIN. *The Present Age, from 1914*. Cresset Pr., 1939; McBride, 1940.

—— *The Structure of the Novel*. Hogarth Press, 1928, 1947. *See* "Remarks on the Novel," *Symposium*, 1 (Jan., 1930), 84-96 (by F. Cudworth Flint), 96-105 (by David Garnett), 106-114 (by Lionel Trilling). (A review of Muir's *Structure of the Novel* and Grabo's *Technique of the Novel*.)

—— "The Novel and the Modern World," *Horizon*, 2 (Nov., 1940), 246-253.

—— *Transition: Essays on Contemporary Literature*. Viking, 1926.

MULLER, H. J. *Modern Fiction*. Funk & Wagnalls, 1937.

MUNSON, GORHAM. *Destinations: A Canvass of American Literature Since 1900*. J. H. Sears, 1928.

MURRY, J. M. *Aspects of Literature*. Collins, 1920; Knopf, 1921; Cape, 1936.

MYERS, WALTER L. *The Later Realism: A Study of Characterization in the British Novel*. Univ. of Chicago Pr., 1927.

NEIDER, CHARLES. Introduction, *Short Novels of the Masters*. Rinehart, 1948.

NEWBY, P. H. *The Novel, 1945-1950*. Longmans, 1951.

New Directions (annual). New Directions Pr., No. 13, 1951.

NICHOLSON, NORMAN. *Man & Literature*. Macmillan, 1943.

NORRIS, FRANK. *The Responsibilities of the Novelist, and Other Literary Essays*. Doubleday Page, 1903.

The Novel of Tomorrow and the Scope of Fiction. By Twelve American Novelists. Bobbs-Merrill, 1922.

O'BRIEN, E. J. *The Advance of the American Short Story*. Dodd, 1931 (Rev. ed.).

O'CONNOR, W. VAN, editor. *Forms of Modern Fiction*. Univ. of Minnesota Pr., 1948.

O'FAOLAIN, SEAN. "It No Longer Matters, or The Death of the English Novel," *Criterion*, 15 (Oct., 1935), 49-56.

O'FAOLAIN, SEAN. "The Modern Novel." *Virginia Quar. Rev.*, 11 (July, 1935), 339-351.

——"The Secret of the Short Story," *United Nations World*, 3 (Mar., 1949), 37-38.

ORAGE, A. R. *Readers and Writers: 1917-1921*. Knopf, 1922.

ORTEGA Y GASSET, JOSÉ. *The Dehumanization of Art and Notes on the Novel*. Princeton Univ. Pr., 1948.

ORWELL, GEORGE. *Critical Essays*. Secker & Warburg, 1946. Repr. as *Dickens, Dali, and Others*. Reynal & Hitchcock, 1946.

OVERTON, GRANT. *An Hour of the American Novel*. Lippincott, 1929.

—— *The Philosophy of Fiction*. Appleton, 1928.

PARRINGTON, V. L. *Main Currents in American Thought*. Harcourt, 1930. Vol. III.

PARRY, ALBERT. *Garrets and Pretenders*. Covici, Friede, 1933.

PATTEE, F. L. *The New American Literature*. Century, 1930.

PHILLIPS, WILLIAM. Introduction, *Great American Short Novels*. Dial Pr., 1946.

PHILLIPS, WILLIAM, AND RAHV, PHILIP, editors. *The Partisan Reader*. Dial Pr., 1946.

POLLOCK, T. C. *The Nature of Literature*. Princeton Univ. Pr., 1942.

PRITCHETT, V. S., "The Future of English Fiction," *Partisan Rev.*, 15 (Oct., 1948), 1063-1070.

—— *In My Good Books*. Chatto & Windus, 1942.

—— *The Living Novel: A Journey of Rediscovery*. Chatto & Windus, 1946, 1949; Reynal & Hitchcock, 1947.

QUINN, ARTHUR HOBSON. *American Fiction*. Appleton Century, 1936.

—— *The Literature of the American People, An Historical and Critical Survey*. Appleton-Century-Crofts, 1951.

QUINN, KERKER, AND SHATTUCK, CHARLES, editors. *Accent Anthology*. Harcourt, 1946.

RAHV, PHILIP. *Image and Idea*. New Directions Pr., 1949. (See pages 231-243 of this book for an excerpt.)

—— editor, *The Partisan Reader*. Dial Pr., 1946.

RAJAN, B., editor. *The Novelist as Thinker: (Focus Four)*. Dobson, 1947.

RANSOM, J. C. "Characters and Character," *American Rev.*, 6 (Jan., 1937), 271-288.

—— "The Content of the Novel," *American Rev.*, 7 (June, 1936), 301-318.

—— "Fiction Harvest," *Southern Rev.*, 2 (Autumn, 1936), 399-418.

—— editor, *The Kenyon Critics: Studies in Modern Literature from The Kenyon Review*. World Publishing, 1951.

—— "The Understanding of Fiction." *Kenyon Rev.*, 12 (Spring, 1950), 189-218.

READ, HERBERT. "The Modern Novel," *Reason and Romanticism*. Faber & Gwyer, 1926. Chap. 11.

RICKWORD, C. H. "A Note on Fiction," *Towards Standards of Criticism*, edited by F. R. Leavis. Wishart, 1933. Pp. 29-43. Repr. from *The Calendar of Modern Letters*, 3 (1926-27), 226-233. Repr. in *Forms of Modern Fiction*, edited by W. Van O'Connor. Univ. of Minnesota Pr., 1948. Pp. 294-305.

RICKWORD, EDGELL, editor. *Scrutinies, II*. Wishart, 1931.

RIDING, LAURA. *Contemporaries and Snobs*. Doubleday, 1928.

ROSENFELD, PAUL. *Men Seen*. Dial Pr., 1925.

—— *Port of New York*. Harcourt, 1924.

ROTHENSTEIN, WILLIAM. *Men and Memories: 1900-1922*. Coward McCann, 1932. Vol. II.

ROURKE, CONSTANCE. *American Humor*. Harcourt, 1931.

ROUSE, BLAIR. "A Selective and Critical Bibliography of Studies in Prose Fiction," *Journal of English and Germanic Philology*, 49 (July, 1950), 358-387. (Annual compilation.)

SACKVILLE-WEST, E. *Inclinations*. Secker & Warburg, 1950.

SAMPSON, GEORGE. *The Concise History of English Literature*. Macmillan, 1942.

SANDBURG, CARL. *Homefront Memo*. Harcourt, 1943.

SAVAGE, D. S. *The Withered Branch*. Eyre & Spottiswoode, 1950.

SCHORER, MARK. "Fiction and the 'Analogical Matrix,'" *Kenyon Rev.*, 11 (Autumn, 1949), 539-560. (See pages 83-98 of this book.)

SEAVER, EDWIN. "What is a Proletarian Novel?" *Partisan Rev.*, 2 (Apr., 1935), 5-15.

"Shapers of the Modern Novel: A Catalogue of an Exhibition," *Princeton Univ. Library Chronicle*, 11 (Spring, 1950), 134-141.

SHERMAN, S. P. *The Main Stream*. Scribner's, 1927.

SITWELL, OSBERT. "The Modern Novel: Its Cause and Cure," in *Trio*, by Edith, Osbert, and Sacheverell Sitwell. Macmillan, 1938.

SLOCHOWER, HARRY. *No Voice is Wholly Lost*. Creative Age Pr., 1945; Dobson, 1947.

SMITH, HENRY NASH. *Virgin Land*. Harvard Univ. Pr., 1951.

SNELL, GEORGE. *The Shapers of American Fiction: 1798-1947*. Dutton, 1947.

SPENCER, BENJAMIN T. "An American Literature Again," *Sewanee Rev.*, 57 (Spring, 1949), 56-72.

—— "Wherefore This Southern Fiction?" *Sewanee Rev.*, 47 (Autumn, 1939), 500-512.

SQUIRE, J. G., AND OTHERS. *Contemporary American Authors*. Holt, 1928.

STAFFORD, JEAN. "The Psychological Novel," *Kenyon Rev.*, 10 (Spring, 1948), 214-227.

STALLMAN, R. W., editor. *The Critic's Notebook*. Univ. of Minnesota Pr., 1950. Bibliography, pp. 255-293.

—— *Critiques and Essays in Criticism: 1920-1948*. Ronald Pr., 1949. Bibliography, pp. 519-571.

STARRETT, VINCENT. *Buried Caesars: Essays in Literary Appreciation*. Covici, Friede, 1923.

STEGNER, WALLACE. "Fiction: A Lens on Life," *Sat. Rev. Lit.*, 33 (Apr. 22, 1950), 9-10, 32-34.

—— "New Climates for the Writer," *New York Times Book Rev.*, March 7, 1948, pp. 1, 20.

STEIN, GERTRUDE. *The Autobiography of Alice B. Toklas*. Random House, 1933.

—— *Four in America*. With an Introduction by T. N. Wilder. Yale Univ. Pr., 1947.

—— *Portraits and Prayers*. Random House, 1934.

STOLL, E. E. *From Shakespeare to Joyce*. Doubleday Doran, 1944.

SWINNERTON, FRANK. *The Georgian Scene: A Literary Panorama*. Farrar & Rinehart, 1934.

TATE, ALLEN, editor. *A Southern Vanguard*. Prentice-Hall, 1947.

TAYLOR, W. F. *A History of American Letters*. American Book, 1936. Bibliography by Harry Hartwick (on modern authors), pp. 556 ff.

TINDALL, W. Y. *Forces in Modern British Literature*. Knopf, 1947.

—— "Many-Leveled Fiction: Virginia Woolf to Ross Lockridge," *College English*, 10 (Nov., 1948), 65-71.

Tradition and Experiment in Present-Day Literature. Oxford Univ. Pr., 1929. See "Experiment in Fiction."

TRILLING, LIONEL. "Contemporary American Literature in its Relation to Ideas," *The American Writer and the European Tradition*, ed. by Margaret Denny and William Gilman. Univ. of Minnesota Pr., 1950.

—— *The Liberal Imagination*. Viking, 1950.

—— "Some Tendencies of the Novel," *Symposium*, 1 (Jan., 1930), 106-14.

TURNELL, MARTIN. *The Novel in France*. Hamish Hamilton, 1950.

VAN DOREN, CARL. *The American Novel: 1789-1939*. Macmillan, 1940.

—— *Contemporary American Novelists*. 1900-1920. Macmillan, 1922, 1931.

VAN DOREN, CARL AND MARK. *American and British Literature Since 1890*. Century Co., 1925.

VAN DOREN, MARK. *The Private Reader*. Holt, 1942.

VERSCHOYLE, DEREK, editor. *The English Novelists*. Harcourt, 1936.

WAGENKNECHT, EDWARD. *Cavalcade of the English Novel*. Holt, 1943.

WALCUTT, C. C. "The Regional Novel and its Failure," *Arizona Quar.*, 1 (1945), 17-27.

WALPOLE, HUGH, AND OTHERS. *Tendencies of the Modern Novel.* Peter Smith, 1934;
Allen & Unwin, 1935.

WARD, A. C. *American Literature, 1880-1930.* Methuen, 1932; Dial Pr., 1932.

—— *Twentieth Century Literature,* 1901-1940. Methuen, 1940.

WARFEL, HARRY. *American Novelists of Today.* American Book, 1951.

WARREN, AUSTIN, AND WELLEK, RENÉ. "The Nature and Modes of Fiction," *Theory of
Literature.* Harcourt, 1949. Chap. XVI. Bibliography, pp. 375-378.

WELTY, EUDORA. "Department of Amplification," *New Yorker,* 24 (Jan. 1, 1949), 50-51.

—— "The Reading of Short Stories," *Atlantic,* 183 (Feb., Mar., 1949), 54-58, 46-49.

WEST, ALICK. *Crisis and Criticism.* Lawrence & Wishart, 1937.

WEST, RAY B., JR. "A Note on American Fiction," *Western Rev.,* 11 (Autumn, 1946),
45-48; 12 (Autumn, 1947), 58-62.

WEST, RAY B., JR., AND STALLMAN, R. W. *The Art of Modern Fiction.* Rinehart, 1949.

WEST, REBECCA. *The Strange Necessity.* Doubleday, 1928.

WHARTON, EDITH. "Visibility in Fiction," *Life & Letters,* 2 (Apr., 1929), 263-272.

WHIPPLE, T. K. *Spokesmen.* Appleton, 1928.

—— *Study Out the Land.* Univ. of California Pr., 1943.

WHITEFORD, R. N. *Motives in English Fiction.* 1918.

WICKHAM, H. *The Impuritans.* Dial Pr., 1929.

WILLIAMS, ORLO. *Some Great English Novels: Studies in the Art of Fiction.* Macmillan, 1926.

WILSON, EDMUND. *Axel's Castle.* Scribner's, 1931.

—— *The Boys in the Back Room.* Colt, 1941.

—— *Classics and Commercials: A Literary Chronicle of the Forties.* Farrar, Straus,
1950.

WINTERS, YVOR. *Maule's Curse: Seven Studies.* New Directions Pr., 1938.

WOLFE, THOMAS. "The Story of a Novel," *Sat. Rev. Lit.,* 13 (Dec. 14, 1935), 3-4,
12, 14, 16; 13 (Dec. 21, 1935), 3-4, 15; 13 (Dec. 28, 1935), 3-4, 14-16.

WOOLF, VIRGINIA. "Character in Fiction," *Criterion,* 2 (July, 1924), 409-430.

—— *The Common Reader.* Hogarth Pr., 1925, 1929. *The Second Common Reader.*
Hogarth Pr., Harcourt, 1932. Combined edition, Harcourt, 1947. See for "Modern
Fiction," pp. 207-218, in *The Common Reader,* 1925.

—— "The Leaning Tower," *Folios of New Writing.* Hogarth Press, 1940.

—— "Letter to a Young Poet," *Yale Rev.,* 21 (June, 1932).

ZABEL, M. D., editor. *Literary Opinion in America.* Harper, 1937. Rev. ed., 1951.

II. TOPIC CHECKLISTS

1. PROBLEMS OF THE ARTIST AND HIS SOCIETY

ALDRIDGE, JOHN W. *After the Lost Generation.* McGraw-Hill, 1951.

BARZUN, JACQUES. "Artist Against Society." *Partisan Rev.,* 19 (Jan., 1952), 60-77.

BLACKMUR, R. P. "The Economy of the American Writer," *Sewanee Rev.,* 53 (April-
June, 1945), 175-185.

—— "A Featherbed for Critics: Notes on the Profession of Writing," *The Expense of
Greatness.* Arrow Editions, 1940. Pp. 277-305.

BOAS, GEORGE. *Wingless Pegasus.* Johns Hopkins Univ. Pr., 1950.

BROOKS, VAN WYCK. "Primary Literature and Coterie Literature," *The Opinions of
Oliver Allston.* Dutton, 1941.

COWLEY, MALCOLM, *Exile's Return.* Norton, 1934; rev. ed. Viking, 1951.

—— "How the Writer Lives." *The Writer,* 64 (June, 1951), 181-183.

DeVOTO, BERNARD. *The Literary Fallacy.* Little Brown, 1944.

ELIOT, T. S. "The Man of Letters and the Future of Europe," *Sewanee Rev.,* 53
(Summer, 1945), 333-342.

FARRELL, J. T. *The Fate of Writing in America.* New Directions Pr., 1946. (Pamphlet.)

—— *The League of Frightened Philistines.* Vanguard Pr.; Routledge, 1945.

—— *Literature and Morality.* Vanguard Pr., 1947.

FOX, RALPH. *The Novel and the People.* Lawrence & Wishart, 1937; International Publishers, 1945.

—— *Writers in Arms.* Lawrence & Wishart, 1937.

GREENBERG, CLEMENT. "Avant-Garde and Kitsch," *The Partisan Reader,* edited by William Phillips and Philip Rahv. Dial Pr., 1946. Pp. 378-392.

GUERARD, ALBERT. *Literature and Society.* Lothrop Lee & Shepard, 1935.

HENDERSON, PHILIP. *Literature and a Changing Civilisation.* Lane (Bodley Head), 1935.

HYMAN, S. E. AND LEWIS, R. W. B. "Two Views on the American Writer," *Hudson Rev.,* 2 (Winter, 1950), 600-619.

JOSEPHSON, MATTHEW. *Portrait of the Artist as American.* Harcourt, 1930.

LEAVIS, F. R. *Mass Civilization and Minority Culture.* Minority Pr., 1930.

LEAVIS, Q. D. *Fiction and the Reading Public.* Chatto & Windus, 1932.

LEVIN, HARRY. "America Discovers Bohemia," *Atlantic,* 180 (Sept., 1947), 68 ff.

LEWIS, WYNDHAM. "The Objective of Art in Our Time," in *Wyndham Lewis the Artist.* Laidlaw, 1939.

MACLEISH, ARCHIBALD. *The Irresponsibles.* Duell Sloan, 1940.

MAUGHAM, W. SOMERSET. *Cakes and Ale.* Triangle Books, 1930, 1941. Pp. 305-308.

MITCHELL, EDWIN. *The Art of Authorship.* Loring & Mussey, 1935.

MORRIS, GEORGE. "Some Personal Letters to American Artists," *The Partisan Reader,* edited by William Phillips and Philip Rahv. Dial Pr., 1946. Pp. 585-590.

PARRY, ALBERT. *Garrets and Pretenders: A History of Bohemianism in America.* Covici, Friede, 1933.

PHILLIPS, WILLIAM. "The Intellectuals' Tradition," *The Partisan Reader,* edited by William Phillips and Philip Rahv. Dial Pr., 1946. Pp. 484-493.

PORTER, KATHERINE ANNE. Introduction, *A Curtain of Green,* by Eudora Welty. Doubleday, 1941.

PRYCE-JONES, ALAN. "The Novelist in a World Awry," *New York Times Book Rev.,* Dec. 10, 1950, pp. 1, 22.

RAHV, PHILIP. "The Cult of Experience in American Writing," *Partisan Rev.,* 7 (Nov.-Dec., 1940), 412-424. Reprinted in *Image and Idea.* New Directions Pr., 1949. (See pages 231-243 of this book.)

—— "Proletarian Literature: A Political Autopsy," *Southern Rev.,* 4 (Winter, 1939), 616-628.

READ, HERBERT. *Art and Society.* Heinemann; Macmillan, 1937.

ROURKE, CONSTANCE. *American Humor: A Study of the National Character.* Harcourt, 1931.

SCHUCKING, LEVIN. *The Sociology of Literary Taste.* Oxford Univ. Pr., 1944.

"The Situation in American Writing: Seven Questions." *Partisan Rev.,* 6 (Summer, 1939), 25-27. Dos Passos, 26-27; Tate, 28-30; Farrell, 30-33; Fearing, 33-35; Porter, 31-39; Stevens, 39-40; Gertrude Stein, 40-41; William Carlos Williams, 41-44; John Peale Bishop, 44-46; Rosenberg, 47-49; Henry Miller, 50-51. Repr. in *The Partisan Reader,* edited by William Phillips and Philip Rahv. Dial Pr., 1946. Pp. 596-628.

SPENDER, STEPHEN. "The American Writer." *New Directions,* 12. New Directions Pr., 1950.

—— "Modern Writers in the World of Necessity," *Partisan Rev.,* 12 (Summer, 1945), 352-360.

"The State of American Writing, 1948: A Symposium," *Partisan Rev.,* 15 (Aug., 1948), 855-893.

TRILLING, LIONEL. "Art and Fortune," *Partisan Rev.*, 15 (Dec., 1948), 1271-1292. Reprinted in *The Liberal Imagination*. Viking, 1950. (See pages 526-543 of this book.)

TROTSKY, LEON. *Literature and Revolution*. International Publishers, 1925.

TURNELL, MARTIN. "The Writer and Social Strategy," *Partisan Rev.*, 18 (Mar.-Apr., 1951), 167-182.

WEST, R. B., JR. "Literature and the American Writer," *Western Rev.*, 14 (Summer, 1950), 242, 244, 315-318.

2. WRITERS ON THEIR CRAFT

ANDERSON, SHERWOOD. *A Story Teller's Story*. Viking, 1924.

—— *Sherwood Anderson's Notebook*. Boni & Liveright, 1926.

—— *Memoirs*. Harcourt, 1942. See esp. pp. 341 ff.

BENNETT, ARNOLD. *The Journal of Arnold Bennett*. Viking, 1933.

BENTLEY, PHYLLIS. *Some Observations on the Art of Narrative*. Macmillan, 1947.

BRANDE, DOROTHEA. *Becoming a Writer*. Harcourt, 1934.

BRICKELL, HERSCHEL, editor. *Writers on Writing*. Doubleday, 1949.

CABELL, J. B. *Some of Us*. McBride, 1930.

CATHER, WILLA. *On Writing*. Knopf, 1949.

CHEKHOV, ANTON. *Notebooks of Anton Chekhov*, translated by Leonard Woolf. Huebsch, 1921.

—— *Letters on the Short Story, the Drama and Other Literary Topics, by Anton Chekhov*, selected and edited by Louis Friedland. Minton Balch, 1924.

—— *The Personal Papers of Anton Chekhov*, edited by Matthew Josephson. Lear Publishers, 1948. See James T. Farrell: "On the Letters of Anton Chekhov," *University Rev.*, 9 (Spring, 1943), 167-173.

Conrad to a Friend (Letters from Conrad to Richard Curle). Doubleday Page, 1928.

Conrad's Prefaces to His Work. With an Essay by Edward Garnett. Dent, 1937.

Joseph Conrad: Life and Letters, edited by G. Jean-Aubry. Two vols. Doubleday Page, 1927.

Letters From Conrad 1895 to 1924, edited with Introduction and Notes by Edward Garnett. Bobbs-Merrill, 1928; The Nonesuch Pr., n. d.

Letters of Joseph Conrad to Marguerite Poradowska: 1898-1920. Translated from the French by John Gee and Paul Sturm. Yale Univ. Pr., 1940.

DREISER, THEODORE. *A Book about Myself*. Boni & Liveright, 1922. Re-issued as *Newspaper Days*, 1931.

FORSTER, E. M. *Aspects of the Novel*. Harcourt, 1927, 1947.

—— "Credo: What I Believe," *London Mercury*, 38 (Sept., 1938), 397-404.

GALLICO, PAUL. *Confessions of a Story Writer*. Knopf, 1946.

GLASGOW, ELLEN. "One Way to Write Novels," *Sat. Rev. Lit.*, 11 (Dec. 8, 1934), 335, 344, 350.

—— *A Certain Measure: An Interpretation of Prose Fiction*. Harcourt, 1938; McLeod, 1943.

GRAVES, ROBERT. *Occupation: Writer*. Creative Age Pr., 1950.

HARDING, R. M. *An Anatomy of Inspiration*. Cambridge Univ. Pr., 1940; Heffer, 1948.

HARDY, THOMAS. *The Early Life: 1840-1891*, by Florence Emily Hardy. Macmillan, 1928. *The Later Years of Thomas Hardy: 1892-1928*, by Florence Emily Hardy. Macmillan, 1930.

HULL, HELEN, editor. *The Writer's Book*. Harper, 1950.

JAMES, HENRY. *The Art of Fiction and Other Essays*, edited by Morris Roberts. Oxford Univ. Pr., 1948.

—— *The Art of the Novel*. Introduction by R. P. Blackmur. Scribner's, 1934.

—— *The Letters of Henry James*, edited by Percy Lubbock. Scribner's, 1920.

JAMES, HENRY. *The Notebooks of Henry James,* edited by F. O. Matthiessen and K. B. Murdock. Oxford Univ. Pr., 1947.

JAMESON, STORM. *The Novel in Contemporary Life.* The Writer, Inc., 1938.

—— *The Writer's Situation and Other Essays.* Macmillan, 1950.

KIPLING, RUDYARD. *Something of Myself.* Macmillan, 1937.

D. H. Lawrence's Letters to Bertrand Russell, edited, with an introduction, by Harry T. Moore. Gotham, 1948.

Letters of Composers, edited by G. Norman and L. Shrifte. Knopf, 1946.

The Letters of T. E. Lawrence, edited by David Garnett. Doubleday Doran, 1939.

MANSFIELD, KATHERINE. *The Journal of Katherine Mansfield,* edited by J. M. Murry. Knopf, 1927.

—— *The Letters of Katherine Mansfield,* edited by J. M. Murry. Knopf, 1929. Two vols.

—— *Novels and Novelists,* edited by J. M. Murry. Knopf, 1930.

MAUGHAM, W. SOMERSET. *The Summing Up.* Literary Guild, 1938.

—— *A Writer's Notebook.* Doubleday, 1949; Heinemann, 1949.

MONTAGUE, C. E. *A Writer's Notes on his Trade.* Chatto & Windus, 1930.

NATHAN, G. J. *The Intimate Notebooks of George Jean Nathan.* Knopf, 1932.

NORRIS, FRANK. "The Novel with a 'Purpose,'" *The World's Work,* 4 (May, 1902), 2117-2119.

—— *The Responsibilities of the Novelist.* Doubleday Page, 1903.

PIERCY, JOSEPHINE. *Modern Writers at Work.* Macmillan, 1931.

POUND, EZRA AND FORD MADOX FORD: "Conversation on Writing," *Western Rev.,* 12 (Autumn, 1947), 17-19.

STALLMAN, R. W., editor. *The Critic's Notebook.* Univ. of Minnesota Pr., 1950.

VAN GELDER, ROBERT, editor. *Writers and Writing.* Scribner's, 1946.

WELTY, EUDORA. "The Reading and Writing of Short Stories," *Atlantic,* 183 (Feb., 1949), 54-58; 183 (Mar., 1949), 46-49.

WEST, REBECCA. *The Strange Necessity.* Garden City, 1928.

WHARTON, EDITH. *A Backward Glance.* Appleton Century, 1934.

—— *The Writing of Fiction.* Scribner's, 1925.

WOLFE, THOMAS. "Portrait of a Literary Critic," *The Hills Beyond.* Sun Dial Pr., 1943.

—— *The Story of a Novel.* Scribner's, 1936.

3. THE ARTIST AND THE CREATIVE PROCESS

ALEXANDER, SAMUEL. *Art and the Material.* Manchester Univ. Pr., 1925.

ANDERSON, SHERWOOD. *Sherwood Anderson's Memoirs.* Harcourt, 1942.

AUDEN, W. H. "Psychology and Art," *The Arts To-Day,* edited by Geoffrey Grigson. Lane (Bodley Head), 1935, 1937. Pp. 1-21.

AUSTIN, MARY. "Automatism in Writing," *Unpartisan Review,* 14 (1920), 336-347.

BARRETT, WILLIAM. "Writers and Madness," *Partisan Rev.,* 14 (Jan.-Feb., 1947), 5-22.

BARTLETT, PHYLLIS BROOKS. *Poems in Process.* Oxford Univ. Pr., 1951.

BAUDOUIN, CHARLES. *Psychoanalysis and Aesthetics.* Allen & Unwin, 1924.

BELGION, MONTGOMERY. "The Expression of Emotion," *Southern Rev.,* 3 (Spring, 1938), 783-789.

BELL, CLIVE. *Art.* Chatto & Windus, 1914, 1947.

BERGLER, EDMUND. "Psychology of Writers," *Psychoan. Rev.,* 31 (1944), 40-70.

BRICKELL, HERSCHEL, editor. *Writers on Writing.* Doubleday, 1949.

BROOKS, CLEANTH. "The Place of Creative Writing in the Study of Literature." *Association of American Colleges Bulletin,* 34 (May, 1948), 225-33.

BULLOUGH, EDWARD. "Mind and Medium in Art," *British Journal of Psychology,* 11 (1920-21), 26-46.

BURKE, KENNETH. "The Poetic Process," *Counter-Statement*. Harcourt, 1931. Pp. 57-78.

CHANDLER, A. R. *Beauty and Human Nature: Elements of Psychological Aesthetics.* Appleton Century, 1934.

COLLINGWOOD, R. G. *The Principles of Art.* Clarendon Pr., 1938. Chap. viii.

DELACROIX, EUGÈNE. *The Journal*, translated by Walter Pach. Covici, Friede, 1937; Crown, 1947.

DELACROIX, HENRÏ, *Psychologie de l'art.* Paris, 1927.

DELL, FLOYD. "A Literary Self-Analysis," *Modern Quar.*, 4 (June-Sept., 1927), 148 ff.

DEWEY, JOHN. *Art as Experience.* Minton Balch, 1934. Chaps. IV, V.

DOSTOEVSKY, F. M. *The Diary of a Writer.* Capell's, 1950.

EASTMAN, MAX. *The Literary Mind.* Scribner's, 1935. Part IV, Chap. 1.

ELIOT, T. S. *The Sacred Wood.* Methuen, 1920, 1928; Knopf, 1921, 1930.

FREUD, SIGMUND. *Leonardo Da Vinci: A Study in Psychosexuality*, translated by A. A. Brill. Random House, 1947.

———*Stravrogrin's Confession*, by F. M. Dostoevsky. With a Psychological Study by Sigmund Freud. Lear Publishers, 1947.

GARRISON, ROGER. *A Creative Approach to Writing.* Holt, 1951.

GLASGOW, ELLEN. *A Certain Measure: An Interpretation of Prose Fiction.* Harcourt, 1938; McLeod, 1943.

———"One Way to Write Novels." *Sat. Rev. Lit.*, 11 (Dec. 8, 1934), 335, 344, 350.

GOLDWATER, ROBERT, AND TREVES, MARC, editors. *Artists on Art.* Pantheon Books, 1945.

GOTSHALK, D. W. "The Creative Process," *Art and the Social Order.* Univ. of Chicago Pr., 1947. Chap. III.

GRAVES, ROBERT. *Occupation Writer.* Creative Age Pr., 1950.

GREENE, GRAHAM, BOWEN, ELIZABETH, AND PRITCHETT, V. S. *Why Do I Write?: An Exchange of Views.* With an introduction by V. S. Pritchett. Chatto & Windus, 1948.

GREENE, T. M. *The Arts and the Art of Criticism.* Princeton Univ. Pr., 1940. Chaps. XII, XV.

HARDING, R. M. "An Essay on the Creative Mood," *An Anatomy of Inspiration.* Heffer, 1948. Pp. 113-144.

HOFFMAN, FREDERICK. *Freudianism and the Literary Mind.* Louisiana State Univ. Pr., 1945. Bibliography.

HOGREFE, PEARL. *The Process of Creative Writing.* Harper, 1947.

HUXLEY, ALDOUS. *Music at Night.* Chatto & Windus, 1931. Pp. 258-269.

———*The Olive Tree.* Harper, 1937. Esp. pp. 215-216.

KRUTCH, J. W. *Experience and Art.* Harrison Smith, 1932.

LAWRENCE, D. H. *Phoenix: Posthumous Papers*, edited by E. McDonald. Heinemann; Viking, 1936.

LOWES, JOHN. *The Road to Xanadu: A Study in the Ways of the Imagination.* Constable, 1927; Houghton, 1927.

MACGILLIVRAY, ARTHUR, S. J. "Hopkins and Creative Writing," in *Immortal Diamond*, edited by Norman Weyand, S. J. Sheed & Ward, 1949. Pp. 51-72.

MALRAUX, ANDRÉ. *The Psychology of Art.* Pantheon Books, 1950, 2 vols.; Vol. III, 1951.

MARCH, HAROLD. *The Two Worlds of Marcel Proust.* Univ. of Pennsylvania Pr., 1948. Chap. VI.

MATTHIESSEN, F. O. *American Renaissance.* Oxford Univ. Pr., 1941.

MAUGHAM, W. SOMERSET. *Cakes and Ale.* Triangle Books, 1930, 1941. Pp. 305-308.

———*The Summing Up.* Literary Guild, 1938.

MILLER, HENRY. "Reflections on Writing," *Horizon*, 1 (July, 1940), 472-481.

MORGAN, D. N. "Psychology and Art Today: A Summary and Critique," *Jour. Aesthetics & Art Criticism*, 9 (Dec., 1950), 81-96.

MORRIS, BERTRAM. *Aesthetic Process.* Northwestern Univ. Pr., 1943.

MUNRO, THOMAS. "Methods in the Psychology of Art," *Jour. Aesthetics & Art Criticism*, 7 (Mar., 1948).

MURRAY, H. A. "Personality and Creative Imagination," *English Institute Annual*. Columbia Univ. Pr., 1942.

NEWMAN, ERNEST. *The Unconscious Beethoven*. Knopf, 1927.

NICHOLS, ROBERT. "Birth of a Poem," *An Anatomy of Inspiration*. Heffer, 1948. Pp. 147-168.

NIXON, H. K. *Psychology for the Writer*. Harper, 1928.

PARKER, DE WITT. *The Analysis of Art*. Yale Univ. Pr., 1926. Chap. II.

Poets at Work. Essays by W. H. Auden, Karl Shapiro, Rudolf Arnheim, Donald A. Stauffer. Introduction by Charles D. Abbott. Harcourt, 1948.

PUTNAM, BRENDA. *The Sculptor's Way*. Rinehart, 1939.

RADER, M. M., editor. *A Modern Book of Aesthetics*. Holt, 1935. Chap. III.

RANK, OTTO. *Art and Artist: Creative Urge and Personality Development*, translated by C. F. Atkinson. Knopf, 1932.

REID, LOUIS. *A Study in Aesthetics*. Macmillan, 1931.

RICHARDS, I. A. *Principles of Literary Criticism*. Kegan Paul, 1924; Harcourt, 1925, 1929.

—— "The Poetic Experience," *Science and Poetry*. Norton, 1926.

—— *Coleridge on Imagination*. Kegan Paul, 1934; Harcourt, 1935, 1950.

RIDING, LAURA, AND GRAVES, ROBERT. "The Making of the Poem," *A Survey of Modernist Poetry*. Heinemann, 1927; Doubleday Doran, 1928. Pp. 131-154.

ROBERTS, MICHAEL. *Critique of Poetry*. Cape, 1934.

SAYERS, DOROTHY. *The Mind of the Maker*. Harcourt, 1942.

SCHNEIDER, ELISABETH. *Aesthetic Motive*. Macmillan, 1939.

SCHOEN, MAX. *Art and Beauty*. Macmillan, 1932. Esp. pp. 54-55.

SITWELL, EDITH. "Some Notes on the Making of a Poem," *Orpheus, a Symposium of the Arts*, edited by John Lehmann. New Directions Pr., 1948. Pp. 69-75.

SMITH, LOGAN PEARSALL. *Unforgotten Years*. Little Brown, 1939. Esp. pp. 207-208.

SPENDER, STEPHEN. "The Making of a Poem," in *Critiques and Essays in Criticism*, edited by R. W. Stallman. Ronald Pr., 1949. Reprinted from *Partisan Rev.*, 13 (Summer, 1946).

STALLMAN, R. W., editor. *The Critic's Notebook*. Univ. of Minnesota Pr., 1950. Bibliography, pp. 255-293.

—— editor. *Critiques and Essays in Criticism: 1920-1948*. Ronald Pr., 1949. Bibliography, pp. 519-571.

STEGNER, WALLACE. "A Problem in Fiction," *Pacific Spectator*, 3 (Autumn, 1949), 368-375.

STEIN, LEO. *The A-B-C of Aesthetics*. Liveright, 1927.

STEKEL, WILHELM. "Poetry and Neurosis," *Psychoan. Rev.*, 10 (1923), 73-96; 90-208, 316-328, 457-466.

TATE, ALLEN. "Narcissus as Narcissus," *On the Limits of Poetry*. Morrow Pr., 1948.

"The Teaching and Study of Writing (A Symposium)," *Western Rev.*, 14 (Spring, 1950), 165-179. (By Allen Tate, Eudora Welty, Malcolm Cowley, and others.)

TRILLING, LIONEL. "The Legacy of Freud: Literary and Aesthetic," *Kenyon Rev.*, 2 (1940), 152-173.

—— "A Note on Art and Neurosis," *Partisan Rev.*, 12 (Winter, 1945), 41-48. *See* Davis, R. G.: "Art and Anxiety," *Partisan Rev.* 12 (Summer, 1945), 310-321.

TSANOFF, RADOSLAV. "On the Psychology of Poetic Construction," *American Journal of Psychology*, 25 (1914), 528-537.

VAN GELDER, ROBERT. *Writers and Writing*. Scribner's, 1946.

VIVAS, ELISEO. "The Objective Correlative of T. S. Eliot," *Critiques & Essays in Criticism*, edited by R. W. Stallman. Ronald Pr., 1949. Pp. 389-400.

WHEELOCK, JOHN HALL, editor. *Editor to Author: The Letters of Maxwell E. Perkins*. Scribner's, 1950.

WILENSKI, R. H. *French Painting.* Hale, Cushman, Flint, 1931. Esp. p. 118.

WILLIAMS, CHARLES. *Reason and Beauty in the Poetic Mind.* Clarendon Pr., 1933.

WILSON, EDMUND. "Philoctetes: The Wound and the Bow," *The Wound and the Bow.* Oxford Univ. Pr., 1947. Chap. VII.

ZWEIG, STEFAN. *Balzac.* Viking, 1946.

4. THE CRAFT OF FICTION: TECHNIQUE AND STYLE

AMES, VAN METER. "The Technique of the Novel," *Aesthetics of the Novel.* Univ. of Chicago Pr., 1928.

BABER, A. L. "The Structure of the Modern Short Story," *College English,* 7 (Nov., 1945) , 86-92.

BATES, H. E. *The Modern Short Story.* The Writer Inc., 1950.

BECK, WARREN. "Art and Formula in the Short Story," *College English,* 5 (Nov., 1943) , 55-62.

BERKELMAN, ROBERT G. "How to Put Words on Paper," *Sat. Rev. Lit.* 28 (Dec. 29, 1945) , 18-19.

BISHOP, J. P. "Reflections on Style," *Hudson Rev.,* 1 (Summer, 1948) , 207-220.

BLACKMUR, R. P. "Notes on Four Categories," *Sewanee Rev.,* 54 (Autumn, 1946) , 576-590.

BOWLING, LAWRENCE. "What is the Stream of Consciousness Technique?" *P.M.L.A.,* 65 (June, 1950) , 333-345.

BROOKS, CLEANTH, AND WARREN, ROBERT PENN. *Understanding Fiction,* Crofts, 1943.

BROWER, R. A. *The Fields of Light.* Oxford Univ. Pr., 1951.

BULLOUGH, EDWARD. "Psychic Distance as a Factor in Art and an Aesthetic Principle," *British Journal of Psychology,* 5 (1912-13), 87-118. Repr. in *A Modern Book of Aesthetics,* edited by M. M. Rader. Holt, 1935.

BURACK, A. S. *The Craft of Novel Writing.* The Writer, Inc., 1948.

BURKE, KENNETH. *Counter-Statement.* Harcourt, 1931.

—— "Style," *Permanence and Change.* New Republic Books, 1935. Pp. 71-82.

—— "Three Definitions," *Kenyon Rev.,* 13 (Spring, 1951), 173-192.

BURLINGAME, ROGER. *Of Making Many Books.* Scribner's, 1946.

CAMPBELL, W. S. *Professional Writing.* Macmillan, 1947.

—— *Writing: Advice and Devices.* Doubleday, 1950.

CAZAMIAN, LOUIS. "The Method of Discontinuity in Modern Art and Literature," *Criticism in the Making.* Macmillan, 1929. Pp. 63-80.

COX, SIDNEY. *Indirections: For Those Who Want to Write.* Knopf, 1947.

DAICHES, DAVID. "Problems for Modern Novelists," *Accent,* 3 (Spring, Summer, 1943), 144-152, 231-239. Repr. in *Accent Anthology,* edited by Kerker Quinn and Charles Shattuck. Harcourt, 1946.

DERLETH, AUGUST. *Writing Fiction.* The Writer, Inc., 1946.

DEVOTO, BERNARD. "The Invisible Novelist," *Pacific Spectator,* 4 (Winter, 1950) , 30-45.

—— *The World of Fiction.* Houghton, 1950.

DOBRÉE, BONAMY. *Modern Prose Style.* Oxford Univ. Pr., 1946.

DREW, ELIZABETH. "A Note on Technique," *The Modern Novel.* Harcourt, 1926. Pp. 243-262.

ELTON, WILLIAM. *A Glossary of the New Criticism.* Poetry: A Magazine of Verse, 1949. (Pamphlet.)

ELWOOD, MAREN. *Characters Make Your Story.* The Writer, Inc., 1942.

FLESCH, RUDOLF. *The Art of Readable Writing.* Harper, 1949.

FORD, F. M. "Techniques," *Southern Rev.,* 1 (July, 1935) , 20-35.

"Form in Literature," *Times Lit. Suppl.* Mar. 25, 1944, p. 147. (Menander's Mirror.)

FORSTER, E. M. *Aspects of the Novel.* Harcourt, 1927, 1947.

FRANK, JOSEPH. "Spatial Form in Modern Literature," *Sewanee Rev.*, 53 (Spring, 1945), 221-240. Sections 2 and 3 in following issues. Repr. in *Criticism*, edited by Mark Schorer and others. Harcourt, 1948. Repr. in *Critiques and Essays in Criticism: 1920-1948*, edited by R. W. Stallman. Ronald Pr., 1949. (See pages 43-66 of this book for sections 2 and 3.)

FREDERICK, JOHN. "New Techniques in the Novel." *English Jour.*, 24 (May, 1935), 355-363.

FRYE, NORTHROP. "The Four Forms of Fiction," *Hudson Rev.*, 2 (Winter, 1950), 582-99.

GRAVES, ROBERT, AND HODGE, ALAN. *The Reader Over Your Shoulder: A Handbook for Writers of English Prose*. Cape, 1943, 1947; Macmillan, 1947.

HAINES, GEORGE. "Forms of Imaginative Prose: 1900-1940," *Southern Rev.*, 7 (Spring, 1942), 755-775.

HATCHER, ANNA G. "Voir as a Modern Novelistic Device," *Philological Quar.*, 23 (1944), 354-374.

HEARN, LAFCADIO. "On Composition," in *Readings for Creative Writers*, edited by George W. Williams. Harper, 1938. Pp. 98-112.

HOFFMAN, ARTHUR S., editor. *Fiction Writing Self-taught*. The Writer, Inc., 1939.

KEMPTON, K. P. *The Short Story*. Harvard Univ. Pr., 1947.

KOMROFF, MANUEL. *How to Write a Novel*. Simon & Schuster, 1950.

KREY, LAURA. "Time and the English Novel," in *Twentieth Century English*, edited by W. S. Knickerbocker. Philosophical Library, 1946. Pp. 401-415.

LUBBOCK, PERCY. *The Craft of Fiction*. Cape; Scribner's, 1921, 1929; Peter Smith, 1947.

LYNES, CARLOS, JR. "André Gide and the Problem of Form in the Novel," *Southern Rev.*, 7 (Summer, 1941), 161-173.

McHUGH, VINCENT. *Primer of the Novel*. Random House, 1950.

MIRRIELEES, EDITH R. *The Story Writer*. Little Brown, 1939.

—— *Writing the Short Story*. Doubleday, 1929.

MUIR, EDWIN. *The Structure of the Novel*. Hogarth Pr., 1928.

MUNSON, GORHAM B. *Style and Form in American Prose*. Doubleday, 1929.

—— *The Written Word*. Creative Age Pr., 1949.

MURRY, J. M. *The Problem of Style*. Oxford Univ. Pr., 1922.

O'BRIEN, EDWARD J. *The Advance of the American Short Story*. Dodd, Mead, 1931.

O'CONNOR, W. VAN, editor. *Forms of Modern Fiction*. Univ. of Minnesota Pr., 1948.

O'FAOLAIN, SEAN. *The Short Story*. Collins, 1948; Devin-Adair, 1951.

ORVIS, MARY. *The Art of Writing Fiction*. Prentice-Hall, 1948. Bibliography, pp. 240-243.

PATER, WALTER. *Appreciations: With an Essay on Style*. Macmillan, 1927.

PATTEE, FREDERICK LEWIS. *The Development of the American Short Story*. Harper, 1923.

PENTON, BRIAN. "Notes on Form in the Novel," in *Scrutinies, II*. Collected by Edgell Rickword. Wishart, 1931. Pp. 236-262.

READ, HERBERT. *English Prose Style*. Bell, 1942.

RODITI, EDOUARD. "Trick Perspectives," *Virginia Quar. Rev.*, 20 (Oct., 1944), 545-549.

SAINTSBURY, GEORGE. "Technique," *Dial*, 80 (April, 1926), 273-278.

SCHORER, MARK. "Technique as Discovery," *Hudson Rev.*, 1 (Spring, 1948), 67-87. Repr. in *Forms of Modern Fiction*, edited by W. Van O'Connor. Univ. of Minnesota Pr., 1948. Pp. 9-29. (See pages 67-82 of this book.)

SEWELL, ELIZABETH. *The Structure of the Novel*. Routledge and Kegan Paul, 1951.

STEVENSON, ROBERT LOUIS. "On Some Technical Elements of Style in Literature," in *Readings for Creative Writers*, edited by George G. Williams. Harper, 1938. Pp. 128-142.

SWINNERTON, FRANK. "Variations of Form in the Novel," *Essays and Studies by Members of the English Association*. Clarendon Pr., 1938. Vol. XXIII. Pp. 79-92.

TATE, ALLEN. "The Post of Observation in Fiction," *Maryland Quar.*, 2 (1944), 61-64.

TATE, ALLEN. "Techniques of Fiction," *Sewanee Rev.*, 52 (1944), 210-225. Repr. in *Forms of Modern Fiction*, edited by W. Van O'Connor. Univ. of Minnesota Pr., 1948. Pp. 30-45. (See pages 31-42 of this book.)

TATE, ALLEN, AND GORDON, CAROLINE. *The House of Fiction*. Scribner's, 1950.

"The Teaching and Study of Writing: A Symposium." *Western Rev.*, 14 (Spring, 1950).

WARREN, AUSTIN, AND WELLEK, RENÉ. *Theory of Literature*. Harcourt, 1949. Bibliography, pp. 347-387.

WENGER, J. "Speed as Technique in the Novels of Balzac," *P.M.L.A.*, 55 (1940), 241-252.

WEST, R. B., JR., AND STALLMAN, R. W. *The Art of Modern Fiction*, Rinehart, 1949. (With critical glossary and explications.)

WILLIAMS, GEORGE G. *Readings for Creative Writers*. Harper, 1938.

WOOLF, VIRGINIA. "Character in Fiction," *Criterion*, 2 (July, 1924), 409-430.

5. REALISM AND NATURALISM

ADAMS, J. D. *The Writer's Responsibility*. Secker & Warburg, 1946.

ARAGON, LOUIS. "The Return to Reality," *International Lit.*, 1 (Jan., 1936), 100-105.

BABBITT, IRVING. *The New Laokoon*. Houghton, 1910. Pp. 186-217.

BAKER, ERNEST. *The History of the English Novel*. H. F. & G. Witherby, 1937.

BAKER, HOWARD. "The Contemporary Short Story," *Southern Rev.*, 2 (Winter, 1938), 576-596.

——— "An Essay on Fiction With Examples," *Southern Rev.*, 7 (Autumn, 1941), 385-406.

BEACH, J. W. *American Fiction: 1920-1940*. Macmillan, 1941, 1948.

——— *The Twentieth Century Novel*. Appleton Century, 1932.

BREWSTER, DOROTHY, AND BURRELL, ANGUS. *Dead Reckonings in Fiction*. Longmans Green, 1924. Repr. (revised and extended) as *Modern Fiction*. Columbia Univ. Pr., 1934.

CANBY, H. S. "An Open Letter to the Realists," *Sat. Rev. Lit.*, 30 (May 3, 1947).

CHAMBERLAIN, JOHN. *Farewell to Reform*. John Day Co., 1932.

COMMAGER, HENRY STEELE. *The American Mind*. Yale Univ. Press, 1950.

Comparative Literature, 3 (Summer, 1951): A Symposium on Realism, arranged by Harry Levin.

COWLEY, MALCOLM, " 'Not Men': A Natural History of American Naturalism," *Kenyon Rev.*, 9 (Summer, 1947), 414-435. (See pages 370-387 of this book.)

DAICHES, DAVID. *The Novel and the Modern World*. Univ. of Chicago Pr., 1939.

DEWEY, JOHN. "Anti-Naturalism in Extremis," *The Partisan Reader*, edited by William Phillips and Philip Rahv. Dial Pr., 1946. Pp. 514-528.

FARRELL, JAMES T. "Some Observations on Naturalism, So Called, in Fiction," *Antioch Rev.*, 10 (June, 1950), 247-264.

FRIERSON, W. C., AND EDWARDS, HERBERT. "The Impact of French Naturalism on American Critical Opinion: 1871-1892," *P.M.L.A.*, 63 (Sept., 1948), 1007-1016.

GLASGOW, ELLEN. *A Certain Measure*. McLeod; Harcourt, 1943.

HANSEN, AGNES. *Twentieth Century Forces in European Fiction*. American Library Association, 1934.

HATCHER, HARLAN. *Creating the Modern American Novel*. Farrar & Rinehart, 1935; Williams & Norgate, 1936.

HENDRY, IRENE. "The Regional Novel," *Sewanee Rev.*, 53 (Winter, 1945), 84-102.

KAZIN, ALFRED. "American Naturalism: Reflections from Another Era." *The American Writer and the European Tradition*, edited by Margaret Denny and W. H. Gilman. Univ. of Minnesota Pr., 1950. Pp. 121-131.

——— "The Revival of Naturalism," *On Native Grounds*. Reynal and Hitchcock, 1942. Chap. 13.

KRIKORIAN, Y., editor. *Naturalism and the Human Spirit.* Columbia Univ. Pr., 1944.
LANGER, SUSANNE. *Philosophy in a New Key.* Oxford Univ. Pr.; Harvard Univ. Pr., 1942.
Literary History of the United States, edited by Robert Spiller, Willard Thorp, and others. Macmillan, 1948. Vol. II, pp. 878-898.
LOOMIS, ROGER SHERMAN. "A Defense of Naturalism," *International Journal of Ethics,* 29 (Jan., 1919), 188-201.
LOVETT, ROBERT. "A Note on English Realism," *Contemporary American Criticism,* edited by James C. Bowman. Holt, 1926. Pp. 185-191.
LUKÁCS, GEORGE. *Studies in European Realism.* Hillway Publishing Co., 1950.
MIZENER, ARTHUR. "*The Fathers* and Realistic Fiction," *Accent,* 7 (Winter, 1947). 101-109.
MULLER, HERBERT. *Modern Fiction.* Funk & Wagnalls, 1937. Pp. 44-45, and *passim.*
MYERS, WALTER. *The Later Realism: A Study of Characterization in the British Novel.* Univ. of Chicago Pr., 1927.
O'CONNOR, W. VAN, editor. *Forms of Modern Fiction.* Univ. of Minnesota Pr., 1948. Pp. 16, 24, 26, 142, 163, 170, 172, 173, 182, 188, 252 f., 254 ff., 258, 259, 261, 283, 284, 285.
PARRINGTON, V. L. *Main Currents in American Thought.* Harcourt, 1930. Vol. III.
RAHV, PHILIP. "Notes on the Decline of Naturalism," *Image and Idea.* New Directions Pr., 1949. Pp. 128 ff. (See pages 415-423 of this book.)
"Realism." *Dictionary of World Literature.* Philosophical Library, 1943. Pp. 470-471.
SNELL, GEORGE. "Naturalism Nascent," *The Shapers of American Fiction.* Dutton, 1947.
STAUFFER, RUTH. *Joseph Conrad: His Romantic Realism.* Four Seas Co., 1923.
UZZELL, T. H. "Modern Innovators," *College English,* 7 (Nov., 1945), 59-65.
VAN DOREN, CARL. "Emergence of Naturalism," *The American Novel.* Macmillan, 1940. Pp. 225-244.
WALCUTT, C. C. "The Naturalism of *Vandover and the Brute,*" *Forms of Modern Fiction,* edited by W. Van O'Connor. Univ. of Minnesota Pr., 1948. Pp. 254-268.
—— "The 'Naturalistic Novel'," *Quarterly Rev. of Lit.,* 3 (Oct., 1946), 167-179.
—— "The Regional Novel and its Failure," *Arizona Quar.,* 1 (1945), 17-27.
WALPOLE, HUGH. *Joseph Conrad.* Holt, 1916. Pp. 108-110.
WARREN, ROBERT PENN. "T. S. Stribling: A Paragraph in the History of Critical Realism," *American Rev.,* 2 (Feb., 1934), 463-486.
WEINBERG, BERNARD. *French Realism: The Critical Reaction, 1830-70.* Univ. of Chicago Pr., 1937.
WERFEL, FRANZ. "Realism and Inwardness," *American Bookman,* 1 (Fall, 1944).
WHARTON, EDITH. "Visibility in Fiction," *Life & Letters,* 2 (Apr., 1929), 263-272.
WHEELWRIGHT, PHILIP. "The Failure of Naturalism," *Kenyon Rev.,* 3 (1941), 460-472.

6. SYMBOLISM AND MYTH

ALDRIDGE, JOHN W. "The Metaphorical World of Truman Capote," *Western Rev.* 15 (Summer, 1951), pp. 247-260.
ALLEN, DON CAMERON. "Symbolic Color in the Literature of the English Renaissance," *Philological Quar.,* 15 (1936), 81-92.
ARVIN, NEWTON. *Herman Melville.* Sloane Associates, 1950.
BEARDSLEY, M. C. "Dostoevsky's Metaphor of the Underground," *Journal of the History of Ideas,* 3 (1942).
BELGION, MONTGOMERY. "Heterodoxy on *Moby Dick?*" *Sewanee Rev.,* 55 Winter, 1947), 108-125.
BISHOP, J. P. "The Myth and Modern Literature," *Collected Essays,* edited by Edmund Wilson. Scribner's, 1948. Pp. 122-128.
BLACKMUR, R. P. *The Expense of Greatness.* Arrow Editions, 1940.

BLACKMUR, R. P. "Notes on Four Categories in Criticism," *Sewanee Rev.*, 54 (Autumn, 1946), 589 ff.

BODKIN, MAUD. *Archetypal Patterns in Poetry.* Clarendon Pr., 1934, 1948.

BROOKS, CLEANTH, AND WARREN, R. P. *Understanding Fiction.* Crofts, 1943.

BURKE, KENNETH. *Counter-Statement.* Harcourt, 1931. Pp. 193-232, and *passim.*

―― "Four Master Tropes," *A Grammar of Motives.* Prentice-Hall, 1945. Pp. 503-517.

CAMPBELL, JOSEPH. *The Hero with a Thousand Faces.* Pantheon Books, 1949.

CASSIRER, ERNST. *An Essay on Man.* Yale Univ. Press, 1944. Pp. 32, 36 ff.

CATER, CATHERINE. "Myth and the Contemporary Southern Novelist." *Midwest Jour.*, 2 (Winter, 1949), 1-8.

CHASE, RICHARD. *Herman Melville: A Critical Study.* Macmillan, 1949.

―― "Notes on the Study of Myth," *Partisan Rev.*, 13 (Summer, 1946), 338-346.

―― *Quest for Myth.* Louisiana State Univ. Pr., 1949.

COLLINGWOOD, R. G. *The Principles of Art.* Clarendon Pr., 1938. Chap. 2.

DAICHES, DAVID. *The Novel and the Modern World.* Univ. of Chicago Pr., 1939.

DONNELLY, DOROTHY. *The Golden Well.* Sheed & Ward, 1950.

DOWNS, B. W. "Ibsen's Use of Symbols," *Ibsen, A Study of Six Plays.* Cambridge Univ. Pr., 1950.

ELIOT, T. S. "*Ulysses,* Order and Myth," *Dial,* 75 (Nov. 19, 1923), 480-483. Repr. in *Forms of Modern Fiction,* edited by W. Van O'Connor. Univ. of Minnesota Pr., 1948. (See pages 424-426 of this book.)

FEIBLEMAN, JAMES. *Aesthetics.* Duell Sloan, 1949.

FERGUSSON, FRANCIS. *The Idea of a Theatre.* Princeton Univ. Pr., 1949.

FOSS, MARTIN. *Symbol and Metaphor in Human Experience.* Princeton Univ. Pr., 1949.

FRAZER, SIR JAMES. *The Golden Bough: A Study in Magic and Religion.* Macmillan, 1922, 1940.

FRYE, NORTHROP. "The Archetypes of Literature," *Kenyon Rev.*, 13 (Winter, 1951), 92-110.

GIVENS, SEON, editor. *James Joyce: Two Decades of Criticism.* Vanguard, 1949. Pp. 27-46, 132-175.

GRAVES, ROBERT. "The Language of Myth," *Hudson Rev.*, 4 (Spring, 1951), 5-21.

HAMILL, ELIZABETH. *These Modern Writers: An Introduction for Modern Readers.* Georgian House (Melbourne), 1946. Chap. 2.

HERTZ, RICHARD. *Chance and Symbol.* Univ. of Chicago Pr., 1948.

HINKS, ROGER. *Myth and Allegory in Ancient Art.* Warburg Institute, 1939.

HOOKE, SAMUEL H. *Myth and Ritual.* Oxford Univ. Pr., 1933.

HUNGERFORD, EDWARD. *Shores of Darkness.* Columbia Univ. Pr., 1941.

JELLIFFE, SMITH ELY. "Paleopsychology ... the Origin and Evolution of Symbolic Function," *Psychoan. Rev.*, 10 (1923), 121-139.

JUNG, C. G., AND KERENYI, C. *Essays on a Science of Mythology.* Pantheon Books, 1950.

―― *The Imperial Theme.* Oxford Univ. Pr., 1931.

KNIGHT, G. W. *The Imperial Throne.* Oxford Univ. Pr., 1931.

―― *The Wheel of Fire.* Oxford Univ. Pr., 1930; Methuen, 1949.

LANGER, S. K. *Philosophy in a New Key.* Oxford Univ. Pr., Harvard Univ. Pr., 1942.

LEWIS, C. S. *The Allegory of Love.* Clarendon Pr., 1936.

MAGNY, CLAUDE-EDMONDE. *Les Sandales d'Empédocles.* Éditions de la Baconnière. (Neuchâtel, Switzerland), 1945.

MATTHIESSEN, F. O. *The American Renaissance.* Oxford Univ. Press, 1941.

McLUHAN, H. M. "The Southern Quality," *Sewanee Rev.*, 55 (July-Sept., 1947), 357-383.

MULLER, H. J. "Impressionism in Fiction," *American Scholar*, 7 (Summer, 1938), 355-367.

―― *Modern Fiction.* Funk & Wagnalls, 1937.

NEIDER, CHARLES. *The Frozen Sea: A Study of Franz Kafka.* Oxford Univ. Pr., 1948.

NEIDER, CHARLES. Introduction, *Short Novels of the Masters*. Rinehart, 1949.

NIEBUHR, REINHOLD. "The True Value of Myths," *The Nature of Religious Experience: Essays in Honor of Douglas C. Macintosh*. Harper, 1937.

OPEL, HAROLD. "The Double Symbol," *Amer. Lit.*, 23 (Mar., 1951), 2-6.

ORVIS, MARY B. *The Art of Writing Fiction*. Prentice-Hall, 1948. Chap. 13.

PRESCOTT, F. C. *Poetry and Myth*. Macmillan, 1927.

RAGLAN, LORD. *The Hero: A Study in Tradition, Myth, and Drama*. Oxford Univ. Pr., 1937.

RAHV, PHILIP. *Image and Idea*. New Directions Pr., 1949.

RICE, P. B. "Thomas Mann and the Religious Revival," *Kenyon Rev.*, 7 (1945), 374-376.

RICHARDS, I. A. *Coleridge on Imagination*. Kegan Paul, 1926. Repr. in part in *Critiques and Essays in Criticism: 1920-1948*, edited by R. W. Stallman. Ronald Pr., 1949.

SALINAS, PEDRO. " 'Don Quixote' and the Novel," *Nation*, 166 (Dec. 20, 1947), 682-683.

SANTAYANA, GEORGE. *Interpretations of Poetry and Religion*. Scribner's, 1900.

SHORT, RAY. "Melville as Symbolist," *Univ. of Kansas City Rev.*, 15 (Autumn, 1948), 38-46.

STOLL, E. E. "Symbolism in *Moby Dick*," *Jour. Hist. of Ideas*, 12 (June, 1951), 440-465.

"SYMBOLISM." *Dictionary of World Literature*. Philosophical Library, 1943. Pp. 564-568.

TROY, WILLIAM. "Thomas Mann: Myth and Reason," *Partisan Rev.*, 5 (1938), 51-64.

TURNELL, MARTIN. *The Novel in France*. Hamish Hamilton, 1950.

URBAN, W. M. "The Principles of Symbolism," *Language and Reality*. Macmillan, 1939.

WARNER, REX. *The Cult of Power: Selected Essays*. Lane, 1946; Lippincott, 1947.

WARREN, A. AND WELLEK, R. *Theory of Literature*. Harcourt, 1949.

WARREN, R. P. *The Rime of the Ancient Mariner: An Essay*. Reynal & Hitchcock, 1946.

WEST, R. B., JR., AND STALLMAN, R. W. *The Art of Modern Fiction*. Rinehart, 1949.

WESTON, JESSIE. *From Ritual to Romance*. Cambridge Univ. Pr., 1920.

WHEELWRIGHT, PHILIP. "Notes on Mythopoeia," *Sewanee Rev.*, 59 (Autumn, 1951), 574-592.

WHITEHEAD, A. N. *Symbolism: Its Meaning and Effect*. Macmillan, 1927.

WILSON, EDMUND. *Axel's Castle: A Study of Imaginative Literature of 1870-1930*. Scribner's, 1931; 1947.

WIMSATT, W. K. JR. "Symbol and Metaphor," *Rev. of Metaphysics*, 4 (Dec., 1950), 279-290.

WRIGHT, L. B. "Myth-Makers and the South's Dilemma," *A Southern Vanguard*, edited by Allen Tate. Prentice-Hall, 1947. Pp. 136-147.

ZABEL, M. D., editor. *Literary Opinion in America*. Harper, 1937. Rev. ed., 1951.

III. AUTHOR CHECKLISTS

SHERWOOD ANDERSON

ANDERSON, SHERWOOD. Introduction: *Free, and Other Stories*, by Theodore Dreiser. Boni & Liveright, 1918.

—— "Letters of Sherwood Anderson," *Berkeley*, No. 1 (Oct., 1947), 1-4.

—— *Memoirs*. Harcourt, 1942.

—— *Notebook*. Boni & Liveright, 1926.

—— *A Story Teller's Story*. Viking, 1924.

   On Anderson: Adams, J. D. *The Writer's Responsibility*. Secker & Warburg, 1946. Pp. 75-79, and *passim*.

Anderson, Margaret. *My Thirty Years' War.* Covici, Friede, 1930.

Beach, J. W. *The Outlook for American Prose.* Univ. of Chicago Pr., 1926. Pp. 247-280.

Berland, Alwyn. "Comment: Sherwood Anderson and the Pathetic Grotesque," *Western Rev.,* 15 (Winter, 1951). 135-139.

Bourne, Randolph S. *History of a Literary Radical and Other Essays.* Huebsch, 1920.

Boynton, Percy. *More Contemporary Americans.* Univ. of Chicago Pr., 1927. Pp. 157-177.

Brooks, Cleanth, and Warren, Robert Penn. "I Want to Know Why," *Understanding Fiction.* Crofts, 1943. Pp. 335-350.

Calverton, V. F. "Sherwood Anderson," *Modern Quar.,* 2 (Autumn, 1924), 82-118.

Chase, Cleveland B. *Sherwood Anderson.* McBride & Co., 1927.

Collins, Joseph. *Taking the Literary Pulse.* George H. Doran, 1924. Pp. 29-47.

Fadiman, Clifton. "Sherwood Anderson: The Search for Salvation," *Nation,* 135 (Nov. 9, 1932), 454-456.

Fagin, N. B. *The Phenomenon of Sherwood Anderson.* Johns Hopkins Univ. Pr., 1927. Bibliography, pp. 153-156.

Farrar, John, editor. *The Literary Spotlight.* George H. Doran, 1924. Pp. 232-240.

Frank, Waldo. *Salvos.* Boni, 1924. Pp. 31-40.

Garnett, Edward. *Friday Nights.* Knopf, 1922. Pp. 342-346.

Gregory, A. "Sherwood Anderson, *Dial,* 75 (Sept., 1923), 243-246.

Gregory, Horace. Introduction, *The Portable Sherwood Anderson.* Viking, 1949.

Hansen, Harry. *Midwest Portraits.* Harcourt, 1923. Pp. 111-179.

Hartwick, Harry. *The Foreground of American Fiction.* American Book, 1934. Pp. 111-137.

Hatcher, Harlan. *Creating the Modern American Novel.* Farrar & Rinehart, 1935; Williams & Norgate, 1936. Pp. 155-171.

Hicks, Granville. *The Great Tradition.* Macmillan, 1933. Pp. 226-236.

Hoffman, Frederick. *Freudianism and the Literary Mind.* Louisiana State Univ. Pr., 1945. Chap. VIII.

Howe, Irving. "The Book of the Grotesque," *Partisan Rev.,* 18 (Jan.-Feb., 1951), 32-40.

_____ *Sherwood Anderson.* Sloane Assoc., 1951.

_____ "Sherwood Anderson: An American as Artist," *Kenyon Rev.,* 13 (Spring, 1951), 193-203.

_____ "Sherwood Anderson and D. H. Lawrence." *Furioso,* 5 (Autumn, 1950), 21-33.

_____ "Sherwood Anderson: The Unavailable Self (rev. of *The Sherwood Anderson Reader*)," *Partisan Rev.,* 15 (Apr., 1948), 492-499.

Kazin, Alfred. *On Native Grounds.* Reynal & Hitchcock, 1942. See index.

Lewis, Wyndham. *Men Without Art.* Cassell; Harcourt, 1934.

_____ *Paleface.* Chatto & Windus, 1929. (See index.)

Lovett, Robert M. "Sherwood Anderson," *New Rep.,* 89 (1936), 103-105.

_____ "Sherwood Anderson, American," *Virginia Quar. Rev.,* 17 (1941), 379-388.

_____ "The Promise of Sherwood Anderson," *Dial,* 72 (Jan., 1922), 79-83. Repr. in *Literary Opinion in America,* edited by M. D. Zabel. Harper, 1951. Pp. 478-484.

Michaud, Regis. *The American Novel of To-day.* Little Brown, 1928. Pp. 154-199.

"My Brother Sherwood Anderson," *Sat. Rev. Lit.,* 31 (Sept. 4, 1948), pp. 6-7, 26-27.

O'Brien, E. J. *The Advance of the American Short Story*. Dodd, 1931. (Rev. ed.) Pp. 247-261.

Phillips, William. "How Sherwood Anderson Wrote *Winesburg, Ohio*," *Am. Lit.*, 23 (March, 1951), 7-30.

Rosenfeld, Paul. *Port of New York*. Harcourt, 1924. Pp. 175-198.

—— Introduction, *The Sherwood Anderson Reader*. Houghton, 1947.

Schevill, James. *Sherwood Anderson: His Life and Work*. Univ. of Denver Pr., 1951.

"Sherwood Anderson in Retrospect," *New Rep.* (Aug. 15, 1949), 18-19.

Smith, R. "Sherwood Anderson," *Sewanee Rev.*, 37 (Oct., 1929), 159-163.

Trilling, Diana. Introduction, *The Portable Sherwood Anderson*. Viking, 1949.

Trilling, Lionel. "Sherwood Anderson," *Kenyon Rev.*, 3 (Summer, 1941), 293-302. (See pages 319-327 of this book.)

—— *The Liberal Imagination*. Viking, 1950.

Van Doren, Carl. "Sinclair Lewis and Sherwood Anderson," *Century*, 110 (July, 1925), 362-369.

Werth, Alexander. "Sherwood Anderson," *New Age*, 35 (1924), 94-95.

West, Rebecca. *The Strange Necessity*. Doubleday, 1928. Pp. 281-290.

Wheelock, John Hall, editor. *Editor to Author: The Letters of Maxwell E. Perkins*. Scribner's, 1950.

Whipple, T. K. *Spokesman*. Appleton Century, 1928. Pp. 115-138.

Wickham, H. *The Impuritans*. Dial Pr., 1929. Pp. 268-282.

JOSEPH CONRAD

CONRAD, JOSEPH. *Last Essays*. Dent, 1926.

—— *Notes on Conrad, with Some Unpublished Letters*, edited by Arthur Symons. Myers, 1925.

—— *Notes on Life and Letters*. Dent, 1921.

—— *A Personal Record*. Dent, 1912.

—— *Conrad to a Friend: 150 Selected Letters from Joseph Conrad to Richard Curle*. Doubleday Page, 1928.

—— *Conrad's Prefaces to His Works*, with an introductory essay by Edward Garnett. Dent, 1937.

—— *Letters from Conrad 1895 to 1924*, edited with Introduction and Notes by Edward Garnett. Bobbs-Merrill, 1928; The Nonesuch Pr., n. d.

—— *Letters of Joseph Conrad to Marguerite Poradowska: 1898-1920*. Translated from the French by John Gee and Paul Sturm. Yale Univ. Pr., 1940.

—— *The Life and Letters of Joseph Conrad*, edited by G. Jean-Aubry. Doubleday Page, 1927. Two vols.

On Conrad: Adams, J. D. Introduction, *Lord Jim*. Random House (Modern Library, 1931); Doubleday, 1943.

—— "Speaking of Books," *New York Times Book Rev.*, Jan. 25, 1948, p. 2.

Altick, Richard. *The Scholar Adventurers*. Macmillan, 1950.

Ames, Van Meter. *Aesthetics of the Novel*. Univ. of Chicago Pr., 1928. Pp. 177-181 and *passim*.

Babb, J. T. "A Check List of Additions to a Conrad Memorial Library, 1929-1938," *Yale Univ. Library Gazette*, 13 (1938), 30-40.

Baker, Ernest. *History of the English Novel*. H. F. & G. Witherby, 1937.

Bancroft, W. W. *Joseph Conrad: His Philosophy of Life*. Stratford Co., 1933.

Beach, J. W. *American Fiction: 1920-1940*. Macmillan, 1941, 1948. Pp. 99, and *passim*.

—— "Impressionism: Conrad," *The Twentieth Century Novel*. Appleton Century, 1932. Pp. 337-366.

—— *The Outlook for American Prose*. Univ. of Chicago Pr., 1926. Pp. 171-172, 265-266, and *passim*.

Bendz, E. P. *Joseph Conrad: An Appreciation.* N. J. Gumpert (Gothenberg), 1923.

Binse, H. L. "Polish Picture," *Commonweal,* 42 (Apr. 27, 1945), 43-45.

Bluth, Raphael. "Joseph Conrad et Dostoievski: le problème du crime et du châtiment," *Vie Intellectuelle,* 12 (1931), 320-339.

Bradbrook, M. C. *Joseph Conrad: Poland's English Genius.* Cambridge Univ. Pr.; Macmillan, 1941, 1942.

Brewster, D., and Burrell, A. "Conrad's *Nostromo:* Twenty Years After," *Dead Reckonings in Fiction.* Longmans, Green and Co., 1924. Pp. 101-128. Repr. as *Modern Fiction.* Columbia Univ. Pr., 1934.

Brown, E. K. "James and Conrad," *Yale Rev.,* 35 (Dec., 1945), 265-285.

Carroll, Wesley. "The Fiction of Joseph Conrad." Cornell Univ. Dissertation, 1934. (Unpublished.)

Clemens, Florence. "Conrad's Malaysia," *College English,* 2 (Jan., 1941), 338-346.

Conrad, Jessie. *Joseph Conrad as I Knew Him.* Heinemann, 1926.

Crankshaw, Edward. *Joseph Conrad: Some Aspects of the Art of the Novel.* John Lane (Bodley Head), 1936.

—— "Joseph Conrad and To-day." *National Rev.,* 128 (March, 1947), 224-230.

Cross, Wilbur. *Four Contemporary Novelists.* Macmillan, 1930.

—— "The Illusions of Joseph Conrad," *Yale Rev.,* 17 (Oct., 1927), 464-482.

—— "Lawrence Sterne in Respect to Conrad," *Yale Rev.,* 15 (Oct., 1925).

Curle, Richard. *Joseph Conrad: A Study.* Doubleday Page, 1914.

—— "Joseph Conrad: Ten Years After," *Virginia Quar. Rev.,* 10 (July, 1934), 420-435.

—— *Joseph Conrad: The Last Twelve Years.* Sampson Low, 1928.

Cushwa, F. W. *An Introduction to Conrad.* Odyssey Pr., 1933.

Cutler, F. W. "Why Marlow?" *Sewanee Rev.,* 26 (1918), 28-38.

Daiches, David. *The Novel and the Modern World.* Univ. of Chicago Pr., 1939. Pp. 48-64.

Davidson, Donald. "Joseph Conrad's Directed Indirections." *Sewanee Rev.,* 33 (1925), 163-177.

Dean, L. F. "Tragic Pattern in Conrad's *Heart of Darkness." College English,* 6 (Nov., 1944), 100-104.

Drabowski, M. "Interview with Joseph Conrad," *Amer. Scholar,* 13 (July, 1944), 371-375.

Drew, Elizabeth. "Joseph Conrad," *The Modern Novel,* Harcourt, 1926. Pp. 223-240.

Fernández, Ramón. "The Art of Conrad," *Messages.* Harcourt, 1927. Pp. 139-151.

Fletcher, J. V. "Ethical Symbolism in Conrad," *College English,* 2 (Oct., 1940), 19-21.

Follett, Wilson. *Joseph Conrad.* Doubleday Page, 1915, Holt, 1919.

Ford, F. M. "Conrad and the Sea," *Portraits from Life.* Houghton, 1937. Pp. 57-69.

—— *Joseph Conrad: A Personal Remembrance.* Little Brown, 1924.

—— "On Conrad's Vocabulary." *Bookman,* 67 (June, 1928), 405-408.

—— "Technique," *Southern Rev.,* 1 (July, 1935), 20-35.

—— "Three Americans and a Pole," *Scribner's,* 90 (Oct., 1931), 379-386.

—— "Working with Conrad," *Yale Rev.,* (June, 1929), 699-715.

Forster, E. M. *Abinger Harvest.* Edward Arnold, 1936; Harcourt, 1936. Pp. 136-141.

Galsworthy, John. *Two Essays on Conrad, with the Story of a Remarkable Friendship,* by Richard Curle. Freelands, 1930.

Garland, Hamlin. *My Friendly Contemporaries.* Macmillan, 1932.

Garnett, Edward. Introduction, *Conrad's Prefaces*. Dent, 1937.
—— "Mr. Joseph Conrad," *Friday Nights*. Knopf, 1922. Pp. 83-101.
"The Ghost of Thomas Hardy." *Times Lit. Suppl.*, July 14, 1950. P. 435.
Gordan, J. D. *Joseph Conrad: The Making of a Novelist*. Harvard University Pr., 1940. Bibliography.
Guerard, Albert, Jr. *Joseph Conrad*. New Directions Pr., 1947.
—— "A Perspective on Conrad," *Western Rev.*, 14 (Winter, 1950), 151-153.
—— *Thomas Hardy*. Harvard Univ. Pr., 1950.
Haines, George. "Forms of Imaginative Prose: 1900-1940," *Southern Rev.*, 7 (Spring, 1942), 755.
Hall, James. "My Conrad," *Atlantic*, 169 (May, 1942), 583-587.
Halle, Louis. "Joseph Conrad: An Enigma Decided," *Sat. Rev. Lit.*, 30 (May 22, 1949), 7-8.
Hanley, J. "Minority Report," *Fortnightly Rev.*, 159 (June, 1943), 419-422.
Haugh, Robert. "Joseph Conrad and Revolution," *College English*, 10 (Feb., 1949), 273-277.
Hicks, Granville. "Conrad After Five Years," *New Rep.*, 61 (Jan. 8, 1930), 192-194.
Hoare, Dorothy. *Some Studies in the Modern Novel*. Chatto & Windus, 1938.
"Hommage à Joseph Conrad." *Nouvelle Revue Française*, 135 (1924), 649-806. (Nouvelle Série.)
Hoppe, A. J. Introduction, *The Conrad Companion*. Phoenix House, 1947.
Hueffer, F. M. "Mr. Joseph Conrad and Anglo-Saxondom," *Thus to Revisit*. Dutton; Chapman and Hall, 1921. Chap. 8 in Part II. (Ford Madox Ford.)
James, Henry. "The New Novel," *Notes on Novelists*. Dent; Scribner's, 1914.
Knight, Grant. *The Novel in English*. Farrar & Rinehart, 1935.
Leavis, F. R. "Joseph Conrad," *Scrutiny*, 10 (June, 1941; Oct., 1941), 22-51, 157-182. Repr. in *The Great Tradition*. Chatto & Windus, 1948; Stewart, 1949. Pp. 173-226. (See pages 106-128 of this book.)
Mann, Thomas. *Past Masters and Other Papers*, by Thomas Mann. Secker & Warburg; Knopf, 1933.
McCullough, Bruce. *Representative English Novelists: Defoe to Conrad*. Harper, 1946.
Megroz, R. L. *Joseph Conrad's Mind and Method*. Faber & Faber, 1931.
Mencken, H. L. "Freudian Autopsy Upon a Genius," *American Mercury*, 23 (June, 1931), 251-253.
—— "Joseph Conrad," *Prejudices*, Fifth Series. 1926. Pp. 34-41. Repr. in *A Mencken Chrestomathy*. Knopf, 1949. Pp. 518-522.
—— "Theodore Dreiser," in *The Shock of Recognition*, edited by Edmund Wilson. Doubleday, 1943. Pp. 1173, 1175, 1177, 1178.
Morf, Gustav. *The Polish Heritage of Joseph Conrad*. Sampson Low, 1930.
Morris, R. L. "The Classical References in Conrad's Fiction," *College English*, 7 (Mar., 1946), 312-318.
Muller, H. J. *Modern Fiction*. Funk & Wagnalls, 1937. Pp. 244-261.
Orvis, Mary. *The Art of Writing Fiction*. Prentice-Hall, 1948.
Pritchett, V. S. "Conrad: The Exile, the Isolated Man," *New Statesman*, 40 (July 15, 1950), 72-73.
Proust, Marcel. *An English Tribute to Joseph Conrad and Others*. Boni & Liveright, 1923.
Retinger, J. H. *Conrad and His Contemporaries*. Roy, 1943.
Roditi, Edouard. "Trick Perspectives," *Virginia Quar. Rev.*, 20 (Oct., 1944), 545-549.
Shand, John. "Some Notes on Joseph Conrad," *Criterion*, 3 (Oct. 1924), 6-14.
Stallman, R. W. "Conrad and the *Secret Sharer*," *Accent*, 9 (Spring, 1949),

131-144. Repr. in revised form in *The Art of Modern Fiction*, by R. B. West Jr. and R. W. Stallman. Rinehart, 1949.

—— "Life, Art, and 'The Secret Sharer,'" *Forms of Modern Fiction*, edited by W. Van O'Connor. Univ. of Minnesota Pr., 1948. Pp. 229-242.

Stauffer, Ruth. *Joseph Conrad: His Romantic Realism*. Four Seas Co., 1922.

Stawell, F. M. "Conrad," *Essays and Studies of the English Association*. Clarendon Pr., Vol. VI (1920), pp. 88-111.

Stegner, Wallace. "Variations on a Theme by Conrad," *Yale Rev.*, 39 (Spring, 1950), 512-523.

Swinnerton, Frank. *The Georgian Scene*. Farrar & Rinehart, 1934. Pp. 146-155, and *passim*.

Symons, Arthur. *Dramatis Personae*. Bobbs-Merrill, 1923.

—— editor. *Notes on Conrad, with Some Unpublished Letters*. Myers, 1925.

Thompson, Alan. "The Humanism of Joseph Conrad," *Sewanee Rev.*, 37 (Apr., 1929), 204-220.

Van Doren, Carl and Mark. *American and British Literature Since 1890*. Century, 1925. Pp. 177-181 and *passim*.

Wagenknecht, Edward. "'Pessimism' in Hardy and Conrad," *College English*, 3 (1942), 546-554.

Walpole, Hugh. *Joseph Conrad*. Holt, 1916.

—— *Tendencies of the Modern Novel*. Peter Smith, 1934; Allen, 1935.

Warner, Oliver. *Joseph Conrad*. Longmans Green, 1950.

Warren, Robert Penn. "Nostromo," *Sewanee Rev.*, 59 (Summer, 1951), 363-391. Repr. as Introduction to *Nostromo*. Random House (Modern Library), 1951.

Webster, H. T. "Conrad's Changes in Narrative Conception in the Manuscript of *Typhoon* and Other Stories and *Victory*," *P.M.L.A.*, 64 (Dec., 1949), 953-963.

—— "Joseph Conrad: A Reinterpretation of Five Novels," *College English*, 7 (Dec., 1945), 125-134.

West, R. B., Jr., and Stallman, R. W. *The Art of Modern Fiction*. Rinehart, 1949. Pp. 490-500, 607-621.

Whiting, G. W. "Conrad's Revision of Six of His Short Stories," *P.M.L.A.*, 48 (1933), 552-557.

—— "Conrad's Revision of 'The Lighthouse' in *Nostromo*," *P.M.L.A.*, 52 (1937), 1183-1190.

Williams, Orlo. *Some Great English Novels: Studies in the Art of Fiction*. Macmillan, 1926.

Woolf, Virginia. "Joseph Conrad," *The Common Reader*. Hogarth Pr., 1925, 1929; Harcourt, 1925. Pp. 282-291.

Wright, W. F. "Conrad's 'The Rescue' from Serial to Book," *Research Studies, State College of Washington*, 13 (Dec., 1945). Pp. 203-224.

—— "How Conrad Tells a Story," *Prairie Schooner*, 21 (1947), 290-295.

—— "Joseph Conrad's Critical Views," *Research Studies, State College of Washington*, 12 (1944), 155-175.

—— *Romance and Tragedy in Joseph Conrad*. Univ. of Nebraska Pr., 1949.

Young, Vernon. "Joseph Conrad," *Hudson Rev.*, 2 (Spring, 1949), 5-20.

Zabel, M. D. "Conrad: Chance and Recognition," *Sewanee Rev.*, 53 (Jan., 1945), 1-22. (See pages 270-285 of this book.)

—— "Conrad in His Age," *New Rep.*, 106 (Nov. 16, 1942).

—— "Conrad: Nel Mezzo del Cammin," *New Rep.*, 103 (Dec. 23, 1940), 873-874.

—— "Conrad: The Secret Sharer," *New Rep.*, 104 (Apr. 21, 1941), 567-568, 570-574.

—— Introduction: *The Portable Conrad*. Viking, 1947. See *Nation*, 166 (Jan. 3, 1946).

Zabel, M. D. Introduction: *The Nigger of the 'Narcissus.'* Harper, 1951.
—— Introduction: *Under Western Eyes.* New Directions Pr., 1951.

STEPHEN CRANE

On Crane: Baker, Ernest. *History of the English Novel.* H. F. & G. Witherby, 1937.
Beer, Thomas. *Stephen Crane: A Study in American Letters.* Knopf, 1923. Repr. in *Hanna, Crane, and the Mauve Decade.* Knopf, 1941.
Berryman, John. *Stephen Crane.* Sloane Associates, 1950; Methuen, 1951.
Bushman, John Conrad. "The Fiction of Stephen Crane and Its Critics." Univ. of Illinois Dissertation, 1943. (Unpublished.)
Chamberlain, John. *Farewell to Reform.* John Day Co., 1932.
Conrad, Joseph. In *A Personal Record.* Dent, 1912. P. 103.
—— "A Note Without Dates," in *Notes on Life and Letters.* Dent, 1921.
—— Introduction to *Stephen Crane,* by Thomas Beer. Knopf, 1923. Repr. in *Hanna, Crane, and the Mauve Decade,* by Thomas Beer. Knopf, 1941. Pp. 211-234.
—— Preface to *The Red Badge of Courage.* Heinemann, 1925. Repr. as "His War Book," in *Last Essays.* Dent, 1926. Pp. 175-183.
—— *Joseph Conrad: Life & Letters,* edited by G. Jean-Aubry. Doubleday Page, 1927. Vol. I. Pp. 211, 270, 274.
Cowie, Alexander. *The Rise of the American Novel.* American Book, 1948.
Cowley, Malcolm. " 'Not Men': A Natural History of American Naturalism," *Kenyon Rev.,* 9 (Summer, 1947), 414-435.
Follett, Wilson, editor. *The Work of Stephen Crane.* 12 vols. *See* introductions by Joseph Hergesheimer, vol. 1; Willa Cather, vol. 9; H. L. Mencken, vol. 10. Knopf, 1925-27.
Ford, F. M. "Henry James, Stephen Crane and the Main Stream," *Thus to Revisit.* Chapman and Hall; Dutton, 1921. (Hueffer, Ford Madox.)
—— *Portraits from Life.* Houghton, 1937.
—— "Technique," *Southern Rev.,* 1 (July, 1935), 20-35. (On James, Conrad, and Crane.)
Garnett, Edward. "Stephen Crane and His Work," *Friday Nights: Literary Criticisms and Appreciations.* First Series. Knopf, 1922. (Reprints the *Academy* article of 1898.) Pp. 201-217.
Gibson, William. Introduction: *Stephen Crane: Selected Prose and Poetry.* Rinehart Editions, 1950.
Hartwick, Harry. *The Foreground of American Fiction.* American Book, 1934. Pp. 21-44 and *passim.*
Hatcher, Harlan. *Creating the Modern American Novel.* Farrar & Rinehart, 1935; Williams & Norgate, 1936. Pp. 12-20.
Hicks, Granville. *The Great Tradition.* Macmillan, 1933. Pp. 159-163 and *passim.*
Josephson, Matthew. *Portrait of the Artist as American.* Harcourt, 1930. Pp. 232-264.
Kazin, Alfred. *On Native Grounds.* Reynal & Hitchcock, 1942.
Lewisohn, Ludwig. *Expression in America.* Harper, 1932.
Loggins, Vernon. *I Hear America: Literature in the United States Since 1900.* Crowell, 1937.
Mencken, H. L. "Stephen Crane," in *A Mencken Chrestomathy.* Knopf, 1949 Pp. 496-497.
Munson, G. B. *Style and Form in American Prose.* Doubleday Doran, 1929.
Nye, Russell. "Stephen Crane as Social Critic," *Modern Quar.,* 11 (Summer, 1940), 48-54.

Pritchett, V. S. *The Living Novel.* Chatto & Windus, 1946, 1949; Reynal & Hitchcock, 1947. Pp. 166-178.

Quinn, A. H. *American Fiction.* Appleton Century, 1936.

Schoberlin, Melvin. Introduction, *The Sullivan County Sketches of Stephen Crane.* Syracuse Univ. Pr., 1949.

Schroeder, John. "Stephen Crane Embattled," *Univ. Kansas City Rev.,* 17 (Winter, 1950), 119-129.

Snell, George. "Naturalism Nascent: Crane and Norris," *The Shapers of American Fiction.* Dutton, 1947. Pp. 223-233.

Spiller, Robert. "Stephen Crane," *Literary History of the United States,* edited by Robert Spiller, Willard Thorp, and Others. Vol. II, Ch. 62, sec. 3. Macmillan, 1948. *See also* Bibliography, III, pp. 458-461.

Stallman, R. W. Introduction: *The Red Badge of Courage.* Random House (Modern Library), 1951. (See pages 244-269 of this book.)

—— editor. *The Stephen Crane Reader.* Knopf, Heinemann, 1952.

Tate, Allen, and Gordon, Caroline. *The House of Fiction.* Scribner's, 1950. Pp. 308-312.

Van Doren, Carl. *The American Novel: 1780-1939.* Macmillan, 1940. Pp. 236, and *passim.*

—— Introduction: *Twenty Stories* (by Stephen Crane), edited by Carl Van Doren. Knopf, 1940.

Van Doren, Carl and Mark. *American and British Literature Since 1890.* Century Co., 1925.

Webster, H. T. "Wilbur F. Hinman's *Corporal Si Klegg* and Stephen Crane's *Red Badge of Courage,*" *American Lit.,* 11 (Nov., 1939), 285-293.

Wells, H. G. "Stephen Crane from an English Viewpoint," *North Amer. Rev.,* 171 (Aug., 1900), 233-242. Repr. in *The Shock of Recognition,* edited by Edmund Wilson. Doubleday Doran, 1943.

West, R. B. Jr., and Stallman, R. W. *The Art of Modern Fiction.* Rinehart, 1949. Pp. 53-58.

Whitehead, Jean. "The Art of Stephen Crane," Cornell Univ. Dissertation, 1944. (Unpublished.)

Williams, A. W., and Starrett, Vincent. *Stephen Crane: A Bibliography.* John Valentine, 1948. Introduction, pp. 7-12.

JOHN DOS PASSOS

On Dos Passos: Adams, J. D. *The Writer's Responsibility.* Secker & Warburg, 1946. Pp. 79-83 and *passim.*

Aldridge, John W. "Dos Passos," *After the Lost Generation.* McGraw-Hill, 1951. Pp. 59-81.

Beach, J. W. *American Fiction: 1920-1940.* Macmillan, 1941, 1948. Pp. 25-68.

—— "Dos Passos," *Sewanee Rev.,* 56 (Spring, 1948), 406 ff.

Bishop, J. P. "Three Brilliant Young Novelists," *Collected Essays,* edited by Edmund Wilson. Scribner's, 1948. Pp. 229-232.

Calmer, A. "John Dos Passos," *Sewanee Rev.,* 40 (Sept., 1932), 341-349.

Cowley, Malcolm. "John Dos Passos: The Poet and the World," *New Rep.,* 70 (Apr., 27, 1932), 303-305; 88 (Sept. 9, 1936), 34. Repr. in *Literary Opinion in America,* edited by M. D. Zabel. Harper, 1937. Pp. 494-505. Rev. ed., 1951.

Frohock, W. M. *The Novel of Violence in America, 1920-1950.* Southern Methodist Univ. Pr., 1950.

Gold, Michael. "The Education of John Dos Passos," *English Journal,* 22 (Feb., 1933), 87-97.

Hartwick, Harry. *The Foreground of American Fiction.* American Book Co., 1934. Pp. 262-293.

Hatcher, Harlan. *Creating the Modern American Novel*. Farrar and Rinehart, 1935; Williams & Norgate, 1936. Pp. 132-139.

Hicks, Granville. "John Dos Passos," *Bookman*, 75 (Apr., 1932), 32-42.

—— "John Dos Passos," *The Great Tradition*. Macmillan, 1933. Pp. 287-291.

—— "Politics and John Dos Passos," *Antioch Rev.*, 10 (Spring, 1950), 85-98.

Kallich, Martin. "John Dos Passos: Liberty and the Father-Image," *Antioch Rev.*, 10 (Spring, 1950), 99-106.

Kazin, Alfred. *On Native Grounds*. Reynal & Hitchcock, 1942. Pp. 341-359.

Lewis, Sinclair. "Manhattan at Last!" *Sat. Rev. Lit.*, 2 (Dec. 25, 1925), 361.

Schappes, Morris. "Review of *1919*," *Symposium*, 3 (July, 1932), 380-386.

Schwartz, Delmore. "John Dos Passos and the Whole Truth," *Southern Rev.*, 4 (Autumn, 1938), 351-367. (See pages 176-189 of this book.)

Snell, George. "John Dos Passos: Literary Collectivist." *The Shapers of American Fiction*. Dutton, 1947.

Trilling, Lionel. "The America of John Dos Passos," *Partisan Rev.*, 4 (Apr., 1938), 26-32.

THEODORE DREISER

DREISER, THEODORE. *A Book About Myself*. Boni & Liveright, 1922. Reissued as *Newspaper Days*. 1931.

—— *Dawn*. Constable, 1931.

On Dreiser: Adams, J. D. *The Writer's Responsibility*. Secker & Warburg, 1946. Pp. 62-89.

Beach, J. W. *The Outlook for American Prose*. Univ. of Chicago Pr., 1926. Pp. 177-196.

—— *The Twentieth Century Novel*. Appleton Century, 1932. Pp. 321-331.

Bourne, Randolph S. "The Art of Theodore Dreiser," *Dial*, 62 (June 14, 1917), 507-509. Repr. in *History of a Literary Radical*. Huebsch, 1920. Pp. 195-204.

Boynton, Percy. *Some Contemporary Americans*. Univ. of Chicago Pr., 1924. Pp. 126-144.

Cabell, J. B. *Some of Us*. McBride, 1930. Pp. 75-88.

Chamberlain, John. *Farewell to Reform*. John Day Co., 1932.

Cowie, Alexander. *The Rise of the American Novel*. American Book, 1948.

Cowley, Malcolm. "The Slow Triumph of Sister Carrie," *New Rep.*, 116 (June 23, 1947), 24, 25, 26, 27.

Duffus, R. L. "'Dreiser," *American Mercury*, 7 (Jan., 1926), 71-76.

Edgar, Pelham. *The Art of the Novel*. Macmillan, 1933. Pp. 244-254.

Fadiman, Clifton. "Dreiser and the American Dream," *Nation*, 135 (Oct. 19, 1932), 364-365.

Farrell, J. T. *Literature and Morality*. Vanguard Pr., 1947.

Ford, Ford Madox. *Portraits from Life*. Houghton, 1937. Pp. 164-182.

Frank, Waldo. *Time Exposures*. Boni & Liveright, 1926. Pp. 159-164.

Hartwick, Harry. *The Foreground of American Fiction*. American Book, 1934. Pp. 85-110.

Hatcher, Harlan. *Creating the Modern American Novel*. Farrar and Rinehart, 1935; Williams & Norgate, 1936. Pp. 34-57.

Hicks, Granville. *The Great Tradition*. Macmillan, 1933. Pp. 226-236.

Huth, John Jr. "Theodore Dreiser, Success Monger." *Colophon*, n. s., 3 (Winter, 1938), 120-133.

—— "Dreiser and Success: An Additional Note." *Colophon*, 3 (Summer, 1938), 406-410.

Jones, L. "An American Tragedy," *Current Reviews*, edited by L. W. Smith. 1926. Pp. 203-212.

Josephson, Matthew. *Portrait of the Artist as American*. Harcourt, 1930.

Kazin, Alfred. *On Native Grounds.* Reynal & Hitchcock, 1942. Pp. 83-90 and *passim.*

Lewisohn, Ludwig. *Expression in America.* Harper, 1932.

Matthiessen, F. O. "Dreiser's Politics," *Tomorrow*, 10 (Jan., 1951), 10-21.

—— *Theodore Dreiser.* Sloane Associates, 1951.

Mayberry, George. "Dreiser: 1871-1945." *New Rep.*, 114 (Jan. 14, 1946), 56.

McDonald, E. D. "Dreiser Before *Sister Carrie*," *Bookman*, 67 (June, 1928), 369-374.

Mencken, H. L. "Dreiser," *A Mencken Chrestomathy.* Knopf, 1949. Pp. 501-505.

—— "The Dreiser Bugaboo," *The Seven Arts*, 2 (Aug., 1917), 507-517.

—— "Theodore Dreiser," *A Book of Prefaces.* Knopf, 1917. Repr. in *The Shock of Recognition*, edited by Edmund Wilson. Doubleday, 1943. Pp. 1160-1228. (See pages 388-401 of this book.)

Michaud, Regis. *The American Novel To-day.* Little Brown, 1931. Pp. 71-127.

Morris, L. R. *Postscript to Yesterday.* Random House, 1947. Pp. 107-133.

Munson, Gorham B. *Destinations.* J. H. Sears & Co., 1928. Pp. 41-56.

Nathan, G. J. *The Intimate Notebooks of George Jean Nathan.* Knopf, 1932. Pp. 38-53.

Orton, Vrest. *Dreiserana.* Chocorna Bibliographies, 1929.

Parrington, V. L. *Main Currents in American Thought.* Harcourt, 1930. Vol. III, pp. 354-359.

Powys, J. C. "Theodore Dreiser," *Little Rev.*, 2 (Nov., 1915), 7-13.

Quinn, A. H. *American Fiction.* Appleton Century, 1936.

Richards, Grant. *Author Hunting by an Old Literary Sportsman.* Musson, 1934. Pp. 165-206.

Schneider, Isador. "Theodore Dreiser," *Sat. Rev. Lit.*, 10 (Mar. 10, 1934), 533-535.

Shafer, Robert. "An American Tragedy," in *Humanism and America*, edited by Norman Foerster. Farrar & Rinehart, 1930. Pp. 149-169.

Sherman, S. P. *The Main Stream.* Scribner's, 1927. Pp. 134-144.

—— *On Contemporary Literature.* Smith, 1931. Pp. 86-101.

Smith, E. H. "Dreiser—After Twenty Years," *Bookman*, 53 (Mar., 1921), 27-39.

Snell, George. "Theodore Dreiser: Philosopher." *The Shapers of American Fiction.* Dutton, 1947. Pp. 233-248.

Spiller, Robert. "Theodore Dreiser," *Literary History of the United States*, edited by Robert Spiller, Willard Thorp, and Others. Macmillan, 1948. Vol. II, pp. 1197-1207.

Van Doren, Carl. *The American Novel.* Macmillan, 1940.

—— *Contemporary American Novelists.* Macmillan, 1925. Pp. 74-83.

Waldman, M. "Theodore Dreiser," in *Contemporary American Authors*, edited by J. C. Squire and Others. Holt, 1928. Pp. 97-118.

Walker, C. R. "How Big is Dreiser?" *Bookman*, 63 (Apr., 1926), 146-149.

Ward, A. C. *American Literature: 1880-1930.* Dial Pr., Methuen, 1932.

JAMES T. FARRELL

FARRELL, JAMES T. *The Fate of Writing in America.* New Directions Pr., 1946. (Pamphlet.)

—— *The League of Frightened Philistines.* Vanguard Pr., 1945.

—— *Literature and Morality.* Vanguard Pr., 1947.

—— *A Note on Literary Criticism.* Vanguard Pr., 1936.

On Farrell: Adams, J. D. *The Writer's Responsibility.* Secker & Warburg, 1946. Pp. 95-98 and *passim.*

Beach, J. W. *American Fiction: 1920-1940.* Macmillan, 1941, 1948. Pp. 273-305. (See pages 402-414 of this book.)

Carghill, Oscar. *Intellectual America.* Macmillan, 1941.

DeVoto, Bernard. *The Literary Fallacy.* Little Brown, 1944. Pp. 95-123.

Frohock, W. H. "James Farrell: The Precise Content," *Southwest Rev.,* 35 (1950), 39-48. Repr. in *The Novel of Violence in America: 1920-1950.* Southern Methodist Univ. Pr., 1950. Pp. 69-85.

Kazin, Alfred. *On Native Grounds.* Reynal & Hitchcock, 1942.

Morris, L. R. "Seven Pillars of Wisdom," *Postscript to Yesterday.* Random House, 1947. Pp. 134-171.

Snell, George. "James T. Farrell and the Poverty of Spirit." *The Shapers of American Fiction.* Dutton, 1947. Pp. 288-300.

Van Gelder, Robert, editor. *Writers and Writing.* Scribner's, 1946. Pp. 278-282.

Willingham, Calder. "A Note on James T. Farrell," *Quar. Rev. Lit.,* 2 (Winter, 1944), 120-124.

WILLIAM FAULKNER

FAULKNER, WILLIAM. Introduction: *Sanctuary.* Random House (Modern Library).

On Faulkner: Adams, J. D. *The Shape of Books to Come.* Viking, 1945. Pp. 91-95. Repr. as *The Writer's Responsibility,* Secker & Warburg, 1946.

Aiken, Conrad. "William Faulkner; the Novel as Form." *Atlantic,* 164 (Nov., 1939), 650-654.

Arthos, John. "Ritual and Humor in the Writings of William Faulkner," *Accent,* 9 (Autumn, 1948), 17-31.

Beach, Joseph Warren. "William Faulkner: The Haunted South"; "William Faulkner: Virtuoso," *American Fiction, 1920-1940.* Macmillan, 1941, 1948. Pp. 123-143; 147-169.

Beck, Warren. "Faulkner and the South," *Antioch Rev.,* 1 (Mar., 1941), 82-94.

—— "Faulkner's Point of View," *College English,* 2 (May, 1941), 736-749.

—— "William Faulkner's Style," *American Prefaces,* 6 (Spring, 1941), 195-211.

Benét, W. R. "Faulkner as Poet," *Sat. Rev. Lit.,* 9 (Apr. 29, 1933), 565.

Bergel, Lienhard. "Faulkner's *Sanctuary,*" *Explicator,* 6 (Dec., 1947), item 20.

Bowling, Lawrence Edward. "Faulkner: Technique of *The Sound and the Fury,*" *Kenyon Rev.,* 10 (Autumn, 1948), 552-566.

Boyle, Kay. "Tattered Banners," *New Rep.,* 94 (Mar. 9, 1938), 136-137.

Boynton, Percy. *America in Contemporary Fiction.* Univ. of Chicago Pr., 1940. Pp. 91-112.

Brooks, Cleanth. "*Absalom, Absalom!:* The Definition of Innocence," *Sewanee Rev.,* 59 (Autumn, 1951), 543-558.

Brooks, Cleanth and Warren, Robert Penn. "A Rose for Emily," *Understanding Fiction.* Crofts, 1943. Pp. 409-414.

Brooks, Van Wyck. "Fashions in Defeatism," *Sat. Rev. Lit.,* 23 (Mar. 22, 1941), 3.

Burgum, E. B. "William Faulkner's Patterns of American Decadence," *The Novel and the World's Dilemma.* Oxford Univ. Pr., 1947. Pp. 205-222.

Buttitta, Anthony. "William Faulkner: That Writin' Man of Oxford," *Sat. Rev. Lit.,* 18 (May 21, 1938), 6-8.

Calverton, V. F. "William Faulkner: Southerner at Large," *Modern Monthly,* 10 (Mar., 1938), 11-12.

Campbell, Harry M. "Experiment and Achievement: *As I Lay Dying* and *The Sound and the Fury,*" *Sewanee Rev.,* 51 (Apr., 1943), 305-320.

—— "Structural Devices in the Works of Faulkner," *Perspective,* 3 (Winter, 1950), 209-226.

Campbell, Harry, and Foster, Ruel. *William Faulkner: A Critical Appraisal.* Univ. of Oklahoma Pr., 1951.

Canby, H. S. "The School of Cruelty," *Sat. Rev. Lit.*, 7 (Mar. 21, 1931), 673-674.
—— *Seven Years' Harvest*. Farrar & Rinehart, 1936. Pp. 79-83. See also *Designed for Reading*, edited by H. S. Canby and others. Macmillan, 1934. Pp. 42-47.
Cargill, O. "Primitivists," *Intellectual America*. Macmillan, 1941. Pp. 311-398. Esp. pp. 370-386.
Cecchi, Emilio. "William Faulkner," *Pan*, 2 (May, 1934), 64-70.
Chase, Richard. "The Stone and the Crucifixion: Faulkner's *Light in August*," *Kenyon Rev.*, 10 (Autumn, 1948), 539-551. (See pages 190-199 of this book.)
Cochran, L. "William Faulkner, Literary Tyro of Mississippi." *Commercial Appeal*, Nov. 6, 1932, mag. sec., p. 4.
Coindreau, Maurice. "Quadrille américain," *Les Œuvres nouvelles*. Éditions de la Maison Française, 1946. Vol. I, pp. 137-181.
Cowley, Malcolm. "Faulkner by Daylight," *New Rep.*, 102 (Apr. 15, 1940), 510.
—— "Poe in Mississippi," *New Rep.*, 89 (Nov. 4, 1936), 22.
—— William Faulkner Revisited," *Sat. Rev. Lit.*, 28 (Apr. 14, 1945), 13-16.
—— "William Faulkner's Legend of the South," *Sewanee Rev.*, 53 (Summer, 1945), 343-361. Repr. in *A Southern Vanguard*, edited by Allen Tate. Prentice-Hall, 1947. Pp. 13-27. (See pages 427-446 of this book.)
—— Introduction: *The Portable Faulkner*. Viking, 1946. (See pages 427-446 of this book.)
Daniel, Robert. *A Catalogue of the Writings of William Faulkner*. Yale Univ. Library, 1942.
——, and Longley, John L. Jr. "Faulkner's Critics: A Selective Bibliography," *Perspective*, 3 (Winter, 1950), 202-208. (I have drawn from this checklist for a few items and more extensively from the bibliography in *William Faulkner*, edited by F. J. Hoffman and Olga Vickery [1951].)
DeVoto, Bernard. "Witchcraft in Mississippi." *Sat. Rev. Lit.*, 15 (Oct. 31, 1936), 3-4, 14. Repr. in *Minority Report*. Little Brown, 1940. Pp. 209-218.
Edgar, Pelham. *Art of the Novel*. Macmillan, 1933. Pp. 338-351.
Fadiman, Clifton. "Faulkner, Extra-Special, Double-Distilled." *New Yorker* (Oct. 31, 1936).
—— "The World of William Faulkner," *Nation*, 132 (Apr. 15, 1931), 422-423.
Fiedler, Leslie. "William Faulkner: An American Dickens," *Commentary*, 10 (Oct., 1950), 384-387.
Foster, Ruel. "Dream as Symbolic Act in Faulkner," *Perspective*, 2 (Summer, 1949), 179-194.
Franc, M. "Prokosch non ama Faulkner." *La Friera Letteraria* (Italy), No. 3 (Jan. 15, 1950).
Frohock, W. M. "William Faulkner: the Private versus the Public Vision," *Southwest Rev.*, 34 (1949), 281-294. Repr. in *The Novel of Violence in America, 1920-1950*. Southern Methodist Univ. Pr., 1950. Pp. 101-124.
Geismar, Maxwell. "William Faulkner: The Negro and the Female," *Writers in Crisis*. Houghton, 1942. Pp. 141-183.
—— "Ex-Aristocrat's Emotional Education," *Sat. Rev. Lit.*, 31 (Sept. 25, 1948), 8-9.
Glicksberg, Charles. "The World of William Faulkner," *Arizona Quar. Rev.*, 5 (Spring, 1949), 46-58.
Gordon, Caroline. "Notes on Faulkner and Flaubert," *Hudson Rev.*, 1 (Summer, 1948), 222-232.
Green, A. W. "William Faulkner at Home," *Sewanee Rev.*, 40 (July, 1932), 294-306.
Greene, Graham. "The Furies in Mississippi." *London Mercury*, 35 (Mar., 1937), 517-518.
Hardwick, Elizabeth. "Faulkner and the South Today," *Partisan Rev.*, 15 (1948), 1130-1135.

Hartwick, Harry. *The Foreground of American Fiction*. American Book, 1934. Pp. 160-166.

Hatcher, Harlan. *Creating the Modern American Novel*. Farrar & Rinehart, 1935; Williams & Norgate, 1936. Pp. 234-243.

Henderson, Philip. *The Novel To-Day*. Lane (Bodley Head), 1936.

Hicks, Granville. "The Past and Future of William Faulkner," *Bookman*, 74 (Sept., 1931), 17-24.

—— "The Trumpet Call," *The Great Tradition*. Macmillan, 1933. Pp. 257-292. Esp. pp. 262-268.

Hirshleifer, Phyllis. "As Whirlwinds in the South," *Perspective*, 2 (Summer, 1949), 225-238.

Hoffman, F. J., and Vickery, Olga, editors. *William Faulkner: Two Decades of Criticism*. Michigan State College Pr., 1951. Bibliography, pp. 269-280.

Hopper, Vincent. "Faulkner's Paradise Lost." *Virginia Quar. Rev.*, 23 (Summer, 1947), 405-420.

Howe, Irving. "William Faulkner and the Quest for Freedom," *Tomorrow*, 9 (Dec., 1949), 54-56.

Hudson, Tommy. "William Faulkner: Mystic and Traditionalist," *Perspective*, 3 (Autumn, 1950), 227-235.

Huxley, Julian. "The Analysis of Fame," *Sat. Rev. Lit.*, 12 (May 11, 1935), 12.

Jackson, James. "Delta Cycle." *Chimera*, 5 (Autumn, 1946), 3-14.

Janson, Åke. "William Faulkner." *Bonniers Litterära Magasin* (Stockholm), 10 (Dec., 1950), 734-739.

Johnson. C. W. M. "Faulkner's 'A Rose for Emily'." *Expl.* 6. (May, 1948), item 45.

Kazin, Alfred. "Faulkner: The Rhetoric and the Agony," *Virginia Quar. Rev.*, 18 (July, 1942), 153-167. Repr. in *On Native Grounds*. Reynal & Hitchcock, 1942. Pp. 453-484.

Kohler, Dayton. "William Faulkner and the Social Conscience," *English Journal*, 38 (Dec., 1949), 545-553. In *College English*, 11 (1949), 119-127.

Kronenberger, Louis. "Faulkner's Dismal Swamp," *Nation*, 146 (1938), 212, 214.

—— "The World of William Faulkner," *Nation*, 150 (Apr. 13, 1940), 481-482.

Kubie, L. S. "William Faulkner's *Sanctuary*: An Analysis," *Sat. Rev. Lit.*, 11 (Oct. 20, 1934), 218, 224-226.

LaBudde, Kenneth. "Cultural Primitivism in William Faulkner's 'The Bear,' " *American Quar.*, 2 (Winter, 1950), 322-328.

Lewis, Wyndham. "A Moralist with a Corn-Cob, A Study of William Faulkner," *Life & Letters*, 10 (June, 1934), 312-328. Repr. in *Men Without Art*. Cassell; Harcourt, 1934. Pp. 42-64.

Loggins, V. "Cleaving to the Dream," *I Hear America*. Crowell, 1937. Pp. 71-112.

Longley, J. L. Jr. "The Problem of Evil in Three Novels of William Faulkner." Univ. of Tennessee, M. A. dissertation (unpublished).

Lytle, Andrew. "Regeneration for the Man." *Sewanee Rev.*, 57 (Winter, 1949), 120-127.

Maclachlan, John. "William Faulkner and the Southern Folk," *Southern Folklore Quar.*, 9 (1945), 153-167.

Magny, Claude-Edmonde. *Les Sandales d'Empédocles*. Éditions de la Baconnière (Neuchâtel, Switzerland), 1945.

—— *L'Age du roman américain*. Éditions du Seuil, 1948. Pp. 196-243.

McCole, C. J. *Lucifer at Large*. Longmans Green, 1937. Pp. 203-222.

McIlwaine, (Ardy) Shields. "Naturalistic Modes: the Gothic, the Ribald, and the Tragic: William Faulkner and Erskine Caldwell," *The Southern Poor-White*. Univ. of Oklahoma Pr., 1939. Pp. 217-240.

Morris, L. R. "Seven Pillars of Wisdom," in *Postscript to Yesterday*. Random House, 1947. Pp. 134-171.

Muller, H. J. *Modern Fiction*. Funk & Wagnalls, 1937. Pp. 405-407.

Nicholson, Norman. "William Faulkner." *New Spirit*, edited by Ernest Martin. Dobson, 1946. Pp. 32-41.

O'Donnell, George. "Faulkner's Mythology," *Kenyon Rev.*, 1 (Summer, 1939), 285-299.

—— Reply to H. M. Campbell's "Experiment and Achievement," *Sewanee Rev.*, 51 (July, 1943), 446-447.

Perspective, 2 (Summer, 1949). "William Faulkner Issue." And see also *Perspective*, 3 (Autumn, 1950). "Faulkner No. 2."

Peyre, Henri. "American Literature Through French Eyes," *Virginia Quar. Rev.*, 23 (Summer, 1947), 421-437.

Poirier, William. " 'Strange Gods' in Jefferson, Mississippi: Analysis of *Absalom, Absalom!*" in *William Faulkner*, edited by F. J. Hoffman and Olga Vickery. Univ. of Oklahoma Pr., 1951. Pp. 217-243.

Powell, Sumner. "William Faulkner Celebrates Easter," *Perspective*, 2 (Summer, 1949), 195-218.

Randall, Julia. "Some Notes on *As I Lay Dying*," *Hopkins Rev.*, 4 (Summer, 1951), 47-51.

Rascoe, Burton. "Faulkner's New York Critics," *American Mercury*, 50 (1940), 243-247.

Redman, B. R. "Faulkner's Double Novel," *Sat. Rev. Lit.*, 19 (Jan. 21, 1939), 5.

Rosenfeld, Isaac. "Faulkner and His Contemporaries," *Partisan Rev.*, 18 (Jan., 1951), 106-112, 114.

Roth, Russell. "The Brennan Papers: Faulkner in Manuscript," *Perspective*, 2 (Summer, 1949), 219-224.

—— "William Faulkner: The Pattern of Pilgrimage," *Perspective* 2 (Summer, 1949), 246-254.

Rovere, Richard. Introduction, *Light in August*. Random House (Modern Library), 1950. Pp. v-xiv.

Sartre, Jean-Paul. "Sartoris." *Nouvelle Revue Française*, 50 (Feb., 1938), 323-328.

—— "La Temporalité chez Faulkner." *Situations*, 1 (1947), 70-81.

—— "Time in Faulkner: *The Sound and the Fury*," in *William Faulkner*, edited by F. Hoffman and Olga Vickery. Univ. of Oklahoma Pr., 1951. Pp. 180-188.

Schappes, Morris. "Faulkner as a Poet," *Poetry*, 43 (Oct., 1933), 48-52.

Schwartz, Delmore. "The Fiction of William Faulkner." *Southern Rev.*, 7 (Summer, 1941), 145-160.

Scott, Evelyn. *On William Faulkner's "The Sound and the Fury."* Cape, 1929. (Pamphlet).

Smith, Bradley. "The Faulkner Country," in *'48*, 2 (May, 1948), 85-94.

Smith, Marshall. "Faulkner of Mississippi." *Bookman*, 74 (Dec., 1931), 411-417.

Snell, George. "William Faulkner," *Western Rev.*, 11 (Autumn, 1946), 29-41. Repr. in *The Shapers of American Fiction*. Dutton, 1947. Pp. 87-104.

Spencer, Benjamin. "Wherefore This Southern Fiction?" *Sewanee Rev.*, 47 (1939), 500-513.

Spender, Stephen. *The Destructive Element*. Cape, 1935.

Spiller, Robert, Thorp, Willard, and Others, editors. *Literary History of the United States*. Macmillan, 1948. Vol. III, pp. 1304-1306.

Sylvester, Harry. "The Dark, Bright World of Faulkner," *New York Times Book Rev.*, Aug. 20, 1950, p. 1.

Tate, Allen, and Gordon, Caroline. *The House of Fiction*. Scribner's, 1950. Pp. 531-534.

Thompson, A. R. "The Cult of Cruelty." *Bookman,* 74 (Jan., 1932), 477-487.

"Town A-building," *Time,* 31 (Feb. 21, 1938), 79.

Trilling, Lionel. "Contemporary American Literature in Its Relation to Ideas." *The American Writer and the European Tradition,* edited by Margaret Denny and W. H. Gilman. Univ. of Minnesota Pr., 1950. Pp. 132-153.

Van Doren, Carl. *The American Novel: 1789-1939.* Macmillan, 1940. Pp. 354-356.

Vickery, Olga. *"As I Lay Dying," Perspective,* 3 (Autumn, 1950), 179-191. Repr. in *William Faulkner,* edited by F. J. Hoffman and Olga Vickery. Univ. of Oklahoma Pr., 1951. Pp. 189-205.

Waldman, Milton. "Tendencies of the Modern Novel, America," *Fortnightly Rev.,* 140 (Dec., 1933), 709-725.

Ward, A. C. *American Literature, 1880-1930.* Methuen, 1932. Pp. 153-156.

Warren, Robert Penn. "Cowley's Faulkner." *New Rep.,* 115 (Aug. 12, 1946), 176-180.

—— "The Redemption of Temple Drake." *New York Times Book Rev.,* Sept. 30, 1951, pp. 1, 31.

—— "The Snopes World," *Kenyon Rev.,* 3 (Spring, 1941), 253-257.

—— "William Faulkner," *Forms of Modern Fiction,* edited by W. Van O'Connor. University of Minnesota Pr., 1948. Pp. 125-143.

Welty, Eudora. "Department of Amplification," *New Yorker,* 24 (Jan. 1, 1949), 50-51.

—— "In Yoknapatawpha," *Hudson Rev.,* 1 (Winter, 1949), 596-598.

West, R. B. Jr. "Atmosphere and Theme in Faulkner's 'A Rose for Emily,' " *Perspective,* 2 (Summer, 1949), 239-245.

—— "Faulkner's 'A Rose for Emily'." *Expl.,* 7 (Oct., 1948), item 8.

West, R. B. Jr., and Stallman, R. W. *The Art of Modern Fiction.* Rinehart, 1949. Pp. 270-276.

Whan, Edgar. *"Absalom, Absalom!* as Gothic Myth," *Perspective,* 3 (Autumn, 1950), 192-201.

Whittemore, Reed. "Notes on Mr. Faulkner," *Furioso,* 2 (Summer, 1947), 18-25.

Wilson, Edmund. *Classics and Commercials.* Farrar Straus, 1950. Pp. 460-470.

Wilson, James. "The Novel in the South," *Sat. Rev. Lit.,* 26 (Jan. 23, 1943), 11.

F. Scott Fitzgerald

Fitzgerald, F. Scott. *The Crack-Up,* edited by Edmund Wilson. New Directions, 1945.

On Fitzgerald: Adams, J. D. *The Writer's Responsibility.* Secker & Warburg, 1946. Pp. 92-94 and *passim.*

Aldridge, John W. "Fitzgerald," *After the Lost Generation.* McGraw-Hill, 1951. Pp. 44-58.

Baldwin, C. C. *The Men Who Make Our Novels.* Rev. ed., Moffat Yard, 1914. Rev. ed., 1924.

Barrett, William. "Fitzgerald and America," *Partisan Rev.,* 18 (May-June, 1951), 345-353.

Benét, W. R. "An Admirable Novel," *Sat. Rev. Lit.,* 1 (May 9, 1925), 739-740.

Berryman, John. "F. Scott Fitzgerald," *Kenyon Rev.,* 8 (Winter, 1946), 103-112.

Bishop, J. P. *Collected Essays,* edited by Edmund Wilson. Scribner's, 1948. Pp. 229-232. *See* also pp. 67-68.

Boyd, Ernest. *Portraits: Real and Imaginary.* George H. Doran, 1924. Pp. 217-226.

Cowley, Malcolm, editor. *The Short Stories of F. Scott Fitzgerald.* Scribner's, 1951.

Embler, Weller. "F. Scott Fitzgerald and the Future," *Chimera*, 4 (Autumn, 1945), 48-55. Repr. in *F. Scott Fitzgerald: The Man and His Work*, edited by Alfred Kazin. World Publishing Co., 1951. Pp. 212-219.

Farrar, John, editor. *The Literary Spotlight*. George H. Doran, 1924. Pp. 125-134.

Fussell, Edwin. "The Stature of Scott Fitzgerald." *Kenyon Rev.*, 13 (Summer, 1951), 530-534.

Hatcher, Harlan. *Creating the Modern American Novel*. Farrar & Rinehart, 1935; Williams & Norgate, 1936. Pp. 72-82.

Hoffman, Frederick. "Points of Moral Reference: A Comparative Study of Edith Wharton and F. Scott Fitzgerald." *English Institute Essays*, 1949. Columbia Univ. Pr., 1950.

Kazin, Alfred. *F. Scott Fitzgerald, The Man and His Work*. World Publishing Co., 1951.

—— *On Native Grounds*. Reynal & Hitchcock, 1942.

Geismar, Maxwell. *Writers in Crisis: 1925-1940*. Houghton, 1942.

—— *The Last of the Provincials: The American Novel: 1915-1925*. Houghton, 1948.

Leighton, Lawrence. "An Autopsy and a Prescription." *Hound & Horn*, 5 (July, 1932), 519-539.

MacKendrick, Paul. "The Great Gatsby and Trimalchio." *Classical Jour.*, 45 (Apr., 1950), 307-314.

Mizener, Arthur. *The Far Side of Paradise*. Houghton Mifflin, 1951; Eyre & Spottiswoode, 1951.

—— "Fitzgerald in the Twenties," *Partisan Rev.*, 17 (Jan., 1950), 7-34.

—— "Scott Fitzgerald and the Imaginative Possession of American Life," *Sewanee Rev.*, 54 (Jan., 1946), 66-86. (See pages 286-302 of this book for slightly different form.)

Piper, Henry Dan. "Fitzgerald's Cult of Disillusion," *American Quar.*, 3 (Spring, 1951), 69-80.

"Power Without Glory" (rev. of *The Crack-Up*), *Times Lit. Suppl.* (Jan. 20, 1950), p. 40.

Rosenfeld, Paul. *Men Seen*. Dial Pr., 1925. Pp. 215-224.

Ross, Alan. "Rumble Among the Drums," *Horizon*, 108 (Dec., 1948), 420 ff.

Thurber, James. " 'Scott in Thorns,' " *The Reporter*, 4 (Apr. 17, 1951), 35-38.

Trilling, Lionel. Introduction. *The Great Gatsby*. New Directions Pr. (n. d.)

—— *The Liberal Imagination*. Viking, 1950.

Troy, William. "Scott Fitzgerald—the Authority of Failure," *Accent*, 6 (Autumn, 1945), 56-60. Repr. in *Accent Anthology*. Repr. in *F. Scott Fitzgerald: The Man and His Work*, edited by Alfred Kazin. World Publishing Co., 1951. Pp. 187-193.

Wanning, Andrew. "Fitzgerald and His Brethren," *Partisan Rev.*, 12 (Fall, 1945), 545-551.

Weir, Charles. " 'An Invite with Gilded Edges,' A Study of F. Scott Fitzgerald," *Virginia Quarterly Rev.*, 20 (1944). Repr. in *F. Scott Fitzgerald: The Man and His Work*, edited by Alfred Kazin. World Publishing Co., 1951. Pp. 133-145.

Wheelock, John Hall, editor. *Editor to Author: The Letters of Maxwell E. Perkins*. Scribner's, 1950.

E. M. FORSTER

FORSTER, E. M. *Aspects of the Novel*. Harcourt, 1927, 1947.

—— "Credo: What I Believe," *London Mercury*, 38 (Sept., 1938), 397-404.

On Forster: "Aspects of E. M. Forster," *Dublin Review*, 439 (Oct., 1946), 109-134.

Beach, Joseph Warren. *The Twentieth Century Novel.* Appleton Century, 1932.

Belgion, Montgomery. "The Diabolism of Mr. E. M. Forster," *Criterion,* 14 (Oct., 1934-July, 1935), 54-73.

Bentley, Phyllis. "The Novels of E. M. Forster," *College English,* 9 (Apr., 1948), 349-356.

Brown, E. K. "The Revival of E. M. Forster," *Yale Rev.,* 33 (Summer, 1944), 668-681. Repr. in *Forms of Modern Fiction,* edited by W. Van O'Connor. Univ. of Minnesota Pr., 1948. Pp. 161-174.

Cecil, David. "Virginia Woolf, and E. M. Forster," *Poets and Story-Tellers.* Macmillan, 1948. Pp. 156-201.

Connolly, Cyril. *Enemies of Promise.* Routledge, 1938; Macmillan, 1948.

Dobrée, Bonamy. *The Lamp and the Lute.* Clarendon Pr., 1929. Pp. 66-85.

Drew, Elizabeth. *The Modern Novel.* Harcourt, 1926.

Edgar, Pelham. *The Art of the Novel.* Macmillan, 1933.

Gould, Gerald. *The English Novel of Today.* Castle, 1924.

Haines, Helen. *What's in a Novel.* Columbia Univ. Pr., 1942.

Hoare, D. M. *Some Studies of the Modern Novel.* Chatto & Windus, 1938. Pp. 68 ff.

Holt, Lee. "E. M. Forster and Samuel Butler," *P.M.L.A.,* 61 (Sept., 1946), 804-819.

Isherwood, Christopher. *Lions and Shadows.* Hogarth Pr., 1938.

Jones, E. B. "E. M. Forster and Virginia Woolf," *English Novelists,* edited by D. Verschoyle. Harcourt, 1936. Pp. 281-287.

Knight, Grant. *The Novel in English.* Farrar & Rinehart, 1931; R. R. Smith, 1935.

Leavis, F. R. "E. M. Forster," *Scrutiny,* 7 (Sept., 1938), 185-202. Repr. in *The Importance of Scrutiny,* edited by Eric Bentley. Stewart, 1948. Pp. 295 ff.

Macaulay, Rose. *The Writings of E. M. Forster.* Hogarth Pr.; Harcourt, 1938.

Mansfield, Katherine. *Novels and Novelists,* edited by J. M. Murry. Knopf, 1930.

McLuhan, H. M. "Kipling and Forster," *Sewanee Rev.,* 52 (Summer, 1944), 332-343.

Muller, H. J. *Modern Fiction.* Funk & Wagnalls, 1937.

Ransom, J. C. "E. M. Forster," *Kenyon Rev.,* 5 (Autumn, 1943), 618-623. (Editorial.)

Richards, I. A. "A Passage to Forster," *Forum,* 78 (Dec., 1927), 914-920.

Savage, D. S. "E. M. Forster," *Rocky Mountain Rev.,* 10 (Summer, 1946), 190-204.

—— *The Withered Branch.* Eyre & Spottiswoode, 1950. Pp. 44-69.

Swinnerton, Frank. *The Georgian Scene.* Farrar & Rinehart, 1934.

Traversi, D. A. "The Novels of E. M. Forster," *Arena,* No. 1 (Apr., 1937).

Trilling, Lionel. *E. M. Forster.* New Directions Pr., 1943.

—— "E. M. Forster and the Liberal Tradition," *Kenyon Rev.,* 4 (Spring, 1942), 160-173.

Waggoner, H. H. "Exercises in Perspective," *Chimera,* 3 (Summer, 1945), 3-14.

Warren, Austin. "The Novels of E. M. Forster," *American Rev.,* 9 (Summer, 1937), 226-251. Repr. in *Rage for Order: Essays in Criticism.* Univ. of Chicago Pr., 1948. Pp. 119-141. (See pages 474-487 of this book.)

Woolf, Virginia. *The Death of the Moth.* Harcourt, 1942.

Zabel, M. D. "E. M. Forster," *Nation,* 147 (Oct. 22, 1938), 412-413.

ERNEST HEMINGWAY

HEMINGWAY, ERNEST. Correspondence. *Hound & Horn,* 6 (Oct.-Dec., 1932), 135.

—— Introduction. *In Sicily,* by Elio Vittorini. New Directions Pr., 1949.

A SELECTED BIBLIOGRAPHY 589

HEMINGWAY, ERNEST. Introduction, *Men at War*. Crown Publishers, 1942.

—— "Monologue to the Maestro," *Esquire*, 4 (Oct., 1925), 21 ff.

On Hemingway: Adams, J. D. *The Writer's Responsibility*. Secker & Warburg, 1946. Pp. 105-113 and *passim*.

Aldridge, John W. "Hemingway," *After the Lost Generation*. McGraw-Hill, 1951. Pp. 23-43.

Angstrom, Alfred. "Dante, Flaubert, and 'The Snows of Kilimanjaro,'" *Mod. Language Notes*, 65 (1950), 203-205.

Baker, Carlos. "Twenty-five Years of a Hemingway Classic," *New York Times Book Rev.*, Apr. 29, 1951, pp. 5, 30. (On *The Sun Also Rises*.)

Barea, Arturo. "Not Spain but Hemingway," *Horizon*, 3 (May, 1941), 350-361.

Beach, Joseph Warren. "Empirical Ethics," and "The Esthetic of Simplicity," *American Fiction, 1920-1940*. Macmillan, 1941, 1948.

—— "How Do You Like It Now, Gentlemen?" *Sewanee Rev.*, 59 (Spring, 1951), 311-328.

Bishop, John Peale. "Homage to Hemingway," *New Rep.*, 89 (Nov. 11, 1936), 39-42. Repr. in *The Collected Essays of John Peale Bishop*, edited by Edmund Wilson. Scribner's, 1948. Pp. 37-46.

—— "The Missing All," *Virginia Quar. Rev.*, 13 (Summer, 1947), 106-121. Repr. in *The Collected Essays of John Peale Bishop*, edited by Edmund Wilson. Scribner's, 1948. Pp. 66-77.

Blackmur, R. P. "Notes on the Novel: 1936," *Expense of Greatness*. Arrow Editions, 1940.

Brooks, Cleanth, and Warren, Robert Penn. " 'The Killers,' " *American Prefaces*, 7 (Spring, 1942), 195-209. Repr. in *Understanding Fiction*. Crofts, 1943.

Burgum, Edwin Berry. "Ernest Hemingway and the Psychology of the Lost Generation," *The Novel and the World's Dilemma*. Oxford Univ. Pr., 1947.

Calverton, V. F. "Ernest Hemingway: Primevalite," *Modern Monthly*, 10 (Dec., 1937), 6-7.

—— "Steinbeck, Hemingway and Faulkner," *Mod. Quar.*, 11 (Fall, 1939), 36-44.

Canby, H. S. "Farewell to the Nineties," *Sat. Rev. Lit.*, 10 (Oct 28, 1933), 217.

Cohn, Louis H. *Bibliography of Ernest Hemingway*. Random House, 1931.

—— "A Note on Ernest Hemingway." *Colophon*, 1 (Summer, 1935), 119-122.

Coindreau, Maurice. "Ernest Hemingway." *La Nouvelle Revue Française*, 26 (Mar., 1938), 501-504.

Comfort, Alex. *The Novel & Our Time*. Dent; Alan Swallow Pr., 1948.

Cowley, Malcolm. "Ernest Hemingway: A Farewell to Spain," *New Rep.*, 73 (Nov. 30, 1932), 76-77. Repr. in *Literary Opinion in America*, edited by M. D. Zabel. Harper, 1937. Pp. 506-511.

——Introduction, *The Portable Hemingway*. Viking, 1943.

Daiches, David. "Hemingway," *College English*, 2 (May, 1941), 725 ff.

Daniel, Robert. "Hemingway and His Heroes." *Queen's Quar.*, 54 (Winter, 1947-48), 471-485.

Dewing, A. "The Mistake About Hemingway," *North Amer. Rev.*, 232 (Oct., 1931), 364-371.

Eastman, Max. "Bull in the Afternoon," *New Rep.*, 75 (June 7, 1933), 94-97.

Fadiman, Clifton. "Ernest Hemingway, An American Byron," *Nation*, 136 (Jan. 18, 1933), 63-64.

Farrell, James T. *The League of Frightened Philistines*. Vanguard Pr., 1945.

Fenimore, Edward. "English and Spanish in *For Whom the Bell Tolls*," *Journal of English Literary History*, 10 (June, 1943).

Ford, Ford Madox. Introduction, *A Farewell to Arms*. Random House, 1932.

Ford, Terrence. "The Trailer of Mr. Hemingway." *Bookman*, 76 (Feb., 1933), 140. (Parody.)

Frankenberg, Lloyd. "Themes and Characters in Hemingway's Latest Period," *Southern Rev.*, 7 (Spring, 1942), 776-788.

Frohock, W. M. *The Novel of Violence in America, 1920-1950*. Southern Methodist Univ. Pr., 1950.

Galantière, L. "The Brushwood Boy at the Front," *Hound & Horn*, 3 (Jan.-Mar., 1930), 259-262.

Geismar, Maxwell. "Hemingway," *Writers in Crisis*. Houghton, 1942.

Gordon, Caroline. "Notes on Hemingway and Kafka," *Sewanee Rev.*, 5 (Apr.-June, 1949), 215-226.

Hartwick, Harry. *The Foreground of American Fiction*. American Book, 1934. Pp. 151-159.

Hatcher, Harlan. *Creating the Modern American Novel*. Farrar & Rinehart, 1935; Williams & Norgate, 1936. Pp. 228-233.

Hemphill, George. "Hemingway and James," *Kenyon Rev.*, 11 (Winter, 1949), 50-60.

Herrick, Robert. "What is Dirt?" *Bookman*, 70 (Nov., 1929), 258-262.

Hicks, Granville. *The Great Tradition*. Macmillan, 1933. Pp. 273-276.

Isherwood, Christopher. "Hemingway, Death and the Devil," *Decision*, 1 Jan., 1941), 58-60.

Jameson, Storm. "The Craft of the Novelist," *English Rev.*, 58 (Jan., 1934), 28-43.

Johnson, Edgar. "Farewell the Separate Peace: The Rejections of Ernest Hemingway." *Sewanee Rev.*, 48 (Summer, 1940). Repr. in *F. Scott Fitzgerald: The Man and His Work*, edited by Alfred Kazin. World Publishing, 1951. Pp. 205-211.

Kashkeen, J. "Ernest Hemingway," *International Lit.*, 5 (1945).

Kazin, Alfred. "Into the Thirties: All the Lost Generations," *On Native Grounds*. Reynal & Hitchcock, 1942.

Kirstein, Louis. "The Canon of Death," *Hound & Horn*, 6 (Jan.-Mar., 1933), 336-341.

Leighton, Lawrence. "An Autopsy and a Prescription," *Hound & Horn*, 5 (July-Sept., 1932), 519-539.

Lewis, Wyndham. "The Dumb Ox: A Study of Ernest Hemingway," *American Rev.*, 3 (June, 1934), 289-312.

—— *Men Without Art*. Cassell; Harcourt, 1934.

Littell, Robert. "Notes on Hemingway," *New Rep.*, 51 (Aug. 10, 1927), 303-306.

Lovett, Robert. "Ernest Hemingway," *English Journal*, 21 (Oct., 1932), 609-617.

Matthews, T. S. "Nothing Ever Happens to the Brave," *New Rep.*, 60 (Oct. 9, 1929), 208-210.

McCaffery, John, editor. *Ernest Hemingway: The Man and His Work*. World Publishing, 1950. (Essays by Bishop, Burgum, Eastman, Farrell, Kazin, Elliot Paul, Schwartz, Stein, and others.) Rev'd by Granville Hicks: "The Critics," *New York Times Book Rev.*, Oct. 15, 1950, pp. 5, 32.

Mellers, W. H. "The Ox in Spain" (review of *For Whom the Bell Tolls*), *Scrutiny*, 10 (June, 1941), 93-99.

Muller, Herbert. "Apostles of the Lost Generation," *Modern Fiction: A Study of Values*. Funk & Wagnalls, 1937.

O'Hara, John. "The Author's Name is Hemingway" (rev. of *Across the River and into the Trees*), *New York Times Book Rev.*, Sept. 10, 1950, pp. 1, 30-31.

Orvis, M. B. *The Art of Writing Fiction*. Prentice-Hall, 1948. Pp. 129-132.

Paul, Elliot. "Hemingway and the Critics," *Sat. Rev. Lit.*, 17 (Nov. 6, 1937), 3-4.

Praz, Mario. "Hemingway in Italy," *Partisan Rev.*, 15 (Oct., 1948), 1086-1100.

Rahv, Philip. *Image and Idea*. New Directions Pr., 1949.

—— "The Social Muse and the Great Kudu," *Partisan Rev.*, 4 (Dec., 1937).

Redman, Ben Ray. "The Champ and His Critics." *Sat. Rev. Lit.*, 33 (Oct. 28, 1950), 15-16, 38.

Rosenfeld, Isaac. "A Farewell to Hemingway," *Kenyon Rev.*, 13 (Winter, 1951), 147-155.

Ross, Lillian. "How Do You Like It Now, Gentlemen?" (Profiles.) *New Yorker*, (May 13, 1950), 36, 38-40, 42-56.

Samuels, Lee. *A Hemingway Check List*. Scribner's, 1951.

Savage, D. S. "Hemingway," *Hudson Rev.*, 1 (Autumn, 1948), 380-401.

—— "Hemingway," *The Withered Branch*. Eyre and Spottiswoode, 1950. Pp. 23-43.

Schwartz, Delmore. "Ernest Hemingway's Literary Situation," *Southern Rev.*, (Spring, 1938), 769-789. Repr. in *Ernest Hemingway: The Man and His Work*, edited by John McCaffery. World Publishing, 1950.

Seward, William Jr. "Ernest Hemingway's *Across the River and Into the Trees*." *Norfolk Virginian-Pilot*, Sept. 10, 1950, p. 4.

Slochower, H. "Hemingway and Huxley," *No Voice is Wholly Lost*. Creative Age Press, 1945. Pp. 32 ff. Dobson, 1946.

Snell, George. *The Shapers of American Fiction*. Dutton, 1947.

Spender, Stephen. *The Destructive Element*. Cape, 1935.

Stein, Gertrude. *The Autobiography of Alice B. Toklas*. Random House, 1933.

—— "Ernest Hemingway and the Postwar Decade," *Atlantic*, 152 (Aug., 1933), 197-208.

Tate, Allen, and Gordon, Caroline. *The House of Fiction*. Scribner's, 1950. Pp. 419-423.

Trilling, Lionel. "An American in Spain," *The Partisan Reader*, edited by William Phillips and Philip Rahv. Dial Pr., 1946. Pp. 639-644.

—— "Contemporary American Literature in Its Relation to Ideas." *The American Writer and the European Tradition*, edited by Margaret Denny and W. H. Gilman. University of Minnesota Pr., 1950. Pp. 132-153.

—— "Hemingway and His Critics," *Partisan Rev.*, 6 (Winter, 1939), 52-60.

Van Doren, Carl. *The American Novel, 1789-1939*. Macmillan, 1940. Pp. 334-348.

Ward, A. C. *American Literature: 1880-1930*. Dial Pr.; Methuen, 1932.

Warren, Robert Penn. Introduction, *A Farewell to Arms*. Scribner's, 1949. (See pages 447-473 of this book.)

—— "Hemingway," *Kenyon Rev.*, 9 (Winter, 1947), 1-28.

West, R. B. Jr. "Ernest Hemingway," *Sewanee Rev.*, 53 (Jan., 1945), 120-135. Repr. in *Forms of Modern Fiction*, edited by W. Van O'Connor. University of Minnesota Pr., 1948.

—— "Ernest Hemingway: Death in the Evening," *Antioch Rev.*, 4 (Dec., 1944), 569 ff.

West, R. B. Jr., and Stallman, R. W. *The Art of Modern Fiction*. Rinehart, 1949. Pp. 259-262, 622-634.

Wheelock, John Hall, editor. *Editor to Author: The Letters of Maxwell E. Perkins*. Scribner's, 1950.

White, E. B. "Across the Street and Into the Grille," *New Yorker*, 26 (Oct. 14, 1950), 28. (Parody.)

Wilson, Edmund. "Hemingway: Gauge of Morale," *The Wound and the Bow*. Houghton, 1941; Oxford Univ. Pr., 1947. Pp. 214 ff.

—— Introduction, *In Our Time*. Scribner's, 1931.

—— "The Sportsman's Tragedy," *New Rep.*, 53 (Dec. 14, 1927), 102-103.

Young, Philip. *Ernest Hemingway*. Rinehart Editions, 1952.

A SELECTED BIBLIOGRAPHY

Aldous Huxley

On Huxley: Baker, Howard. "In Praise of the Novel: The Fiction of Huxley, Steinbeck and Others." *Southern Rev.*, 5 (Spring, 1940), 793 ff.

Bald, R. C. "Aldous Huxley as a Borrower," *College English*, 2 (Jan., 1942), 183-187.

Butts, Mary. In *Scrutinies II*, edited by Edgell Rickword. Wishart, 1931. Pp. 74-98.

Daiches, David. "Aldous Huxley." *The Novel and the Modern World*. Univ. of Chicago Pr., 1939. Pp. 188-210.

Estrich, Helen. "Jesting Pilate Tells the Answer: Aldous Huxley," *Sewanee Rev.*, 47 (Jan., 1939), 63-81.

Hamill, Elizabeth. *These Modern Writers*. Georgia House (Melbourne), 1946. Chap. 7.

Hoffman, Frederick. "Aldous Huxley and the Novel of Ideas," *Forms of Modern Fiction*, edited by W. Van O'Connor. University of Minnesota Pr., 1948. Pp. 189-200.

Lovett, Robert. "Vanity Fair Up-to-Date," *New Rep.*, 57 (Dec. 5, 1928), 75-76. Repr. in *Literary Opinion in America*, edited by M. D. Zabel. Harper, 1937. Pp. 332-336. Rev. ed., 1951.

Rolo, Charles, editor. Introduction to *The World of Aldous Huxley*. Harper, 1947.

Savage, D. S. "Aldous Huxley and the Dissociation of Personality," in *The Withered Branch*. Eyre & Spottiswoode, 1950; repr. in *The Novelist as Thinker (Focus Four)*, edited by B. Rajan. Dobson, 1947. Pp. 9-34. Repr. from *Sewanee Rev.*, 55 (Autumn, 1947). (See pages 340-361 of this book.)

Slochower, Harry. *No Voice is Wholly Lost*. Creative Age Pr., 1945; Dobson, 1946.

Watts, Harold. Introduction, *Point Counter Point*. Harper, 1947.

Henry James

James, Henry. *The Art of Fiction and Other Essays*, edited by Morris Roberts. Oxford Univ. Pr., 1948.

—— *The Art of the Novel: Critical Prefaces of Henry James*, edited by R. P. Blackmur. Scribner's, 1934.

—— *Henry James's Criticism*, edited by Morris Roberts. Harvard Univ. Pr., 1929.

—— *The Letters*, edited by Percy Lubbock. Scribner's, 1920. 2 vols.

—— *The Notebooks of Henry James*, edited by F. O. Matthiessen and K. B. Murdock. Oxford Univ. Pr., 1947.

On James: Adams, J. D. *The Writer's Responsibility*. Secker & Warburg, 1946. Pp. 44 ff. and *passim*.

Anderson, Quentin. "Henry James and the New Jerusalem," *Kenyon Rev.*, 8 (Autumn, 1946), 515-566.

—— "Henry James, His Symbolism and His Critics," *Scrutiny*, 15 (Dec., 1947), 12-19.

—— "The Two Henry Jameses," *Scrutiny*, 14 (Sept., 1947), 242-252.

Andreas, Osborn. *Henry James and the Expanding Horizon*. Univ. of Washington Pr., 1949.

Auden, W. H. Introduction, *The American Scene*. Scribner's, 1946.

—— "Henry James and the Artist in America," *Harper's*, 197 (July, 1948), 36-40.

Barrett, Laurence. "Young Henry James, Critic," *American Lit.*, 20 (Jan., 1949), 385-400.

Barzun, Jacques. "James as Melodramatist," *Kenyon Rev.*, 5 (Autumn, 1943), 508-521.

Beach, Joseph Warren. *The Method of Henry James.* Yale Univ. Pr., 1918.

—— "The Sacred and Solitary Refuge," *Furioso*, 3 (Winter, 1947), 23-37. Repr. as "The Witness of the Notebooks," *Forms of Modern Fiction*, edited by W. Van O'Connor. University of Minnesota Pr., 1948. Pp. 46-60.

Berland, Alwyn. "Henry James," *Univ. of Kansas City Rev.*, 17 (Winter, 1950), 94-108.

Berryman, John. "Henry James," *Sewanee Rev.*, 53 (Spring, 1945), 291-297.

Berti, Luigi. "Saggio su Henry James." *Inventario*, 1 (Autumn, 1946-47), 78-88.

Bethurum, Dorothy. "Morality and Henry James," *Sewanee Rev.*, 31 (July, 1932), 324-330.

Bewley, Marius. "Appearance and Reality in Henry James," *Scrutiny*, 17 (Summer, 1950), 90-114.

—— "Maisie, Miles and Flora, The Jamesian Innocents: A Rejoinder," *Scrutiny*, 17 (Autumn, 1950), 255-263.

—— "Correspondence: The Relation between William and Henry James," *Scrutiny*, 17 (Mar., 1951), 331-334.

—— "James's Debt to Hawthorne (I): *The Blithedale Romance* and *The Bostonians*," *Scrutiny*, 16 (Sept., 1949), 178-196. *See also:* Leon Edel and Bewley, "Correspondence," *Scrutiny*, 17 (Spring, 1950), 53-61.

—— "James's Debt to Hawthorne (II): *The Marble Faun* and *The Wings of the Dove*," *Scrutiny*, 16 (Winter, 1949), 301-318.

—— "James's Debt to Hawthorne (III): The American Problem," *Scrutiny*, 17 (Spring, 1950) 14-32.

Blackmur, R. P. "The Critical Prefaces of Henry James," *Hound & Horn*, 7 (Apr.-May, 1934), 444-477. Repr. in *The Art of the Novel*. Scribner's, 1934. In *Double Agent*. Arrow Editions, 1935. Pp. 234-268.

—— "Henry James," in *Literary History of the United States, Vol. II*, edited by Robert Spiller, Willard Thorp, and Others. Macmillan, 1948.

—— "In the Country of the Blue," *Kenyon Rev.*, 5 (Autumn, 1943), 595-617. Repr. in *The Question of Henry James*, edited by F. W. Dupee. Holt, 1945. Pp. 191-211. (See pages 303-318 of this book.)

—— "The Loose and Baggy Monsters of Henry James," *Accent*, 11 (Summer, 1951), 129-146.

—— "The Sacred Fount," *Kenyon Rev.*, 4 (Autumn, 1942), 328-352.

Bogan, Louise. "Silver Clue," *Nation*, 159 (Dec. 23, 1944), 775-776.

Bosanquet, Theodora. *Henry James at Work*. Hogarth Pr., 1924.

—— "Henry James at Work," *Hogarth Essays*. Doubleday Doran, 1928. Pp. 243-276.

Brooks, Van Wyck. "Henry James: The American Scene," *Dial*, 75 (July, 1923), 29-42.

—— "Henry James: An International Episode," *Dial*, 75 (1923), 226-238.

—— "Henry James as Reviewer." *Sketches in Criticism*. Dutton, 1932. Pp. 190-196.

—— *New England: Indian Summer, 1865-1915*. Dutton, 1940. Pp. 224, 249, 276-295, 395-408.

—— *The Pilgrimage of Henry James*. Dutton, 1925.

Brown, E. K. "James and Conrad," *Yale Rev.*, 35 (1946), 265-285.

—— "Two Formulas for Fiction: Henry James and H. G. Wells," *College English*, 8 (Oct., 1946), 7-17.

Burgum, E. B. *The Novel and the World's Dilemma*. Oxford Univ. Pr., 1947.

Burnham, D. "View of America," (review of *The American Scene*), *Commonweal*, 45 (Oct. 25, 1946), 36-40.

Burnham, D. "Fiction is Art, Plus," *Commonweal*, 48 (1948), 106-109.

Canby, Henry Seidel. "The Return of Henry James," *Sat. Rev. Lit.*, 31 (Jan. 24, 1948), 9-10, 34-35.

—— "The Timelessness of Henry James," *Sat. Rev. Lit.*, 28 (Oct. 20, 1945), 9.

Cantwell, Robert. "No Landmarks," *Symposium*, 4 (Jan., 1933), 70-84. Repr. in *Literary Opinion in America*, edited by M. D. Zabel. Harper, 1937. Pp. 530-541. Rev. ed., 1951.

Conrad, Joseph. "Henry James," *Notes on Life and Letters*. Dent, 1921.

Cowie, Alexander. *The Rise of the American Novel*. American Book, 1948. Pp. 702-742.

Cowley, Malcolm. "Return of Henry James," *New Rep.*, 112 (Jan. 22, 1945), 121-122.

—— "Two Henry Jameses," *New Rep.*, 112 (Feb. 5, 1945), 177-178.

Daiches, David. "Sense and Technique," *Kenyon Rev.*, 5 (Autumn, 1943), 569-579.

Dunbar, Viola. "The Revision of *Daisy Miller*." *Mod. Language Notes*, 65 (May, 1950), 311-317.

Dupee, F. W. *Henry James*. Sloane Assoc., 1951.

—— "Henry James and the Play," *Nation*, 171 (July 8, 1950), 40-41.

—— "Henry James in the Great Grey Babylon," *Partisan Rev.*, 18 (Mar.-Apr., 1951), 183-190.

—— editor. *The Question of Henry James*. Holt, 1945.

Edel, Leon, editor. *The Complete Plays of Henry James*. Lippincott, 1950.

Edgar, Pelham. *Henry James: Man and Author*. Macmillan, 1933.

Eliot, T. S. "Henry James," *The Shock of Recognition*, edited by Edmund Wilson. Doubleday, 1943.

—— "Henry James," *The Question of Henry James*, edited by F. W. Dupee. Holt, 1945. Pp. 108-119.

Evans, Oliver. "James's Air of Evil: 'The Turn of the Screw,'" *Partisan Rev.*, (Feb., 1949), 175-187.

Fadiman, Clifton. Introduction. *The Short Novels of Henry James*. Random House, 1945.

Falk, Robert. "Henry James's Romantic 'Vision of the Real' in the 1870's." *Essays Critical and Historical: Dedicated to Lily B. Campbell*. By Members of the Departments of English, University of California. University of California Pr., 1950.

Fergusson, Francis. "The Drama in *The Golden Bowl*," *Hound & Horn*, 7 (Apr.-May, 1934), 407-413.

—— "James's Idea of Dramatic Form," *Kenyon Rev.*, 4 (Autumn, 1943), 495-507.

Foley, Richard N. *Criticism in American Periodicals of the Works of Henry James from 1866-1916*. Catholic University Press, 1944.

Ford, F. M. "Henry James," *Portraits from Life*. Houghton, 1937. Pp. 1-20.

—— "The Old Man," *The Question of Henry James*, edited by F. W. Dupee. Holt, 1945. Pp. 47-53.

—— "Techniques," *Southern Rev.*, 1 (July, 1935), 20-35.

See Hueffer.

Forster, E. M. *Aspects of the Novel*. Harcourt, 1927, 1947. Pp. 30-31, 218-234.

Frierson, W. C. "Henry James's Version of the Experimental Novel," *The English Novel in Transition*. Univ. of Oklahoma Press, 1942.

Gettman, Royal A. "Henry James's Revision of *The American*," *American Lit.*, 16 (Jan., 1945), 279-295.

Gide, André. "Henry James," *Yale Rev.*, 19 (Spring, 1930).

Greene, Graham. Introduction, *The Portrait of a Lady*. Oxford Univ. Pr., 1948. Rev'd. by F. R. Leavis. *Scrutiny*, 15 (Summer, 1948), 235-241.

Gretton, M. S. "Mr. Henry James and his Prefaces." *Cont. Rev.*, 101 (Jan., 1918), 68-78.

Grossman, J. "Face in the Mountain," *Nation*, 161 (Sept. 8, 1945), 230-232.

Hamilton, Eunice. "Biographical and Critical Studies of Henry James, 1941-1948." *American Lit.*, 20 (Jan., 1949), 424-435.

Hartwick, Harry. *The Foreground of American Fiction*. American Book, 1934. Pp. 341-368.

Havens, Raymond. "Henry James' 'The Impressions of a Cousin.'" *Mod. Language Notes*, 65 (May, 1950), 317-319.

Hays, H. R. "Henry James, The Satirist," *Hound & Horn*, 7 (Apr.-May, 1934), 514-522.

Heilman, Robert. "'The Turn of the Screw' as Poem," *Univ. of Kansas City Rev.*, 14 (Summer, 1948), 272-289. Repr. in *The Story*, edited by Mark Schorer. Prentice-Hall, 1950. Pp. 586-606.

Hemphill, George. "Hemingway and James," *Kenyon Rev.*, 11 (Winter, 1949), 50-60.

"Henry James Reprints," *Times Lit. Suppl.*, Feb. 5, 1949, p. 96. *See* Mar. 12, 1949. P. 169.

Hicks, Granville. *The Great Tradition*. Macmillan, 1933. Pp. 105-123.

Hoare, Dorothy. *Some Studies in the Modern Novel*. Chatto & Windus, 1938. Pp. 17 ff.

Hoskins, Katherine. "Henry James and the Future of the Novel," *Sewanee Rev.*, 54 (Jan., 1946), 87-101.

Hound & Horn, 7 (Apr.-May, 1934), "Henry James Issue."

Hoxie, Elizabeth F. "Mrs. Grundy Adopts Daisy Miller," *New England Quar.*, 19 (1945), 474-484.

Hueffer, F. M. [Ford Madox Ford] *Henry James: A Critical Study*. Secker, n.d.

—— *Thus to Revisit*. Dutton, 1921. Part 2, Chap. 9.

Josephson, Matthew. *Portrait of the Artist as American*. Harcourt, 1930.

Kane, R. J. "Hawthorne's 'The Prophetic Pictures' and James' 'The Liar.'" *Mod. Language Notes*, 65 (Apr., 1950), 257-258.

Kazin, Alfred. *On Native Grounds*. Reynal & Hitchcock, 1942.

—— "Our Passion is our Task." *New Rep.*, 108 (Feb. 15, 1943), 215-218.

Kelley, Cornelia. *The Early Development of Henry James*. Univ. Illinois Studies in Language and Literature, 15 (1930).

Kenton, Edna. "*The Ambassadors*: Project of a Novel," *Hound & Horn*, 7 (Apr.-May, 1934), 541-562.

—— "Henry James in the World," *Hound & Horn*, 7 (Apr.-May, 1934), 506-513.

Kenyon Review, 5 (Autumn, 1943), "The Henry James Number."

Kerner, David. "A Note on 'The Beast in the Jungle,'" *Univ. of Kansas City Rev.*, 17 (Winter, 1950), 109-118.

Knight, Grant C. *The Novel in English*. Farrar & Rinehart, 1931; R. R. Smith, 1935. Pp. 95 ff.

Knights, L. C. "Henry James and the Trapped Spectator," *Southern Rev.*, 4 (Winter, 1939), 600-615. Repr. in *Explorations*. Chatto & Windus, 1946. Pp. 155-169.

Krutch, J. W. *The Modern Temper: A Study and a Confession*. Harcourt, 1929. Pp. 155 ff.

Leavis, F. R. "The Appreciation of Henry James" (review of *Henry James: the Major Phase*), *Scrutiny*, 14 (Spring, 1947), 229-237.

—— *The Great Tradition*. Chatto & Windus, 1948; Stewart, 1949.

—— "Henry James and the Function of Criticism," *Scrutiny*, 15 (Spring, 1948), 98-105.

—— "Henry James's First Novel" (review of *Roderick Hudson*), *Scrutiny*, 14 (Sept., 1947), 295-301.

Leavis, F. R. "James's *What Maisie Knew:* A Disagreement," *Scrutiny,* 17 (Summer, 1950), 115-128.

—— "The Novel as Dramatic Poem: *The Europeans,*" *Scrutiny,* 15 (Summer, 1948), 209-221.

——"*The Portrait of a Lady* Reprinted," *Scrutiny,* 15 (Summer, 1948), 235-241.

Leavis, Q. D., "Henry James: The Stories" (review of *Fourteen Stories* by H. *James*), *Scrutiny,* 14, (Spring, 1947), 223-229.

—— "Henry James's *Heiress:* the Importance of Edith Wharton," *Scrutiny,* 7 (Dec., 1938), 261-276.

—— "The Institution of Henry James" (review of F. W. Dupee's *The Question of Henry James*), *Scrutiny,* 15 (Dec., 1947), 68-75.

Leighton, Lawrence. "Armor Against Time," *Hound & Horn,* 7 (Apr.-May, 1934), 373-384.

Lerner, Daniel. "The Influence of Turgenev on Henry James," *Slavonic Year Book,* 20 (1941), 28-54.

Lerner, Daniel, and Cargill, Oscar. "Henry James at the Grecian Urn." *P.M.L.A.,* 66 (June, 1951), 316-331.

Lewis, Wyndham. *Men Without Art.* Cassell; Harcourt, 1934.

Littell, Philip. "Henry James as Critic." *New Rep.,* 1 (Nov. 21, 1914), 26-28.

Lubbock, Percy. *The Craft of Fiction.* Cape; Scribner's, 1921, 1929; Peter Smith, 1947.

Mackenzie, Compton. "Henry James," *Life & Letters To-day,* 39 (Dec., 1943), 147-155.

Marsh, Edward. "James: Auto-Critic." *Bookman,* 30 (Oct., 1909), 138-143.

Matthews, Brander. "Henry James, Book Reviewer." *New York Times Book Rev.,* June 12, 1921.

Matthiessen, F. O. Introduction, *The American Novels and Stories of Henry James.* Knopf, 1947.

—— *The American Renaissance.* Oxford Univ. Pr., 1941.

—— *Henry James: The Major Phase.* Oxford Univ. Pr., 1946.

—— "Henry James's Portrait of the Artist," *Partisan Rev.,* 11 (Winter, 1944), 71-87. Repr. as the Introduction to *Stories of Writers and Artists.* New Directions Pr. (n.d.)

—— *The James Family.* Knopf, 1947.

—— "Not Quite the Real Thing," *New Rep.,* 113 (Dec. 3, 1945), 766.

—— "The Painter's Sponge and Varnish Bottle," *American Bookman,* 1 (Winter, 1944), 49-68. Repr. in *Henry James: The Major Phase.* Oxford Univ. Pr., 1946.

——, editor. *Stories of Writers & Artists.* New Directions Pr., n.d.

Matthiessen, F. O. and Murdock, Kenneth B., editors. *The Notebooks of Henry James.* Oxford Univ. Pr., 1947.

Maurois, André. "Ecrivains américains." *Revue de Paris,* 54 (Apr., 1947), 9-24.

McCullough, Bruce. *Representative English Novelists.* Harper, 1946.

McElderry, B. R., Jr. "Henry James and 'The Whole Family,'" *Pacific Spectator,* 4 (Summer, 1950), 352-360.

Mencken, H. L. *A Mencken Chrestomathy.* Knopf, 1949. Pp. 500-501.

Michaud, Regis. *The American Novel To-day.* Little, Brown, 1931. Chap. 3.

Moore, Marianne. "Henry James as a Characteristic American," *Hound & Horn,* 7 (Apr., 1934), 363-372. Repr. in *Literary Opinion in America,* edited by M. D. Zabel. Harper, 1937. Rev. ed., 1951.

Morris, L. R. *Postscript to Yesterday.* Random House, 1947. Pp. 89-106.

Munson, Gorham. "The Real Thing: A Parable for Writers of Fiction." *Univ. Kansas City Rev.,* 16 (Summer, 1950), 261-264.

Neff, John. "Henry James the Reporter." *New Mexico Quar.*, 8 (Feb., 1938), 9-14.

Nowell-Smith, Simon. *The Legend of the Master.* Scribner's, 1948.

Nuhn, Ferner. "The Enchanted Kingdom of Henry James," *The Wind Blew from the East.* Harper, 1942. Pp. 87-163.

Oliver, Clinton. "Henry James as Social Critic," *Antioch Rev.*, 7 (Summer, 1947), 243-258.

Pacey, W. C. D. "Henry James and His French Contemporaries," *American Lit.*, 13 (1941), 240-256.

Palache, John. "The Critical Faculty of Henry James," *Univ. California Chronicle*, 26 (Oct., 1924), 399-410.

Parkes, Henry B. "The James Brothers," *Sewanee Rev.*, 56 (1948), 323-328.

Peacock, Ronald. *The Poet in the Theater.* Routledge, 1946.

Phillips, LeRoy. *Bibliography of the Writings of Henry James.* Coward McCann, 1930.

Porter, Katherine Anne. "The Days Before," *Kenyon Rev.*, 5 (Autumn, 1943), 481-494.

Pound, Ezra. "Henry James and Remy de Gourmont," *Make It New.* Yale Univ. Pr., 1935. Pp. 251-333.

——— *Instigations.* Boni, 1929.

Qvamme, B. "Henry James." *Edda* (Oslo), 44 (Jan.-June, 1944), 73-85.

Rahv, Philip. "Attitudes Toward Henry James," *New Rep.*, 108 (Feb. 15, 1943). 220-224. Repr. in *Image and Idea.* New Directions Pr., 1949. Pp. 63-70.

——— "The Heiress of All the Ages," *Partisan Rev.*, 10 (May-June, 1943), 227-247. Repr. in *Image and Idea.* New Directions Pr., 1949. Pp. 42-62.

——— Introduction. *The Great Short Novels of Henry James.* Dial Pr., 1944.

Raleigh, John. "Henry James: the Poetics of Empiricism." *P.M.L.A.*, 66 (Mar., 1951), 107-123.

Read, Herbert. "Henry James," *Collected Essays in Literary Criticism.* Faber & Faber, 1938. Pp. 354-366.

Reed, Glenn. "Another Turn on James's 'The Turn of the Screw.' " *American Lit.*, 20 (Jan., 1949), 413-423.

Richardson, Lyon. "Bibliography of Henry James," *The Question of Henry James,* edited by F. W. Dupee. Holt, 1945. Pp. 281-298.

——— editor. *Henry James: Representative Selections.* American Book, 1941. Bibliography.

Roberts, Morris. "Henry James and the Art of Foreshortening," *Rev. of English Studies*, 22 (July, 1946), 207-214.

——— *Henry James's Criticism.* Harvard Univ. Pr., 1929.

——— "Henry James's Final Period," *Yale Rev.*, 37 (1947), 60-67.

Roellinger, Francis. "Psychical Research and 'The Turn of the Screw.' " *American Lit.*, 20 (Jan., 1949), 401-412.

Rosenzweig, Saul. "The Ghost of Henry James," *Partisan Rev.*, 11 (Fall, 1944), 436-455.

Rourke, Constance. "The American," in *The Question of Henry James,* edited by F. W. Dupee. Holt, 1945. Pp. 138-159.

Rouse, Blair. "Charles Dickens and Henry James: Two Approaches to the Art of Fiction," *Nineteenth-Century Fiction*, 5 (Sept., 1950), 151-157.

Sackville-West, Edward. "James: An American in Europe." *Sat. Rev. Lit.*, 34 (Jan. 20, 1951), 24-25.

Schroeder, John. "The Mothers of Henry James." *American Lit.*, 22 (Jan., 1951), 424-431.

Short, R. W. "The Sentence Structure of Henry James," *American Lit.*, 18 (1946), 71-88.

Short, R. W. "Some Critical Terms of Henry James," *P.M.L.A.*, 65 (Sept., 1950), 667-680.

"The Significance of Henry James," *Times Lit. Suppl.* (Jan. 6, 1927).

Smith, F. E. " 'The Beast in the Jungle': The Limits of Method," *Perspective*, 1 (Autumn, 1947), 33-40.

Smith, Janet Adam, editor. *Henry James and Robert Louis Stevenson*. Macmillan, 1949.

Snell, George. *The Shapers of American Fiction*. Dutton, 1947. Pp. 129 ff.

Specker, Heidi. "The Change of Emphasis in the Criticism of Henry James." *Eng. Stud.*, 29 (Apr., 1948), 33-47.

Spender, Stephen. "The School of Experience in the Early Novels," *Hound & Horn*, 7 (Apr.-May, 1934), 417-433. Repr. in *The Destructive Element*. Cape, 1935; Houghton, 1936.

—— "A World Where the Victor Belonged to the Spoils," *New York Times Book Rev.*, Mar. 12, 1944, p. 3.

Spiller, Robert, et al. *Literary History of the United States: Vol. II*. Macmillan, 1948. III, bibliography, pp. 584-590.

Stein, Gertrude. *Four in America*. Yale Univ. Pr., 1947. Pp. 119-159.

Stevenson, Elizabeth. *The Crooked Corridor: A Study of Henry James*. Macmillan, 1949.

Stewart, Randall. "Moral Aspects of Henry James's International Situation," *University Rev.*, 9 (1943), 109-113.

Stone, Edward. "Henry James's First Novel." *Boston Public Lib. Quar.*, 2 (Apr., 1950), 167-171.

—— "A Further Note on *Daisy Miller*," *Philological Quar.*, 29 (Spring, 1950), 213-216.

—— "Henry James's Last Novel." *Philological Quar.*, 2 (Oct., 1950), 348-353.

"Symposium: In Honor of William and Henry James," *New Rep.*, 108 (Feb. 15, 1943), 215-230.

Tate, Allen. "Three Commentaries: Poe, James and Joyce," *Sewanee Rev.*, 58 (Winter, 1950), 1-15.

Tate, Allen, and Gordon, Caroline. *The House of Fiction*. Scribner's, 1950. Pp. 228-231.

Tintner, Adeline R. "The Spoils of Henry James," *P.M.L.A.*, 61 (1946), 239-251.

Trilling, Lionel. "The Princess Casamassima," *Horizon*, 17 (1948), 265-295. Repr. as the Introduction to *The Princess Casamassima*. Macmillan, 1948.

—— *The Liberal Imagination*. Viking, 1950.

Troy, William. "The Altar of Henry James," *New Rep.*, 108 (Feb. 15, 1943), 228-230.

Vivas, Eliseo. "Henry and William (Two Notes)," *Kenyon Rev.*, 5 (Autumn, 1943), 540-594.

Wade, Allan. *The Scenic Art*. Rutgers Univ. Pr., 1948.

Wagenknecht, Edward. "Our Contemporary Henry James," *College English*, 10 (1948), 123-132.

Walpole, Sir Hugh. "Henry James: A Personal Reminiscence," *Horizon*, 1 (Feb., 1940), 74-80.

Ward, A. C. *American Literature: 1880-1930*. Dial Pr.; Methuen, 1932.

Warren, Austin. "James and His Secret," *Sat Rev. Lit.*, 8 (May 28, 1932), 759.

—— "Myth and Dialectic in the Later Novels," *Kenyon Rev.*, 5 (Autumn, 1943), 551-568. Repr. as "Henry James: Symbolic Imagery in the Later Novels," in *Rage for Order*, Univ. of Chicago Pr., 1948. Pp. 142-161.

—— Repr. in *The Kenyon Critics*, edited by John Crowe Ransom, World Publishing, 1951. Pp. 42-57.

West, R. B. Jr., and Stallman, R. W. *The Art of Modern Fiction*. Rinehart, 1949. Pp. 209-217, 583-593.

West, Rebecca. *The Strange Necessity*. Doubleday, 1928.

Wharton, Edith. *A Backward Glance*. Appleton-Century, 1934.

Williams, Orlo. " 'The Ambassadors,' " *Criterion*, 8 (Sept., 1928), 47-64.

Wilson, Edmund. "The Ambiguity of Henry James," *Hound & Horn*, 7 (Apr.-May, 1934), 385-406. Repr. in *The Triple Thinkers*. Oxford Univ. Pr., 1948. Pp. 88-132. *See* Robert Heilman: " 'The Turn of the Screw' as Poem," *Univ. of Kansas City Rev.*, 14 (Summer, 1948), 277-289. Repr. in *Forms of Modern Fiction*. Univ. of Minnesota Pr., 1948. Pp. 211-228. *See* Robert Heilman: "The Freudian Reading of 'The Turn of the Screw,' " *Mod. Language Notes*, 42 (Nov., 1947), 433-445. *See* E. E. Stoll: "Symbolism in Coleridge," *P.M.L.A.*, 63 (Mar., 1948), 214-233, and "Mr. Edmund Wilson and 'The Turn of the Screw,' " *Mod. Language Notes*, 62 (May, 1947), 331 ff. *See also* Yvor Winters: *In Defense of Reason*. Wm. Morrow Pr., 1947. Pp. 317 ff. *See* Robert Wolff: "The Genesis of 'The Turn of the Screw,' " *American Lit.*, 13 (Mar., 1941), 1-18. *See* F. X. Roellinger: "Psychological Research and 'The Turn of the Screw,' " *American Lit.*, 20 (Jan., 1949), 400-412. *See* Glenn Reed: "Another Turn on James's 'The Turn of the Screw,' " *American Lit.*, 20 (Jan., 1949), 413-423.

—— "The Exploration of Henry James," *New Rep.*, 50 (Mar. 16, 1927), 112-113.

—— "The Last Phase of Henry James," *Partisan Rev.*, 4 (Feb., 1938), 3-8.

—— "Vogue of Henry James," *New Yorker*, 20 (Nov. 25, 1944), 92.

—— "New Documents on the Jameses," *New Yorker*, 23 (Dec. 13, 1947), 133-136.

Wilson, J. S. "Henry James and Herman Melville," *Virginia Quar. Rev.*, 21 (Apr., 1945), 281-286.

Winters, Yvor. "Henry James and the Relation of Morals to Manners." *American Rev.*, 9 (Oct., 1937), 482-503.

—— *Maule's Curse: Seven Studies*. New Directions Pr., 1938. Pp. 300-343.

Wolff, R. E. "The Genesis of 'The Turn of the Screw,' " *American Lit.*, 13 (Mar., 1941), 1-8.

Wyatt, Edith. "Henry James: An Impression," *Great Companions*. Appleton, 1917. Pp. 83-99.

Young, Robert. "An Error in *The Ambassadors*." *American Lit.*, 22 (Nov., 1950), 245-253.

Young, V. A. "The Question of Henry James," *Arizona Quar.*, 1 (Winter, 1945), 57-62.

Zabel, M. D. "Henry James' Place," *Nation*, 156 (Apr. 24, 1943), 596.

—— "The Poetics of Henry James," *Poetry*, 45 (Feb., 1935), 270-276. Repr. in *The Question of Henry James*, edited by W. F. Dupee. Holt, 1945. Pp. 212-217.

—— editor. *The Portable Henry James*. Viking, 1951.

JAMES JOYCE

On Joyce: Bernbaum, Ernest. "The Crucial Question Regarding *Finnegans Wake*," *College English*, 7 (Dec., 1945), 151-154.

Bishop, J. P. "Finnegans Wake," *Collected Essays*, edited by Edmund Wilson. Scribner's, 1948. Pp. 146-165.

Block, H. M. "The Critical Theory of James Joyce," *Journal of Aesthetics*, 8 (Mar., 1950), 172-184.

Brion, Marcel. "The Idea of Time in the Work of James Joyce," *Transition*, 5 (Mar., 1928).

Brooks, Cleanth, and Warren, Robert Penn. "Araby," *Understanding Fiction*. Crofts, 1943. Pp. 420-424.

Budgen, Frank. "James Joyce," *Horizon*, 3 (Feb., 1941), 104-109.

Budgen, Frank. *James Joyce and the Making of Ulysses.* Harrison Smith and Robert Haas, 1934.

Campbell, Joseph. "Finnegan the Wake," *Chimera,* 4 (Spring, 1946), 63-80. Repr. in *James Joyce: Two Decades of Criticism,* edited by Seon Givens. Vanguard Pr., 1948. Pp. 368-389.

Campbell, Joseph, and Robinson, H. M. *A Skeleton Key to Finnegans Wake.* Harcourt, 1944.

Cantwell, Robert. "Brightness Falls From the Air," *New Rep.,* 87 (Aug. 5, 1936), 375-377.

Collins, Ben. "Joyce's Haveth Childers Everywhere." *Explicator,* 10 (Dec., 1951), item 21.

Colum, Mary. *Life and the Dream.* Doubleday, 1947.

Connolly, Cyril. "The Position of Joyce," *Life and Letters,* 2 (Apr., 1929), 273-290. Repr. in *The Condemned Playground: Essays 1927-1944.* Routledge & Kegan Paul, 1945; Macmillan, 1946. Pp. 1-15.

Daiches, David. *The Novel and the Modern World.* Univ. of Chicago Pr., 1939. Pp. 101-118, 119-134, 135-157.

—— "James Joyce: The Artist as Exile," *Forms of Modern Fiction,* edited by W. Van O'Connor. University of Minnesota Pr., 1948. Pp. 61-72.

Damon, S. Foster. "The Odyssey in Dublin," *Hound & Horn,* 3 (Oct.-Dec., 1930), 7-44. Repr. (With a "Postscript, 1947") in *James Joyce: Two Decades of Criticism,* edited by Seon Givens. Vanguard Pr., 1948. Pp. 203-242.

Duff, Charles. *James Joyce and the Plain Reader.* Harmsworth, 1932.

Duncan, Edward. "Unsubstantial Father: A Study of the 'Hamlet' Symbolism in Joyce's *Ulysses,*" *Univ. of Toronto Quar.,* 19 (Jan., 1950), 126-140.

Edel, Leon. *James Joyce: The Last Journey.* The Gotham Book Mart, 1947.

Edwards, Calvin. "The Hamlet Motif in Joyce's *Ulysses,*" *Western Rev.,* 15 (Autumn, 1950), 5-13.

Eliot, T. S. *After Strange Gods.* Faber & Faber; Harcourt, 1934. Pp. 35 ff.

—— Introduction, *Introducing James Joyce: A Selection.* Faber & Faber, 1942.

—— "*Ulysses,* Order, and Myth," *Dial,* 75 (Nov., 1923), 480-483. Repr. in *Forms of Modern Fiction,* edited by W. Van O'Connor. University of Minnesota Pr., 1948. Pp. 120-124. Repr. in *James Joyce: Two Decades of Criticism,* edited by Seon Givens. Vanguard Pr., 1948. Pp. 198-202. (See pages 424-426 of this book.)

Ellmann, Richard. "Joyce and Yeats," *Kenyon Rev.,* 12 (Autumn, 1950), 618-638.

Farrell, James T. "Joyce's *A Portrait of the Artist as a Young Man,*" *The League of Frightened Philistines.* Vanguard Pr., 1945. Repr. (with a "Postscript on *Stephen Hero*") in *James Joyce: Two Decades of Criticism,* edited by Seon Givens. Vanguard Pr., 1948. Pp. 175-197.

—— "*Exiles* and Ibsen," *James Joyce: Two Decades of Criticism,* edited by Seon Givens. Vanguard Pr., 1948. Pp. 95-131.

Fergusson, Francis. Introduction, *Exiles,* by James Joyce. New Directions Pr., 1947.

Gilbert, Stuart. *James Joyce's "Ulysses."* Faber & Faber, 1930.

Givens, Seon, editor. *James Joyce: Two Decades of Criticism.* Vanguard Pr., 1948. Bibliography.

Gogarty, Oliver St. John. *As I Was Going Down Sackville Street.* Reynal & Hitchcock, 1937.

—— *Mourning Becomes Mrs. Spendlove.* Creative Age Pr., 1948.

Golding, Louis. *James Joyce.* Butterworth, 1933.

Gorman, Herbert. *James Joyce.* Farrar, 1940; Rinehart, 1940, 1948.

Halper, Nathan. "James Joyce and the Russian General." *Partisan Rev.,* 18 (July, 1951), 424-431.

Hamill, Elizabeth. *These Modern Writers: An Introduction for Modern Readers.* Georgian House (Melbourne), 1946. Chap. 7.

Hanley, Miles L. *Word Index to James Joyce's "Ulysses."* 1944, 2d ed. (Mimeographed pamphlet, Madison, Wisconsin.)

Hendry, Irene. "Joyce's Epiphanies," *Sewanee Rev.,* 54 (Summer, 1946), 449-467. Repr. in *James Joyce: Two Decades of Criticism,* edited by Seon Givens. Vanguard Pr., 1948. Pp. 27-46. (See pages 129-142 of this book.)

Higgins, Aidau. "Aspects of James Joyce," *Fortnightly Rev.,* 112 new series (Apr., 1951), 264-270.

Hoare, Dorothy M. *Some Studies in the Modern Novel.* Chatto & Windus, 1938. Pp. 133-148.

Hoffman, Frederick J. "Infroyce." *Freudianism and the Literary Mind.* Louisiana State Univ. Pr., 1945. Repr. in *James Joyce: Two Decades of Criticism,* edited by Seon Givens. Vanguard Pr., 1948. Pp. 390-435.

Hutchins, Patricia. "James Joyce on View," *Life & Letters,* 64 (Feb. 13, 1950), 123.

"James Joyce Issue," *Transition,* 9 (Mar., 1932).

Jolas, Eugene. "My Friend James Joyce," *Partisan Reader,* edited by William Phillips and Philip Rahv. Dial Pr., 1946. Pp. 457-468. Repr. in *James Joyce: Two Decades of Criticism,* edited by Seon Givens. Vanguard Pr., 1948. Pp. 3-18.

—— editor. *Our Exagmination Round his Factification for Incamination of Work in Progress.* Shakespeare & Co., 1929. Repr. as *An Exagmination of James Joyce.* New Directions Pr., 1939.

Jolas, Maria, editor. *James Joyce Yearbook.* Paris, 1949.

Joyce, Stanislaus. "James Joyce: A Memoir," *Hudson Rev.,* 2 (Winter, 1950), 485-515.

Kain, Richard M. *Fabulous Voyager, James Joyce's "Ulysses."* Univ. of Chicago Pr., 1947.

Kelly, R. G. "James Joyce: A Partial Explanation," *P.M.L.A.,* 65 (Mar., 1949), 26-39.

Kenner, Hugh. "Baker St. to Eccles St.," *Hudson Rev.,* 1 (Winter, 1949), 481-500.

—— "A Communication on James and Stanislaus Joyce," *Hudson Rev.,* 3 (Spring, 1950), 157-160.

—— "Joyce and Ibsen's Naturalism," *Sewanee Rev.,* 59 (Jan.-Mar., 1951), 75-96.

—— "The *Portrait* in Perspective," *Kenyon Rev.,* 10 (Summer, 1948), 361-381. Repr. in *James Joyce: Two Decades of Criticism,* edited by Seon Givens. Vanguard Pr., 1948. Pp. 132-174.

Klein, A. M. "The Black Panther—A Study of Joyce," *Accent,* 10 (Spring, 1950), 139-154.

Larbaud, Valéry. "The 'Ulysses' of James Joyce," *Criterion,* 1 (Oct., 1922), 94-103.

Leavis, F. R. "Joyce and 'The Revolution of the Word'" (critical commentary and review of Joyce's *Work in Progress*), *Scrutiny,* 2 (Sept., 1933), 193-201.

Levin, Harry. "Joyce's Sentimental Journey Through France and Italy," *Yale Rev.,* 38 (Summer, 1949), 664-672.

—— "On First Looking Into *Finnegans Wake,*" *New Directions in Prose and Poetry.* New Directions Pr., 1939.

—— (ed.). Introduction, *The Portable James Joyce.* Viking, 1947.

—— *James Joyce, A Critical Introduction.* New Directions Pr., 1941. (See pages 143-159 of this book for section 2, Part II.)

Levin, Richard, and Shattuck, Charles. "First Flight to Ithaca—A New Reading of Joyce's *Dubliners,*" *Accent,* 4 (Winter, 1944), 75-100. Repr. in

James Joyce: Two Decades of Criticism, edited by Seon Givens. Vanguard Pr., 1948. Pp. 47-94.

Lewis, Wyndham. *Time and the Western Man.* Chatto & Windus, 1927.

Lindsay, Jack. "James Joyce," *Scrutinies II,* edited by Edgell Rickword. Wishart, 1931. Pp. 100-121.

Miller, Henry. *The Cosmological Eye.* New Directions Pr., 1939.

Monnier, Adrienne. "Joyce's *Ulysses* and the French Public," *Kenyon Rev.,* 8 (Summer, 1946), 430-444.

More, Paul Elmer. "James Joyce," *American Rev.,* 5 (1935), 129-157.

Muir, Edwin. "James Joyce: The Meaning of *Ulysses,*" *Calendar of Modern Letters,* 1 (July, 1925), 347-355.

Nicholson, Norman. *Man & Literature.* Macmillan, 1943.

O'Hegarty, P. S. "Bibliography of Joyce," *Dublin Rev.,* 436 (Jan., 1946).

Parker, Alan. *James Joyce: A Bibliography.* F. W. Faxon Co., 1948.

Pound, Ezra. "James Joyce et Pécuchet," *Polite Essays.* Faber & Faber, 1937. Pp. 82-97.

Prescott, Joseph. "James Joyce: A Study in Words." *P.M.L.A.,* 54 (Mar., 1939), 304-315.

—— "Homer's *Odyssey* and Joyce's *Ulysses.*" *Mod. Language Quar.,* 3 (Sept., 1942), 427-444.

—— "James Joyce." *Encyclopaedia Britannica* (1947). Vol. 13, pp. 159-160.

Ransom, J. C. "The Aesthetic of *Finnegans Wake,*" *Kenyon Rev.,* 1 (Oct., 1939), 424-428.

Robinson, H. M., and Campbell, Joseph. "Unlocking the Door to Joyce," *Sat. Rev. Lit.,* 26 (June 19, 1943), pp. 4, 5, 6, 28.

Rothman, Nathan. "Thomas Wolfe and James Joyce," *A Southern Vanguard,* edited by Allen Tate. Prentice-Hall, 1947. Pp. 52-77.

Savage, D. S. "James Joyce," *The Withered Branch.* Eyre and Spottiswoode, 1950. Pp. 156-200.

Schorer, Mark. "Technique as Discovery," Hudson Rev., 1 (Spring, 1948), 67-87. Repr. in *Forms of Modern Fiction,* edited by W. Van O'Connor. University of Minnesota Pr., 1948. Pp. 9-29.

Smith, P. J. *A Key to the "Ulysses" of James Joyce.* Covici, Friede, 1934.

"Special James Joyce Number," *Envoy,* 5 (Apr., 1951).

Spencer, Theodore. "*Stephen Hero:* The Unpublished Manuscript of James Joyce's *A Portrait of the Artist as a Young Man,*" *Southern Rev.,* 7 (Summer, 1941), 174-186. Repr. as the Introduction to *Stephen Hero.* New Directions Pr., 1944.

Stoll, E. E. *From Shakespeare to Joyce.* Doubleday Doran, 1944.

Strong, L. A. G. "James Joyce," *The English Novelists,* edited by Derek Verschoyle. Harcourt, 1936.

—— "James Joyce and the New Fiction." *Amer. Mercury,* 35 (Aug., 1935), 433-437.

—— *The Sacred River.* Pellegrini and Cudahy, 1951.

Stuart, Michael. "Mr. Joyce's Word—Creatures," *Symposium,* 2 (Oct., 1931), 459-468.

Taplin, Walter. "James Joyce Wrote English," *The Critic,* 1 (Spring, 1947), 11-17.

Tate, Allen. "Three Commentaries: Poe, James and Joyce," *Sewanee Rev.,* 58 (Winter, 1950), 1-15.

Tate, Allen, and Gordon, Caroline. *The House of Fiction.* Scribner's, 1950. Pp. 279-282.

Thompson, Francis. "A Portrait of the Artist Asleep," *Western Rev.,* 14 (Summer, 1950), 245-253.

Tindall, W. Y. "Dante and Mrs. Bloom." *Accent,* 11 (Spring, 1951), 85-92.

Tindall, W. Y. *James Joyce: His Way of Interpreting the Modern World.* Scribner's, 1950.

Waldock, A. J., Howarth, R. G., and Dobson, E. J. *Some Developments in English Literature. A Series of ... Lectures on James Joyce, Edith Sitwell, T. S. Eliot.* Sidney, 1935; Williams & Norgate, 1937.

West, Rebecca. "The Strange Case of James Joyce." *Bookman,* 68 (1928), 9-23.

—— *The Strange Necessity.* Doubleday, 1928.

Wilder, T. N. *James Joyce: 1882-1941.* Limited ed., Aurora, N. Y., 1944.

Williams, Raymond. "The *Exiles* of James Joyce," *Politics and Letters,* 1 (Summer, 1948), 13-21.

Wilson, Edmund. "The Dream of H. C. Earwicker," *The Wound and the Bow.* Oxford Univ. Pr., 1947. Repr. in *James Joyce: Two Decades of Criticism,* edited by Seon Givens. Vanguard Pr., 1948. Pp. 319-342. (See pages 160-175 of this book.)

—— "James Joyce," *Axel's Castle.* Scribner's, 1931. Pp. 191-236.

D. H. LAWRENCE

LAWRENCE, D. H. *Assorted Articles.* Secker & Warburg; Knopf, 1930.

—— *D. H. Lawrence's Letters to Bertrand Russell,* edited and with an introduction by Harry T. Moore. Gotham Book Mart, 1948.

—— *The Letters,* edited by Aldous Huxley. Heinemann; Viking, 1932, 1937.

—— *Phoenix: Posthumous Papers,* edited by E. McDonald. Heinemann; Viking, 1936.

—— *Studies in Classic American Literature.* Boni, 1923. Repr. in *The Shock of Recognition,* edited by Edmund Wilson. Doubleday, 1943.

On Lawrence: Aldington, Richard. *D. H. Lawrence.* Chatto & Windus, 1930.

Alexander, H. "Lawrence and Huxley," *Queen's Quar.,* 42 (Feb., 1935), 96-108.

Anderson, Sherwood. "A Man's Mind," *New Rep.,* 63 (May, 1930), 22-23.

——Auden, W. H. "Some Notes on D. H. Lawrence," *Nation,* 164 (Apr., 1947), 482-484.

Bentley, Eric. *A Century of Hero Worship.* Lippincott, 1944.

Bishop, J. P. *Collected Essays,* edited by Edmund Wilson. Scribner's, 1948.

Blackmur, R. P. "D. H. Lawrence and Expressive Form," *Double Agent,* Arrow Editions, 1935. Pp. 103-120.

Brett, Dorothy. *Lawrence and Brett.* Lippincott, 1933.

Burgum, E. B. *The Novel and the World's Dilemma.* Oxford Univ. Pr., 1947.

Burrell, Angus. "D. H. Lawrence: *Sons and Lovers,*" *Modern Fiction.* Columbia Univ. Pr., 1934. Pp. 137-154. First issued as *Dead Reckonings in Fiction,* by Dorothy Brewster and Angus Burrell. Longmans Green, 1924.

Bynner, Witter. *Journey with Genius: Recollections and Reflections Concerning the D. H. Lawrences.* John Day, 1951.

Carswell, Catherine. *The Savage Pilgrimage.* Harcourt, 1932.

Carter, Frederick. *The Dragon of Revelation.* Harmsworth, 1931.

—— *D. H. Lawrence and the Body Mystical.* Archer, 1932.

Collins, Clifford. "The Letters of D. H. Lawrence," *Politics & Letters,* 1 (Summer, 1947), 6-12.

Coombes, H. "D. H. Lawrence Placed" (letter), *Scrutiny,* 16 (March, 1949), 44-48.

—— *Lawrence and Apocalypse.* Heinemann, 1933.

Dobrée, Bonamy. *The Lamp and the Lute.* Clarendon Pr., 1929. Pp. 86 ff.

Eliot, T. S. *After Strange Gods.* Faber & Faber; Harcourt, 1934. Pp. 35 ff.

Fergusson, Francis. "D. H. Lawrence's Sensibility," *Forms of Modern Fiction.* University of Minnesota Pr., 1948. Pp. 72-79. Repr. from *Hound & Horn,* 4 (1933). (See pages 328-339 of this book.)

Ford, F. M. "D. H. Lawrence," *Portraits From Life*. Houghton, 1937. Pp. 70-89.
—— *Return to Yesterday*. Liveright, 1932.
Fox, Ralph. *The Novel and the People*. Lawrence & Wishart, 1937; International Publishers, 1945.
Fraenkel, Michael. *Death is Not Enough*. Daniel, 1936.
Garnett, Edward. "Mr. D. H. Lawrence," *Friday Nights*. Knopf, 1922. Pp. 145-160.
Ghiselin, Brewster. "D. H. Lawrence," *Western Rev.*, 11 (Spring, 1947), 150-159.
Greene, Thomas. "Lawrence and the Quixotic Hero," *Sewanee Rev.*, 59 (Autumn, 1951), 559-573.
Gregory, Horace. "D. H. Lawrence: Posthumous Reputation," *Makers and Ancestors*. Covici, Friede, 1937.
—— *Pilgrim of the Apocalypse: A Critical Study*. Viking, 1933.
Hamill, Elizabeth. *These Modern Writers: An Introduction for Modern Readers*. Georgian House (Melbourne), 1946. Chap. 6.
Hoare, Dorothy. "The Novels of D. H. Lawrence," *Some Studies in the Modern Novel*. Chatto & Windus, 1938.
Hoffman, Frederick. *Freudianism and the Literary Mind*. Louisiana State Univ. Pr., 1945.
—— "From Surrealism to *The Apocalypse*: A Development in Twentieth Century Irrationalism," *English Lit. Hist.*, 15 (June, 1948), 147-165.
Howe, Irving. "Sherwood Anderson and D. H. Lawrence." *Furioso*, 5 (Fall, 1950), 21-33.
Huxley, Aldous. Introduction, *The Letters of D. H. Lawrence*. Heinemann, 1932.
—— *The Olive Tree*. Harper, 1937. Pp. 215-216.
Kenmare, Dallas. *Fire-Bird: A Study of D. H. Lawrence*. James Barrie, 1951.
Kingsmill, Hugh. *The Life of D. H. Lawrence*. Dodge, 1938.
Krutch, J. W. "D. H. Lawrence: The Man and His Work," *Nation*, 130 (Mar. 19, 1930), 320.
Lawrence, Frieda. *Not I, But the Wind*. Rydal Pr.; Viking; Dodge Publishing, 1934.
Leavis, F. R. *D. H. Lawrence*. Minority Pr., 1932.
—— In *Importance of Scrutiny*, edited by Eric Bentley. Stewart, 1948. Pp. 338-343.
—— "The Novel as Dramatic Poem: 'St. Mawr,'" *Scrutiny*, 17 (Spring, 1949), 38-53.
Lewis, Wyndham. *Men Without Art*. Cassell; Harcourt, 1934.
Luhan, Mabel Dodge. *Lorenzo in Taos*. Knopf, 1932.
MacCarthy, Desmond. *Criticism*. Putnam, 1932.
Malraux, André. "Preface to *Lady Chatterley's Lover*," *Criterion*, 12 (Jan., 1933), 215-219.
McDonald, D. *A Bibliography of the Writings of D. H. Lawrence*. Foreword by D. H. Lawrence. Centaur Book, 1925.
—— *A Bibliography of the Writings, 1925-1930*. Centaur Book, 1931.
Megroz, R. L. *Five Novelist Poets of To-day*. Joiner, 1933.
Merrild, Knud. *A Poet and Two Painters: A Memoir of D. H. Lawrence*. Viking Pr., 1939.
Moore, Harry T. "Another Side of D. H. Lawrence," *Reading and Collecting*, 1 (April, 1937), 506.
—— Introduction. *D. H. Lawrence's Letters to Bertrand Russell*. Gotham Book Mart, 1948.
—— "New Light on D. H. Lawrence," *Spectator* (London, Sept. 29, 1950).
—— "The Great Unread," *Sat. Rev. Lit.*, 21 (Mar. 2, 1940) 8.

Moore, Harry T. *The Life and Works of D. H. Lawrence.* Twayne Publishers, 1951; Allen & Unwin, 1951.
—— "The Status of D. H. Lawrence," *New Republic* 97 (Dec. 21, 1938), 210-211.
—— "Why Not Read Lawrence Too?" *Portfolio* 5 (Vol. 2; Washington and Paris, Spring, 1947).
Muller, Herbert. *Modern Fiction.* Funk & Wagnalls, 1937.
Murry, J. M. *D. H. Lawrence.* Cambridge Univ. Pr., 1930.
—— *The Son of Woman: The Story of D. H. Lawrence.* Cape, 1931. Rev'd by T. S. Eliot in *Criterion*, 10 (July, 1931), 768-774.
—— *Reminiscences of D. H. Lawrence.* Cape, 1933.
—— *The Autobiography of John Middleton Murry: Between Two Worlds.* Cape, 1935; Messner, 1936.
New Adelphi, 3 (June-Aug., 1930), "D. H. Lawrence Issue."
Nicholson, Norman. *Man & Literature.* Macmillan, 1943.
Parkes, H. B. "D. H. Lawrence and Irving Babbitt." *Adelphi*, 9 (Mar., 1935), 328-331.
Phoenix, edited by J. P. Cooney. I (1938). Contains "An Open Letter to Mr. Tindall," by Frieda Lawrence; article by Henry Miller; poems and stories by D. H. Lawrence; etc.
Potter, Stephen. *D. H. Lawrence: A First Study.* Cape; Harrison Smith, 1930.
Quennell, Peter. "The Later Period of D. H. Lawrence," *Scrutinies, II*, edited by Edgell Rickword. Wishart, 1931. Pp. 124 ff.
Roberts, J. H. "Huxley and Lawrence," *Virg. Quar. Rev.*, 13 (Autumn, 1937), 546-557.
Rosenfeld, Paul. "D. H. Lawrence," *New Rep.*, 62 (Mar. 26, 1930), 155-56.
Savage, D. S. "D. H. Lawrence: A Study in Dissolution," *The Personal Principle.* Routledge, 1944.
Swinnerton, Frank. *The Georgian Scene.* Farrar & Rinehart, 1934. Pp. 401-415 and *passim*.
T., E. *D. H. Lawrence: A Personal Record.* Cape, 1935; Knight Publ., 1936.
Tate, Allen, and Gordon, Caroline. *The House of Fiction.* Scribner's, 1950. Pp. 348-351.
Tedlock, E. W. Jr., editor. *The Frieda Lawrence Collection of D. H. Lawrence's Manuscripts.* Univ. of New Mexico Pr., 1948.
Thomas, John Heywood. "The Perversity of D. H. Lawrence," *Criterion*, 10 (Oct., 1950), 5-22.
Tindall, W. Y. *D. H. Lawrence and Susan His Cow.* Columbia Univ. Pr., 1939.
—— *Forces in Modern British Literature.* Knopf, 1947.
Tiverton, William. *D. H. Lawrence and Human Existence.* Foreword by T. S. Eliot. Rockliff; Philosophical Library, 1951.
Trilling, Diana. Introduction. *The Portable D. H. Lawrence.* Viking, 1947.
Trilling, Lionel. "D. H. Lawrence," *Symposium*, 1 (July, 1930), 361-370.
Troy, William. "The D. H. Lawrence Myth," *The Partisan Reader*, edited by William Phillips and Philip Rahv. Dial Pr., 1946. Pp. 336-347.
Vivas, Eliseo, "Lawrence's Problems," *Kenyon Rev.*, 3 (Winter, 1941), 83-94.
West, Anthony. *D. H. Lawrence.* Arthur Barker, 1951.
West, Rebecca. *D. H. Lawrence.* Secker & Warburg, 1930.
White, William. *D. H. Lawrence Bibliography.* Wayne Univ. Pr., 1951.
Woolf, Virginia. *The Common Reader.* Combined edition. Harcourt, 1947.

KATHERINE ANNE PORTER

PORTER, KATHERINE ANNE. Introduction: *Flowering Judas.* Random House (Modern Library).

On Porter: Baker, Howard. "Some Notes on New Fiction," *Southern Rev.*, 1 (July, 1935), 178-191

Brooks, Cleanth, and Warren, Robert Penn. "Old Mortality," *Understanding Fiction*. Crofts, 1943. Pp. 529-535.

Buckman, Gertrude. "Miss Porter's New Stories," *Partisan Rev.*, 12 (Winter, 1945), 134 ff.

Hartley, Lodwick. "Katherine Anne Porter," *Sewanee Rev.*, 48 (Apr.-June, 1940), 206-216.

Herbst, Josephine. "Miss Porter and Miss Stein," *Partisan Rev.*, 15 (May, 1948), 568-572.

Kazin, Alfred. *On Native Grounds*. Reynal & Hitchcock, 1942. Pp. 248, 466.

Marshall, Margaret. "Writers in the Wilderness: Katherine Anne Porter," *Nation*, 150 (Apr. 13, 1940), 473-475.

Tate, Allen. "A Fully Matured Art," *Nation*, 131 (Oct. 1, 1930), 352-353.

Warren, R. P. "Katherine Anne Porter," *Kenyon Rev.*, 4 (Winter, 1942), 29-42.

West, R. B. Jr. "Katherine Anne Porter: Symbol and Theme in 'Flowering Judas,' " *Accent*, 7 (Spring, 1947), 182-188. Repr. in *The Art of Modern Fiction*, by R. B. West Jr., and R. W. Stallman. Rinehart, 1949. Pp. 287-292. (See pages 217-230 of this book.)

Wilson, Edmund. *Classics and Commercials*. Farrar Straus, 1950.

ROBERT PENN WARREN

On Warren: Baker, J. E. "Irony in Fiction: *All the King's Men*," *College English*, 9 (Dec., 1947), 122-130.

Bentley, Eric. "The Meaning of Robert Penn Warren's Novels," *Kenyon Rev.*, 10 (Summer, 1948), 407-424. Repr. in *Forms of Modern Fiction*, edited by W. Van O'Connor. University of Minnesota Pr., 1948. Pp. 269-286.

Brantley, Frederick. "The Achievement of Robert Penn Warren." *Modern American Poetry*, edited by B. Rajan. Dobson, 1950. Pp. 66-80.

Daniels, Jonathan. "Scraping the Bottom of Southern Life," (rev. of *At Heaven's Gate*), *Sat. Rev. Lit.*, 26 (Aug. 21, 1943) , p. 6.

Dillin, Edward. "Mighty Like Despair" (rev. of *At Heaven's Gate*), *Commonweal*, 38 (Aug. 6, 1943), 398 ff.

Frank, Joseph. "Romanticism and Reality in Robert Penn Warren," *Hudson Rev.*, 4 (Summer, 1951), 248-258.

Frohock, W. M. "Mr. Warren's Albatross." *Southwest Rev.*, 36 (Winter, 1951), 48-59.

Garrigue, Jean. "Many Ways of Evil" (rev. of *At Heaven's Gate*), *Kenyon Rev.*, 6 (Winter, 1944), 135-138.

Girault, Norton R. "The Narrator's Mind as Symbol: An Analysis of *All the King's Men*," *Accent*, 7 (Summer, 1947), 220-234. (See pages 200-216 of this book.)

Heilman, Robert. "Melpomene as Wallflower; or the Reading of Tragedy," *Sewanee Rev.*, 55 (Winter, 1947), 154-166.

Hendry, Irene. "The Regional Novel: The Example of Robert Penn Warren," *Sewanee Rev.*, 53 (Winter, 1945), 84-102.

Humbolt, Charles. "The Lost Cause of Robert Penn Warren." *Masses & Mainstream*, 1 (July, 1948), 8-23.

Hynes, Sam. "R. P. Warren: The Symbolic Journey," *Univ. Kansas City Rev.*, 17 (Summer, 1951), 279-285.

Mizener, Arthur. "Amphibium in Old Kentucky." *Kenyon Rev.*, 12 (Autumn, 1950), 697-701.

O'Connor, W. Van. "Robert Penn Warren's Short Fiction," *Western Rev.*, 12 (Summer, 1948), 251-253.

Stallman, R. W. "Robert Penn Warren: A Checklist of His Critical Writings."
Univ. Kansas City Rev., 14 (Autumn, 1947), 78-83.

EUDORA WELTY

On Welty: Brooks, Cleanth, and Warren, Robert Penn. "Old Mr. Marblehall,"
Understanding Fiction. Crofts, 1948. Pp. 479-480.

Glenn, Eunice. "Fantasy in the Fiction of Eudora Welty," in *A Southern Vanguard,* edited by Allen Tate. Prentice-Hall, 1947. Pp. 78-91. (See pages
506-517 of this book.)

Porter, Katherine Anne. Introduction, *A Curtain of Green,* by Eudora Welty.
Doubleday, 1941.

Van Gelder, Robert, editor. *Writers and Writing.* Scribner's, 1946. Pp. 287-290.

Warren, Robert Penn. "The Love and the Separateness in Miss Welty," *Kenyon Rev.*, 6 (Spring, 1944), 246-259.

West, R. B. Jr., and Stallman, R. W. *The Art of Modern Fiction.* Rinehart,
1949. Pp. 403-408.

THOMAS WOLFE

WOLFE, THOMAS. *A Western Journal.* University of Pittsburgh Pr., 1950.

—— "Portrait of a Literary Critic," in *The Hills Beyond.* Sun Dial Pr., 1943.

—— "Something of My Life." *Sat. Rev. Lit.,* 31 (Feb. 7, 1948), 6-8.

—— "What a Writer Reads." *Book Buyer,* 1 (Dec., 1935), 13-14.

On Wolfe: Adams, J. D. *The Writer's Responsibility.* Secker & Warburg, 1946.
Pp. 99-103 and *passim.*

Ames, R. S. "Wolfe, Wolfe!" *Amer. Spectator,* 3 (Jan., 1935), 5-6.

Armstrong, Anne. "As I Saw Thomas Wolfe," *Arizona Quar.,* 1 (Spring, 1945).

Bates, E. S. "Thomas Wolfe." *Modern Quar.,* 11 (Fall, 1938), 86-88.

Beach, J. W. "Thomas Wolfe: The Search for a Father," *American Fiction:
1920-1940.* Macmillan, 1941, 1948. Pp. 173-215.

Bishop, J. P. "The Sorrows of Thomas Wolfe," *Kenyon Rev.,* 1 (Winter, 1939),
7-17. Repr. in *The Collected Essays of John Peale Bishop,* edited by
Edmund Wilson. Scribner's, 1948. Pp. 129-137. (See pages 362-369 of this
book.)

Blackmur, R. P. "Notes on the Novel: 1936," *Expense of Greatness.* Arrow
Editions, 1940.

Bridges, A. P. "Thomas Wolfe," *Sat. Rev. Lit.,* 11 (Apr. 6, 1935), 599, 609.

Burgum, E. B. *The Novel and the World's Dilemma.* Oxford Univ. Pr., 1947.

—— "Thomas Wolfe's Discovery of America," *Virginia Quar. Rev.,* 22 (Summer, 1946).

Canby, H. S. "The River of Youth," *Sat. Rev. Lit.,* 11 (Mar. 9, 1935), 529-530.

Church, Margaret. "Thomas Wolfe: Dark Time," *P.M.L.A.,* 64 (Dec., 1949),
629-638.

Cowley, Malcolm. "Thomas Wolfe's Legacy," *New Rep.,* 99 (July 19, 1939),
311-312.

Cross, Neal. "Thomas Wolfe: If I am Not Better," *Pacific Spectator,* 4 (Autumn, 1950), 488-496.

Geismar, Maxwell. Introduction, *The Portable Thomas Wolfe.* Viking.

—— *Writers in Crisis.* Houghton, 1942. Chap. 5.

Jack, Peter Monro. "Remembering Thomas Wolfe." *New York Times Book
Rev.,* Oct. 2, 1938. Pp. 2, 28.

Johnson, P. H. *Hungry Gulliver.* Scribner's, 1948.

Kazin, Alfred. *On Native Grounds.* Reynal & Hitchcock, 1942. Pp. 118, 370,
and *passim.* Chap. 15.

Muller, Herbert. *Thomas Wolfe.* New Directions Pr., 1947.

Preston, G. R. Jr. *Thomas Wolfe: A Bibliography*. C. S. Boesen, 1943.

Rothman, Nathan. "Thomas Wolfe and James Joyce," *A Southern Vanguard*, edited by Allen Tate. Prentice-Hall, 1947. Pp. 52-77.

Snell, George. "The Education of Thomas Wolfe." *The Shapers of American Fiction*. Dutton, 1947. Pp. 173-187.

Solon, S. L. "The Ordeal of Thomas Wolfe," *Modern Quar.*, 11 (Winter, 1939), 45-53.

Warren, R. P. "The Hamlet of Thomas Wolfe," *American Rev.*, 5 (Sept., 1935), 191-208. Repr. in *Literary Opinion in America*, edited by M. D. Zabel. Harper, 1937. Pp. 359-372. 1951, Rev. ed.

VIRGINIA WOOLF

WOOLF, VIRGINIA. *The Common Reader*. Hogarth Pr., 1925, 1929.

—— *The Second Common Reader*. Hogarth Pr.; Harcourt, 1932, 1947.

On Woolf: Aiken, Conrad. "The Novel as a Work of Art" (*To the Lighthouse*), *Dial*, 83 (July, 1927), 41-44.

Beach, J. W. *The Twentieth Century Novel*. Appleton Century, 1932. Pp. 485-500.

—— "Virginia Woolf," *English Journal*, 26 (Oct., 1937), 603-612.

Beck, Warren. "For Virginia Woolf," *American Prefaces*, 7 (Summer, 1942), 316-327. Repr. in *Forms of Modern Fiction*, edited by W. Van O'Connor. University of Minnesota Pr., 1948. Pp. 243-253.

Bell, Clive. "Virginia Woolf," *Dial*, 76 (Dec., 1924), 451-465.

Bennett, Arnold. *Savour of Life: Essays in Gusto*. Doubleday Doran, 1928. Pp. 293-313.

Bennett, Joan. *Virginia Woolf: Her Art as a Novelist*. Harcourt, 1945.

Blackstone, Bernard. *Virginia Woolf*. Hogarth Pr., 1948; Harcourt, 1949.

Bowen, Elizabeth. "The Achievement of Virginia Woolf," *New York Times Book Rev.*, June 26, 1949, pp. 1, 21.

Brace, Marjorie. "Understanding Solid Objects: The Pagan World of Virginia Woolf," *Accent Anthology*, edited by Kerker Quinn. Harcourt, 1946. Pp. 489-495.

Bradbrook, M. C. "Notes on the Style of Mrs. Woolf," *Scrutiny*, 1 (May, 1932), 33-38.

Brooks, B. G. "Virginia Woolf," *Nineteenth Century and After*, 130 (Dec., 1941), 334-340.

Burgum, E. B. *The Novel and the World's Dilemma*. Oxford Univ. Pr., 1947.

—— "Virginia Woolf and the Empty Room," *Antioch Rev.*, 7 (Dec., 1943), 596-611.

Burra, Peter. "Virginia Woolf," *Nineteenth Century and After*, 115 (Jan., 1934), 112-125.

Cecil, David. "Virginia Woolf and E. M. Forster," *Poets and Story-Tellers*. Macmillan, 1948. Pp. 156-201.

Chambers, R. L. *The Novels of Virginia Woolf: A Critical Study*. Oliver & Boyd, 1947.

Cowley, Malcolm. "England Under Glass," *New Rep.*, 105 (Oct. 6, 1941), 440.

Cunliffe, J. W. *English Novelists in the Twentieth Century*. Macmillan, 1933. Pp. 201-258.

Daiches, David. "Virginia Woolf," *The Novel and the Modern World*. Univ. of Chicago Pr., 1939. Pp. 158-187. (See pages 488-505 of this book.)

—— *Virginia Woolf*. New Directions Pr., 1942.

Derbyshire, S. H. "An Analysis of Mrs. Woolf's *To the Lighthouse*," *College English*, 3 (Jan., 1942), 353-360.

Drew, Elizabeth. *The Modern Novel*. Harcourt, 1926. Pp. 254-262.

Edgar, Pelham. *Art of the Novel.* Macmillan, 1933. Pp. 320-337.

Empson, William. "Virginia Woolf," *Scrutinies II,* edited by Edgell Rickword. Wishart, 1931.

Forster, E. M. "The Novels of Virginia Woolf," *Criterion,* 4 (Apr., 1926), 277-286. Repr. in *Yale Rev.,* 15 (Apr., 1926), 505-514.

—— "The Early Novels of Virginia Woolf," *Abinger Harvest.* Harcourt, 1936. Pp. 106-114.

—— "The Art of Virginia Woolf," *Atlantic,* 170 (Sept., 1942), 82-90.

—— *Aspects of the Novel.* Harcourt, 1927; 1947. Pp. 34-37.

Grabo, Carl. *The Technique of the Novel.* Scribner's, 1928. Pp. 297-306.

Grant, Duncan. "Virginia Woolf," *Horizon,* 3 (June, 1941), 402-406.

Gregory, Horace. *The Shield of Achilles.* Harcourt, 1944. Pp. 188-193.

Hamill, Elizabeth. "Katherine Mansfield and Virginia Woolf," *These Modern Writers: An Introduction for Modern Readers.* Georgian House (Melbourne), 1946. Chap. 8.

Henderson, Philip. *The Novel Today.* Lane (Bodley Head), 1936. Pp. 87-91.

Hoare, Dorothy M. *Some Studies in the Modern Novel.* Chatto & Windus, 1938. Pp. 36-67.

Holtby, W. *Virginia Woolf.* Wishart, 1932.

Johnson, R. B. *Some Contemporary Novelists: Women.* Parsons, 1920. Pp. 147-160.

Jones, E. B. "E. M. Forster and Virginia Woolf," *English Novelists,* edited by Derek Verschoyle. Harcourt, 1936. Pp. 281-287.

Josephson, Matthew. "Virginia Woolf and the Modern Novel," *New Rep.,* 66 (Apr. 15, 1931), 239-241.

Kronenberger, L. "Virginia Woolf as Critic," *Nation,* 155 (Oct. 17, 1942), 382-385.

Lawrence, M. A. *School of Femininity.* Stokes, 1936. Pp. 339-382.

Leavis, F. R. "After *To the Lighthouse*" (rev. of *Between the Acts*), *Scrutiny,* 10 (January, 1942), 295-298.

Leavis, Q. D. "Caterpillars of the Commonwealth Unite," *The Importance of Scrutiny,* edited by Eric Bentley. Stewart, 1948. Pp. 382-391.

Lewis, Wyndham. "Virginia Woolf," *Men Without Art.* Cassell, 1934. Pp. 158-171.

Mansfield, Katherine. *Novels and Novelists,* edited by J. M. Murry. Knopf, 1930.

Mellers, W. H. "Mrs. Woolf and Life" (rev. of *The Years*), *Scrutiny,* 6 June, 1937, 71-75. Repr. in *The Importance of Scrutiny,* edited by Eric Bentley. Stewart, 1948. Pp. 378-382.

—— "Virginia Woolf: The Last Phase," *Kenyon Rev.,* 4 (Autumn, 1942), 381-387.

Monroe, N. E. "Experimental Humanism in Virginia Woolf," *The Novel and Society.* University of North Carolina Pr., 1941. Pp. 188-224.

—— "The Inception of Mrs. Woolf's Art," *College English,* 2 (Dec., 1940), 217-230.

Muir, Edwin. *The Structure of the Novel.* Hogarth Pr., 1928, 1947. Pp. 131-133.

—— "Virginia Woolf," *Bookman,* 74 (Dec., 1931), 362-367.

—— "Virginia Woolf," *Nation,* 122 (June 30, 1926), 721-723.

—— "Virginia Woolf," *Transition: Essays on Contemporary Literature.* Viking, 1926. Pp. 67-82.

Muller, H. J. "Virginia Woolf and Feminine Fiction," *Modern Fiction.* Funk & Wagnalls, 1937. Pp. 317-328.

Newton, D. *Virginia Woolf.* Melbourne Univ. Pr., 1942.

Overcarsh, F. L., "Virginia Woolf," *Accent,* 10 (Winter, 1950), 107-122.

Quennell, Peter. "A Letter on Virginia Woolf," *Hogarth Letters No. 2.* Hogarth Pr., 1932.

Rahv, Philip. "Mrs. Woolf and Mrs. Brown," *Image and Idea.* New Directions Pr., 1949. Pp. 139-143.

Read, Herbert. *Reason and Romanticism.* Faber & Guyer, 1926. Chap. 11.

Roberts, John. "Toward Virginia Woolf," *Virginia Quar. Rev.,* 10 (Oct., 1934), 587-602.

—— "End of the English Novel?" *Virginia Quar. Rev.,* 13 (1937), 437-439.

—— "'Vision and Design' in Virginia Woolf," *P.M.L.A.,* 61 (Sept., 1946), 835-847.

Russell, H. K. "Virginia Woolf's *To the Lighthouse,*" *Explicator,* 8 (Mar., 1950).

Savage, D. S. "The Mind of Virginia Woolf," *South Atlantic Quar.,* 46 (Oct., 1947), 556-573.

—— "Virginia Woolf," *The Withered Branch.* Eyre and Spottiswoode, 1950. Pp. 70-105.

Schorer, Mark. "The Chronicle of Doubt," *Virginia Quar. Rev.,* 18 (Spring, 1942), 200-215.

Smart, J. A. "Virginia Woolf," *Dalhousie Rev.,* 21 (1921), 37-50.

Spencer, Theodore. "Mrs. Woolf's Novels," *New Rep.,* 113 (Dec. 3, 1945), 758.

Tindall, W. Y. *Forces in Modern British Literature.* Knopf, 1947. Pp. 283-317.

—— "Many-Leveled Fiction: Virginia Woolf to Ross Lockridge," *College English,* 10 (Nov., 1948), 65-71.

Toynbee, Philip. "Virginia Woolf: A Study of Three Experimental Novels," *Horizon,* 14 (Nov., 1946), 290-304.

Troy, William. "Virginia Woolf: The Poetic Style," Part I, *Symposium,* 3 (January, 1932), 53-63. Part II, *Symposium,* 3 (Apr., 1932), 153-166. Repr. in *Literary Opinion in America,* edited by M. D. Zabel. Harper, 1937, 340-358. 1951, rev. ed.

Turnell, M. "Virginia Woolf," *Horizon,* 3 (July, 1942).

"Virginia Woolf" (tributes by four authors), *Horizon,* 3 (May, 1941).

—— Eliot, T. S. Pp. 313-316.

—— Macaulay, Rose. Pp. 316-318.

—— West, V. S. Pp. 318-323.

—— Plomer, William. Pp. 323-327.

Wagenknecht, Edward. *Cavalcade of the English Novel.* Holt, 1943. Pp. 505-532.

West, Rebecca. "Autumn and Virginia Woolf," *Ending in Earnest.* Doubleday Doran, 1931. Pp. 208-213.

Wilson, J. S. "Time and Virginia Woolf," *Virginia Quar. Rev.,* 18 (Spring, 1942), 267-276.

Wright, Nathalie. *"Mrs. Dalloway:* A Study in Composition," *College English,* 5 (Apr., 1944), 351-358.